GOTHIC TALES

SIR ARTHUR CONAN DOYLE was born in Edinburgh in 1859 to Irish Catholic parents. He was educated at Stonyhurst, the Jesuit College, and studied Medicine at Edinburgh University, graduating in 1881. He practised medicine at Southsea in the 1880s as well as in a Greenland whaler, a West African trader, and (after twenty years' retirement) a Boer War hospital. His literary career began in 1879 with the publication of a short story in *Chambers's Journal*, and the first Sherlock Holmes adventure, *A Study in Scarlet*, was published in 1887. A master of short fiction, Doyle was one of the most important writers of the Gothic shirt story at time when this genre was at its most important and influential. Doyle's Gothic tales draw on his enormously wide range of interests, and cover the full panoply of Gothic subgenres, including medical horror, Egyptomaniac stories, ghosts, and spiritualism. He also wrote historical and colonial novels including those that revolved around Brigadier Gerard and Napoleon. He ran unsuccessfully for Parliament and became a leading public figure, as an enthusiastic cricketer, an activist against miscarriages of justice, and the foremost English publicist of spiritualism. He was knighted in 1902 and died at Crowborough, Sussex, in 1930.

DARRYL JONES is Professor in English at Trinity College Dublin, where he has taught since 1994. His publications include *Horror: A Thematic History in Fiction and Film* (2002) and *Jane Austen* (2004). He has edited *Horror Stories: Classic Tales from Hoffmann to Hodgson* (2014), and M. R. James's *Collected Ghost Stories* (2013) for Oxford World's Classics.

OXFORD WORLD'S CLASSICS

For over 100 years Oxford World's Classics have brought readers closer to the world's great literature. Now with over 700 titles—from the 4,000-year-old myths of Mesopotamia to the twentieth century's greatest novels—the series makes available lesser-known as well as celebrated writing.

The pocket-sized hardbacks of the early years contained introductions by Virginia Woolf, T. S. Eliot, Graham Greene, and other literary figures which enriched the experience of reading. Today the series is recognized for its fine scholarship and reliability in texts that span world literature, drama and poetry, religion, philosophy and politics. Each edition includes perceptive commentary and essential background information to meet the changing needs of readers.

OXFORD WORLD'S CLASSICS

=

ARTHUR CONAN DOYLE

Gothic Tales

=

Edited with an Introduction and Notes by
DARRYL JONES

OXFORD
UNIVERSITY PRESS

OXFORD
UNIVERSITY PRESS

Great Clarendon Street, Oxford, OX2 6DP,
United Kingdom

Oxford University Press is a department of the University of Oxford.
It furthers the University's objective of excellence in research, scholarship,
and education by publishing worldwide. Oxford is a registered trade mark of
Oxford University Press in the UK and in certain other countries

First published 2016
First published as an Oxford World's Classics paperback 2018

Impression: 1

Published in the United States of America by Oxford University Press
198 Madison Avenue, New York, NY 10016, United States of America

British Library Cataloguing in Publication Data

Data available

Library of Congress Cataloging in Publication Data

Data available

ISBN 978-0-19-873430-7

Printed in Great Britain by
Clays Ltd, St Ives plc

ACKNOWLEDGEMENTS

I would like to begin by thanking my editors at OUP. Judith Luna's enthusiasm for the subject, and her habitual patience and wisdom, have meant a great deal to me. My thanks also to Luciana O'Flaherty for seeing the project through to completion, and for her understanding towards my cavalier attitude to the specifics of deadlines. My thanks to the librarians of the British Library and Trinity College Dublin for their help and advice.

I would also like to thank Ailise Bulfin, Con Casey, Valeria Cavalli, Clare Clarke, John Connolly, Nick Daly, Ruth Doherty, Mary Donnelly, Christine Ferguson, Laura Habbe, Kate Hebblethwaite, Douglas Kerr, Miles Link, Roger Luckhurst, Elizabeth McCarthy, Bernice Murphy, Helen Conrad O'Briain, Deaglán Ó Dongháile, Eve Patten, Catherine Phelps, and Conor Reid, all of whom, whether they know it or not, have helped to make this book what it is. Particular thanks go as ever to Jarlath Killeen for his friendship, knowledge, and support over many years.

This book is dedicated with love to Margaret Robson and Morgan Jones, my family.

CONTENTS

INTRODUCTION

Readers who are unfamiliar with the stories may prefer to treat the Introduction as an Afterword.

ARTHUR CONAN DOYLE is the greatest genre writer Britain has ever produced. Over the course of a long and very prolific career he earned enormous popularity and public acclaim, some degree of political influence, a knighthood, a very large amount of money, and towards the end of his life no little scorn and ridicule. He was a forceful personality: a big man, proud of his physique—'strong and active', he called himself[1]—and a man of considerable intelligence, of boundless energy, and of unassailable self-confidence. These were qualities which he brought to bear on a variety of endeavours, but especially upon the writing of fiction, of which he produced a great amount in an astounding variety of genres.

Writers are not always the best judges of their own work. To a significant degree, Doyle owed his fame and success to the creation of Sherlock Holmes, a true literary immortal whose international celebrity and marketability show no signs of dwindling. Doyle is unquestionably one of the most important writers in the history of crime fiction. And yet Holmes was increasingly a source of irritation to his creator, who was convinced that his real talents lay elsewhere. As far as he was concerned, his lasting achievements were in the genre of historical fiction. Looking back on his career in his 1924 autobiography, *Memories and Adventures*, Doyle identified the fourteenth-century historical romances *The White Company* (1891) and *Sir Nigel* (1906) as 'the most complete, satisfying thing that I have ever done. All things find their level, but I believe that if I had never touched Holmes, who has tended to obscure my higher work, my position in literature would at the present moment be a more commanding one.'[2]

As well as being a hyper-successful crime writer and a somewhat frustrated historical novelist, Doyle was also a great writer of imperial

---

[1] Arthur Conan Doyle, *The Crowborough Edition*, xxiv. *Memories and Adventures* (Garden City, NY, 1930), 242.   [2] Doyle, *Memories and Adventures*, 86.

adventure fiction, notably with the first of the Professor Challenger
novels, *The Lost World* (1912). He wrote pirate stories (the 'Captain
Sharkey' series), and with his boxing stories made a distinguished
contribution to sporting fiction. While a combination of public clamour and financial wisdom saw him returning intermittently to Holmes
across his career—reluctantly acknowledging that 'I do not wish to be
ungrateful to Holmes, who has been a good friend to me in many
ways'[3]—there was one genre which he revisited again and again, with
great enthusiasm. Arthur Conan Doyle was a major figure in the great
period of the history of the Gothic tale.[4]

Dismissed for much of the twentieth century as a cheap brand of
populist melodrama, over recent decades the Gothic has become
understood as a major cultural mode for the articulation of uncer-
tainty and anxiety.[5] With its characteristic tensions between past and
present, rational scientific naturalism and the irrational and supernatural, centre and periphery, the country and the city, the Gothic
drew together many of Doyle's concerns.[6] It provided him with
a vehicle to express his divided national identity and double consciousness. It gave form to his anxieties, unarticulable in official public discourse, about the moral mission of the British Empire. It allowed him
to explore, from the very beginning of his writing career, those possibilities of metaphysics and extreme states of being, disallowed within
the realist economy of orthodox literary fiction. 'We have in our
police reports realism pushed to its extreme limits', Dr Watson suggests.[7] The Gothic tale allowed Doyle's imagination to venture far
beyond even these limits. The range of stories in this volume is com-
pendious, taking in the full panoply of the Victorian Gothic imagination's preoccupations—spiritualism, supernaturalism, and the occult;

---

[3] Doyle, *Memories and Adventures*, 117.

[4] Much has been written on the Gothic tale and Victorian periodical culture. See, for
example, Darryl Jones, 'Introduction' to *Horror Stories: Classic Tales from Hoffmann to
Hodgson*, ed. with an introduction and notes by Jones (Oxford, 2014), pp. xi–xxx.

[5] For important foundational works of modern Gothic interpretation, see, for example,
David Punter, *The Literature of Terror* (London, 1979); Fred Botting, *Gothic* (London,
1996). For an excellent modern introductory critical study, see Nick Groom, *The Gothic:
A Very Short Introduction* (Oxford, 2012). For the best overview of nineteenth-century
Gothic, see Jarlath Killeen, *Gothic Literature 1825–1914* (Cardiff, 2009).

[6] For a similar argument to this, see Catherine Wynne, *The Colonial Conan Doyle:
British Imperialism, Irish Nationalism, and the Gothic* (Westport, Conn., 2002), 2–3.

[7] Doyle, 'A Case of Identity', in *Sherlock Holmes: The Complete Short Stories* (London,
1928), 56.

colonial, Egyptomaniac, and yellow peril horrors; medical and surgical horrors; psychological tales of madness, obsession, and murder; tales of precognition and the uncanny.

Doyle was fortunate to be writing at a time when the literary marketplace was especially amenable to his own particular talents. The hegemony of the classic Victorian 'three-decker' novel came to a crashing end in the 1890s: by 1897, the number of three-volume novels published annually in Britain had fallen to four.[8] The three-decker novel was the distinctive product of an effective cartel of publishers and librarians, which kept the prices of novels artificially—and ultimately unsustainably—high. Into the vacuum created by the demise of the three-decker poured a great number of new periodicals, most notably the *Strand Magazine* (founded 1891), but also *The Idler* (1892), the *Pall Mall Magazine* (1893, and itself an offshoot of the *Pall Mall Gazette*, founded 1865), *The Windsor* (1895), *Pearson's* (1896), and many others.[9] Aimed squarely at a popular readership, these periodicals were the major vehicle for the development and publication of the genre short story. More than this, *Blackwood's Edinburgh Magazine*, the first of the great nineteenth-century periodicals, founded as far back as 1817, had soon discovered a lucrative market for sensational horror fiction—a market which continued throughout the century's flourishing periodical culture, and intensified with the welter of new arrivals in the 1890s.[10]

Doyle's connection with the periodicals was intimate. It was to the *Strand Magazine*, most particularly, that he owed his success. His agent, A. P. Watt, sent one of his short stories, 'The Voice of Science', to Herbert Greenhough Smith, editor of the newly founded periodical: it was published in the third edition of the *Strand* (March 1891), and marked the beginning of a long and mutually fruitful relationship between the author and the magazine.[11] Four months later, in July 1891, the *Strand* published the first Holmes short story, 'A Scandal

---

[8] Peter Keating, *The Haunted Study: A Social History of the English Novel 1875–1914* (London, 1989), 26. See pp. 9–91 for a general account of the literary marketplace in the late Victorian and Edwardian periods, on which I draw heavily in this section.

[9] Keating, *The Haunted Study*, 35.

[10] See Chris Baldick and Robert Mighall, 'Introduction', to *Tales of Terror from Blackwood's Magazine*, ed. with an introduction and notes by Baldick and Mighall (Oxford, 1995), pp. vii–xviii.

[11] Andrew Lycett, *Conan Doyle: The Man Who Created Sherlock Holmes* (London, 2007), 170.

in Bohemia', and Arthur Conan Doyle was a literary celebrity. No
fewer than fifteen of the stories in this volume were first published
in the *Strand*. The great majority of the others—all but one, in fact
('The Third Generation')—were published in *The Idler*, *Pearson's*,
the *Cornhill Magazine*, or in one of a number of other magazines
or newspapers. In writing his Gothic tales for the periodicals,
then, Doyle was continuing a significant nineteenth-century literary
tradition.

At the same time that he was making a name for himself as a writer,
Doyle also made himself, very insistently, into a public figure, in
a manner which suggests that an acknowledged place of influence
within the public sphere was central to his conception of himself.
Indeed, as Douglas Kerr suggests, Doyle may well have been 'Britain's
last national writer'.[12] He was, firstly, a committed correspondent to
the press. As the editors of his letters, John Michael Gibson and
Richard Lancelyn Green, assert, 'Probably no other writer has ever
before revealed quite such a range of interests or believed so fervently
that he had the ear of society, and therefore the right to address it
on a variety of topics, as did Arthur Conan Doyle.'[13] His first published story, 'The Mystery of Sasassa Valley', appeared in *Chambers's
Magazine* in September 1879, the selfsame month in which the *British
Medical Journal* published his first letter—an extraordinary document in which the 20-year-old medical student discusses the results
of a course of self-experimentation, having systematically poisoned
himself with gelsemium ('a motor paralyser', notes Doyle, with effects
that included 'headache, with diarrhoea and extreme lassitude').[14]
   Though fortuitous, the simultaneous appearance of the story and
the letter was not exactly happenstance, as Doyle clearly understood
writing fiction and taking public positions to be related activities,
each one enabling the other. From 1879 right up to his death in 1930,
he was keen to communicate, with great certainty and to a mass audience, his opinions on a wide variety of subjects, on which he generally

[12] Douglas Kerr, *Conan Doyle: Writing, Profession and Practice* (Oxford, 2013), 1.
[13] John Michael Gibson and Richard Lancelyn Green, 'Introduction' to Arthur
Conan Doyle, *The Unknown Conan Doyle: Letters to the Press*, ed. Gibson and Green
(London, 1986), 1.
[14] Doyle, 'Gelseminum [*sic*] as a Poison', in *Letters to the Press*, 13.

took an uncompromising stance. Irish Home Rule, the Contagious Diseases Act, the Boer War, organized religion, trade protectionism, volunteer militias, mounted riflemen, massacres in the Congo, the desirability of a Channel Tunnel, German atrocities in the Great War, the need for reprisal against Zeppelin attacks, the reality of spiritualism. On these and numerous other subjects, the British public was never in doubt as to what Arthur Conan Doyle thought. He was in fact a frustrated politician, having twice stood unsuccessfully for parliament on a Liberal Unionist ticket in Scottish constituencies, in the 1900 and 1905 elections, and used his fame as a platform from which to express his social and political views.

But the habitual confidence of his public utterances concealed, perhaps deliberately, contradictions beneath. One of the most fascinating things about Doyle is that he was such a conflicted, or even a divided, figure. He was by training a doctor, completely aware of the significance of scientific naturalism and, in the figure of Sherlock Holmes, the creator of the foremost literary rationalist: a brilliant applied experimenter (and, like his creator, not past experimenting on himself) and thoroughgoing materialist. And yet he was also increasingly drawn to spiritualism, for which he became a high-profile advocate, to the point, many observers believed, of utter self-damaging credulity. The educational institutions with which he was closely associated themselves express this duality, as he moved from the ultramontane anti-modernity of the Jesuit academy Stonyhurst to the Enlightenment scientism of Edinburgh University medical school. He later wrote with characteristically divided feelings about his Jesuit education: 'Nothing can exceed the uncompromising bigotry of the Jesuit theology, or their apparent ignorance of how it shocks the modern conscience', he maintained, while acknowledging of the Jesuits that 'In all ways, save their theology, they were admirable'.[15] His Irish Catholic background (on both sides of the family) and his Liberal Unionist politics were in direct conflict with one another, to the extent that he reversed his views on Irish Home Rule, which he came to support in the 1910s. Andrew Lycett, one of Doyle's biographers, understands these dualities as the key to grasping his subject as a writer and a man, and traces them back to his home city of Edinburgh, 'a city of dramatic contrasts, made tolerable by thoughtful accommodation'.[16]

---

[15] *Memories and Adventures*, 16.   [16] Lycett, *Conan Doyle*, 3.

It is a city whose very geography is almost Freudian: a planned, rational, orderly, neoclassical New Town paired with a dark, rambling—and in the nineteenth century occasionally dangerous—Old Town, like the conscious and unconscious minds. It is the city which produced one of the great Gothic parables of the divided self, Robert Louis Stevenson's *Strange Case of Dr Jekyll and Mr Hyde*, published in 1886, shortly after Doyle's graduation from Edinburgh Medical School—itself the setting for another of Stevenson's dualistic Gothic tales of public virtue and private vice, 'The Bodysnatcher' (1884). This kind of conflict and duality is a central component of Victorian Gothic, and so it is no surprise that Doyle should be drawn to the form, and should return to it so frequently across the course of his career.

Doyle's Gothic fiction often seeks out remote landscapes on the margins of British polity. Holmes is a fundamentally urban creation. His sensibilities are entirely metropolitan—he hates and fears rural life: 'the lowest and vilest alleys in London do not present a more dreadful record of sin than does the smiling and beautiful countryside'.[17] *The Hound of the Baskervilles* (1902), perpetually on the verge of turning into a full-blooded Gothic novel, transforms remote Dartmoor into a phantasmagoric locale, 'like some fantastic landscape in a dream': 'all things are possible upon the moor', says the criminal mastermind Stapleton.[18] But this was hardly Doyle's first fictional visit to Dartmoor. One of his very earliest stories, 'The Winning Shot' (1883), is set in Toynby Hall, on the very edge of 'the great wilderness of Dartmoor, which stretched away to the horizon' (p. 34). To this far-flung spot, as though irresistibly drawn, comes the Swedish occultist and necromancer Dr Octavius Gaster, who makes a dramatic appearance at dusk high on a rock in a 'charnel-house place' on the moor, where the water sounds 'like the gurgling in the throat of a dying man' (p. 36). Gaster is a kind of vampire: 'There was something about

---

[17] 'The Copper Beeches', in *Sherlock Holmes: The Complete Short Stories*, 286.

[18] *The Hound of the Baskervilles*, in *Sherlock Holmes: The Complete Long Stories* (London, 1929), 329, 345. Working from Doyle's 1901 diaries, Christopher Frayling has suggested that Dartmoor was literally an imaginative locale for Doyle, who may not have gone there until after he wrote *The Hound of the Baskervilles*, but rather drew from his reading of Sabine Baring-Gould's *A Book of Dartmoor* (1900). See Frayling, 'Nothing But a Hound Dog', in *Inside the Bloody Chamber: On Angela Carter, the Gothic, and Other Weird Tales* (London, 2015), 193–212.

his angular proportions and the bloodless face which, taken in conjunction with the black cloak which fluttered from his shoulders, irresistibly reminded me of a bloodsucking species of bat' (p. 37). In a manner characteristic of much classic nineteenth-century Gothic, from *Frankenstein* to 'William Wilson' to *Dr Jekyll and Mr Hyde* to *The Picture of Dorian Gray*, 'The Winning Shot' is a tale of the divided self. Gaster recites a spell from an ancient Arabic grimoire which enables him to split his rival Charley Pillar in two, causing Charley to shoot his own double, and thus to kill himself. All things are indeed possible on the moor.

An explicit echo of Dr Gaster returns in a different form in 'The Surgeon of Gaster Fell' (1890), another Gothic tale of occultists on the moors, whose very title suggests a paired relationship with 'The Winning Shot'. This is also a story which, if not straightforwardly autobiographical, certainly weaves together elements from Doyle's life. Like the slightly earlier 'Uncle Jeremy's Household' (1887), 'The Surgeon of Gaster Fell' takes place on the fells of north-east Yorkshire, an area which Doyle knew well: both these stories are based around fictionalized versions of the Yorkshire village of Masongill, where his mother lived from 1882 until 1917. In 'The Surgeon of Gaster Fell', James Upperton, a demobbed soldier, comes to the 'Bleak and windswept...harsh and forbidding...lonely and secluded' village of Kirkby-Malthouse seeking solitude in which to pursue his 'mystic studies' into the possibility of human immortality to be found in ancient Egyptian and Neoplatonic works (pp. 166, 167). Upperton's neighbours—the local doctor and his beautiful sister—have come to Gaster Fell to keep a family secret: their father, an exhausted Birmingham GP, has developed homicidal mania, and so his family have locked him away here, far from society. This is a grotesque refiguring of Doyle's own family history. His father, the artist Charles Altamont Doyle, may not have been a homicidal maniac, but he was a chronic alcoholic prone to episodes of mental breakdown, who had a tendency, in Lycett's words, to 'violent and abusive' behaviour, and spent the last years of his life in a series of mental asylums, where he was certainly classed in official documentation as a 'lunatic'.[19] The story of a doctor being summoned to care for a genteel lunatic is one to which Doyle returns several times. In his autobiographical novel *The Stark Munro Letters* (1895), young

---

[19] Lycett, *Conan Doyle*, 109, 160.

Dr Munro at one point gets a job caring for the Honourable James Derwent, whose mental condition turns him into 'a foul-tongued rough'.[20] In the interview for the job, his prospective employer insists on asking for his height and weight, as the doctor will need to be sufficiently physically robust to restrain the lunatic if necessary. This very same episode is recycled for the Gothic tale 'The Beetle-Hunter' (1898), in which a newly qualified doctor answers a newspaper advertisement looking for 'a medical man...of strong physique, of steady nerves, and of a resolute nature' (p. 303) and finds himself caring for a distinguished aristocratic entomologist who has, once again, succumbed to homicidal mania.

Understandably, Doyle was highly reluctant publicly to discuss his father's history. His autobiography makes no explicit mention of Charles Altamont Doyle's alcoholism or his insanity:

My father's health had utterly broken; he had to retire to that convalescent house in which the last twenty years of his life were spent.... My father's life was full of the tragedy of unfulfilled promise and undeveloped gifts. He had his weaknesses, as all of us have ours, but he also had some remarkable and outstanding virtues.[21]

In ways that were perhaps unknown to himself, the Gothic, with its ability to explore extreme states of being and to give oblique articulation to the unspeakable, provided Doyle with a vehicle to explore the psychological consequences of this 'tragedy of unfulfilled promise'.

In December 1899, Doyle found himself in Hounslow, 'standing in a long queue of men who were waiting to enlist in the Middlesex Yeomanry'.[22] The Boer War had recently broken out in South Africa, and he was keen to enlist, but the regimental colonel, seeing in front of him a man of 40 with no military training or experience, had other ideas. And so, rather than serving as a soldier, Doyle travelled to Bloemfontein to work as a doctor in a military hospital set up on a racecourse. There, he had to deal with a virulent outbreak of enteric fever which cost 5,000 lives: this, he recalled, was 'death in its vilest

---

[20] Doyle, *The Stark Munro Letters: Being a series of sixteen letters written by J. Stark Munro, M.B., to his friend and former fellow student, Herbert Swanborough, of Lowell, Massachusetts, during the years 1881–1884* (London, 1895), 73.

[21] *Memories and Adventures*, 28.   [22] *Memories and Adventures*, 168.

and filthiest forms... the disease causes constant pollution, and this pollution of the most dangerous kind, with the vilest effluvia'.[23]

On returning to Britain, his first literary response to his experiences was not, as might perhaps be expected, a Gothic tale, but a history of the war, *The Great Boer War* (1900). The book was controversial, not least in its justification of British concentration camps. One piece of hostile criticism in particular stuck in the author's mind: 'Doyle's book makes the impression that it was ordered or influenced by the English Jingo party.'[24] His response to criticism of the British conduct of the Boer War was an inspired exercise in propaganda, *The War in South Africa: Its Cause and Conduct*, a mass-circulation 6,000-word pamphlet. Doyle oversaw a vigorous campaign of subscriptions to ensure that the pamphlet was translated as quickly as possible into as many languages as possible, and in February 1902 wrote proudly to *The Times* that it was in the process of being translated not only into Dutch (for obvious reasons, as the Boers were the descendants of Dutch settlers), but also into German, French, Norwegian, Italian, Spanish, Russian, Hungarian, Portuguese, and Welsh.[25] It was for the success of this campaign—for services not to literature but to military propaganda—that Arthur Conan Doyle was knighted by King Edward VII in 1902.

Doyle may not have been a jingoist, exactly, but he was a British imperialist to his bones. In fact, if one were to single out the major, recurring explicit theme and preoccupation of his writing and thought, it would be his unwavering belief in and support for the British Empire. 'I am an Imperialist,' he wrote to the *Irish Times* in 1912, 'because I believe the whole to be greater than the part, and I would always willingly sacrifice any part if I thought it to the advantage of the whole.'[26] The British Empire underlay his own consciousness and sense of self, his national and supranational identity: 'The Empire is in no sense an English thing. Scotch and Irish have combined in the

---

[23] *Memories and Adventures*, 178–9.   [24] *Memories and Adventures*, 215.

[25] ' "The Cause and Conduct of the War" ', *The Times*, 4 February 1902, in *Letters to the Press*, 85–7. The Welsh translation was felt to be necessary because 'the vernacular press of the principality was almost entirely pro-Boer, and the Welsh people had the most distorted information as to the cause for which their fellow-countrymen fought so bravely in the field': *Memories and Adventures*, 219.

[26] 'Home Rule: Letter to R. J. Kelly of Dublin', *Irish Times*, 4 April 1912, in *Letters to the Press*, 164.

building of it, and have an equal pride and interest in its immense future.'[27] In 1924, musing on a visit to Canada, he wrote rapturously of the future of the Empire, which will 'remain exactly as it is for the remainder of the century':

[Canadian] imperialism is as warm or warmer than our own. And everywhere there is a consciousness of the glory of the Empire, its magnificent future, and the wonderful possibilities of those great nations all growing up under the same flag and with the same language and destinies.[28]

Unquestionably, Doyle viewed imperial warfare as a kind of *Boys' Own* adventure. 'The British officer at his best', he came to realize, was really 'a large edition of the public schoolboy'.[29] During his Boer War time in Bloemfontein, he journeyed out onto the veldt, where he discovered the corpse of a nameless Australian soldier: 'So he met his end—somebody's boy. Fair fight, open air, and a great cause—I know no better death.'[30] Consistently throughout his letters Doyle bemoans the reluctance of the British Empire to propagandize on its own behalf. He himself exhibited no such reluctance, and was, as we have seen, a highly effective propagandist, for whom fiction was a potent tool. *The White Company* and *Sir Nigel* are extended paeans to martial prowess. Near the beginning of *The Lost World*, the journalist Malone, chastised by his beloved Gladys, who wants to love 'a man of great deeds and strange experiences' like Sir Richard Burton or Henry Morton Stanley, is told by his editor that 'The big blank spaces on the map are all being filled in, and there's no room for romance anywhere'.[31] *The Lost World* does explicitly what many of Doyle's writings do by implication: it reinscribes a space for romance onto an increasingly utilitarian map of the world.

A few years before his Boer War adventure, in 1896 Doyle had found himself visiting Egypt, and while he was there had wangled a press pass to cover a Mahdist uprising in Nubia, 'the next adventure which was opening up before both us and the British Empire'.[32] Doyle's fiction had already touched on Mahdism—Bellingham, the occult Egyptologist villain of 'Lot No. 249' (1892), is forced to leave

[27] 'On Ireland and the Empire', *Freeman's Journal*, Dublin, 3 August 1914, in *Letters to the Press*, 207.   [28] *Memories and Adventures*, 344.

[29] *Memories and Adventures*, 151.   [30] *Memories and Adventures*, 196.

[31] Doyle, *The Lost World* (London, 1912), 13, 19.

[32] *Memories and Adventures*, 147.

England in disgrace and 'was last heard of in the Soudan' (p. 240), presumably meddling in a Mahdist insurrection, while the Fenian conscripts of 'The Green Flag' (1893) ultimately recognize where their allegiances lie, and die a heroic death defending the Empire in Sudan. The 1896 adventure provided Doyle with fresh imperial material, and led to the publication of the autobiographical 'The Three Correspondents' (1896), the extraordinarily pro-imperialist novel *The Tragedy of the Korosko* (1898, but serialized in 1897), and 'The Debut of Bimbashi Joyce' (1900), another tale of an Irish soldier coming good in Egypt and the Sudan. The Mahdist wars of the 1890s were to culminate in the Battle of Omdurman on 2 September 1898, the most one-sided massacre in British imperial history, in which the Maxim guns of the British army cut down 10,000 Mahdist soldiers, many of whom were armed only with assegai spears. This was not, it should be noted, how Doyle himself saw events:

The Arab of the Soudan is a desperate fanatic who rushes to death with the frenzy of a madman and longs for close quarters where he can bury his spear in the body of his foeman, even though he carries several bullets in him before he reaches him.[33]

As Sven Lindqvist notes, it was to prevent such wounded death-charges that the exploding dumdum bullet was developed, 'named after the factory outside Dum Dum in Calcutta, and patented in 1897.... The use of dumdum bullets between "civilized" states was prohibited. They were reserved for big-game hunting and colonial wars.'[34] Doyle himself raises the use of exploding bullets in his defence of the British conduct of the Boer War, noting 'that the British, whose wars are usually against savages, had prepared huge quantities of soft-nosed [dumdum] bullets.... It is only just to say, however, that they were never intended to be used against white races.'[35]

But Doyle's assertive public confidence in the civilizing mission of the British Empire is not borne out by a reading of the Gothic tales, whose sensibilities are more modern—or, at least, the stories seem more amenable to modern sensibilities. These tales are full of anxieties about the vengeful or monstrous capabilities and consequences

[33] *Memories and Adventures*, 149.
[34] Sven Lindqvist, *'Exterminate All the Brutes'*, trans. Joan Tate (New York, 1996), 52.
[35] Doyle, 'Dr Conan Doyle on his Defence', *Daily News*, 31 January 1902, in *Letters to the Press*, 84.

of imperialism. In a manner unusually explicit for Doyle, the super-natural tale ' "De Profundis" ' (1892) opens with a recognition that for the success of 'the great, broadcast British Empire ... a price must be paid, and the price is a grievous one. As the beast of old must have one young, human life as a tribute every year, so to our Empire we throw from day to day the pick and flower of our youth' (p. 201). The Empire, then, is a monster devouring the nation's young.

In a further, recurring exploration of this Gothic image, one group of Doyle's stories deals with exotic creatures wreaking havoc either in the colonies, or, worse, on British soil: as Christopher Frayling notes, Doyle was much given to tales of 'biology run amok', and particularly of 'monstrous beasts giving nightmares to the aristocracy of deep England'.[36] These tales are Doyle's most idiosyncratic contribution to fictional explorations of the common *fin-de-siècle* cultural anxiety of reverse colonization, which saw a series of Continental, orien-tal, imperial, or interplanetary Others wreaking havoc upon British soil. In 1897 alone—the year of Queen Victoria's Diamond Jubilee, which might be said to mark the high point of British imperialism—three canonical works of reverse colonization were published: Bram Stoker's *Dracula*, Richard Marsh's *The Beetle*, and (in serial form) H. G. Wells's *The War of the Worlds*. A number of Doyle's stories from the 1890s—'The Ring of Thoth', 'Lot No. 249', 'The Case of Lady Sannox', 'The Fiend of the Cooperage', 'The Brazilian Cat', 'The Brown Hand'—as well as numerous of the Holmes stories—notably *The Sign of Four* (1890) and 'The Speckled Band' (1892)—are classic tales of colonial horror, shot through with a variety of imperial anxieties.

Fresh out of medical school in the early 1880s, and looking for occupation and adventure, the young Doyle signed as ship's doctor on a couple of sea voyages that were straight out of the imperial adventure romance. In 1880, he spent several months upon the whal-ing ship *Hope*, working the far northern waters around Greenland: 'a region of romance,' he was to recall many years later, where 'You stand on the very brink of the unknown ... a land which the maps know not'.[37] More influential for Doyle was his voyage to West Africa

---

[36] Christopher Frayling, 'Introduction' to Doyle, *The Hound of the Baskervilles*, ed. with an introduction and notes by Frayling (London, 2001), p. xxii.

[37] *Memories and Adventures*, 47.

on board the *Mayumba* in 1881–2, which was to provide him with the genesis of a decades-long imaginative and political engagement with the region. His initial response to Africa, as recalled in his autobiography, is clearly spoken through by the classic racist discourse of the 'civilizing mission' of European colonialism. Africa is a savage and exotic land:

The natives were all absolute savages, offering up human sacrifices to snakes and crocodiles. The captain had heard the screams of the victims and seen them dragged down to the water's edge, while on another occasion he had seen the protruding skull of a man who had been buried in an antheap. It is all very well to make game of the missionaries, but how are such people ever to be improved if it were not for the labours of devoted men?[38]

All of which sounds as though it might have come straight out of the report for the Society for the Suppression of Savage Customs which Kurtz has prepared in Conrad's *Heart of Darkness* (1899), and whose mad logic drives him to the notorious conclusion, 'Exterminate all the brutes!' But the truth of Doyle's engagement with West Africa was more nuanced. One of the *Mayumba*'s passengers was Henry Highland Garnet, an African American diplomat, and 'The most intelligent and well-read man whom I met on the Coast'. Garnet educated Doyle in the complexities of European–African cultural exchanges:

'The only way to explore Africa [he told Doyle] is to go without arms and with few servants. You would not like it in England if a body of men came armed to the teeth and marched through your land. The Africans are quite as sensitive.' It was the method of Livingstone as against the method of Stanley. The former takes the braver and better man.[39]

Doyle's first fictional engagement with the implications of this journey was the riotously imaginative 'J. Habakuk Jephson's Statement' (1884), which weaves together the mystery of the *Mary Celeste*—discovered floating crewless in the North Atlantic in 1872—and the founding of the West African Republic of Liberia by freed American slaves in 1847 into a tale of a murderous African American separatist, Septimus Goring. Goring explains his political intentions to the narrator, the abolitionist Doctor Jephson: 'I determined to find some

---

[38] *Memories and Adventures*, 54.   [39] *Memories and Adventures*, 57.

bold free black people and throw in my lot with them, to cultivate their latent powers and to form a nucleus of a great coloured nation' (p. 88). Cast adrift in the Atlantic at the end of the story, Jephson is picked up 'by the British and African Steam Navigation Company's boat *Monrovia*' (p. 90), named in honour of the capital of Liberia.

Journeying through the 'Dark and terrible mangrove swamps' of Creek Town, a former slave port on the Nigerian coast, 'where nothing that is not horrible could exist . . . a foul place', Doyle recalled glimpsing a native monster: 'Once in an isolated tree standing in a flood, I saw an evil-looking snake, worm-coloured and about three feet long.'[40] This episode underwent an extraordinary Gothic transformation to become one of Doyle's most remarkable tales of colonial anxiety, 'The Fiend of the Cooperage' (1897), in which a giant West African python which is consistently imagined in terms of 'queer Voodoo tales' and 'Voodoo devilry' (pp. 296, 301) horribly kills Walker, a colonial agent of 'good stiff Unionist' politics and a 'decent, God-fearing, nineteenth-century, Primrose-League Englishman' (p. 301). Walker's colleague, the 'rank Radical' Dr Severall, a supporter of Irish Home Rule, explains that their outpost is situated 'just upon the edge of the great unknown . . . an undiscovered country', the home of exotic fauna: 'That is the Gaboon country—the land of the great apes' (pp. 292, 293). '[T]he great python of the Gaboon' (p. 301), the story's titular fiend, emerges out of the African unknown to wreak revenge upon the colonizing Englishman.

The threatening or vengeful colonial serpent is an image which Doyle deployed several times, perhaps most famously in 'The Adventure of the Speckled Band' (1892), which he himself considered to be the best of the Holmes stories.[41] Earlier still is 'Uncle Jeremy's Household' (1887), one of his most explicit tales of colonial retribution, in which 'Miss Warrender', in reality a Thug princess dispossessed by the British on account of her father's role in the 1857 First War of Indian Independence, comes to work as a governess in a remote house on the Yorkshire moors: 'She is the child of an Indian chieftain, whose wife was an Englishwoman. He was killed in the mutiny, fighting against us, and his estates being seized by Government, his

---

[40] *Memories and Adventures*, 55.
[41] Doyle, *The Adventures of Sherlock Holmes*, ed. with an introduction and notes by Richard Lancelyn Green (Oxford, 1998), 361.

daughter, then fifteen, was left almost destitute' (p. 115). 'Miss Warrender' is joined on the moors by a Thug strangler, come to carry out her murderous bidding, who is explicitly rendered as a human snake:

As I gazed I became conscious that down this luminous branch something was crawling—a flickering, inchoate something, almost indistinguishable from the branch itself, and yet slowly and steadily writhing its way down it.... It was a human being—a man—the Indian whom I had seen in the village. With his arms and legs twined round the great limb, he was shuffling his way down as silently and almost as rapidly as one of his native snakes. (p. 146)

Lawrence, the narrator of 'Uncle Jeremy's Household', is a close counterpart of the Arthur Conan Doyle of the 1880s—he is a student, 'working hard for the final examination which should make me a qualified medical man', at that time living 'in lodgings in London' (p. 114), but whose connections bring him out to the moors—as we have seen, a common location for Doyle's early stories in particular, and a place of which he had direct personal experience. Lawrence is clearly intoxicated by the beautiful Indian governess, who brings 'the brilliance of the tropics in the cold English dwelling-house' (p. 126), and the narrative of 'Uncle Jeremy's Household' cannot bring itself to condemn her actions outright. Her victim is the vile blackmailer Copperthorne, who is trying to inveigle his way into the possession of Uncle Jeremy's fortune. She exits the story, and Lawrence's life, on 'the 7.20 London train, and was safe in the metropolis before any search could be made for her' (p. 147). She will make her way back to India, Lawrence speculates, 'to join her scattered tribesmen' (p. 148) and take up her birthright as queen of the Thugs.

The fact that Severall and Walker, the colonial agents of 'The Fiend of the Cooperage', 'talk Home Rule for two solid hours every evening' (p. 292) in their West African outpost suggests a very real connection in Doyle's imagination between the local concerns of his own Irish family background on the one hand and the global anxieties of 'the great, broadcast British Empire' on the other. Doyle, as we have seen, twice stood for Parliament on a Liberal Unionist platform, in opposition to Gladstone's Home Rule policies, and, as Catherine Wynne has argued, 'the Irish question' runs like a thread throughout his works, which frequently turn on the 'often-troubled convergence of Irish nationalism and British imperialism'.[42] Irish nationalism and British imperialism form two halves of one of Doyle's most intriguing and deep-seated dualities. This is, in fact, a feature of 'The Winning Shot', Doyle's most explicit tale of the double: Colonel Pillar, the doomed Charley's father, spends his time cursing Gladstone's 'Liberal administration' for its Irish policies, to such an extent that his son fears that 'that Irish question will get into his system and finish him off' (p. 33). Indeed, it is entirely plausible that Irish nationalism is written into one half of the most celebrated of all of Doyle's doubles, Holmes and Moriarty. Is Moriarty an Irishman? His surname is certainly an Anglicization of the Irish Ó Muircheartaigh; his second-in-command, Colonel Sebastian Moran, also has an Irish surname; and *The Valley of Fear* (1915) reveals his close connections with Irish–American criminal organizations.

In *Memories and Adventures*, Doyle recalls how, as a young man returning from studying at the Stella Matutina academy in Feldkirch on the Austian Tyrol (a biographical episode recycled in Gothic form in the story 'A Pastoral Horror'), he stopped off to visit his great-uncle Michael Conan in his Paris apartment. Doyle remembered this visit warmly. Conan was a graduate of Trinity College Dublin, an Irish nationalist, and 'a man of distinction, an intellectual Irishman of the type which originally founded the Sinn Fein movement'. He and the young Arthur found they had much in common: Michael was 'a dear old volcanic Irishman... I am built rather on his lines of body and mind than any of the Doyles. We made a true friendship.'[43] Doyle stayed for a month in his great uncle's apartment on Avenue de Wagram, itself later recycled as the location for one of his most ghoulish tales, 'The Leather Funnel'.

For much of his life, Doyle's public pronouncements consistently expressed his vision of an Ireland firmly situated within the Union. 'The Irish question is upon us once more,' he wrote to his would-be constituents in the Border Burghs seat in the 1905 election. 'My views upon it are the same as in Central Edinburgh in 1900.... I will never consent to a separate legislature for Ireland.'[44] Nevertheless, Doyle's public standing also brought him into contact with men

[42] Wynne, *The Colonial Conan Doyle*, 2.   [43] *Memories and Adventures*, 17–18.
[44] 'To the Electors of the Border Burghs', *Border Telegraph*, 9 January 1906, in *Letters to the Press*, 113.

whose commitment to the Irish nationalist cause was to cost them their lives: the bestselling novelist turned Sinn Fein politician, Erskine Childers, and the colonial administrator turned nationalist revolutionary, Roger Casement. His friendship with Casement, in particular, changed things, and turned Doyle into a supporter of Irish Home Rule.[45] Doyle's change of heart began with his involvement in the campaign against atrocities in the Congo, which Casement, who had served there as a British consul, brought to light in a sensational 1905 report which listed the appalling acts of wholesale massacre and brutality committed by King Leopold's administration. Never one to resist involvement in a cause, Doyle found himself drawn into the activities of the Congo Reform Association, founded in Dublin in 1903 by Casement and the Anglo-French journalist and politician Edmund Dene Morel. These activities culminated for Doyle in the publication of *The Crime of the Congo* in 1909, which presented the case against Leopold in the most sensational and uncompromising terms:

never before has there been such a mixture of wholesale expropriation and wholesale massacre all done under an odious guise of philanthropy and with the lowest commercial motive as a reason. It is this sordid cause and unctious [*sic*] hypocrisy which makes this crime unparalleled in its horror.[46]

In a companion article written in *The Times*, Doyle described the Congo atrocities as 'the greatest crime which has ever been committed in the history of the world'.[47] 'Leopold of Belgium', Doyle came to realize, was 'an incarnate devil who through motives of greed carried murder and torture though a large section of Africa'.[48]

It was his experiences in the Congo, Casement claimed, which gave him the insight he needed into the reality of colonialism, and thus transformed him from a British imperialist to an Irish nationalist: 'In these lonely Congo lands,' he wrote, 'I found Leopold, I found also myself, the incorrigible Irishman'; 'it was only', he wrote elsewhere,

---

[45] For a similar argument to the one I make here, and using some of the same sources, see Wynne, *The Colonial Conan Doyle*, 103–5.

[46] Doyle, *The Crime of the Congo* (New York, 1909), p. iii.

[47] Doyle, 'England and the Congo', *The Times*, 18 August 1909, in *Letters to the Press*, 138.

[48] Doyle, *The Vital Message* (1919), in *The New Revelation and the Vital Message* (London, 1981), 78.

'because I was an Irishman that I could understand *fully*, I think, the whole scheme of wrongdoing at work in the Congo'.[49] Though less extreme, Doyle's own thought followed some of the same lines, drawing him irresistibly towards Irish Home Rule. At the beginning of *The Crime of the Congo*, Doyle acknowledges that Leopold's activities are not historically *sui generis*, and in doing so his gaze alights on Ireland: 'There have been great expropriations like that of the Normans in England or of the English in Ireland.'[50] Doyle took advice from Casement, and from his mother, before going public with his new-found belief in Irish Home Rule, which he did in a series of pamphlets and letters published in 1911, most notably the official Liberal Party pamphlet *Why He is Now in Favour of Home Rule*.[51]

Doyle's belief in Home Rule did not, however, modify his publicly stated faith in the British Empire: 'I think', he wrote to the *Belfast Telegraph*, 'that a solid loyal Ireland is the one thing which the Empire needs to make it impregnable.'[52] However, the signs of this new-found ambivalence are visible in his fiction of the period, provided one knows where, and how, to look. *The Lost World*, published in 1912, is, we have seen, ostensibly one of Doyle's most straightforwardly imperialist works. And yet one of its heroes, the big-game hunter and imperial fixer Lord John Roxton, is closely modelled on Casement, who followed his Congo report with another, this time into the atrocities committed against the Putomayo Indians in Peru by the rubber industry—a campaign for which Casement was knighted in 1911. Clearly writing under Casement's influence, in the midst of a series of pieces on Irish Home Rule, Doyle wrote a letter on the subject to the *Daily News* in March 1912, entitled 'Rubber Atrocities'.[53] *The Lost World* closes with two related images: a pterodactyl flying across the London skies (monstrous beasts at large in England!) and the Irish journalist-narrator Malone taking Roxton's 'brown hand', off for another adventure.[54]

[49] For these quotations, see Wynne, *The Colonial Conan Doyle*, 105–6.

[50] Doyle, *The Crime of the Congo*, p. iii.

[51] Doyle, *Why He is Now in Favour of Home Rule* (Liberal Publication Department Leaflet no. 2399; London, 1911).

[52] Doyle, 'Conan Doyle and Home Rule: How I Stand in the Matter', *Belfast Evening Telegraph*, 22 September 1911, in *Letters to the Press*, 157.

[53] Doyle, 'Rubber Atrocities', *Daily News*, 5 March 1912, in *Letters to the Press*, 162–3.

[54] *The Lost World*, 319.

The Lost World, with its allosaurus and iguanodons, is Doyle's most sustained exercise in the representation of monstrous fauna. But it is not the only work of this kind from around this time. In some ways even more interesting is 'The Terror of Blue John Gap' (1910). Here, the beast is not a product of colonialism wreaking retribution on British soil, but an aboriginal English creature. This is a gigantic cave bear which emerges from the Derbyshire Peak District to cause havoc:

This place had then developed a fauna and flora of its own, including such monsters as the one which I had seen, which may well have been the old cave-bear, enormously enlarged and modified by its new environment. For countless æons the internal and the external creation had been kept apart, growing steadily away from each other. Then there had come some rift in the depths of the mountain which had enabled one creature to wander up and ... to reach the open air. (pp. 444–5)

By 1910, Doyle had come to realize that monsters could be home-grown.[55]

It is, perhaps, possible to imagine an Arthur Conan Doyle fully committed to the cause of Irish nationalism, and perhaps too, like Casement and Childers, willing to give his life for this cause. But that is not what happened. Instead, Doyle's last decades were consumed almost entirely by one overwhelming subject: spiritualism.

The spiritualist movement of the late nineteenth century was, Doyle came to believe, 'by far the greatest religious event since the death of Christ. ... [It was] an enormous new development, the greatest in this history of mankind.'[56] Such statements, and they are not uncommon in his later work, seem downright absurd to twenty-first-century ears, and certainly did enormous damage to Doyle's reputation in the last years of his life. But it is important to realize that they arise out of a perfectly comprehensible context, and that while Doyle may have expressed them with characteristically extreme certainty,

---

[55] Doyle was not the only writer with Irish connections to explore the possibilities of a distinctively British horror in the Derbyshire Peak District during this period. Bram Stoker's last novel, *The Lair of the White Worm* (1911), has an identical location to 'The Terror of Blue John Gap', and draws heavily on Stoker's own researches into a distinctively British folkloric tradition.   [56] Doyle, *The New Revelation*, 58.

and at a far later date than perhaps he should have, these were not particularly unusual views for a person of Doyle's generation.

It is impossible, in fact, to understand the intellectual culture of Victorian Britain, the culture which formed Doyle's sensibilities, without understanding spiritualism—the belief in the survival of the human personality after death, and that the dead were continually attempting to make contact with the living, still interested in our activities and our well-being—along with the distinct but overlapping practices of psychical research and occultism. Towards the end of the second volume of his monumental *The History of Spiritualism* (1926), Doyle offers the following definition of the reality of spiritualism:

The spiritual heavens, then, would appear to be sublimated and ethereal reproductions of earth and of earth life under higher and better conditions.... The body carries on with its spiritual and intellectual qualities unchanged by the transition from one room of the great universal mansion to the next one.[57]

As Janet Oppenheim writes in *The Other World*, her definitive history of the subject, in the last decades of the nineteenth century the spiritualists' 'concerns and aspirations placed them—far from the lunatic fringe of society—squarely amidst the cultural, intellectual, and emotional moods of the era'.[58] This is an important point. The Western intelligentsia, at least, tends to see itself as inhabiting a secular modernity characterized, to use Max Weber's famous phrase, by *Entzauberung* (disenchantment): in 1917 Weber wrote that 'the fate of our times is characterized by rationalism and intellectualization and, above all, by the "disenchantment of the world" '.[59] In the closing decades of the nineteenth century, spiritualism was taken very seriously by some very serious people. The Society for Psychical Research (SPR), of which Doyle was a member, was founded in Trinity College, Cambridge, in 1891 by a group of researchers which included Henry

---

[57] Doyle, *The History of Spiritualism* (London, 1926), ii. 284.

[58] Janet Oppenheim, *The Other World: Spiritualism and Psychical Research in England, 1850–1914* (Cambridge, 1985), 4.

[59] Max Weber, 'Science as a Vocation', in *Max Weber: Essays in Sociology*, trans. and ed. H. H. Gerth and C. Wright Mills (Oxford and New York, 1958), 155. For an analysis of the significance of *Entzauberung* to the spiritualist movement, on which I draw here, see Alex Owen, *The Place of Enchantment: British Occultism and the Culture of the Modern* (Chicago and London, 2004), 10–16.

Sidgwick, Knightsbridge Professor of Philosophy and Fellow of Trinity, and Frederic W. H. Myers, also formerly a Fellow of Trinity. As Roger Luckhurst notes, both Sidgwick and Myers were extraordinarily well connected, with ties of blood, marriage, and friendship to the late Victorian social and intellectual elite. Sidgwick to the Balfour and Benson families (prime ministers, archbishops of Canterbury, the heads of Cambridge colleges), Myers to George Eliot and William James. Both had associations with Tennyson. Gladstone, Tennyson, and Ruskin were all allied to the SPR, whose early presidents included Sidgwick himself, A. J. Balfour, William James, and Henri Bergson.[60] This was no marginal group.

Doyle did not formally announce himself as a spiritualist until the publication of *The New Revelation* in 1918, but anyone paying attention to his writing career would have been able to trace this as an important, or perhaps a central, interest in his fiction from the very beginning. Spiritualism was a major source for his Gothic imagination—and vice versa. In his fiction of the 1880s and early 1890s, 'The Winning Shot', 'The Surgeon of Gaster Fell', 'Lot No. 249', and '"De Profundis"' are heavily influenced by his growing interest in spiritualism and the occult. His third novel, *The Mystery of Cloomber* (1889), combines occultism and colonial revenge in a tale of Indian Yogis possessed of esoteric knowledge who remorselessly pursue General Heatherstone to his death in 'the Hole of Cree', a bottomless chasm on the Scottish borders, in retribution for the General's killing of their spiritual leader, 'Goolab Shah, the arch adept', in the Afghan wars.[61] The novel, full of theosophical disquisitions, closes with a lengthy 'Addendum' on 'The Occult Philosophy', which acknowledges its author's reading of the works of the esoteric writer Alfred Percy Sinnett, most particularly *The Occult World* (1883). On joining the SPR in 'about 1891', Doyle recalled, 'I read that monumental book [Frederic] Myers' *Human Personality*, a great root book from which a whole world of knowledge will grow.'[62]

From the beginning, then, Doyle's Gothic tales enact his struggle to reconcile his growing acceptance of the reality of the spirit world with his formal professional training in medicine and science. As

[60] Roger Luckhurst, *The Invention of Telepathy, 1870–1901* (Oxford, 2002), 54–6.
[61] Doyle, *The Mystery of Cloomber* (London, 1896), 114.
[62] Doyle, *The New Revelation*, 21.

a number of commentators have noted, spiritualism was the nineteenth century's most characteristic response to the materialism suggested by the publication of Darwin's *On the Origin of Species* in 1859, and the more widespread rise of scientific naturalism from the 1870s, which completely rejected any metaphysical basis for existence.[63] This tension between materialism and metaphysics, which is there throughout Doyle's writings, is revealed most clearly in two of his less-well-known longer works of the 1890s, the 1894 novella *The Parasite* and the autobiographical *Stark Munro Letters*. The narrator of *The Parasite*, Austin Gilroy, is a young professor of physiology and a self-proclaimed 'materialist...a rank one', who initially boasts that 'my brain is soaked with exact knowledge. I have trained myself to deal only with fact and with proof. Surmise and fancy have no place in my scheme of thought.'[64] Gilroy is taught a comprehensive lesson in metaphysics at the hands of the West Indian mesmerist and supernaturalist Miss Penelosa. *Stark Munro* reads like a tormented work of epistemological self-questioning, whose narrator, a thinly fictionalized version of Doyle himself, constantly interrupts his own narrative with lengthy disquisitions which attempt to reconcile his rejection of conventional organized religion—'I have mastered the principles of several religions. They have all shocked me by the violence which I should have to do to my reason to accept the dogmas of any of them'—with his awareness of the limits of scientific naturalism: 'I know nothing more unbearable than the complacent type of scientist who knows very exactly all that he does know, but has not imagination enough to understand what a speck his little accumulation of doubtful erudition is when compared with the immensity of our ignorance.'[65]

Doyle was not alone in these doubts and questions. This tension between materialism and metaphysics is, in fact, a characteristic of the Victorian and Edwardian supernatural tale more generally. Doyle's very close contemporary, the great English ghost-story writer M. R. James, believed that this was the key to the success of the genre: 'It is

---

[63] See e.g. Oppenheim, *Other World*, 1–4; Luckhurst, *Invention of Telepathy*, 9–59. For Victorian scientific naturalism, see e.g. Bernard Lightman and Gowan Dawson (eds.), *Victorian Scientific Naturalism: Community, Identity, Continuity* (Chicago, 2014).

[64] Doyle, *The Parasite*, in *The Crowborough Edition*, xxiii. *The Parasite, The Captain of the Pole-Star, Other Tales* (Garden City, NY, 1930), 4.

[65] Doyle, *The Stark Munro Letters*, 16, 280.

not amiss sometimes to leave a loophole for a natural explanation; but, I would say, let the loophole be so narrow as not to be quite practicable.'[66] This is exactly the narrow loophole which Doyle exploits in '"De Profundis"', which closes by positing two competing explanations for the emergence of John Vansittart's body, apparently leaping out of its watery grave to greet his wife as she sails to meet him in Madeira. Either, the narrator suggests, this tale serves 'to support the recent theory of telepathy...[which] I hold...to be proved' (p. 209), or else 'the surgeon tells me that the leaden weight was not too firmly fixed, and that seven days bring about changes which fetch a body to the surface. Coming from the depth to which the weight would have sunk it, he explains that it might well attain such a velocity as to carry it clear of the water. Such is my own explanation of the matter' (p. 209). The loophole, however, seems to grow narrower and narrower as Doyle's career progresses: the enraged unicorn summoned in the séance in 'Playing with Fire' (1900) might be a delusion, but there seems little doubt about the Indian revenant of 'The Brown Hand' (1899) or the past visions of 'The Silver Mirror' (1909) and 'Through the Veil' (1910), and none at all about the afterlife testimony of 'How It Happened' (1913) or the undead pugilist of 'The Bully of Brocas Court' (1921).

This, of course, accounts for Doyle's increasing frustration with Sherlock Holmes, a thoroughgoing scientific materialist with whom he was indelibly associated, from whom he could not unchain himself, and whose rationalism was central to his appeal. Professor Challenger, the evolutionary biologist of *The Lost World*, was certainly marshalled for the spiritualist cause: the late Challenger novel *The Land of Mist* (1926) is an almost unreadable exercise in spiritualist fiction, the product of a writer who seems, almost for the only time, adrift from his mooring as a genre professional who knows what his audience wants. But Challenger was no Holmes. *The Hound of the Baskervilles*, though it deploys the imagery of the Gothic to great effect, transforms Holmes into a sceptical psychical researcher, of the kind the later Doyle of *The History of Spiritualism* was to deplore, roundly debunking the Great Grimpen Mire's supernatural demon hound. One of

---

[66] M. R. James, Introduction to V. H. Collins (ed.), *Ghosts and Marvels* (Oxford, 1924), in *Collected Ghost Stories*, ed. with an introduction and notes by Darryl Jones (Oxford, 2011), 407.

the very last Holmes stories, 'The Sussex Vampire', written long after Doyle's public conversion to spiritualism, opens with Holmes contemptuously denying the possibility of the supernatural: 'Rubbish, Watson, rubbish! What have we to do with walking corpses who can only be held in their grave by stakes driven through their hearts? It's pure lunacy.... This Agency stands flat-footed upon the ground, and there it must remain. The world is big enough for us. No ghosts need apply.'[67]

Scientific materialism itself, Doyle came to believe, was at the root of all the problems of modernity. This is a subject to which he returns again and again in his major works on spiritualism of the late 1910s and 1920s. It is important to stress that, while he had imaginatively engaged with spiritualism as far back as the early 1880s, Doyle does not explicitly declare himself a spiritualist until 1918, toward the close of the Great War. The connections between spiritualism and the War were, for Doyle, vividly real. The war was brought about by 'the organized materialism of Germany', since 'when religion is dead, materialism becomes active, and what active materialism may produce has been seen in Germany'.[68] The outbreak of the war saw Doyle conducting a press campaign in characteristically bellicose mode, fulminating publicly against 'Germany's "Policy of Murder"', advocating the shaming of 'shirkers' into compulsory national service, and lobbying for remorseless reprisals against Zeppelin raids.[69] But the war brought its traumatic consequences to Doyle, too. His oldest son, Kingsley, died from pneumonia as a consequence of being wounded in action in 1918, while his beloved younger brother, Innes, who survived the war with a promotion to adjutant-general, died in the influenza pandemic of 1919. He also lost two brothers-in-law and two nephews.

If Doyle was interested in spiritualism before the war, he was committed to it afterwards. Indeed, it is little wonder that, like so many others, he should have sought solace in spiritualism, a creed which taught that death is not the end and that the dead are still with us,

[67] Doyle, 'The Sussex Vampire', in *Sherlock Holmes: The Complete Short Stories*, 1179.

[68] Doyle, *The Vital Message*, 79, 149.

[69] See e.g. 'Germany's "Policy of Murder"', *New York Times*, 6 February 1915, in *Letters to the Press*, 216–19; 'Compulsory National Service', *Daily Chronicle, 23 August 1915*, in *Letters to the Press*, 223–6; 'Reprisal', *The Times*, 15 October 1915, in *Letters to the Press*, 226–7.

essentially unchanged in personality and attachments, still solicitous of our welfare. There is a very strong element of wish-fulfilment to the spiritualism of the Great War. 'The body', he wrote in 1919, 'is a perfect thing. This is a matter of consequence when many of our heroes have been mutilated in wars. One cannot mutilate the etheric body, and it always remains intact.' The next world, Doyle saw, 'is a place of joy and laughter. There are games and sports of all sorts, though none which cause pain to lower life.'[70] Both Kingsley and Innes communicated posthumously with Doyle in some of the many seances he attended, passing on their assurances that all was well. By the time of *The History of Spiritualism*, having dwelled publicly on the issue for the better part of a decade, Doyle was very explicit about the intimate connection between spiritualism and the war: 'Many people had never heard of Spiritualism until the period that began in 1914, when into so many homes the Angel of Death entered suddenly.'[71]

Doyle was hardly the only writer of his generation or his genre to recoil from the terror of modernity in the wake of the Great War. M. R. James, traumatized beyond endurance by the deaths of so many of his Cambridge University colleagues and students, retreated into the perpetual childhood afforded him by a sinecure as provost of Eton College, where he had been very happy as a boy. As Doyle's writing progresses through the early decades of the twentieth century, a recurrent, and very particular, note of anxiety enters into his stories. In 'How It Happened' (1913), a motorist loses control of his car and hurtles downhill to his death. In 'The Horror of the Heights' (1913), an aviator discovers a hostile new ecosystem high in the stratosphere. In 'The Nightmare Room' (1921), a disturbing domestic scenario is gradually revealed in all its horror as a film set. In 'The Lift' (1922), a group of tourists find themselves suspended in an elevator high above the ground, at the mercy of a homicidal religious maniac. Increasingly, as Arthur Conan Doyle grew older, it was the modern world itself which he found most terrifying.

---

[70] Doyle, *The Vital Message*, 124–5.
[71] Doyle, *The History of Spiritualism*, ii. 224.

NOTE ON THE TEXT

THE majority of the stories here are taken from *The Conan Doyle Stories* (London: John Murray, 1929), part of a multi-volume edition of his work which Conan Doyle oversaw for publication at the end of his life. The texts for those stories not collected for this edition are taken from their first periodical publications, with the exception of 'John Barrington Cowles', which is taken from *The Captain of the 'Polestar' and Other Tales* (London: Longmans, Green and Co., 1892).

SELECT BIBLIOGRAPHY

Biographies and Critical Studies of Arthur Conan Doyle

Edwards, Owen Dudley, *The Quest for Sherlock Holmes: A Biographical Study of Arthur Conan Doyle* (Edinburgh, 1983). Seminal work of biographical criticism, full of fascinating insights.

Kerr, Douglas, *Conan Doyle: Writing, Profession and Practice* (Oxford, 2013).

Lellenberg, John, Stashower, Daniel, and Foley, Charles (eds.), *Arthur Conan Doyle: A Life in Letters* (London, 2007).

Lycett, Andrew, *Conan Doyle: The Man Who Created Sherlock Holmes* (London, 2007). The best modern biography of ACD.

Rodin, Alvin E., and Key, Jack D., *The Medical Casebook of Doctor Arthur Conan Doyle* (Malabar, Fla., 1984). Deals with ACD as a physician and surgeon.

Wynne, Catherine, *The Colonial Conan Doyle: British Imperialism, Irish Nationalism, and the Gothic* (Westport, Conn., 2002). Brilliant postcolonial study of ACD's work.

The Gothic and Popular Fiction

Arata, Stephen J., *Fictions of Loss in the Victorian Fin de Siècle: Identity and Empire* (Cambridge, 1996).

Bloom, Clive (ed.), *Gothic Horror* (London, 1998).

Botting, Fred, *Gothic* (London, 1996).

Brantlinger, Patrick, *Rule of Darkness: British Literature and Imperialism 1830–1900* (Ithaca, NY, 1988).

Daly, Nicholas, *Modernism, Romance and the Fin de Siècle: Popular Fiction and British Culture, 1880–1914* (Cambridge, 1999).

Keating, Peter, *The Haunted Study: A Social History of the English Novel 1875–1914* (London, 1989).

Killeen, Jarlath, *Gothic Literature, 1825–1914* (Cardiff, 2009).

Luckhurst, Roger, *The Mummy's Curse: The True History of a Dark Fantasy* (Oxford, 1914).

Spiritualism

Luckhurst, Roger, *The Invention of Telepathy, 1870–1901* (Oxford, 2002).

Ferguson, Christine, *Determined Spirits: Eugenics, Heredity and Racial Regeneration in Anglo-American Spiritualist Writing, 1848–1930* (Edinburgh, 2012).

Oppenheim, Janet, *The Other World: Spiritualism and Psychical Research in England, 1850–1914* (Cambridge, 1985).

Owen, Alex, *The Place of Enchantment: British Occultism and the Culture of the Modern* (Chicago and London, 2004).

CHRONOLOGY OF ARTHUR CONAN DOYLE

Life	Cultural and Historical Background
1859 ACD born in Edinburgh on 22 May	Work begins on Suez Canal; Henri Bergson, Knut Hamsen, and Alfred Dreyfus born. Charles Darwin, *The Origin of Species*; George Eliot, *Adam Bede*; Edward Fitzgerald, *The Rubáiyát of Omar Khayyám*; John Stuart Mill, *On Liberty*; Samuel Smiles, *Self Help*.
1870 Enters Stonyhurst Academy.	Death of Charles Dickens; Franco-Prussian War (1870–1). Verne, *Twenty-Thousand Leagues Under the Sea*.
1875 Enters Stella Matutina school, Feldkirch, Austria.	Edgar Wallace, Edgar Rice Burroughs, and Alcister Crowley born.
1876 Enters Edinburgh University Medical School.	Alexander Graham Bell patents telephone. Cesare Lombroso, *The Criminal Man*.
1878 Works as a doctor's assistant in Sheffield, Shropshire, and Birmingham; writes first (unpublished) novel, *The Narrative of John Smith*.	Death of Pope Pius IX, Joseph Stalin born. Thomas Hardy, *The Return of the Native*; Leo Tolstoy, *Anna Karenina*.
1879 First story, 'The Mystery of Sasassa Valley', published in *Chambers's Journal*.	Edison produces electric light bulb; Anglo-Zulu War. Mark Twain, *Tom Sawyer*.
1880 Ship's doctor on Greenland whaler *Hope*; 'The American's Tale'.	Second Afghan War; First Boer War; Lytton Strachey, Sean O'Casey, and Oswald Spengler born. Dostoevsky, *The Brothers Karamazov*; Lew Wallace, *Ben-Hur*.
1881 Voyage to West Africa as ship's doctor on board the *Mayumba*.	Robert Louis Stevenson, 'The Body Snatcher' and *Treasure Island*; death of Dostoevsky and Benjamin Disraeli.
1882 Sets up medical practice in Southsea.	Death of Charles Darwin; Society for Psychical Research founded.
1883 'The Captain of the "Polestar" '; 'The Winning Shot'.	Sax Rohmer and Franz Kafka born; death of Karl Marx.
1884 'John Barrington Cowles'; 'J. Habakuk Jephson's Statement'.	Siege of Khartoum begins.

Life	*Cultural and Historical Background*
1885 Marries Louise Hawkins; writes MD thesis on syphilis.	Leopold II of Belgium establishes Congo Free State; Louis Pasteur produces rabies vaccine; General Charles Gordon killed in Khartoum; D. H. Lawrence born. H. Rider Haggard, *King Solomon's Mines*; Mark Twain, *Huckleberry Finn*.
1887 'Uncle Jeremy's Household'; *A Study in Scarlet* published in *Beeton's Christmas Annual*.	Hermetic Order of the Golden Dawn founded. Rider Haggard, *She*; Boris Karloff born.
1890 Studies opthalmology in Vienna; 'A Pastoral Horror'; 'The Ring of Thoth'; 'The Surgeon of Gaster Fell'.	H. P. Lovecraft born. William Morris, *News from Nowhere*; William James, *Principles of Psychology*.
1891 Moves to London to set up practice as ophthalmic surgeon in Upper Wimpole Street; 'A Scandal in Bohemia', first Holmes story, published in the *Strand*; gives up medical practice and moves to Norwood.	Death of Herman Melville and Madame Blavatsky. Oscar Wilde, *The Picture of Dorian Gray*.
1892 ' "De Profundis" '; 'Lot No. 249'; 'The Los Amigos Fiasco'; *The Adventures of Sherlock Holmes*.	Gladstone becomes prime minister for third time; Basil Rathbone born; Dimitri Ivanovski discovers the virus. Max Nordau, *Degeneration*.
1893 'The Case of Lady Sannox'; death of Sherlock Holmes in 'The Final Problem'.	Sigmund Freud and Josef Breuer, *Studies in Hysteria*.
1894 'The Lord of Château Noir'; 'The Third Generation'; *The Memoirs of Sherlock Holmes*.	Death of Robert Louis Stevenson. Arthur Machen, *The Great God Pan*; Rudyard Kipling, *Jungle Books*; Alfred Dreyfus arrested and convicted of treason; Martial Bourdin attempts to blow up Greenwich Observatory.
1897 Meets Jean Leckie, his future second wife; 'The Fiend of the Cooperage'; 'The Striped Chest'.	Stoker, *Dracula*; Marsh, *The Beetle*; Wells, *The Invisible Man*.
1898 'The Beetle-Hunter'; 'The Brazilian Cat'; 'The New Catacomb'; 'The Retirement of Signor Lambert'; 'The Sealed Room'; *The Tragedy of the Korosko*.	Spanish–American War. Wells, *War of the Worlds*; Wilde, *The Ballad of Reading Gaol*; Henry James, *The Turn of the Screw*; Conrad's 'Heart of Darkness' in *Blackwood's Magazine*.

	Life	*Cultural and Historical Background*
1899	'The Brown Hand'.	Second Boer War; Boxer Rebellion. Sigmund Freud, *The Interpretation of Dreams*; Jorge Luis Borges born.
1900	ACD volunteers as medic in Boer War, and published *The Great Boer War*; stands as a Liberal Unionist candidate for Edinburgh Central constituency; 'Playing with Fire'.	British Labour Party founded; death of Oscar Wilde.
1901	*The Hound of the Baskervilles* begins publication in the *Strand*.	Death of Queen Victoria.
1902	Knighted by King Edward VII; *The War in South Africa—Its Cause and Conduct*.	End of Boer War; coronation of Edward VII.
1903	'The Leather Funnel'.	George Orwell born. Henry James, *The Ambassadors*; Erskine Childers, *The Riddle of the Sands*; Joseph Conrad, *Typhoon*.
1905	*The Return of Sherlock Holmes*.	Trans-Siberian Railway opens; death of Jules Verne and Henry Irving; Albert Einstein, Theory of Special Relativity.
1906	Death of Louise Conan Doyle; stands as Liberal Unionist candidate in Hawick Burghs constituency; *Sir Nigel*.	San Francisco earthquake; Robert E. Howard and Samuel Beckett born.
1907	Marries Jean Leckie.	W. H. Auden born. Conrad, *The Secret Agent*; Rudyard Kipling wins Nobel Prize for Literature.
1908	Moves to Crowborough, Sussex; 'The Pot of Caviare'.	Ford Model T goes on sale. E. M. Foster, *A Room with a View*; Kenneth Grahame, *The Wind in the Willows*.
1909	'The Silver Mirror'; *The Crime of the Congo*.	Louis Bleriot flies across English Channel. Wells, *Tono-Bungay*.
1910	'The Terror of Blue John Gap'; 'Through the Veil'.	Mexican Revolution; first horror film released, an adaptation of *Frankenstein*; death of Mark Twain and Leo Tolstoy. Gaston Leroux, *The Phantom of the Opera*; Forster, *Howards End*.
1911	Converts to Irish Home Rule.	Stoker, *The Lair of the White Worm*; M. R. James, *More Ghost Stories of an Antiquary*; Conrad, *Under Western Eyes*; Einstein, General Theory of Relativity.

Life	*Cultural and Historical Background*
1912 *The Lost World.*	Republic of China formed; sinking of RMS *Titanic*; Woodrow Wilson elected US president; Scott Expedition to South Pole ends in disaster. Carl Jung, *Psychology of the Unconscious*; death of Bram Stoker.
1913 'How It Happened'; 'The Horror of the Heights'.	Freud, *Totem and Taboo*; D. H. Lawrence, *Sons and Lovers*; Marcel Proust, *Swann's Way*.
1914 *The Valley of Fear* begins publication in the *Strand*.	First World War begins; assassination of Archduke Franz Ferdinand of Austria; Irish Home Rule. James Joyce, *Dubliners*; Edgar Rice Burroughs, *Tarzan of the Apes*; Wyndham Lewis, *BLAST*, vol. i.
1918 Death of eldest son Kingsley from pneumonia after being wounded in battle; *The New Revelation*, first book on spiritualism.	First World War ends; influenza pandemic kills *c.*100,000,000 worldwide. Lytton Strachey, *Eminent Victorians*.
1919 Death of younger brother Innes; *The Vital Message*.	Benito Mussolini founds Italian Fascist movement; Amritsar Massacre; Treaty of Versailles; Irish War of Independence. M. R. James, *A Thin Ghost and Others*; Freud, 'The Uncanny'.
1921 'The Nightmare Room'; 'The Bully of Brocas Court'; death of mother Mary Doyle.	Irish War of Independence ends. Ludwig Wittgenstein, *Tractatus Logico-Philosophicus*.
1922 'The Lift'; *The Coming of the Fairies*.	Irish Civil War begins; death of Michael Collins and Erskine Childers; BBC formed. Joyce, *Ulysses*; T. S. Eliot, *The Waste Land*.
1924 *Memories and Adventures*.	Death of Lenin; Stalin assumes power in Russia.
1926 *The History of Spiritualism*, 2 vols.; *The Land of Mist*.	John Logie Baird demonstrates television; General Strike. A. A. Milne, *Winnie-the-Pooh*; T. E. Lawrence, *The Seven Pillars of Wisdom*.
1927 *The Casebook of Sherlock Holmes*.	Virginia Woolf, *To the Lighthouse*; J. W. Dunne, *An Experiment with Time*.
1930 Arthur Conan Doyle dies in Crowborough on 7 July.	Haile Selassie crowned emperor of Abyssinia; Mahatma Gandhi initiates Indian civil disobedience; death of D. H. Lawrence. William Faulkner, *As I Lay Dying*; Dashiell Hammett, *The Maltese Falcon*.

THE TALES

THE AMERICAN'S TALE

'It air strange, it air,' he was saying as I opened the door of the room where our social little semi-literary society met; 'but I could tell you queerer things than that 'ere—almighty queer things. You can't learn everything out of books, sirs, nohow. You see it ain't the men as can string English together and as has had good eddications as finds themselves in the queer places I've been in. They're mostly rough men, sirs, as can scarce speak aright, far less tell with pen and ink the things they've seen; but if they could they'd make some of your European's har riz with astonishment. They would, sirs, you bet!'

His name was Jefferson Adams, I believe; I know his initials were J.A., for you may see them yet deeply whittled on the right-hand upper panel of our smoking-room door. He left us this legacy, and also some artistic patterns done in tobacco juice upon our Turkey carpet; but beyond these reminiscences our American storyteller has vanished from our ken. He gleamed across our ordinary quiet conviviality like some brilliant meteor, and then was lost in the outer darkness. That night, however, our Nevada friend was in full swing; and I quietly lit my pipe and dropped into the nearest chair, anxious not to interrupt his story.

'Mind you,' he continued, 'I hain't got no grudge against your men of science. I likes and respects a chap as can match every beast and plant, from a huckleberry to a grizzly with a jaw-breakin' name; but if you wants real interestin' facts, something a bit juicy, you go to your whalers and your frontiersmen, and your scouts and Hudson Bay men,* chaps who mostly can scarce sign their names.'

There was a pause here, as Mr Jefferson Adams produced a long cheroot and lit it. We preserved a strict silence in the room, for we had already learned that on the slightest interruption our Yankee drew himself into his shell again. He glanced round with a self-satisfied smile as he remarked our expectant looks, and continued through a halo of smoke

'Now which of you gentlemen has ever been in Arizona? None, I'll warrant. And of all English or Americans as can put pen to paper, how many has been in Arizona? Precious few, I calc'late. I've been there, sirs, lived there for years; and when I think of what I've seen there, why, I can scarce get myself to believe it now.

'Ah, there's a country! I was one of Walker's filibusters,* as they chose to call us; and after we'd busted up, and the chief was shot, some on us made tracks and located down there. A reg'lar English and American colony, we was, with our wives and children, and all complete. I reckon there's some of the old folk there yet, and that they hain't forgotten what I'm agoing to tell you. No, I warrant they hain't, never on this side of the grave, sirs.

'I was talking about the country, though; and I guess I could astonish you considerable if I spoke of nothing else. To think of such a land being built for a few "Greasers"* and half-breeds! It's a misusing of the gifts of Providence, that's what I calls it. Grass as hung over a chap's head as he rode through it, and trees so thick that you couldn't catch a glimpse of blue sky for leagues and leagues, and orchids like umbrellas! Maybe some on you has seen a plant as they calls the "fly-catcher," in some parts of the States?'

'Dianœa muscipula,'* murmured Dawson, our scientific man *par excellence*.

'Ah, "Die near a municipal," that's him! You'll see a fly stand on that 'ere plant, and then you'll see the two sides of a leaf snap up together and catch it between them, and grind it up and mash it to bits, for all the world like some great sea squid with its beak; and hours after, if you open the leaf, you'll see the body lying half-digested, and in bits. Well, I've seen those flytraps in Arizona with leaves eight and ten feet long, and thorns or teeth a foot or more; why, they could—But darn it, I'm going too fast!

'It's about the death of Joe Hawkins I was going to tell you; 'bout as queer a thing, I reckon, as ever you heard tell on. There wasn't nobody in Montana as didn't know of Joe Hawkins—"Alabama" Joe, as he was called there. A reg'lar out and outer,* he was, 'bout the darndest skunk as ever man clapt eyes on. He was a good chap enough, mind ye, as long as you stroked him the right way; but rile him anyhow, and he were worse nor a wild-cat. I've seen him empty his six-shooter into a crowd as chanced to jostle him agoing into Simpson's bar when there was a dance on; and he bowied Tom Hooper 'cause he spilt his liquor over his weskit by mistake. No, he didn't stick at murder, Joe didn't; and he weren't a man to be trusted further nor you could see him.

'Now at the time I tell on, when Joe Hawkins was swaggerin' about the town and layin' down the law with his shootin'-irons, there was an Englishman there of the name of Scott—Tom Scott, if I rec'lects aright. This chap Scott was a thorough Britisher (beggin' the present company's pardon), and yet he didn't freeze much to the British set there, or they didn't freeze much to him. He was a quiet simple man, Scott was—rather too quiet for a rough set like that; sneakin' they called him, but he weren't that. He kept hisself mostly apart, an' didn't interfere with nobody so long as he were left alone. Some said as how he'd been kinder ill-treated at home—been a Chartist,* or something of that sort, and had to up stick and run; but he never spoke of it hisself, an' never complained. Bad luck or good, that chap kept a stiff lip on him.

'This chap Scott was a sort o' butt among the men about Montana, for he was so quiet an' simple-like. There was no party either to take up his grievances; for, as I've been saying, the Britishers hardly counted him one of them, and many a rough joke they played on him. He never cut up rough, but was polite to all hisself. I think the boys got to think he hadn't much grit in him till he showed 'em their mistake.

'It was in Simpson's bar as the row got up, an' that led to the queer thing I was going to tell you of. Alabama Joe and one or two other rowdies were dead on the Britishers in those days, and they spoke their opinions pretty free, though I warned them as there'd be an almighty muss. That partic'lar night Joe was nigh half drunk, an' he swaggered about the town with his six-shooter, lookin' out for a quarrel. Then he turned into the bar where he know'd he'd find some o' the English as ready for one as he was hisself. Sure enough, there was half a dozen lounging about, an' Tom Scott standin' alone before the stove. Joe sat down by the table, and put his revolver and bowie* down in front of him. "Them's my arguments, Jeff," he says to me, "if any white-livered Britisher dares give me the lie." I tried to stop him, sirs; but he weren't a man as you could easily turn, an' he began to speak in a way as no chap could stand. Why, even a "Greaser" would flare up if you said as much of Greaser-land! There was a commotion at the bar, an' every man laid his hands on his wepins; but afore they could draw we heard a quiet voice from the stove: "Say your prayers, Joe Hawkins; for, by Heaven, you're a dead man!" Joe turned round, and looked like grabbin' at his iron;* but it weren't no manner of use. Tom Scott was standing up, covering him with his Derringer;* a smile on his white face, but the very devil shining in his eye. "It ain't that the old country has used me over-well," he says, "but no man shall speak agin it afore me, and live." For a second or two I could see his finger tighten round the trigger, an' then he gave a laugh, an' threw the pistol on the floor. "No," he says, "I can't shoot a half-drunk man. Take your dirty life, Joe, an' use it better nor you have done. You've been nearer the grave this night than you will be agin until your time comes. You'd best make tracks now, I guess. Nay, never look black at me, man; I'm not afeard at your shootin'-iron. A bully's nigh always a coward." And he swung contemptuously round, and relit his half-smoked pipe from the stove; while Alabama slunk out o' the bar, with the laughs of the Britishers ringing in his ears. I saw his face as he passed me, and on it I saw murder, sirs— murder, as plain as ever I seed anything in my life.

'I stayed in the bar after the row, and watched Tom Scott as he shook hands with the men about. It seemed kinder queer to me to see him smilin' and cheerful-like; for I knew Joe's bloodthirsty mind, and that the Englishman had small chance of ever seeing the morning. He lived in an out-of-the-way sort of place, you see, clean off the trail, and had to pass through the Flytrap Gulch to get to it. This here gulch was a marshy gloomy place, lonely enough during the day even; for it were always a creepy sort o' thing to see the great eight- and ten-foot leaves snapping up if aught touched them; but at night there were never a soul near. Some parts of the marsh, too, were soft and deep, and a body thrown in would be gone by the morning. I could see Alabama Joe crouchin' under the leaves of the great Flytrap in the darkest part of the gulch, with a scowl on his face and a revolver in his hand; I could see it, sirs, as plain as with my two eyes.

''Bout midnight Simpson shuts up his bar, so out we had to go. Tom Scott started off for his three-mile walk at a slashing pace. I just dropped him a hint as he passed me, for I kinder liked the chap. "Keep your Derringer loose in your belt, sir," I says, "for you might chance to need it." He looked round at me with his quiet smile, and then I lost sight of him in the gloom. I never thought to see him again. He'd hardly gone afore Simpson comes up to me and says, "There'll be a nice job in the Flytrap Gulch to-night, Jeff; the boys say that Hawkins started half an hour ago to wait for Scott and shoot him on sight. I calc'late the coroner'll be wanted to-morrow."

'What passed in the gulch that night? It were a question as were asked pretty free next morning. A half-breed was in Ferguson's store after daybreak, and he said as he'd chanced to be near the gulch 'bout one in the morning. It warn't easy to get at his story, he seemed so uncommon scared; but he told us, at last, as he'd heard the fearfulest screams in the stillness of the night. There weren't no shots, he said, but scream after scream, kinder muffled, like a man with a serapé* over his head, an' in mortal pain. Abner Brandon and me, and a few more, was in the store at the time; so we mounted and rode out to Scott's house, passing through the gulch on the way. There weren't nothing partic'lar to be seen there—no blood nor marks of a fight, nor nothing; and when we gets up to Scott's house, out he comes to meet us as fresh as a lark. "Hullo, Jeff!" says he, "no need for the pistols after all. Come in an' have a cocktail, boys." "Did ye see or hear nothing as ye came home last night?" says I. "No," says he; "all was quiet enough. An owl kinder moaning in the Flytrap Gulch—that was all. Come, jump off and have a glass." "Thank ye," says Abner. So off we gets, and Tom Scott rode into the settlement with us when we went back.

'An allfired commotion was on in Main-street as we rode into it. The 'Merican party seemed to have gone clean crazed. Alabama Joe was gone, not a darned particle of him left. Since he went out to the gulch nary eye had seen him. As we got off our horses there was a considerable crowd in front of Simpson's, and some ugly looks at Tom Scott, I can tell you. There was a clickin' of pistols, and I saw as Scott had his hand in his bosom too. There weren't a single English face about. "Stand aside, Jeff Adams," says Zebb Humphrey, as great a scoundrel as ever lived, "you hain't got no hand in this game. Say, boys, are we, free Americans, to be murdered by any darned Britisher?" It was the quickest thing as ever I seed. There was a rush an' a crack; Zebb was down, with Scott's ball in his thigh, and Scott hisself was on the ground with a dozen men holding him. It weren't no use struggling, so he lay quiet. They seemed a bit uncertain what to do with him at first, but then one of Alabama's special chums put them up to it. "Joe's gone," he said; "nothing ain't surer nor that, an' there lies the man as killed him. Some on you knows as Joe went on business to the gulch last night; he never came back. That 'ere Britisher passed through after he'd gone; they'd had a row, screams is heard 'mong the great flytraps. I say agin he has played poor Joe some o' his sneakin'

tricks, an' thrown him into the swamp. It ain't no wonder as the body
is gone. But air we to stan' by and see English murderin' our own
chums? I guess not. Let Judge Lynch* try him, that's what I say."
"Lynch him!" shouted a hundred angry voices—for all the rag-tag
an' bobtail o' the settlement was round us by this time. "Here, boys,
fetch a rope, and swing him up. Up with him over Simpson's door!"
"See here though," says another, coming forrards; "let's hang him by
the great flytrap in the gulch. Let Joe see as he's revenged, if so be as
he's buried 'bout theer." There was a shout for this, an' away they
went, with Scott tied on his mustang in the middle, and a mounted
guard, with cocked revolvers, round him; for we knew as there was
a score or so Britishers about, as didn't seem to recognise Judge
Lynch, and was dead on a free fight.

'I went out with them, my heart bleedin' for Scott, though he
didn't seem a cent put out, he didn't. He were game to the backbone.
Seems kinder queer, sirs, hangin' a man to a flytrap; but our'n were
a reg'lar tree, and the leaves like a brace of boats with a hinge between
'em and thorns at the bottom.

'We passed down the gulch to the place where the great one grows,
and there we seed it with the leaves, some open, some shut. But we
seed something worse nor that. Standin' round the tree was some
thirty men, Britishers all, an' armed to the teeth. They was waitin' for
us evidently, an' had a businesslike look about 'em, as if they'd come
for something and meant to have it. There was the raw material there
for about as warm a scrimmidge as ever I seed. As we rode up, a great
red-bearded Scotchman—Cameron were his name—stood out afore
the rest, his revolver cocked in his hand. "See here, boys," he says,
"you've got no call to hurt a hair of that man's head. You hain't proved
as Joe is dead yet; and if you had, you hain't proved as Scott killed
him. Anyhow, it were in self-defence; for you all know as he was lying
in wait for Scott, to shoot him on sight; so I say agin, you hain't got no
call to hurt that man; and what's more, I've got thirty six-barrelled
arguments against your doin' it." "It's an interestin' pint, and worth
arguin' out," said the man as was Alabama Joe's special chum. There
was a clickin' of pistols, and a loosenin' of knives, and the two parties
began to draw up to one another, an' it looked like a rise in the mor-
tality of Montana. Scott was standing behind with a pistol at his ear if
he stirred, lookin' quiet and composed as having no money on the
table, when sudden he gives a start an' a shout as rang in our ears like

a trumpet. "Joe!" he cried, "Joe! Look at him! In the flytrap!" We all turned an' looked where he was pointin'. Jerusalem! I think we won't get that picter out of our minds agin. One of the great leaves of the flytrap, that had been shut and touchin' the ground as it lay, was slowly rolling back upon its hinges. There, lying like a child in its cradle, was Alabama Joe in the hollow of the leaf. The great thorns had been slowly driven through his heart as it shut upon him. We could see as he'd tried to cut his way out, for there was a slit in the thick fleshy leaf, an' his bowie was in his hand; but it had smothered him first. He'd lain down on it likely to keep the damp off while he were awaitin' for Scott, and it had closed on him as you've seen your little hothouse ones do on a fly; an' there he were as we found him, torn and crushed into pulp by the great jagged teeth of the man-eatin' plant. There, sirs, I think you'll own as that's a curious story.'

'And what became of Scott?' asked Jack Sinclair.

'Why, we carried him back on our shoulders, we did, to Simpson's bar, and he stood us liquors round. Made a speech too—a darned fine speech—from the counter. Somethin' about the British lion an' the 'Merican cagle walkin' arm in arm for ever an' a day. And now, sirs, that yarn was long, and my cheroot's out, so I reckon I'll make tracks afore it's later;' and with a 'Good-night!' he left the room.

*   *   *

'A most extraordinary narrative!' said Dawson. 'Who would have thought a Diancea had such power!'

'Deuced rum yarn!' said young Sinclair.

'Evidently a matter-of-fact truthful man,' said the doctor.

'Or the most original liar that ever lived,' said I.

I wonder which he was.

THE CAPTAIN OF THE 'POLESTAR'

[Being an extract from the singular journal of JOHN M'ALISTER RAY, student of medicine.]

SEPTEMBER 11*th*.—Lat. 81° 40′ N.; long. 2° E.* Still lying-to amid enormous ice-fields. The one which stretches away to the north of us, and to which our ice-anchor is attached, cannot be smaller than an English county. To the right and left unbroken sheets extend to the horizon. This morning the mate reported that there were signs of pack ice to the southward. Should this form of sufficient thickness to bar our return, we shall be in a position of danger, as the food, I hear, is already running somewhat short. It is late in the season, and the nights are beginning to reappear. This morning I saw a star twinkling just over the fore-yard, the first since the beginning of May. There is considerable discontent among the crew, many of whom are anxious to get back home to be in time for the herring season, when labour always commands a high price upon the Scotch coast. As yet their displeasure is only signified by sullen countenances and black looks, but I heard from the second mate this afternoon that they contemplated sending a deputation to the captain to explain their grievance. I much doubt how he will receive it, as he is a man of fierce temper, and very sensitive about anything approaching to an infringement of his rights. I shall venture after dinner to say a few words to him upon the subject. I have always found that he will tolerate from me what he would resent from any other member of the crew. Amsterdam Island, at the north-west corner of Spitzbergen,* is visible upon our starboard quarter—a rugged line of volcanic rocks, intersected by white seams, which represent glaciers. It is curious to think that at the present moment there is probably no human being nearer to us than the Danish settlements in the south of Greenland— a good nine hundred miles as the crow flies. A captain takes a great responsibility upon himself when he risks his vessel under such circumstances. No whaler* has ever remained in these latitudes till so advanced a period of the year.

9 P.M.—I have spoken to Captain Craigie, and though the result has been hardly satisfactory, I am bound to say that he listened to

what I had to say very quietly and even deferentially. When I had finished he put on that air of iron determination which I have frequently observed upon his face, and paced rapidly backwards and forwards across the narrow cabin for some minutes. At first I feared that I had seriously offended him, but he dispelled the idea by sitting down again, and putting his hand upon my arm with a gesture which almost amounted to a caress. There was a depth of tenderness too in his wild dark eyes which surprised me considerably. 'Look here, Doctor,' he said, 'I'm sorry I ever took you—I am indeed—and I would give fifty pounds this minute to see you standing safe upon the Dundee* quay. It's hit or miss with me this time. There are fish to the north of us. How dare you shake your head, sir, when I tell you I saw them blowing from the masthead?'—this in a sudden burst of fury, though I was not conscious of having shown any signs of doubt. 'Two-and-twenty fish in as many minutes as I am a living man, and not one under ten foot.[1] Now, Doctor, do you think I can leave the country when there is only one infernal strip of ice between me and my fortune? If it came on to blow from the north to-morrow we could fill the ship and be away before the frost could catch us. If it came on to blow from the south—well, I suppose the men are paid for risking their lives, and as for myself it matters but little to me, for I have more to bind me to the other world than to this one. I confess that I am sorry for *you*, though. I wish I had old Angus Tait who was with me last voyage, for he was a man that would never be missed, and you—you said once that you were engaged, did you not?'

'Yes,' I answered, snapping the spring of the locket which hung from my watch-chain, and holding up the little vignette of Flora.

'Curse you!' he yelled, springing out of his seat, with his very beard bristling with passion. 'What is your happiness to me? What have I to do with her that you must dangle her photograph before my eyes?' I almost thought that he was about to strike me in the frenzy of his rage, but with another imprecation he dashed open the door of the cabin and rushed out upon deck, leaving me considerably astonished at his extraordinary violence. It is the first time that he has ever shown me anything but courtesy and kindness. I can hear him pacing excitedly up and down overhead as I write these lines.

[1] A whale is measured among whalers not by the length of its body, but by the length of its whalebone.

I should like to give a sketch of the character of this man, but it seems presumptuous to attempt such a thing upon paper, when the idea in my own mind is at best a vague and uncertain one. Several times I have thought that I grasped the clue which might explain it, but only to be disappointed by his presenting himself in some new light which would upset all my conclusions. It may be that no human eye but my own shall ever rest upon these lines, yet as a psychological study I shall attempt to leave some record of Captain Nicholas Craigie.

A man's outer case generally gives some indication of the soul within. The captain is tall and well-formed, with dark, handsome face, and a curious way of twitching his limbs, which may arise from nervousness, or be simply an outcome of his excessive energy. His jaw and whole cast of countenance is manly and resolute, but the eyes are the distinctive feature of his face. They are of the very darkest hazel, bright and eager, with a singular mixture of recklessness in their expression, and of something else which I have sometimes thought was more allied with horror than any other emotion. Generally the former predominated, but on occasions, and more particularly when he was thoughtfully inclined, the look of fear would spread and deepen until it imparted a new character to his whole countenance. It is at these times that he is most subject to tempestuous fits of anger, and he seems to be aware of it, for I have known him lock himself up so that no one might approach him until his dark hour was passed. He sleeps badly, and I have heard him shouting during the night, but his cabin is some little distance from mine, and I could never distinguish the words which he said.

This is one phase of his character, and the most disagreeable one. It is only through my close association with him, thrown together as we are day after day, that I have observed it. Otherwise he is an agreeable companion, well-read and entertaining, and as gallant a seaman as ever trod a deck. I shall not easily forget the way in which he handled the ship when we were caught by a gale among the loose ice at the beginning of April. I have never seen him so cheerful, and even hilarious, as he was that night, as he paced backwards and forwards upon the bridge amid the flashing of the lightning and the howling of the wind. He has told me several times that the thought of death was a pleasant one to him, which is a sad thing for a young man to say; he cannot be much more than thirty, though his hair and moustache are already slightly grizzled. Some great sorrow must have overtaken him and blighted his whole life. Perhaps I should be the same if I lost my Flora—God knows! I think if it were not for her that I should care very little whether the wind blew from the north or the south to-morrow. There, I hear him come down the companion, and he has locked himself up in his room, which shows that he is still in an unamiable mood. And so to bed, as old Pepys* would say, for the candle is burning down (we have to use them now since the nights are closing in), and the steward has turned in, so there are no hopes of another one.

September 12th.—Calm, clear day, and still lying in the same position. What wind there is comes from the south-east, but it is very slight. Captain is in a better humour, and apologised to me at breakfast for his rudeness. He still looks somewhat distrait,* however, and retains that wild look in his eyes which in a Highlander would mean that he was 'fey'*—at least so our chief engineer remarked to me, and he has some reputation among the Celtic portion of our crew as a seer and expounder of omens.

It is strange that superstition should have obtained such mastery over this hard-headed and practical race. I could not have believed to what an extent it is carried had I not observed it for myself. We have had a perfect epidemic of it this voyage, until I have felt inclined to serve out rations of sedatives and nerve-tonics with the Saturday allowance of grog. The first symptom of it was that shortly after leaving Shetland the men at the wheel used to complain that they heard plaintive cries and screams in the wake of the ship, as if something were following it and were unable to overtake it. This fiction has been kept up during the whole voyage, and on dark nights at the beginning of the seal-fishing it was only with great difficulty that men could be induced to do their spell. No doubt what they heard was either the creaking of the rudder-chains, or the cry of some passing sea-bird. I have been fetched out of bed several times to listen to it, but I need hardly say that I was never able to distinguish anything unnatural. The men, however, are so absurdly positive upon the subject that it is hopeless to argue with them. I mentioned the matter to the captain once, but to my surprise he took it very gravely, and indeed appeared to be considerably disturbed by what I told him. I should have thought that he at least would have been above such vulgar delusions.

All this disquisition upon superstition leads me up to the fact that Mr Manson, our second mate, saw a ghost last night—or, at least, says that he did, which of course is the same thing. It is quite refreshing to have some new topic of conversation after the eternal routine of bears and whales which has served us for so many months. Manson swears the ship is haunted, and that he would not stay in her a day if he had any other place to go to. Indeed the fellow is honestly frightened, and I had to give him some chloral and bromide of potassium* this morning to steady him down. He seemed quite indignant when I suggested that he had been having an extra glass the night before, and I was obliged to pacify him by keeping as grave a countenance as possible during his story, which he certainly narrated in a very straightforward and matter-of-fact way.

'I was on the bridge,' he said, 'about four bells in the middle watch,* just when the night was at its darkest. There was a bit of a moon, but the clouds were blowing across it so that you couldn't see far from the ship. John M'Leod, the harpooner, came aft from the fo'c'sle-head* and reported a strange noise on the starboard bow. I went forrard and we both heard it, sometimes like a bairn crying and sometimes like a wench in pain. I've been seventeen years to the country and I never heard seal, old or young, make a sound like that. As we were standing there on the fo'c'sle-head the moon came out from behind a cloud, and we both saw a sort of white figure moving across the icefield in the same direction that we had heard the cries. We lost sight of it for a while, but it came back on the port bow, and we could just make it out like a shadow on the ice. I sent a hand aft for the rifles, and M'Leod and I went down on to the pack, thinking that maybe it might be a bear. When we got on the ice I lost sight of M'Leod, but I pushed on in the direction where I could still hear the cries. I followed them for a mile or maybe more, and then running round a hummock I came right on to the top of it standing and waiting for me seemingly. I don't know what it was. It wasn't a bear, anyway. It was tall and white and straight, and if it wasn't a man nor a woman, I'll stake my davy* it was something worse. I made for the ship as hard as I could run, and precious glad I was to find myself aboard. I signed articles to do my duty by the ship, and on the ship I'll stay, but you don't catch me on the ice again after sundown.'

That is his story, given as far as I can in his own words. I fancy what he saw must, in spite of his denial, have been a young bear erect upon its hind legs, an attitude which they often assume when alarmed. In the uncertain light this would bear a resemblance to a human figure, especially to a man whose nerves were already somewhat shaken. Whatever it may have been, the occurrence is unfortunate, for it has produced a most unpleasant effect upon the crew. Their looks are more sullen than before, and their discontent more open. The double grievance of being debarred from the herring fishing and of being detained in what they choose to call a haunted vessel, may lead them to do something rash. Even the harpooners, who are the oldest and steadiest among them, are joining in the general agitation.

Apart from this absurd outbreak of superstition, things are looking rather more cheerful. The pack which was forming to the south of us has partly cleared away, and the water is so warm as to lead me to believe that we are lying in one of those branches of the gulfstream which run up between Greenland and Spitzbergen. There are numerous small Medusæ and sea-lemons* about the ship, with abundance of shrimps, so that there is every possibility of 'fish' being sighted. Indeed one was seen blowing about dinner-time, but in such a position that it was impossible for the boats to follow it.

September 13th.—Had an interesting conversation with the chief mate, Mr Milne, upon the bridge. It seems that our captain is as great an enigma to the seamen, and even to the owners of the vessel, as he has been to me. Mr Milne tells me that when the ship is paid off, upon returning from a voyage, Captain Craigie disappears, and is not seen again until the approach of another season, when he walks quietly into the office of the company, and asks whether his services will be required. He has no friend in Dundee, nor does anyone pretend to be acquainted with his early history. His position depends entirely upon his skill as a seaman, and the name for courage and coolness which he had earned in the capacity of mate, before being entrusted with a separate command. The unanimous opinion seems to be that he is not a Scotchman, and that his name is an assumed one. Mr Milne thinks that he has devoted himself to whaling simply for the reason that it is the most dangerous occupation which he could select, and that he courts death in every possible manner. He mentioned several instances of this, one of which is rather curious, if true. It seems that on one occasion he did not put in an appearance at the office, and a substitute had to be selected in his place. That was at the time of the last Russian and Turkish War.* When he turned up again next spring he had a puckered wound in the side of his neck which he used to endeavour to conceal with his cravat. Whether the mate's inference that he had been engaged in the war is true or not I cannot say. It was certainly a strange coincidence.

The wind is veering round in an easterly direction, but is still very slight. I think the ice is lying closer than it did yesterday. As far as the eye can reach on every side there is one wide expanse of spotless white, only broken by an occasional rift or the dark shadow of a hummock. To the south there is the narrow lane of blue water which is our sole means of escape, and which is closing up every day. The captain is taking a heavy responsibility upon himself. I hear that the tank of potatoes has been finished, and even the biscuits are running short, but he preserves the same impassable* countenance, and spends the greater part of the day at the crow's nest, sweeping the horizon with his glass. His manner is very variable, and he seems to avoid my society, but there has been no repetition of the violence which he showed the other night.

7.30 P.M.—My deliberate opinion is that we are commanded by a madman. Nothing else can account for the extraordinary vagaries of Captain Craigie. It is fortunate that I have kept this journal of our voyage, as it will serve to justify us in case we have to put him under any sort of restraint, a step which I should only consent to as a last resource. Curiously enough it was he himself who suggested lunacy and not mere eccentricity as the secret of his strange conduct. He was standing upon the bridge about an hour ago, peering as usual through his glass, while I was walking up and down the quarter-deck. The majority of the men were below at their tea, for the watches have not been regularly kept of late. Tired of walking, I leaned against the bulwarks, and admired the mellow glow cast by the sinking sun upon the great ice-fields which surround us. I was suddenly aroused from the reverie into which I had fallen by a hoarse voice at my elbow, and starting round I found that the captain had descended and was standing by my side. He was staring out over the ice with an expression in which horror, surprise, and something approaching to joy were contending for the mastery. In spite of the cold, great drops of perspiration were coursing down his forehead, and he was evidently fearfully excited. His limbs twitched like those of a man upon the verge of an epileptic fit, and the lines about his mouth were drawn and hard.

'Look!' he gasped, seizing me by the wrist, but still keeping his eyes upon the distant ice, and moving his head slowly in a horizontal direction, as if following some object which was moving across the field of

vision. 'Look! There, man, there! Between the hummocks! Now coming out from behind the far one! You see her—you *must* see her!
There still! Flying from me, by God, flying from me—and gone!'

He uttered the last two words in a whisper of concentrated agony
which shall never fade from my remembrance. Clinging to the
ratlines* he endeavoured to climb up upon the top of the bulwarks as
if in the hope of obtaining a last glance at the departing object. His
strength was not equal to the attempt, however, and he staggered back
against the saloon skylights, where he leaned panting and exhausted.
His face was so livid that I expected him to become unconscious, so
lost no time in leading him down the companion, and stretching him
upon one of the sofas in the cabin. I then poured him out some
brandy, which I held to his lips, and which had a wonderful effect
upon him, bringing the blood back into his white face and steadying
his poor shaking limbs. He raised himself up upon his elbow, and
looking round to see that we were alone, he beckoned to me to come
and sit beside him.

'You saw it, didn't you?' he asked, still in the same subdued awesome
tone so foreign to the nature of the man.

'No, I saw nothing.'

His head sank back again upon the cushions. 'No, he wouldn't
without the glass,' he murmured. 'He couldn't. It was the glass that
showed her to me, and then the eyes of love—the eyes of love. I say,
Doc, don't let the steward in! He'll think I'm mad. Just bolt the door,
will you!'

I rose and did what he had commanded.

He lay quiet for a while, lost in thought apparently, and then raised
himself up upon his elbow again, and asked for some more brandy.

'You don't think I am, do you, Doc?' he asked, as I was putting the
bottle back into the after-locker. 'Tell me now, as man to man, do you
think that I am mad?'

'I think you have something on your mind,' I answered, 'which is
exciting you and doing you a good deal of harm.'

'Right there, lad!' he cried, his eyes sparkling from the effects of
the brandy. 'Plenty on my mind—plenty! But I can work out the latitude and the longitude, and I can handle my sextant and manage my
logarithms. You couldn't prove me mad in a court of law, could you,
now?' It was curious to hear the man lying back and coolly arguing
out the question of his own sanity.

'Perhaps not,' I said; 'but still I think you would be wise to get home as soon as you can, and settle down to a quiet life for a while.'

'Get home, eh?' he muttered, with a sneer upon his face. 'One word for me and two for yourself, lad. Settle down with Flora—pretty little Flora. Are bad dreams signs of madness?'

'Sometimes,' I answered.

'What else? What would be the first symptoms?'

'Pains in the head, noises in the ears, flashes before the eyes, delusions——'

'Ah! what about them?' he interrupted. 'What would you call a delusion?'

'Seeing a thing which is not there is a delusion.'

'But she *was* there!' he groaned to himself. 'She *was* there!' and rising, he unbolted the door and walked with slow and uncertain steps to his own cabin, where I have no doubt that he will remain until to-morrow morning. His system seems to have received a terrible shock, whatever it may have been that he imagined himself to have seen. The man becomes a greater mystery every day, though I fear that the solution which he has himself suggested is the correct one, and that his reason is affected. I do not think that a guilty conscience has anything to do with his behaviour. The idea is a popular one among the officers, and, I believe, the crew; but I have seen nothing to support it. He has not the air of a guilty man, but of one who has had terrible usage at the hands of fortune, and who should be regarded as a martyr rather than a criminal.

The wind is veering round to the south to-night. God help us if it blocks that narrow pass which is our only road to safety! Situated as we are on the edge of the main Arctic pack, or the 'barrier' as it is called by the whalers, any wind from the north has the effect of shredding out the ice around us and allowing our escape, while a wind from the south blows up all the loose ice behind us, and hems us in between two packs. God help us, I say again!

September 14*th.*—Sunday, and a day of rest. My fears have been confirmed, and the thin strip of blue water has disappeared from the southward. Nothing but the great motionless ice-fields around us, with their weird hummocks and fantastic pinnacles. There is a deathly silence over their wide expanse which is horrible. No lapping of the waves now, no cries of seagulls or straining of sails, but one deep universal silence in which the murmurs of the seamen, and the creak of their boots upon the white shining deck, seem discordant and out of place. Our only visitor was an Arctic fox, a rare animal upon the pack, though common enough upon the land. He did not come near the ship, however, but after surveying us from a distance fled rapidly across the ice. This was curious conduct, as they generally know nothing of man, and being of an impulsive nature, become so familiar that they are easily captured. Incredible as it may seem, even this little incident produced a bad effect upon the crew. 'Yon puir beastie kens mair, ay, an' sees mair nor you nor me!'* was the comment of one of the leading harpooners, and the others nodded their acquiescence. It is vain to attempt to argue against such puerile superstition. They have made up their minds that there is a curse upon the ship, and nothing will ever persuade them to the contrary.

The captain remained in seclusion all day except for about half an hour in the afternoon, when he came out upon the quarter-deck. I observed that he kept his eye fixed upon the spot where the vision of yesterday had appeared, and was quite prepared for another outburst, but none such came. He did not seem to see me, although I was standing close beside him. Divine service was read as usual, by the chief engineer. It is a curious thing that in whaling vessels the Church of England Prayer-book is always employed, although there is never a member of that Church among either officers or crew. Our men are all Roman Catholics or Presbyterians, the former predominating. Since a ritual is used which is foreign to both, neither can complain that the other is preferred to them, and they listen with all attention and devotion, so that the system has something to recommend it.

A glorious sunset, which made the great fields of ice look like a lake of blood. I have never seen a finer and at the same time more weird effect. Wind is veering round. If it will blow twenty-four hours from the north all will yet be well.

September 15*th*.—To-day is Flora's birthday. Dear lass! it is well that she cannot see her boy, as she used to call me, shut up among the ice-fields with a crazy captain and a few weeks' provisions. No doubt she scans the shipping list in the *Scotsman** every morning to see if we are reported from Shetland. I have to set an example to the men and look cheery and unconcerned; but God knows, my heart is very heavy at times.

The thermometer is at nineteen Fahrenheit to-day. There is but little wind, and what there is comes from an unfavourable quarter.

Captain is in an excellent humour; I think he imagines he has seen
some other omen or vision, poor fellow, during the night, for he came
into my room early in the morning, and stooping down over my bunk,
whispered, 'It wasn't a delusion, Doc; it's all right!' After breakfast he
asked me to find out how much food was left, which the second mate
and I proceeded to do. It is even less than we had expected. Forward
they have half a tank full of biscuits, three barrels of salt meat, and
a very limited supply of coffee beans and sugar. In the after-hold and
lockers there are a good many luxuries, such as tinned salmon, soups,
haricot mutton,* etc., but they will go a very short way among a crew
of fifty men. There are two barrels of flour in the store-room, and an
unlimited supply of tobacco. Altogether there is about enough to keep
the men on half rations for eighteen or twenty days—certainly not
more. When we reported the state of things to the captain, he ordered
all hands to be piped,* and addressed them from the quarter-deck.
I never saw him to better advantage. With his tall, well-knit figure, and
dark animated face, he seemed a man born to command, and he discussed the situation in a cool sailor-like way which showed that while
appreciating the danger he had an eye for every loophole of escape.

   'My lads,' he said, 'no doubt you think I brought you into this fix,
if it is a fix, and maybe some of you feel bitter against me on account
of it. But you must remember that for many a season no ship that
comes to the country has brought in as much oil-money as the old
Polestar, and every one of you has had his share of it. You can leave
your wives behind you in comfort, while other poor fellows come back
to find their lassies on the parish.* If you have to thank me for the one
you have to thank me for the other, and we may call it quits. We've
tried a bold venture before this and succeeded, so now that we've tried
one and failed we've no cause to cry out about it. If the worst comes
to the worst, we can make the land across the ice, and lay in a stock of
seals which will keep us alive until the spring. It won't come to that,
though, for you'll see the Scotch coast again before three weeks are
out. At present every man must go on half rations, share and share
alike, and no favour to any. Keep up your hearts and you'll pull
through this as you've pulled through many a danger before.' These
few simple words of his had a wonderful effect upon the crew. His
former unpopularity was forgotten, and the old harpooner whom
I have already mentioned for his superstition, led off three cheers,
which were heartily joined in by all hands.

September 16*th.*—The wind has veered round to the north during the night, and the ice shows some symptoms of opening out. The men are in a good humour in spite of the short allowance upon which they have been placed. Steam is kept up in the engine-room, that there may be no delay should an opportunity for escape present itself. The captain is in exuberant spirits, though he still retains that wild 'fey' expression which I have already remarked upon. This burst of cheerfulness puzzles me more than his former gloom. I cannot understand it. I think I mentioned in an early part of this journal that one of his oddities is that he never permits any person to enter his cabin, but insists upon making his own bed, such as it is, and performing every other office for himself. To my surprise he handed me the key to-day and requested me to go down there and take the time by his chronometer while he measured the altitude of the sun at noon. It is a bare little room, containing a washing-stand and a few books, but little else in the way of luxury, except some pictures upon the walls. The majority of these are small cheap oleographs,* but there was one water-colour sketch of the head of a young lady which arrested my attention. It was evidently a portrait, and not one of those fancy types of female beauty which sailors particularly affect. No artist could have evolved from his own mind such a curious mixture of character and weakness. The languid, dreamy eyes, with their drooping lashes, and the broad, low brow, unruffled by thought or care, were in strong contrast with the clean-cut, prominent jaw, and the resolute set of the lower lip. Underneath it in one of the corners was written, 'M.B., æt.* 19.' That anyone in the short space of nineteen years of existence could develop such strength of will as was stamped upon her face seemed to me at the time to be well-nigh incredible. She must have been an extraordinary woman. Her features have thrown such a glamour over me that, though I had but a fleeting glance at them, I could, were I a draughtsman, reproduce them line for line upon this page of the journal. I wonder what part she has played in our captain's life. He has hung her picture at the end of his berth, so that his eyes continually rest upon it. Were he a less reserved man I should make some remark upon the subject. Of the other things in his cabin there was nothing worthy of mention—uniform coats, a camp-stool, small looking-glass, tobacco-box, and numerous pipes, including an oriental hookah—which, by the by, gives some colour to Mr Milne's story about his participation in the war, though the connection may seem rather a distant one.

11.20 P.M.—Captain just gone to bed after a long and interesting conversation on general topics. When he chooses he can be a most fascinating companion, being remarkably well-read, and having the power of expressing his opinion forcibly without appearing to be dogmatic. I hate to have my intellectual toes trod upon. He spoke about the nature of the soul, and sketched out the views of Aristotle and Plato* upon the subject in a masterly manner. He seems to have a leaning for metempsychosis and the doctrines of Pythagoras.* In discussing them we touched upon modern spiritualism, and I made some joking allusion to the impostures of Slade,* upon which, to my surprise, he warned me most impressively against confusing the innocent with the guilty, and argued that it would be as logical to brand Christianity as an error because Judas, who professed that religion, was a villain. He shortly afterwards bade me good night and retired to his room.

The wind is freshening up, and blows steadily from the north. The nights are as dark now as they are in England. I hope to-morrow may set us free from our frozen fetters.

September 17*th.*—The Bogie* again. Thank Heaven that I have strong nerves! The superstition of these poor fellows, and the circumstantial accounts which they give, with the utmost earnestness and self-conviction, would horrify any man not accustomed to their ways. There are many versions of the matter, but the sum-total of them all is that something uncanny has been flitting round the ship all night, and that Sandie M'Donald of Peterhead* and 'lang' Peter Williamson of Shetland saw it, as also did Mr Milne on the bridge—so, having three witnesses, they can make a better case of it than the second mate did. I spoke to Milne after breakfast, and told him that he should be above such nonsense, and that as an officer he ought to set the men a better example. He shook his weather-beaten head ominously, but answered with characteristic caution, 'Mebbe, aye, mebbe na, Doctor,' he said, 'I didna ca' it a ghaist. I canna' say I preen my faith in seabogles an' the like, though there's a mony as claims to ha' seen a' that and waur.* I'm no easy feared, but maybe your ain bluid would run a bit cauld, mun, if instead o' speerin' aboot it in daylicht ye were wi' me last night, an' seed an awfu' like shape, white an' gruesome, whiles here, whiles there, an' it greetin' and ca'ing in the darkness like a bit lambie that hae lost its mither. Ye would na' be sae ready to put it a' doon to auld wives' clavers* then, I'm thinkin'.' I saw it was hopeless to reason with him, so contented myself with begging him as a personal favour to call me up the next time the spectre appeared—a request to which he acceded with many ejaculations expressive of his hopes that such an opportunity might never arise.

As I had hoped, the white desert behind us has become broken by many thin streaks of water which intersect it in all directions. Our latitude to-day was 80° 52' N., which shows that there is a strong southerly drift upon the pack. Should the wind continue favourable it will break up as rapidly as it formed. At present we can do nothing but smoke and wait and hope for the best. I am rapidly becoming a fatalist. When dealing with such uncertain factors as wind and ice a man can be nothing else. Perhaps it was the wind and sand of the Arabian deserts which gave the minds of the original followers of Mahomet their tendency to bow to kismet.

These spectral alarms have a very bad effect upon the captain. I feared that it might excite his sensitive mind, and endeavoured to conceal the absurd story from him, but unfortunately he overheard one of the men making an allusion to it, and insisted upon being informed about it. As I had expected, it brought out all his latent lunacy in an exaggerated form. I can hardly believe that this is the same man who discoursed philosophy last night with the most critical acumen and coolest judgment. He is pacing backwards and forwards upon the quarter-deck like a caged tiger, stopping now and again to throw out his hands with a yearning gesture, and stare impatiently out over the ice. He keeps up a continual mutter to himself, and once he called out, 'But a little time, love—but a little time!' Poor fellow, it is sad to see a gallant seaman and accomplished gentleman reduced to such a pass, and to think that imagination and delusion can cow a mind to which real danger was but the salt of life. Was ever a man in such a position as I, between a demented captain and a ghost-seeing mate? I sometimes think I am the only really sane man aboard the vessel— except perhaps the second engineer, who is a kind of ruminant, and would care nothing for all the fiends in the Red Sea so long as they would leave him alone and not disarrange his tools.

The ice is still opening rapidly, and there is every probability of our being able to make a start to-morrow morning. They will think I am inventing when I tell them at home all the strange things that have befallen me.

12 P.M.—I have been a good deal startled, though I feel steadier

now, thanks to a stiff glass of brandy. I am hardly myself yet, however, as this handwriting will testify. The fact is, that I have gone through a very strange experience, and am beginning to doubt whether I was justified in branding everyone on board as madmen because they professed to have seen things which did not seem reasonable to my understanding. Pshaw! I am a fool to let such a trifle unnerve me; and yet, coming as it does after all these alarms, it has an additional significance, for I cannot doubt either Mr Manson's story or that of the mate, now that I have experienced that which I used formerly to scoff at.

After all it was nothing very alarming—a mere sound, and that was all. I cannot expect that anyone reading this, if anyone ever should read it, will sympathise with my feelings, or realize the effect which it produced upon me at the time. Supper was over, and I had gone on deck to have a quiet pipe before turning in. The night was very dark—so dark that, standing under the quarter-boat,* I was unable to see the officer upon the bridge. I think I have already mentioned the extraordinary silence which prevails in these frozen seas. In other parts of the world, be they ever so barren, there is some slight vibration of the air—some faint hum, be it from the distant haunts of men, or from the leaves of the trees or the wings of the birds, or even the faint rustle of the grass that covers the ground. One may not actively perceive the sound, and yet if it were withdrawn it would be missed. It is only here in these Arctic seas that stark, unfathomable stillness obtrudes itself upon you all in its gruesome reality. You find your tympanum* straining to catch some little murmur, and dwelling eagerly upon every accidental sound within the vessel. In this state I was leaning against the bulwarks when there arose from the ice almost directly underneath me a cry, sharp and shrill, upon the silent air of the night, beginning, as it seemed to me, at a note such as prima donna never reached, and mounting from that ever higher and higher until it culminated in a long wail of agony, which might have been the last cry of a lost soul. The ghastly scream is still ringing in my ears. Grief, unutterable grief, seemed to be expressed in it, and a great longing, and yet through it all there was an occasional wild note of exultation. It shrilled out from close beside me, and yet as I glared into the darkness I could discern nothing. I waited some little time, but without hearing any repetition of the sound, so I came below, more shaken than I have ever been in my life before. As I came down the companion I met Mr Milne coming up to relieve the watch. 'Weel, Doctor,' he said, 'maybe that's auld wives' clavers tae? Did ye no hear it skirling?* Maybe that's a supersteetion? What d'ye think o't noo?' I was obliged to apologise to the honest fellow, and acknowledge that I was as puzzled by it as he was. Perhaps to-morrow things may look different. At present I dare hardly write all that I think. Reading it again in days to come, when I have shaken off all these associations, I should despise myself for having been so weak.

September 18th.—Passed a restless and uneasy night, still haunted by that strange sound. The captain does not look as if he had had much repose either, for his face is haggard and his eyes bloodshot. I have not told him of my adventure of last night, nor shall I. He is already restless and excited, standing up, sitting down, and apparently utterly unable to keep still.

A fine lead appeared in the pack this morning, as I had expected, and we were able to cast off our ice-anchor, and steam about twelve miles in a west-sou'-westerly direction. We were then brought to a halt by a great floe as massive as any which we have left behind us. It bars our progress completely, so we can do nothing but anchor again and wait until it breaks up, which it will probably do within twenty-four hours, if the wind holds. Several bladder-nosed seals* were seen swimming in the water, and one was shot, an immense creature more than eleven feet long. They are fierce, pugnacious animals, and are said to be more than a match for a bear. Fortunately they are slow and clumsy in their movements, so that there is little danger in attacking them upon the ice.

The captain evidently does not think we have seen the last of our troubles, though why he should take a gloomy view of the situation is more than I can fathom, since everyone else on board considers that we have had a miraculous escape, and are sure now to reach the open sea.

'I suppose you think it's all right now, Doctor?' he said, as we sat together after dinner.

'I hope so,' I answered.

'We mustn't be too sure—and yet no doubt you are right. We'll all be in the arms of our own true loves before long, lad, won't we? But we mustn't be too sure—we mustn't be too sure.'

He sat silent a little, swinging his leg thoughtfully backwards and forwards. 'Look here,' he continued; 'it's a dangerous place this, even at its best—a treacherous, dangerous place. I have known men cut off very suddenly in a land like this. A slip would do it sometimes—a single slip, and down you go through a crack, and only a bubble on the green water to show where it was that you sank. It's a queer thing,' he continued with a nervous laugh, 'but all the years I've been in this country I never once thought of making a will—not that I have anything to leave in particular, but still when a man is exposed to danger he should have everything arranged and ready—don't you think so?'

'Certainly,' I answered, wondering what on earth he was driving at.

'He feels better for knowing it's all settled,' he went on. 'Now if anything should ever befall me, I hope that you will look after things for me. There is very little in the cabin, but such as it is I should like it to be sold, and the money divided in the same proportion as the oil-money among the crew. The chronometer I wish you to keep yourself as some slight remembrance of our voyage. Of course all this is a mere precaution, but I thought I would take the opportunity of speaking to you about it. I suppose I might rely upon you if there were any necessity?'

'Most assuredly,' I answered; 'and since you are taking this step, I may as well——'

'You! you!' he interrupted. *'You're* all right. What the devil is the matter with *you?* There, I didn't mean to be peppery, but I don't like to hear a young fellow, that has hardly began life, speculating about death. Go up on deck and get some fresh air into your lungs instead of talking nonsense in the cabin, and encouraging me to do the same.'

The more I think of this conversation of ours the less do I like it. Why should the man be settling his affairs at the very time when we seem to be emerging from all danger? There must be some method in his madness. Can it be that he contemplates suicide? I remember that upon one occasion he spoke in a deeply reverent manner of the heinousness of the crime of self-destruction. I shall keep my eye upon him, however, and though I cannot obtrude upon the privacy of his cabin, I shall at least make a point of remaining on deck as long as he stays up.

Mr Milne pooh-poohs my fears, and says it is only the 'skipper's little way.' He himself takes a very rosy view of the situation. According to him we shall be out of the ice by the day after to-morrow, pass Jan Meyen* two days after that, and sight Shetland in little more than a week. I hope he may not be too sanguine. His opinion may be fairly balanced against the gloomy precautions of the captain, for he is an

old and experienced seaman, and weighs his words well before uttering them.

* * *

The long-impending catastrophe has come at last, I hardly know
what to write about it. The captain is gone. He may come back to us
again alive, but I fear me* I fear me. It is now seven o'clock of the
morning of the 19th of September. I have spent the whole night
traversing the great ice-floe in front of us with a party of seamen in
the hope of coming upon some trace of him, but in vain. I shall try to
give some account of the circumstances which attended upon his disappearance. Should anyone ever chance to read the words which I put
down, I trust they will remember that I do not write from conjecture
or from hearsay, but that I, a sane and educated man, am describing
accurately what actually occurred before my very eyes. My inferences
are my own, but I shall be answerable for the facts.

The captain remained in excellent spirits after the conversation
which I have recorded. He appeared to be nervous and impatient,
however, frequently changing his position, and moving his limbs in
an aimless choreic* way which is characteristic of him at times. In
a quarter of an hour he went upon deck seven times, only to descend
after a few hurried paces. I followed him each time, for there was
something about his face which confirmed my resolution of not letting him out of my sight. He seemed to observe the effect which his
movements had produced, for he endeavoured by an overdone hilar-
ity, laughing boisterously at the very smallest of jokes, to quiet my
apprehensions.

After supper he went on to the poop* once more, and I with him.
The night was dark and very still, save for the melancholy soughing
of the wind among the spars. A thick cloud was coming up from the
northwest, and the ragged tentacles which it threw out in front of it
were drifting across the face of the moon, which only shone now and
again through a rift in the wrack. The captain paced rapidly backwards and forwards, and then seeing me still dogging him, he came
across and hinted that he thought I should be better below—which,
I need hardly say, had the effect of strengthening my resolution to
remain on deck.

I think he forgot about my presence after this, for he stood silently
leaning over the taffrail* and peering out across the great desert of

snow, part of which lay in shadow, while part glittered mistily in the moonlight. Several times I could see by his movements that he was referring to his watch, and once he muttered a short sentence, of which I could only catch the one word 'ready.' I confess to having felt an eerie feeling creeping over me as I watched the loom of his tall figure through the darkness, and noted how completely he fulfilled the idea of a man who is keeping a tryst. A tryst with whom? Some vague perception began to dawn upon me as I pieced one fact with another, but I was utterly unprepared for the sequel.

By the sudden intensity of his attitude I felt that he saw something. I crept up behind him. He was staring with an eager questioning gaze at what seemed to be a wreath of mist, blown swiftly in a line with the ship. It was a dim nebulous body, devoid of shape, sometimes more, sometimes less apparent, as the light fell on it. The moon was dimmed in its brilliancy at the moment by a canopy of thinnest cloud, like the coating of an anemone.

'Coming, lass, coming,' cried the skipper, in a voice of unfathomable tenderness and compassion, like one who soothes a beloved one by some favour long looked for, and as pleasant to bestow as to receive.

What followed happened in an instant. I had no power to interfere. He gave one spring to the top of the bulwarks, and another which took him on to the ice, almost to the feet of the pale misty figure. He held out his hands as if to clasp it, and so ran into the darkness with outstretched arms and loving words. I still stood rigid and motionless, straining my eyes after his retreating form, until his voice died away in the distance. I never thought to see him again, but at that moment the moon shone out brilliantly through a chink in the cloudy heaven, and illuminated the great field of ice. Then I saw his dark figure already a very long way off, running with prodigious speed across the frozen plain. That was the last glimpse which we caught of him—perhaps the last we ever shall. A party was organized to follow him, and I accompanied them, but the men's hearts were not in the work, and nothing was found. Another will be formed within a few hours. I can hardly believe I have not been dreaming, or suffering from some hideous nightmare, as I write these things down.

7.30 P.M.—Just returned dead beat and utterly tired out from a second unsuccessful search for the captain. The floe is of enormous extent, for though we have traversed at least twenty miles of its surface, there has been no sign of its coming to an end. The frost has been so severe of late that the overlying snow is frozen as hard as granite, otherwise we might have had the footsteps to guide us. The crew are anxious that we should cast off and steam round the floe and so to the southward, for the ice has opened up during the night, and the sea is visible upon the horizon. They argue that Captain Craigie is certainly dead, and that we are all risking our lives to no purpose by remaining when we have an opportunity of escape. Mr Milne and I have had the greatest difficulty in persuading them to wait until to-morrow night, and have been compelled to promise that we will not under any circumstances delay our departure longer than that. We propose therefore to take a few hours' sleep, and then to start upon a final search.

September 20th, evening.—I crossed the ice this morning with a party of men exploring the southern part of the floe, while Mr Milne went off in a northerly direction. We pushed on for ten or twelve miles without seeing a trace of any living thing except a single bird, which fluttered a great way over our heads, and which by its flight I should judge to have been a falcon. The southern extremity of the ice-field tapered away into a long narrow spit which projected out into the sea. When we came to the base of this promontory, the men halted, but I begged them to continue to the extreme end of it, that we might have the satisfaction of knowing that no possible chance had been neglected.

We had hardly gone a hundred yards before M'Donald of Peterhead cried out that he saw something in front of us, and began to run. We all got a glimpse of it and ran too. At first it was only a vague darkness against the white ice, but as we raced along together it took the shape of a man, and eventually of the man of whom we were in search. He was lying face downwards upon a frozen bank. Many little crystals of ice and feathers of snow had drifted on to him as he lay, and sparkled upon his dark seaman's jacket. As we came up some wandering puff of wind caught these tiny flakes in its vortex, and they whirled up into the air, partially descended again, and then, caught once more in the current, sped rapidly away in the direction of the sea. To my eyes it seemed but a snow-drift, but many of my companions averred that it started up in the shape of a woman, stooped over the corpse and kissed it, and then hurried away across the floe. I have learned never to ridicule any man's opinion, however strange it may seem. Sure it is that Captain Nicholas Craigie had met with no painful end, for there was a bright smile upon his blue pinched features, and his hands were still outstretched as though grasping at the strange visitor which had summoned him away into the dim world that lies beyond the grave.

We buried him the same afternoon with the ship's ensign around him, and a thirty-two pound shot at his feet. I read the burial service, while the rough sailors wept like children, for there were many who owed much to his kind heart, and who showed now the affection which his strange ways had repelled during his lifetime. He went off the grating with a dull, sullen splash, and as I looked into the green water I saw him go down, down, down until he was but a little flickering patch of white hanging upon the outskirts of eternal darkness. Then even that faded away, and he was gone. There he shall lie, with his secret and his sorrows and his mystery all still buried in his breast, until that great day when the sea shall give up its dead, and Nicholas Craigie come out from among the ice with the smile upon his face, and his stiffened arms outstretched in greeting. I pray that his lot may be a happier one in that life than it has been in this.

I shall not continue my journal. Our road to home lies plain and clear before us, and the great ice-field will soon be but a remembrance of the past. It will be some time before I get over the shock produced by recent events. When I began this record of our voyage I little thought of how I should be compelled to finish it. I am writing these final words in the lonely cabin, still starting at times and fancying I hear the quick nervous step of the dead man upon the deck above me. I entered his cabin to-night, as was my duty, to make a list of his effects in order that they might be entered in the official log. All was as it had been upon my previous visit, save that the picture which I have described as having hung at the end of his bed had been cut out of its frame, as with a knife, and was gone. With this last link in a strange chain of evidence I close my diary of the voyage of the *Polestar*.

[NOTE by Dr John M'Alister Ray, senior.—I have read over the strange events connected with the death of the captain of the *Polestar*, as narrated in the journal of my son. That everything occurred exactly as he describes it I have the fullest confidence, and, indeed, the most positive certainty, for I know him to be a strong-nerved and unimaginative man, with the strictest regard for veracity. Still, the story is, on the face of it, so vague and so improbable, that I was long opposed to its publication. Within the last few days, however, I have had independent testimony upon the subject which throws a new light upon it. I had run down to Edinburgh to attend a meeting of the British Medical Association, when I chanced to come across Dr P——, an old college chum of mine, now practising at Saltash, in Devonshire.* Upon my telling him of this experience of my son's, he declared to me that he was familiar with the man, and proceeded, to my no small surprise, to give me a description of him, which tallied remarkably well with that given in the journal, except that he depicted him as a younger man. According to his account, he had been engaged to a young lady of singular beauty residing upon the Cornish coast. During his absence at sea his betrothed had died under circumstances of peculiar horror.]

THE WINNING SHOT

⧫⧫⧫

'**C**AUTION.—The public are hereby cautioned against a man calling himself Octavius Gaster. He is to be recognised by his great height, his flaxen hair, and deep scar upon his left cheek, extending from the eye to the angle of the mouth. His predilection for bright colours—green neckties, and the like—may help to identify him. A slightly foreign accent is to be detected in his speech. This man is beyond the reach of the law, but is more dangerous than a mad dog. Shun him as you would shun the pestilence that walketh at noonday.* Any communications as to his whereabouts will be thankfully acknowledged by A.C.U., Lincoln's Inn,* London.'

This is a copy of an advertisement which may have been noticed by many readers in the columns of the London morning papers during the early part of the present year. It has, I believe, excited considerable curiosity in certain quarters, and many guesses have been hazarded as to the identity of Octavius Gaster and the nature of the charge brought against him. When I state that the 'caution' has been inserted by my elder brother, Arthur Cooper Underwood, barrister-at-law, upon my representations, it will be acknowledged that I am the most fitting person to enter upon an authentic explanation.

Hitherto the horror and vagueness of my suspicion, combined with my grief at the loss of my poor darling on the very eve of our wedding, have prevented me from revealing the events of last August to anyone save my brother.

Now, however, looking back, I can fit in many little facts almost unnoticed at the time, which form a chain of evidence that, though worthless in a court of law, may yet have some effect upon the mind of the public.

I shall therefore relate, without exaggeration or prejudice, all that occurred from the day upon which this man, Octavius Gaster, entered Toynby Hall up to the great rifle competition. I know that many people will always ridicule the supernatural, or what our poor intellects choose to regard as supernatural, and that the fact of my being a woman will be thought to weaken my evidence. I can only plead that

I have never been weak-minded or impressionable, and that other people formed the same opinions of Octavius Gaster that I did.

Now to the story.

It was at Colonel Pillar's place at Roborough,* in the pleasant county of Devon, that we spent our autumn holidays. For some months I had been engaged to his eldest son Charley, and it was hoped that the marriage might take place before the termination of the Long Vacation.*

Charley was considered 'safe' for his degree, and in any case was rich enough to be practically independent, while I was by no means penniless.

The old Colonel was delighted at the prospect of the match, and so was my mother; so that look what way we would, there seemed to be no cloud above our horizon.

It was no wonder, then, that that August was a happy one. Even the most miserable of mankind would have laid his woes aside under the genial influence of the merry household at Toynby Hall.

There was Lieutenant Daseby, 'Jack,' as he was invariably called, fresh home from Japan in Her Majesty's ship *Shark*, who was on the same interesting footing with Fanny Pillar, Charley's sister, as Charley was with me, so that we were able to lend each other a certain moral support.

Then there was Harry, Charley's younger brother, and Trevor, his bosom friend at Cambridge.

Finally there was my mother, dearest of old ladies, beaming at us through her gold-rimmed spectacles, anxiously smoothing every little difficulty in the way of the two young couples, and never weary of detailing to them *her* own doubts and fears and perplexities when that gay young blood, Mr Nicholas Underwood, came a-wooing into the provinces, and forswore Crockford's and Tattersall's* for the sake of the country parson's daughter.

I must not, however, forget the gallant old warrior who was our host; with his time-honoured jokes, and his gout, and his harmless affectation of ferocity.

'I don't know what's come over the governor lately,' Charley used to say. 'He has never cursed the Liberal Administration* since you've been here, Lottie; and my belief is that unless he has a good blow-off, that Irish question* will get into his system and finish him.'

Perhaps in the privacy of his own apartment the veteran used to make up for his self-abnegation during the day.

He seemed to have taken a special fancy to me, which he showed in a hundred little attentions.

'You're a good lass,' he remarked one evening, in a very port-winey whisper. 'Charley's a lucky dog, egad! and has more discrimination than I thought. Mark my words, Miss Underwood, you'll find that young gentleman isn't such a fool as he looks!'

With which equivocal compliment the Colonel solemnly covered his face with his handkerchief, and went off into the land of dreams.

* * *

How well I remember the day that was the commencement of all our miseries!

Dinner was over, and we were in the drawing-room, with the windows open to admit the balmy southern breeze.

My mother was sitting in the corner, engaged on a piece of fancy-work, and occasionally purring forth some truism which the dear old soul believed to be an entirely original remark, and founded exclusively upon her own individual experiences.

Fanny and the young lieutenant were billing and cooing upon the sofa, while Charley paced restlessly about the room.

I was sitting by the window, gazing out dreamily at the great wilderness of Dartmoor, which stretched away to the horizon, ruddy and glowing in the light of the sinking sun, save where some rugged tor stood out in bold relief against the scarlet background.

'I say,' remarked Charley, coming over to join me at the window, 'it seems a positive shame to waste an evening like this.'

'Confound the evening!' said Jack Daseby.

'You're always victimising yourself to the weather. Fan and I ar'n't going to move off this sofa—are we, Fan?'

That young lady announced her intention of remaining by nestling among the cushions, and glancing defiantly at her brother.

'Spooning is a demoralising thing—isn't it, Lottie?' said Charley, appealing laughingly to me.

'Shockingly so,' I answered.

'Why, I can remember Daseby here when he was as active a young fellow as any in Devon; and just look at him now! Fanny, Fanny, you've got a lot to answer for!'

'Never mind him, my dear,' said my mother, from the corner. 'Still, my experience has always shown me that moderation is an excellent thing for young people. Poor dear Nicholas used to think so too. He would never go to bed of a night until he had jumped the length of the hearthrug. I often told him it was dangerous; but he *would* do it, until one night he fell on the fender and snapped the muscle of his leg, which made him limp till the day of his death, for Doctor Pearson mistook it for a fracture of the bone, and put him in splints, which had the effect of stiffening his knee. They did say that the doctor was almost out of his mind at the time from anxiety, brought on by his younger daughter swallowing a halfpenny, and that that was what caused him to make the mistake.'

My mother had a curious way of drifting along in her conversation, and occasionally rushing off at a tangent, which made it rather difficult to remember her original proposition. On this occasion Charley had, however, stowed it away in his mind as likely to admit of immediate application.

'An excellent thing, as you say, Mrs Underwood,' he remarked; 'and we have not been out to-day. Look here, Lottie, we have an hour of daylight yet. Suppose we go down and have a try for a trout, if your mamma does not object.'

'Put something round your throat, dear,' said my mother, feeling that she had been outmanœuvred.

'All right, dear,' I answered; 'I'll just run up and put on my hat.'

'And we'll have a walk back in the gloaming,'* said Charley, as I made for the door.

When I came down, I found my lover waiting impatiently with his fishing basket in the hall.

We crossed the lawn together, and passed the open drawing-room windows, where three mischievous faces were looking at us.

'Spooning is a terribly demoralising thing,' remarked Jack, reflectively staring up at the clouds.

'Shocking,' said Fan; and all three laughed until they woke the sleeping Colonel, and we could hear them endeavouring to explain the joke to that ill-used veteran, who apparently obstinately refused to appreciate it.

We passed down the winding lane together, and through the little wooden gate, which opens on to the Tavistock* road.

Charley paused for a moment after we had emerged and seemed irresolute which way to turn.

Had we but known it, our fate depended upon that trivial question.

'Shall we go down to the river, dear,' he said, 'or shall we try one of the brooks upon the moor?'*

'Whichever you like?' I answered.

'Well, I vote that we cross the moor. We'll have a longer walk back that way,' he added, looking down lovingly at the little white-shawled figure beside him.

The brook in question runs through a most desolate part of the country. By the path it is several miles from Toynby Hall; but we were both young and active, and struck out across the moor, regardless of rocks and furze-bushes.

Not a living creature did we meet upon our solitary walk, save a few scraggy Devonshire sheep, who looked at us wistfully, and followed us for some distance, as if curious as to what could possibly have induced us to trespass upon their domains.

It was almost dark before we reached the little stream, which comes gurgling down through a precipitous glen, and meanders away to help to form the Plymouth 'leat.'*

Above us towered two great columns of rock, between which the water trickled to form a deep, still pool at the bottom. This pool had always been a favourite spot of Charley's, and was a pretty cheerful place by day; but now, with the rising moon reflected upon its glassy waters, and throwing dark shadows from the overhanging rocks, it seemed anything rather than the haunt of a pleasure-seeker.

'I don't think, darling, that I'll fish, after all,' said Charley, as we sat down together on a mossy bank. 'It's a dismal sort of place, isn't it?'

'Very,' said I, shuddering.

'We'll just have a rest, and then we will walk back by the pathway. You're shivering. You're not cold, are you?'

'No,' said I, trying to keep up my courage; 'I'm not cold, but I'm rather frightened, though it's very silly of me.'

'By jove!' said my lover, 'I can't wonder at it, for I feel a bit depressed myself. The noise that water makes is like the gurgling in the throat of a dying man.'

'Don't, Charley; you frighten me!'

'Come, dear, we mustn't get the blues,' he said, with a laugh, trying lo reassure me. 'Let's run away from this charnel-house place, and— Look!—see!—good gracious! what is that?'

Charley had staggered back, and was gazing upwards with a pallid face.

I followed the direction of his eyes, and could scarcely suppress a scream.

I have already mentioned that the pool by which we were standing lay at the foot of a rough mound of rocks. On the top of this mound, about sixty feet above our heads, a tall dark figure was standing looking down, apparently, into the rugged hollow in which we were.

The moon was just topping the ridge behind, and the gaunt, angular outlines of the stranger stood out hard and clear against its silvery radiance.

There was something ghastly in the sudden and silent appearance of this solitary wanderer, especially when coupled with the weird nature of the scene.

I clung to my lover in speechless terror, and glared up at the dark figure above us.

'Hullo, you sir!' cried Charley, passing from fear into anger, as Englishmen generally do. 'Who are you, and what the devil are you doing?'

'Oh! I thought it, I thought it!' said the man who was overlooking us, and disappeared from the top of the hill.

We heard him scrambling about among the loose stones, and in another moment he emerged upon the banks of the brook and stood facing us.

Weird as his appearance had been when we first caught sight of him, the impression was intensified rather than removed by a closer acquaintance.

The moon shining full upon him revealed a long, thin face of ghastly pallor, the effect being increased by its contrast with the flaring green necktie which he wore.

A scar upon his cheek had healed badly and caused a nasty pucker at the side of his mouth, which gave his whole countenance a most distorted expression, more particularly when he smiled.

The knapsack on his back and stout staff in his hand announced him to be a tourist, while the easy grace with which he raised his hat on perceiving the presence of a lady showed that he could lay claim to the *savoir faire* of a man of the world.

There was something in his angular proportions and the bloodless face which, taken in conjunction with the black cloak which fluttered from his shoulders, irresistibly reminded me of a bloodsucking species of bat which Jack Daseby had brought from Japan upon his previous voyage, and which was the bugbear of the servants' hall at Toynby.

'Excuse my intrusion,' he said, with a slightly foreign lisp, which imparted a peculiar beauty to his voice. 'I should have had to sleep on the moor had I not had the good fortune to fall in with you.'

'Confound it, man!' said Charley; 'why couldn't you shout out, or give some warning? You quite frightened Miss Underwood when you suddenly appeared up there.'

The stranger once more raised his hat as he apologised to me for having given me such a start.

'I am a gentleman from Sweden,' he continued, in that peculiar intonation of his, 'and am viewing this beautiful land of yours. Allow me to introduce myself as Doctor Octavius Gaster. Perhaps you could tell me where I may sleep, and how I can get from this place, which is truly of great size?'

'You're very lucky in falling in with us,' said Charley. 'It is no easy matter to find your way upon the moor.'

'That can I well believe,' remarked our new acquaintance.

'Strangers have been found dead on it before now,' continued Charley. 'They lose themselves, and then wander in a circle until they fall from fatigue.'

'Ha, ha!' laughed the Swede; 'it is not I, who have drifted in an open boat from Cape Blanco to Canary,* that will starve upon an English moor. But how may I turn to seek an inn?'

'Look here!' said Charley, whose interest was excited by the stranger's allusion, and who was at all times the most open-hearted of men. 'There's not an inn for many a mile round; and I daresay you have had a long day's walk already. Come home with us, and my father, the Colonel, will be delighted to see you and find you a spare bed.'

'For this great kindness how can I thank you?' returned the traveller. 'Truly, when I return to Sweden, I shall have strange stories to tell of the English and the hospitality!'

'Nonsense!' said Charley. 'Come, we will start at once, for Miss Underwood is cold. Wrap the shawl well round your neck, Lottie, and we will be home in no time.'

We stumbled along in silence, keeping as far as we could to the rugged pathway, sometimes losing it as a cloud drifted over the face of the moon, and then regaining it further on with the return of the light.

The stranger seemed buried in thought, but once or twice I had the impression that he was looking hard at me through the darkness as we strode along together.

'So', said Charley at last, breaking the silence, 'you drifted about in an open boat, did you?'

'Ah, yes,' answered the stranger; 'many strange sights have I seen, and many perils undergone, but none worse than that. It is, however, too sad a subject for a lady's ears. She has been frightened once to-night.'

'Oh, you needn't be afraid of frightening me now,' said I, as I leaned on Charley's arm.

'Indeed there is but little to tell, and yet is it sorrowful.

'A friend of mine, Karl Osgood of Upsala,* and myself started on a trading venture. Few white men had been among the wandering Moors at Cape Blanco, but nevertheless we went, and for some months lived well, selling this and that, and gathering much ivory and gold.

'' Tis a strange country, where is neither wood nor stone, so that the huts are made from the weeds of the sea.

'At last, just as what we thought was a sufficiency, the Moors conspired to kill us, and came down against us in the night.

'Short was our warning, but we fled to the beach, launched a canoe and put out to sea, leaving everything behind.

'The Moors chased us, but lost us in the darkness; and when day dawned the land was out of sight.

'There was no country where we could hope for food nearer than Canary, and for that we made.

'I reached it alive, though very weak and mad; but poor Karl died the day before we sighted the islands.

'I gave him warning!

'I cannot blame myself in the matter.

'I said, "Karl, the strength that you might gain by eating them would be more than made up for by the blood that you would lose!"

'He laughed at my words, caught the knife from my belt, cut them off and eat them; and he died.'

'Eat what?' asked Charley.

'His ears!' said the stranger.

We both looked round at him in horror.

There was no suspicion of a smile or joke upon his ghastly face.

'He was what you call headstrong,' he continued, 'but he should

have known better than to do a thing like that. Had he but used his
will he would have lived as I did.'

'And you think a man's will can prevent him from feeling hungry?'
said Charley.

'What can it not do?' returned Octavius Gaster, and relapsed into
a silence which was not broken until our arrival in Toynby Hall.

Considerable alarm had been caused by our nonappearance, and
Jack Daseby was just setting off with Charley's friend Trevor in search
of us. They were delighted, therefore, when we marched in upon them,
and considerably astonished at the appearance of our companion.

'Where the deuce did you pick up that second-hand corpse?' asked
Jack, drawing Charley aside into the smoking-room.

'Shut up, man; he'll hear you,' growled Charley. 'He's a Swedish
doctor on a tour, and a deuced good fellow. He went in an open boat
from What's-it's-name to another place. I've offered him a bed for the
night.'

'Well, all I can say is,' remarked Jack, 'that his face will never be his
fortune.'

'Ha, ha! Very good! very good!' laughed the subject of the remark,
walking calmly into the room, to the complete discomfiture of the
sailor. 'No, it will never, as you say, in this country be my fortune,'—
and he grinned until the hideous gash across the angle of his mouth
made him look more like the reflection in a broken mirror than anything else.

'Come upstairs and have a wash; I can lend you a pair of slippers,'
said Charley; and hurried the visitor out of the room to put an end to
a somewhat embarrassing situation.

Colonel Pillar was the soul of hospitality, and welcomed Doctor
Gaster as effusively as if he had been an old friend of the family.

'Egad, sir,' he said, 'the place is your own; and as long as you care
to stop you are very welcome. We're pretty quiet down here, and
a visitor is an acquisition.'

My mother was a little more distant. 'A very well informed young
man, Lottie,' she remarked to me; 'but I wish he would wink his eyes
more. I don't like to see people who never wink their eyes. Still, my
dear, my life has taught me one great lesson, and that is that a man's
looks are of very little importance compared with his actions.'

With which brand new and eminently original remark, my mother
kissed me and left me to my meditations.

Whatever Doctor Octavius Gaster might be physically, he was certainly a social success.

By next day he had so completely installed himself as a member of the household that the Colonel would not hear of his departure.

He astonished everybody by the extent and variety of his knowl edge. He could tell the veteran considerably more about the Crimea* than he knew himself; he gave the sailor information about the coast of Japan; and even tackled my athletic lover upon the subject of rowing, discoursing about levers of the first order, and fixed points and fulcra, until the unhappy Cantab* was fain to drop the subject.

Yet all this was done so modestly and even deferentially, that no one could possibly feel offended at being beaten upon their own ground. There was a quiet power about everything he said and did which was very striking.

I remember one example of this, which impressed us all at the time.

Trevor had a remarkably savage bulldog, which, however fond of its master, fiercely resented any liberties from the rest of us. This animal was, it may be imagined, rather unpopular, but as it was the pride of the student's heart it was agreed not to banish it entirely, but to lock it up in the stable and give it a wide berth.

From the first, it seemed to have taken a decided aversion to our visitor, and showed every fang in its head whenever he approached it.

On the second day of his visit we were passing the stable in a body, when the growls of the creature inside arrested Doctor Gaster's attention.

'Ha!' he said. 'There is that dog of yours, Mr Trevor, is it not?'

'Yes; that's Towzer,' assented Trevor.

'He is a bulldog, I think? What they call the national animal of England on the Continent?'

'Pure-bred,' said the student, proudly.

'They are ugly animals—very ugly! Would you come into the stable and unchain him, that I may see him to advantage. It is a pity to keep an animal so powerful and full of life in captivity.'

'He's rather a nipper,' said Trevor, with a mischievous expression in his eye; 'but I suppose you are not afraid of a dog?'

'Afraid?—no. Why should I be afraid?'

The mischievous look on Trevor's face increased as he opened the stable door. I heard Charley mutter something to him about its being past a joke, but the other's answer was drowned by the hollow growling from inside.

The rest of us retreated to a respectable distance, while Octavius Gaster stood in the open doorway with a look of mild curiosity upon his pallid face.

'And those,' he said, 'that I see so bright and red in the darkness— are those his eyes?'

'Those are they,' said the student, as he stooped down and un- buckled the strap.

'Come here!' said Octavius Gaster.

The growling of the dog suddenly subsided into a long whimper, and instead of making the furious rush that we expected, he rustled among the straw as if trying to huddle into a corner.

'What the deuce is the matter with him?' exclaimed his perplexed owner.

'Come here!' repeated Gaster, in sharp metallic accents, with an indescribable air of command in them. 'Come here!'

To our astonishment, the dog trotted out and stood at his side, but looking as unlike the usually pugnacious Towzer as is possible to con- ceive. His ears were drooping, his tail limp, and he altogether pre- sented the very picture of canine humiliation.

'A very fine dog, but singularly quiet,' remarked the Swede, as he stroked him down.

'Now, sir, go back!'

The brute turned and slunk back into its corner. We heard the rat- tling of its chain as it was being fastened, and next moment Trevor came out of the stable-door with blood dripping from his finger.

'Confound the beast!' he said. 'I don't know what can have come over him. I've had him three years, and he never bit me before.'

I fancy—I cannot say it for certain—but I fancy that there was a spasmodic twitching of the cicatrix* upon our visitor's face, which betokened an inclination to laugh.

Looking back, I think that it was from that moment that I began to have a strange indefinable fear and dislike of the man.

* * *

Week followed week, and the day fixed for my marriage began to draw near.

Octavius Gaster was still a guest at Toynby Hall, and, indeed, had so ingratiated himself with the proprietor that any hint at departure was laughed to scorn by that worthy soldier.

'Here you've come, sir, and here you'll stay; you shall, by Jove!'

Whereat Octavius would smile and shrug his shoulders and mutter something about the attractions of Devon, which would put the Colonel in a good humour for the whole day afterwards.

My darling and I were too much engrossed with each other to pay very much attention to the traveller's occupations. We used to come upon him sometimes in our rambles through the woods, sitting reading in the most lonely situations.

He always placed the book in his pocket when he saw us approaching. I remember on one occasion, however, that we stumbled upon him so suddenly that the volume was still lying open before him.

'Ah, Gaster,' said Charley, 'studying, as usual! What an old bookworm you are! What's the book? Ah, a foreign language; Swedish, I suppose?'

'No, it is not Swedish,' said Gaster; 'it is Arabic.'

'You don't mean to say you know Arabic?'

'Oh, very well—very well indeed!'

'And what's it about?' I asked, turning over the leaves of the musty old volume.

'Nothing that would interest one so young and fair as yourself, Miss Underwood,' he answered, looking at me in a way which had become habitual to him of late. 'It treats of the days when mind was stronger than what you call matter; when great spirits lived that were able to exist without these coarse bodies of ours, and could mould all things to their so-powerful wills.'

'Oh, I see; a kind of ghost story,' said Charley. 'Well, adieu; we won't keep you from your studies.'

We left him sitting in the little glen still absorbed in his mystical treatise. It must have been imagination which induced me, on turning suddenly round half an hour later, to think that I saw his familiar figure glide rapidly behind a tree.

I mentioned it to Charley at the time, but he laughed my idea to scorn.

* * *

I alluded just now to a peculiar manner which this man Gaster had of looking at me. His eyes seemed to lose their usual steely expression when he did so, and soften into something which might be almost called caressing. They seemed to influence me strangely, for I could always tell, without looking at him, when his gaze was fixed upon me.

Sometimes I fancied that this idea was simply due to a disordered nervous system or morbid imagination; but my mother dispelled that delusion from my mind.

'Do you know,' she said, coming into my bedroom one night, and carefully shutting the door behind her, 'if the idea was not so utterly preposterous, Lottie, I should say that that Doctor was madly in love with you?'

'Nonsense, 'ma!' said I, nearly dropping my candle in my consternation at the thought.

'I really think so, Lottie,' continued my mother. 'He's got a way of looking which is very like that of your poor dear father, Nicholas, before we were married. Something of this sort, you know.'

And the old lady cast an utterly heart-broken glance at the bed-post.

'Now, go to bed,' said I, 'and don't have such funny ideas. Why, poor Doctor Gaster knows that I am engaged as well as you do.'

'Time will show,' said the old lady, as she left the room; and I went to bed with the words still ringing in my ears.

Certainly, it is a strange thing that on that very night a thrill which I had come to know well ran through me, and awakened me from my slumbers.

I stole softly to the window, and peered out through the bars of the Venetian blinds, and there was the gaunt, vampire-like figure of our Swedish visitor standing upon the gravel-walk, and apparently gazing up at my window.

It may have been that he detected the movement of the blind, for, lighting a cigarette, he began pacing up and down the avenue.

I noticed that at breakfast next morning he went out of his way to explain the fact that he had been restless during the night, and had steadied his nerves by a short stroll and a smoke.

After all, when I came to consider it calmly, the aversion which I had against the man and my distrust of him were founded on very scanty grounds. A man might have a strange face, and be fond of curious literature, and even look approvingly at an engaged young lady, without being a very dangerous member of society.

I say this to show that even up to that point I was perfectly unbiased and free from prejudice in my opinion of Octavius Gaster.

*　*　*

'I say!' remarked Lieutenant Daseby, one morning; 'what do you think of having a picnic to-day?'

'Capital!' ejaculated everybody.

'You see, they are talking of commissioning the old *Shark* soon, and Trevor here will have to go back to the mill, We may all well compress as much fun as we can into the time.'

'What is it that you call nicpic?' asked Doctor Gaster.

'It's another of our English institutions for you to study,' said Charley. 'It's our version of a *fête champêtre*.'*

'Ah, I see! That will be very jolly!' acquiesced the Swede.

'There are half a dozen places we might go to,' continued the Lieutenant. 'There's the Lover's Leap, or Black Tor, or Beer Ferris Abbey.'*

'That's the best,' said Charley. 'Nothing like ruins for a picnic.'

'Well the Abbey be it. How far is it?'

'Six miles,' said Trevor.

'Seven by the road,' remarked the Colonel, with military exactness. 'Mrs Underwood and I shall stay at home, and the rest of you can fit into the waggonette. You'll all have to chaperon each other.'

I need hardly say that this motion was carried also without a division.

'Well,' said Charley, 'I'll order the trap to be round in half an hour, so you'd better all make the best of your time. We'll want salmon, and salad, and hard-boiled eggs, and liquor, and any number of things. I'll look after the liquor department. What will you do, Lottie?'

'I'll take charge of the china,' I said.

'I'll bring the fish,' said Daseby.

'And I the vegetables,' added Fan.

'What will you do, Gaster?' asked Charley.

'Truly,' said the Swede, in his strange, musical accents, 'but little is left for me to do. I can, however, wait upon the ladies, and I can make what you call a salad.'

'You'll be more popular in the latter capacity than in the former,' said I, laughingly.

'Ah, you say so,' he said, turning sharp round upon me, and flushing up to his flaxen hair. 'Yes. Ha! ha! Very good!'

And with a discordant laugh, he strode out of the room.

'I say, Lottie,' remonstrated my lover, 'you've hurt the fellow's feelings.'

'I'm sure I didn't mean to,' I answered. 'If you like I'll go after him and tell him so.'

'Oh, leave him alone,' said Daseby. 'A man with a mug like that has no right to be so touchy. He'll come round right enough.'

It was true that I had not had the slightest intention of offending Gaster, still I felt pained at having annoyed him.

After I had stowed away the knives and plates into the hamper, I found that the others were still busy at their various departments. The moment seemed a favourable one for apologising for my thoughtless remark, so without saying anything to anyone, I slipped away and ran down the corridor in the direction of our visitor's room.

I suppose I must have tripped along very lightly, or it may have been the rich thick matting of Toynby Hall—certain it is that Mr Gaster seemed unconscious of my approach.

His door was open, and as I came up to it and caught sight of him inside, there was something so strange in his appearance that I paused, literally petrified for the moment with astonishment.

He had in his hand a small slip from a newspaper which he was reading, and which seemed to afford him considerable amusement. There was something horrible too in this mirth of his, for though he writhed his body about as if with laughter, no sound was emitted from his lips.

His face, which was half-turned towards me, wore an expression upon it which I had never seen on it before; I can only describe it as one of savage exultation.

Just as I was recovering myself sufficiently to step forward and knock at the door, he suddenly, with a last convulsive spasm of merriment, dashed down the piece of paper upon the table and hurried out by the other door of his room, which led through the billiard-room to the hall.

I heard his steps dying away in the distance, and peeped once more into his room.

What could be the joke that had moved this stern man to mirth? Surely some masterpiece of humour.

Was there ever a woman whose principles were strong enough to overcome her curiosity?

Looking cautiously round to make sure that the passage was empty, I slipped into the room and examined the paper which he had been reading.

It was a cutting from an English journal, and had evidently been long carried about and frequently perused, for it was almost illegible in places. There was, however, as far as I could see, very little to provoke laughter in its contents. It ran, as well as I can remember, in this way:

'Sudden Death in the Docks.—The master of the bark-rigged steamer Olga, from Tromsberg,* was found lying dead in his cabin on Wednesday afternoon. Deceased was, it seems, of a violent disposition, and had had frequent altercations with the surgeon of the vessel. On this particular day he had been more than usually offensive, declaring that the surgeon was a necromancer and worshipper of the devil. The latter retired on deck to avoid further persecution. Shortly afterwards the steward had occasion to enter the cabin, and found the captain lying across the table quite dead. Death is attributed to heart disease, accelerated by excessive passion. An inquest will be held to-day.'

And this was the paragraph which this strange man had regarded as the height of humour!

I hurried downstairs, astonishment, not un-mixed with repugnance, predominating in my mind. So just was I, however, that the dark inference which has so often occurred to me since never for one moment crossed my mind. I looked upon him as a curious and rather repulsive enigma—nothing more.

When I met him at the picnic, all remembrance of my unfortunate speech seemed to have vanished from his mind. He made himself as agreeable as usual, and his salad was pronounced a *chef-d'œuvre*,* while his quaint little Swedish songs and his tales of all climes and countries alternately thrilled and amused us. It was after luncheon, however, that the conversation turned upon a subject which seemed to have special charms for his daring mind.

I forget who it was that broached the question of the supernatural. I think it was Trevor, by some story of a hoax which he had perpetrated at Cambridge. The story seemed to have a strange effect upon Octavius Gaster, who tossed his long arms about in impassioned invective as he ridiculed those who dared to doubt about the existence of the unseen.

'Tell me,' he said, standing up in his excitement, 'which among you has ever known what you call an instinct to fail. The wild bird has an instinct which tells it of the solitary rock upon the so boundless sea on which it may lay its egg, and is it disappointed? The swallow turns to the south when the winter is coming, and has its instinct ever led it astray? And shall this instinct which tells us of the unknown spirits around us, and which pervades every untaught child and every race so savage, be wrong? I say, never!'

'Go it, Gaster!' cried Charley.

'Take your wind and have another spell,' said the sailor.

'No, never,' repeated the Swede, disregarding our amusement. 'We can see that matter exists apart from mind; then why should not mind exist apart from matter?'

'Give it up,' said Daseby.

'Have we not proofs of it?' continued Gaster, his gray eyes gleaming with excitement. 'Who that has read Steinberg's book upon spirits, or that by the eminent American, Madame Crowe, can doubt it? Did not Gustav von Spee meet his brother Leopold in the streets of Strasbourg, the same brother having been drowned three months before in the Pacific? Did not Home,* the spiritualist, in open daylight, float above the housetops of Paris? Who has not heard the voices of the dead around him? I myself—'

'Well, what of yourself?' asked half a dozen of us, in a breath.

'Bah! it matters nothing,' he said, passing his hand over his forehead, and evidently controlling himself with difficulty. 'Truly, our talk is too sad for such an occasion.' And, in spite of all our efforts, we were unable to extract from Gaster any relation of his own experiences of the supernatural.

It was a merry day. Our approaching dissolution seemed to cause each one to contribute his utmost to the general amusement. It was settled that after the coming rifle match Jack was to return to his ship and Trevor to his university. As to Charley and myself, we were to settle down into a staid respectable couple.

The match was one of our principal topics of conversation. Shooting had always been a hobby of Charley's, and he was the captain of the Roborough company of Devon volunteers, which boasted some of the crack shots of the county. The match was to be against a picked team of regulars from Plymouth, and as they were no despicable opponents, the issue was considered doubtful. Charley had evidently set his heart on winning, and descanted long and loudly on the chances.

'The range is only a mile from Toynby Hall,' he said, 'and we'll all drive over, and you shall see the fun. You'll bring me luck, Lottie,' he whispered, 'I know you will.'

Oh, my poor lost darling, to think of the luck that I brought you!

There was one dark cloud to mar the brightness of that happy day.

I could not hide from myself any longer the fact that my mother's suspicions were correct, and that Octavius Gaster loved me.

Throughout the whole of the excursion his attentions had been most assiduous, and his eyes hardly ever wandered away from me. There was a manner, too, in all that he said which spoke louder than words.

I was on thorns lest Charley should perceive it, for I knew his fiery temper; but the thought of such treachery never entered the honest heart of my lover.

He did once look up with mild surprise when the Swede insisted on relieving me of a fern which I was carrying; but the expression faded away into a smile at what he regarded as Gaster's effusive good-nature. My own feeling in the matter was pity for the unfortunate foreigner, and sorrow that I should have been the means of rendering him unhappy.

I thought of the torture it must be for a wild, fierce spirit like his to have a passion gnawing at his heart which honour and pride would alike prevent him from ever expressing in words. Alas! I had not counted upon the utter recklessness and want of principle of the man; but it was not long before I was undeceived.

There was a little arbour at the bottom of the garden, over-grown with honeysuckle and ivy, which had long been a favourite haunt of Charley and myself. It was doubly dear to us from the fact that it was here, on the occasion of my former visit, that words of love had first passed between us.

After dinner on the day following the picnic I sauntered down to this little summer-house, as was my custom. Here I used to wait until Charley, having finished his cigar with the other gentlemen, would come down and join me.

On that particular evening he seemed to be longer away than usual. I waited impatiently for his coming, going to the door every now and then to see if there were any signs if his approach.

I had just sat down again after one of those fruitless excursions, when I heard the tread of a male foot upon the gravel, and a figure emerged from among the bushes.

I sprang up with a glad smile, which changed to an expression of bewilderment, and even fear, when I saw the gaunt, pallid face of Octavius Gaster peering in at me.

There was certainly something about his actions which would have inspired distrust in the mind of anyone in my position. Instead of greeting me, he looked up and down the garden, as if to make sure that we were entirely alone. He then stealthily entered the arbour, and seated himself upon a chair, in such a position that he was between me and the doorway.

'Do not be afraid,' he said, as he noticed my scared expression. 'There is nothing to fear. I do but come that I may have talk with you.'

'Have you seen Mr Pillar?' I asked, trying hard to seem at my ease.

'Ha! Have I seen your Charley?' he answered, with a sneer upon the last words. 'Are you then so anxious that he come? Can no one speak to thee but Charley, little one?'

'Mr Gaster,' I said, 'you are forgetting yourself.'

'It is Charley, Charley, ever Charley!' continued the Swede, disregarding my interruption. 'Yes, I have seen Charley. I have told him that you wait upon the bank of the river, and he has gone thither upon the wings of love.'

'Why have you told him this lie?' I asked, still trying not to lose my self-control.

'That I might see you; that I might speak to you. Do you, then, love him so? Cannot the thought of glory, and riches, and power, above all that the mind can conceive, win you from this first maiden fancy of yours? Fly with me, Charlotte, and all this, and more, shall be yours! Come!'

And he stretched his long arms out in passionate entreaty.

Even at that moment the thought flashed through my mind of how like they were to the tentacles of some poisonous insect.

'You insult me, sir!' I cried, rising to my feet. 'You shall pay heavily for this treatment of an unprotected girl!'

'Ah, you say it,' he cried, 'but you mean it not. In your heart so tender there is pity left for the most miserable of men. Nay, you shall not pass me—you shall hear me first!'

'Let me go, sir!'

'Nay; you shall not go until you tell me if nothing that I can do may win your love.'

'How dare you speak so?' I almost screamed, losing all my fear in my indignation. 'You, who are the guest of my future husband! Let me tell you, once and for all, that I had no feeling towards you before save one of repugnance and contempt, which you have now converted into positive hatred!'

'And is it so?' he gasped, tottering backwards towards the doorway, and putting his hand up to his throat as if he found a difficulty in uttering the words. 'And has my love won hatred in return? Ha!' he continued, advancing, his face within a foot of mine as I cowered away from his glassy eyes. 'I know it now. It is this—it is this!' and he struck the horrible cicatrix on his face with his clenched hand. 'Maids love not such faces as this! I am not smooth, and brown, and curly like this Charley—this brainless school-boy; this human brute who cares but for his sport and his—'

'Let me pass!' I cried, rushing at the door.

'No; you shall not go—you shall not!' he hissed, pushing me backwards.

I struggled furiously to escape from his grasp. His long arms seemed to clasp me like bars of steel. I felt my strength going, and was making one last despairing effort to shake myself loose, when some irresistible power from behind tore my persecutor away from me and hurled him backwards on to the gravel walk.

Looking up, I saw Charley's towering figure and square shoulders in the doorway.

'My poor darling!' he said, catching me in his arms. 'Sit here—here in the angle. There is no danger now. I shall be with you in a minute.'

'Don't Charley, don't!' I murmured, as he turned to leave me.

But he was deaf to my entreaties, and strode out of the arbour.

I could not see either him or his opponent from the position in which he had placed me, but I heard every word that was spoken.

'You villain!' said a voice that I could hardly recognise as my lover's. 'So this is why you put me on a wrong scent?'

'That is why,' answered the foreigner, in a tone of easy indifference.

'And this is how you repay our hospitality, you infernal scoundrel!'

'Yes; we amuse ourselves in your so beautiful summer-house.'

'We! You are still on my ground and my guest, and I would wish to keep my hands from you; but, by heavens—'

Charley was speaking very low and in gasps now.

'Why do you swear? What is it, then?' asked the languid voice of Octavius Gaster.

'If you dare to couple Miss Underwood's name with this business, and insinuate that—'

'Insinuate? I insinuate nothing. What I say I say plain for all the world to hear. I say that this so chaste maiden did herself ask—'

I heard the sound of a heavy blow, and a great rattling of the gravel.

I was too weak to rise from where I lay, and could only clasp my hands together and utter a faint scream.

'You cur!' said Charley. 'Say as much again, and I'll stop your mouth for all eternity!'

There was a silence, and then I heard Gaster speaking in a husky, strange voice.

'You have struck me!' he said; 'you have drawn my blood!'

'Yes; I'll strike you again if you show your cursed face within these grounds. Don't look at me so! You don't suppose your hankey-pankey* tricks can frighten me?'

An indefinable dread came over me as my lover spoke. I staggered to my feet and looked out at them, leaning against the door-way for support.

Charley was standing erect and defiant, with his young head in the air, like one who glories in the cause for which he battles.

Octavius Gaster was opposite him, surveying him with pinched lips and a baleful look in his cruel eyes. The blood was running freely from a deep gash on his lip, and spotting the front of his green neck-tie and white waistcoat. He perceived me the instant I emerged from the arbour.

'Ha, ha!' he cried, with a demoniacal burst of laughter. 'She comes! The bride! She comes! Room for the bride! Oh, happy pair, happy pair!'

And with another fiendish burst of merriment he turned and disappeared over the crumbling wall of the garden with such rapidity that he was gone before we had realised what it was that he was about to do.

'Oh, Charley,' I said, as my lover came back to my side, 'you've hurt him!'

'Hurt him! I should hope I have! Come, darling, you are frightened and tired. He did not injure you, did he?'

'No; but I feel rather faint and sick.'

'Come, we'll walk slowly to the house together. The rascal! It was cunningly and deliberately planned, too. He told me he had seen you down by the river, and I was going down when I met young Stokes, the keeper's son, coming back from fishing, and he told me that there was nobody there. Somehow, when Stokes said that, a thousand little things flashed into my mind at once, and I became in a moment so convinced of Gaster's villainy that I ran as hard as I could to the arbour.'

'Charley,' I said, clinging to my lover's arm, 'I fear he will injure you in some way. Did you see the look in his eyes before he leaped the wall?'

'Pshaw!' said Charley. 'All these foreigners have a way of scowling and glaring when they are angry, but it never comes to much.'

'Still, I am afraid of him,' said I, mournfully, as we went up the steps together, 'and I wish you had not struck him.'

'So do I,' Charley answered; 'for he was our guest, you know, in spite of his rascality. However, it's done now and it can't be helped, as the cook says in "Pickwick,"* and really it was more than flesh and blood could stand.'

I must run rapidly over the events of the next few days. For me, at least, it was a period of absolute happiness. With Gaster's departure a cloud seemed to be lifted off my soul, and a depression which had weighed upon the whole household completely disappeared.

Once more I was the light-hearted girl that I had been before the foreigner's arrival. Even the Colonel forgot to mourn over his absence, owing to the all-absorbing interest in the coming competition in which his son was engaged.

It was our main subject of conversation and bets were freely offered by the gentlemen on the success of the Roborough team, though no one was unprincipled enough to seem to support their antagonists by taking them.

Jack Daseby ran down to Plymouth, and 'made a book on the event' with some officers of the Marines, which he did in such an extraordinary way that we reckoned that in case of Roborough winning, he would lose seventeen shillings; while, should the other contingency occur, he would be involved in hopeless liabilities.

Charley and I had tacitly agreed not to mention the name of Gaster, nor to allude in any way to what had passed.

On the morning after our scene in the garden, Charley had sent a servant up to the Swede's room with instructions to pack up any things he might find there, and leave them at the nearest inn.

It was found, however, that all Gaster's effects had been already removed, though how and when was a perfect mystery to the servants.

I know of few more attractive spots than the shooting-range at

Roborough. The glen in which it is situated is about half a mile long and perfectly level, so that the targets were able to range from two to seven hundred yards, the further ones simply showing as square white dots against the green of the rising hills behind.

The glen itself is part of the great moor and its sides, sloping gradually up, lose themselves in the vast rugged expanse. Its symmetrical character suggested to the imaginative mind that some giant of old had made an excavation in the moor with a titanic cheese-scoop, but that a single trial had convinced him of the utter worthlessness of the soil.

He might even be imagined to have dropped the despised sample at the mouth of the cutting which he had made, for there was a considerable elevation there, from which the riflemen were to fire, and thither we bent our steps on that eventful afternoon.

Our opponents had arrived there before us, bringing with them a considerable number of naval and military officers, while a long line of nondescript vehicles showed that many of the good citizens of Plymouth had seized the opportunity of giving their wives and families an outing on the moor.

An enclosure for ladies and distinguished guests had been erected on the top of the hill, which, with the marquee and refreshment tents, made the scene a lively one.

The country people had turned out in force, and were excitedly staking their half-crowns upon their local champions, which were as enthusiastically taken up by the admirers of the regulars.

Through all this scene of bustle and confusion we were safely conveyed by Charley, aided by Jack and Trevor, who finally deposited us in a sort of rudimentary grandstand, from which we could look round at our ease on all that was going on.

We were soon, however, so absorbed in the glorious view, that we became utterly unconscious of the betting and pushing and chaff of the crowd in front of us.

Away to the south we could see the blue smoke of Plymouth curling up into the calm summer air, while beyond that was the great sea, stretching away to the horizon, dark and vast, save where some petulant wave dashed it with a streak of foam, as if rebelling against the great peacefulness of nature.

From the Eddystone to the Start* the long rugged line of the Devonshire coast lay like a map before us.

I was still lost in admiration when Charley's voice broke half-reproachfully on my ear.

'Why, Lottie,' he said, 'you don't seem to take a bit of interest in it!'

'Oh, yes I do, dear,' I answered. 'But the scenery is so pretty, and the sea is always a weakness of mine. Come and sit here, and tell me all about the match until now we are to know whether you are winning or losing.'

'I've just been explaining it,' answered Charley. 'But I'll go over it again.'

'Do, like a darling,' said I; and settled myself down to mark, learn, and inwardly digest.

'Well,' said Charley, 'there are ten men on each side. We shoot alternately; first, one of our fellows, then one of them, and so on—you understand?'

'Yes, I understand that.'

'First we fire at the two hundred yards range—those are the targets nearest of all. We fire five shots each at those. Then we fire five shots at the ones at five hundred yards—those middle ones; and then we finish up by firing at the seven hundred yards range—you see the target far over there on the side of the hill. Whoever makes the most points wins. Do you grasp it now?'

'Oh, yes; that's very simple,' I said.

'Do you know what a bull's eye is?' asked my lover.

'Some sort of sweetmeat,* isn't it?' I hazarded.

Charley seemed amazed at the extent of my ignorance. 'That's the bull's-eye,' he said; 'that dark spot in the centre of the target. If you hit that, it counts five. There is another ring, which you can't see, drawn round that, and if you get inside of it, it is called a 'centre,' and counts four. Outside that, again, is called an 'outer,' and only gives you three. You can tell where the shot has hit, for the marker puts out a coloured disc, and covers the place.'

'Oh, I understand it all now,' said I, enthusiastically. 'I'll tell you what I'll do Charley; I'll mark the score on a bit of paper every shot that is fired, and then I'll always know how Roborough is getting on!'

'You can't do better,' he laughed as he strode off to get his men together, for a warning bell signified that the contest was about to begin.

There was a great waving of flags and shouting before the ground could be got clear, and then I saw a little cluster of red-coats lying upon the greensward, while a similar group, in grey, took up their position to the left of them.

'Pang!' went a rifle-shot, and the blue smoke came curling up from the grass.

Fanny shrieked, while I gave a cry of delight, for I saw the white disc go up, which proclaimed a 'bull,' and the shot had been fired by one of the Roborough men. My elation was, however, promptly checked by the answering shot which put down five to the credit of the regulars. The next was also a 'bull,' which was speedily cancelled by another. At the end of the competition at the short range each side had scored forty-nine out of a possible fifty, and the question of supremacy was as undecided as ever.

'It's getting exciting,' said Charley, lounging over the stand. 'We begin shooting at the five hundred yards in a few minutes.'

'Oh, Charley,' cried Fanny in high excitement, 'don't you go and miss, whatever you do!'

'I won't if I can help it,' responded Charley, cheerfully.

'You made a "bull" every time just now,' I said.

'Yes, but it's not so easy when you've got your sights up. However, we'll do our best, and we can't do more. They've got some terribly good long-range men among them. Come over here, Lottie, for a moment.'

'What is it, Charley?' I asked, as he led me away from the others. I could see by the look in his face that something was troubling him.

'It's that fellow,' growled my lover. 'What the deuce does he want to come here for? I hoped we had seen the last of him!'

'What fellow?' I gasped, with a vague apprehension at my heart.

'Why, that infernal Swedish fellow, Gaster!'

I followed the direction of Charley's glance, and there, sure enough, standing on a little knoll close to the place where the riflemen were lying, was the tall, angular figure of the foreigner.

He seemed utterly unconscious of the sensation which his singular appearance and hideous countenance excited among the burly farmers around him; but was craning his long neck about, this way and that, as if in search of somebody.

As we watched him, his eye suddenly rested upon us, and it seemed to me that, even at that distance, I could see a spasm of hatred and triumph pass over his livid features.

A strange foreboding came over me, and I seized my lover's hand in both my own.

'Oh, Charley,' I cried, 'don't—don't go back to the shooting! Say you are ill—make some excuse, and come away!'

'Nonsense, lass!' said he, laughing heartily at my terror. 'Why, what in the world are you afraid of?'

'Of him!' I answered.

'Don't be so silly, dear. One would think he was a demi-god to hear the way in which you talk of him. But there! that's the bell, and I must be off.'

'Well, promise, at least, that you will not go near him?' I cried, following Charley.

'All right—all right!' said he.

And I had to be content with that small concession.

The contest at the five hundred yards range was a close and exciting one. Roborough led by a couple of points for some time, until a series of 'bulls' by one of the crack marksmen of their opponents turned the tables upon them.

At the end of it was found that the volunteers were three points to the bad—a result which was hailed by cheers from the Plymouth contingent and by long faces and black looks among the dwellers on the moor.

During the whole of this competition Octavius Gaster had remained perfectly still and motionless upon the top of the knoll on which he had originally taken up his position.

It seemed to me that he knew little of what was going on, for his face was turned away from the marksmen, and he appeared to be gazing into the distance.

Once I caught sight of his profile, and thought that his lips were moving rapidly as if in prayer, or it may have been the shimmer of the hot air of the almost Indian summer which deceived me. It was, however, my impression at the time.

And now came the competition at the longest range of all, which was to decide the match.

The Roborough men settled down steadily to their task of making up the lost ground; while the regulars seemed determined not to throw away a chance by over-confidence.

As shot after shot was fired, the excitement of the spectators became so great that they crowded round the marksmen, cheering enthusiastically at every 'bull.'

We ourselves were so far affected by the general contagion that we left our harbour of refuge, and submitted meekly to the pushing and rough ways of the mob, in order to obtain a nearer view of the champions and their doings.

The military stood at seventeen when the volunteers were at sixteen, and great was the despondency of the rustics.

Things looked brighter, however, when the two sides tied at twenty-four, and brighter still when the steady shooting of the local team raised their score to thirty-two against thirty of their opponents.

There were still, however, the three points which had been lost at the last range to be made up for.

Slowly the score rose, and desperate were the efforts of both parties to pull off the victory.

Finally, a thrill ran through the crowd when it was known that the last red-coat had fired, while one volunteer was still left, and that the soldiers were leading by four points.

Even *our* unsportsman-like minds were worked into a state of all-absorbing excitement by the nature of the crisis which now presented itself.

If the last representative of our little town could but hit the bull's-eye the match was won.

The silver cup, the glory, the money of our adherents, all depended upon that single shot.

The reader will imagine that my interest was by no means lessened when, by dint of craning my neck and standing on tiptoe, I caught sight of my Charley coolly shoving a cartridge into his rifle, and realised that it was upon his skill that the honour of Roborough depended.

It was this, I think, which lent me strength to push my way so vigorously through the crowd that I found myself almost in the first row and commanding an excellent view of the proceedings.

There were two gigantic farmers on each side of me, and while we were waiting for the decisive shot to be fired, I could not help listening to the conversation, which they carried on in broad Devon, over my head.

'Mun's a rare ugly 'un,' said one.

'He is that,' cordially assented the other.

'See to mun's een?'

'Eh, Jock; see to mun's moo',* rayther!—Blessed if he bean't foamin' like Farmer Watson's dog—t' bull pup whot died mad o' the hydropathics.'*

I turned round to see the favoured object of these flattering comments and my eyes fell upon Doctor Octavius Gaster, whose presence I had entirely forgotten in my excitement.

His face was turned towards me; but he evidently did not see me, for his eyes were bent with unswerving persistence upon a point midway apparently between the distant targets and himself.

I have never seen anything to compare with the extraordinary concentration of that stare, which had the effect of making his eyeballs appear gorged and prominent, while the pupils were contracted to the finest possible point.

Perspiration was running freely down his long, cadaverous face, and, as the farmer had remarked, there were some traces of foam at the corners of his mouth. The jaw was locked, as if with some fierce effort of the will which demanded all the energy of his soul.

To my dying day that hideous countenance shall never fade from my remembrance nor cease to haunt me in my dreams. I shuddered, and turned away my head in the vain hope that perhaps the honest farmer might be right, and mental disease be the cause of all the vagaries of this extraordinary man.

A great stillness fell upon the whole crowd as Charley, having loaded his rifle, snapped up the breech cheerily, and proceeded to lie down in his appointed place.

'That's right, Mr Charles, sir—that's right!' I heard old McIntosh, the volunteer sergeant, whisper as I passed. 'A cool head and a steady hand, that's what does the trick, sir!'

My lover smiled round at the gray-headed soldier as he lay down upon the grass, and then proceeded to look along the sight of his rifle amid a silence in which the faint rustling of the breeze among the blades of grass was distinctly audible.

For more than a minute he hung upon his aim. His finger seemed to press the trigger, and every eye was fixed upon the distant target, when suddenly, instead of firing, the rifleman staggered up to his knees, leaving his weapon upon the ground.

To the surprise of everyone, his face was deadly pale, and perspiration was standing on his brow.

'I say, McIntosh,' he said, in a strange, gasping voice, 'is there any-body standing between the target and me?'

'Between, sir? No, not a soul, sir,' answered the astonished sergeant.

'There, man, there!' cried Charley, with fierce energy, seizing him by the arm, and pointing in the direction of the target, 'Don't you see him there, standing right in the line of fire?'

'There's no one there!' shouted half a dozen voices.

'No one there? Well, it must have been my imagination,' said Charley, passing his hand slowly over his forehead. 'Yet I could have sworn—Here, give me the rifle!'

He lay down again, and having settled himself into position, raised his weapon slowly to his eye. He had hardly looked along the barrel before he sprang up again with a loud cry.

'There!' he cried; 'I tell you I see it! A man dressed in volunteer uniform, and very like myself—the image of myself. Is this a conspiracy?' he continued, turning fiercely on the crowd. 'Do you tell me none of you see a man resembling myself walking from that target, and not two hundred yards from me as I speak?'

I should have flown to Charley's side had I not known how he hated feminine interference, and anything approaching to a scene. I could only listen silently to his strange wild words.

'I protest against this!' said an officer coming forward. 'This gentleman must really either take his shot, or we shall remove our men off the field and claim the victory.'

'But I'll shoot *him*!' gasped poor Charley.

'Humbug!' 'Rubbish!' 'Shoot him, then!' growled half a score of masculine voices.

'The fact is,' lisped one of the military men in front of me to another, 'the young fellow's nerves ar'n't quite equal to the occasion, and he feels it, and is trying to back out.'

The imbecile young lieutenant little knew at this point how a feminine hand was longing to stretch forth and deal him a sounding box on the ears.

'It's Martell's three-star brandy,* that's what it is,' whispered the other. 'The "devils," don't you know. I've had 'em myself, and know a case when I see it.'

This remark was too recondite for my understanding, or the speaker would have run the same risk as his predecessor.

'Well, are you going to shoot or not?' cried several voices.

'Yes, I'll shoot,' groaned Charley—'I'll shoot *him* through! It's murder—sheer *murder*!'

I shall never forget the haggard look which he cast round at the crowd. 'I'm aiming *through* him, McIntosh,' he murmured, as he lay down on the grass and raised the gun for the third time to his shoulder.

There was one moment of suspense, a spurt of flame, the crack of a rifle, and a cheer which echoed across the moor, and might have been heard in the distant village.

'Well done, lad—well done!' shouted a hundred honest Devonshire voices, as the little white disc came out from behind the marker's shield and obliterated the dark 'bull' for the moment, proclaiming that the match was won.

'Well done, lad! It's Maister Pillar, of Toynby Hall. Here, let's gie mun a lift, carry mun home, for the honour o' Roborough. Come on, lads! There mun is on the grass. Wake up, Sergeant McIntosh. What be the matter with thee? Eh? What?'

A deadly stillness came over the crowd, and then a low incredulous murmur, changing to one of pity, with whispers of 'leave her alone, poor lass leave her to hersel'!'—and then there was silence again, save for the moaning of a woman, and her short, quick cries of despair.

For, reader, my Charley, my beautiful, brave Charley, was lying cold and dead upon the ground, with the rifle still clenched in his stiffening fingers.

I heard kind words of sympathy. I heard Lieutenant Daseby's voice, broken with grief, begging me to control my sorrow, and felt his hand, as he gently raised me from my poor boy's body. This I can remember, and nothing more, until my recovery from my illness, when I found myself in the sick-room at Toynby Hall, and learned that three restless, delirious weeks had passed since that terrible day.

Stay!—do I remember nothing else?

Sometimes I think I do. Sometimes I think I can recall a lucid interval in the midst of my wanderings. I seem to have a dim recollection of seeing my good nurse go out of the room—of seeing a gaunt, bloodless face peering in through the half-open window, and of hearing a voice which said, 'I have dealt with thy so beautiful lover, and I have yet to deal with thee.' The words come back to me with a familiar ring, as if they had sounded in my ears before, and yet it may have been but a dream.

'And this is all!' you say. 'It is for this that a hysterical woman hunts down a harmless *savant* in the advertisement columns of the newspapers! On this shallow evidence she hints at crimes of the most monstrous description!'

Well, I cannot expect that these things should strike you as they struck me. I can but say that if I were upon a bridge with Octavius Gaster standing at one end, and the most merciless tiger that ever prowled in an Indian jungle at the other, I should fly to the wild beast for protection.

For me, my life is broken and blasted. I care not how soon it may end, but if my words shall keep this man out of one honest household, I have not written in vain.

* * *

Within a fortnight after writing this narrative, my poor daughter disappeared. All search has failed to find her. A porter at the railway station has deposed to having seen a young lady resembling her description get into a first-class carriage with a tall, thin gentleman. It is, however, too ridiculous to suppose that she can have eloped after her recent grief, and without my having had any suspicions. The detectives are, however, working out the clue.—EMILY UNDERWOOD

J. HABAKUK JEPHSON'S STATEMENT

IN the month of December in the year 1873, the British ship *Dei Gratia** steered into Gibraltar, having in tow the derelict brigantine *Marie Celeste*,* which had been picked up in latitude 38° 40′, longitude 17° 15′ W. There were several circumstances in connection with the condition and appearance of this abandoned vessel which excited considerable comment at the time, and aroused a curiosity which has never been satisfied. What these circumstances were was summed up in an able article which appeared in the *Gibraltar Gazette*.* The curious can find it in the issue for January 4, 1874, unless my memory deceives me. For the benefit of those, however, who may be unable to refer to the paper in question, I shall subjoin a few extracts which touch upon the leading features of the case.

'We have ourselves,' says the anonymous writer in the *Gazette*, 'been over the derelict *Marie Celeste*, and have closely questioned the officers of the *Dei Gratia* on every point which might throw light on the affair. They are of opinion that she had been abandoned several days, or perhaps weeks, before being picked up. The official log, which was found in the cabin, states that the vessel sailed from Boston to Lisbon, starting upon October 16.* It is, however, most imperfectly kept, and affords little information. There is no reference to rough weather, and, indeed, the state of the vessel's paint and rigging excludes the idea that she was abandoned for any such reason. She is perfectly watertight. No signs of a struggle or of violence are to be detected, and there is absolutely nothing to account for the disappearance of the crew. There are several indications that a lady was present on board, a sewing-machine being found in the cabin and some articles of female attire. These probably belonged to the captain's wife, who is mentioned in the log as having accompanied her husband. As an instance of the mildness of the weather, it may be remarked that a bobbin of silk was found standing upon the sewing-machine, though the least roll of the vessel would have precipitated it to the floor. The boats were intact and slung upon the davits;* and the cargo, consisting of tallow and American clocks, was untouched. An old-fashioned sword of curious workmanship was discovered among some lumber in the forecastle, and this weapon is said to exhibit a longitudinal striation* on the steel, as if it had been recently wiped. It has been placed in the hands of the police, and submitted to Dr Monaghan, the analyst, for inspection. The result of his examination has not yet been published. We may remark, in conclusion, that Captain Dalton, of the *Dei Gratia*, an able and intelligent seaman, is of opinion that the *Marie Celeste* may have been abandoned a considerable distance from the spot at which she was picked up, since a powerful current runs up in that latitude from the African coast. He confesses his inability, however, to advance any hypothesis which can reconcile all the facts of the case. In the utter absence of a clue or grain of evidence, it is to be feared that the fate of the crew of the *Marie Celeste* will be added to those numerous mysteries of the deep which will never be solved until the great day when the sea shall give up its dead. If crime has been committed, as is much to be suspected, there is little hope of bringing the perpetrators to justice.'

I shall supplement this extract from the *Gibraltar Gazette* by quoting a telegram from Boston, which went the round of the English papers, and represented the total amount of information which had been collected about the *Marie Celeste*. 'She was,' it said, 'a brigantine of 170 tons burden, and belonged to White, Russell & White, wine importers, of this city. Captain J. W. Tibbs* was an old servant of the firm, and was a man of known ability and tried probity. He was accompanied by his wife, aged thirty-one, and their youngest child, five years old. The crew consisted of seven hands, including two coloured seamen, and a boy. There were three passengers, one of whom was the well-known Brooklyn specialist on consumption, Dr Habakuk Jephson, who was a distinguished advocate for Abolition in the early days of the movement, and whose pamphlet, entitled "Where is thy Brother?" exercised a strong influence on public opinion before the war.* The other passengers were Mr J. Harton, a writer in the employ of the firm, and Mr Septimius Goring, a half-caste gentleman, from New Orleans. All investigations have failed to throw any light upon the fate of these fourteen human beings. The loss of Dr Jephson will be felt both in political and scientific circles.'

I have here epitomised,* for the benefit of the public, all that has been hitherto known concerning the *Marie Celeste* and her crew, for the past ten years have not in any way helped to elucidate the mystery. I have now taken up my pen with the intention of telling all that

I know of the ill-fated voyage. I consider that it is a duty which I owe to society, for symptoms which I am familiar with in others lead me to believe that before many months my tongue and hand may be alike incapable of conveying information. Let me remark, as a preface to my narrative, that I am Joseph Habakuk Jephson, Doctor of Medicine of the University of Harvard, and ex-Consulting Physician of the Samaritan Hospital of Brooklyn.

Many will doubtless wonder why I have not proclaimed myself before, and why I have suffered so many conjectures and surmises to pass unchallenged. Could the ends of justice have been served in any way by my revealing the facts in my possession I should unhesitatingly have done so. It seemed to me, however, that there was no possibility of such a result; and when I attempted, after the occurrence, to state my case to an English official, I was met with such offensive incredulity that I determined never again to expose myself to the chance of such an indignity. I can excuse the discourtesy of the Liverpool magistrate, however, when I reflect upon the treatment which I received at the hands of my own relatives, who, though they knew my unimpeachable character, listened to my statement with an indulgent smile as if humouring the delusion of a monomaniac.* This slur upon my veracity led to a quarrel between myself and John Vanburger, the brother of my wife, and confirmed me in my resolution to let the matter sink into oblivion—a determination which I have only altered through my son's solicitations. In order to make my narrative intelligible, I must run lightly over one or two incidents in my former life which throw light upon subsequent events. My father, William K. Jephson, was a preacher of the sect called Plymouth Brethren, and was one of the most respected citizens of Lowell.* Like most of the other Puritans of New England, he was a determined opponent of slavery, and it was from his lips that I received those lessons which tinged every action of my life. While I was studying medicine at Harvard University, I had already made a mark as an advanced Abolitionist; and when, after taking my degree, I bought a third share of the practice of Dr Willis, of Brooklyn, I managed, in spite of my professional duties, to devote a considerable time to the cause which I had at heart, my pamphlet, 'Where is thy Brother?' (Swarburgh, Lister & Co., 1859)* attracting considerable attention.

When the war broke out I left Brooklyn and accompanied the 113th New York Regiment through the campaign. I was present at the second battle of Bull's Run and at the battle of Gettysburg. Finally, I was severely wounded at Antietam,* and would probably have perished on the field had it not been for the kindness of a gentleman named Murray, who had me carried to his house and provided me with every comfort. Thanks to his charity, and to the nursing which I received from his black domestics, I was soon able to get about the plantation with the help of a stick. It was during this period of convalescence that an incident occurred which is closely connected with my story.

Among the most assiduous of the negresses who had watched my couch during my illness there was one old crone who appeared to exert considerable authority over the others. She was exceedingly attentive to me, and I gathered from the few words that passed between us that she had heard of me, and that she was grateful to me for championing her oppressed race.

One day as I was sitting alone in the verandah, basking in the sun, and debating whether I should rejoin Grant's* army, I was surprised to see this old creature hobbling towards me. After looking cautiously around to see that we were alone, she fumbled in the front of her dress, and produced a small chamois leather bag which was hung round her neck by a white cord.

'Massa,' she said, bending down and croaking the words into my ear, 'me die soon. Me very old woman. Not stay long on Massa Murray's plantation.'

'You may live a long time yet, Martha,' I answered. 'You know I am a doctor. If you feel ill let me know about it and I will try to cure you.'

'No wish to live—wish to die. I'm gwine to join the heavenly host.' Here she relapsed into one of those half-heathenish rhapsodies in which negroes indulge. 'But, massa, me have one thing must leave behind me when I go. No able to take it with me across the Jordan.* That one thing very precious, more precious and more holy than all thing else in the world. Me, a poor old black woman, have this because my people, very great people, 'spose they was back in the old country. But you cannot understand this same as black folk could. My fader give it me, and his fader give it him, but now who shall I give it to? Poor Martha hab no child, no relation, nobody. All round I see black man very bad man. Black woman very stupid woman. Nobody worthy of the stone. And so I say, Here is Massa Jephson who write books and fight for coloured folk—he must be a good man, and he shall have it though he is white man, and nebber can know what it mean or where it came from.' Here the old woman fumbled in the chamois leather bag and pulled out a flattish black stone with a hole through the middle of it. 'Here, take it,' she said, pressing it into my hand; 'take it. No harm nebber come from anything good. Keep it safe—nebber lose it!' and with a warning gesture the old crone hobbled away in the same cautious way as she had come, looking from side to side to see if we had been observed.

I was more amused than impressed by the old woman's earnestness, and was only prevented from laughing during her oration by the fear of hurting her feelings. When she was gone I took a good look at the stone which she had given me. It was intensely black, of extreme hardness, and oval in shape—just such a flat stone as one would pick up on the seashore if one wished to throw a long way. It was about three inches long, and an inch and a half broad at the middle, but rounded off at the extremities. The most curious part about it was several well-marked ridges which ran in semicircles over its surface, and gave it exactly the appearance of a human ear. Altogether I was rather interested in my new possession and determined to submit it, as a geological specimen, to my friend Professor Shroeder of the New York Institute* upon the earliest opportunity. In the meantime I thrust it into my pocket, and rising from my chair started off for a short stroll in the shrubbery, dismissing the incident from my mind.

As my wound had nearly healed by this time, I took my leave of Mr Murray shortly afterwards. The Union armies were everywhere victorious and converging on Richmond,* so that my assistance seemed unnecessary, and I returned to Brooklyn. There I resumed my practice, and married the second daughter of Josiah Vanburger, the well-known wood engraver. In the course of a few years I built up a good connection and acquired considerable reputation in the treatment of pulmonary complaints. I still kept the old black stone in my pocket, and frequently told the story of the dramatic way in which I had become possessed of it. I also kept my resolution of showing it to Professor Shroeder, who was much interested both by the anecdote and the specimen. He pronounced it to be a piece of meteoric stone, and drew my attention to the fact that its resemblance to an ear was not accidental, but that it was most carefully worked into that shape. A dozen little anatomical points showed that the worker had been as accurate as he was skilful. 'I should not wonder,' said the Professor, 'if it were broken off from some larger statue, though how such hard

material could be so perfectly worked is more than I can understand.
If there is a statue to correspond I should like to see it!' So I thought
at the time, but I have changed my opinion since.

The next seven or eight years of my life were quiet and uneventful.
Summer followed spring, and spring followed winter, without any variation in my duties. As the practice increased I admitted J. S. Jackson
as partner, he to have one-fourth of the profits. The continued strain
had told upon my constitution, however, and I became at last so unwell
that my wife insisted upon my consulting Dr Kavanagh Smith, who
was my colleague at the Samaritan Hospital. That gentleman examined me, and pronounced the apex of my left lung to be in a state of
consolidation,* recommending me at the same time to go through
a course of medical treatment and to take a long sea-voyage.

My own disposition, which is naturally restless, predisposed me
strongly in favour of the latter piece of advice, and the matter was
clinched by my meeting young Russell, of the firm of White, Russell
& White, who offered me a passage in one of his father's ships, the
Marie Celeste, which was just starting from Boston. 'She is a snug
little ship,' he said, 'and Tibbs, the captain, is an excellent fellow.
There is nothing like a sailing ship for an invalid.' I was very much of
the same opinion myself, so I closed with the offer on the spot.

My original plan was that my wife should accompany me on my
travels. She has always been a very poor sailor, however, and there
were strong family reasons against her exposing herself to any risk at
the time, so we determined that she should remain at home. I am not
a religious or an effusive man; but oh, thank God for that! As to leaving my practice, I was easily reconciled to it, as Jackson, my partner,
was a reliable and hard-working man.

I arrived in Boston on October 12, 1873, and proceeded immediately to the office of the firm in order to thank them for their courtesy.
As I was sitting in the counting-house waiting until they should be at
liberty to see me, the words *Marie Celeste* suddenly attracted my
attention. I looked round and saw a very tall, gaunt man, who was
leaning across the polished mahogany counter asking some questions
of the clerk at the other side. His face was turned half towards me, and
I could see that he had a strong dash of negro blood in him, being
probably a quadroon* or even nearer akin to the black. His curved
aquiline nose and straight lank hair showed the white strain; but the
dark, restless eye, sensuous mouth, and gleaming teeth all told of his

African origin. His complexion was of a sickly, unhealthy yellow, and as his face was deeply pitted with small-pox, the general impression was so unfavourable as to be almost revolting. When he spoke, however, it was in a soft, melodious voice, and in well-chosen words, and he was evidently a man of some education.

'I wished to ask a few questions about the *Marie Celeste*,' he repeated, leaning across to the clerk. 'She sails the day after to-morrow, does she not?'

'Yes, sir,' said the young clerk, awed into unusual politeness by the glimmer of a large diamond in the stranger's shirt front.

'Where is she bound for?'

'Lisbon.'

'How many of a crew?'

'Seven, sir.'

'Passengers?'

'Yes, two. One of our young gentlemen, and a doctor from New York.'

'No gentleman from the South?' asked the stranger eagerly.

'No, none, sir.'

'Is there room for another passenger?'

'Accommodation, for three more,' answered the clerk.

'I'll go,' said the quadroon decisively; 'I'll go, I'll engage my passage at once. Put it down, will you—Mr Septimius Goring, of New Orleans.'

The clerk filled up a form and handed it over to the stranger, pointing to a blank space at the bottom. As Mr Goring stooped over to sign it I was horrified to observe that the fingers of his right hand had been lopped off, and that he was holding the pen between his thumb and the palm. I have seen thousands slain in battle, and assisted at every conceivable surgical operation, but I cannot recall any sight which gave me such a thrill of disgust as that great brown sponge-like hand with the single member protruding from it. He used it skilfully enough, however, for, dashing off his signature, he nodded to the clerk and strolled out of the office just as Mr White sent out word that he was ready to receive me.

I went down to the *Marie Celeste* that evening, and looked over my berth, which was extremely comfortable considering the small size of the vessel. Mr Goring, whom I had seen in the morning, was to have the one next mine. Opposite was the captain's cabin and a small berth for Mr John Harton, a gentleman who was going out in the interests of the firm. These little rooms were arranged on each side of the passage which led from the main-deck to the saloon. The latter was a comfortable room, the panelling tastefully done in oak and mahogany, with a rich Brussels carpet* and luxurious settees. I was very much pleased with the accommodation, and also with Tibbs the captain, a bluff, sailor-like fellow, with a loud voice and hearty manner, who welcomed me to the ship with effusion, and insisted upon our splitting a bottle of wine in his cabin. He told me that he intended to take his wife and youngest child with him on the voyage, and that he hoped with good luck to make Lisbon in three weeks. We had a pleasant chat and parted the best of friends, he warning me to make the last of my preparations next morning, as he intended to make a start by the mid-day tide, having now shipped all his cargo. I went back to my hotel, where I found a letter from my wife awaiting me, and, after a refreshing night's sleep, returned to the boat in the morning. From this point I am able to quote from the journal which I kept in order to vary the monotony of the long sea-voyage. If it is somewhat bald in places I can at least rely upon its accuracy in details, as it was written conscientiously from day to day.

October 16th.—Cast off our warps* at half-past two and were towed out into the bay, where the tug left us, and with all sail set we bowled along at about nine knots an hour. I stood upon the poop* watching the low land of America sinking gradually upon the horizon until the evening haze hid it from my sight. A single red light, however, continued to blaze balefully behind us, throwing a long track like a trail of blood upon the water, and it is still visible as I write, though reduced to a mere speck. The captain is in a bad humour, for two of his hands disappointed him at the last moment, and he was compelled to ship a couple of negroes who happened to be on the quay. The missing men were steady, reliable fellows, who had been with him several voyages, and their non-appearance puzzled as well as irritated him. Where a crew of seven men have to work a fair-sized ship the loss of two experienced seamen is a serious one, for though the negroes may take a spell at the wheel or swab the decks, they are of little or no use in rough weather. Our cook is also a black man, and Mr Septimius Goring has a little darkie servant, so that we are rather a piebald community. The accountant, John Harton, promises to be an acquisition, for he is a cheery, amusing young fellow. Strange how little wealth has to do with happiness! He has all the world before him and is seeking his fortune in a far land, yet he is as transparently happy as a man can be. Goring is rich, if I am not mistaken, and so am I; but I know that I have a lung, and Goring has some deeper trouble still, to judge by his features. How poorly do we both contrast with the careless, penniless clerk!

October 17th. Mrs Tibbs appeared upon the deck for the first time this morning —a cheerful, energetic woman, with a dear little child just able to walk and prattle. Young Harton pounced on it at once, and carried it away to his cabin, where no doubt he will lay the seeds of future dyspepsia* in the child's stomach. Thus medicine doth make cynics of us all! The weather is still all that could be desired, with a fine fresh breeze from the west-sou'-west. The vessel goes so steadily that you would hardly know that she was moving were it not for the creaking of the cordage,* the bellying of the sails, and the long white furrow in our wake. Walked the quarter-deck all morning with the captain, and I think the keen fresh air has already done my breathing good, for the exercise did not fatigue me in any way. Tibbs is a remarkably intelligent man, and we had an interesting argument about Maury's observations* on ocean currents, which we terminated by going down into his cabin to consult the original work. There we found Goring, rather to the captain's surprise, as it is not usual for passengers to enter that sanctum unless specially invited. He apologised for his intrusion, however, pleading his ignorance of the usages of ship life; and the good-natured sailor simply laughed at the incident, begging him to remain and favour us with his company. Goring pointed to the chronometers, the case of which he had opened, and remarked that he had been admiring them. He has evidently some practical knowledge of mathematical instruments, as he told at a glance which was the most trustworthy of the three, and also named their price within a few dollars. He had a discussion with the captain too upon the variation of the compass, and when we came back to the ocean currents he showed a thorough grasp of the subject. Altogether he rather improves upon acquaintance, and is a man of decided culture and refinement. His voice harmonises with his conversation, and both are the very antithesis of his face and figure.

The noonday observation shows that we have run two hundred and twenty miles. Towards evening the breeze freshened up, and the first mate ordered reefs to be taken in the topsails and top-gallant sails* in expectation of a windy night. I observe that the barometer has fallen to twenty-nine. I trust our voyage will not be a rough one, as I am a poor sailor, and my health would probably derive more harm than good from a stormy trip, though I have the greatest confidence in the captain's seamanship and in the soundness of the vessel. Played cribbage with Mrs Tibbs after supper, and Harton gave us a couple of tunes on the violin.

October 18*th.*—The gloomy prognostications of last night were not fulfilled, as the wind died away again and we are lying now in a long greasy swell, ruffled here and there by a fleeting catspaw* which is insufficient to fill the sails. The air is colder than it was yesterday, and I have put on one of the thick woollen jerseys which my wife knitted for me. Harton came into my cabin in the morning, and we had a cigar together. He says that he remembers having seen Goring in Cleveland, Ohio, in '69. He was, it appears, a mystery then as now, wandering about without any visible employment, and extremely reticent on his own affairs. The man interests me as a psychological study. At breakfast this morning I suddenly had that vague feeling of uneasiness which comes over some people when closely stared at, and, looking quickly up, I met his eyes bent upon me with an intensity which amounted to ferocity, though their expression instantly softened as he made some conventional remark upon the weather. Curiously enough, Harton says that he had a very similar experience yesterday upon deck. I observe that Goring frequently talks to the coloured seamen as he strolls about—a trait which I rather admire, as it is common to find half-breeds ignore their dark strain and treat their black kinsfolk with greater intolerance than a white man would do. His little page is devoted to him, apparently, which speaks well for his treatment of him. Altogether, the man is a curious mixture of incongruous qualities, and unless I am deceived in him will give me food for observation during the voyage.

The captain is grumbling about his chronometers, which do not register exactly the same time. He says it is the first time that they have ever disagreed. We were unable to get a noonday observation on account of the haze. By dead reckoning, we have done about a hundred and seventy miles in the twenty-four hours. The dark seamen have proved, as the skipper prophesied, to be very inferior hands, but as they can both manage the wheel well they are kept steering, and so leave the more experienced men to work the ship. These details are trivial enough, but a small thing serves as food for gossip aboard ship.

The appearance of a whale in the evening caused quite a flutter among us. From its sharp back and forked tail, I should pronounce it to have been a rorqual, or 'finner,'* as they are called by the fishermen.

October 19*th.*—Wind was cold, so I prudently remained in my cabin all day, only creeping out for dinner. Lying in my bunk I can without moving, reach my books, pipes, or anything else I may want, which is one advantage of a small apartment. My old wound began to ache a little to-day, probably from the cold. Read *Montaigne's Essays*✻ and nursed myself. Harton came in in the afternoon with Doddy, the captain's child, and the skipper himself followed, so that I held quite a reception.

October 20*th and* 21*st.*—Still cold, with a continual drizzle of rain, and I have not been able to leave the cabin. This confinement makes me feel weak and depressed. Goring came in to see me, but his company did not tend to cheer me up much, as he hardly uttered a word, but contented himself with staring at me in a peculiar and rather irritating manner. He then got up and stole out of the cabin without saying anything. I am beginning to suspect that the man is a lunatic. I think I mentioned that his cabin is next to mine. The two are simply divided by a thin wooden partition which is cracked in many places, some of the cracks being so large that I can hardly avoid, as I lie in my bunk, observing his motions in the adjoining room. Without any wish to play the spy, I see him continually stooping over what appears to be a chart and working with a pencil and compasses. I have remarked the interest he displays in matters connected with navigation, but I am surprised that he should take the trouble to work out the course of the ship. However, it is a harmless amusement enough, and no doubt he verifies his results by those of the captain.

I wish the man did not run in my thoughts so much. I had a nightmare on the night of the 20th, in which I thought my bunk was a coffin, that I was laid out in it, and that Goring was endeavouring to nail up the lid, which I was frantically pushing away. Even when I woke up, I could hardly persuade myself that I was not in a coffin. As a medical man, I know that a nightmare is simply a vascular derangement of the cerebral hemispheres,* and yet in my weak state I cannot shake off the morbid impression which it produces.

October 22*nd.*—A fine day, with hardly a cloud in the sky, and a fresh breeze from the sou'-west which wafts us gaily on our way. There has evidently been some heavy weather near us, as there is a tremendous swell on, and the ship lurches until the end of the fore-yard nearly touches the water. Had a refreshing walk up and down the quarter-deck, though I have hardly found my sea-legs yet. Several small birds—chaffinches,* I think—perched in the rigging.

4.40 P.M.—While I was on deck this morning I heard a sudden explosion from the direction of my cabin, and, hurrying down, found that I had very nearly met with a serious accident. Goring was clean-ing a revolver, it seems, in his cabin, when one of the barrels which he thought was unloaded went off. The ball passed through the side par-tition and imbedded itself in the bulwarks in the exact place where my head usually rests. I have been under fire too often to magnify trifles, but there is no doubt that if I had been in the bunk it must have killed me. Goring, poor fellow, did not know that I had gone on deck that day, and must therefore have felt terribly frightened. I never saw such emotion in a man's face as when, on rushing out of his cabin with the smoking pistol in his hand, he met me face to face as I came down from deck. Of course, he was profuse in his apologies, though I simply laughed at the incident.

11 P.M.—A misfortune has occurred so unexpected and so hor-rible that my little escape of the morning dwindles into insignificance. Mrs Tibbs and her child have disappeared—utterly and entirely dis-appeared. I can hardly compose myself to write the sad details. About half-past eight Tibbs rushed into my cabin with a very white face and asked me if I had seen his wife. I answered that I had not. He then ran wildly into the saloon and began groping about for any trace of her, while I followed him, endeavouring vainly to persuade him that his fears were ridiculous. We hunted over the ship for an hour and a half without coming on any sign of the missing woman or child. Poor Tibbs lost his voice completely from calling her name. Even the sail-ors, who are generally stolid enough, were deeply affected by the sight of him as he roamed bareheaded and dishevelled about the deck, searching with feverish anxiety the most impossible places, and returning to them again and again with a piteous pertinacity.* The last time she was seen was about seven o'clock, when she took Doddy on to the poop to give him a breath of fresh air before putting him to bed. There was no one there at the time except the black seaman at the wheel, who denies having seen her at all. The whole affair is wrapped in mystery. My own theory is that while Mrs Tibbs was holding the child and standing near the bulwarks it gave a spring and

fell overboard, and that in her convulsive attempt to catch or save it, she followed it. I cannot account for the double disappearance in any other way. It is quite feasible that such a tragedy should be enacted without the knowledge of the man at the wheel, since it was dark at the time, and the peaked skylights of the saloon screen the greater part of the quarter-deck. Whatever the truth may be it is a terrible catastrophe, and has cast the darkest gloom upon our voyage. The mate has put the ship about, but of course there is not the slightest hope of picking them up. The captain is lying in a state of stupor in his cabin. I gave him a powerful dose of opium in his coffee that for a few hours at least his anguish may be deadened.

October 23rd.—Woke with a vague feeling of heaviness and misfortune, but it was not until a few moments' reflection that I was able to recall our loss of the night before. When I came on deck I saw the poor skipper standing gazing back at the waste of waters behind us which contains everything dear to him upon earth. I attempted to speak to him, but he turned brusquely away, and began pacing the deck with his head sunk upon his breast. Even now, when the truth is so clear, he cannot pass a boat or an unbent sail without peering under it. He looks ten years older than he did yesterday morning. Harton is terribly cut up, for he was fond of little Doddy, and Goring seems sorry too. At least he has shut himself up in his cabin all day, and when I got a casual glance at him his head was resting on his two hands as if in a melancholy reverie. I fear we are about as dismal a crew as ever sailed. How shocked my wife will be to hear of our disaster! The swell has gone down now, and we are doing about eight knots with all sail set and a nice little breeze. Hyson is practically in command of the ship, as Tibbs, though he does his best to bear up and keep a brave front, is incapable of applying himself to serious work.

October 24th.—Is the ship accursed? Was there ever a voyage which began so fairly and which changed so disastrously? Tibbs shot himself through the head during the night. I was awakened about three o'clock in the morning by an explosion, and immediately sprang out of bed and rushed into the captain's cabin to find out the cause, though with a terrible presentiment in my heart. Quickly as I went, Goring went more quickly still, for he was already in the cabin stooping over the dead body of the captain. It was a hideous sight, for the whole front of his face was blown in, and the little room was swimming in blood. The pistol was lying beside him on the floor, just as it had dropped from his hand. He had evidently put it to his mouth before pulling the trigger. Goring and I picked him reverently up and laid him on his bed. The crew had all clustered into his cabin, and the six white men were deeply grieved, for they were old hands who had sailed with him many years. There were dark looks and murmurs among them too, and one of them openly declared that the ship was haunted. Harton helped to lay the poor skipper out, and we did him up in canvas between us. At twelve o'clock the fore-yard was hauled aback, and we committed his body to the deep, Goring reading the Church of England burial service. The breeze has freshened up, and we have done ten knots all day and sometimes twelve. The sooner we reach Lisbon and get away from this accursed ship the better pleased shall I be. I feel as though we were in a floating coffin. Little wonder that the poor sailors are superstitious when I, an educated man, feel it so strongly.

October 25th.—Made a good run all day. Feel listless and depressed.

October 26th.—Goring, Harton, and I had a chat together on deck in the morning. Harton tried to draw Goring out as to his profession, and his object in going to Europe, but the quadroon parried all his questions and gave us no information. Indeed, he seemed to be slightly offended by Harton's pertinacity, and went down into his cabin. I wonder why we should both take such an interest in this man! I suppose it is his striking appearance, coupled with his apparent wealth, which piques our curiosity. Harton has a theory that he is really a detective, that he is after some criminal who has got away to Portugal, and that he chooses this peculiar way of travelling that he may arrive unnoticed and pounce upon his quarry unawares. I think the supposition is rather a far-fetched one, but Harton bases it upon a book which Goring left on deck, and which he picked up and glanced over. It was a sort of scrap-book, it seems, and contained a large number of newspaper cuttings. All these cuttings related to murders which had been committed at various times in the States during the last twenty years or so. The curious thing which Harton observed about them, however, was that they were invariably murders the authors of which had never been brought to justice. They varied in every detail, he says, as to the manner of execution and the social status of the victim, but they uniformly wound up with the same for-mula that the murderer was still at large, though, of course, the police had every reason to expect his speedy capture. Certainly the incident seems to support Harton's theory, though it may be a mere whim of Goring's, or, as I suggested to Harton, he may be collecting materials for a book which shall outvie De Quincy.* In any case it is no business of ours.

October 27th, 28th.—Wind still fair, and we are making good progress. Strange, how easily a human unit may drop out of its place and be forgotten! Tibbs is hardly ever mentioned now; Hyson has taken possession of his cabin, and all goes on as before. Were it not for Mrs Tibbs's sewing-machine upon a side-table we might forget that the unfortunate family had ever existed. Another accident occurred on board to-day, though fortunately not a very serious one. One of our white hands had gone down the afterhold* to fetch up a spare coil of rope, when one of the hatches which he had removed came crashing down on the top of him. He saved his life by springing out of the way, but one of his feet was terribly crushed, and he will be of little use for the remainder of the voyage. He attributes the accident to the carelessness of his negro companion, who had helped him to shift the hatches. The latter, however, puts it down to the roll of the ship. Whatever be the cause, it reduces our short-handed crew still further. This run of ill-luck seems to be depressing Harton, for he has lost his usual good spirits and joviality. Goring is the only one who preserves his cheerfulness. I see him still working at his chart in his own cabin. His nautical knowledge would be useful should anything happen to Hyson—which God forbid!

October 29th, 30th.—Still bowling along with a fresh breeze. All quiet and nothing of note to chronicle.

October 31st.—My weak lungs, combined with the exciting episodes of the voyage, have shaken my nervous system so much that the most trivial incident affects me. I can hardly believe that I am the same man who tied the external iliac artery,* an operation requiring the nicest precision, under a heavy rifle fire at Antietam. I am as nervous as a child. I was lying half dozing last night about four bells in the middle watch* trying in vain to drop into a refreshing sleep. There was no light inside my cabin, but a single ray of moonlight streamed in through the port-hole, throwing a silvery flickering circle upon the door. As I lay I kept my drowsy eyes upon this circle, and was conscious that it was gradually becoming less well-defined as my senses left me, when I was suddenly recalled to full wakefulness by the appearance of a small dark object in the very centre of the luminous disc. I lay quietly and breathlessly watching it. Gradually it grew larger and plainer, and then I perceived that it was a human hand which had been cautiously inserted through the chink of the half-closed door—a hand which, as I observed with a thrill of horror, was not provided with fingers. The door swung cautiously backwards, and Goring's head followed his hand. It appeared in the centre of the moonlight, and was framed as it were in a ghastly uncertain halo, against which his features showed out plainly. It seemed to me that I had never seen such an utterly fiendish and merciless expression upon a human face. His eyes were dilated and glaring, his lips drawn back so as to show his white fangs, and his straight black hair appeared to bristle over his low forehead like the hood of a cobra. The sudden and noiseless apparition had such an effect upon me that I sprang up in bed trembling in every limb, and held out my hand towards my revolver. I was heartily ashamed of my hastiness when he explained the object of his intrusion, as he immediately did in the most courteous language. He had been suffering from toothache, poor fellow! and had come in to beg some laudanum,* knowing that I possessed a medicine chest. As to a sinister expression he is never a beauty, and what with my state of nervous tension and the effect of the shifting moonlight it was easy to conjure up something horrible. I gave him twenty drops, and he went off again, with many expressions of gratitude. I can hardly say how much this trivial incident affected me. I have felt unstrung all day.

A week's record of our voyage is here omitted, as nothing eventful occurred during the time, and my log consists merely of a few pages of unimportant gossip.

November 7th.—Harton and I sat on the poop all the morning, for the weather is becoming very warm as we come into southern latitudes. We reckon that we have done two-thirds of our voyage. How glad we shall be to see the green banks of the Tagus,* and leave this unlucky ship for ever! I was endeavouring to amuse Harton to-day and to while away the time by telling him some of the experiences of my past life. Among others I related to him how I came into the possession of my black stone, and as a finale I rummaged in the side pocket of my old shooting coat and produced the identical object in question. He and I were bending over it together, I pointing out to him the curious ridges upon its surface, when we were conscious of a shadow falling between us and the sun, and looking round saw Goring standing behind us glaring over our shoulders at the stone. For some reason or other he appeared to be powerfully excited, though he was evidently trying to control himself and to conceal his emotion. He pointed once or twice at my relic with his stubby thumb before he could recover himself sufficiently to ask what it was and how I obtained it—a question put in such a brusque manner that I should have been offended had I not known the man to be an eccentric. I told him the story very much as I had told it to Harton. He listened with the deepest interest and then asked me if I had any idea what the stone was. I said I had not, beyond that it was meteoric. He asked me if I had ever tried its effect upon a negro. I said I had not. 'Come,' said he, 'we'll see what our black friend at the wheel thinks of it.' He took the stone in his hand and went across to the sailor, and the two examined it carefully. I could see the man gesticulating and nodding his head excitedly as if making some assertion, while his face betrayed the utmost astonishment, mixed, I think, with some reverence. Goring came across the deck to us presently, still holding the stone in his hand. 'He says it is a worthless, useless thing,' he said, 'and fit only to be chucked overboard,' with which he raised his hand and would most certainly have made an end of my relic, had the black sailor behind him not rushed forward and seized him by the wrist. Finding himself secured Goring dropped the stone and turned away with a very bad grace to avoid my angry remonstrances at his breach of faith. The black picked up the stone and handed it to me with a low bow and every sign of profound respect. The whole affair is inexplicable. I am rapidly coming to the conclusion that Goring is a maniac or something very near one. When I compare the effect produced by the stone upon the sailor, however, with the respect shown to Martha on the plantation, and the surprise of Goring on its first production, I cannot but come to the conclusion that I have really got hold of some powerful talisman which appeals to the whole dark race. I must not trust it in Goring's hands again.

November 8*th*, 9*th*.—What splendid weather we are having! Beyond one little blow, we have had nothing but fresh breezes the whole voyage. These two days we have made better runs than any hitherto. It is a pretty thing to watch the spray fly up from our prow as it cuts through the waves. The sun shines through it and breaks it up into a number of miniature rainbows—'sun-dogs,' the sailors call them. I stood on the fo'c'sle-head* for several hours to-day watching the effect, and surrounded by a halo of prismatic colours. The steersman has evidently told the other blacks about my wonderful stone, for I am treated by them all with the greatest respect. Talking about optical phenomena, we had a curious one yesterday evening which was pointed out to me by Hyson. This was the appearance of a triangular well-defined object high up in the heavens to the north of us. He explained that it was exactly like the Peak of Teneriffe* as seen from a great distance—the peak was, however, at that moment at least five hundred miles to the south. It may have been a cloud, or it may have been one of those strange reflections of which one reads. The weather is very warm. The mate says that he never knew it so warm in these latitudes. Played chess with Harton in the evening.

November 10*th*.—It is getting warmer and warmer. Some land birds came and perched in the rigging to-day, though we are still a considerable way from our destination. The heat is so great that we are too lazy to do anything but lounge about the decks and smoke. Goring came over to me to-day and asked me some more questions about my stone; but I answered him rather shortly, for I have not quite forgiven him yet for the cool way in which he attempted to deprive me of it.

November 11*th*, 12*th*.—Still making good progress. I had no idea Portugal was ever as hot as this, but no doubt it is cooler on land. Hyson himself seemed surprised at it, and so do the men.

November 13*th*.—A most extraordinary event has happened, so extraordinary as to be almost inexplicable. Either Hyson has blundered wonderfully, or some magnetic influence has disturbed our instruments. Just about daybreak the watch on the fo'c'sle-head shouted out that he heard the sound of surf ahead, and Hyson thought he saw the loom of land. The ship was put about, and, though no lights were seen, none of us doubted that we had struck the Portuguese coast a little sooner than we had expected. What was our surprise to see the scene which was revealed to us at break of day! As far as we could look on either side was one long line of surf, great, green billows rolling in and breaking into a cloud of foam. But behind the surf what was there! Not the green banks nor the high cliffs of the shores of Portugal, but a great sandy waste which stretched away and away until it blended with the skyline. To right and left, look where you would, there was nothing but yellow sand, heaped in some places into fantastic mounds, some of them several hundred feet high, while in other parts were long stretches as level apparently as a billiard board. Harton and I, who had come on deck together, looked at each other in astonishment, and Harton burst out laughing. Hyson is exceedingly mortified at the occurrence, and protests that the instruments have been tampered with. There is no doubt that this is the mainland of Africa, and that it was really the Peak of Teneriffe which we saw some days ago upon the northern horizon. At the time when we saw the land birds we must have been passing some of the Canary Islands. If we continued on the same course, we are now to the north of Cape Blanco,* near the unexplored country which skirts the great Sahara. All we can do is to rectify our instruments as far as possible and start afresh for our destination.

8.30 P.M.—Have been lying in a calm all day. The coast is now about a mile and a half from us. Hyson has examined the instruments, but cannot find any reason for their extraordinary deviation.

This is the end of my private journal, and I must make the remainder of my statement from memory. There is little chance of my being mistaken about facts, which have seared themselves into my recollection. That very night the storm which had been brewing so long burst over us, and I came to learn whither all those little incidents were tending which I had recorded so aimlessly. Blind fool that I was not to have seen it sooner! I shall tell what occurred as precisely as I can.

I had gone into my cabin about half-past eleven, and was preparing to go to bed, when a tap came at my door. On opening it I saw Goring's little black page, who told me that his master would like to have a word with me on deck. I was rather surprised that he should want me at such a late hour, but I went up without hesitation. I had hardly put my foot on the quarter-deck before I was seized from behind, dragged down upon my back, and a handkerchief slipped round my mouth. I struggled as hard as I could, but a coil of rope was rapidly and firmly wound round me, and I found myself lashed to the davit of one of the boats, utterly powerless to do or say anything, while the point of a knife pressed to my throat warned me to cease my struggles. The night was so dark that I had been unable hitherto to recognize my assailants, but as my eyes became accustomed to the gloom, and the moon broke out through the clouds that obscured it, I made out that I was surrounded by the two negro sailors, the black cook, and my fellow-passenger, Goring. Another man was crouching on the deck at my feet, but he was in the shadow and I could not recognize him.

All this occurred so rapidly that a minute could hardly have elapsed from the time I mounted the companion until I found myself gagged and powerless. It was so sudden that I could scarce bring myself to realize it, or to comprehend what it all meant. I heard the gang round me speaking in short, fierce whispers to each other, and some instinct told me that my life was the question at issue. Goring spoke authoritatively and angrily—the others doggedly and all together, as if disputing his commands. Then they moved away in a body to the opposite side of the deck, where I could still hear them whispering, though they were concealed from my view by the saloon skylights.

All this time the voices of the watch on deck chatting and laughing at the other end of the ship were distinctly audible, and I could see them gathered in a group, little dreaming of the dark doings which were going on within thirty yards of them. Oh! That I could have given them one word of warning, even though I had lost my life in doing it! but it was impossible. The moon was shining fitfully through the scattered clouds, and I could see the silvery gleam of the surge, and beyond it the vast weird desert with its fantastic sand-hills. Glancing down, I saw that the man who had been crouching on the deck was still lying there, and as I gazed at him a flickering ray of moonlight fell full upon his upturned face. Great heaven! even now, when more than twelve years have elapsed, my hand trembles as I write that, in spite of distorted features and projecting eyes, I recognized the face of Harton, the cheery young clerk who had been my companion during the voyage. It needed no medical eye to see that he was quite dead, while the twisted handkerchief round the neck, and the gag in his mouth, showed the silent way in which the hell-hounds had done their work. The clue which explained every event of our voyage came upon me like a flash of light as I gazed on poor Harton's corpse. Much was dark and unexplained, but I felt a great dim perception of the truth.

I heard the striking of a match at the other side of the skylights, and then I saw the tall, gaunt figure of Goring standing up on the bulwarks and holding in his hands what appeared to be a dark lantern. He lowered this for a moment over the side of the ship, and, to my inexpressible astonishment, I saw it answered instantaneously by a flash among the sand-hills on shore, which came and went so rapidly, that unless I had been following the direction of Goring's gaze, I should never have detected it. Again he lowered the lantern, and

again it was answered from the shore. He then stepped down from
the bulwarks, and in doing so slipped, making such a noise, that for
a moment my heart bounded with the thought that the attention of
the watch would be directed to his proceedings. It was a vain hope.
The night was calm and the ship motionless, so that no idea of duty
kept them vigilant, Hyson, who after the death of Tibbs was in command of both watches, had gone below to snatch a few hours' sleep,
and the boatswain, who was left in charge, was standing with the
other two men at the foot of the foremast. Powerless, speechless,
with the cords cutting into my flesh and the murdered man at my feet,
I awaited the next act in the tragedy.

The four ruffians were standing up now at the other side of the
deck. The cook was armed with some sort of a cleaver, the others had
knives, and Goring had a revolver. They were all leaning against the
rail and looking out over the water as if watching for something. I saw
one of them grasp another's arm and point as if at some object, and
following the direction I made out the loom of a large moving mass
making towards the ship. As it emerged from the gloom I saw that it
was a great canoe crammed with men and propelled by at least a score
of paddles. As it shot under our stern the watch caught sight of it also,
and raising a cry hurried aft. They were too late, however. A swarm of
gigantic negroes clambered over the quarter, and led by Goring swept
down the deck in an irresistible torrent. All opposition was overpow-
ered in a moment, the unarmed watch were knocked over and bound,
and the sleepers dragged out of their bunks and secured in the same
manner. Hyson made an attempt to defend the narrow passage leading to his cabin, and I heard a scuffle, and his voice shouting for assistance. There was none to assist, however, and he was brought on to the
poop with the blood streaming from a deep cut in his forehead. He
was gagged like the others, and a council was held upon our fate by
the negroes. I saw our black seamen pointing towards me and making
some statement, which was received with murmurs of astonishment
and incredulity by the savages. One of them then came over to me,
and plunging his hand into my pocket took out my black stone and
held it up. He then handed it to a man who appeared to be a chief, who
examined it as minutely as the light would permit, and muttering
a few words passed it on to the warrior beside him, who also scrutin-
ized it and passed it on until it had gone from hand to hand round
the whole circle. The chief then said a few words to Goring in the

native tongue, on which the quadroon addressed me in English. At this moment I seem to see the scene. The tall masts of the ship with the moonlight streaming down, silvering the yards and bringing the network of cordage into hard relief; the group of dusky warriors leaning on their spears; the dead man at my feet; the line of white-faced prisoners, and in front of me the loathsome half-breed, looking in his white linen and elegant clothes a strange contrast to his associates.

'You will bear me witness,' he said in his softest accents, 'that I am no party to sparing your life. If it rested with me you would die as these other men are about to do. I have no personal grudge against either you or them, but I have devoted my life to the destruction of the white race, and you are the first that has ever been in my power and has escaped me. You may thank that stone of yours for your life. These poor fellows reverence it, and indeed if it really be what they think it is they have cause. Should it prove when we get ashore that they are mistaken, and that its shape and material is a mere chance, nothing can save your life. In the meantime we wish to treat you well, so if there are any of your possessions which you would like to take with you, you are at liberty to get them.' As he finished he gave a sign, and a couple of the negroes unbound me, though without removing the gag. I was led down into the cabin, where I put a few valuables into my pockets, together with a pocket-compass and my journal of the voyage. They then pushed me over the side into a small canoe, which was lying beside the large one, and my guards followed me, and shoving off began paddling for the shore. We had got about a hundred yards or so from the ship when our steersman held up his hand, and the paddlers paused for a moment and listened. Then on the silence of the night I heard a sort of dull, moaning sound, followed by a succession of splashes in the water. That is all I know of the fate of my poor shipmates. Almost immediately afterwards the large canoe followed us, and the deserted ship was left drifting about—a dreary spectre-like hulk. Nothing was taken from her by the savages. The whole fiendish transaction was carried through as decorously and temperately as though it were a religious rite.

The first grey of daylight was visible in the east as we passed through the surge and reached the shore. Leaving half a dozen men with the canoes, the rest of the negroes set off through the sand-hills, leading me with them, but treating me very gently and respectfully. It was difficult walking, as we sank over our ankles into the loose, shifting sand at every step, and I was nearly dead beat by the time we reached the native village, or town rather, for it was a place of considerable dimensions. The houses were conical structures not unlike bee-hives, and were made of compressed seaweed cemented over with a rude form of mortar, there being neither stick nor stone upon the coast nor anywhere within many hundreds of miles. As we entered the town an enormous crowd of both sexes came swarming out to meet us, beating tom-toms and howling and screaming. On seeing me they redoubled their yells and assumed a threatening attitude, which was instantly quelled by a few words shouted by my escort. A buzz of wonder succeeded the war-cries and yells of the moment before, and the whole dense mass proceeded down the broad central street of the town, having my escort and myself in the centre.

My statement hitherto may seem so strange as to excite doubt in the minds of those who do not know me, but it was the fact which I am now about to relate which caused my own brother-in-law to insult me by disbelief. I can but relate the occurrence in the simplest words, and trust to chance and time to prove their truth. In the centre of this main street there was a large building, formed in the same primitive way as the others, but towering high above them; a stockade of beautifully polished ebony rails was planted all round it, the framework of the door was formed by two magnificent elephant's tusks sunk in the ground on each side and meeting at the top, and the aperture was closed by a screen of native cloth richly embroidered with gold. We made our way to this imposing-looking structure, but on reaching the opening in the stockade, the multitude stopped and squatted down upon their hams, while I was led through into the enclosure by a few of the chiefs and elders of the tribe, Goring accompanying us, and in fact directing the proceedings. On reaching the screen which closed the temple—for such it evidently was—my hat and my shoes were removed, and I was then led in, a venerable old negro leading the way carrying in his hand my stone, which had been taken from my pocket. The building was only lit up by a few long slits in the roof, through which the tropical sun poured, throwing broad golden bars upon the clay floor, alternating with intervals of darkness.

The interior was even larger than one would have imagined from the outside appearance. The walls were hung with native mats, shells, and other ornaments, but the remainder of the great space was quite empty, with the exception of a single object in the centre. This was the figure of a colossal negro, which I at first thought to be some real king or high priest of titanic size, but as I approached it I saw by the way in which the light was reflected from it that it was a statue admirably cut in jet-black stone. I was led up to this idol, for such it seemed to be, and looking at it closer I saw that though it was perfect in every other respect, one of its ears had been broken short off. The grey-haired negro who held my relic mounted upon a small stool, and stretching up his arm fitted Martha's black stone on to the jagged surface on the side of the statue's head. There could not be a doubt that the one had been broken off from the other. The parts dovetailed together so accurately that when the old man removed his hand the ear stuck in its place for a few seconds before dropping into his open palm. The group round me prostrated themselves upon the ground at the sight with a cry of reverence, while the crowd outside, to whom the result was communicated, set up a wild whooping and cheering.

In a moment I found myself converted from a prisoner into a demi-god. I was escorted back through the town in triumph, the people pressing forward to touch my clothing and to gather up the dust on which my foot had trod. One of the largest huts was put at my disposal, and a banquet of every native delicacy was served me. I still felt, however, that I was not a free man, as several spearmen were placed as a guard at the entrance of my hut. All day my mind was occupied with plans of escape, but none seemed in any way feasible. On the one side was the great arid desert stretching away to Timbuctoo,* on the other was a sea untraversed by vessels. The more I pondered over the problem the more hopeless did it seem. I little dreamed how near I was to its solution.

Night had fallen, and the clamour of the negroes had died gradually away. I was stretched on the couch of skins which had been provided for me, and was still meditating over my future, when Goring walked stealthily into the hut. My first idea was that he had come to complete his murderous holocaust by making away with me, the last survivor, and I sprang up upon my feet, determined to defend myself to the last. He smiled when he saw the action, and motioned me down again while he seated himself upon the other end of the couch.

'What do you think of me?' was the astonishing question with which he commenced our conversation.

'Think of you!' I almost yelled. 'I think you the vilest, most unnatural renegade that ever polluted the earth. If we were away from these black devils of yours I would strangle you with my hands!'

'Don't speak so loud,' he said, without the slightest appearance of irritation. 'I don't want our chat to be cut short. So you would strangle me, would you!' he went on, with an amused smile. 'I suppose I am returning good for evil, for I ham I mm in limp you to escape.'

'You!' I gasped incredulously.

'Yes, I,' he continued. 'Oh, there is no credit to me in the matter. I am quite consistent. There is no reason why I should not be perfectly candid with you. I wish to be king over these fellows—not a very high ambition, certainly, but you know what Cæsar said about being first in a village in Gaul.* Well, this unlucky stone of yours has not only saved your life, but has turned all their heads so that they think you are come down from heaven, and my influence will be gone until you are out of the way. That is why I am going to help you to escape, since I cannot kill you'—this in the most natural and dulcet voice, as if the desire to do so were a matter of course.

'You would give the world to ask me a few questions,' he went on, after a pause; 'but you are too proud to do it. Never mind, I'll tell you one or two things, because I want your fellow white men to know them when you go back—if you are lucky enough to get back. About that cursed stone of yours, for instance. These negroes, or at least so the legend goes, were Mahometans originally. While Mahomet himself was still alive, there was a schism among his followers,* and the smaller party moved away from Arabia, and eventually crossed Africa. They took away with them, in their exile, a valuable relic of their old faith in the shape of a large piece of the black stone of Mecca.* The stone was a meteoric one, as you may have heard, and in its fall upon the earth it broke into two pieces. One of these pieces is still at Mecca. The larger piece was carried away to Barbary,* where a skilful worker modelled it into the fashion which you saw to-day. These men are the descendants of the original seceders from Mahomet, and they have brought their relic safely through all their wanderings until they settled in this strange place, where the desert protects them from their enemies.'

'And the ear?' I asked, almost involuntarily.

'Oh, that was the same story over again. Some of the tribe wandered away to the south a few hundred years ago, and one of them, wishing to have good luck for the enterprise, got into the temple at night and carried off one of the ears. There has been a tradition among the negroes ever since that the ear would come back some day. The fellow who carried it was caught by some slaver, no doubt, and that was how it got into America, and so into your hands—and you have had the honour of fulfilling the prophecy.'

He paused for a few minutes, resting his head upon his hands, waiting apparently for me to speak. When he looked up again, the whole expression of his face had changed. His features were firm and set, and he changed the air of half-levity with which he had spoken before for one of sternness and almost ferocity.

'I wish you to carry a message back,' he said, 'to the white race, the great dominating race whom I hate and defy. Tell them that I have battened on their blood for twenty years, that I have slain them until even I became tired of what had once been a joy, that I did this unnoticed and unsuspected in the face of every precaution which their civilization could suggest. There is no satisfaction in revenge when your enemy does not know who has struck him. I am not sorry, therefore, to have you as a messenger. There is no need why I should tell you how this great hate became born in me. See this,' and he held up his mutilated hand; 'that was done by a white man's knife. My father was white, my mother was a slave. When he died she was sold again, and I, a child then, saw her lashed to death to break her of some of the little airs and graces which her late master had encouraged in her. My young wife, too, oh, my young wife!' a shudder ran through his whole frame. 'No matter! I swore my oath, and I kept it. From Maine to Florida, and from Boston to San Francisco, you could track my steps by sudden deaths which baffled the police. I warred against the whole white race as they for centuries had warred against the black one. At last, as I tell you, I sickened of blood. Still, the sight of a white face was abhorrent to me, and I determined to find some bold free black people and to throw in my lot with them, to cultivate their latent powers and to form a nucleus for a great coloured nation. This idea possessed me, and I travelled over the world for two years seeking for what I desired. At last I almost despaired of finding it. There was no hope of regeneration in the slave-dealing Soudanese, the debased Fantee, or the Americanized negroes of Liberia.* I was returning from my quest when chance brought me in contact with this magnificent tribe of dwellers in the desert, and I threw in my lot with them. Before doing so, however, my old instinct of revenge prompted me to make one last visit to the United States, and I returned from it in the *Marie Celeste*.

'As to the voyage itself, your intelligence will have told you by this time that, thanks to my manipulation, both compasses and chronometers were entirely untrustworthy. I alone worked out the course with correct instruments of my own, while the steering was done by my black friends under my guidance. I pushed Tibbs's wife overboard. What! You look surprised and shrink away. Surely you had guessed that by this time. I would have shot you that day through the partition, but unfortunately you were not there. I tried again afterwards, but you were awake. I shot Tibbs. I think the idea of suicide was carried out rather neatly. Of course when once we got on the coast the rest was simple. I had bargained that all on board should die; but that stone of yours upset my plans. I also bargained that there should be no plunder. No one can say we are pirates. We have acted from principle, not from any sordid motive.'

I listened in amazement to the summary of his crimes which this strange man gave me, all in the quietest and most composed of voices, as though detailing incidents of every-day occurrence. I still seem to see him sitting like a hideous nightmare at the end of my couch, with the single rude lamp flickering over his cadaverous features.

'And now,' he continued, 'there is no difficulty about your escape. These stupid adopted children of mine will say that you have gone back to heaven from whence you came. The wind blows off the land. I have a boat all ready for you, well stored with provisions and water. I am anxious to be rid of you, so you may rely that nothing is neglected. Rise up and follow me.'

I did what he commanded, and he led me through the door of the hut. The guards had either been withdrawn, or Goring had arranged matters with them. We passed unchallenged through the town and across the sandy plain. Once more I heard the roar of the sea, and saw the long white line of the surge. Two figures were standing upon the shore arranging the gear of a small boat. They were the two sailors who had been with us on the voyage.

'See him safely through the surf,' said Goring. The two men sprang in and pushed off, pulling me in after them. With mainsail and jib we ran out from the land and passed safely over the bar. Then my two companions without a word of farewell sprang overboard, and I saw their heads like black dots on the white foam as they made their way back to the shore, while I scudded away into the blackness of the night. Looking back I caught my last glimpse of Goring. He was standing upon the summit of a sand-hill, and the rising moon behind him threw his gaunt angular figure into hard relief. He was waving his arms frantically to and fro; it may have been to encourage me on my way, but the gestures seemed to me at the time to be threatening ones, and I have often thought that it was more likely that his old savage instinct had returned when he realized that I was out of his power. Be that as it may, it was the last that I ever saw or ever shall see of Septimius Goring.

There is no need for me to dwell upon my solitary voyage. I steered as well as I could for the Canaries, but was picked up upon the fifth day by the British and African Steam Navigation Company's boat *Monrovia*. Let me take this opportunity of tendering my sincerest thanks to Captain Stornoway and his officers for the great kindness which they showed me from that time till they landed me in Liverpool, where I was enabled to take one of the Guion boats to New York.

From the day on which I found myself once more in the bosom of my family I have said little of what I have undergone. The subject is still an intensely painful one to me, and the little which I have dropped has been discredited. I now put the facts before the public as they occurred, careless how far they may be believed, and simply writing them down because my lung is growing weaker, and I feel the responsibility of holding my peace longer. I make no vague statement. Turn to your map of Africa. There above Cape Blanco, where the land trends away north and south from the westernmost point of the continent, there it is that Septimius Goring still reigns over his dark subjects, unless retribution has overtaken him; and there, where the long green ridges run swiftly in to roar and hiss upon the hot yellow sand, it is there that Harton lies with Hyson and the other poor fellows who were done to death in the *Marie Celeste*.

JOHN BARRINGTON COWLES

IT might seem rash of me to say that I ascribe the death of my poor friend, John Barrington Cowles, to any preternatural agency. I am aware that in the present state of public feeling a chain of evidence would require to be strong indeed before the possibility of such a conclusion could be admitted.

I shall therefore merely state the circumstances which led up to this sad event as concisely and as plainly as I can, and leave every reader to draw his own deductions. Perhaps there may be some one who can throw light upon what is dark to me.

I first met Barrington Cowles when I went up to Edinburgh University to take out medical classes there. My landlady in Northumberland Street* had a large house, and, being a widow without children, she gained a livelihood by providing accommodation for several students.

Barrington Cowles happened to have taken a bedroom upon the same floor as mine, and when we came to know each other better we shared a small sitting-room, in which we took our meals. In this manner we originated a friendship which was unmarred by the slightest disagreement up to the day of his death.

Cowles' father was the colonel of a Sikh regiment* and had remained in India for many years. He allowed his son a handsome income, but seldom gave any other sign of parental affection—writing irregularly and briefly.

My friend, who had himself been born in India, and whose whole disposition was an ardent tropical one, was much hurt by this neglect. His mother was dead, and he had no other relation in the world to supply the blank.

Thus he came in time to concentrate all his affection upon me, and to confide in me in a manner which is rare among men. Even when a stronger and deeper passion came upon him, it never infringed upon the old tenderness between us.

Cowles was a tall, slim young fellow, with an olive, Velasquez-like* face, and dark, tender eyes. I have seldom seen a man who was more likely to excite a woman's interest, or to captivate her imagination.

His expression was, as a rule, dreamy, and even languid; but if in conversation a subject arose which interested him he would be all animation in a moment. On such occasions his colour would heighten, his eyes gleam, and he could speak with an eloquence which would carry his audience with him.

In spite of these natural advantages he led a solitary life, avoiding female society, and reading with great diligence. He was one of the foremost men of his year, taking the senior medal for anatomy, and the Neil Arnott prize for physics.*

How well I can recollect the first time we met her! Often and often I have recalled the circumstances, and tried to remember what the exact impression was which she produced on my mind at the time. After we came to know her my judgment was warped, so that I am curious to recollect what my unbiassed instincts were. It is hard, however, to eliminate the feelings which reason or prejudice afterwards raised in me.

It was at the opening of the Royal Scottish Academy* in the spring of 1879. My poor friend was passionately attached to art in every form, and a pleasing chord in music or a delicate effect upon canvas would give exquisite pleasure to his highly-strung nature. We had gone together to see the pictures, and were standing in the grand central *salon*, when I noticed an extremely beautiful woman standing at the other side of the room. In my whole life I have never seen such a classically perfect countenance. It was the real Greek type*—the forehead broad, very low, and as white as marble, with a cloudlet of delicate locks wreathing round it, the nose straight and clean cut, the lips inclined to thinness, the chin and lower jaw beautifully rounded off, and yet sufficiently developed to promise unusual strength of character.

But those eyes—those wonderful eyes! If I could but give some faint idea of their varying moods, their steely hardness, their feminine softness, their power of command, their penetrating intensity suddenly melting away into an expression of womanly weakness—but I am speaking now of future impressions!

There was a tall, yellow-haired young man with this lady, whom I at once recognised as a law student with whom I had a slight acquaintance.

Archibald Reeves—for that was his name—was a dashing, handsome young fellow, and had at one time been a ringleader in every university escapade; but of late I had seen little of him, and the report was that he was engaged to be married. His companion was, then,

I presumed, his *fiancée*. I seated myself upon the velvet settee in the centre of the room, and furtively watched the couple from behind my catalogue.

The more I looked at her the more her beauty grew upon me. She was somewhat short in stature, it is true; but her figure was perfec-tion, and she wore her dress in such a fashion that it was only by actual comparison that one would have known her to be under the medium height.

As I kept my eyes upon them, Reeves was called away for some reason, and the young lady was left alone. Turning her back to the pictures, she passed the time until the return of her escort in taking a deliberate survey of the company, without paying the least heed to the fact that a dozen pair of eyes, attracted by her elegance and beauty, were bent curiously upon her. With one of her hands holding the red silk cord which railed off the pictures, she stood languidly moving her eyes from face to face with as little self-consciousness as if she were looking at the canvas creatures behind her. Suddenly, as I watched her, I saw her gaze become fixed, and, as it were, intense. I followed the direction of her looks, wondering what could have attracted her so strongly.

John Barrington Cowles was standing before a picture—one, I think, by Noel Paton*—I know that the subject was a noble and ethereal one. His profile was turned towards us, and never have I seen him to such advantage. I have said that he was a strikingly handsome man, but at that moment he looked absolutely magnificent. It was evident that he had momentarily forgotten his surroundings, and that his whole soul was in sympathy with the picture before him. His eyes sparkled, and a dusky pink shone through his clear olive cheeks. She continued to watch him fixedly, with a look of interest upon her face, until he came out of his reverie with a start, and turned abruptly round, so that his gaze met hers. She glanced away at once, but his eyes remained fixed upon her for some moments. The picture was forgotten already, and his soul had come down to earth once more.

We caught sight of her once or twice before we left, and each time I noticed my friend look after her. He made no remark, however, until we got out into the open air, and were walking arm-in-arm along Princes Street.*

'Did you notice that beautiful woman, in the dark dress, with the white fur?' he asked.

'Yes, I saw her,' I answered.

'Do you know her?' he asked eagerly. 'Have you any idea who she is?'

'I don't know her personally,' I replied. 'But I have no doubt I could find out all about her, for I believe she is engaged to young Archie Reeves, and he and I have a lot of mutual friends.'

'Engaged!' ejaculated Cowles.

'Why, my dear boy,' I said, laughing, 'you don't mean to say you are so susceptible that the fact that a girl to whom you never spoke in your life is engaged is enough to upset you?'

'Well, not exactly to upset me,' he answered, forcing a laugh. 'But I don't mind telling you, Armitage, that I never was so taken by any one in my life. It wasn't the mere beauty of the face—though that was perfect enough—but it was the character and the intellect upon it. I hope, if she is engaged, that it is to some man who will be worthy of her.'

'Why,' I remarked, 'you speak quite feelingly. It is a clear case of love at first sight, Jack. However, to put your perturbed spirit at rest, I'll make a point of finding out all about her whenever I meet any fellow who is likely to know.'

Barrington Cowles thanked me, and the conversation drifted off into other channels. For several days neither of us made any allusion to the subject, though my companion was perhaps a little more dreamy and distraught than usual. The incident had almost vanished from my remembrance, when one day young Brodie, who is a second cousin of mine, came up to me on the university steps with the face of a bearer of tidings.

'I say,' he began, 'you know Reeves, don't you?'

'Yes. What of him?'

'His engagement is off.'

'Off!' I cried. 'Why, I only learned the other day that it was on.'

'Oh, yes—it's all off. His brother told me so. Deucedly mean of Reeves, you know, if he has backed out of it, for she was an uncommonly nice girl.'

'I've seen her,' I said; 'but I don't know her name.'

'She is a Miss Northcott, and lives with an old aunt of hers in Abercrombie Place.* Nobody knows anything about her people, or where she comes from. Anyhow, she is about the most unlucky girl in the world, poor soul!'

'Why unlucky?'

'Well, you know, this was her second engagement,' said young Brodie, who had a marvellous knack of knowing everything about everybody. 'She was engaged to Prescott—William Prescott, who died. That was a very sad affair. The wedding day was fixed, and the whole thing looked as straight as a die when the smash came.'

'What smash?' I asked, with some dim recollection of the circumstances.

'Why, Prescott's death. He came to Abercrombie Place one night, and stayed very late. No one knows exactly when he left, but about one in the morning a fellow who knew him met him walking rapidly in the direction of the Queen's Park.* He bade him good night, but Prescott hurried on without heeding him, and that was the last time he was ever seen alive. Three days afterwards his body was found floating in St Margaret's Loch, under St Anthony's Chapel.* No one could ever understand it, but of course the verdict brought it in as temporary insanity.'

'It was very strange,' I remarked.

'Yes, and deucedly rough on the poor girl,' said Brodie. 'Now that this other blow has come it will quite crush her. So gentle and ladylike she is too!'

'You know her personally, then!' I asked.

'Oh, yes, I know her. I have met her several times. I could easily manage that you should be introduced to her.'

'Well,' I answered, 'it's not so much for my own sake as for a friend of mine. However, I don't suppose she will go out much for some little time after this. When she does I will take advantage of your offer.'

We shook hands on this, and I thought no more of the matter for some time.

The next incident which I have to relate as bearing at all upon the question of Miss Northcott is an unpleasant one. Yet I must detail it as accurately as possible, since it may throw some light upon the sequel. One cold night, several months after the conversation with my second cousin which I have quoted above, I was walking down one of the lowest streets in the city on my way back from a case which I had been attending. It was very late, and I was picking my way among the dirty loungers who were clustering round the doors of a great gin-palace,* when a man staggered out from among them, and held out his hand to me with a drunken leer. The gaslight fell full upon his face, and, to my intense astonishment, I recognised in the degraded creature before me my former acquaintance, young Archibald Reeves, who had once been famous as one of the most dressy and particular men in the whole college. I was so utterly surprised that for a moment I almost doubted the evidence of my own senses; but there was no mistaking those features, which, though bloated with drink, still retained something of their former comeliness. I was determined to rescue him, for one night at least, from the company into which he had fallen.

'Holloa, Reeves!' I said. 'Come along with me. I'm going in your direction.'

He muttered some incoherent apology for his condition, and took my arm. As I supported him towards his lodgings I could see that he was not only suffering from the effects of a recent debauch, but that a long course of intemperance had affected his nerves and his brain. His hand when I touched it was dry and feverish, and he started from every shadow which fell upon the pavement. He rambled in his speech, too, in a manner which suggested the delirium of disease rather than the talk of a drunkard.

When I got him to his lodgings I partially undressed him and laid him upon his bed. His pulse at this time was very high, and he was evidently extremely feverish. He seemed to have sunk into a doze; and I was about to steal out of the room to warn his landlady of his condition, when he started up and caught me by the sleeve of my coat.

'Don't go!' he cried. 'I feel better when you are here. I am safe from her then.'

'From her!' I said. 'From whom?'

'Her! her!' he answered peevishly. 'Ah! you don't know her. She is the devil! Beautiful—beautiful; but the devil!'

'You are feverish and excited,' I said. 'Try and get a little sleep. You will wake better.'

'Sleep!' he groaned. 'How am I to sleep when I see her sitting down yonder at the foot of the bed with her great eyes watching and watching hour after hour? I tell you it saps all the strength and manhood out of me. That's what makes me drink. God help me—I'm half drunk now!'

'You are very ill,' I said, putting some vinegar to his temples;* 'and you are delirious. You don't know what you say.'

'Yes, I do,' he interrupted sharply, looking up at me. 'I know very well what I say. I brought it upon myself. It is my own choice. But I couldn't—no, by heaven, I couldn't—accept the alternative. I couldn't keep my faith to her. It was more than man could do.'

I sat by the side of the bed, holding one of his burning hands in mine, and wondering over his strange words. He lay still for some time, and then, raising his eyes to me, said in a most plaintive voice—

'Why did she not give me warning sooner? Why did she wait until I had learned to love her so?'

He repeated this question several times, rolling his feverish head from side to side, and then he dropped into a troubled sleep. I crept out of the room, and, having seen that he would be properly cared for, left the house. His words, however, rang in my ears for days afterwards, and assumed a deeper significance when taken with what was to come.

My friend, Barrington Cowles, had been away for his summer holidays, and I had heard nothing of him for several months. When the winter session came on, however, I received a telegram from him, asking me to secure the old rooms in Northumberland Street for him, and telling me the train by which he would arrive. I went down to meet him, and was delighted to find him looking wonderfully hearty and well.

'By the way,' he said suddenly, that night, as we sat in our chairs by the fire, talking over the events of the holidays, 'you have never congratulated me yet!'

'On what, my boy?' I asked.

'What! Do you mean to say you have not heard of my engagement?'

'Engagement! No!' I answered. 'However, I am delighted to hear it, and congratulate you with all my heart.'

'I wonder it didn't come to your ears,' he said. 'It was the queerest thing. You remember that girl whom we both admired so much at the Academy?'

'What!' I cried, with a vague feeling of apprehension at my heart. 'You don't mean to say that you are engaged to her?'

'I thought you would be surprised,' he answered. 'When I was staying with an old aunt of mine in Peterhead,* in Aberdeenshire, the Northcotts happened to come there on a visit, and as we had mutual friends we soon met. I found out that it was a false alarm about her being engaged, and then—well, you know what it is when you are thrown into the society of such a girl in a place like Peterhead. Not, mind you,' he added, 'that I consider I did a foolish or hasty thing. I have never regretted it for a moment. The more I know Kate the more I admire her and love her. However, you must be introduced to her, and then you will form your own opinion.'

I expressed my pleasure at the prospect, and endeavoured to speak as lightly as I could to Cowles upon the subject, but I felt depressed and anxious at heart. The words of Reeves and the unhappy fate of young Prescott recurred to my recollection, and though I could assign no tangible reason for it, a vague, dim fear and distrust of the woman took possession of me. It may be that this was foolish prejudice and superstition upon my part, and that I involuntarily contorted her future doings and sayings to fit into some half-formed wild theory of my own. This has been suggested to me by others as an explanation of my narrative. They are welcome to their opinion if they can reconcile it with the facts which I have to tell.

I went round with my friend a few days afterwards to call upon Miss Northcott. I remember that, as we went down Abercrombie Place, our attention was attracted by the shrill yelping of a dog—which noise proved eventually to come from the house to which we were bound. We were shown upstairs, where I was introduced to old Mrs Merton, Miss Northcott's aunt, and to the young lady herself. She looked as beautiful as ever, and I could not wonder at my friend's infatuation. Her face was a little more flushed than usual, and she held in her hand a heavy dog-whip, with which she had been chastising a small Scotch terrier, whose cries we had heard in the street. The poor brute was cringing up against the wall, whining piteously, and evidently completely cowed.

'So Kate,' said my friend, after we had taken our seats, 'you have been falling out with Carlo* again.'

'Only a very little quarrel this time,' she said, smiling charmingly. 'He is a dear, good old fellow, but he needs correction now and then.' Then, turning to me, 'We all do that, Mr Armitage, don't we? What a capital thing if, instead of receiving a collective punishment at the end of our lives, we were to have one at once, as the dogs do, when we did anything wicked. It would make us more careful, wouldn't it?'

I acknowledged that it would.

'Supposing that every time a man misbehaved himself a gigantic hand were to seize him, and he were lashed with a whip until he fainted'—she clenched her white fingers as she spoke, and cut out viciously with the dog-whip—'it would do more to keep him good than any number of high-minded theories of morality.'

'Why, Kate,' said my friend, 'you are quite savage to-day.'

'No, Jack,' she laughed. 'I'm only propounding a theory for Mr Armitage's consideration.'

The two began to chat together about some Aberdeenshire reminiscence, and I had time to observe Mrs Merton, who had remained silent during our short conversation. She was a very strange-looking old lady. What attracted attention most in her appearance was the utter want of colour which she exhibited. Her hair was snow-white, and her face extremely pale. Her lips were bloodless, and even her eyes were of such a light tinge of blue that they hardly relieved the general pallor. Her dress was a grey silk, which harmonised with her general appearance. She had a peculiar expression of countenance, which I was unable at the moment to refer to its proper cause.

She was working at some old-fashioned piece of ornamental needlework, and as she moved her arms her dress gave forth a dry, melancholy rustling, like the sound of leaves in the autumn. There was something mournful and depressing in the sight of her. I moved my chair a little nearer, and asked her how she liked Edinburgh, and whether she had been there long.

When I spoke to her she started and looked up at me with a scared look on her face. Then I saw in a moment what the expression was which I had observed there. It was one of fear—intense and overpowering fear. It was so marked that I could have staked my life on the woman before me having at some period of her life been subjected to some terrible experience or dreadful misfortune.

'Oh, yes, I like it,' she said, in a soft, timid voice; 'and we have been here long—that is, not very long. We move about a great deal.' She spoke with hesitation, as if afraid of committing herself.

'You are a native of Scotland, I presume?' I said.

'No—that is, not entirely. We are not natives of any place. We are cosmopolitan, you know.' She glanced round in the direction of Miss Northcott as she spoke, but the two were still chatting together near the window. Then she suddenly bent forward to me, with a look of intense earnestness upon her face, and said—

'Don't talk to me any more, please. She does not like it, and I shall suffer for it afterwards. Please, don't do it.'

I was about to ask her the reason for this strange request, but when she saw I was going to address her, she rose and walked slowly out of the room. As she did so I perceived that the lovers had ceased to talk, and that Miss Northcott was looking at me with her keen, grey eyes.

'You must excuse my aunt, Mr Armitage,' she said; 'she is odd, and easily fatigued. Come over and look at my album.'

We spent some time examining the portraits. Miss Northcott's father and mother were apparently ordinary mortals enough, and I could not detect in either of them any traces of the character which showed itself in their daughter's face. There was one old daguerreo-type,* however, which arrested my attention. It represented a man of about the age of forty, and strikingly handsome. He was clean shaven, and extraordinary power was expressed upon his prominent lower jaw and firm, straight mouth. His eyes were somewhat deeply set in his head, however, and there was a snake-like flattening at the upper part of his forehead, which detracted from his appearance. I almost invol-untarily, when I saw the head, pointed to it, and exclaimed—

'There is your prototype in your family, Miss Northcott.'

'Do you think so?' she said. 'I am afraid you are paying me a very bad compliment. Uncle Anthony was always considered the black sheep of the family.'

'Indeed,' I answered; 'my remark was an unfortunate one, then.'

'Oh, don't mind that,' she said; 'I always thought myself that he was worth all of them put together. He was an officer in the Forty-first Regiment,* and he was killed in action during the Persian War*—so he died nobly, at any rate.'

'That's the sort of death I should like to die,' said Cowles, his dark eyes flashing, as they would when he was excited; 'I often wish I had taken to my father's profession instead of this vile pill-compounding drudgery.'

'Come, Jack, you are not going to die any sort of death yet,' she said, tenderly taking his hand in hers.

I could not understand the woman. There was such an extraordin-ary mixture of masculine decision and womanly tenderness about her, with the consciousness of something all her own in the back-ground, that she fairly puzzled me. I hardly knew, therefore, how to answer Cowles when, as we walked down the street together, he asked the comprehensive question—

'Well, what do you think of her?'

'I think she is wonderfully beautiful,' I answered guardedly.

'That, of course,' he replied irritably. 'You knew that before you came!'

'I think she is very clever too,' I remarked.

Barrington Cowles walked on for some time, and then he suddenly turned on me with the strange question

'Do you think she is cruel? Do you think she is the sort of girl who would take a pleasure in inflicting pain?'

'Well, really,' I answered, 'I have hardly had time to form an opinion.'

We then walked on for some time in silence.

'She is an old fool,' at length muttered Cowles. 'She is mad.'

'Who is?' I asked.

'Why, that old woman—that aunt of Kate's —Mrs Merton, or whatever her name is.'

Then I knew that my poor colourless friend had been speaking to Cowles, but he never said anything more as to the nature of her communication.

My companion went to bed early that night, and I sat up a long time by the fire, thinking over all that I had seen and heard. I felt that there was some mystery about the girl—some dark fatality so strange as to defy conjecture. I thought of Prescott's interview with her before their marriage, and the fatal termination of it. I coupled it with poor drunken Reeves' plaintive cry, 'Why did she not tell me sooner?' and with the other words he had spoken. Then my mind ran over Mrs Merton's warning to me, Cowles' reference to her, and even the episode of the whip and the cringing dog.

The whole effect of my recollections was unpleasant to a degree, and yet there was no tangible charge which I could bring against the woman. It would be worse than useless to attempt to warn my friend until I had definitely made up my mind what I was to warn him against. He would treat any charge against her with scorn. What could I do? How could I get at some tangible conclusion as to her character and antecedents? No one in Edinburgh knew them except as recent acquaintances. She was an orphan, and as far as I knew she had never disclosed where her former home had been. Suddenly an idea struck me. Among my father's friends there was a Colonel Joyce, who had served a long time in India upon the staff, and who would be likely to know most of the officers who had been out there since the

Mutiny.* I sat down at once, and, having trimmed the lamp, proceeded to write a letter to the Colonel. I told him that I was very
curious to gain some particulars about a certain Captain Northcott,
who had served in the Forty-first Foot, and who had fallen in the
Persian War. I described the man as well as I could from my recollection of the daguerreotype, and then, having directed the letter, posted
it that very night, after which, feeling that I had done all that could be
done, I retired to bed, with a mind too anxious to allow me to sleep.

PART II

I got an answer from Leicester, where the Colonel resided, within two
days. I have it before me as I write, and copy it verbatim.

'DEAR BOB,' it said, 'I remember the man well. I was with him at
Calcutta, and afterwards at Hyderabad.* He was a curious, solitary
sort of mortal; but a gallant soldier enough, for he distinguished himself at Sobraon,* and was wounded, if I remember right. He was not
popular in his corps—they said he was a pitiless, cold-blooded fellow,
with no geniality in him. There was a rumour, too, that he was a devil-
worshipper, or something of that sort, and also that he had the evil
eye, which, of course, was all nonsense. He had some strange theories,
I remember, about the power of the human will and the effects of
mind upon matter.*

'How are you getting on with your medical studies? Never forget,
my boy, that your father's son has every claim upon me, and that if
I can serve you in any way I am always at your command.—Ever
affectionately yours,

EDWARD JOYCE.

'*P.S.*—By the way, Northcott did not fall in action. He was killed
after peace was declared in a crazy attempt to get some of the eternal
fire from the sun-worshippers' temple.* There was considerable mystery about his death.'

I read this epistle over several times—at first with a feeling of satisfaction, and then with one of disappointment. I had come on some
curious information, and yet hardly what I wanted. He was an eccentric man, a devil-worshipper, and rumoured to have the power of the

evil eye. I could believe the young lady's eyes, when endowed with that cold, grey shimmer which I had noticed in them once or twice, to be capable of any evil which human eye ever wrought; but still the superstition was an effete* one. Was there not more meaning in that sentence which followed—'He had theories of the power of the human will and of the effect of mind upon matter'. I remember having once read a quaint treatise, which I had imagined to be mere charlatanism at the time, of the power of certain human minds, and of effects produced by them at a distance. Was Miss Northcott endowed with some exceptional power of the sort? The idea grew upon me, and very shortly I had evidence which convinced me of the truth of the supposition.

It happened that at the very time when my mind was dwelling upon this subject, I saw a notice in the paper that our town was to be visited by Dr Messinger, the well-known medium and mesmerist. Messinger was a man whose performance, such as it was, had been again and again pronounced to be genuine by competent judges. He was far above trickery, and had the reputation of being the soundest living authority upon the strange pseudo-sciences of animal magnetism and electro-biology.* Determined, therefore, to see what the human will could do, even against all the disadvantages of glaring footlights and a public platform, I took a ticket for the first night of the performance, and went with several student friends.

We had secured one of the side boxes, and did not arrive until after the performance had begun. I had hardly taken my seat before I recognised Barrington Cowles, with his *fiancée* and old Mrs Merton, sitting in the third or fourth row of the stalls. They caught sight of me at almost the same moment, and we bowed to each other. The first portion of the lecture was somewhat commonplace, the lecturer giving tricks of pure legerdemain,* with one or two manifestations of mesmerism, performed upon a subject whom he had brought with him. He gave us an exhibition of clairvoyance too, throwing his subject into a trance, and then demanding particulars as to the movements of absent friends, and the whereabouts of hidden objects, all of which appeared to be answered satisfactorily. I had seen all this before, however. What I wanted to see now was the effect of the lecturer's will when exerted upon some independent member of the audience.

He came round to that as the concluding exhibition in his performance. 'I have shown you,' he said, 'that a mesmerised subject is entirely dominated by the will of the mesmeriser. He loses all power of volition, and his very thoughts are such as are suggested to him by the master-mind. The same end may be attained without any preliminary process. A strong will can, simply by virtue of its strength, take possession of a weaker one, even at a distance, and can regulate the impulses and the actions of the owner of it. If there was one man in the world who had a very much more highly-developed will than any of the rest of the human family, there is no reason why he should not be able to rule over them all, and to reduce his fellow-creatures to the condition of automatons. Happily there is such a dead level of mental power, or rather of mental weakness, among us that such a catastrophe is not likely to occur; but still within our small compass there are variations which produce surprising effects. I shall now single out one of the audience, and endeavour 'by the mere power of will' to compel him to come upon the platform, and do and say what I wish. Let me assure you that there is no collusion, and that the subject whom I may select is at perfect liberty to resent to the uttermost any impulse which I may communicate to him.'

With these words the lecturer came to the front of the platform, and glanced over the first few rows of the stalls. No doubt Cowles' dark skin and bright eyes marked him out as a man of a highly nervous temperament, for the mesmerist picked him out in a moment, and fixed his eyes upon him. I saw my friend give a start of surprise, and then settle down in his chair, as if to express his determination not to yield to the influence of the operator. Messinger was not a man whose head denoted any great brain-power, but his gaze was singularly intense and penetrating. Under the influence of it Cowles made one or two spasmodic motions of his hands, as if to grasp the sides of his seat, and then half rose, but only to sink down again, though with an evident effort. I was watching the scene with intense interest, when I happened to catch a glimpse of Miss Northcott's face. She was sitting with her eyes fixed intently upon the mesmerist, and with such an expression of concentrated power upon her features as I have never seen on any other human countenance. Her jaw was firmly set, her lips compressed, and her face as hard as if it were a beautiful sculpture cut out of the whitest marble. Her eyebrows were drawn down, however, and from beneath them her grey eyes seemed to sparkle and gleam with a cold light.

I looked at Cowles again, expecting every moment to see him rise and obey the mesmerist's wishes, when there came from the platform a short, gasping cry as of a man utterly worn out and prostrated by a prolonged struggle. Messinger was leaning against the table, his hand to his forehead, and the perspiration pouring down his face. 'I won't go on,' he cried, addressing the audience. 'There is a stronger will than mine acting against me. You must excuse me for to-night.' The man was evidently ill, and utterly unable to proceed, so the curtain was lowered and the audience dispersed, with many comments upon the lecturer's sudden indisposition.

I waited outside the hall until my friend and the ladies came out. Cowles was laughing over his recent experience.

'He didn't succeed with me, Bob,' he cried triumphantly, as he shook my hand. 'I think he caught a Tartar* that time.'

'Yes,' said Miss Northcott, 'I think that Jack ought to be very proud of his strength of mind; don't you, Mr Armitage?'

'It took me all my time, though,' my friend said seriously. 'You can't conceive what a strange feeling I had once or twice. All the strength seemed to have gone out of me—especially just before he collapsed himself.'

I walked round with Cowles in order to see the ladies home. He walked in front with Mrs Merton, and I found myself behind with the young lady. For a minute or so I walked beside her without making any remark, and then I suddenly blurted out, in a manner which must have seemed somewhat brusque to her—

'You did that, Miss Northcott.'

'Did what?' she asked sharply.

'Why, mesmerised the mesmeriser—I suppose that is the best way of describing the transaction.'

'What a strange idea!' she said, laughing. 'You give me credit for a strong will then?'

'Yes,' I said. 'For a dangerously strong one.'

'Why dangerous?' she asked, in a tone of surprise.

'I think,' I answered, 'that any will which can exercise such power is dangerous—for there is always a chance of its being turned to bad uses.'

'You would make me out a very dreadful individual, Mr Armitage,' she said; and then looking up suddenly in my face—'You have never liked me. You are suspicious of me and distrust me, though I have never given you cause.'

The accusation was so sudden and so true that I was unable to find any reply to it. She paused for a moment, and then said in a voice which was hard and cold—

'Don't let your prejudice lead you to interfere with me, however, or say anything to your friend, Mr Cowles, which might lead to a difference between us. You would find that to be very bad policy.'

There was something in the way she spoke which gave an indescribable air of a threat to these few words.

'I have no power,' I said, 'to interfere with your plans for the future. I cannot help, however, from what I have seen and heard, having fears for my friend.'

'Fears!' she repeated scornfully. 'Pray what have you seen and heard. Something from Mr Reeves, perhaps—I believe he is another of your friends?'

'He never mentioned your name to me,' I answered, truthfully enough. 'You will be sorry to hear that he is dying.' As I said it we passed by a lighted window, and I glanced down to see what effect my words had upon her. She was laughing—there was no doubt of it; she was laughing quietly to herself. I could see merriment in every feature of her face. I feared and mistrusted the woman from that moment more than ever.

We said little more that night. When we parted she gave me a quick, warning glance, as if to remind me of what she had said about the danger of interference. Her cautions would have made little difference to me could I have seen my way to benefiting Barrington Cowles by anything which I might say. But what could I say? I might say that her former suitors had been unfortunate. I might say that I believed her to be a cruel-hearted woman. I might say that I considered her to possess wonderful, and almost preternatural powers. What impression would any of these accusations make upon an ardent lover— a man with my friend's enthusiastic temperament? I felt that it would be useless to advance them, so I was silent.

And now I come to the beginning of the end. Hitherto much has been surmise and inference and hearsay. It is my painful task to relate now, as dispassionately and as accurately as I can, what actually occurred under my own notice, and to reduce to writing the events which preceded the death of my friend.

Towards the end of the winter Cowles remarked to me that he intended to marry Miss Northcott as soon as possible—probably some time in the spring. He was, as I have already remarked, fairly well off, and the young lady had some money of her own, so that there was no pecuniary reason for a long engagement. 'We are going to take a little house out at Corstorphine,'* he said, 'and we hope to see your face at our table, Bob, as often as you can possibly come.' I thanked him, and tried to shake off my apprehensions, and persuade myself that all would yet be well.

It was about three weeks before the time fixed for the marriage, that Cowles remarked to me one evening that he feared he would be late that night. 'I have had a note from Kate,' he said, 'asking me to call about eleven o'clock to-night, which seems rather a late hour, but perhaps she wants to talk over something quietly after old Mrs Merton retires.'

It was not until after my friend's departure that I suddenly recollected the mysterious interview which I had been told of as preceding the suicide of young Prescott. Then I thought of the ravings of poor Reeves, rendered more tragic by the fact that I had heard that very day of his death. What was the meaning of it all? Had this woman some baleful secret to disclose which must be known before her marriage? Was it some reason which forbade her to marry? Or was it some reason which forbade others to marry her? I felt so uneasy that I would have followed Cowles, even at the risk of offending him, and endeavoured to dissuade him from keeping his appointment, but a glance at the clock showed me that I was too late.

I was determined to wait up for his return, so I piled some coals upon the fire and took down a novel from the shelf. My thoughts proved more interesting than the book, however, and I threw it on one side. An indefinable feeling of anxiety and depression weighed upon me. Twelve o'clock came, and then half-past, without any sign of my friend. It was nearly one when I heard a step in the street outside, and then a knocking at the door. I was surprised, as I knew that my friend always carried a key—however, I hurried down and undid the latch. As the door flew open I knew in a moment that my worst apprehensions had been fulfilled. Barrington Cowles was leaning against the railings outside with his face sunk upon his breast, and his whole attitude expressive of the most intense despondency. As he passed in he gave a stagger, and would have fallen had I not thrown my left arm around him. Supporting him with this, and holding the lamp in my other hand, I led him slowly upstairs into our sitting-room. He sank down upon the sofa without a word. Now that I could get a good view of him, I was horrified to see the change which had come over him. His face was deadly pale, and his very lips were bloodless. His cheeks and forehead were clammy, his eyes glazed, and his whole expression altered. He looked like a man who had gone through some terrible ordeal, and was thoroughly unnerved.

'My dear fellow, what is the matter?' I asked, breaking the silence. 'Nothing amiss, I trust? Are you unwell?'

'Brandy!' he gasped. 'Give me some brandy!'

I took out the decanter, and was about to help him, when he snatched it from me with a trembling hand, and poured out nearly half a tumbler of the spirit. He was usually a most abstemious man, but he took this off at a gulp without adding any water to it. It seemed to do him good, for the colour began to come back to his face, and he leaned upon his elbow.

'My engagement is off, Bob,' he said, trying to speak calmly, but with a tremor in his voice which he could not conceal. 'It is all over.'

'Cheer up!' I answered, trying to encourage him. 'Don't get down on your luck. How was it? What was it all about?'

'About?' he groaned, covering his face with his hands. 'If I did tell you, Bob, you would not believe it. It is too dreadful—too horrible—unutterably awful and incredible! O Kate, Kate!' and he rocked himself to and fro in his grief; 'I pictured you an angel and I find you a——'

'A what?' I asked, for he had paused.

He looked at me with a vacant stare, and then suddenly burst out, waving his arms: 'A fiend!' he cried. 'A ghoul from the pit!* A vampire soul behind a lovely face! Now, God forgive me!' he went on in a lower tone, turning his face to the wall; 'I have said more than I should. I have loved her too much to speak of her as she is. I love her too much now.'

He lay still for some time, and I had hoped that the brandy had had the effect of sending him to sleep, when he suddenly turned his face towards me.

'Did you ever read of wehr-wolves?'* he asked.

I answered that I had.

'There is a story,' he said thoughtfully, 'in one of Marryat's books,* about a beautiful woman who took the form of a wolf at night and devoured her own children. I wonder what put that idea into Marryat's head?'

He pondered for some minutes, and then he cried out for some more brandy. There was a small bottle of laudanum* upon the table, and I managed, by insisting upon helping him myself, to mix about half a drachm* with the spirits. He drank it off, and sank his head once more upon the pillow. 'Anything better than that,' he groaned. 'Death is better than that. Crime and cruelty; cruelty and crime. Anything is better than that,' and so on, with the monotonous refrain, until at last the words became indistinct, his eyelids closed over his weary eyes, and he sank into a profound slumber. I carried him into his bedroom without arousing him; and making a couch for myself out of the chairs, I remained by his side all night.

In the morning Barrington Cowles was in a high fever. For weeks he lingered between life and death. The highest medical skill of Edinburgh was called in, and his vigorous constitution slowly got the better of his disease. I nursed him during this anxious time; but through all his wild delirium and ravings he never let a word escape him which explained the mystery connected with Miss Northcott. Sometimes he spoke of her in the tenderest words and most loving voice. At others he screamed out that she was a fiend, and stretched out his arms, as if to keep her off. Several times he cried that he would not sell his soul for a beautiful face, and then he would moan in a most piteous voice, 'But I love her—I love her for all that, I shall never cease to love her.'

When he came to himself he was an altered man. His severe illness had emaciated him greatly, but his dark eyes had lost none of their brightness. They shone out with startling brilliancy from under his dark, overhanging brows. His manner was eccentric and variable— sometimes irritable, sometimes recklessly mirthful, but never natural. He would glance about him in a strange, suspicious manner, like one who feared something, and yet hardly knew what it was he dreaded. He never mentioned Miss Northcott's name—never until that fatal evening of which I have now to speak.

In an endeavour to break the current of his thoughts by frequent change of scene, I travelled with him through the highlands of Scotland, and afterwards down the east coast. In one of these peregrinations of ours we visited the Isle of May, an island near the mouth of the Firth of Forth,* which, except in the tourist season, is singularly barren and desolate. Beyond the keeper of the lighthouse there are only one or two families of poor fisher-folk, who sustain a precarious existence by their nets, and by the capture of cormorants and solan geese.* This grim spot seemed to have such a fascination for Cowles that we engaged a room in one of the fishermen's huts, with the intention of passing a week or two there. I found it very dull, but the loneliness appeared to be a relief to my friend's mind. He lost the look of apprehension which had become habitual to him, and became something like his old self. He would wander round the island all day, looking down from the summit of the great cliffs which gird it round, and watching the long green waves as they came booming in and burst in a shower of spray over the rocks beneath.

One night—I think it was our third or fourth on the island— Barrington Cowles and I went outside the cottage before retiring to rest, to enjoy a little fresh air, for our room was small, and the rough lamp caused an unpleasant odour. How well I remember every little circumstance in connection with that night! It promised to be tempestuous, for the clouds were piling up in the north-west, and the dark wrack* was drifting across the face of the moon, throwing alternate belts of light and shade upon the rugged surface of the island and the restless sea beyond.

We were standing talking close by the door of the cottage, and I was thinking to myself that my friend was more cheerful than he had been since his illness, when he gave a sudden, sharp cry, and looking round at him I saw, by the light of the moon, an expression of unutterable horror come over his features. His eyes became fixed and staring, as if riveted upon some approaching object, and he extended his long thin forefinger, which quivered as he pointed.

'Look there!' he cried. 'It is she! It is she! You see her there coming down the side of the brae.'* He gripped me convulsively by the wrist as he spoke. 'There she is, coming towards us!'

'Who?' I cried, straining my eyes into the darkness.

'She—Kate—Kate Northcott!' he screamed. 'She has come for me. Hold me fast, old friend. Don't let me go!'

'Hold up, old man,' I said, clapping him on the shoulder. 'Pull yourself together; you are dreaming; there is nothing to fear.'

'She is gone!' he cried, with a gasp of relief. 'No, by heaven! there she is again, and nearer—coming nearer. She told me she would come for me, and she keeps her word.'

'Come into the house,' I said. His hand, as I grasped it, was as cold as ice.

'Ah, I knew it!' he shouted. 'There she is, waving her arms. She is beckoning to me. It is the signal. I must go. I am coming, Kate; I am coming!'

I threw my arms around him, but he burst from me with superhuman strength, and dashed into the darkness of the night. I followed him, calling to him to stop, but he ran the more swiftly. When the moon shone out between the clouds I could catch a glimpse of his dark figure, running rapidly in a straight line, as if to reach some definite goal. It may have been imagination, but it seemed to me that in the flickering light I could distinguish a vague something in front of him— a shimmering form which eluded his grasp and led him onwards. I saw his outlines stand out hard against the sky behind him as he surmounted the brow of a little hill, then he disappeared, and that was the last ever seen by mortal eye of Barrington Cowles.

The fishermen and I walked round the island all that night with lanterns, and examined every nook and corner without seeing a trace of my poor lost friend. The direction in which he had been running terminated in a rugged line of jagged cliffs overhanging the sea. At one place here the edge was somewhat crumbled, and there appeared marks upon the turf which might have been left by human feet. We lay upon our faces at this spot, and peered with our lanterns over the edge, looking down on the boiling surge two hundred feet below. As we lay there, suddenly, above the beating of the waves and the howling of the wind, there rose a strange wild screech from the abyss below. The fishermen—a naturally superstitious race—averred that it was the sound of a woman's laughter, and I could hardly persuade them to continue the search. For my own part I think it may have been the cry of some sea-fowl startled from its nest by the flash of the lantern. However that may be, I never wish to hear such a sound again.

And now I have come to the end of the painful duty which I have undertaken. I have told as plainly and as accurately as I could the story of the death of John Barrington Cowles, and the train of events which preceded it. I am aware that to others the sad episode seemed commonplace enough. Here is the prosaic account which appeared in the *Scotsman** a couple of days afterwards:—

'*Sad Occurrence on the Isle of May.*—The Isle of May has been the scene of a sad disaster. Mr John Barrington Cowles, a gentleman well known in University circles as a most distinguished student, and the present holder of the Neil Arnott prize for physics, has been recruiting his health in this quiet retreat. The night before last he suddenly left his friend, Mr Robert Armitage, and he has not since been heard

of. It is almost certain that he has met his death by falling over the
cliffs which surround the island. Mr Cowles' health has been failing
for some time, partly from over-study and partly from worry connected with family affairs. By his death the University loses one of
her most promising alumni.'

I have nothing more to add to my statement. I have unburdened my
mind of all that I know. I can well conceive that many, after weighing
all that I have said, will see no ground for an accusation against Miss
Northcott. They will say that, because a man of a naturally excitable
disposition says and does wild things, and even eventually commits
self-murder after a sudden and heavy disappointment, there is no
reason why vague charges should be advanced against a young lady.
To this, I answer that they are welcome to their opinion. For my own
part, I ascribe the death of William Prescott, of Archibald Reeves, and
of John Barrington Cowles to this woman with as much confidence as
if I had seen her drive a dagger into their hearts.

You ask me, no doubt, what my own theory is which will explain all
these strange facts. I have none, or, at best, a dim and vague one. That
Miss Northcott possessed extraordinary powers over the minds, and
through the minds over the bodies, of others, I am convinced, as well
as that her instincts were to use this power for base and cruel purposes. That some even more fiendish and terrible phase of character
lay behind this—some horrible trait which it was necessary for her to
reveal before marriage—is to be inferred from the experience of her
three lovers, while the dreadful nature of the mystery thus revealed
can only be surmised from the fact that the very mention of it drove
from her those who had loved her so passionately. Their subsequent
fate was, in my opinion, the result of her vindictive remembrance of
their desertion of her, and that they were forewarned of it at the time
was shown by the words of both Reeves and Cowles. Above this, I can
say nothing. I lay the facts soberly before the public as they came
under my notice. I have never seen Miss Northcott since, nor do I wish
to do so. If by the words I have written I can save any one human
being from the snare of those bright eyes and that beautiful face, then
I can lay down my pen with the assurance that my poor friend has not
died altogether in vain.

UNCLE JEREMY'S HOUSEHOLD

I

My life has been a somewhat chequered one, and it has fallen to my lot during the course of it to have had several unusual experiences. There is one episode, however, which is so surpassingly strange that whenever I look back to it it reduces the others to insignificance. It looks up out of the mists of the past, gloomy and fantastic, overshadowing the eventless years which preceded and which followed it.

It is not a story which I have often told. A few, but only a few, who know me well have heard the facts from my lips. I have been asked from time to time by these to narrate them to some assemblage of friends, but I have invariably refused, for I have no desire to gain a reputation as an amateur Munchausen.* I have yielded to their wishes, however, so far as to draw up this written statement of the facts in connection with my visit to Dunkelthwaite.*

Here is John Thurston's first letter to me. It is dated April 1862. I take it from my desk and copy it as it stands:

'My dear Lawrence, —if you knew my utter loneliness and complete *ennui* I am sure you would have pity upon me and come up to share my solitude. You have often made vague promises of visiting Dunkelthwaite and having a look at the Yorkshire Fells.* What time could suit you better than the present? Of course I understand that you are hard at work, but as you are not actually taking out classes you can read just as well here as in Baker Street.* Pack up your books, like a good fellow, and come along! We have a snug little room, with writing-desk and armchair, which will just do for your study. Let me know when we may expect you.

'When I say that I am lonely I do not mean that there is any lack of people in the house. On the contrary, we form rather a large household. First and foremost, of course, comes my poor Uncle Jeremy, garrulous and imbecile, shuffling about in his list slippers, and composing, as is his wont, innumerable bad verses. I think I told you when last we met of that trait in his character. It has attained such a pitch that he has an amanuensis, whose sole duty it is to copy down and preserve these effusions. This fellow, whose name is Copperthorne, has become as necessary to the old man as his foolscap or as the "Universal Rhyming Dictionary."* I can't say I care for him myself, but then I have always shared Caesar's prejudice against lean men*—though, by the way, little Julius was rather inclined that way himself if we may believe the medals. Then we have the two children of my Uncle Samuel, who were adopted by Jeremy—there were three of them, but one has gone the way of all flesh*—and their governess, a stylish-looking brunette with Indian blood in her veins. Besides all these, there are three maidservants and the old groom, so you see we have quite a little world of our own in this out-of-the-way corner. For all that, my dear Hugh, I long for a familiar face and for a congenial companion. I am deep in chemistry myself, so I won't interrupt your studies. Write by return to your isolated friend,

'JOHN H. THURSTON.'

At the time that I received this letter I was in lodgings in London, and was working hard for the final examination which should make me a qualified medical man. Thurston and I had been close friends at Cambridge before I took to the study of medicine, and I had a great desire to see him again. On the other hand, I was rather afraid that, in spite of his assurances, my studies might suffer by the change. I pictured to myself the childish old man, the lean secretary, the stylish governess, the two children, probably spoiled and noisy, and I came to the conclusion that when we were all cooped together in one country house there would be very little room for quiet reading. At the end of two days' cogitation I had almost made up my mind to refuse the invitation, when I received another letter from Yorkshire even more pressing than the first.

'We expect to hear from you by every post,' my friend said, 'and there is never a knock that I do not think it is a telegram announcing your train. Your room is all ready, and I think you will find it comfortable. Uncle Jeremy bids me say how very happy he will be to see you. He would have written, but he is absorbed in a great epic poem of five thousand lines or so, and he spends his day trotting about the rooms, while Copperthorne stalks behind him like the monster in Frankenstein, with notebook and pencil, jotting down the words of wisdom as they drop from his lips. By the way, I think I mentioned the brunettish governess to you. I might throw her out as a bait to you if you retain your taste for ethnological studies. She is the child of an Indian chieftain, whose wife was an Englishwoman. He was killed in the mutiny,* fighting against us, and, his estates being seized by Government, his daughter, then fifteen, was left almost destitute. Some charitable German merchant in Calcutta adopted her, it seems, and brought her over to Europe with him together with his own daughter. The latter died, and then Miss Warrender—as we call her, after her mother—answered uncle's advertisement; and here she is. Now, my dear boy, stand not upon the order of your coming, but come at once.'

There were other things in this second letter which prevent me from quoting it in full.

There was no resisting the importunity of my old friend, so, with many inward grumbles, I hastily packed up my books, and, having telegraphed overnight, started for Yorkshire the first thing in the morning. I well remember that it was a miserable day, and that the journey seemed to be an interminable one as I sat huddled up in a corner of the draughty carriage, revolving in my mind many problems of surgery and of medicine. I had been warned that the little wayside station of Ingleton, some fifteen miles from Carnforth,* was the nearest to my destination, and there I alighted just as John Thurston came dashing down the country road in a high dog-cart. He waved his whip enthusiastically at the sight of me, and pulling up his horse with a jerk, sprang out and on to the platform.

'My dear Hugh,' he cried, 'I'm so delighted to see you! It's so kind of you to come!' He wrung my hand until my arm ached.

'I'm afraid you'll find me very bad company now that I am here,' I answered; 'I am up to my eyes in work.'

'Of course, of course,' he said, in his good-humoured way. 'I reckoned on this. We'll have time for a crack at the rabbits for all that. It's a longish drive, and you must be bitterly cold, so let's start for home at once.'

We rattled off along the dusty road.

'I think you'll like your room,' my friend remarked. 'You'll soon find yourself at home. You know it is not often that I visit Dunkelthwaite myself, and I am only just beginning to settle down and get my laboratory into working order. I have been here a fortnight. It's an open secret that I occupy a prominent position in old Uncle Jeremy's will, so my father thought it only right that I should come up and do the polite. Under the circumstances I can hardly do less than put myself out a little now and again.'

'Certainly not,' I said.

'And besides, he's a very good old fellow. You'll be amused at our ménage. A princess for governess—it sounds well, doesn't it? I think our imperturbable secretary is somewhat gone in that direction. Turn up your coat-collar, for the wind is very sharp.'

The road ran over a succession of low bleak hills, which were devoid of all vegetation save a few scattered gorse-bushes and a thin covering of stiff wiry grass, which gave nourishment to a scattered flock of lean, hungry-looking sheep. Alternately we dipped down into a hollow or rose to the summit of an eminence from which we could see the road winding as a thin white track over successive hills beyond. Every here and there the monotony of the landscape was broken by jagged scarps, where the grey granite peeped grimly out, as though nature had been sorely wounded until her gaunt bones protruded through their covering. In the distance lay a range of mountains, with one great peak shooting up from amongst them coquettishly draped in a wreath of clouds which reflected the ruddy light of the setting sun.

'That's Ingleborough,' my companion said, indicating the mountain with his whip, 'and these are the Yorkshire Fells. You won't find a wilder, bleaker place in all England. They breed a good race of men. The raw militia who beat the Scotch chivalry at the Battle of the Standard* came from this part of the country. Just jump down, old fellow and open the gate.'

We had pulled up at a place where a long moss-grown wall ran parallel to the road. It was broken by a dilapidated iron gate, flanked by two pillars, on the summit of which were stone devices which appeared to represent some heraldic animal, though wind and rain had reduced them to shapeless blocks. A ruined cottage, which may have served at some time as a lodge, stood on one side. I pushed the gate open and we drove up a long, winding avenue, grass-grown and uneven, but lined by magnificent oaks, which shot their branches so thickly over us that the evening twilight deepened suddenly into darkness.

'I'm afraid our avenue won't impress you much,' Thurston said, with a laugh. 'It's one of the old man's whims to let nature have her way in everything. Here we are at last at Dunkelthwaite.'

As he spoke we swung round a curve in the avenue marked by a patriarchal oak which towered high above the others, and came upon a great square whitewashed house with a lawn in front of it. The lower part of the building was all in shadow, but up at the top a row of blood-shot windows glimmered out at the setting sun. At the sound of the wheels an old man in livery ran out and seized the horse's head when we pulled up.

'You can put her up, Elijah,' my friend said, as we jumped down. 'Hugh, let me introduce you to my Uncle Jeremy.'

'How d'ye do? How d'ye do?' cried a wheezy cracked voice, and looking up I saw a little red-faced man who was standing waiting for us in the porch. He wore a cotton cloth tied round his head after the fashion of Pope* and other eighteenth-century celeb-rities, and was further distinguished by a pair of enormous slippers. These contrasted so strangely with his thin spindle shanks that he appeared to be wearing snowshoes, a resemblance which was height-ened by the fact that when he walked he was compelled to slide his feet along the ground in order to retain his grip of these unwieldly appendages.

'You must be tired, sir. Yes, and cold, sir,' he said, in a strange jerky way, as he shook me by the hand. 'We must be hospitable to you, we must indeed. Hospitality is one of the old-world virtues which we still retain. Let me see, what are those lines? "Ready and strong the Yorkshire arm, but oh, the Yorkshire heart is warm?" Neat and terse, sir. That comes from one of my poems. What poem is it, Copperthorne?'

'"The Harrying of Borrodaile",'* said a voice behind him, and a tall long-visaged man stepped forward into the circle of light which was thrown by the lamp above the porch. John introduced us, and I remember that his hand as I shook it was cold and unpleasantly clammy.

This ceremony over, my friend led the way to my room, passing through many passages and corridors connected by old-fashioned and irregular staircases. I noticed as I passed the thickness of the walls and the strange slants and angles of the ceilings, suggestive of mys-terious spaces above. The chamber set apart for me proved, as John had said, to be a cheery little sanctum with a crackling fire and a well-stocked bookcase. I began to think as I pulled on my slippers that I might have done worse after all than accept this Yorkshire invitation.

II

When we descended to the dining-room the rest of the household had already assembled for dinner. Old Jeremy, still wearing his quaint headgear, sat at the head of the table. Next to him, on his right, sat a very dark young lady with black hair and eyes, who was introduced to me as Miss Warrender. Beside her were two pretty children, a boy and a girl, who were evidently her charges. I sat opposite her, with Copperthorne on my left, while John faced his uncle. I can almost fancy now that I can see the yellow glare of the great oil lamp throwing Rembrandt-like lights and shades* upon the ring of faces, some of which were soon to have so strange an interest for me.

It was a pleasant meal, apart from the excellence of the viands and the fact that the long journey had sharpened my appetite. Uncle Jeremy overflowed with anecdote and quotation, delighted to have found a new listener. Neither Miss Warrender nor Copperthorne spoke much, but all that the latter said bespoke the thoughtful and educated man. As to John, he had so much to say of college reminiscences and subsequent events that I fear his dinner was a scanty one.

When the dessert was put on the table Miss Warrender took the children away, and Uncle Jeremy withdrew into the library, where we could hear the dull murmur of his voice as he dictated to his amanuensis. My old friend and I sat for some time before the fire discussing the many things which had happened to both of us since our last meeting.

'And what do you think of our household?' he asked at last, with a smile.

I answered that I was very much interested with what I had seen of it. 'Your uncle,' I said, 'is quite a character. I like him very much.'

'Yes; he has a warm heart behind all his peculiarities. Your coming seems to have cheered him up, for he's never been quite himself since little Ethel's death. She was the youngest of Uncle Sam's children, and came here with the others, but she had a fit or something in the shrubbery a couple of months ago. They found her lying dead there in the evening. It was a great blow to the old man.'

'It must have been to Miss Warrender too?' I remarked.

'Yes; she was very much cut up. She had only been here a week or two at the time. She had driven over to Kirby Lonsdale* that day to buy something.'

'I was very much interested,' I said, 'in all that you told me about her. You were not chaffing, I suppose!'

'No, no; it's true as gospel. Her father was Achmet Genghis Khan, a semi-independent chieftain somewhere in the Central Provinces. He was a bit of a heathen fanatic in spite of his Christian wife, and he became chummy with the Nana, and mixed himself up in the Cawnpore business,* so Government came down heavily on him.'

'She must have been quite a woman before she left her tribe,' I said. 'What view of religion does she take? Does she side with her father or mother?'

'We never press that question,' my friend answered. 'Between ourselves, I don't think she's very orthodox. Her mother must have been a good woman, and besides teaching her English, she is a good French scholar, and plays remarkably well. Why, there she goes!'

As he spoke the sound of a piano was heard from the next room, and we both paused to listen. At first the player struck a few isolated notes, as though uncertain how to proceed. Then came a series of clanging chords and jarring discords, until out of the chaos there suddenly swelled a strange barbaric march, with blare of trumpet and crash of cymbal. Louder and louder it pealed forth in a gust of wild melody, and then died away once more into the jerky chords which had preceded it. Then we heard the sound of the shutting of the piano, and the music was at an end.

'She does that every night,' my friend remarked; 'I suppose it is some Indian reminiscence. Picturesque, don't you think so? Now don't stay here longer than you wish. Your room is ready whenever you would like to study.'

I took my companion at his word and left him with his uncle and Copperthorne, who had returned into the room, while I went upstairs and read Medical Jurisprudence for a couple of hours. I imagined that I should see no more of the inhabitants of Dunkelthwaite that night, but I was mistaken, for about ten o'clock Uncle Jeremy thrust his little red face into the room.

'All comfortable?' he asked.

'Excellent, thanks,' I answered.

'That's right. Keep at it. Sure to succeed,' he said, in his spasmodic way. 'Good night!'

'Good night!' I answered.

'Good night!' said another voice from the passage; and looking out
I saw the tall figure of the secretary gliding along at the old man's
heels like a long dark shadow.

I went back to my desk and worked for another hour, after which
I retired to bed, where I pondered for some time before I dropped to
sleep over the curious household of which I had become a member.

III

I was up betimes in the morning and out on the lawn, where I found
Miss Warrender, who was picking primroses and making them into
a little bunch for the breakfast-table. I approached her before she saw
me, and I could not help admiring the beautiful litheness of her figure
as she stooped over the flowers. There was a feline grace about her
every movement such as I never remember to have seen in any woman.
I recalled Thurston's words as to the impression which she had made
upon the secretary, and ceased to wonder at it. As she heard my step,
she stood up and turned her dark handsome face towards me.

'Good morning, Miss Warrender,' I said. 'You are an early riser,
like myself.'

'Yes,' she answered. 'I have always been accustomed to rise at
daybreak.'

'What a strange, wild view!' I remarked, looking out over the wide
stretch of fells. 'I am a stranger to this part of the country, like yourself. How do you like it?'

'I don't like it,' she said, frankly. 'I detest it. It is cold and bleak and
wretched. Look at these'—holding up her bunch of primroses—
'they call these things flowers. They have not even a smell.'

'You have been used to a more genial climate and a tropical
vegetation?'

'Oh, then, Mr Thurston has been telling you about me,' she said,
with a smile. 'Yes, I have been used to something better than this.'

We were standing together when a shadow fell between us, and
looking round I found that Copperthorne was standing close behind
us. He held out his thin white hand to me with a constrained smile.

'You seem to be able to find your way about already,' he remarked, glancing backwards and forwards from my face to that of Miss Warrender. 'Let me hold your flowers for you, miss.'

'No, thank you,' the other said, coldly. 'I have picked enough and am going inside.'

She swept past him and across the lawn to the house. Copperthorne looked after her with a frowning brow.

'You are a student of medicine, Mr Lawrence?' he said, turning towards me and stamping one of his feet up and down in a jerky, nervous fashion, as he spoke.

'Yes, I am.'

'Oh, we have heard of you students of medicine,' he cried in a raised voice, with a little crackling laugh. 'You are dreadful fellows, are you not? We have heard of you. There is no standing against you.'

'A medical student, sir,' I answered, 'is usually a gentleman.'

'Quite so,' he said, in a changed voice. 'Of course I was only joking.' Nevertheless I could not help noticing that at breakfast he kept his eyes persistently fixed upon me while Miss Warrender was speaking, and if I chanced to make a remark he would flash a glance round at her as though to read in our faces what our thoughts were of each other. It was clear that he took a more than common interest in the beautiful governess, and it seemed to me to be equally evident that his feelings were by no means reciprocated.

We had an illustration that morning of the simple nature of these primitive Yorkshire folk. It appears that the housemaid and the cook, who sleep together, were alarmed during the night by something which their superstitious minds contorted into an apparition. I was sitting after breakfast with Uncle Jeremy, who, with the help of continual promptings from his secretary, was reciting some Border poetry,* when there was a tap at the door and the housemaid appeared. Close at her heels came the cook, buxom but timorous, the two mutually encouraging and abetting each other. They told their story in a strophe and antistrophe, like a Greek chorus,* Jane talking until her breath failed, when the narrative was taken up by the cook, who, in turn, was supplanted by the other. Much of what they said was almost unintelligible to me owing to their extraordinary dialect, but I could make out the main thread of their story. It appears that in the early morning the cook had been awakened by something touching her face, and starting up had seen a shadowy figure standing by her bed, which figure had at once glided noiselessly from the room. The house-maid was awakened by the cook's cry, and averred stoutly that she had seen the apparition. No amount of cross-examination or reasoning could shake them, and they wound up by both giving notice, which was a practical way of showing that they were honestly scared. They seemed considerably indignant at our want of belief, and ended by bouncing out of the room, leaving Uncle Jeremy angry, Copperthorne contemptuous, and myself very much amused.

I spent nearly the whole of the second day of my visit in my room, and got over a considerable amount of work. In the evening John and I went down to the rabbit-warren with our guns. I told John as we came back of the absurd scene with the servants in the morning, but it did not seem to strike him in the same ridiculous light that it had me.

'The fact is,' he said, 'in very old houses like ours, where you have the timber rotten and warped, you get curious effects sometimes which predispose the mind to superstition. I have heard one or two things at night during this visit which might have frightened a nervous man, and still more an uneducated servant. Of course all this about apparitions is mere nonsense, but when once the imagination is excited there's no checking it.'

'What have you heard, then?' I asked with interest.

'Oh, nothing of any importance,' he answered. 'Here are the youngsters and Miss Warrender. We mustn't talk about these things before her, or else we shall have her giving warning too, and that would be a loss to the establishment.'

She was sitting on a little stile which stood on the outskirts of the wood which surrounds Dunkelthwaite, and the two children were leaning up against her, one on either side, with their hands clasped round her arms, and their chubby faces turned up to hers. It was a pretty picture and we both paused to look at it. She had heard our approach, however, and springing lightly down she came towards us, with the two little ones toddling behind her.

'You must aid me with the weight of your authority,' she said to John. 'These little rebels are fond of the night air and won't be persuaded to come indoors.'

'Don't want to come,' said the boy, with decision. 'Want to hear the rest of the story.'

'Yes—the 'tory,' lisped the younger one.

'You shall hear the rest of the story to-morrow if you are good. Here is Mr Lawrence, who is a doctor—he will tell you how bad it is for little boys and girls to be out when the dew falls.'

'So you have been hearing a story?' John said as we moved on together.

'Yes such a good story!' the little chap said with enthusiasm. 'Uncle Jeremy tells us stories, but they are in po'try and they are not nearly so nice as Miss Warrender's stories. This one was about elephants—'

'And tigers—and gold—' said the other.

'Yes, and wars and fighting, and the king of the Cheroots—'

'Rajpoots,* my dear,' said the governess.

'And the scattered tribes that know each other by signs, and the man that was killed in the wood. She knows splendid stories. Why don't you make her tell you some, Cousin John?'

'Really, Miss Warrender, you have excited our curiosity,' my companion said. 'You must tell us of these wonders.'

'They would seem stupid enough to you,' she answered, with a laugh. 'They are merely a few reminiscences of my early life.'

As we strolled along the pathway which led through the wood we met Copperthorne coming from the opposite direction.

'I was looking for you all,' he said, with an ungainly attempt at geniality. 'I wanted to tell you that it was dinner-time.'

'Our watches told us that,' said John, rather ungraciously as I thought.

'And you have been all rabbiting together?' the secretary continued, as he stalked along beside us.

'Not all,' I answered. 'We met Miss Warrender and the children on our way back.'

'Oh, Miss Warrender came to meet you as you came back!' said he. This quick contortion of my words, together with the sneering way in which he spoke, vexed me so much that I should have made a sharp rejoinder had it not been for the lady's presence.

I happened to turn my eyes towards the governess at the moment, and I saw her glance at the speaker with an angry sparkle in her eyes which showed that she shared my indignation. I was surprised, however, that same night when about ten o'clock I chanced to look out of the window of my study, to see the two of them walking up and down in the moonlight engaged in deep conversation. I don't know how it was, but the sight disturbed me so much that after several fruitless attempts to continue my studies I threw my books aside and gave up work for the night. About eleven I glanced out again, but they were gone, and shortly afterwards I heard the shuffling step of Uncle Jeremy, and the firm heavy footfall of the secretary, as they ascended the staircase which led to their bedrooms upon the upper floor.

IV

John Thurston was never a very observant man, and I believe that before I had been three days under his uncle's roof I knew more of what was going on there than he did. My friend was ardently devoted to chemistry, and spent his days happily among his test-tubes and solutions, perfectly contented so long as he had a congenial companion at hand to whom he could communicate his results. For myself, I have always had a weakness for the study and analysis of human character, and I found much that was interesting in the microcosm in which I lived. Indeed, I became so absorbed in my observations that I fear my studies suffered to a considerable extent.

In the first place, I discovered beyond all doubt that the real master of Dunkelthwaite was not Uncle Jeremy, but Uncle Jeremy's amanuensis. My medical instinct told me that the absorbing love of poetry, which had been nothing more than a harmless eccentricity in the old man's younger days, had now become a complete monomania, which filled his mind to the exclusion of every other subject. Copperthorne, by humouring his employer upon this one point until he had made himself indispensable to him, had succeeded in gaining complete power over him in everything else. He managed his money matters and the affairs of the house unquestioned and uncontrolled. He had sense enough, however, to exert his authority so lightly that it galled no one's neck, and therefore excited no opposition. My friend, busy with his distillations and analyses, was never allowed to realise that he was really a nonentity in the establishment.

I have already expressed my conviction that though Copperthorne had some tender feeling for the governess, she by no means favoured his addresses. After a few days I came to think, however, that there existed besides this unrequited affection some other link which bound the pair together. I had seen him more than once assume an air towards

her which can only be described as one of authority. Two or three
times also I had observed them pacing the lawn and conversing earnestly in the early hours of the night. I could not guess what mutual
understanding existed between them, and the mystery piqued my
curiosity.

It is proverbially easy to fall in love in a country house, but my
nature has never been a sentimental one, and my judgment was not
warped by any such feeling towards Miss Warrender. On the contrary, I set myself to study her as an entomologist might a specimen,
critically, but without bias. With this object I used to arrange my
studies in such a way as to be free at the times when she took the children out for exercise, so that we had many walks together, and I gained
a deeper insight into her character than I should otherwise have done.

She was fairly well read, and had a superficial acquaintance with
several languages, as well as a great natural taste for music. Underneath
this veneer of culture, however, there was a great dash of the savage in
her nature. In the course of her conversation she would every now and
again drop some remark which would almost startle me by its primi
tive reasoning, and by its disregard for the conventionalities of civilisation. I could hardly wonder at this, however, when I reflected that she
had been a woman before she left the wild tribe which her father ruled.

I remember one instance which struck me as particularly characteristic, in which her wild original habits suddenly asserted themselves. We were walking along the country road, talking of Germany,
in which she had spent some months, when she suddenly stopped
short and laid her finger upon her lips. 'Lend me your stick!' she said,
in a whisper. I handed it to her, and at once, to my astonishment, she
darted lightly and noiselessly through a gap in the hedge, and bending her body, crept swiftly along under the shelter of a little knoll.
I was still looking after her in amazement, when a rabbit rose suddenly in front of her and scuttled away. She hurled the stick after it
and struck it, but the creature made good its escape, though trailing
one leg behind it.

She came back to me exultant and panting. 'I saw it move among
the grass,' she said. 'I hit it.'

'Yes, you hit it. You broke its leg,' I said, somewhat coldly.

'You hurt it,' the little boy cried, ruefully.

'Poor little beast!' she exclaimed, with a sudden change in her
whole manner. 'I am sorry I harmed it.' She seemed completely cast

down by the incident, and spoke little during the remainder of our walk. For my own part I could not blame her much. It was evidently an outbreak of the old predatory instinct of the savage, though with a somewhat incongruous effect in the case of a fashionably dressed young lady on an English high road.

John Thurston made me peep into her private sitting-room one day when she was out. She had a thousand little Indian knickknacks there which showed that she had come well-laden from her native land. Her Oriental love for bright colours had exhibited itself in an amusing fashion. She had gone down to the market town and bought numerous sheets of pink and blue paper, and these she had pinned in patches over the sombre covering which had lined the walls before. She had some tinsel too, which she had put up in the most conspicuous places. The whole effect was ludicrously tawdry and glaring, and yet there seemed to me to be a touch of pathos in this attempt to reproduce the brilliance of the tropics in the cold English dwelling-house.

During the first few days of my visit the curious relationship which existed between Miss Warrender and the secretary had simply excited my curiosity, but as the weeks passed and I became more interested in the beautiful Anglo-Indian a deeper and more personal feeling took possession of me. I puzzled my brains as to what tie could exist between them. Why was it that while she showed every symptom of being averse to his company during the day she should walk about with him alone after nightfall? Could it be that the distaste which she showed for him before others was a blind to conceal her real feelings? Such a supposition seemed to involve a depth of dissimulation in her nature which appeared to be incompatible with her frank eyes and clear-cut proud features. And yet, what other hypothesis could account for the power which he most certainly exercised over her?

This power showed itself in many ways, but was exerted so quietly and silently that none but a close observer could have known that it existed. I have seen him glance at her with a look so commanding, and, as it seemed to me, so menacing, that next moment I could hardly believe that his white impassive face could be capable of so intense an expression. When he looked at her in this manner she would wince and quiver as though she had been in physical pain. 'Decidedly,' I thought, 'it is fear and not love which produces such effects.'

I was so interested in the question that I spoke to my friend John about it. He was in his little laboratory at the time, and was deeply immersed in a series of manipulations and distillations, which ended in the production of an evil-smelling gas, which set us both coughing and choking. I took advantage of our enforced retreat into the fresh air to question him upon one or two points on which I wanted information.

'How long did you say that Miss Warrender had been with your uncle?' I asked.

John looked at me slyly, and shook his acid-stained finger.

'You seem to be wonderfully interested about the daughter of the late lamented Achmet Genghis,' he said.

'Who could help it?' I answered, frankly. 'I think she is one of the most romantic characters I ever met.'

'Take care of the studies, my boy,' John said, paternally. 'This sort of thing doesn't do before examinations.'

'Don't be ridiculous!' I remonstrated. 'Any one would think that I was in love with Miss Warrender to hear the way in which you talk. I look on her as an interesting psychological problem, nothing more.'

'Quite so—an interesting psychological problem, nothing more.'

John seemed to have some of the vapours of the gas still hanging about his system, for his manner was decidedly irritating.

'To revert to my original question,' I said. 'How long has she been here?'

'About ten weeks.'

'And Copperthorne?'

'Over two years.'

'Do you imagine that they could have known each other before?'

'Impossible!' said John, with decision. 'She came from Germany. I saw the letter from the old merchant, in which he traced her previous life. Copperthorne has always been in Yorkshire except for two years at Cambridge. He had to leave the university under a cloud.'

'What sort of a cloud?'

'Don't know,' John answered. 'They kept it very quiet. I fancy Uncle Jeremy knows. He's very fond of taking rapscallions up and giving them what he calls another start. Some of them will give him a start some of these fine days.'

'And so Copperthorne and Miss Warrender were absolute strangers until the last few weeks?'

'Quite so; and now I think we can go back and analyse the sediment.'

'Never mind the sediment,' I cried, detaining him. 'There's more I want to talk to you about. If these two have only known each other for this short time, how has he managed to gain his power over her?'

John stared at me open-eyed.

'His power?' he said.

'Yes, the power which he exercises over her.'

'My dear Hugh,' my friend said, gravely, 'I'm not in the habit of thus quoting Scripture, but there is one text which occurs irresistibly to my mind, and that is, that "Much learning hath made thee mad."* You've been reading too hard.'

'Do you mean to say,' I cried, 'that you have never observed that there is some secret understanding between your uncle's governess and his amanuensis?'

'Try bromide of potassium,'* said John. 'It's very soothing in twenty-grain doses.'

'Try a pair of spectacles,' I retorted, 'you most certainly need them;' with which parting shot I turned on my heel and went off in high dudgeon. I had not gone twenty yards down the gravel walk of the garden before I saw the very couple of whom we had just been speaking. They were some little way off, she leaning against the sundial, he standing in front of her and speaking earnestly, with occasional jerky gesticulations. With his tall, gaunt figure towering above her, and the spasmodic motions of his long arms, he might have been some great bat fluttering over a victim. I remember that that was the simile which rose in my mind at the time, heightened perhaps by the suggestion of shrinking and of fear which seemed to me to lie in every curve of her beautiful figure.

The little picture was such an illustration of the text upon which I had been preaching, that I had half a mind to go back to the laboratory and bring the incredulous John out to witness it. Before I had time to come to a conclusion, however, Copperthorne caught a glimpse of me, and turning away, he strolled slowly in the opposite direction into the shrubbery, his companion walking by his side and cutting at the flowers as she passed with her sunshade.

I went up to my room after this small episode with the intention of pushing on with my studies, but do what I would my mind wandered away from my books in order to speculate upon this mystery.

I had learned from John that Copperthorne's antecedents were not of the best, and yet he had obviously gained enormous power over his almost imbecile employer. I could understand this fact by observing the infinite pains with which he devoted himself to the old man's hobby, and the consummate tact with which he humoured and encouraged his strange poetic whims. But how could I account for the to me equally obvious power which he wielded over the governess? She had no whims to be humoured. Mutual love might account for the tie between them, but my instinct as a man of the world and as an observer of human nature told me most conclusively that no such love existed. If not love, it must be fear—a supposition which was favoured by all that I had seen.

What, then, had occurred during these two months to cause this high-spirited, dark-eyed princess to fear the white-faced Englishman with the soft voice and the gentle manner? That was the problem which I set myself to solve with an energy and earnestness which eclipsed my ardour for study, and rendered me superior to the terrors of my approaching examination.

I ventured to approach the subject that same afternoon to Miss Warrender, whom I found alone in the library, the two little children having gone to spend the day in the nursery of a neighbouring squire.

'You must be rather lonely when there are no visitors,' I remarked. 'It does not seem to be a very lively part of the country.'

'Children are always good companions,' she answered. 'Nevertheless I shall miss both Mr Thurston* and yourself very much when you go.'

'I shall be sorry when the time comes,' I said. 'I never expected to enjoy this visit as I have done; still you won't be quite companionless when we are gone, you'll always have Mr Copperthorne.'

'Yes; we shall always have Mr Copperthorne.' She spoke with a weary intonation.

'He's a pleasant companion,' I remarked; 'quiet, well informed, and amiable. I don't wonder that old Mr Thurston is so fond of him.'

As I spoke in this way I watched my companion intently. There was a slight flush on her dark cheeks, and she drummed her fingers impatiently against the arms of the chair.

'His manner may be a little cold sometimes—' I was continuing, but she interrupted me, turning on me furiously, with an angry glare in her black eyes.

'What do you want to talk to me about him for?' she asked.

'I beg pardon,' I answered, submissively, 'I did not know it was a forbidden subject.'

'I don't wish ever to hear his name,' she cried, passionately. 'I hate it and I hate him. Oh, if I had only some one who loved me—that is, as men love away over the seas in my own land, I know what I should say to him.'

'What would you say?' I asked, astonished at this extraordinary outburst.

She leaned forward until I seemed to feel the quick pants of her warm breath upon my face.

'Kill Copperthorne,' she said. 'That is what I should say to him. Kill Copperthorne. Then you can come and talk of love to me.'

Nothing can describe the intensity of fierceness with which she hissed these words out from between her white teeth.

She looked so venomous as she spoke that I involuntarily shrank away from her. Could this pythoness be the demure young lady who sat every day so primly and quietly at the table of Uncle Jeremy? I had hoped to gain some insight into her character by my leading question, but I had never expected to conjure up such a spirit as this. She must have seen the horror and surprise which was depicted on my face, for her manner changed and she laughed nervously.

'You must really think me mad,' she said. 'You see it is the Indian training breaking out again. We do nothing by halves over there—either loving or hating.'

'And why is it that you hate Mr Copperthorne?' I asked.

'Ah, well,' she answered, in a subdued voice, 'perhaps hate is rather too strong a term after all. Dislike would be better. There are some people you cannot help having an antipathy to, even though you are unable to give any exact reason.'

It was evident that she regretted her recent outburst and was endeavouring to explain it away.

As I saw that she wished to change the conversation, I aided her to do so, and made some remark about a book of Indian prints which she had taken down before I came in, and which still lay upon her lap. Uncle Jeremy's collection was an extensive one, and was particularly rich in works of this class.

'They are not very accurate,' she said, turning over the many-coloured leaves. 'This is good, though,' she continued, picking out a picture of a chieftain clad in chain mail with a picturesque turban upon his head. 'This is very good indeed. My father was dressed like that when he rode down on his white charger and led all the warriors of the Dooab to do battle with the Feringhees.* My father was chosen out from amongst them all, for they knew that Achmet Genghis Khan was a great priest as well as a great soldier. The people would be led by none but a tried Borka.* He is dead now, and of all those who followed his banner there are none who are not scattered or slain, whilst I his daughter, am a wanderer in a far land.

'No doubt you will go back to India some day,' I said, in a somewhat feeble attempt at consolation.

She turned the pages over listlessly for a few moments without answering. Then she gave a sudden little cry of pleasure as she paused at one of the prints.

'Look at this,' she cried, eagerly. 'It is one of our wanderers. He is a Bhuttotee.* It is very like.'

The picture which excited her so was one which represented a particularly uninviting-looking native with a small instrument which looked like a miniature pickaxe in one hand, and a striped handkerchief or roll of linen in the other.

'That handkerchief is his roomal,'* she said. 'Of course he wouldn't go about with it openly like that, nor would he bear the sacred axe, but in every other respect he is as he should be. Many a time have I been with such upon the moonless nights when the Lughaees were on ahead and the heedless stranger heard the Pilhaoo* away to the left and knew not what it might mean. Ah! that was a life that was worth the living!'

'And what may a roomal be—and the Lughaee and all the rest of it?' I asked.

'Oh, they are Indian terms,' she answered, with a laugh. 'You would not understand them.'

'But,' I said, 'this picture is marked as Dacoit,* and I always thought that a Dacoit was a robber.'

'That is because the English know no better,' she observed. 'Of course, Dacoits are robbers, but they call many people robbers who are not really so. Now this man is a holy man and in all probability a Gooroo.'*

She might have given me more information upon Indian manners and customs, for it was a subject upon which she loved to talk; but suddenly as I watched her I saw a change come over her face, and she gazed with a rigid stare at the window behind me. I looked round, and there peering stealthily round the corner at us was the face of the amanuensis. I confess that I was startled myself at the sight, for, with its corpse-like pallor, the head might have been one which had been severed from his shoulders. He threw open the sash when he saw that he was observed.

'I'm sorry to interrupt you,' he said, looking in, 'but don't you think, Miss Warrender, that it is a pity to be boxed up on such a fine day in a close room? Won't you come out and take a stroll?'

Though his words were courteous they were uttered in a harsh and almost menacing voice, so as to sound more like a command than a request. The governess rose, and without protest or remark glided away to put on her bonnet. It was another example of Copperthorne's authority over her. As he looked in at me through the open window a mocking smile played about his thin lips, as though he would have liked to have taunted me with this display of his power. With the sun shining in behind him he might have been a demon in a halo. He stood in this manner for a few moments gazing in at me with concentrated malice upon his face. Then I heard his heavy footfall scrunching along the gravel path as he walked round in the direction of the door.

V

For some days after the interview in which Miss Warrender confessed her hatred of the secretary, things ran smoothly at Dunkelthwaite. I had several long conversations with her as we rambled about the woods and fields with the two little children, but I was never able to bring her round to the subject of her outburst in the library, nor did she tell me anything which threw any light at all upon the problem which interested me so deeply. Whenever I made any remark which might lead in that direction she either answered me in a guarded manner or else discovered suddenly that it was high time that the children were back in their nursery, so that I came to despair of ever learning anything from her lips.

During this time I studied spasmodically and irregularly. Occasionally old Uncle Jeremy would shuffle into my room with a roll of manuscript in his hand, and would read me extracts from his great epic poem. Whenever I felt in need of company I used to go a-visiting to John's laboratory, and he in his turn would come to my chamber if he were lonely. Sometimes I used to vary the monotony of my studies by taking my books out into an arbour in the shrubbery and working there during the day. As to Copperthorne, I avoided him as much as possible, and he, for his part, appeared to be by no means anxious to cultivate my acquaintance.

One day about the second week in June, John came to me with a telegram in his hand and look of considerable disgust upon his face. 'Here's a pretty go!' he cried. 'The governor wants me to go up at once and meet him in London. It's some legal business, I suppose. He was always threatening to set his affairs in order, and now he has got an energetic fit and intends to do it.'

'I suppose you won't be gone long?' I said.

'A week or two perhaps. It's rather a nuisance, just when I was in a fair way towards separating that alkaloid.'*

'You'll find it there when you come back,' I said laughing. 'There's no one here who is likely to separate it in your absence.'

'What bothers me most is leaving you here,' he continued. 'It seems such an inhospitable thing to ask a fellow down to a lonely place like this and then to run away and leave him.'

'Don't you mind about me,' I answered, 'I have too much to do to be lonely. Besides, I have found attractions in this place which I never expected. I don't think any six weeks of my life have ever passed more quickly than the last.'

'Oh, they passed quickly, did they?' said John, and sniggered to himself. I am convinced that he was still under the delusion that I was hopelessly in love with the governess.

He went off that day by the early train, promising to write and tell us his address in town, for he did not know yet at which hotel his father would put up. I little knew what a difference this trifle would make, nor what was to occur before I set eyes upon my friend once more. At the time I was by no means grieved at his departure. It brought the four of us who were left into closer apposition, and seemed to favour the solving of that problem in which I found myself from day to day becoming more interested.

About a quarter of a mile from the house of Dunkelthwaite there is a straggling little village of the same name, consisting of some twenty or thirty slate-roofed cottages, with an ivy-clad church hard by and the inevitable beerhouse. On the afternoon of the very day on which John left us, Miss Warrender and the two children walked down to the post-office there, and I volunteered to accompany them.

Copperthorne would have liked well to have either prevented the excursion or to have gone with us, but fortunately Uncle Jeremy was in the throes of composition, and the services of his secretary were indispensable to him. It was a pleasant walk, I remember, for the road was well shaded by trees, and the birds were singing merrily overhead. We strolled along together, talking of many things, while the little boy and girl ran on, laughing and romping.

Before you get to the post-office you have to pass the beerhouse already mentioned. As we walked down the village street we became conscious that a small knot of people had assembled in front of this building. There were a dozen or so ragged boys and draggle-tailed girls, with a few bonnetless women, and a couple of loungers from the bar—probably as large an assemblage as ever met together in the annals of that quiet neighbourhood. We could not see what it was that was exciting their curiosity, but the children scampered on and quickly returned brimful of information.

'Oh, Miss Warrender,' Johnnie cried, as he dashed up, panting and eager, 'there's a black man there like the ones you tell us stories about!'

'A gipsy, I suppose,' I said.

'No, no,' said Johnnie, with decision; 'he is blacker than that, isn't he, May?'

'Blacker than that,' the little girl echoed.

'I suppose we had better go and see what this wonderful apparition is,' I said.

As I spoke I glanced at my companion. To my surprise, she was very pale, and her great black eyes appeared to be luminous with suppressed excitement.

'Aren't you well?' I asked.

'Oh, yes. Come on!' she cried, eagerly, quickening her step; 'come on!'

It was certainly a curious sight which met our eyes when we joined the little circle of rustics. It reminded me of the description of the opium-eating Malay whom De Quincey* saw in the farmhouse in Scotland. In the centre of the circle of homely Yorkshire folk there stood an Oriental wanderer, tall, lithe, and graceful, his linen clothes stained with dust and his brown feet projecting through his rude shoes. It was evident that he had travelled far and long. He had a heavy stick in his hand, on which he leaned, while his dark eyes looked thoughtfully away into space, careless apparently of the throng around him. His picturesque attire, with his coloured turban and swarthy face, had a strange and incongruous effect amongst all the prosaic surroundings.

'Poor fellow!' Miss Warrender said to me, speaking in an excited, gasping voice. 'He is tired and hungry, no doubt, and cannot explain his wants. I will speak to him,' and, going up to the Indian, she said a few words in his native dialect.

Never shall I forget the effect which those few syllables produced. Without a word the wanderer fell straight down upon his face on the dusty road and absolutely grovelled at the feet of my companion. I had read of Eastern forms of abasement when in the presence of a superior, but I could not have imagined that any human could have expressed such abject humility as was indicated in this man's attitude.

Miss Warrender spoke again in a sharp and commanding voice, on which he sprang to his feet and stood with his hands clasped and his eyes cast down, like a slave in the presence of his mistress. The little crowd, who seemed to think that the sudden prostration had been the prelude to some conjuring feat or acrobatic entertainment, looked on amused and interested.

'Should you mind walking on with the children and posting the letters?' the governess said. 'I should like to have a word with this man.'

I complied with her request, and when I returned in a few minutes the two were still conversing. The Indian appeared to be giving a narrative of his adventures or detailing the causes of his journey, for he spoke rapidly and excitedly, with quivering fingers and gleaming eyes. Miss Warrender listened intently, giving an occasional start or exclamation, which showed how deeply the man's statement interested her.

'I must apologise for detaining you so long in the sun,' she said, turning to me at last. 'We must go home, or we shall be late for dinner.'

With a few parting sentences, which sounded like commands, she left her dusky acquaintance still standing in the village street, and we strolled homewards with the children.

'Well?' I asked, with natural curiosity, when we were out of earshot of the visitors. 'Who is he, and what is he?'

'He comes from the Central Provinces, near the land of the Mahrattas.* He is one of us. It has been quite a shock to me to meet a fellow-countryman so unexpectedly; I feel quite upset.'

'It must have been pleasant for you,' I remarked.

'Yes, very pleasant,' she said, heartily.

'And why did he fall down like that?'

'Because he knew me to be the daughter of Achmet Genghis Khan,' she said, proudly.

'And what chance has brought him here?'

'Oh, it's a long story,' she said, carelessly. 'He has led a wandering life. How dark it is in this avenue, and how the great branches shoot across! If you were to crouch on one of those you could drop down on the back of any one who passed, and they would never know that you were there until they felt your fingers on their throat.'

'What a horrible idea!' I exclaimed.

'Gloomy places always give me gloomy thoughts,' she said, lightly. 'By the way, I want you to do me a favour, Mr Lawrence.'

'What is that?' I asked.

'Don't say anything at the house about this poor compatriot of mine. They might think him a rogue and a vagabond, you know, and order him to be driven from the village.'

'I'm sure Mr Thurston would do nothing so unkind.'

'No; but Mr Copperthorne might.'

'Just as you like,' I said; 'but the children are sure to tell.'

'No, I think not,' she answered.

I don't know how she managed to curb their little prattling tongues, but they certainly preserved silence upon the point, and there was no talk that evening of the strange visitor who had wandered into our little hamlet.

I had a shrewd suspicion that this stranger from the tropics was no chance wanderer, but had come to Dunkelthwaite upon some set errand. Next day I had the best possible evidence that he was still in the vicinity, for I met Miss Warrender coming down the garden walk with a basketful of scraps of bread and of meat in her hand. She was in the habit of taking these leavings to sundry old women in the neighbourhood, so I offered to accompany her.

'Is it old Dame Venables or old Dame Taylforth to-day?' I asked.

'Neither one nor the other,' she said, with a smile. 'I'll tell you the truth, Mr Lawrence, because you have always been a good friend to me, and I feel I can trust you. These scraps are for my poor country-man. I'll hang the basket here on this branch, and he will get it.'

'Oh, he's still about, then,' I observed.

'Yes, he's still in the neighbourhood.'

'You think he will find it?'

'Oh, trust him for that,' she said. 'You don't blame me for helping him, do you? You would do the same if you lived among Indians and suddenly came upon an Englishman. Come to the hothouse and look at the flowers.'

We walked round to the conservatory together. When we came back the basket was still hanging to the branch, but the contents were gone. She took it down with a laugh and carried it in with her.

It seemed to me that since this interview with her countryman the day before her spirits had become higher and her step freer and more elastic. It may have been imagination, but it appeared to me also that she was not as constrained as usual in the presence of Copperthorne, and that she met his glances more fearlessly, and was less under the influence of his will.

And now I am coming to that part of this statement of mine which describes how I first gained an insight into the relation which existed between those two strange mortals, and learned the terrible truth about Miss Warrender, or of the Princess Achmet Genghis, as I should prefer to call her, for assuredly she was the descendant of the fierce fanatical warrior rather than of her gentle mother.

To me the revelation came as a shock, the effect of which I can never forget. It is possible that in the way in which I have told the story, emphasising those facts which had a bearing upon her, and omitting those which had not, my readers have already detected the strain which ran in her blood. As for myself, I solemnly aver that up to the last moment I had not the smallest suspicion of the truth. Little did I know what manner of woman this was, whose hand I pressed in friendship, and whose voice was music to my ears. Yet it is my belief, looking back, that she was really well disposed to me, and would not willingly have harmed me.

It was in this manner that the revelation came about. I think I have mentioned that there was a certain arbour in the shrubbery in which I was accustomed to study during the daytime. One night, about ten o'clock, I found on going to my room that I had left a book on gynæcology in this summer-house, and as I intended to do a couple of hours' work before turning in, I started off with the intention of getting it. Uncle Jeremy and the servants had already gone to bed, so I slipped downstairs very quietly and turned the key gently in the front door. Once in the open air, I hurried rapidly across the lawn, and so into the shrubbery, with the intention of regaining my property and returning as rapidly as possible.

I had hardly passed the little wooden gate and entered the plantation before I heard the sound of talking, and knew that I had chanced to stumble upon one of those nocturnal conclaves which I had observed from my window. The voices were those of the secretary and of the governess, and it was clear to me, from the direction in which they sounded, that they were sitting in the arbour and conversing together without any suspicion of the presence of a third person. I have ever held that eavesdropping, under any circumstances, is a dishonourable practice, and curious as I was to know what passed between these two, I was about to cough or give some other signal of my presence, when suddenly I heard some words of Copperthorne's which brought me to a halt with every faculty overwhelmed with horrified amazement.

'They'll think he died of apoplexy,' were the words which sounded clearly and distinctly through the peaceful air in the incisive tones of the amanuensis.

I stood breathless, listening with all my ears. Every thought of announcing my presence had left me. What was the crime which these ill-assorted conspirators were hatching upon this lovely summer's night.

I heard the deep sweet tones of her voice, but she spoke so rapidly, and in such a subdued manner, that I could not catch the words. I could tell by the intonation that she was under the influence of deep emotion. I drew nearer on tip-toe, with my ears straining to catch every sound. The moon was not up yet, and under the shadows of the trees it was very dark. There was little chance of my being observed.

'Eaten his bread, indeed!' the secretary said, derisively. 'You are not usually so squeamish. You did not think of that in the case of little Ethel.'

'I was mad! I was mad!' she ejaculated in a broken voice. 'I had prayed much to Buddha and to the great Bhowanee,* and it seemed to me that in this land of unbelievers it would be a great and glorious thing for me, a lonely woman, to act up to the teachings of my great father. There are few women who are admitted into the secrets of our faith, and it was but by an accident that the honour came upon me. Yet, having once had the path pointed out to me, I have walked straight and fearlessly, and the great Gooroo Ramdeen Singh* has said that even in my fourteenth year I was worthy to sit upon the cloth of the Tupounee* with the other Bhuttotees. Yet I swear by the sacred pickaxe that I have grieved much over this, for what had the poor child done that she should be sacrificed!'

'I fancy that my having caught you has had more to do with your repentance than the moral aspect of the case,' Copperthorne said, with a sneer. 'I may have had my misgivings before, but it was only when I saw you rising up with the handkerchief in your hand that I knew for certain that we were honoured by the presence of a Princess of the Thugs.* An English scaffold would be rather a prosaic end for such a romantic being.'

'And you have used your knowledge ever since to crush all the life out of me,' she said, bitterly. 'You have made my existence a burden to me.'

'A burden to you!' he said, in an altered voice. 'You know what my feelings are towards you. If I have occasionally governed you by the fear of exposure it was only because I found you were insensible to the milder influence of love.'

'Love!' she cried, bitterly. 'How could I love a man who held a shameful death for ever before my eyes. But let us come to the point. You promise me my unconditional liberty if I do this one thing for you?'

'Yes,' Copperthorne answered; 'you may go where you will when this is done. I shall forget what I saw here in the shrubbery.'

'You swear it?'

'Yes, I swear it.'

'I would do anything for my freedom,' she said.

'We can never have such a chance again,' Copperthorne cried. 'Young Thurston is gone, and this friend of his sleeps heavily, and is too stupid to suspect. The will is made out in my favour, and if the old man dies every stock and stone of the great estate will be mine.'

'Why don't you do it yourself, then?' she asked.

'It's not in my line,' he said. 'Besides, I have not got the knack. That roomal, or whatever you call it, leaves no mark. That's the advantage of it.'

'It is an accursed thing to slay one's benefactor.'

'But it is a great thing to serve Bhowanee, the goddess of murder. I know enough of your religion to know that. Would not your father do it if he were here?'

'My father was the greatest of all the Borkas of Jublepore,'* she said, proudly. 'He has slain more than there are days in the year.'

'I wouldn't have met him for a thousand pounds,' Copperthorne remarked, with a laugh. 'But what would Achmet Genghis Khan say now if he saw his daughter hesitate with such a chance before her of serving the gods? You have done excellently so far. He may well have smiled when the infant soul of young Ethel was wafted up to this god or ghoul of yours. Perhaps this is not the first sacrifice you have made. How about the daughter of this charitable German merchant? Ah, I see in your face that I am right again! After such deeds you do wrong to hesitate now when there is no danger and all shall be made easy to you. Besides that, the deed will free you from your existence here, which cannot be particularly pleasant with a rope, so to speak, round your neck the whole time. If it is to be done it must be done at once. He might rewrite his will at any moment, for he is fond of the lad, and is as changeable as a weather-cock.'

There was a long pause, and a silence so profound that I seemed to hear my own heart throbbing in the darkness.

'When shall it be done?' she asked at last.

'Why not to-morrow night?'

'How am I to get to him?'

'I shall leave his door open,' Copperthorne said. 'He sleeps heavily, and I shall leave a night-light burning, so that you may see your way.'

'And afterwards?'

'Afterwards you will return to your room. In the morning it will be discovered that our poor employer has passed away in his sleep. It will also be found that he has left all his worldly goods as a slight return for the devoted labours of his faithful secretary. Then the services of Miss Warrender the governess being no longer required, she may go back to her beloved country or to anywhere else that she fancies. She can run away with Mr John Lawrence, student of medicine, if she pleases.'

'You insult me,' she said, angrily; and then, after a pause. 'You must meet me to-morrow night before I do this.'

'Why so?' he asked.

'Because there may be some last instructions which I may require.'

'Let it be here, then, at twelve,' he said.

'No, not here. It is too near the house. Let us meet under the great oak at the head of the avenue.'

'Where you will,' he answered, sulkily; 'but mind, I'm not going to be with you when you do it.'

'I shall not ask you,' she said, scornfully. 'I think we have said all that need be said to-night.'

I heard the sound of one or other of them rising to their feet, and though they continued to talk I did not stop to hear more, but crept quietly out from my place of concealment and scudded across the dark lawn and in through the door, which I closed behind me. It was only when I had regained my room and had sunk back into my arm-chair that I was able to collect my scattered senses and to think over the terrible conversation to which I had listened. Long into the hours of the night I sat motionless, meditating over every word that I had heard and endeavouring to form in my mind some plan of action for the future.

VI

The Thugs! I had heard of the wild fanatics of that name who are found in the central part of India, and whose distorted religion represents murder as being the highest and purest of all the gifts which a mortal can offer to the Creator. I remember an account of them which I had read in the works of Colonel Meadows Taylor,* of their secrecy, their organisation, their relentlessness, and the terrible power which their homicidal craze has over every other mental or moral faculty. I even recalled now that the roomal—a word which I had heard her mention more than once—was the sacred handkerchief with which they were wont to work their diabolical purpose. She was already a woman when she had left them, and being, according to her own account, the daughter of their principal leader, it was no wonder that the varnish of civilisation had not eradicated all her early impressions or prevented the breaking out of occasional fits of fanaticism. In one of these apparently she had put an end to poor Ethel, having carefully prepared an alibi to conceal her crime, and it was Copperthorne's acci-dental discovery of this murder which gave him his power over his strange associate. Of all deaths that by hanging is considered among these tribes to be the most impious and degrading, and her knowledge that she had subjected herself to this death by the law of the land was evidently the reason why she had found herself compelled to subject her will and tame her imperious nature when in the presence of the amanuensis.

As to Copperthorne himself, as I thought over what he had done, and what he proposed to do, a great horror and loathing filled my whole soul. Was this his return for the kindness lavished upon him by the poor old man? He had already cozened* him into signing away his estates, and now, for fear some prickings of conscience should cause him to change his mind, he had determined to put it out of his power ever to write a codicil. All this was bad enough, but the acme of all seemed to be that, too cowardly to effect his purpose with his own hand, he had made use of this unfortunate woman's horrible conceptions of religion in order to remove Uncle Jeremy in such a way that no suspicion could possibly fall upon the real culprit. I determined in my mind that, come what might, the amanuensis should not escape from the punishment due to his crimes.

But what was I to do? Had I known my friend's address I should have telegraphed for him in the morning, and he could have been back in Dunkelthwaite before nightfall. Unfortunately John was the worst of correspondents, and though he had been gone for some days we had had no word yet of his whereabouts. There were three maid-servants in the house, but no man, with the exception of old Elijah; nor did I know of any upon whom I could rely in the neighbourhood. This, however, was a small matter, for I knew that in personal strength I was more than a match for the secretary, and I had confidence enough in myself to feel that my resistance alone would prevent any possibility of the plot being carried out.

The question was, what were the best steps for me to take under the circumstances? My first impulse was to wait until morning, and then to quietly go or send to the nearest police-station and summon a couple of constables. I could then hand Copperthorne and his female accomplice over to justice and narrate the conversation which I had overheard. On second thoughts this plan struck me as being a very impracticable one. What grain of evidence had I against them except my story? which, to people who did not know me, would certainly appear a very wild and improbable one. I could well imagine too the plausible voice and imperturbable manner with which Copperthorne would oppose the accusation, and how he would dilate upon the ill-will which I bore both him and his companion on account of their mutual affection. How easy it would be for him to make a third person believe that I was trumping up a story in the hope of injuring a rival, and how difficult for me to make any one credit that this clerical-looking gentleman and this stylishly-dressed young lady were two beasts of prey who were hunting in couples! I felt that it would be a great mistake for me to show my hand before I was sure of the game.

The alternative was to say nothing and to let things take their course, being always ready to step in when the evidence against the conspirators appeared to be conclusive. This was the course which recommended itself to my young adventurous disposition, and it also appeared to be the one most likely to lead to conclusive results. When at last at early dawn I stretched myself upon my bed and I had fully made up my mind to retain my knowledge in my own breast, and to trust to myself entirely for the defeat of the murderous plot which I had overheard.

Old Uncle Jeremy was in high spirits next morning after breakfast, and insisted upon reading aloud a scene from Shelley's 'Cenci,'* a work for which he had a profound admiration. Copperthorne sat silent and inscrutable by his side, save when he threw in a suggestion or uttered an exclamation of admiration. Miss Warrender appeared to be lost in thought, and it seemed to me more than once that I saw tears in her dark eyes. It was strange for me to watch the three of them and to think of the real relation in which they stood to each other. My heart warmed towards my little red-faced host with the quaint head-gear and the old-fashioned ways. I vowed to myself that no harm should befall him while I had power to prevent it.

The day wore along slowly and drearily. It was impossible for me to settle down to work, so I wandered restlessly about the corridors of the old-fashioned house and over the garden. Copperthorne was with Uncle Jeremy upstairs, and I saw little of him. Twice when I was striding up and down outside I perceived the governess coming with the children in my direction, but on each occasion I avoided her by hurrying away. I felt that I could not speak to her without showing the intense horror with which she inspired me, and so betraying my knowledge of what had transpired the night before. She noticed that I shunned her, for at luncheon, when my eyes caught hers for a moment, she flashed across a surprised and injured glance, to which, however, I made no response.

The afternoon post brought a letter from John telling us that he was stopping at the Langham.* I knew that it was now impossible for him to be of any use to me in the way of sharing the responsibility of whatever might occur, but I nevertheless thought it my duty to tele-graph to him and let him know that his presence was desirable. This involved a long walk to the station, but that was useful as helping me to while away the time, and I felt a weight off my mind when I heard the clicking of the needles which told me that my message was flying upon its way.

When I reached the avenue gate on my return from Ingleton I found our old serving-man Elijah standing there, apparently in a violent passion.

'They says as one rat brings others,' he said to me, touching his hat, 'and it seems as it be the same with they darkies.'

He had always disliked the governess on account of what he called her 'uppish ways.'

'What's the matter, then?' I asked.

'It's one o' they furriners a-hidin' and a-prowlin',' said the old man. 'I seed him here among the bushes, and I sent him off wi' a bit o' my mind. Lookin' after the hens as like as not, or maybe wantin' to burn the house and murder us all in our beds. I'll go down to the vil-lage, Muster Lawrence, and see what he's after,' and he hurried away in a paroxysm of senile anger.

This little incident made a considerable impression on me, and I thought seriously over it as I walked up the long avenue. It was clear that the wandering Hindoo was still hanging about the premises. He was a factor whom I had forgotten to take into account. If his com-patriot enlisted him as an accomplice in her dark plans, it was possible that the three of them might be too many for me. Still it appeared to me to be improbable that she should do so, since she had taken such pains to conceal his presence from Copperthorne.

I was half tempted to take Elijah into my confidence, but on second thoughts I came to the conclusion that a man of his age would be worse than useless as an ally.

About seven o'clock I was going up to my room when I met the sec-retary, who asked me whether I could tell him where Miss Warrender was. I answered that I had not seen her.

'It's a singular thing,' he said, 'that no one has seen her since dinner-time. The children don't know where she is. I particularly want to speak to her.'

He hurried on with an agitated and disturbed expression upon his features.

As to me, Miss Warrender's absence did not seem a matter of surprise. No doubt she was out in the shrubbery somewhere, nerving herself for the terrible piece of work which she had undertaken to do. I closed my door behind me and sat down, with a book in my hand, but with my mind too much excited to comprehend the contents. My plan of campaign had been already formed I determined to be within sight of their trysting place, to follow them, and to interfere at the moment when my interference would have most effect. I had chosen a thick, knobby stick, dear to my student heart, and with this I knew that I was master of the situation, for I had ascertained that Copperthorne had no firearms.

I do not remember any period of my life when the hours passed so slowly as did those which I spent in my room that night. Far away I heard the mellow tones of the Dunkelthwaite clock as it struck the hours of eight and then of nine, and then, after an interminable pause, of ten. After that it seemed as though time had stopped altogether as I paced my little room, fearing and yet longing for the hour as men will when some great ordeal has to be faced. All things have an end, however, and at last there came pealing through the still night air the first clear stroke which announced the eleventh hour. Then I rose, and, putting on my soft slippers, I seized my stick and slipped quietly out of my room and down the creaking old-fashioned staircase. I could hear the stertorous* snoring of Uncle Jeremy upon the floor above. I managed to feel my way to the door through the darkness, and having opened it passed out into the beautiful starlit night.

I had to be very careful of my movements, because the moon shone so brightly that it was almost as light as day. I hugged the shadow of the house until I reached the garden hedge, and then, crawling down in its shelter, I found myself safe in the shrubbery in which I had been the night before. Through this I made my way, treading very cautiously and gingerly, so that not a stick snapped beneath my feet. In this way I advanced until I found myself among the brushwood at the edge of the plantation and within full view of the great oak-tree which stood at the upper end of the avenue.

There was someone standing under the shadow of the oak. At first I could hardly make out who it was, but presently the figure began to move, and, coming out into a silvery patch where the moon shone down between two branches, looked impatiently to left and to right. Then I saw that it was Copperthorne, who was waiting alone. The governess apparently had not yet kept her appointment.

As I wished to hear as well as to see, I wormed my way along under the dark shadows of the trunks in the direction of the oak. When I stopped I was not more than fifteen paces from the spot where the tall gaunt figure of the amanuensis looked grim and ghastly in the shifting light. He paced about uneasily, now disappearing in the shadow, now reappearing in the silvery patches where the moon broke through the covering above him. It was evident from his movements that he was puzzled and disconcerted at the non-appearance of his accomplice. Finally he stationed himself under a great branch which concealed his figure, while from beneath it he commanded a view of the gravel drive which led down from the house, and along which, no doubt, he expected Miss Warrender to come.

I was still lying in my hiding-place, congratulating myself inwardly at having gained a point from which I could hear all without risk of discovery, when my eye lit suddenly upon something which made my heart rise to my mouth and almost caused me to utter an ejaculation which would have betrayed my presence.

I have said that Copperthorne was standing immediately under one of the great branches of the oak-tree. Beneath this all was plunged in the deepest shadow, but the upper part of the branch itself was silvered over by the light of the moon. As I gazed I became conscious that down this luminous branch something was crawling—a flickering, inchoate something, almost indistinguishable from the branch itself, and yet slowly and steadily writhing its way down it. My eyes, as I looked, became more accustomed to the light, and then this indefinite something took form and substance. It was a human being—a man—the Indian whom I had seen in the village. With his arms and legs twined round the great limb, he was shuffling his way down as silently and almost as rapidly as one of his native snakes.

Before I had time to conjecture the meaning of his presence he was directly over the spot where the secretary stood, his bronzed body showing out hard and clear against the disc of moon behind him. I saw him take something from round his waist, hesitate for a moment, as though judging his distance, and then spring downwards, crashing through the intervening foliage. There was a heavy thud, as of two bodies falling together, and then there rose on the night air a noise as of some one gargling his throat, followed by a succession of croaking sounds, the remembrance of which will haunt me to my dying day.

Whilst this tragedy had been enacted before my eyes its entire unex-
pectedness and its horror had bereft me of the power of acting in any
way. Only those who have been in a similar position can imagine the
utter paralysis of mind and body which comes upon a man in such
straits, and prevents him from doing the thousand and one things which
may be suggested afterwards as having been appropriate to the occasion. When those notes of death, however, reached my ears I shook off
my lethargy and ran forward with a loud cry from my place of concealment. At the sound the young Thug sprang from his victim with a snarl
like a wild beast driven from a carcase, and made off down the avenue
at such a pace that I felt it to be impossible for me to overtake him. I ran
to the secretary and raised his head. His face was purple and horribly
distorted. I loosened his shirt-collar and did all I could to restore him,
but it was useless. The roomal had done its work, and he was dead.

I have little more to add to this strange tale of mine. If I have been
somewhat long-winded in the telling of it, I feel that I owe no apology
for that, for I have simply set the successive events down in a plain
unvarnished fashion, and the narrative would be incomplete without
any one of them. It transpired afterwards that Miss Warrender had
caught the 7.20 London train, and was safe in the metropolis before
any search could be made for her. As to the messenger of death whom
she had left behind to keep her appointment with Copperthorne
under the old oak-tree, he was never either heard of or seen again.
There was a hue and cry over the whole countryside, but nothing
came of it. No doubt the fugitive passed the days in sheltered places,
and travelled rapidly at night, living on such scraps as can sustain an
Oriental, until he was out of danger.

John Thurston returned next day, and I poured all the facts into his
astonished ears. He agreed with me that it was best perhaps not to
speak of what I knew concerning Copperthorne's plans and the reasons which kept him out so late upon that summer's night. Thus even
the county police have never known the full story of that strange tragedy, and they certainly never shall, unless, indeed, the eyes of some
of them should chance to fall upon this narrative. Poor Uncle Jeremy
mourned the loss of his secretary for months, and many were the
verses which he poured forth in the form of epitaphs and of 'In
Memoriam' poems. He has been gathered to his fathers himself since
then, and the greater part of his estate has, I am glad to say, descended
to the rightful heir, his nephew.

There is only one point on which I should like to make a remark. How was it that the wandering Thug came to Dunkelthwaite? This question has never been cleared up; but I have not the slightest doubt in my own mind, nor I think can anyone have who considers the facts of the case, that there was no chance about his appearance. The sect in India were a large and powerful body, and when they came to look around for a fresh leader, they naturally bethought them of the beautiful daughter of their late chief. It would be no difficult matter to trace her to Calcutta, to Germany, and finally to Dunkelthwaite. He had come, no doubt, with the message that she was not forgotten in India, and that a warm welcome awaited her if she chose to join her scattered tribesmen. This may seem far-fetched, but it is the opinion which I have always entertained upon the matter.

I began this statement by a quotation from a letter, and I shall end it by one. This was from an old friend, Dr B. C. Haller,* a man of encyclopædic knowledge, and particularly well versed in Indian manners and customs. It is through his kindness that I am able to reproduce the various native words which I heard from time to time from the lips of Miss Warrender, but which I should not have been able to recall to my memory had he not suggested them to me. This is a letter in which he comments upon the matter, which I had mentioned to him in conversation some time previously:

'My dear Lawrence,—I promised to write to you *re* Thuggee, but my time has been so occupied that it is only now that I can redeem my pledge. I was much interested in your unique experience, and should much like to have further talk with you upon the subject. I may inform you that it is most unusual for a woman to be initiated into the mysteries of Thuggee, and it arose in this case probably from her having accidently or by design tasted the sacred goor,* which was the sacrifice offered by the gang after each murder. Any one doing this must become an acting Thug, whatever the rank, sex, or condition. Being of noble blood she would then rapidly pass through the different grades of Tilhaee, or scout, Lughaee, or grave-digger, Shumsheea, or holder of the victim's hands, and finally of Bhuttotee, or strangler. In all this she would be instructed by her Gooroo, or spiritual adviser, whom she mentions in your account as having been her own father, who was a Borka, or an expert Thug. Having once attained this position, I do not wonder that her fanatical instincts broke out at times.

The Pilhaoo which she mentions in one place was the omen on the left hand, which, if it is followed by the Thibaoo,* or omen on the right, was considered to be an indication that all would go well. By the way, you mention that the old coachman saw the Hindoo lurking about among the bushes in the morning. Do you know what he was doing? I am very much mistaken if he was not digging Copperthorne's grave, for it is quite opposed to Thug customs to kill a man without having some receptacle prepared for his body. As far as I know only one English officer in India has ever fallen a victim to the fraternity, and that was Lieutenant Monsell, in 1812.* Since then Colonel Sleeman* has stamped it out to a great extent, though it is unquestionable that it flourishes far more than the authorities suppose. Truly "the dark places of the earth are full of cruelty," and nothing but the Gospel will ever effectually dispel that darkness. You are very welcome to publish these few remarks if they seem to you to throw any light upon your narrative.

'Yours very sincerely,
'B. C. HALLER.'

THE RING OF THOTH

⟨⟨⟨⟩⟩⟩

M R JOHN VANSITTART SMITH, FRS, of 147A Gower Street,*
was a man whose energy of purpose and clearness of thought
might have placed him in the very first rank of scientific observers.
He was the victim, however, of a universal ambition which prompted
him to aim at distinction in many subjects rather than pre-eminence
in one. In his early days he had shown an aptitude for zoology and for
botany which caused his friends to look upon him as a second Darwin,
but when a professorship was almost within his reach he had suddenly
discontinued his studies and turned his whole attention to chemistry.
Here his researches upon the spectra of the metals had won him his
fellowship in the Royal Society; but again he played the coquette with
his subject, and after a year's absence from the laboratory he joined
the Oriental Society, and delivered a paper on the Hieroglyphic and
Demotic inscriptions of El Kab,* thus giving a crowning example
both of the versatility and of the inconstancy of his talents.

The most fickle of wooers, however, is apt to be caught at last, and
so it was with John Vansittart Smith. The more he burrowed his way
into Egyptology the more impressed he became by the vast field
which it opened to the inquirer, and by the extreme importance of
a subject which promised to throw a light upon the first germs of
human civilisation and the origin of the greater part of our arts and
sciences. So struck was Mr Smith that he straightway married an
Egyptological young lady who had written upon the sixth dynasty,*
and having thus secured a sound base of operations he set himself to
collect materials for a work which should unite the research of Lepsius
and the ingenuity of Champollion.* The preparation of this *magnum
opus* entailed many hurried visits to the magnificent Egyptian collections of the Louvre,* upon the last of which, no longer ago than the
middle of last October, he became involved in a most strange and
noteworthy adventure.

The trains had been slow and the Channel had been rough, so that
the student arrived in Paris in a somewhat befogged and feverish condition. On reaching the Hôtel de France, in the Rue Laffitte,* he had
thrown himself upon a sofa for a couple of hours, but finding that he

was unable to sleep, he determined, in spite of his fatigue, to make his way to the Louvre, settle the point which he had come to decide, and take the evening train back to Dieppe. Having come to his conclusion, he donned his greatcoat, for it was a raw rainy day, and made his way across the Boulevard des Italiens and down the Avenue de l'Opéra.* Once in the Louvre he was on familiar ground, and he speedily made his way to the collection of papyri which it was his intention to consult.

The warmest admirers of John Vansittart Smith could hardly claim for him that he was a handsome man. His high-beaked nose and prominent chin had something of the same acute and incisive character which distinguished his intellect. He held his head in a birdlike fashion, and birdlike, too, was the pecking motion with which, in conversation, he threw out his objections and retorts. As he stood, with the high collar of his greatcoat raised to his ears, he might have seen from the reflection in the glass-case before him that his appearance was a singular one. Yet it came upon him as a sudden jar when an English voice behind him exclaimed in very audible tones, 'What a queer-looking mortal!'

The student had a large amount of petty vanity in his composition which manifested itself by an ostentatious and overdone disregard of all personal considerations. He straightened his lips and looked rigidly at the roll of papyrus, while his heart filled with bitterness against the whole race of travelling Britons.

'Yes,' said another voice, 'he really is an extraordinary fellow.'

'Do you know,' said the first speaker, 'one could almost believe that by the continual contemplation of mummies the chap has become half a mummy himself?'

'He has certainly an Egyptian cast of countenance,' said the other.

John Vansittart Smith spun round upon his heel with the intention of shaming his countrymen by a corrosive remark or two. To his surprise and relief, the two young fellows who had been conversing had their shoulders turned towards him, and were gazing at one of the Louvre attendants who was polishing some brass-work at the other side of the room.

'Carter will be waiting for us at the Palais Royal,'* said one tourist to the other, glancing at his watch, and they clattered away, leaving the student to his labours.

'I wonder what these chatterers call an Egyptian cast of countenance,' thought John Vansittart Smith, and he moved his position

slightly in order to catch a glimpse of the man's face. He started as his
eyes fell upon it. It was indeed the very face with which his studies
had made him familiar. The regular statuesque features, broad brow,
well-rounded chin, and dusky complexion were the exact counterpart of the innumerable statues, mummy-cases, and pictures which
adorned the walls of the apartment. The thing was beyond all coincidence. The man must be an Egyptian. The national angularity of the
shoulders and narrowness of the hips were alone sufficient to identify
him.

John Vansittart Smith shuffled towards the attendant with some
intention of addressing him. He was not light of touch in conversation, and found it difficult to strike the happy mean between the
brusqueness of the superior and the geniality of the equal. As he came
nearer, the man presented his side face to him, but kept his gaze still
bent upon his work. Vansittart Smith, fixing his eyes upon the fellow's
skin, was conscious of a sudden impression that there was something
inhuman and preternatural about its appearance. Over the temple
and cheek-bone it was as glazed and as shiny as varnished parchment.
There was no suggestion of pores. One could not fancy a drop of
moisture upon that arid surface. From brow to chin, however, it was
cross-hatched by a million delicate wrinkles, which shot and interlaced as though Nature in some Maori mood* had tried how wild and
intricate a pattern she could devise.

'Où est la collection de Memphis?'* asked the student, with the
awkward air of a man who is devising a question merely for the purpose
of opening a conversation.

'C'est là,' replied the man brusquely, nodding his head at the other
side of the room.

'Vous êtes un Egyptien, n'est-ce pas?' asked the Englishman.

The attendant looked up and turned his strange dark eyes upon his
questioner. They were vitreous,* with a misty dry shininess, such as
Smith had never seen in a human head before. As he gazed into them
he saw some strong emotion gather in their depths, which rose and
deepened until it broke into a look of something akin both to horror
and to hatred.

'Non, monsieur; je suis français.' The man turned abruptly and
bent low over his polishing. The student gazed at him for a moment
in astonishment, and then turning to a chair in a retired corner behind
one of the doors he proceeded to make notes of his researches among

the papyri. His thoughts, however, refused to return into their natural groove. They would run upon the enigmatical attendant with the sphinx-like face and the parchment skin.

'Where have I seen such eyes?' said Vansittart Smith to himself. 'There is something saurian about them, something reptilian. There's the membrana nictitans* of the snakes,' he mused, bethinking himself of his zoological studies. 'It gives a shiny effect. But there was something more here. There was a sense of power, of wisdom — so I read them — and of weariness, utter weariness, and ineffable despair. It may be all imagination, but I never had so strong an impression. By Jove, I must have another look at them!' He rose and paced round the Egyptian rooms, but the man who had excited his curiosity had disappeared.

The student sat down again in his quiet corner, and continued to work at his notes. He had gained the information which he required from the papyri, and it only remained to write it down while it was still fresh in his memory. For a time his pencil travelled rapidly over the paper, but soon the lines became less level, the words more blurred, and finally the pencil tinkled down upon the floor, and the head of the student dropped heavily forward upon his chest. Tired out by his journey, he slept so soundly in his lonely post behind the door that neither the clanking civil guard, nor the footsteps of sightseers, nor even the loud hoarse bell which gives the signal for closing, were sufficient to arouse him.

Twilight deepened into darkness, the bustle from the Rue de Rivoli waxed and then waned, distant Notre Dame* clanged out the hour of midnight, and still the dark and lonely figure sat silently in the shadow. It was not until close upon one in the morning that, with a sudden gasp and an intaking of the breath, Vansittart Smith returned to consciousness. For a moment it flashed upon him that he had dropped asleep in his study-chair at home. The moon was shining fitfully through the unshuttered window, however, and as his eye ran along the lines of mummies and the endless array of polished cases, he remembered clearly where he was and how he came there. The student was not a nervous man. He possessed that love of a novel situation which is peculiar to his race. Stretching out his cramped limbs, he looked at his watch, and burst into a chuckle as he observed the hour. The episode would make an admirable anecdote to be introduced into his next paper as a relief to the graver and heavier speculations.

He was a little cold, but wide awake and much refreshed. It was no wonder that the guardians had overlooked him, for the door threw its heavy black shadow right across him.

The complete silence was impressive. Neither outside nor inside was there a creak or a murmur. He was alone with the dead men of a dead civilisation. What though the outer city reeked of the garish nineteenth century! In all this chamber there was scarce an article, from the shrivelled ear of wheat to the pigment-box of the painter, which had not held its own against four thousand years. Here was the flotsam and jetsam washed up by the great ocean of time from that far-off empire. From stately Thebes, from lordly Luxor, from the great temples of Heliopolis,* from a hundred rifled tombs, these relics had been brought. The student glanced round at the long-silent figures who flickered vaguely up through the gloom, at the busy toilers who were now so restful, and he fell into a reverent and thoughtful mood. An unwonted sense of his own youth and insignificance came over him. Leaning back in his chair, he gazed dreamily down the long vista of rooms, all silvery with the moonshine, which extend through the whole wing of the widespread building. His eyes fell upon the yellow glare of a distant lamp.

John Vansittart Smith sat up on his chair with his nerves all on edge. The light was advancing slowly towards him, pausing from time to time, and then coming jerkily onwards. The bearer moved noiselessly. In the utter silence there was no suspicion of the pat of a footfall. An idea of robbers entered the Englishman's head. He snuggled up farther into the corner. The light was two rooms off. Now it was in the next chamber, and still there was no sound. With something approaching to a thrill of fear the student observed a face, floating in the air as it were, behind the flare of the lamp. The figure was wrapped in shadow, but the light fell full upon the strange, eager face. There was no mistaking the metallic, glistening eyes and the cadaverous skin. It was the attendant with whom he had conversed.

Vansittart Smith's first impulse was to come forward and address him. A few words of explanation would set the matter clear, and lead doubtless to his being conducted to some side-door from which he might make his way to his hotel. As the man entered the chamber, however, there was something so stealthy in his movements, and so furtive in his expression, that the Englishman altered his intention. This was clearly no ordinary official walking the rounds. The fellow wore felt-soled slippers, stepped with a rising chest, and glanced quickly from left to right, while his hurried, gasping breathing thrilled the flame of his lamp. Vansittart Smith crouched silently back into the corner and watched him keenly, convinced that his errand was one of secret and probably sinister import.

There was no hesitation in the other's movements. He stepped lightly and swiftly across to one of the great cases, and, drawing a key from his pocket, he unlocked it. From the upper shelf he pulled down a mummy, which he bore away with him, and laid it with much care and solicitude upon the ground. By it he placed his lamp, and then squatting down beside it in Eastern fashion he began with long, quivering fingers to undo the cerecloths* and bandages which girt it round. As the crackling rolls of linen peeled off one after the other, a strong aromatic odour filled the chamber, and fragments of scented wood and of spices pattered down upon the marble floor.

It was clear to John Vansittart Smith that this mummy had never been unswathed before. The operation interested him keenly. He thrilled all over with curiosity, and his bird-like head protruded farther and farther from behind the door. When, however, the last roll had been removed from the four-thousand-year-old head, it was all that he could do to stifle an outcry of amazement. First, a cascade of long, black, glossy tresses poured over the workman's hands and arms. A second turn of the bandage revealed a low, white forehead, with a pair of delicately arched eyebrows. A third uncovered a pair of bright, deeply fringed eyes, and a straight, well-cut nose, while a fourth and last showed a sweet, full, sensitive mouth, and a beautifully curved chin. The whole face was one of extraordinary loveliness, save for the one blemish that in the centre of the forehead there was a single irregular, coffee-coloured splotch. It was a triumph of the embalmer's art. Vansittart Smith's eyes grew larger and larger as he gazed upon it, and he chirruped in his throat with satisfaction.

Its effect upon the Egyptologist was as nothing, however, compared with that which it produced upon the strange attendant. He threw his hands up into the air, burst into a harsh clatter of words, and then, hurling himself down upon the ground beside the mummy, he threw his arms round her, and kissed her repeatedly upon the lips and brow. 'Ma petite!' he groaned in French. 'Ma pauvre petite!'* His voice broke with emotion, and his innumerable wrinkles quivered and writhed, but the student observed in the lamp-light that his shining eyes were still dry and tearless as two beads of steel. For some minutes he lay, with a twitching face, crooning and moaning over the beautiful head. Then he broke into a sudden smile, said some words in an unknown tongue, and sprang to his feet with the vigorous air of one who has braced himself for an effort.

In the centre of the room there was a large, circular case which contained, as the student had frequently remarked, a magnificent collection of early Egyptian rings and precious stones. To this the attendant strode, and, unlocking it, threw it open. On the ledge at the side he placed his lamp, and beside it a small, earthenware jar which he had drawn from his pocket. He then took a handful of rings from the case, and with a most serious and anxious face he proceeded to smear each in turn with some liquid substance from the earthen pot, holding them to the light as he did so. He was clearly disappointed with the first lot, for he threw them petulantly back into the case and drew out some more. One of these, a massive ring with a large crystal set in it, he seized and eagerly tested with the contents of the jar. Instantly he uttered a cry of joy, and threw out his arms in a wild gesture which upset the pot and set the liquid streaming across the floor to the very feet of the Englishman. The attendant drew a red handkerchief from his bosom, and, mopping up the mess, he followed it into the corner, where in a moment he found himself face to face with his observer.

'Excuse me,' said John Vansittart Smith, with all imaginable politeness; 'I have been unfortunate enough to fall asleep behind this door.'

'And you have been watching me?' the other asked in English, with a most venomous look on his corpse-like face.

The student was a man of veracity. 'I confess,' said he, 'that I have noticed your movements, and that they have aroused my curiosity and interest in the highest degree.'

The man drew a long, flamboyant-bladed knife from his bosom. 'You have had a very narrow escape,' he said; 'had I seen you ten minutes ago, I should have driven this through your heart. As it is, if you touch me or interfere with me in any way you are a dead man.'

'I have no wish to interfere with you,' the student answered. 'My presence here is entirely accidental. All I ask is that you will have the extreme kindness to show me out through some side-door.' He spoke with great suavity, for the man was still pressing the tip of his dagger against the palm of his left hand, as though to assure himself of its sharpness, while his face preserved its malignant expression.

'If I thought——' said he. 'But no, perhaps it is as well. What is your name?'

The Englishman gave it.

'Vansittart Smith,' the other repeated. 'Are you the same Vansittart Smith who gave a paper in London upon El Kab? I saw a report of it. Your knowledge of the subject is contemptible.'

'Sir!' cried the Egyptologist.

'Yet it is superior to that of many who make even greater pretensions. The whole keystone of our old life in Egypt was not the inscriptions or monuments of which you make so much, but was our hermetic philosophy* and mystic knowledge of which you say little or nothing.'

'Our old life!' repeated the scholar, wide-eyed; and then suddenly, 'Good God, look at the mummy's face!'

The strange man turned and flashed his light upon the dead woman, uttering a long, doleful cry as he did so. The action of the air had already undone all the art of the embalmer. The skin had fallen away, the eyes had sunk inwards, the discoloured lips had writhed away from the yellow teeth, and the brown mark upon the forehead alone showed that it was indeed the same face which had shown such youth and beauty a few short minutes before.

The man flapped his hands together in grief and horror. Then mastering himself by a strong effort he turned his hard eyes once more upon the Englishman.

'It does not matter,' he said, in a shaking voice. 'It does not really matter. I came here to-night with the fixed determination to do something. It is now done. All else is as nothing. I have found my quest. The old curse is broken. I can rejoin her. What matter about her inanimate shell so long as her spirit is awaiting me at the other side of the veil!'

'These are wild words,' said Vansittart Smith. He was becoming more and more convinced that he had to do with a madman.

'Time presses, and I must go,' continued the other. 'The moment is at hand for which I have waited this weary time. But I must show you out first. Come with me.'

Taking up the lamp, he turned from the disordered chamber, and led the student swiftly through the long series of the Egyptian, Assyrian, and Persian apartments. At the end of the latter he pushed open a small door let into the wall and descended a winding, stone stair. The Englishman felt the cold, fresh air of the night upon his brow. There was a door opposite him which appeared to communicate with the street. To the right of this another door stood ajar, throwing a spurt of yellow light across the passage. 'Come in here!' said the attendant shortly.

Vansittart Smith hesitated. He had hoped that he had come to the end of his adventure. Yet his curiosity was strong within him. He could not leave the matter unsolved, so he followed his strange companion into the lighted chamber.

It was a small room, such as is devoted to a *concierge*. A wood fire sparkled in the grate. At one side stood a truckle bed,* and at the other a coarse, wooden chair, with a round table in the centre, which bore the remains of a meal. As the visitor's eye glanced round he could not but remark with an ever-recurring thrill that all the small details of the room were of the most quaint design and antique workmanship. The candlesticks, the vases upon the chimney-piece, the fire-irons, the ornaments upon the walls, were all such as he had been wont to associate with the remote past. The gnarled heavy-eyed man sat himself down upon the edge of the bed, and motioned his guest into the chair.

'There may be design in this,' he said, still speaking excellent English. 'It may be decreed that I should leave some account behind as a warning to all rash mortals who would set their wits up against workings of Nature. I leave it with you. Make such use as you will of it. I speak to you now with my feet upon the threshold of the other world.

'I am, as you surmised, an Egyptian—not one of the down-trodden race of slaves who now inhabit the Delta of the Nile, but a survivor of that fiercer and harder people who tamed the Hebrew, drove the Ethiopian back into the southern deserts, and built those mighty works which have been the envy and the wonder of all after generations. It was in the reign of Tuthmosis,* sixteen hundred years before the birth of Christ, that I first saw the light. You shrink away from me. Wait, and you will see that I am more to be pitied than to be feared.

'My name was Sosra. My father had been the chief priest of Osiris in the great temple of Abaris, which stood in those days upon the Bubastic* branch of the Nile. I was brought up in the temple and was trained in all those mystic arts which are spoken of in your own Bible.* I was an apt pupil. Before I was sixteen I had learned all which the wisest priest could teach me. From that time on I studied Nature's secrets for myself, and shared my knowledge with no man.

'Of all the questions which attracted me there were none over which I laboured so long as over those which concern themselves with the nature of life. I probed deeply into the vital principle. The aim of medicine had been to drive away disease when it appeared. It seemed to me that a method might be devised which should so fortify the body as to prevent weakness or death from ever taking hold of it. It is useless that I should recount my researches. You would scarce comprehend them if I did. They were carried out partly upon animals, partly upon slaves, and partly on myself. Suffice it that their result was to furnish me with a substance which, when injected into the blood, would endow the body with strength to resist the effects of time, of violence, or of disease. It would not indeed confer immortality, but its potency would endure for many thousands of years. I used it upon a cat, and afterwards drugged the creature with the most deadly poisons. That cat is alive in Lower Egypt at the present moment. There was nothing of mystery or magic in the matter. It was simply a chemical discovery, which may well be made again.

'Love of life runs high in the young. It seemed to me that I had broken away from all human care now that I had abolished pain and driven death to such a distance. With a light heart I poured the accursed stuff into my veins. Then I looked round for someone whom I could benefit. There was a young priest of Thoth, Parmes by name, who had won my goodwill by his earnest nature and his devotion to his studies. To him I whispered my secret, and at his request I injected him with my elixir. I should now, I reflected, never be without a companion of the same age as myself.

'After this grand discovery I relaxed my studies to some extent, but Parmes continued his with redoubled energy. Every day I could see him working with his flasks and his distiller in the Temple of Thoth, but he said little to me as to the result of his labours. For my own part, I used to walk through the city and look around me with exultation as I reflected that all this was destined to pass away, and that only I should remain. The people would bow to me as they passed me, for the fame of my knowledge had gone abroad.

'There was war at this time, and the Great King had sent down his soldiers to the eastern boundary to drive away the Hyksos.* A Governor, too, was sent to Abaris, that he might hold it for the King. I had heard much of the beauty of the daughter of this Governor, but one day as I walked out with Parmes we met her, borne upon the shoulders of her slaves. I was struck with love as with lightning. My heart went out from me. I could have thrown myself beneath the feet of her bearers. This was my woman. Life without her was impossible. I swore by the head of Horus* that she should be mine. I swore it to the Priest of Thoth. He turned away from me with a brow which was as black as midnight.

'There is no need to tell you of our wooing. She came to love me even as I loved her. I learned that Parmes had seen her before I did, and had shown her that he, too, loved her, but I could smile at his passion, for I knew that her heart was mine. The white plague had come upon the city and many were stricken, but I laid my hands upon the sick and nursed them without fear or scathe. She marvelled at my daring. Then I told her my secret, and begged her that she would let me use my art upon her.

' "Your flower shall then be unwithered, Atma," I said. "Other things may pass away, but you and I, and our great love for each other, shall outlive the tomb of King Chefru."*

'But she was full of timid, maidenly objections. "Was it right?" she asked, "was it not a thwarting of the will of the gods? If the great Osiris had wished that our years should be so long, would he not himself have brought it about?"

'With fond and loving words I overcame her doubts, and yet she hesitated. It was a great question, she said. She would think it over for this one night. In the morning I should know of her resolution. Surely one night was not too much to ask. She wished to pray to Isis for help in her decision.

'With a sinking heart and a sad foreboding of evil I left her with her tirewomen.* In the morning, when the early sacrifice was over, I hurried to her house. A frightened slave met me upon the steps. Her mistress was ill, she said, very ill. In a frenzy I broke my way through the attendants, and rushed through hall and corridor to my Atma's chamber. She lay upon her couch, her head high upon the pillow, with a pallid face and a glazed eye. On her forehead there blazed a single angry, purple patch. I knew that hell-mark of old. It was the scar of the white plague,* the sign-manual of death.

'Why should I speak of that terrible time? For months I was mad, fevered, delirious, and yet I could not die. Never did an Arab thirst after the sweet wells as I longed after death. Could poison or steel have shortened the thread of my existence, I should soon have rejoined my love in the land with the narrow portal,* I tried, but it was of no avail. The accursed influence was too strong upon me. One night as I lay upon my couch, weak and weary, Parmes, the priest of Thoth, came to my chamber. He stood in the circle of the lamplight, and he looked down upon me with eyes which were bright with a mad joy.

' Why did you let the maiden die?" he asked; "why did you not strengthen her as you strengthened me?"

' "I was too late," I answered. "But I had forgot. You also loved her. You are my fellow in misfortune. Is it not terrible to think of the centuries which must pass ere we look upon her again? Fools, fools, that we were to take death to be our enemy!"

' "You may say that," he cried with a wild laugh; "the words come well from your lips. For me they have no meaning."

' "What mean you?" I cried, raising myself upon my elbow. "Surely, friend, this grief has turned your brain." His face was aflame with joy, and he writhed and shook like one who hath a devil.

' "Do you know whither I go?" he asked.

' "Nay," I answered, "I cannot tell."

' "I go to her," said he. "She lies embalmed in the farther tomb by the double palm-tree beyond the city wall."

' "Why do you go there?" I asked.

' "To die!" he shrieked, "to die! I am not bound by earthen fetters."

' "But the elixir is in your blood," I cried.

' "I can defy it," said he; "I have found a stronger principle which will destroy it. It is working in my veins at this moment, and in an hour I shall be a dead man. I shall join her, and you shall remain behind."

'As I looked upon him I could see that he spoke words of truth. The light in his eye told me that he was indeed beyond the power of the elixir.

' "You will teach me!" I cried.

' "Never!" he answered.

' "I implore you, by the wisdom of Thoth, by the majesty of Anubis!"*

' "It is useless," he said coldly.

' "Then I will find it out," I cried.

' "You cannot," he answered; "it came to me by chance. There is one ingredient which you can never get. Save that which is in the ring of Thoth, none will ever more be made."

' "In the ring of Thoth!" I repeated, "where then is the ring of Thoth?"

' "That also you shall never know," he answered. "You won her love. Who has won in the end? I leave you to your sordid earth life. My chains are broken. I must go!" He turned upon his heel and fled from the chamber. In the morning came the news that the Priest of Thoth was dead.

'My days after that were spent in study. I must find this subtle poison which was strong enough to undo the elixir. From early dawn to midnight I bent over the test-tube and the furnace. Above all, I collected the papyri and the chemical flasks of the Priest of Thoth. Alas! they taught me little. Here and there some hint or stray expression would raise hope in my bosom, but no good ever came of it. Still, month after month, I struggled on. When my heart grew faint I would make my way to the tomb by the palm-trees. There, standing by the dead casket from which the jewel had been rifled, I would feel her sweet presence, and would whisper to her that I would rejoin her if mortal wit could solve the riddle.

'Parmes had said that his discovery was connected with the ring of Thoth. I had some remembrance of the trinket. It was a large and weighty circlet, made, not of gold, but of a rarer and heavier metal brought from the mines of Mount Harbal.* Platinum, you call it. The ring had, I remembered, a hollow crystal set in it, in which some few drops of liquid might be stored. Now, the secret of Parmes could not have to do with the metal alone, for there were many rings of that metal in the Temple. Was it not more likely that he had stored his precious poison within the cavity of the crystal? I had scarce come to this conclusion before, in hunting through his papers, I came upon one which told me that it was indeed so, and that there was still some of the liquid unused.

'But how to find the ring? It was not upon him when he was stripped for the embalmer. Of that I made sure. Neither was it among his private effects. In vain I searched every room that he had entered, every box and vase and chattel that he had owned. I sifted the very sand of the desert in the places where he had been wont to walk; but, do what I would, I could come upon no traces of the ring of Thoth. Yet it may be that my labours would have overcome all obstacles had it not been for a new and unlooked-for misfortune.

'A great war had been waged against the Hyksos, and the Captains

of the Great King had been cut off in the desert, with all their bow-
men and horsemen. The shepherd tribes were upon us like the locusts
in a dry year. From the wilderness of Shur to the great, bitter lake*
there was blood by day and fire by night. Abaris was the bulwark of
Egypt, but we could not keep the savages back. The city fell. The
Governor and the soldiers were put to the sword, and I, with many
more, was led away into captivity.

'For years and years I tended cattle in the great plains by the
Euphrates.* My master died, and his son grew old, but I was still as
far from death as ever. At last I escaped upon a swift camel, and made
my way back to Egypt. The Hyksos had settled in the land which they
had conquered, and their own King ruled over the country. Abaris
had been torn down, the city had been burned, and of the great
Temple there was nothing left save an unsightly mound. Everywhere
the tombs had been rifled and the monuments destroyed. Of my
Atma's grave no sign was left. It was buried in the sands of the desert,
and the palm-trees which marked the spot had long disappeared. The
papers of Parmes and the remains of the Temple of Thoth were either
destroyed or scattered far and wide over the deserts of Syria. All
search after them was vain.

'From that time I gave up all hope of ever finding the ring or discovering the subtle drug. I set myself to live as patiently as might be
until the effect of the elixir should wear away. How can you understand how terrible a thing time is, you who have experience only of the
narrow course which lies between the cradle and the grave! I know
it to my cost, I who have floated down the whole stream of history.
I was old when Ilium fell. I was very old when Herodotus* came to
Memphis. I was bowed down with years when the new gospel came
upon earth. Yet you see me much as other men are, with the cursed
elixir still sweetening my blood, and guarding me against that which
I would court. Now, at last, at last I have come to the end of it!

'I have travelled in all lands and I have dwelt with all nations. Every
tongue is the same to me. I learned them all to help pass the weary time.
I need not tell you how slowly they drifted by, the long dawn of modern
civilization, the dreary middle years, the dark times of barbarism.
They are all behind me now. I have never looked with the eyes of love
upon another woman. Atma knows that I have been constant to her.

'It was my custom to read all that the scholars had to say upon
Ancient Egypt. I have been in many positions, sometimes affluent,

sometimes poor, but I have always found enough to enable me to buy the journals which deal with such matters. Some nine months ago I was in San Francisco, when I read an account of some discoveries made in the neighbourhood of Abaris. My heart leapt into my mouth as I read it. It said that the excavator had busied himself in exploring some tombs recently unearthed. In one there had been found an unopened mummy with an inscription upon the outer case setting forth that it contained the body of the daughter of the Governor of the city in the days of Tuthmosis. It added that on removing the outer case there had been exposed a large platinum ring set with a crystal, which had been laid upon the breast of the embalmed woman. This, then, was where Parmes had hid the ring of Thoth. He might well say that it was safe, for no Egyptian would ever stain his soul by moving even the outer case of a buried friend.

'That very night I set off from San Francisco, and in a few weeks I found myself once more at Abaris, if a few sand-heaps and crumbling walls may retain the name of the great city. I hurried to the Frenchmen who were digging there and asked them for the ring. They replied that both the ring and the mummy had been sent to the Boulak Museum at Cairo. To Boulak I went, but only to be told that Mariette Bey* had claimed them and had shipped them to the Louvre. I followed them, and there, at last, in the Egyptian chamber, I came, after close upon four thousand years, upon the remains of my Atma, and upon the ring for which I had sought so long.

'But how was I to lay hands upon them? How was I to have them for my very own? It chanced that the office of attendant was vacant. I went to the Director. I convinced him that I knew much about Egypt. In my eagerness I said too much. He remarked that a Professor's chair would suit me better than a seat in the conciergerie. I knew more, he said, than he did. It was only by blundering, and letting him think that he had over-estimated my knowledge, that I prevailed upon him to let me move the few effects which I have retained into this chamber. It is my first and my last night here.

'Such is my story, Mr Vansittart Smith. I need not say more to a man of your perception. By a strange chance you have this night looked upon the face of the woman whom I loved in those far-off days. There were many rings with crystals in the case, and I had to test for the platinum to be sure of the one which I wanted. A glance at the crystal has shown me that the liquid is indeed within it, and that

I shall at last be able to shake off that accursed health which has been worse to me than the foulest disease. I have nothing more to say to you. I have unburdened myself. You may tell my story or you may withhold it at your pleasure. The choice rests with you. I owe you some amends, for you have had a narrow escape of your life this night. I was a desperate man, and not to be baulked in my purpose. Had I seen you before the thing was done, I might have put it beyond your power to oppose me or to raise an alarm. This is the door. It leads into the Rue de Rivoli. Good night.'

The Englishman glanced back. For a moment the lean figure of Sosra the Egyptian stood framed in the narrow doorway. The next the door had slammed, and the heavy rasping of a bolt broke on the silent night.

It was on the second day after his return to London that Mr John Vansittart Smith saw the following concise narrative in the Paris correspondence of *The Times*: —

'*Curious Occurrence in the Louvre.* — Yesterday morning a strange discovery was made in the principal Eastern chamber. The *ouvriers* who are employed to clean out the rooms in the morning found one of the attendants lying dead upon the floor with his arms round one of the mummies. So close was his embrace that it was only with the utmost difficulty that they were separated. One of the cases containing valuable rings had been opened and rifled. The authorities are of opinion that the man was bearing away the mummy with some idea of selling it to a private collector, but that he was struck down in the very act by long-standing disease of the heart. It is said that he was a man of uncertain age and eccentric habits, without any living relations to mourn over his dramatic and untimely end.'

THE SURGEON OF GASTER FELL

I

HOW THE WOMAN CAME TO KIRKBY-MALHOUSE

ℬLEAK and wind-swept is the little town of Kirkby-Malhouse,*
harsh and forbidding are the fells upon which it stands. It stretches
in a single line of grey-stone, slate-roofed houses, dotted down the
furze-clad slope of the rolling moor.

In this lonely and secluded village, I, James Upperton, found
myself in the summer of '85. Little as the hamlet had to offer, it contained that for which I yearned above all things—seclusion and freedom from all which might distract my mind from the high and weighty
subjects which engaged it. But the inquisitiveness of my landlady
made my lodgings undesirable and I determined to seek new quarters.

As it chanced, I had in one of my rambles come upon an isolated
dwelling in the very heart of these lonely moors, which I at once
determined should be my own. It was a two-roomed cottage, which
had once belonged to some shepherd, but had long been deserted,
and was crumbling rapidly to ruin. In the winter floods, the Gaster
Beck, which runs down Gaster Fell, where the little dwelling stood,
had overswept its banks and torn away a part of the wall. The roof was
in ill case, and the scattered slates lay thick amongst the grass. Yet the
main shell of the house stood firm and true; and it was no great task
for me to have all that was amiss set right.

The two rooms I laid out in a widely different manner—my own
tastes are of a Spartan turn, and the outer chamber was so planned as
to accord with them. An oil-stove by Rippingille of Birmingham* furnished me with the means of cooking; while two great bags, the one of
flour, and the other of potatoes, made me independent of all supplies
from without. In diet I had long been a Pythagorean,* so that the
scraggy, long-limbed sheep which browsed upon the wiry grass by
the Gaster Beck had little to fear from their new companion.
A nine-gallon cask of oil served me as a sideboard; while a square
table, a deal chair and a truckle-bed* completed the list of my domestic
fittings. At the head of my couch hung two unpainted shelves—the

lower for my dishes and cooking utensils, the upper for the few portraits which took me back to the little that was pleasant in the long,
wearisome toiling for wealth and for pleasure which had marked the
life I had left behind.

If this dwelling-room of mine were plain even to squalor, its poverty was more than atoned for by the luxury of the chamber which
was destined to serve me as my study. I had ever held that it was best
for my mind to be surrounded by such objects as would be in harmony with the studies which occupied it, and that the loftiest and
most ethereal conditions of thought are only possible amid surroundings which please the eye and gratify the senses. The room which
I had set apart for my mystic studies was set forth in a style as gloomy
and majestic as the thoughts and aspirations with which it was to har-
monise. Both walls and ceilings were covered with a paper of the richest and glossiest black, on which was traced a lurid and arabesque
pattern of dead gold.* A black velvet curtain covered the single
diamond-paned window; while a thick, yielding carpet of the same
material prevented the sound of my own footfalls, as I paced backward and forward, from breaking the current of my thought. Along
the cornices ran gold rods, from which depended six pictures, all of
the sombre and imaginative caste, which chimed best with my fancy.

And yet it was destined that ere ever I reached this quiet harbour
I should learn that I was still one of humankind, and that it is an ill
thing to strive to break the bond which binds us to our fellows. It was
but two nights before the date I had fixed upon for my change of
dwelling, when I was conscious of a bustle in the house beneath, with
the bearing of heavy burdens up the creaking stair, and the harsh
voice of my landlady, loud in welcome and protestations of joy. From
time to time, amid the whirl of words, I could hear a gentle and softly
modulated voice, which struck pleasantly upon my ear after the long
weeks during which I had listened only to the rude dialect of the
dalesmen. For an hour I could hear the dialogue beneath—the high
voice and the low, with clatter of cup and clink of spoon, until at last
a light, quick step passed my study door, and I knew that my new
fellow-lodger had sought her room.

On the morning after this incident I was up betimes, as is my wont;
but I was surprised, on glancing from my window, to see that our new
inmate was earlier still. She was walking down the narrow pathway,
which zigzags over the fell—a tall woman, slender, her head sunk

upon her breast, her arms filled with a bristle of wild flowers, which she had gathered in her morning rambles. The white and pink of her dress, and the touch of deep red ribbon in her broad, drooping hat, formed a pleasant dash of colour against the dun-tinted landscape. She was some distance off when I first set eyes upon her, yet I knew that this wandering woman could be none other than our arrival of last night, for there was a grace and refinement in her bearing which marked her from the dwellers of the fells. Even as I watched she passed swiftly and lightly down the pathway, and turning through the wicket gate, at the farther end of our cottage garden, she seated herself upon the green bank which faced my window, and strewing her flowers in front of her, set herself to arrange them.

As she sat there, with the rising sun at her back, and the glow of the morning spreading like an aureole around her stately and well-poised head, I could see that she was a woman of extraordinary personal beauty. Her face was Spanish rather than English in its type—oval, olive, with black, sparkling eyes, and a sweetly sensitive mouth. From under the broad straw hat two thick coils of blue-black hair curved down on either side of her graceful, queenly neck. I was surprised, as I watched her, to see that her shoes and skirt bore witness to a journey rather than to a mere morning ramble. Her light dress was stained, wet and bedraggled; while her boots were thick with the yellow soil of the fells. Her face, too, wore a weary expression, and her young beauty seemed to be clouded over by the shadow of inward trouble. Even as I watched her, she burst suddenly into wild weeping, and throwing down her bundle of flowers, ran swiftly into the house.

Distrait* as I was and weary of the ways of the world, I was conscious of a sudden pang of sympathy and grief as I looked upon the spasm of despair which seemed to convulse this strange and beautiful woman. I bent to my books, and yet my thoughts would ever turn to her proud, clear-cut face, her weather-stained dress, her drooping head, and the sorrow which lay in each line and feature of her pensive face.

Mrs Adams, my landlady, was wont to carry up my frugal breakfast; yet it was very rarely that I allowed her to break the current of my thoughts, or to draw my mind by her idle chatter from weightier things. This morning, however, for once, she found me in a listening mood, and with little prompting, proceeded to pour into my ears all that she knew of our beautiful visitor.

'Miss Eva Cameron be her name, sir,' she said: 'but who she be, or where she came fra, I know little more than yoursel'. Maybe it was the same reason that brought her to Kirkby-Malhouse as fetched you there yoursel', sir.'

'Possibly,' said I, ignoring the covert question; 'but I should hardly have thought that Kirkby-Malhouse was a place which offered any great attractions to a young lady.'

'Heh, sir! 'she cried, 'there's the wonder of it. The leddy has just come fra France; and how her folk come to learn of me is just a wonder. A week ago, up comes a man to my door—a fine man, sir, and a gentleman, as one could see with half an eye. 'You are Mrs Adams,' says he. 'I engage your rooms for Miss Cameron,' says he. 'She will be here in a week,' says he; and then off without a word of terms. Last night there comes the young leddy hersel'—soft-spoken and down-cast, with a touch of the French in her speech. But my sakes, sir! I must away and mak' her some tea, for she'll feel lonesome-like, poor lamb, when she wakes under a strange roof.'

II

HOW I WENT FORTH TO GASTER FELL

I was still engaged upon my breakfast when I heard the clatter of dishes and the landlady's footfall as she passed toward her new lodger's room. An instant afterward she had rushed down the passage and burst in upon me with uplifted hand and startled eyes. 'Lord 'a mercy, sir!' she cried, 'and asking your pardon for troubling you, but I'm feared o' the young leddy, sir; she is not in her room.'

'Why, there she is,' said I, standing up and glancing through the casement. 'She has gone back for the flowers she left upon the bank.'

'Oh, sir, see her boots and her dress!' cried the landlady wildly. 'I wish her mother was here, sir—I do. Where she has been is more than I ken, but her bed has not been lain on this night.'

'She has felt restless, doubtless, and went for a walk, though the hour was certainly a strange one.'

Mrs Adams pursed her lip and shook her head. But then as she stood at the casement, the girl beneath looked smilingly up at her and beckoned to her with a merry gesture to open the window.

'Have you my tea there?' she asked in a rich, clear voice, with a touch of the mincing French accent.

'It is in your room, miss.'

'Look at my boots, Mrs Adams!' she cried, thrusting them out from under her skirt. 'These fells of yours are dreadful places— *effroyable**—one inch, two inch; never have I seen such mud! My dress, too—*voilà!*'

'Eh, miss, but you are in a pickle,' cried the landlady, as she gazed down at the bedraggled gown. 'But you must be main weary and heavy for sleep.'

'No, no,' she answered laughingly, 'I care not for sleep. What is sleep? it is a little death—*voilà tout*.* But for me to walk, to run, to breathe the air—that is to live. I was not tired, and so all night I have explored these fells of Yorkshire.'

'Lord 'a mercy, miss, and where did you go?' asked Mrs Adams.

She waved her hand round in a sweeping gesture which included the whole western horizon. 'There,' she cried. 'O comme elles sont tristes et sauvages, ces collines!* But I have flowers here. You will give me water, will you not? They will wither else.' She gathered her treasures in her lap, and a moment later we heard her light, springy footfall upon the stair.

So she had been out all night, this strange woman. What motive could have taken her from her snug room on to the bleak, wind-swept hills? Could it be merely the restlessness, the love of adventure of a young girl? Or was there, possibly, some deeper meaning in this nocturnal journey?

Deep as were the mysteries which my studies had taught me to solve, here was a human problem which for the moment at least was beyond my comprehension. I had walked out on the moor in the forenoon, and on my return, as I topped the brow that overlooks the little town, I saw my fellow-lodger some little distance off amongst the gorse. She had raised a light easel in front of her, and, with papered board laid across it, was preparing to paint the magnificent landscape of rock and moor which stretched away in front of her. As I watched her I saw that she was looking anxiously to right and left. Close by me a pool of water had formed in a hollow. Dipping the cup of my pocket-flask into it, I carried it across to her.

'Miss Cameron, I believe,' said I. 'I am your fellow-lodger. Upperton is my name. We must introduce ourselves in these wilds if we are not to be for ever strangers.'

'Oh, then, you live also with Mrs Adams!' she cried. 'I had thought that there were none but peasants in this strange place.'

'I am a visitor, like yourself,' I answered. 'I am a student, and have come for quiet and repose, which my studies demand.'

'Quiet, indeed!' said she, glancing round at the vast circle of silent moors with the one tiny line of grey cottages which sloped down beneath us.

'And yet not quiet enough,' I answered, laughing, 'for I have been forced to move farther into the fells for the absolute peace which I require.'

'Have you, then, built a house upon the fells?' she asked, arching her eyebrows.

'I have, and hope, within a few days, to occupy it.'

'Ah, but that is *triste*,' she cried. 'And where is it, then, this house which you have built?'

'It is over yonder,' I answered. 'See that stream which lies like a silver band upon the distant moor? It is the Gaster Beck, and it runs through Gaster Fell.'

She started, and turned upon me her great, dark, questioning eyes with a look in which surprise, incredulity, and something akin to horror seemed to be struggling for mastery.

'And you will live on the Gaster Fell?' she cried.

'So I have planned. But what do you know of Gaster Fell, Miss Cameron?' I asked. 'I had thought that you were a stranger in these parts.'

'Indeed, I have never been here before,' she answered, 'but I have heard my brother talk of these Yorkshire moors; and, if I mistake not, I have heard him name this very one as the wildest and most savage of them all.'

'Very likely,' said I carelessly. 'It is indeed a dreary place.'

'Then why live there?' she cried eagerly. 'Consider the loneliness, the barrenness, the want of all comfort and of all aid, should aid be needed.'

'Aid! What aid should be needed on Gaster Fell?'

She looked down and shrugged her shoulders. 'Sickness may come in all places,' said she. 'If I were a man I do not think I would live alone on Gaster Fell.'

'I have braved worse dangers than that,' said I, laughing; 'but I fear that your picture will be spoiled, for the clouds are banking up, and already I feel a few raindrops.'

Indeed, it was high time we were on our way to shelter, for even as I spoke there came the sudden, steady swish of the shower. Laughing merrily, my companion threw her light shawl over her head, and, seizing picture and easel, ran with the lithe grace of a young fawn down the furze-clad slope, while I followed after with camp-stool and paint-box.

* * *

It was the eve of my departure from Kirkby-Malhouse that we sat upon the green bank in the garden, she with dark, dreamy eyes looking sadly out over the sombre fells; while I, with a book upon my knee, glanced covertly at her lovely profile and marvelled to myself how twenty years of life could have stamped so sad and wistful an expression upon it.

'You have read much,' I remarked at last. 'Women have opportunities now such as their mothers never knew. Have you ever thought of going further—or seeking a course of college or even a learned profession?'

She smiled wearily at the thought.

'I have no aim, no ambition,' she said. 'My future is black—confused—a chaos. My life is like to one of these paths upon the fells. You have seen them, Monsieur Upperton. They are smooth and straight and clear where they begin; but soon they wind to left and wind to right, and so mid rocks and crags until they lose themselves in some quagmire. At Brussels my path was straight; but now, *mon Dieu!* who is there can tell me where it leads?'

'It might take no prophet to do that, Miss Cameron,' quoth I, with the fatherly manner which twoscore years may show toward one. 'If I may read your life, I would venture to say that you were destined to fulfil the lot of women—to make some good man happy, and to shed around, in some wider circle, the pleasure which your society has given me since first I knew you.'

'I will never marry,' said she, with a sharp decision, which surprised and somewhat amused me.

'Not marry—and why?'

A strange look passed over her sensitive features, and she plucked nervously at the grass on the bank beside her.

'I dare not,' said she in a voice that quivered with emotion.

'Dare not?'

'It is not for me. I have other things to do. That path of which I spoke is one which I must tread alone.'

'But this is morbid,' said I. 'Why should your lot, Miss Cameron, be separated from that of my own sisters, or the thousand other young ladies whom every season brings out into the world? But perhaps it is that you have a fear and distrust of mankind. Marriage brings a risk as well as a happiness.'

'The risk would be with the man who married me,' she cried. And then in an instant, as though she had said too much, she sprang to her feet and drew her mantle round her. 'The night air is chill, Mr Upperton,' said she, and so swept swiftly away, leaving me to muse over the strange words which had fallen from her lips.

Clearly, it was time that I should go. I set my teeth and vowed that another day should not have passed before I should have snapped this newly formed tie and sought the lonely retreat which awaited me upon the moors. Breakfast was hardly over in the morning before a peasant dragged up to the door the rude hand-cart which was to convey my few personal belongings to my new dwelling. My fellow-lodger had kept her room; and, steeled as my mind was against her influence, I was yet conscious of a little throb of disappointment that she should allow me to depart without a word of farewell. My hand-cart with its load of books had already started, and I, having shaken hands with Mrs Adams, was about to follow it, when there was a quick scurry of feet on the stair, and there she was beside me all panting with her own haste.

'Then you go—you really go?' said she.

'My studies call me.'

'And to Gaster Fell?' she asked.

'Yes; to the cottage which I have built there.'

'And you will live alone there?'

'With my hundred companions who lie in that cart.'

'Ah, books!' she cried, with a pretty shrug of her graceful shoulders. 'But you will make me a promise?'

'What is it?' I asked, in surprise.

'It is a small thing. You will not refuse me?'

'You have but to ask it.'

She bent forward her beautiful face with an expression of the most intense earnestness. 'You will bolt your door at night?' said she; and was gone ere I could say a word in answer to her extraordinary request.

It was a strange thing for me to find myself at last duly installed in my lonely dwelling. For me, now, the horizon was bounded by the barren circle of wiry, unprofitable grass, patched over with furze bushes and scarred by the profusion of Nature's gaunt and granite ribs. A duller, wearier waste I have never seen; but its dullness was its very charm.

And yet the very first night which I spent at Gaster Fell there came a strange incident to lead my thoughts back once more to the world which I had left behind me.

It had been a sullen and sultry evening, with great, livid cloud-banks mustering in the west. As the night wore on, the air within my little cabin became closer and more oppressive. A weight seemed to rest upon my brow and my chest. From far away the low rumble of thunder came moaning over the moor. Unable to sleep, I dressed, and standing at my cottage door, looked on the black solitude which surrounded me.

Taking the narrow sheep path which ran by this stream, I strolled along it for some hundred yards, and had turned to retrace my steps, when the moon was finally buried beneath an ink-black cloud, and the darkness deepened so suddenly that I could see neither the path at my feet, the stream upon my right, nor the rocks upon my left. I was standing groping about in the thick gloom, when there came a crash of thunder with a flash of lightning which lighted up the whole, vast fell, so that every bush and rock stood out clear and hard in the vivid light. It was but for an instant, and yet that momentary view struck a thrill of fear and astonishment through me, for in my very path, not twenty yards before me, there stood a woman, the livid light beating upon her face and showing up every detail of her dress and features.

There was no mistaking those dark eyes, that tall, graceful figure. It was she—Eva Cameron, the woman whom I thought I had for ever left. For an instant I stood petrified, marvelling whether this could indeed be she, or whether it was some figment conjured up by my excited brain. Then I ran swiftly forward in the direction where I had seen her, calling loudly upon her, but without reply. Again I called, and again no answer came back, save the melancholy wail of the owl. A second flash illuminated the landscape, and the moon burst out from behind its cloud. But I could not, though I climbed upon a knoll which overlooked the whole moor, see any sign of this strange, midnight wanderer. For an hour or more I traversed the fell, and at last found myself back at my little cabin, still uncertain as to whether it had been a woman or a shadow upon which I gazed.

III

OF THE GREY COTTAGE IN THE GLEN

It was either on the fourth or the fifth day after I had taken possession
of my cottage that I was astonished to hear footsteps upon the grass
outside, quickly followed by a crack, as from a stick upon the door.
The explosion of an internal machine* would hardly have surprised
or discomfited me more. I had hoped to have shaken off all intrusion
for ever, yet here was somebody beating at my door with as little ceremony as if it had been a village ale-house. Hot with anger, I flung
down my book and withdrew the bolt just as my visitor had raised his
stick to renew his rough application for admittance. He was a tall,
powerful man, tawny-bearded and deep-chested, clad in a loose-
fitting suit of tweed, cut for comfort rather than elegance. As he stood
in the shimmering sunlight, I took in every feature of his face. The
large, fleshy nose; the steady, blue eyes, with their thick thatch of
overhanging brows; the broad forehead, all knitted and lined with
furrows, which were strangely at variance with his youthful bearing.
In spite of his weather-stained felt hat, and the coloured handkerchief
slung round his muscular, brown neck, I could see at a glance he was
a man of breeding and education. I had been prepared for some wandering shepherd or uncouth tramp, but this apparition fairly disconcerted me.

'You look astonished,' said he, with a smile. 'Did you think, then,
that you were the only man in the world with a taste for solitude? You
see that there are other hermits in the wilderness besides yourself.'

'Do you mean to say that you live here?' I asked in no conciliatory
voice.

'Up yonder,' he answered, tossing his head backward. 'I thought as
we were neighbours, Mr Upperton, that I could not do less than look
in and see if I could assist you in any way.'

'Thank you,' I said coldly, standing with my hand upon the latch of
the door. 'I am a man of simple tastes, and you can do nothing for me.
You have the advantage of me in knowing my name.'

He appeared to be chilled by my ungracious manner.

'I learned it from the masons who were at work here,' he said. 'As
for me, I am a surgeon, the surgeon of Gaster Fell. That is the name
I have gone by in these parts, and it serves as well as another.'

'Not much room for practice here?' I observed.

'Not a soul except yourself for miles on either side.'

'You appear to have had need of some assistance yourself,' I remarked, glancing at a broad, white splash, as from the recent action of some powerful acid, upon his sunburnt cheek.

'That is nothing,' he answered, curtly, turning his face half round to hide the mark. 'I must get back, for I have a companion who is waiting for me. If I can ever do anything for you, pray let me know. You have only to follow the beck upward for a mile or so to find my place. Have you a bolt on the inside of your door?'

'Yes,' I answered, rather startled at this question.

'Keep it bolted, then,' he said. 'The fell is a strange place. You never know who may be about. It is as well to be on the safe side. Good-bye.' He raised his hat, turned on his heel and lounged away along the bank of the little stream.

I was still standing with my hand upon the latch, gazing after my unexpected visitor, when I became aware of yet another dweller in the wilderness. Some distance along the path which the stranger was taking there lay a great, grey boulder, and leaning against this was a small, wizened man, who stood erect as the other approached, and advanced to meet him. The two talked for a minute or more, the taller man nodding his head frequently in my direction, as though describing what had passed between us. Then they walked on together, and disappeared in a dip of the fell. Presently I saw them ascending once more some rising ground farther on. My acquaintance had thrown his arm round his elderly friend, either from affection or from a desire to aid him up the steep incline. The square, burly figure and its shrivelled, meagre companion stood out against the skyline, and turning their faces, they looked back at me. At the sight, I slammed the door, lest they should be encouraged to return. But when I peeped from the window some minutes afterward, I perceived that they were gone.

All day I bent over the Egyptian papyrus upon which I was engaged; but neither the subtle reasonings of the ancient philosopher of Memphis,* nor the mystic meaning which lay in his pages, could raise my mind from the things of earth. Evening was drawing in before I threw my work aside in despair. My heart was bitter against this man for his intrusion. Standing by the beck which purled past the door of my cabin, I cooled my heated brow, and thought the matter over. Clearly it was the small mystery hanging over these neighbours of mine which had caused my mind to run so persistently on them. That cleared up, they would no longer cause an obstacle to my studies. What was to hinder me, then, from walking in the direction of their dwelling, and observing for myself, without permitting them to suspect my presence, what manner of men they might be? Doubtless, their mode of life would be found to admit of some simple and prosaic explanation. In any case, the evening was fine, and a walk would be bracing for mind and body. Lighting my pipe, I set off over the moors in the direction which they had taken.

About half-way down a wild glen there stood a small clump of gnarled and stunted oak trees. From behind these, a thin, dark column of smoke rose into the still evening air. Clearly this marked the position of my neighbour's house. Trending away to the left, I was able to gain the shelter of a line of rocks, and so reach a spot from which I could command a view of the building without exposing myself to any risk of being observed. It was a small, slate-covered cottage, hardly larger than the boulders among which it lay. Like my own cabin, it showed signs of having been constructed for the use of some shepherd; but, unlike mine, no pains had been taken by the tenants to improve and enlarge it. Two little peeping windows, a cracked and weather-beaten door, and a discoloured barrel for catching the rainwater, were the only external objects from which I might draw deductions as to the dwellers within. Yet even in these there was food for thought, for as I drew nearer, still concealing myself behind the ridge, I saw that thick bars of iron covered the windows, while the old door was slashed and plated with the same metal. These strange precautions, together with the wild surroundings and unbroken solitude, gave an indescribably ill omen and fearsome character to the solitary building. Thrusting my pipe into my pocket, I crawled upon my hands and knees through the gorse and ferns until I was within a hundred yards of my neighbour's door. There, finding that I could not approach nearer without fear of detection, I crouched down, and set myself to watch.

I had hardly settled into my hiding-place, when the door of the cottage swung open, and the man who had introduced himself to me as the surgeon of Gaster Fell came out, bareheaded, with a spade in his hands. In front of the door there was a small, cultivated patch containing potatoes, peas and other forms of green stuff, and here he proceeded to busy himself, trimming, weeding and arranging, singing the while in a powerful though not very musical voice. He was all engrossed in his work, with his back to the cottage, when there emerged from the half-open door the same attenuated creature whom I had seen in the morning. I could perceive now that he was a man of sixty, wrinkled, bent, and feeble with sparse, grizzled hair, and long, colourless face. With a cringing, sidelong gait, he shuffled toward his companion, who was unconscious of his approach until he was close upon him. His light footfall or his breathing may have finally given notice of his proximity, for the worker sprang round and faced him. Each made a quick step toward the other, as though in greeting, and then—even now I feel the horror of the instant—the tall man rushed upon and knocked his companion to the earth, then whipping up his body, ran with great speed over the intervening ground and disappeared with his burden into the house.

Case-hardened as I was by my varied life, the suddenness and violence of the thing made me shudder. The man's age, his feeble frame, his humble and deprecating manner, all cried shame against the deed. So hot was my anger, that I was on the point of striding up to the cabin, unarmed as I was, when the sound of voices from within showed me that the victim had recovered. The sun had sunk beneath the horizon, and all was grey, save a red feather in the cap of Pennigent.* Secure in the failing light, I approached near and strained my ears to catch what was passing. I could hear the high, querulous voice of the elder man and the deep, rough monotone of his assailant, mixed with a strange metallic jangling and clanking. Presently the surgeon came out, locked the door behind him and stamped up and down in the twilight, pulling at his hair and brandishing his arms, like a man demented. Then he set off, walking rapidly up the valley, and I soon lost sight of him among the rocks.

When his footsteps had died away in the distance, I drew nearer to the cottage. The prisoner within was still pouring forth a stream of words, and moaning from time to time like a man in pain. These words resolved themselves, as I approached, into prayers—shrill, voluble prayers, pattered forth with the intense earnestness of one who sees impending and imminent danger. There was to me something inexpressibly awesome in this gush of solemn entreaty from the lonely sufferer, meant for no human ear, and jarring upon the silence of the night. I was still pondering whether I should mix myself in the affair or not, when I heard in the distance the sound of the surgeon's returning footfall. At that I drew myself up quickly by the iron bars and glanced in through the diamond-paned window. The interior of the cottage was lighted up by a lurid glow, coming from what I afterward discovered to be a chemical furnace. By its rich light I could distinguish a great litter of retorts, test tubes and condensers, which sparkled over the table, and threw strange, grotesque shadows on the wall. On the farther side of the room was a wooden framework resembling a hen-coop, and in this, still absorbed in prayer, knelt the man whose voice I heard. The red glow beating upon his upturned face made it stand out from the shadow like a painting from Rembrandt, showing up every wrinkle upon the parchment-like skin. I had but time for a fleeting glance; then, dropping from the window, I made off through the rocks and the heather, nor slackened my pace until I found myself back in my cabin once more. There I threw myself upon my couch, more disturbed and shaken than I had ever thought to feel again.

Such doubts as I might have had as to whether I had indeed seen my former fellow-lodger upon the night of the thunderstorm were resolved the next morning. Strolling along down the path which led to the fell, I saw in one spot where the ground was soft the impressions of a foot—the small, dainty foot of a well-booted woman. That tiny heel and high instep could have belonged to none other than my companion of Kirkby-Malhouse. I followed her trail for some distance, till it still pointed, so far as I could discern it, to the lonely and ill-omened cottage. What power could there be to draw this tender girl, through wind and rain and darkness, across the fearsome moors to that strange rendezvous?

I have said that a little beck flowed down the valley and past my very door. A week or so after the doings which I have described, I was seated by my window when I perceived something white drifting slowly down the stream. My first thought was that it was a drowning sheep; but picking up my stick, I strolled to the bank and hooked it ashore. On examination it proved to be a large sheet, torn and tattered, with the initials J.C. in the corner. What gave it its sinister significance, however, was that from hem to hem it was all dabbled and discoloured.

Shutting the door of my cabin, I set off up the glen in the direction of the surgeon's cabin. I had not gone far before I perceived the very man himself. He was walking rapidly along the hillside, beating the furze bushes with a cudgel and bellowing like a madman. Indeed, at the sight of him, the doubts as to his sanity which had risen in my mind were strengthened and confirmed.

As he approached I noticed that his left arm was suspended in a sling. On perceiving me he stood irresolute, as though uncertain whether to come over to me or not. I had no desire for an interview with him, however, so I hurried past him, on which he continued on his way, still shouting and striking about with his club. When he had disappeared over the fells, I made my way down to his cottage, determined to find some clue to what had occurred. I was surprised, on reaching it, to find the iron-plated door flung wide open. The ground immediately outside it was marked with the signs of a struggle. The chemical apparatus within and the furniture were all dashed about and shattered. Most suggestive of all, the sinister wooden cage was stained with blood-marks and its unfortunate occupant had disappeared. My heart was heavy for the little man, for I was assured I should never see him in this world more.

There was nothing in the cabin to throw any light upon the identity of my neighbours. The room was stuffed with chemical instruments. In one corner a small book-case contained a choice selection of works of science. In another was a pile of geological specimens collected from the limestone.

I caught no glimpse of the surgeon upon my homeward journey; but when I reached my cottage I was astonished and indignant to find that somebody had entered it in my absence. Boxes had been pulled out from under the bed, the curtains disarranged, the chairs drawn out from the wall. Even my study had not been safe from this rough intruder, for the prints of a heavy boot were plainly visible on the ebony-black carpet.

IV

OF THE MAN WHO CAME IN THE NIGHT

The night set in gusty and tempestuous, and the moon was all girt with ragged clouds. The wind blew in melancholy gusts, sobbing and sighing over the moor, and setting all the gorse bushes a-groaning. From time to time a little sputter of rain pattered up against the window-pane. I sat until near midnight, glancing over the fragment on immortality by Iamblichus, the Alexandrian platonist, of whom the Emperor Julian said that he was posterior to Plato in time but not in genius.* At last, shutting up my book, I opened my door and took a last look at the dreary fell and still more dreary sky. As I protruded my head, a swoop of wind caught me and sent the red ashes of my pipe sparkling and dancing through the darkness. At the same moment the moon shone brilliantly out from between two clouds and I saw, sitting on the hillside, not two hundred yards from my door, the man who called himself the surgeon of Gaster Fell. He was squatted among the heather, his elbows upon his knees, and his chin resting upon his hands, as motionless as a stone, with his gaze fixed steadily upon the door of my dwelling.

At the sight of this ill-omened sentinel, a chill of horror and of fear shot through me, for his gloomy and mysterious associations had cast a glamour round the man, and the hour and place were in keeping with his sinister presence. In a moment, however, a manly glow of resentment and self-confidence drove this petty emotion from my mind, and I strode fearlessly in his direction. He rose as I approached and faced me, with the moon shining on his grave, bearded face and glittering on his eyeballs. 'What is the meaning of this?' I cried, as I came upon him. 'What right have you to play the spy on me?'

I could see the flush of anger rise on his face. 'Your stay in the country has made you forget your manners,' he said. 'The moor is free to all.'

'You will say next that my house is free to all,' I said, hotly. 'You have had the impertinence to ransack it in my absence this afternoon.'

He started, and his features showed the most intense excitement. 'I swear to you that I had no hand in it!' he cried. 'I have never set foot in your house in my life. Oh, sir, sir, if you will but believe me, there is a danger hanging over you, and you would do well to be careful.'

'I have had enough of you,' I said. 'I saw that cowardly blow you struck when you thought no human eye rested upon you. I have been to your cottage, too, and know all that it has to tell. If there is a law in England, you shall hang for what you have done. As to me, I am an old soldier, sir, and I am armed. I shall not fasten my door. But if you or any other villain attempt to cross my threshold it shall be at your own risk.' With these words, I swung round upon my heel and strode into my cabin.

For two days the wind freshened and increased, with constant squalls of rain until on the third night the most furious storm was raging which I can ever recollect in England. I felt that it was positively useless to go to bed, nor could I concentrate my mind sufficiently to read a book. I turned my lamp half down to moderate the glare, and leaning back in my chair, I gave myself up to reverie. I must have lost all perception of time, for I have no recollection how long I sat there on the borderland betwixt thought and slumber. At last, about 3 or possibly 4 o'clock, I came to myself with a start—not only came to myself, but with every sense and nerve upon the strain. Looking round my chamber in the dim light, I could not see anything to justify my sudden trepidation. The homely room, the rain blurred window and the rude wooden door were all as they had been. I had begun to persuade myself that some half-formed dream had sent that vague thrill through my nerves, when in a moment I became conscious of what it was. It was a sound—the sound of a human step outside my solitary cottage.

Amid the thunder and the rain and the wind I could hear it— a dull, stealthy footfall, now on the grass, now on the stones— occasionally stopping entirely, then resumed, and ever drawing nearer. I sat breathlessly, listening to the eerie sound. It had stopped now at my very door, and was replaced by a panting and gasping, as of one who has travelled fast and far.

By the flickering light of the expiring lamp I could see that the latch of my door was twitching, as though a gentle pressure was exerted on it from without. Slowly, slowly, it rose, until it was free of the catch, and then there was a pause of a quarter minute or more, while I still sat silent with dilated eyes and drawn sabre. Then, very slowly, the door began to revolve upon its hinges, and the keen air of the night came whistling through the slit. Very cautiously it was pushed open, so that never a sound came from the rusty hinges. As the aperture enlarged, I became aware of a dark, shadowy figure upon my threshold, and of a pale face that looked in at me. The features were human, but the eyes were not. They seemed to burn through the darkness with a greenish brilliancy of their own; and in their baleful, shifty glare I was conscious of the very spirit of murder. Springing from my chair, I had raised my naked sword, when, with a wild shouting, a second figure dashed up to my door. At its approach my shadowy visitant uttered a shrill cry, and fled away across the fells, yelping like a beaten hound.

Tingling with my recent fear, I stood at my door, peering through the night with the discordant cry of the fugitives still ringing in my ears. At that moment a vivid flash of lightning illuminated the whole landscape and made it as clear as day. By its light I saw far away upon the hillside two dark figures pursuing each other with extreme rapidity across the fells. Even at that distance the contrast between them forbid all doubt as to their identity. The first was the small, elderly man, whom I had supposed to be dead; the second was my neighbour, the surgeon. For an instant they stood out clear and hard in the unearthly light; in the next, the darkness had closed over them, and they were gone. As I turned to re-enter my chamber, my foot rattled against something on my threshold. Stooping, I found it was a straight knife, fashioned entirely of lead, and so soft and brittle that it was a strange choice for a weapon. To render it more harmless, the top had been cut square off. The edge, however, had been assiduously sharpened against a stone, as was evident from the markings upon it, so that it was still a dangerous implement in the grasp of a determined man.

And what was the meaning of it all? you ask. Many a drama which I have come across in my wandering life, some as strange and as striking as this one, has lacked the ultimate explanation which you demand. Fate is a grand weaver of tales; but she ends them, as a rule, in defiance of all artistic laws, and with an unbecoming want of regard for literary propriety. As it happens, however, I have a letter before me as I write which I may add without comment, and which will clear all that may remain dark.

                                                    'Kirkby Lunatic Asylum,
                                                    '*September 4th*, 1885.

'Sir,—I am deeply conscious that some apology and explanation is due to you for the very startling and, in your eyes, mysterious events which have recently occurred, and which have so seriously interfered with the retired existence which you desire to lead. I should have called upon you on the morning after the recapture of my father, but my knowledge of your dislike to visitors and also of—you will excuse my saying it—your very violent temper, led me to think that it was better to communicate with you by letter.

'My poor father was a hard-working general practitioner in Birmingham, where his name is still remembered and respected. About ten years ago he began to show signs of mental aberration, which we were inclined to put down to overwork and the effects of a sunstroke. Feeling my own incompetence to pronounce upon a case of such importance, I at once sought the highest advice in Birmingham and London. Among others we consulted the eminent alienist,* Mr Fraser Brown, who pronounced my father's case to be intermittent in its nature, but dangerous during the paroxysms. "It may take a homicidal, or it may take a religious turn," he said; "or it may prove to be a mixture of both. For months he may be as well as you or me, and then in a moment he may break out. You will incur a great responsibility if you leave him without supervision."

'I need say no more, sir. You will understand the terrible task which has fallen upon my poor sister and me in endeavouring to save my father from the asylum which in his sane moments filled him with horror. I can only regret that your peace has been disturbed by our misfortunes, and I offer you in my sister's name and my own our apologies.

'Yours truly,
'J. Cameron.'

A PASTORAL HORROR

❧

FAR above the level of the Lake of Constance, nestling in a little corner of the Tyrolese Alps, lies the quiet town of Feldkirch. It is remarkable for nothing save for the presence of a large and well-conducted Jesuit school* and for the extreme beauty of its situation. There is no more lovely spot in the whole of the Vorarlberg.* From the hills which rise behind the town, the great lake glimmers some fifteen miles off, like a broad sea of quicksilver. Down below in the plains the Rhine and the Danube prattle along, flowing swiftly and merrily, with none of the dignity which they assume as they grow from brooks into rivers. Five great countries or principalities,— Switzerland, Austria, Baden, Wurtemburg, and Bavaria—are visible from the plateau of Feldkirch.

Feldkirch is the centre of a large tract of hilly and pastoral country. The main road runs through the centre of the town, and then on as far as Anspach,* where it divides into two branches, one of which is larger than the other. This more important one runs through the valleys across Austrian Tyrol into Tyrol proper, going as far, I believe, as the capital of Innsbruck. The lesser road runs for eight or ten miles amid wild and rugged glens to the village of Laden,* where it breaks up into a network of sheep-tracks. In this quiet spot, I, John Hudson, spent nearly two years of my life, from the June of '65 to the March of '67, and it was during that time that those events occurred which for some weeks brought the retired hamlet into an unholy prominence, and caused its name for the first, and probably for the last time, to be a familiar word to the European press. The short account of these incidents which appeared in the English papers was, however, inaccurate and misleading, besides which, the rapid advance of the Prussians, culminating in the battle of Sadowa,* attracted public attention away from what might have moved it deeply in less troublous times. It seems to me that the facts may be detailed now, and be new to the great majority of readers, especially as I was myself intimately connected with the drama, and am in a position to give many particulars which have never before been made public.

And first a few words as to my own presence in this out of the way spot. When the great city firm of Sprynge, Wilkinson, and Spragge failed, and paid their creditors rather less than eighteen-pence in the pound, a number of humble individuals were ruined, including myself. There was, however, some legal objection which held out a chance of my being made an exception to the other creditors, and being paid in full. While the case was being brought out I was left with a very small sum for my subsistance.

I determined, therefore, to take up my residence abroad in the interim, since I could live more economically there, and be spared the mortification of meeting those who had known me in my more prosperous days. A friend of mine had described Laden to me some years before as being the most isolated place which he had ever come across in all his experience, and as isolation and cheap living are usually synonymous, I bethought use of his words. Besides, I was in a cynical humour with my fellow-man, and desired to see as little of him as possible for some time to come. Obeying, then, the guidances of poverty and of misanthropy, I made my way to Laden, where my arrival created the utmost excitement among the simple inhabitants. The manners and customs of the red-bearded Englander, his long walks, his check suit, and the reasons which had led him to abandon his fatherland, were all fruitful sources of gossip to the topers who frequented the Gruner Mann and the Schwartzer Bar*—the two alehouses of the village.

I found myself very happy at Laden. The surroundings were magnificent, and twenty years of Brixton* had sharpened my admiration for nature as an olive improves the flavour of wine. In my youth I had been a fair German scholar, and I found myself able, before I had been many months abroad, to converse even on scientific and abstruse subjects with the new curé of the parish.

This priest was a great godsend to me, for he was a most learned man and a brilliant conversationalist. Father Verhagen—for that was his name—though little more than forty years of age, had made his reputation as an author by a brilliant monograph upon the early Popes—a work which eminent critics have compared favourably with Von Ranke's.* I shrewdly suspect that it was owing to some rather unorthodox views advanced in this book that Verhagen was relegated to the obscurity of Laden. His opinions upon every subject were ultra-Liberal, and in his fiery youth he had been ready to vindicate them, as was proved by a deep scar across his chin, received from a dragoon's sabre in the abortive insurrection at Berlin.* Altogether the man was an interesting one, and though he was by nature somewhat cold and reserved, we soon established an acquaintanceship.

The atmosphere of morality in Laden was a very rarefied one. The position of Intendant* Wurms and his satellites had for many years been a sinecure. Non-attendance at church upon a Sunday or feast-day was about the deepest and darkest of sins which the most advanced of the villagers had attained to. Occasionally some hulking Fritz or Andreas would come lurching home at ten o'clock at night, slightly under the influence of Bavarian beer, and might even abuse the wife of his bosom if she ventured to remonstrate, but such cases were rare, and when they occurred the Ladeners looked at the culprit for some time in a half admiring, half horrified manner, as one who had committed a gaudy sin and so asserted his individuality.

It was in this peaceful village that a series of crimes suddenly broke out which astonished all Europe, and for atrocity and for the mystery which surrounded them surpassed anything of which I have ever heard or read. I shall endeavour to give a succinct account of these events in the order of their sequence, in which I am much helped by the fact that it has been my custom all my life to keep a journal—to the pages of which I now refer.

It was, then, I find upon the 19th of May in the spring of 1866, that my old landlady, Frau Zimmer, rushed wildly into the room as I was sipping my morning cup of chocolate and informed me that a murder had been committed in the village. At first I could hardly believe the news, but as she persisted in her statement, and was evidently terribly frightened, I put on my hat and went out to find the truth. When I came into the main street of the village I saw several men hurrying along in front of me, and following them I came upon an excited group in front of the little Stadthaus or town hall—a barn-like edifice which was used for all manner of public gatherings. They were collected round the body of one Maul, who had formerly been a steward upon one of the steamers running between Lindau and Fredericshaven,* on the Lake of Constance. He was a harmless, inoffensive little man, generally popular in the village, and, as far as was known, without an enemy in the world. Maul lay upon his face, with his fingers dug into the earth, no doubt in his last convulsive struggles, and his hair all matted together with blood, which had streamed down over the collar of his coat. The body had been discovered nearly two hours, but no one appeared to know what to do or whither to convey it. My arrival, however, together with that of the curé, who came almost simultaneously, infused some vigour into the crowd. Under our direction the corpse was carried up the steps, and laid on the floor of the town hall, where, having made sure that life was extinct, we proceeded to examine the injuries, in conjunction with Lieutenant Wurms, of the police. Maul's face was perfectly placid, showing that he had had no thought of danger until the fatal blow was struck. His watch and purse had not been taken. Upon washing the clotted blood from the back of his head a singular triangular wound was found, which had smashed the bone and penetrated deeply into the brain. It had evidently been inflicted by a heavy blow from a sharp-pointed pyramidal instrument. I believe that it was Father Verhagen, the curé, who suggested the probability of the weapon in question having been a short mattock* or small pickaxe, such as are to be found in every Alpine cottage. The Intendant, with praiseworthy promptness, at once obtained one and striking a turnip, produced just such a curious gap as was to be seen in poor Maul's head. We felt that we had come upon the first link of a chain which might guide us to the assassin. It was not long before we seemed to grasp the whole clue.

A sort of inquest was held upon the body that same afternoon, at which Pfiffor, the maire,* presided, the curé, the Intendant, Freckler, of the post office, and myself forming ourselves into a sort of committee of investigation. Any villager who could throw a light upon the case or give an account of the movements of the murdered man upon the previous evening was invited to attend. There was a fair muster of witnesses, and we soon gathered a connected series of facts. At half-past eight o'clock Maul had entered the Gruner Mann public-house, and had called for a flagon of beer. At that time there were sitting in the tap-room Waghorn, the butcher of the village, and an Italian pedlar named Cellini, who used to come three times a year to Laden with cheap jewellery and other wares. Immediately after his entrance the landlord had seated himself with his customers, and the four had spent the evening together, the common villagers not being admitted beyond the bar. It seemed from the evidence of the landlord and of Waghorn, both of whom were most respectable and trustworthy men, that shortly after nine o'clock a dispute arose between the deceased and the pedlar. Hot words had been exchanged, and the Italian had eventually left the room, saying that he would not stay any longer to hear his country decried. Maul remained for nearly an hour, and being somewhat elated at having caused his adversary's retreat, he drank rather more than was usual with him. One witness had met him walking towards his home, about ten o'clock, and deposed to his having been slightly the worse for drink. Another had met him just a minute or so before he reached the spot in front of the Stadthaus where the deed was done. This man's evidence was most important. He swore confidently that while passing the town hall, and before meeting Maul, he had seen a figure standing in the shadow of the building, adding that the person appeared to him, as far as he could make him out, to be not unlike the Italian.

Up to this point we had then established two facts—that the Italian had left the Gruner Mann before Maul, with words of anger on his lips; the second, that some unknown individual had been seen lying in wait on the road which the ex-steward would have to traverse. A third, and most important, was reached when the woman with whom the Italian lodged deposed that he had not returned the night before until half-past ten, an unusually late hour for Laden. How had he employed the time, then, from shortly after nine, when he left the public house, until half-past ten, when he returned to his rooms? Things were beginning to look very black, indeed, against the pedlar.

It could not be denied, however, that there were points in the man's favour, and that the case against him consisted entirely of circumstantial evidence. In the first place, there was no sign of a mattock or any other instrument which could have been used for such a purpose among the Italian's goods; nor was it easy to understand how he could come by any such a weapon, since he did not go home between the time of the quarrel and his final return. Again, as the curé pointed out, since Cellini was a comparative stranger in the village, it was very unlikely that he would know which road Maul would take in order to reach his home. This objection was weakened, however, by the evidence of the dead man's servant, who deposed that the pedlar had been hawking his wares in front of their house the day before, and might very possibly have seen the owner at one of the windows. As to the prisoner himself, his attitude at first had been one of defiance, and even of amusement; but when he began to realise the weight of evidence against him, his manner became cringing, and he wrung his hands hideously, loudly proclaiming his innocence. His defence was that after leaving the inn, he had taken a long walk down the Anspach-road in order to cool down his excitement, and that this was the cause of his late return. As to the murder of Maul, he knew no more about it than the babe unborn.

I have dwelt at some length upon the circumstances of this case, because there are events in connection with it which makes it peculiarly interesting. I intend now to fall back upon my diary, which was very fully kept during this period, and indeed during my whole residence abroad. It will save me trouble to quote from it, and it will be a teacher for the accuracy of facts.

May 20th.—Nothing thought of and nothing talked of but the recent tragedy. A hunt has been made among the woods and along the brook in the hope of finding the weapon of the assassin. The more I think of it, the more convinced I am that Cellini is the man. The fact of the money being untouched proves that the crime was committed from motives of revenge, and who would bear more spite towards poor innocent Maul except the vindictive hot-blooded Italian whom he had just offended. I dined with Pfiffor in the evening, and he entirely agreed with me in my view of the case.

May 21st.—Still no word as far as I can hear which throws any light upon the murder. Poor Maul was buried at twelve o'clock in the neat little village churchyard. The curé led the service with great feeling, and his audience, consisting of the whole population of the village, were much moved, interrupting him frequently by sobs and ejaculations of grief. After the painful ceremony was over I had a short walk with our good priest. His naturally excitable nature has been considerably stirred by recent events. His hand trembles and his face is pale.

'My friend,' said he, taking me by the hand as we walked together, 'you know something of medicine.' (I had been two years at Guy's).* 'I have been far from well of late.'

'It is this sad affair which has upset you,' I said.

'No,' he answered, 'I have felt it coming on for some time, but it has been worse of late. I have a pain which shoots from here to there,' he put his hand to his temples. 'If I were struck by lightning, the sudden shock it causes me could not be more great. At times when I close my eyes flashes of light dart before them, and my ears are for ever ringing. Often I know not what I do. My fear is lest I faint some time when performing the holy offices.'

'You are overworking yourself,' I said, 'you must have rest and strengthening tonics. Are you writing just now? And how much do you do each day?'

'Eight hours,' he answered. 'Sometimes ten, sometimes even twelve, when the pains in my head do not interrupt me.'

'You must reduce it to four,' I said authoritatively. 'You must also take regular exercise. I shall send you some quinine which I have in my trunk, and you can take as much as would cover a gulden* in a glass of milk every morning and night.'

He departed, vowing that he would follow my directions.

I hear from the maire that four policemen are to be sent from Anspach to remove Cellini to a safer gaol.

May 22nd.—To say that I was startled would give but a faint idea of my mental state. I am confounded, amazed, horrified beyond all expression. Another and a more dreadful crime has been committed during the night. Freckler has been found dead in his house—the very Freckler who had sat with me on the committee of investigation the day before. I write these notes after a long and anxious day's work, during which I have been endeavouring to assist the officers of the law. The villagers are so paralysed with fear at this fresh evidence of an assassin in their midst that there would be a general panic but for our exertions. It appears that Freckler, who was a man of peculiar habits, lived alone in an isolated dwelling. Some curiosity was aroused this morning by the fact that he had not gone to his work, and that there was no sign of movement about the house. A crowd assembled, and the doors were eventually forced open. The unfortunate Freckler was found in the bedroom upstairs, lying with his head in the fireplace. He had met his death by an exactly similar wound to that which had proved fatal to Maul, save that in this instance the injury was in front. His hands were clenched, and there was an indescribable look of horror, and, as it seemed to me, of surprise upon his features. There were marks of muddy footsteps upon the stairs, which must have been caused by the murderer in his ascent, as his victim had put on his slippers before retiring to his bedroom. These prints, however, were too much blurred to enable us to get a trustworthy outline of the foot. They were only to be found upon every third step, showing with what fiendish swiftness this human tiger had rushed upstairs in search of his victim. There was a considerable sum of money in the house, but not one farthing had been touched, nor had any of the drawers in the bedroom been opened.

As the dismal news became known the whole population of the village assembled in a great crowd in front of the house—rather,

I think, from the gregariousness of terror than from mere curiosity. Every man looked with suspicion upon his neighbour. Most were silent, and when they spoke it was in whispers, as if they feared to raise their voices. None of these people were allowed to enter the house, and we, the more enlightened members of the community, made a strict examination of the premises. There was absolutely nothing, however, to give the slightest clue as to the assassin. Beyond the fact that he must be an active man, judging from the manner in which he ascended the stairs, we have gained nothing from this second tragedy. Intendant Wurms pointed out, indeed, that the dead man's rigid right arm was stretched out as if in greeting, and that, therefore, it was probable that this late visitor was someone with whom Freckler was well acquainted. This, however, was, to a large extent, conjecture. If anything could have added to the horror created by the dreadful occurrence, it was the fact that the crime must have been committed at the early hour of half-past eight in the evening—that being the time registered by a small cuckoo clock, which had been carried away by Freckler in his fall.

No one, apparently, heard any suspicious sounds or saw any one enter or leave the house. It was done rapidly, quietly, and completely, though many people must have been about at the time. Poor Pfiffor and our good curé are terribly cut up by the awful occurrence, and, indeed, I feel very much depressed myself now that all the excitement is over and the reaction set in. There are very few of the villagers about this evening, but from every side is heard the sound of hammering—the peasants fitting bolts and bars upon the doors and windows of their houses. Very many of them have been entirely unprovided with anything of the sort, nor were they ever required until now. Frau Zimmer has manufactured a huge fastening which would be ludicrous if we were in a humour for laughter.

I hear to-night that Cellini has been released, as, of course, there is no possible pretext for detaining him now; also that word has been sent to all the villages near for any police that can be spared.

My nerves have been so shaken that I remained awake the greater part of the night, reading Gordon's translation of Tacitus* by candle-light. I have got out my navy revolver and cleaned it, so as to be ready for all eventualities.

May 23rd.—The police force has been recruited by three more men from Anspach and two from Thalstadt* at the other side of the hills. Intendant Wurms has established an efficient system of patrols, so that we may consider ourselves reasonably safe. Today has cast no light upon the murders. The general opinion in the village seems to be that they have been done by some stranger who lies concealed among the woods. They argue that they have all known each other since childhood, and that there is no one of their number who would be capable of such actions. Some of the more daring of them have made a hunt among the pine forests to-day, but without success.

May 24th.—Events crowd on apace. We seem hardly to have recovered from one horror when something else occurs to excite the popular imagination. Fortunately, this time it is not a fresh tragedy, although the news is serious enough.

The murderer has been seen, and that upon the public road, which proves that his thirst for blood has not been quenched yet, and also that our reinforcements of police are not enough to guarantee security. I have just come back from hearing Andreas Murch narrate his experience, though he is still in such a state of trepidation that his story is somewhat incoherent. He was belated among the hills, it seems, owing to mist. It was nearly eleven o'clock before he struck the main road about a couple of miles from the village. He confesses that he felt by no means comfortable at finding himself out so late after the recent occurrences. However, as the fog had cleared away and the moon was shining brightly, he trudged sturdily along. Just about a quarter of a mile from the village the road takes a very sharp bend. Andreas had got as far as this when he suddenly heard in the still night the sound of footsteps approaching rapidly round this curve. Overcome with fear, he threw himself into the ditch which skirts the road, and lay there motionless in the shadow, peering over the side. The steps came nearer and nearer, and then a tall dark figure came round the corner at a swinging pace, and passing the spot where the moon glimmered upon the white face of the frightened peasant, halted in the road about twenty yards further on, and began probing about among the reeds on the roadside with an instrument which Andreas Murch recognised with horror as being a long mattock. After searching about in this way for a minute or so, as if he suspected that someone was concealed there, for he must have heard the sound of the footsteps, he stood still leaning upon his weapon. Murch describes him as a tall, thin man, dressed in clothes of a darkish colour. The lower part of his face was swathed in a wrapper of some sort, and the little which was visible appeared to be of a ghastly pallor. Murch could not see enough of his features to identify him, but thinks that it was no one whom he had ever seen in his life before. After standing for some little time, the man with the mattock had walked swiftly away into the darkness, in the direction in which he imagined the fugitive had gone. Andreas, as may be supposed, lost little time in getting safely into the village, where he alarmed the police. Three of them, armed with carbines,* started down the road, but saw no signs of the miscreant. There is, of course, a possibility that Murch's story is exaggerated and that his imagination has been sharpened by fear. Still, the whole incident cannot be trumped up and this awful demon who haunts us is evidently still active.

There is an ill-conditioned fellow named Hiedler, who lives in a hut on the side of the Spiegelberg, and supports himself by chamois* hunting and by acting as guide to the few tourists who find their way here. Popular suspicion has fastened on this man, for no better reason than that he is tall, thin, and known to be rough and brutal. His chalet has been searched to-day, but nothing of importance found. He has, however, been arrested and confined in the same room which Cellini used to occupy.

* * *

At this point there is a gap of a week in my diary, during which time there was an entire cessation of the constant alarms which have harassed us lately. Some explained it by supposing that the terrible unknown had moved on to some fresh and less guarded scene of operations. Others imagine that we have secured the right man in the shape of the vagabond Hiedler. Be the cause what it may, peace and contentment reign once more in the village, and a short seven days have sufficed to clear away the cloud of care from men's brows, though the police are still on the alert. The season for rifle shooting is beginning, and as Laden has, like every other Tyrolese village, butts* of its own, there is a continual pop, pop, all day. These peasants are dead shots up to about four hundred yards. No troops in the world could subdue them among their native mountains.

My friend Verhagen, the curé, and Pfiffor, the maire, used to go down in the afternoon to see the shooting with me. The former says that the quinine has done him much good and that his appetite is improved. We all agree that it is good policy to encourage the amusements of the people so that they may forget all about this wretched business. Vaghorn, the butcher, won the prize offered by the maire. He made five bulls, and what we should call a magpie* out of six shots at 100 yards. This is English prize-medal form.

June 2nd.—Who could have imagined that a day which opened so fairly could have so dark an ending? The early carrier brought me a letter by which I learned that Spragge and Co. have agreed to pay my claim in full, although it may be some months before the money is forthcoming. This will make a difference of nearly £400 a year to me—a matter of moment when a man is in his seven-and-fortieth year.

And now for the grand events of the hour. My interview with the vampire who haunts us, and his attempt upon Frau Bischoff, the landlady of the Gruner Mann—to say nothing of the narrow escape of our good curé. There seems to be something almost supernatural in the malignity of this unknown fiend, and the impunity with which he continues his murderous course. The real reason of it lies in the badly lit state of the place—or rather the entire absence of light—and also in the fact that thick woods stretch right down to the houses on every side, so that escape is made easy. In spite of this, however, he had two very narrow escapes to-night—one from my pistol, and one from the officers of the law. I shall not sleep much, so I may spend half an hour in jotting down these strange doings in my diary. I am no coward, but life in Laden is becoming too much for my nerves. I believe the matter will end in the emigration of the whole population.

To come to my story, then. I felt lonely and depressed this evening, in spite of the good news of the morning. About nine o'clock, just as night began to fall, I determined to stroll over and call upon the curé, thinking that a little intellectual chat might cheer me up. I slipped my revolver into my pocket, therefore—a precaution which I never neglected—and went out, very much against the advice of good Frau Zimmer. I think I mentioned some months ago in my diary that the curé's house is some little way out of the village upon the brow of a small hill. When I arrived there I found that he had gone out—which, indeed, I might have anticipated, for he had complained lately of restlessness at night, and I had recommended him to take a little exercise in the evening. His housekeeper made me very welcome, however, and having lit the lamp, left me in the study with some books to amuse me until her master's return.

I suppose I must have sat for nearly half an hour glancing over an odd volume of Klopstock's* poems, when some sudden instinct caused me to raise my head and look up. I have been in some strange situations in my life, but never have I felt anything to be compared to the thrill which shot through me at that moment. The recollection of it now, hours after the event, makes me shudder. There, framed in one of the panes of the window, was a human face glaring in, from the darkness, into the lighted room—the face of a man so concealed by a cravat and slouch hat that the only impression I retain of it was a pair of wild-beast eyes and a nose which was whitened by being pressed against the glass. It did not need Andreas Murch's description to tell me that at last I was face to face with the man with the mattock. There was murder in those wild eyes. For a second I was so unstrung as to be powerless; the next I cocked my revolver and fired straight at the sinister face. I was a moment too late. As I pressed the trigger I saw it vanish, but the pane through which it had looked was shattered to pieces. I rushed to the window, and then out through the front door, but everything was silent. There was no trace of my visitor. His intention, no doubt, was to attack the curé, for there was nothing to prevent his coming through the folding window had he not found an armed man inside.

As I stood in the cool night air with the curé's frightened house-keeper beside me, I suddenly heard a great hubbub down in the village. By this time, alas! such sounds were so common in Laden that there was no doubting what it foreboded. Some fresh misfortune had occurred there. To-night seemed destined to be a night of horror. My presence might be of use in the village, so I set off there, taking with me the trembling woman, who positively refused to remain behind. There was a crowd round the Gruner Mann public-house, and a dozen excited voices were explaining the circumstances to the curé, who had arrived just before us. It was as I had thought, though happily without the result which I had feared. Frau Bischoff, the wife of the proprietor of the inn, had, it seems, gone some twenty minutes before a few yards from her door to draw some water, and had been at once attacked by a tall disguised man, who had cut at her with some weapon. Fortunately he had slipped, so that she was able to seize him by the wrist and prevent his repeating his attempt, while she screamed for help. There were several people about at the time, who came running towards them, on which the stranger wrested himself free, and dashed off into the woods, with two of our police after him. There is little hope of their overtaking or tracing him, however, in such a dark labyrinth. Frau Bischoff had made a bold attempt to hold the assassin, and declares that her nails made deep furrows in his right wrist. This, however, must be mere conjecture, as there was very little light at the time. She knows no more of the man's features than I do. Fortunately she is entirely unhurt. The curé was horrified when I informed him of the incident at his own house. He was returning from his walk, it appears, when hearing cries in the village, he had hurried down to it. I have not told anyone else of my own adventure, for the people are quite excited enough already.

As I said before, unless this mysterious and bloodthirsty villain is captured, the place will become deserted. Flesh and blood cannot stand such a strain. He is either some murderous misanthrope who has declared a vendetta against the whole human race, or else he is an escaped maniac. Clearly after the unsuccessful attempt upon Frau Bischoff he had made at once for the curé's house, bent upon slaking his thirst for blood, and thinking that its lonely situation gave hope of success. I wish I had fired at him through the pocket of my coat. The moment he saw the glitter of the weapon he was off.

June 3rd.—Everybody in the village this morning has learned about the attempt upon the curé last night. There was quite a crowd at his house to congratulate him on his escape, and when I appeared they raised a cheer and hailed me as the 'tapferer Englander.'* It seems that his narrow shave must have given the ruffian a great start, for a thick woollen muffler was found lying on the pathway leading down to the village, and later in the day the fatal mattock was discovered close to the same place. The scoundrel evidently threw those things down and then took to his heels. It is possible that he may prove to have been frightened away from the neighbourhood altogether. Let us trust so!

June 4th.—A quiet day, which is as remarkable a thing in our annals as an exciting one elsewhere. Wurms has made strict inquiry, but cannot trace the muffler and mattock to any inhabitant. A description of them has been printed, and copies sent to Anspach and neighbouring villages for circulation among the peasants, who may be able to throw some light upon the matter. A thanksgiving service is to be held in the church on Sunday for the double escape of the pastor and of Martha Bischoff. Pfiffer tells me that Herr von Weissendorff, one of the most energetic detectives in Vienna, is on his way to Laden. I see, too, by the English papers sent me, that people at home are interested in the tragedies here, although the accounts which have reached them are garbled and untrustworthy.

How well I can recall the Sunday morning following upon the events which I have described, such a morning as it is hard to find outside the Tyrol! The sky was blue and cloudless, the gentle breeze wafted the balsamic odour of the pine woods through the open windows, and away up on the hills the distant tinkling of the cow bells fell pleasantly upon the ear, until the musical rise and fall which summoned the villagers to prayer drowned their feebler melody. It was hard to believe, looking down that peaceful little street with its quaint top heavy wooden houses and old-fashioned church, that a cloud of crime hung over it which had horrified Europe. I sat at my window watching the peasants passing with their picturesquely dressed wives and daughters on their way to church. With the kindly reverence of Catholic countries, I saw them cross themselves as they went by the house of Freckler and the spot where Maul had met his fate. When the bell had ceased to toll and the whole population had assembled in the church, I walked up there also, for it has always been my custom to join in the religious exercises of any people among whom I may find myself.

When I arrived at the church I found that the service had already begun. I took my place in the gallery which contained the village organ, from which I had a good view of the congregation. In the front seat of all was stationed Frau Bischoff, whose miraculous escape the service was intended to celebrate, and beside her on one side was her worthy spouse, while the maire occupied the other. There was a hush through the church as the curé turned from the altar and ascended the pulpit. I have seldom heard a more magnificent sermon. Father Verhagen was always an eloquent preacher, but on that occasion he surpassed himself. He chose for his text:—'In the midst of life we are in death,' and impressed so vividly upon our minds the thin veil which divides us from eternity, and how unexpectedly it may be rent, that he held his audience spell-bound and horrified. He spoke next with tender pathos of the friends who had been snatched so suddenly and so dreadfully from among us, until his words were almost drowned by the sobs of the women, and, suddenly turning he compared their peaceful existence in a happier land to the dark fate of the gloomy-minded criminal, steeped in blood and with nothing to hope for either in this world or the next—a man solitary among his fellows, with no woman to love him, no child to prattle at his knee, and an endless torture in his own thoughts. So skilfully and so powerfully did he speak that as he finished I am sure that pity for this merciless demon was the prevailing emotion in every heart.

The service was over, and the priest, with his two acolytes before him, was leaving the altar, when he turned, as was his custom, to give his blessing to the congregation. I shall never forget his appearance. The summer sunshine shining slantwise through the single small stained glass window which adorned the little church threw a yellow lustre upon his sharp intellectual features with their dark haggard lines, while a vivid crimson spot reflected from a ruby-coloured mantle in the window quivered over his uplifted right hand. There was a hush as the villagers bent their heads to receive their pastor's blessing—a hush broken by a wild exclamation of surprise from a woman who staggered to her feet in the front pew and gesticulated frantically as she pointed at Father Verhagen's uplifted arm. No need for Frau Bischoff to explain the cause of that sudden cry, for there—there in full sight of his parishioners, were lines of livid scars upon the curé's white wrist—scars which could be left by nothing on earth but a desperate woman's nails. And what woman save her who had clung so fiercely to the murderer two days before!

* * *

That in all this terrible business poor Verhagen was the man most to be pitied I have no manner of doubt. In a town in which there was good medical advice to be had, the approach of the homicidal mania, which had undoubtedly proceeded from over-work and brain worry, and which assumed such a terrible form, would have been detected in time and he would have been spared the awful compunction with which he must have been seized in the lucid intervals between his fits—if, indeed, he had any lucid intervals. How could I diagnose with my smattering of science the existence of such a terrible and insidious form of insanity, especially from the vague symptoms of which he informed me. It is easy now, looking back, to think of many little circumstances which might have put us on the right scent; but what a simple thing is retrospective wisdom! I should be sad indeed if I thought that I had anything with which to reproach myself.

We were never able to discover where he had obtained the weapon with which he had committed his crimes, nor how he managed to secrete it in the interval. My experience proved that it had been his custom to go and come through his study window without disturbing his housekeeper. On the occasion of the attempt on Frau Bischoff he had made a dash for home, and then, finding to his astonishment that his room was occupied, his only resource was to fling away his weapon and muffler, and to mix with the crowd in the village. Being both a strong and an active man, with a good knowledge of the footpaths through the woods, he had never found any difficulty in escaping all observation.

Immediately after his apprehension, Verhagen's disease took an acute form, and he was carried off to the lunatic asylum at Feldkirch. I have heard that some months afterwards he made a determined attempt upon the life of one of his keepers, and afterwards committed suicide. I cannot be positive of this, however, for I heard it quite accidentally during a conversation in a railway carriage.

As for myself, I left Laden within a few months, having received a pleasing intimation from my solicitors that my claim had been paid in full. In spite of my tragic experience there, I had many a pleasing recollection of the little Tyrolese village, and in two subsequent visits I renewed my acquaintance with the maire, the Intendant, and all my old friends, on which occasion, over long pipes and flagons of beer, we have taken a grim pleasure in talking with bated breath of that terrible month in the quiet Vorarlberg hamlet.

'DE PROFUNDIS'

So long as the oceans are the ligaments which bind together the great, broadcast British Empire, so long will there be a dash of romance in our minds. For the soul is swayed by the waters, as the waters are by the moon, and when the great highways of an empire are along such roads as these, so full of strange sights and sounds, with danger ever running like a hedge on either side of the course, it is a dull mind indeed which does not bear away with it some trace of such a passage. And now, Britain lies far beyond herself, for the three-mile limit* of every seaboard is her frontier, which has been won by hammer and loom and pick rather than by arts of war. For it is written in history that neither king nor army can bar the path to the man who, having twopence in his strong box, and knowing well where he can turn it to threepence, sets his mind to that one end. And as the frontier has broadened, the mind of Britain has broadened, too, spreading out until all men can see that the ways of the island are continental, even as those of the Continent are insular.

But for this a price must be paid, and the price is a grievous one. As the beast of old must have one young, human life as a tribute every year, so to our Empire we throw from day to day the pick and flower of our youth. The engine is world-wide and strong, but the only fuel that will drive it is the lives of British men. Thus it is that in the grey, old cathedrals as we look round upon the brasses on the walls, we see strange names, such names as they who reared those walls had never heard, for it is in Peshawur, and Umballah, and Korti, and Fort Pearson* that the youngsters die, leaving only a precedent and a brass behind them. But if every man had his obelisk, even where he lay, then no frontier line need be drawn, for a cordon of British graves would ever show how high the Anglo–Celtic tide had lapped.

This, then, as well as the waters which join us to the world, has done something to tinge us with romance. For when so many have their loved ones over the seas, walking amid hillmen's bullets, or swamp malaria, where death is sudden and distance great, then mind communes with mind, and strange stories arise of dream, presentiment, or vision, where the mother sees her dying son, and is past the first bitterness of her grief ere the message comes which should have broken the news. The learned have of late looked into the matter and have even labelled it with a name;* but what can we know more of it save that a poor, stricken soul, when hard-pressed and driven, can shoot across the earth some ten-thousand-mile-distant picture of its trouble to the mind which is most akin to it. Far be it from me to say that there lies no such power within us, for of all things which the brain will grasp the last will be itself; but yet it is well to be very cautious over such matters, for once at least I have known that which was within the laws of Nature seem to be far upon the further side of them.

John Vansittart was the younger partner of the firm of Hudson and Vansittart, coffee exporters of the Island of Ceylon,* three-quarters Dutchman by descent, but wholly English in his sympathies. For years I had been his agent in London, and when in '72 he came over to England for a three months' holiday, he turned to me for the introductions which would enable him to see something of town and country life. Armed with seven letters he left my offices, and for many weeks scrappy notes from different parts of the country let me know that he had found favour in the eyes of my friends. Then came word of his engagement to Emily Lawson, of a cadet branch of the Hereford Lawsons,* and at the very tail of the first flying rumour the news of his absolute marriage, for the wooing of a wanderer must be short, and the days were already crowding on towards the date when he must be upon his homeward journey. They were to return together to Colombo in one of the firm's own thousand-ton, barque-rigged* sailing ships, and this was to be their princely honeymoon, at once a necessity and a delight.

Those were the royal days of coffee-planting in Ceylon, before a single season and a rotting fungus* drove a whole community through years of despair to one of the greatest commercial victories which pluck and ingenuity ever won. Not often is it that men have the heart when their one great industry is withered to rear up, in a few years, another as rich to take its place, and the tea-fields of Ceylon are as true a monument to courage as is the lion at Waterloo.* But in '72 there was no cloud yet above the skyline, and the hopes of the planters were as high and as bright as the hill-sides on which they reared their crops. Vansittart came down to London with his young and beautiful wife. I was introduced, dined with them, and it was finally arranged that I, since business called me also to Ceylon, should be a fellow-passenger with them on the *Eastern Star*, which was timed to sail on the following Monday.

It was on the Sunday evening that I saw him again. He was shown up into my rooms about nine o'clock at night, with the air of a man who is bothered and out of sorts. His hand, as I shook it, was hot and dry.

'I wish, Atkinson,' said he, 'that you could give me a little lime-juice and water. I have a beastly thirst upon me, and the more I take the more I seem to want.'

I rang and ordered a caraffe and glasses. 'You are flushed,' said I. 'You don't look the thing.'

'No, I'm clean off colour. Got a touch of rheumatism in my back, and don't seem to taste my food. It is this vile London that is choking me. I'm not used to breathing air which has been used up by four million lungs all sucking away on every side of you.' He flapped his crooked hands before his face, like a man who really struggles for his breath.

'A touch of the sea will soon set you right.'

'Yes, I'm of one mind with you there. That's the thing for me. I want no other doctor. If I don't get to sea to-morrow I'll have an illness. There are no two ways about it.' He drank off a tumbler of lime-juice, and clapped his two hands with his knuckles doubled up into the small of his back.

'That seems to ease me,' said he, looking at me with a filmy eye. 'Now I want your help, Atkinson, for I am rather awkwardly placed.'

'As how?'

'This way. My wife's mother got ill and wired for her. I couldn't go—you know best yourself how tied I have been—so she had to go alone. Now I've had another wire to say that she can't come to-morrow, but that she will pick up the ship at Falmouth on Wednesday. We put in there, you know, though I count it hard, Atkinson, that a man should be asked to believe in a mystery, and cursed if he can't do it. Cursed, mind you, no less.' He leaned forward and began to draw a catchy breath like a man who is poised on the very edge of a sob.

Then first it came into my mind that I had heard much of the hard-drinking life of the island, and that from brandy came these wild words and fevered hands. The flushed cheek and the glazing eye were those of one whose drink is strong upon him. Sad it was to see so noble a young man in the grip of that most bestial of all the devils.

'You should lie down,' I said, with some severity.

He screwed up his eyes like a man who is striving to wake himself, and looked up with an air of surprise.

'So I shall presently,' said he, quite rationally. 'I felt quite swimmy just now, but I am my own man again now. Let me see, what was I talking about? Oh ah, of course, about the wife. She joins the ship at Falmouth. Now I want to go round by water. I believe my health depends upon it. I just want a little clean, first-lung air to set me on my feet again. I ask you, like a good fellow, to go to Falmouth* by rail, so that in case we should be late you may be there to look after the wife. Put up at the Royal Hotel,* and I will wire her that you are there. Her sister will bring her down, so that it will be all plain sailing.'

'I'll do it with pleasure,' said I. 'In fact, I would rather go by rail, for we shall have enough and to spare of the sea before we reach Colombo. I believe, too, that you badly need a change. Now, I should go and turn in, if I were you.'

'Yes, I will. I sleep aboard to-night. You know,' he continued, as the film settled down again over his eyes, 'I've not slept well the last few nights. I've been troubled with theolololog—that is to say, theolo-logical—hang it,' with a desperate effort, 'with the doubts of theolo-logicians.* Wondering why the Almighty made us, you know, and why He made our heads swimmy, and fixed little pains into the small of our backs. Maybe I'll do better to-night.' He rose and steadied himself with an effort against the corner of the chair back.

'Look here, Vansittart,' said I gravely, stepping up to him, and lay-ing my hand upon his sleeve, 'I can give you a shakedown* here. You are not fit to go out. You are all over the place. You've been mixing your drinks.'

'Drinks!' He stared at me stupidly.

'You used to carry your liquor better than this.'

'I give you my word, Atkinson, that I have not had a drain for two days. It's not drink. I don't know what it is. I suppose you think this is drink.' He took up my hand in his burning grasp, and passed it over his own forehead.

'Great Lord!' said I.

His skin felt like a thin sheet of velvet beneath which lies a close-packed layer of small shot. It was smooth to the touch at any one place, but to a finger passed along it, rough as a nutmeg-grater.

'It's all right,' said he, smiling at my startled face. 'I've had the prickly heat* nearly as bad.'

'But this is never prickly heat.'

'No, it's London. It's breathing bad air. But to-morrow it'll be all right. There's a surgeon aboard, so I shall be in safe hands. I must be off now.'

'Not you,' said I, pushing him back into a chair. 'This is past a joke You don't move from here until a doctor sees you Just stay where you are.'

I caught up my hat, and rushing round to the house of a neighbouring physician, I brought him back with me. The room was empty and Vansittart gone. I rang the bell. The servant said that the gentleman had ordered a cab the instant that I had left, and had gone off in it. He had told the cabman to drive to the docks.

'Did the gentleman seem ill?' I asked.

'Ill!' The man smiled. 'No, sir, he was singin' his 'ardest all the time.'

The information was not as reassuring as my servant seemed to think, but I reflected that he was going straight back to the *Eastern Star*, and that there was a doctor aboard of her, so that there was nothing which I could do in the matter. None the less, when I thought of his thirst, his burning hands, his heavy eye, his tripping speech, and lastly, of that leprous forehead, I carried with me to bed an unpleasant memory of my visitor and his visit.

At eleven o'clock next day I was at the docks, but the *Eastern Star* had already moved down the river, and was nearly at Gravesend. To Gravesend I went by train, but only to see her topmasts far off, with a plume of smoke from a tug in front of her. I would hear no more of my friend until I rejoined him at Falmouth. When I got back to my offices, a telegram was awaiting me from Mrs Vansittart, asking me to meet her; and next evening found us both at the Royal Hotel, Falmouth, where we were to wait for the *Eastern Star*. Ten days passed, and there came no news of her.

They were ten days which I am not likely to forget. On the very day that the *Eastern Star* had cleared from the Thames, a furious, easterly gale had sprung up, and blew on from day to day for the greater part of a week without the sign of a lull. Such a screaming, raving, long-drawn storm has never been known on the southern coast. From our hotel windows the sea view was all banked in haze, with a little rain-swept half-circle under our very eyes, churned and lashed into one tossing stretch of foam. So heavy was the wind upon the waves that little sea could rise, for the crest of each billow was torn shrieking from it, and lashed broadcast over the bay. Clouds, wind, sea, all were rushing to the west, and there, looking down at this mad jumble of elements, I waited on day after day, my sole companion a white, silent woman, with terror in her eyes, her forehead pressed ever against the window, her gaze from early morning to the fall of night fixed upon that wall of grey haze through which the loom of a vessel might come. She said nothing, but that face of hers was one long wail of fear.

On the fifth day I took counsel with an old seaman. I should have preferred to have done so alone, but she saw me speak with him, and was at our side in an instant, with parted lips and a prayer in her eyes.

'Seven days out from London,' said he, 'and five in the gale. Well, the Channel's swept clear by this wind. There's three things for it. She may have popped into port on the French side. That's like enough.'

'No, no; he knew we were here. He would have telegraphed.'

'Ah, yes, so he would. Well, then, he might have run for it, and if he did that he won't be very far from Madeira* by now. That'll be it, marm, you may depend.'

'Or else? You said there was a third chance.'

'Did I, marm. No, only two, I think. I don't think I said anything of a third. Your ship's out there, depend upon it, away out in the Atlantic, and you'll hear of it time enough, for the weather is breaking. Now don't you fret, marm, and wait quiet and you'll find a real blue Cornish sky to-morrow.'

The old seaman was right in his surmise, for the next day broke calm and bright, with only a low, dwindling cloud in the west to mark the last trailing wreaths of the storm-wrack. But still there came no word from the sea, and no sign of the ship. Three more weary days had passed, the weariest that I have ever spent, when there came a seafaring man to the hotel with a letter. I gave a shout of joy. It was from the captain of the *Eastern Star*. As I read the first lines of it I whisked my hand over it, but she laid her own upon it and drew it away. 'I have seen it,' said she, in a cold, quiet voice. 'I may as well see the rest, too.'

'DEAR SIR,' said the letter,

'Mr Vansittart is down with the small-pox, and we are blown so far on our course that we don't know what to do, he being off his head and unfit to tell us. By dead reckoning we are but three hundred miles from Funchal,* so I take it that it is best that we should push on there, get Mr V. into hospital, and wait in the Bay until you come. There's a sailing-ship due from Falmouth to Funchal in a few days' time, as I understand. This goes by the brig *Marian* of Falmouth, and five pounds is due to the master,

'Yours respectfully,
'JNO. HINES.'

She was a wonderful woman that, only a chit of a girl fresh from school, but as quiet and strong as a man. She said nothing—only pressed her lips together tight, and put on her bonnet.

'You are going out?' I asked.

'Yes.'

'Can I be of use?'

'No; I am going to the doctor's.'

'To the doctor's?'

'Yes. To learn how to nurse a small-pox case.'

She was busy at that all the evening, and next morning we were off with a fine ten-knot breeze in the barque *Rose of Sharon* for Madeira. For five days we made good time, and were no great way from the island; but on the sixth there fell a calm, and we lay without motion on a sea of oil, heaving slowly, but making not a foot of way.

At ten o'clock that night Emily Vansittart and I stood leaning on the starboard railing of the poop, with a full moon shining at our backs, and casting a black shadow of the barque, and of our own two heads, upon the shining water. From the shadow a broadening path of moonshine stretched away to the lonely skyline, flickering and shimmering in the gentle heave of the swell. We were talking with bent heads, chatting of the calm, of the chances of wind, of the look of the sky, when there came a sudden plop, like a rising salmon, and there, in the clear light, John Vansittart sprang out of the water and looked up at us.

I never saw anything clearer in my life than I saw that man. The moon shone full upon him, and he was but three oars' length away. His face was more puffed than when I had seen him last, mottled here and there with dark scabs, his mouth and eyes open as one who is struck with some overpowering surprise. He had some white stuff* streaming from his shoulders, and one hand was raised to his ear, the other crooked across his breast. I saw him leap from the water into the air, and in the dead calm the waves of his coming lapped up against the sides of the vessel. Then his figure sank back into the water again, and I heard a rending, crackling sound like a bundle of brushwood snapping in the fire on a frosty night. There were no signs of him when I looked again, but a swift swirl and eddy on the still sea still marked the spot where he had been. How long I stood there, tingling to my finger-tips, holding up an unconscious woman with one hand, clutching at the rail of the vessel with the other, was more than I could afterwards tell. I had been noted as a man of slow and unresponsive emotions, but this time at least I was shaken to the core. Once and twice I struck my foot upon the deck to be certain that I was indeed the master of my own senses, and that this was not some mad prank of an unruly brain. As I stood, still marvelling, the woman shivered, opened her eyes, gasped, and then standing erect with her hands upon the rail, looked out over the moonlit sea with a face which had aged ten years in a summer night.

'You saw his vision?' she murmured.

'I saw something.'

'It was he! It was John! He is dead!'

I muttered some lame words of doubt.

'Doubtless he died at this hour,' she whispered. 'In hospital at Madeira. I have read of such things. His thoughts were with me. His vision came to me. Oh, my John, my dear, dear, lost John!'

She broke out suddenly into a storm of weeping, and I led her down into her cabin, where I left her with her sorrow. That night a brisk breeze blew up from the east, and in the evening of the next day we passed the two islets of Los Desertos,* and dropped anchor at sundown in the Bay of Funchal. The *Eastern Star* lay no great distance from us, with the quarantine flag flying from her main, and her Jack half-way up her peak.

'You see,' said Mrs Vansittart quickly. She was dry-eyed now, for she had known how it would be.

That night we received permission from the authorities to move on board the *Eastern Star*. The captain, Hines, was waiting upon deck with confusion and grief contending upon his bluff face as he sought for words with which to break this heavy tidings, but she took the story from his lips.

'I know that my husband is dead,' she said. 'He died yesterday night, about ten o'clock, in hospital at Madeira, did he not?'

The seaman stared aghast. 'No, marm, he died eight days ago at sea, and we had to bury him out there, for we lay in a belt of calm, and could not say when we might make the land.'

Well, those are the main facts about the death of John Vansittart, and his appearance to his wife somewhere about lat. 35 N. and long. 15 W.* A clearer case of a wraith has seldom been made out, and since then it has been told as such, and put into print as such, and endorsed by a learned society as such, and so floated off with many others to support the recent theory of telepathy. For myself, I hold telepathy to be proved, but I would snatch this one case from amid the evidence, and say that I do not think that it was the wraith* of John Vansittart, but John Vansittart himself whom we saw that night leaping into the moonlight out of the depths of the Atlantic. It has ever been my belief that some strange chance— one of those chances which seem so improbable and yet so constantly occur—had becalmed us over the very spot where the man had been buried a week before. For the rest, the surgeon tells me that the leaden weight was not too firmly fixed, and that seven days bring about changes which fetch a body to the surface.* Coming from the depth to which the weight would have sunk it, he explains that it might well attain such a velocity as to carry it clear of the water. Such is my own explanation of the matter, and if you ask me what then became of the body, I must recall to you that snapping, crackling sound, with the swirl in the water. The shark is a surface feeder and is plentiful in those parts.

LOT NO. 249

F the dealings of Edward Bellingham with William Monkhouse Lee, and of the cause of the great terror of Abercrombie Smith, it may be that no absolute and final judgment will ever be delivered. It is true that we have the full and clear narrative of Smith himself, and such corroboration as he could look for from Thomas Styles the servant, from the Reverend Plumptree Peterson, Fellow of Old's,* and from such other people as chanced to gain some passing glance at this or that incident in a singular chain of events. Yet, in the main, the story must rest upon Smith alone, and the most will think that it is more likely that one brain, however outwardly sane, has some subtle warp in its texture, some strange flaw in its workings, than that the path of Nature has been overstepped in open day in so famed a centre of learning and light as the University of Oxford. Yet when we think how narrow and how devious this path of Nature is, how dimly we can trace it, for all our lamps of science, and how from the darkness which girds it round great and terrible possibilities loom ever shadowly upwards, it is a bold and confident man who will put a limit to the strange by-paths into which the human spirit may wander.

In a certain wing of what we will call Old College in Oxford there is a corner turret of an exceeding great age. The heavy arch which spans the open door has bent downwards in the centre under the weight of its years, and the grey, lichen-blotched blocks of stone are bound and knitted together with withes and strands of ivy, as though the old mother had set herself to brace them up against wind and weather. From the door a stone stair curves upward spirally, passing two landings, and terminating in a third one, its steps all shapeless and hollowed by the tread of so many generations of the seekers after knowledge. Life has flowed like water down this winding stair, and, waterlike, has left these smooth-worn grooves behind it. From the long-gowned, pedantic scholars of Plantagenet* days down to the young bloods of a later age, how full and strong had been that tide of young, English life. And what was left now of all those hopes, those strivings, those fiery energies, save here and there in some old-world churchyard a few scratches upon a stone, and perchance a handful of dust in a mouldering coffin? Yet here were the silent stair and the grey, old wall, with bend and saltire* and many another heraldic device still to be read upon its surface, like grotesque shadows thrown back from the days that had passed.

In the month of May, in the year 1884, three young men occupied the sets of rooms which opened on to the separate landings of the old stair. Each set consisted simply of a sitting-room and of a bedroom, while the two corresponding rooms upon the ground-floor were used, the one as a coal-cellar, and the other as the living-room of the servant, or scout, Thomas Styles, whose duty it was to wait upon the three men above him. To right and to left was a line of lecture-rooms and of offices, so that the dwellers in the old turret enjoyed a certain seclusion, which made the chambers popular among the more studious undergraduates. Such were the three who occupied them now— Abercrombie Smith above, Edward Bellingham beneath him, and William Monkhouse Lee upon the lowest storey.

It was ten o'clock on a bright, spring night, and Abercrombie Smith lay back in his arm-chair, his feet upon the fender, and his briar-root pipe* between his lips. In a similar chair, and equally at his ease, there lounged on the other side of the fireplace his old school friend Jephro Hastie. Both men were in flannels, for they had spent their evening upon the river, but apart from their dress no one could look at their hard-cut, alert faces without seeing that they were open-air men—men whose minds and tastes turned naturally to all that was manly and robust. Hastie, indeed, was stroke of his college boat, and Smith was an even better oar, but a coming examination had already cast its shadow over him and held him to his work, save for the few hours a week which health demanded. A litter of medical books upon the table, with scattered bones, models, and anatomical plates, pointed to the extent as well as the nature of his studies, while a couple of single-sticks* and a set of boxing-gloves above the mantelpiece hinted at the means by which, with Hastie's help, he might take his exercise in its most compressed and least-distant form. They knew each other very well—so well that they could sit now in that soothing silence which is the very highest development of companionship.

'Have some whisky,' said Abercrombie Smith at last between two cloudbursts. 'Scotch in the jug and Irish in the bottle.'

'No, thanks. I'm in for the sculls.* I don't liquor when I'm training. How about you?'

'I'm reading hard. I think it best to leave it alone.'

Hastie nodded, and they relapsed into a contented silence.

'By the way, Smith,' asked Hastie, presently, 'have you made the acquaintance of either of the fellows on your stair yet?'

'Just a nod when we pass. Nothing more.'

'Hum! I should be inclined to let it stand at that. I know something of them both. Not much, but as much as I want. I don't think I should take them to my bosom if I were you. Not that there's much amiss with Monkhouse Lee.'

'Meaning the thin one?'

'Precisely. He is a gentlemanly little fellow. I don't think there is any vice in him. But then you can't know him without knowing Bellingham.'

'Meaning the fat one?'

'Yes, the fat one. And he's a man whom I, for one, would rather not know.'

Abercrombie Smith raised his eyebrows and glanced across at his companion.

'What's up, then?' he asked. 'Drink? Cards? Cad? You used not to be censorious.'

'Ah! you evidently don't know the man, or you wouldn't ask. There's something damnable about him—something reptilian. My gorge always rises at him. I should put him down as a man with secret vices—an evil liver. He's no fool, though. They say that he is one of the best men in his line that they have ever had in the college.'

'Medicine or classics?'

'Eastern languages. He's a demon at them. Chillingworth met him somewhere above the second cataract last long,* and he told me that he just prattled to the Arabs as if he had been born and nursed and weaned among them. He talked Coptic to the Copts,* and Hebrew to the Jews, and Arabic to the Bedouins, and they were all ready to kiss the hem of his frock-coat. There are some old hermit Johnnies up in those parts who sit on rocks and scowl and spit at the casual stranger. Well, when they saw this chap Bellingham, before he had said five words they just lay down on their bellies and wriggled. Chillingworth said that he never saw anything like it. Bellingham seemed to take it as his right, too, and strutted about among them and talked down to them like a Dutch uncle.* Pretty good for an undergrad. of Old's, wasn't it?'

'Why do you say you can't know Lee without knowing Bellingham?'

'Because Bellingham is engaged to his sister Eveline. Such a bright little girl, Smith! I know the whole family well. It's disgusting to see that brute with her. A toad and a dove, that's what they always remind me of.'

Abercrombie Smith grinned and knocked his ashes out against the side of the grate.

'You show every card in your hand, old chap,' said he. 'What a prejudiced, green-eyed, evil-thinking old man it is! You have really nothing against the fellow except that.'

'Well, I've known her ever since she was as long as that cherry-wood pipe, and I don't like to see her taking risks. And it is a risk. He looks beastly. And he has a beastly temper, a venomous temper. You remember his row with Long Norton?'

'No; you always forget that I am a freshman.'

'Ah, it was last winter. Of course. Well, you know the towpath along by the river. There were several fellows going along it, Bellingham in front, when they came on an old market-woman coming the other way It had been raining—you know what those fields are like when it has rained—and the path ran between the river and a great puddle that was nearly as broad. Well, what does this swine do but keep the path, and push the old girl into the mud, where she and her marketings came to terrible grief. It was a blackguard thing to do, and Long Norton, who is as gentle a fellow as ever stepped, told him what he thought of it. One word led to another, and it ended in Norton laying his stick across the fellow's shoulders. There was the deuce of a fuss about it, and it's a treat to see the way in which Bellingham looks at Norton when they meet now. By Jove, Smith, it's nearly eleven o'clock!'

'No hurry. Light your pipe again.'

'Not I. I'm supposed to be in training. Here I've been sitting gossiping when I ought to have been safely tucked up. I'll borrow your skull, if you can share it. Williams has had mine for a month. I'll take the little bones of your ear, too, if you are sure you won't need them. Thanks very much. Never mind a bag, I can carry them very well under my arm. Good night, my son, and take my tip as to your neighbour.'

When Hastie, bearing his anatomical plunder, had clattered off down the winding stair, Abercrombie Smith hurled his pipe into the wastepaper basket, and drawing his chair nearer to the lamp, plunged into a formidable, green-covered volume, adorned with great, coloured maps of that strange, internal kingdom of which we are the hapless and helpless monarchs. Though a freshman at Oxford, the student was not so in medicine, for he had worked for four years at Glasgow and at Berlin, and this coming examination would place him finally as a member of his profession. With his firm mouth, broad forehead, and clear-cut, somewhat hard-featured face, he was a man who, if he had no brilliant talent, was yet so dogged, so patient, and so strong that he might in the end over-top a more showy genius. A man who can hold his own among Scotchmen and North Germans is not a man to be easily set back. Smith had left a name at Glasgow and at Berlin, and he was bent now upon doing as much at Oxford, if hard work and devotion could accomplish it.

He had sat reading for about an hour, and the hands of the noisy carriage clock upon the side-table were rapidly closing together upon the twelve, when a sudden sound fell upon the student's ear—a sharp, rather shrill sound, like the hissing intake of a man's breath who gasps under some strong emotion. Smith laid down his book and slanted his ear to listen. There was no one on either side or above him, so that the interruption came certainly from the neighbour beneath—the same neighbour of whom Hastie had given so unsavoury an account. Smith knew him only as a flabby, pale-faced man of silent and studious habits, a man whose lamp threw a golden bar from the old turret even after he had extinguished his own. This community in lateness had formed a certain silent bond between them. It was soothing to Smith when the hours stole on towards dawning to feel that there was another so close who set as small a value upon his sleep as he did. Even now, as his thoughts turned towards him, Smith's feelings were kindly. Hastie was a good fellow, but he was rough, strong-fibred, with no imagination or sympathy. He could not tolerate departures from what he looked upon as the model type of manliness. If a man could not be measured by a public-school standard, then he was beyond the pale with Hastie. Like so many who are themselves robust, he was apt to confuse the constitution with the character, to ascribe to want of principle what was really a want of circulation. Smith, with his stronger mind, knew his friend's habit, and made allowance for it now as his thoughts turned towards the man beneath him.

There was no return of the singular sound, and Smith was about to turn to his work once more, when suddenly there broke out in the silence of the night a hoarse cry, a positive scream—the call of a man who is moved and shaken beyond all control. Smith sprang out of his chair and dropped his book. He was a man of fairly firm fibre, but there was something in this sudden, uncontrollable shriek of horror which chilled his blood and pringled* in his skin. Coming in such a place and at such an hour, it brought a thousand fantastic possibilities into his head. Should he rush down, or was it better to wait? He had all the national hatred of making a scene, and he knew so little of his neighbour that he would not lightly intrude upon his affairs. For a moment he stood in doubt and even as he balanced the matter there was a quick rattle of footsteps upon the stairs, and young Monkhouse Lee, half-dressed and as white as ashes, burst into his room.

'Come down!' he gasped. 'Bellingham's ill.'

Abercrombie Smith followed him closely downstairs into the sitting-room which was beneath his own and intent as he was upon the matter in hand, he could not but take an amazed glance around him as he crossed the threshold. It was such a chamber as he had never seen before—a museum rather than a study. Walls and ceiling were thickly covered with a thousand strange relics from Egypt and the East. Tall, angular figures bearing burdens or weapons stalked in an uncouth frieze round the apartments. Above were bull-headed, stork-headed, cat-headed, owl-headed statues,* with viper-crowned, almond-eyed monarchs, and strange, beetle-like deities cut out of the blue Egyptian lapis lazuli.* Horus and Isis and Osiris* peeped down from every niche and shelf, while across the ceiling a true son of Old Nile, a great, hanging-jawed crocodile, was slung in a double noose.

In the centre of this singular chamber was a large, square table, littered with papers, bottles, and the dried leaves of some graceful, palm-like plant. These varied objects had all been heaped together in order to make room for a mummy case, which had been conveyed from the wall, as was evident from the gap there, and laid across the front of the table. The mummy itself, a horrid, black, withered thing, like a charred head on a gnarled bush, was lying half out of the case, with its claw-like hand and bony forearm resting upon the table. Propped up against the sarcophagus was an old, yellow scroll of papyrus, and in front of it, in a wooden arm-chair, sat the owner of the room, his head thrown back, his widely opened eyes directed in a horrified stare to the crocodile above him, and his blue, thick lips puffing loudly with every expiration.

'My God! he's dying!' cried Monkhouse Lee, distractedly.

He was a slim, handsome young fellow, olive-skinned and dark-eyed, of a Spanish rather than of an English type, with a Celtic intensity of manner which contrasted with the Saxon phlegm* of Abercrombie Smith.

'Only a faint, I think,' said the medical student. 'Just give me a hand with him. You take his feet. Now on to the sofa. Can you kick all those little wooden devils off? What a litter it is! Now he will be all right if we undo his collar and give him some water. What has he been up to at all?'

'I don't know. I heard him cry out. I ran up. I know him pretty well, you know. It is very good of you to come down.'

'His heart is going like a pair of castanets,' said Smith, laying his hand on the breast of the unconscious man. 'He seems to me to be frightened all to pieces. Chuck the water over him! What a face he has got on him!'

It was indeed a strange and most repellent face, for colour and outline were equally unnatural. It was white, not with the ordinary pallor of fear, but with an absolutely bloodless white, like the under side of a sole. He was very fat, but gave the impression of having at some time been considerably fatter, for his skin hung loosely in creases and folds, and was shot with a meshwork of wrinkles. Short, stubbly brown hair bristled up from his scalp, with a pair of thick, wrinkled ears protruding at the sides. His light-grey eyes were still open, the pupils dilated and the balls projecting in a fixed and horrid stare. It seemed to Smith as he looked down upon him that he had never seen Nature's danger signals flying so plainly upon a man's countenance, and his thoughts turned more seriously to the warning which Hastie had given him an hour before.

'What the deuce can have frightened him so?' he asked.

'It's the mummy.'

'The mummy? How, then?'

'I don't know. It's beastly and morbid. I wish he would drop it. It's the second fright he has given me. It was the same last winter. I found him just like this, with that horrid thing in front of him.'

'What does he want with the mummy, then?'

'Oh, he's a crank, you know. It's his hobby. He knows more about these things than any man in England. But I wish he wouldn't! Ah, he's beginning to come to.'

A faint tinge of colour had begun to steal back into Bellingham's ghastly cheeks, and his eyelids shivered like a sail after a calm. He clasped and unclasped his hands, drew a long, thin breath between his teeth, and suddenly jerking up his head, threw a glance of recognition around him. As his eyes fell upon the mummy, he sprang off the sofa, seized the roll of papyrus, thrust it into a drawer, turned the key, and then staggered back on to the sofa.

'What's up?' he asked. 'What do you chaps want?'

'You've been shrieking out and making no end of a fuss,' said Monkhouse Lee. 'If our neighbour here from above hadn't come down, I'm sure I don't know what I should have done with you.'

'Ah, it's Abercrombie Smith,' said Bellingham, glancing up at him. 'How very good of you to come in! What a fool I am! Oh, my God, what a fool I am!'

He sank his head on to his hands, and burst into peal after peal of hysterical laughter.

'Look here! Drop it!' cried Smith, shaking him roughly by the shoulder.

'Your nerves are all in a jangle. You must drop these little midnight games with mummies, or you'll be going off your chump. You're all on wires now.'

'I wonder,' said Bellingham, 'whether you would be as cool as I am if you had seen——'

'What then?'

'Oh, nothing. I meant that I wonder if you could sit up at night with a mummy without trying your nerves. I have no doubt that you are quite right. I dare say that I have been taking it out of myself too much lately. But I am all right now. Please don't go, though. Just wait for a few minutes until I am quite myself.'

'The room is very close,' remarked Lee, throwing open the window and letting in the cool night air.

'It's balsamic resin,'* said Bellingham. He lifted up one of the dried palmate leaves from the table and frizzled it over the chimney of the lamp. It broke away into heavy smoke wreaths, and a pungent, biting odour filled the chamber. 'It's the sacred plant—the plant of the priests,' he remarked. 'Do you know anything of Eastern languages, Smith?'

'Nothing at all. Not a word.'

The answer seemed to lift a weight from the Egyptologist's mind.

'By the way,' he continued, 'how long was it from the time that you ran down, until I came to my senses?'

'Not long. Some four or five minutes.'

'I thought it could not be very long,' said he, drawing a long breath. 'But what a strange thing unconsciousness is! There is no measurement to it. I could not tell from my own sensations if it were seconds or weeks. Now that gentleman on the table was packed up in the days of the eleventh dynasty,* some forty centuries ago, and yet if he could find his tongue, he would tell us that this lapse of time has been but a closing of the eyes and a reopening of them. He is a singularly fine mummy, Smith.'

Smith stepped over to the table and looked down with a professional eye at the black and twisted form in front of him. The features, though horribly discoloured, were perfect, and two little nut-like eyes still lurked in the depths of the black, hollow sockets. The blotched skin was drawn tightly from bone to bone, and a tangled wrap of black, coarse hair fell over the ears. Two thin teeth, like those of a rat, overlay the shrivelled lower lip. In its crouching position, with bent joints and craned head, there was a suggestion of energy about the horrid thing which made Smith's gorge rise. The gaunt ribs, with their parchment-like covering, were exposed, and the sunken, leaden-hued abdomen, with the long slit where the embalmer had left his mark;* but the lower limbs were wrapped round with coarse, yellow bandages. A number of little clove-like pieces of myrrh and of cassia* were sprinkled over the body, and lay scattered on the inside of the case.

'I don't know his name,' said Bellingham, passing his hand over the shrivelled head. 'You see the outer sarcophagus with the inscriptions is missing. Lot 249 is all the title he has now. You see it printed on his case. That was his number in the auction at which I picked him up.'

'He has been a very pretty sort of fellow in his day,' remarked Abercrombie Smith.

'He has been a giant. His mummy is six feet seven in length, and that would be a giant over there, for they were never a very robust race. Feel these great, knotted bones, too. He would be a nasty fellow to tackle.'

'Perhaps these very hands helped to build the stones into the pyramids,' suggested Monkhouse Lee, looking down with disgust in his eyes at the crooked, unclean talons.

'No fear. This fellow has been pickled in natron, and looked after in the most approved style. They did not serve hodsmen in that fashion. Salt or bitumen* was enough for them. It has been calculated that this sort of thing cost about seven hundred and thirty pounds in our money. Our friend was a noble at the least. What do you make of that small inscription near his feet, Smith?'

'I told you that I know no Eastern tongue.'

'Ah, so you did. It is the name of the embalmer, I take it. A very conscientious worker he must have been. I wonder how many modern works will survive four thousand years?'

He kept on speaking lightly and rapidly, but it was evident to Abercrombie Smith that he was still palpitating with fear. His hands shook, his lower lip trembled, and look where he would, his eye always came sliding round to his gruesome companion. Through all his fear, however, there was a suspicion of triumph in his tone and manner. His eyes shone, and his footstep, as he paced the room, was brisk and jaunty. He gave the impression of a man who has gone through an ordeal, the marks of which he still bears upon him, but which has helped him to his end.

'You're not going yet?' he cried, as Smith rose from the sofa.

At the prospect of solitude, his fears seemed to crowd back upon him, and he stretched out a hand to detain him.

'Yes, I must go. I have my work to do. You are all right now. I think that with your nervous system you should take up some less morbid study.'

'Oh, I am not nervous as a rule; and I have unwrapped mummies before.'

'You fainted last time,' observed Monkhouse Lee.

'Ah, yes, so I did. Well, I must have a nerve tonic or a course of electricity. You are not going, Lee?'

'I'll do whatever you wish, Ned.'

'Then I'll come down with you and have a shakedown* on your sofa. Good night, Smith. I am so sorry to have disturbed you with my foolishness.'

They shook hands, and as the medical student stumbled up the spiral and irregular stair he heard a key turn in a door, and the steps of his two new acquaintances as they descended to the lower floor.

* * *

In this strange way began the acquaintance between Edward Bellingham and Abercrombie Smith, an acquaintance which the latter, at least, had no desire to push further. Bellingham, however, appeared to have taken a fancy to his rough-spoken neighbour, and made his advances in such a way that he could hardly be repulsed without absolute brutality. Twice he called to thank Smith for his assistance, and many times afterwards he looked in with books, papers and such other civilities as two bachelor neighbours can offer each other. He was, as Smith soon found, a man of wide reading, with catholic tastes and an extraordinary memory. His manner, too, was so pleasing and suave that one came, after a time, to overlook his repellent appearance. For a jaded and wearied man he was no unpleasant companion, and Smith found himself, after a time, looking forward to his visits, and even returning them.

Clever as he undoubtedly was, however, the medical student seemed to detect a dash of insanity in the man. He broke out at times into a high, inflated style of talk which was in contrast with the simplicity of his life.

'It is a wonderful thing,' he cried, 'to feel that one can command powers of good and of evil—a ministering angel or a demon of vengeance.' And again, of Monkhouse Lee, he said,—'Lee is a good fellow, an honest fellow, but he is without strength or ambition. He would not make a fit partner for a man with a great enterprise. He would not make a fit partner for me.'

At such hints and innuendoes stolid Smith, puffing solemnly at his pipe, would simply raise his eyebrow and shake his head, with little interjections of medical wisdom as to earlier hours and fresher air.

One habit Bellingham had developed of late which Smith knew to be a frequent herald of a weakening mind. He appeared to be for ever talking to himself. At late hours of the night, when there could be no visitor with him, Smith could still hear his voice beneath him in a low, muffled monologue, sunk almost to a whisper, and yet very audible in the silence. This solitary babbling annoyed and distracted the student, so that he spoke more than once to his neighbour about it. Bellingham, however, flushed up at the charge, and denied curtly that he had uttered a sound; indeed, he showed more annoyance over the matter than the occasion seemed to demand.

Had Abercrombie Smith had any doubt as to his own ears he had not to go far to find corroboration. Tom Styles, the little wrinkled man-servant who had attended to the wants of the lodgers in the turret for a longer time than any man's memory could carry him, was sorely put to it over the same matter.

'If you please, sir,' said he, as he tidied down the top chamber one morning, 'do you think Mr Bellingham is all right, sir?'

'All right, Styles?'

'Yes sir. Right in his head, sir.'

'Why should he not be, then?'

'Well, I don't know, sir. His habits has changed of late. He's not the same man he used to be, though I make free to say that he was never quite one of my gentlemen, like Mr Hastie or yourself, sir. He's took to talkin' to himself something awful. I wonder it don't disturb you. I don't know what to make of him, sir.'

'I don't know what business it is of yours, Styles.'

'Well, I takes an interest, Mr Smith. It may be forward of me, but I can't help it. I feel sometimes as if I was mother and father to my young gentlemen. It all falls on me when things go wrong and the relations come. But Mr Bellingham, sir. I want to know what it is that walks about his room sometimes when he's out and when the door's locked on the outside.'

'Eh? you're talking nonsense, Styles.'

'Maybe so, sir; but I heard it more'n once with my own ears.'

'Rubbish, Styles.'

'Very good, sir. You'll ring the bell if you want me.'

Abercrombie Smith gave little heed to the gossip of the old man-servant, but a small incident occurred a few days later which left an unpleasant effect upon his mind, and brought the words of Styles forcibly to his memory.

Bellingham had come up to see him late one night, and was entertaining him with an interesting account of the rock tombs of Beni Hassan* in Upper Egypt, when Smith, whose hearing was remarkably acute, distinctly heard the sound of a door opening on the landing below.

'There's some fellow gone in or out of your room,' he remarked.

Bellingham sprang up and stood helpless for a moment, with the expression of a man who is half-incredulous and half-afraid.

'I surely locked it. I am almost positive that I locked it,' he stammered. 'No one could have opened it.'

'Why, I hear someone coming up the steps now,' said Smith.

Bellingham rushed out through the door, slammed it loudly behind him, and hurried down the stairs. About half-way down Smith heard him stop, and thought he caught the sound of whispering. A moment later the door beneath him shut, a key creaked in a lock, and Bellingham, with beads of moisture upon his pale face, ascended the stairs once more, and re-entered the room.

'It's all right,' he said, throwing himself down in a chair. 'It was that fool of a dog. He had pushed the door open. I don't know how I came to forget to lock it.'

'I didn't know you kept a dog,' said Smith, looking very thoughtfully at the disturbed face of his companion.

'Yes, I haven't had him long. I must get rid of him. He's a great nuisance.'

'He must be, if you find it so hard to shut him up. I should have thought that shutting the door would have been enough, without locking it.'

'I want to prevent old Styles from letting him out. He's of some value, you know, and it would be awkward to lose him.'

'I am a bit of a dog-fancier myself,' said Smith, still gazing hard at his companion from the corner of his eyes. 'Perhaps you'll let me have a look at it.'

'Certainly. But I am afraid it cannot be to-night; I have an appointment. Is that clock right? Then I am a quarter of an hour late already. You'll excuse me, I am sure.'

He picked up his cap and hurried from the room. In spite of his appointment, Smith heard him re-enter his own chamber and lock his door upon the inside.

This interview left a disagreeable impression upon the medical student's mind. Bellingham had lied to him, and lied so clumsily that it looked as if he had desperate reasons for concealing the truth. Smith knew that his neighbour had no dog. He knew, also, that the step which he had heard upon the stairs was not the step of an animal. But if it were not, then what could it be? There was old Styles's statement about the something which used to pace the room at times when the owner was absent. Could it be a woman? Smith rather inclined to the view. If so, it would mean disgrace and expulsion to Bellingham if it were discovered by the authorities, so that his anxiety and falsehoods might be accounted for. And yet it was inconceivable that an undergraduate could keep a woman in his rooms without being instantly detected. Be the explanation what it might, there was something ugly about it, and Smith determined, as he turned to his books, to discourage all further attempts at intimacy on the part of his soft-spoken and ill-favoured neighbour.

But his work was destined to interruption that night. He had hardly caught up the broken threads when a firm, heavy footfall came three steps at a time from below, and Hastie, in blazer and flannels, burst into the room

'Still at it!' said he, plumping down into his wonted arm-chair. 'What a chap you are to stew! I believe an earthquake might come and knock Oxford into a cocked hat, and you would sit perfectly placid with your books among the ruins. However, I won't bore you long. Three whiffs of baccy, and I am off.'

'What's the news, then?' asked Smith, cramming a plug of bird's-eye* into his briar with his forefinger.

'Nothing very much. Wilson made 70 for the freshmen against the eleven. They say that they will play him instead of Buddicomb, for Buddicomb is clean off colour. He used to be able to bowl a little, but it's nothing but half-volleys and long hops now.'

'Medium right,' suggested Smith, with the intense gravity which comes upon a 'varsity man when he speaks of athletics.

'Inclining to fast, with a work from leg. Comes with the arm about three inches or so. He used to be nasty on a wet wicket.* Oh, by the way, have you heard about Long Norton?'

'What's that?'

'He's been attacked.'

'Attacked?'

'Yes, just as he was turning out of the High Street,* and within a hundred yards of the gate of Old's.'

'But who——'

'Ah, that's the rub! If you said "what," you would be more grammatical. Norton swears that it was not human, and, indeed, from the scratches on his throat, I should be inclined to agree with him.'

'What, then? Have we come down to spooks?'

Abercrombie Smith puffed his scientific contempt.

'Well no; I don't think that is quite the idea, either. I am inclined to think that if any showman has lost a great ape lately, and the brute is in these parts, a jury would find a true bill* against it. Norton passes that way every night, you know, about the same hour. There's a tree that hangs low over the path—the big elm from Rainy's garden. Norton thinks the thing dropped on him out of the tree. Anyhow, he was nearly strangled by two arms, which, he says, were as strong and as thin as steel bands. He saw nothing; only those beastly arms that tightened and tightened on him. He yelled his head nearly off, and a couple of chaps came running, and the thing went over the wall like a cat. He never got a fair sight of it the whole time. It gave Norton a shake up, I can tell you. I tell him it has been as good as a change at the seaside for him.'

'A garrotter,* most likely,' said Smith.

'Very possibly. Norton says not; but we don't mind what he says. The garrotter had long nails, and was pretty smart at swinging himself over walls. By the way, your beautiful neighbour would be pleased if he heard about it. He had a grudge against Norton, and he's not a man, from what I know of him, to forget his little debts. But hallo, old chap, what have you got in your noddle?'*

'Nothing,' Smith answered curtly.

He had started in his chair, and the look had flashed over his face which comes upon a man who is struck suddenly by some unpleasant idea.

'You looked as if something I had said had taken you on the raw.* By the way, you have made the acquaintance of Master B. since I looked in last, have you not? Young Monkhouse Lee told me something to that effect.'

'Yes; I know him slightly. He has been up here once or twice.'

'Well, you're big enough and ugly enough to take care of yourself. He's not what I should call exactly a healthy sort of Johnny, though, no doubt, he's very clever, and all that. But you'll soon find out for yourself. Lee is all right; he's a very decent little fellow. Well, so long, old chap! I row Mullins for the Vice-Chancellor's pot* on Wednesday week, so mind you come down, in case I don't see you before.'

Bovine Smith laid down his pipe and turned stolidly to his books once more. But with all the will in the world, he found it very hard to keep his mind upon his work. It would slip away to brood upon the man beneath him, and upon the little mystery which hung round his chambers. Then his thoughts turned to this singular attack of which Hastie had spoken, and to the grudge which Bellingham was said to owe the object of it. The two ideas would persist in rising together in his mind, as though there were some close and intimate connection between them. And yet the suspicion was so dim and vague that it could not be put down in words.

'Confound the chap!' cried Smith, as he shied his book on pathology across the room. 'He has spoiled my night's reading, and that's
reason enough, if there were no other, why I should steer clear of him
in the future.'

For ten days the medical student confined himself so closely to his
studies that he neither saw nor heard anything of either of the men
beneath him. At the hours when Bellingham had been accustomed to
visit him, he took care to sport his oak,* and though he more than once
heard a knocking at his outer door, he resolutely refused to answer it.
One afternoon, however, he was descending the stairs when, just as he
was passing it, Bellingham's door flew open, and young Monkhouse
Lee came out with his eyes sparkling and a dark flush of anger upon
his olive cheeks. Close at his heels followed Bellingham, his fat,
unhealthy face all quivering with malignant passion.

'You fool!' he hissed. 'You'll be sorry.'

'Very likely,' cried the other. 'Mind what I say. It's off! I won't hear
of it!'

'You've promised, anyhow.'

'Oh, I'll keep that! I won't speak. But I'd rather little Eva was in her
grave. Once for all, it's off. She'll do what I say. We don't want to see
you again.'

So much Smith could not avoid hearing, but he hurried on, for he
had no wish to be involved in their dispute. There had been a serious
breach between them, that was clear enough, and Lee was going to
cause the engagement with his sister to be broken off. Smith thought of
Hastie's comparison of the toad and the dove, and was glad to think that
the matter was at an end. Bellingham's face when he was in a passion was
not pleasant to look upon. He was not a man to whom an innocent girl
could be trusted for life. As he walked, Smith wondered languidly what
could have caused the quarrel, and what the promise might be which
Bellingham had been so anxious that Monkhouse Lee should keep.

It was the day of the sculling match between Hastie and Mullins,
and a stream of men were making their way down to the banks of the
Isis.* A May sun was shining brightly, and the yellow path was barred
with the black shadows of the tall elm-trees. On either side the grey
colleges lay back from the road, the hoary old mothers of minds looking out from their high, mullioned windows at the tide of young life
which swept so merrily past them. Black-clad tutors, prim officials,
pale, reading men, brown-faced, straw-hatted young athletes in white

sweaters or many-coloured blazers, all were hurrying towards the blue, winding river which curves through the Oxford meadows.

Abercrombie Smith, with the intuition of an old oarsman, chose his position at the point where he knew that the struggle, if there were a struggle, would come. Far off he heard the hum which announced the start, the gathering roar of the approach, the thunder of running feet, and the shouts of the men in the boats beneath him. A spray of half-clad, deep-breathing runners shot past him, and craning over their shoulders, he saw Hastie pulling a steady thirty-six, while his opponent, with a jerky forty,* was a good boat's length behind him. Smith gave a cheer for his friend, and pulling out his watch, was starting off again for his chambers, when he felt a touch upon his shoulder, and found that young Monkhouse Lee was beside him.

'I saw you there,' he said, in a timid, deprecating way. 'I wanted to speak to you, if you could spare me a half-hour. This cottage is mine. I share it with Harrington of King's.* Come in and have a cup of tea.'

'I must be back presently,' said Smith. 'I am hard on the grind at present. But I'll come in for a few minutes with pleasure. I wouldn't have come out only Hastie is a friend of mine.'

'So he is of mine. Hasn't he a beautiful style? Mullins wasn't in it. But come into the cottage. It's a little den of a place, but it is pleasant to work in during the summer months.'

It was a small, square, white building, with green doors and shutters, and a rustic trellis-work porch, standing back some fifty yards from the river's bank. Inside, the main room was roughly fitted up as a study—deal table, unpainted shelves with books, and a few cheap oleographs* upon the wall. A kettle sang upon a spirit-stove, and there were tea things upon a tray on the table.

'Try that chair and have a cigarette,' said Lee. 'Let me pour you out a cup of tea. It's so good of you to come in, for I know that your time is a good deal taken up. I wanted to say to you that, if I were you, I should change my rooms at once.'

'Eh?'

Smith sat staring with a lighted match in one hand and his unlit cigarette in the other.

'Yes; it must seem very extraordinary, and the worst of it is that I cannot give my reasons, for I am under a solemn promise—a very solemn promise. But I may go so far as to say that I don't think

Bellingham is a very safe man to live near. I intend to camp out here as much as I can for a time.'

'Not safe! What do you mean?'

'Ah, that's what I mustn't say. But do take my advice and move your rooms. We had a grand row to-day. You must have heard us, for you came down the stairs.'

'I saw that you had fallen out.'

'He's a horrible chap, Smith. That is the only word for him. I have had doubts about him ever since that night when he fainted—you remember, when you came down. I taxed him to-day, and he told me things that made my hair rise, and wanted me to stand in with him. I'm not straight-laced, but I am a clergyman's son, you know, and I think there are some things which are quite beyond the pale. I only thank God that I found him out before it was too late, for he was to have married into my family.'

'This is all very fine, Lee,' said Abercrombie Smith curtly. 'But either you are saying a great deal too much or a great deal too little.'

'I give you a warning.'

'If there is real reason for warning, no promise can bind you. If I see a rascal about to blow a place up with dynamite no pledge will stand in my way of preventing him.'

'Ah, but I cannot prevent him, and I can do nothing but warn you.'

'Without saying what you warn me against.'

'Against Bellingham.'

'But that is childish. Why should I fear him, or any man?'

'I can't tell you. I can only entreat you to change your rooms. You are in danger where you are. I don't even say that Bellingham would wish to injure you. But it might happen, for he is a dangerous neighbour just now.'

'Perhaps I know more than you think,' said Smith, looking keenly at the young man's boyish, earnest face. 'Suppose I tell you that someone else shares Bellingham's rooms.'

Monkhouse Lee sprang from his chair in uncontrollable excitement.

'You know, then?' he gasped.

'A woman.'

Lee dropped back again with a groan.

'My lips are sealed,' he said. 'I must not speak.'

'Well, anyhow,' said Smith, rising, 'it is not likely that I should allow myself to be frightened out of rooms which suit me very nicely. It would be a little too feeble for me to move out all my goods and chattels because you say that Bellingham might in some unexplained way do me an injury. I think that I'll just take my chance, and stay where I am, and as I see that it's nearly five o'clock, I must ask you to excuse me.'

He bade the young student adieu in a few curt words, and made his way homeward through the sweet spring evening, feeling half-ruffled, half-amused, as any other strong, unimaginative man might who has been menaced by a vague and shadowy danger.

There was one little indulgence which Abercrombie Smith always allowed himself, however closely his work might press upon him. Twice a week, on the Tuesday and the Friday, it was his invariable custom to walk over to Farlingford, the residence of Doctor Plumptree Peterson, situated about a mile and a half out of Oxford. Peterson had been a close friend of Smith's elder brother, Francis, and as he was a bachelor, fairly well-to-do, with a good cellar and a better library, his house was a pleasant goal for a man who was in need of a brisk walk. Twice a week, then, the medical student would swing out there along the dark country roads and spend a pleasant hour in Peterson's comfortable study, discussing, over a glass of old port, the gossip of the 'varsity or the latest developments of medicine or of surgery.

On the day which followed his interview with Monkhouse Lee, Smith shut up his books at a quarter past eight, the hour when he usually started for his friend's house. As he was leaving his room, however, his eyes chanced to fall upon one of the books which Bellingham had lent him, and his conscience pricked him for not having returned it. However repellent the man might be, he should not be treated with discourtesy. Taking the book, he walked downstairs and knocked at his neighbour's door. There was no answer; but on turning the handle he found that it was unlocked. Pleased at the thought of avoiding an interview, he stepped inside, and placed the book with his card upon the table.

The lamp was turned half down, but Smith could see the details of the room plainly enough. It was all much as he had seen it before—the frieze, the animal-headed gods, the hanging crocodile, and the table littered over with papers and dried leaves. The mummy case stood upright against the wall, but the mummy itself was missing. There was no sign of any second occupant of the room, and he felt as he withdrew that he had probably done Bellingham an injustice. Had he a guilty secret to preserve, he would hardly leave his door open so that all the world might enter.

The spiral stair was as black as pitch, and Smith was slowly making his way down its irregular steps, when he was suddenly conscious that something had passed him in the darkness. There was a faint sound, a whiff of air, a light brushing past his elbow, but so slight that he could scarcely be certain of it. He stopped and listened, but the wind was rustling among the ivy outside, and he could hear nothing else.

'Is that you, Styles?' he shouted.

There was no answer, and all was still behind him. It must have been a sudden gust of air, for there were crannies and cracks in the old turret. And yet he could almost have sworn that he heard a footfall by his very side. He had emerged into the quadrangle, still turning the matter over in his head, when a man came running swiftly across the smooth cropped lawn.

'Is that you, Smith?'

'Hullo, Hastie!'

'For God's sake come at once! Young Lee is drowned! Here's Harrington of King's with the news. The doctor is out. You'll do, but come along at once. There may be life in him.'

'Have you brandy?'

'No.'

'I'll bring some. There's a flask on my table.'

Smith bounded up the stairs, taking three at a time, seized the flask, and was rushing down with it, when, as he passed Bellingham's room, his eyes fell upon something which left him gasping and staring upon the landing.

The door, which he had closed behind him, was now open, and right in front of him, with the lamp-light shining upon it, was the mummy case. Three minutes ago it had been empty. He could swear to that. Now it framed the lank body of its horrible occupant, who stood, grim and stark, with his black, shrivelled face towards the door. The form was lifeless and inert, but it seemed to Smith as he gazed that there still lingered a lurid spark of vitality, some faint sign of consciousness in the little eyes which lurked in the depths of the hollow sockets. So astounded and shaken was he that he had forgotten his errand, and was still staring at the lean, sunken figure when the voice of his friend below recalled him to himself.

'Come on, Smith!' he shouted. 'It's life and death, you know. Hurry up! Now, then,' he added, as the medical student reappeared, 'let us do a sprint. It is well under a mile, and we should do it in five minutes. A human life is better worth running for than a pot.'

Neck and neck they dashed through the darkness, and did not pull up until panting and spent, they had reached the little cottage by the river. Young Lee, limp and dripping like a broken water-plant, was stretched upon the sofa, the green scum of the river upon his black hair, and a fringe of white foam upon his leaden-hued lips. Beside him knelt his fellow-student, Harrington, endeavouring to chafe some warmth back into his rigid limbs.

'I think there's life in him,' said Smith, with his hand to the lad's side. 'Put your watch glass to his lips. Yes, there's dimming on it. You take one arm, Hastie. Now work it as I do, and we'll soon pull him round.'

For ten minutes they worked in silence, inflating and depressing the chest of the unconscious man. At the end of that time a shiver ran through his body, his lips trembled, and he opened his eyes. The three students burst out into an irrepressible cheer.

'Wake up, old chap. You've frightened us quite enough.'

'Have some brandy. Take a sip from the flask.'

'He's all right now,' said his companion Harrington. 'Heavens, what a fright I got! I was reading here, and he had gone out for a stroll as far as the river, when I heard a scream and a splash. Out I ran, and by the time I could find him and fish him out, all life seemed to have gone. Then Simpson couldn't get a doctor, for he has a game-leg, and I had to run, and I don't know what I'd have done without you fellows. That's right, old chap. Sit up.'

Monkhouse Lee had raised himself on his hands, and looked wildly about him.

'What's up?' he asked. 'I've been in the water. Ah, yes; I remember.'

A look of fear came into his eyes, and he sank his face into his hands.

'How did you fall in?'

'I didn't fall in.'

'How then?'

'I was thrown in. I was standing by the bank, and something from behind picked me up like a feather and hurled me in. I heard nothing, and I saw nothing. But I know what it was, for all that.'

'And so do I,' whispered Smith.

Lee looked up with a quick glance of surprise.

'You've learned, then?' he said. 'You remember the advice I gave you?'

'Yes, and I begin to think that I shall take it.'

'I don't know what the deuce you fellows are talking about,' said Hastie, 'but I think, if I were you, Harrington, I should get Lee to bed at once. It will be time enough to discuss the why and the wherefore when he is a little stronger. I think, Smith, you and I can leave him alone now. I am walking back to college; if you are coming in that direction, we can have a chat.'

But it was little chat that they had upon their homeward path. Smith's mind was too full of the incidents of the evening, the absence of the mummy from his neighbour's rooms, the step that passed him on the stair, the reappearance— the extraordinary, inexplicable reappearance of the grisly thing—and then this attack upon Lee, corresponding so closely to the previous outrage upon another man against whom Bellingham bore a grudge. All this settled in his thoughts, together with the many little incidents which had previously turned him against his neighbour, and the singular circumstances under which he was first called in to him. What had been a dim suspicion, a vague, fantastic conjecture, had suddenly taken form, and stood out in his mind as a grim fact, a thing not to be denied. And yet, how monstrous it was! how unheard of! how entirely beyond all bounds of human experience. An impartial judge, or even the friend who walked by his side, would simply tell him that his eyes had deceived him, that the mummy had been there all the time, that young Lee had tumbled into the river as any other man tumbles into a river, and the blue pill was the best thing for a disordered liver.* He felt that he would have said as much if the positions had been reversed. And yet he could swear that Bellingham was a murderer at heart, and that he wielded a weapon such as no man had ever used in all the grim history of crime.

Hastie had branched off to his rooms with a few crisp and emphatic comments upon his friend's unsociability, and Abercrombie Smith crossed the quadrangle to his corner turret with a strong feeling of repulsion for his chambers and their associations. He would take Lee's advice, and move his quarters as soon as possible, for how could a man study when his ear was ever straining for every murmur or footstep in the room below? He observed, as he crossed over the lawn, that the light was still shining in Bellingham's window, and as he passed up the staircase the door opened, and the man himself looked out at him. With his fat, evil face he was like some bloated spider fresh from the weaving of his poisonous web.

'Good evening,' said he. 'Won't you come in?'

'No,' cried Smith fiercely.

'No? You are as busy as ever? I wanted to ask you about Lee. I was sorry to hear that there was a rumour that something was amiss with him.'

His features were grave, but there was the gleam of a hidden laugh in his eyes as he spoke. Smith saw it, and he could have knocked him down for it.

'You'll be sorrier still to hear that Monkhouse Lee is doing very well, and is out of all danger,' he answered. 'Your hellish tricks have not come off this time. Oh, you needn't try to brazen it out. I know all about it.'

Bellingham took a step back from the angry student, and half-closed the door as if to protect himself.

'You are mad,' he said. 'What do you mean? Do you assert that I had anything to do with Lee's accident?'

'Yes,' thundered Smith. 'You and that bag of bones behind you; you worked it between you. I tell you what it is, Master B., they have given up burning folk like you, but we still keep a hangman, and, by George! if any man in this college meets his death while you are here, I'll have you up, and if you don't swing for it, it won't be my fault. You'll find that your filthy Egyptian tricks won't answer in England.'

'You're a raving lunatic,' said Bellingham.

'All right. You just remember what I say, for you'll find that I'll be better than my word.'

The door slammed, and Smith went fuming up to his chamber, where he locked the door upon the inside, and spent half the night in smoking his old briar and brooding over the strange events of the evening.

Next morning Abercrombie Smith heard nothing of his neighbour, but Harrington called upon him in the afternoon to say that Lee was almost himself again. All day Smith stuck fast to his work, but in the evening he determined to pay the visit to his friend Doctor Peterson upon which he had started the night before. A good walk and a friendly chat would be welcome to his jangled nerves.

Bellingham's door was shut as he passed, but glancing back when he was some distance from the turret, he saw his neighbour's head at the window outlined against the lamp-light, his face pressed apparently against the glass as he gazed out into the darkness. It was a blessing to be away from all contact with him, if but for a few hours, and Smith stepped out briskly, and breathed the soft spring air into his lungs. The half-moon lay in the west between two Gothic pinnacles, and threw upon the silvered street a dark tracery from the stonework above. There was a brisk breeze, and light, fleecy clouds drifted swiftly across the sky. Old's was on the very border of the town, and in five minutes Smith found himself beyond the houses and between the hedges of a May-scented, Oxfordshire lane.

It was a lonely and little-frequented road which led to his friend's house. Early as it was, Smith did not meet a single soul upon his way. He walked briskly along until he came to the avenue gate, which opened into the long, gravel drive leading up to Farlingford. In front of him he could see the cosy, red light of the windows glimmering through the foliage. He stood with his hand upon the iron latch of the swinging gate, and he glanced back at the road along which he had come. Something was coming swiftly down it.

It moved in the shadow of the hedge, silently and furtively, a dark, crouching figure, dimly visible against the black background. Even as he gazed back at it, it had lessened its distance by twenty paces, and was fast closing upon him. Out of the darkness he had a glimpse of a scraggy neck, and of two eyes that will ever haunt him in his dreams. He turned, and with a cry of terror he ran for his life up the avenue. There were the red lights, the signals of safety, almost within a stone's-throw of him. He was a famous runner, but never had he run as he ran that night.

The heavy gate had swung into place behind him but he heard it dash open again before his pursuer. As he rushed madly and wildly through the night, he could hear a swift, dry patter behind him, and could see, as he threw back a glance, that this horror was bounding like a tiger at his heels, with blazing eyes and one stringy arm outthrown. Thank God, the door was ajar. He could see the thin bar of light which shot from the lamp in the hall. Nearer yet sounded the clatter from behind. He heard a hoarse gurgling at his very shoulder. With a shriek he flung himself against the door, slammed and bolted it behind him, and sank half-fainting on to the hall chair.

'My goodness, Smith, what's the matter?' asked Peterson, appearing at the door of his study.

'Give me some brandy.'

Peterson disappeared, and came rushing out again with a glass and a decanter.

'You need it,' he said, as his visitor drank off what he poured out for him. 'Why, man, you are as white as a cheese.'

Smith laid down his glass, rose up, and took a deep breath.

'I am my own man again now,' said he. 'I was never so unmanned before. But, with your leave, Peterson, I will sleep here to-night, for I don't think I could face that road again except by daylight. It's weak, I know, but I can't help it.'

Peterson looked at his visitor with a very questioning eye.

'Of course you shall sleep here if you wish. I'll tell Mrs Burney to make up the spare bed. Where are you off to now?'

'Come up with me to the window that overlooks the door. I want you to see what I have seen.'

They went up to the window of the upper hall whence they could look down upon the approach to the house. The drive and the fields on either side lay quiet and still, bathed in the peaceful moonlight.

'Well, really, Smith,' remarked Peterson, 'it is well that I know you to be an abstemious man. What in the world can have frightened you?'

'I'll tell you presently. But where can it have gone? Ah, now, look, look! See the curve of the road just beyond your gate.'

'Yes, I see; you needn't pinch my arm off. I saw someone pass. I should say a man, rather thin, apparently, and tall, very tall. But what of him? And what of yourself? You are still shaking like an aspen leaf.'

'I have been within hand-grip of the devil, that's all. But come down to your study, and I shall tell you the whole story.'

He did so. Under the cheery lamp-light with a glass of wine on the table beside him, and the portly form and florid face of his friend in front, he narrated, in their order, all the events, great and small, which had formed so singular a chain, from the night on which he had found Bellingham fainting in front of the mummy case until this horrid experience of an hour ago.

'There now,' he said as he concluded, 'that's the whole, black business. It is monstrous and incredible, but it is true.'

Doctor Plumptree Peterson sat for some time in silence with a very puzzled expression upon his face.

'I never heard of such a thing in my life, never!' he said at last. 'You have told me the facts. Now tell me your inferences.'

'You can draw your own.'

'But I should like to hear yours. You have thought over the matter, and I have not.'

'Well, it must be a little vague in detail, but the main points seem to me to be clear enough. This fellow Bellingham, in his Eastern studies, has got hold of some infernal secret by which a mummy—or possibly only this particular mummy—can be temporarily brought to life. He was trying this disgusting business on the night when he fainted. No doubt the sight of the creature moving had shaken his nerve, even though he had expected it. You remember that almost the first words he said were to call out upon himself as a fool. Well, he got more hard-ened afterwards, and carried the matter through without fainting. The vitality which he could put into it was evidently only a passing thing, for I have seen it continually in its case as dead as this table. He has some elaborate process, I fancy, by which he brings the thing to pass. Having done it, he naturally bethought him that he might use the creature as an agent. It has intelligence and it has strength. For some purpose he took Lee into his confidence; but Lee, like a decent Christian, would have nothing to do with such a business. Then they had a row, and Lee vowed that he would tell his sister of Bellingham's true character. Bellingham's game was to prevent him, and he nearly managed it, by setting this creature of his on his track. He had already tried its powers upon another man—Norton—towards whom he had a grudge. It is the merest chance that he has not two murders upon his soul. Then, when I taxed him with the matter, he had the strongest reasons for wishing to get me out of the way before I could convey my knowledge to anyone else. He got his chance when I went out, for he knew my habits and where I was bound for. I have had a narrow shave, Peterson, and it is mere luck you didn't find me on your doorstep in the morning. I'm not a nervous man as a rule, and I never thought to have the fear of death put upon me as it was to-night.'

'My dear boy, you take the matter too seriously,' said his compan-ion. 'Your nerves are out of order with your work, and you make too much of it. How could such a thing as this stride about the streets of Oxford, even at night, without being seen?'

'It has been seen. There is quite a scare in the town about an escaped ape, as they imagine the creature to be. It is the talk of the place.'

'Well, it's a striking chain of events. And yet, my dear fellow, you must allow that each incident in itself is capable of a more natural explanation.'

'What! even my adventure of to-night?'

'Certainly. You come out with your nerves all unstrung, and your head full of this theory of yours. Some gaunt, half-famished tramp steals after you, and seeing you run, is emboldened to pursue you. Your fears and imagination do the rest.'

'It won't do, Peterson; it won't do.'

'And again, in the instance of your finding the mummy case empty, and then a few moments later with an occupant, you know that it was lamp-light, that the lamp was half turned down, and that you had no special reason to look hard at the case. It is quite possible that you may have overlooked the creature in the first instance.'

'No, no; it is out of the question.'

'And then Lee may have fallen into the river, and Norton been garrotted. It is certainly a formidable indictment that you have against Bellingham; but if you were to place it before a police magistrate, he would simply laugh in your face.'

'I know he would. That is why I mean to take the matter into my own hands.'

'Eh?'

'Yes; I feel that a public duty rests upon me, and, besides, I must do it for my own safety, unless I choose to allow myself to be hunted by this beast out of the college, and that would be a little too feeble. I have quite made up my mind what I shall do. And first of all, may I use your paper and pens for an hour?'

'Most certainly. You will find all that you want upon that side-table.'

Abercrombie Smith sat down before a sheet of foolscap, and for an hour, and then for a second hour his pen travelled swiftly over it. Page after page was finished and tossed aside while his friend leaned back in his arm-chair, looking across at him with patient curiosity. At last with an exclamation of satisfaction, Smith sprang to his feet, gathered his papers up into order, and laid the last one upon Peterson's desk.

'Kindly sign this as a witness,' he said.

'A witness? Of what?'

'Of my signature, and of the date. The date is the most important. Why, Peterson, my life might hang upon it.'

'My dear Smith, you are talking wildly. Let me beg you to go to bed.'

'On the contrary, I never spoke so deliberately in my life. And I will promise to go to bed the moment you have signed it.'

'But what is it?'

'It is a statement of all that I have been telling you to-night. I wish you to witness it.'

'Certainly,' said Peterson, signing his name under that of his companion. 'There you are! But what is the idea?'

'You will kindly retain it, and produce it in case I am arrested.'

'Arrested? For what?'

'For murder. It is quite on the cards. I wish to be ready for every event. There is only one course open to me, and I am determined to take it.'

'For Heaven's sake, don't do anything rash!'

'Believe me, it would be far more rash to adopt any other course. I hope that we won't need to bother you, but it will ease my mind to know that you have this statement of my motives. And now I am ready to take your advice and to go to roost, for I want to be at my best in the morning.'

✢　✢　✢

Abercrombie Smith was not an entirely pleasant man to have as an enemy. Slow and easy-tempered, he was formidable when driven to action. He brought to every purpose in life the same deliberate resoluteness which had distinguished him as a scientific student. He had laid his studies aside for a day, but he intended that the day should not be wasted. Not a word did he say to his host as to his plans, but by nine o'clock he was well on his way to Oxford.

In the High Street he stopped at Clifford's, the gun-maker's, and bought a heavy revolver, with a box of central-fire cartridges.* Six of them he slipped into the chambers, and half-cocking the weapon, placed it in the pocket of his coat. He then made his way to Hastie's rooms, where the big oarsman was lounging over his breakfast, with the *Sporting Times** propped up against the coffee-pot.

'Hullo! What's up?' he asked. 'Have some coffee?'

'No, thank you. I want you to come with me, Hastie, and do what I ask you.'

'Certainly, my boy.'

'And bring a heavy stick with you.'

'Hullo!' Hastie stared. 'Here's a hunting crop that would fell an ox.'

'One other thing. You have a box of amputating knives. Give me the longest of them.'

'There you are. You seem to be fairly on the war trail. Anything else?'

'No; that will do.' Smith placed the knife inside his coat, and led the way to the quadrangle. 'We are neither of us chickens, Hastie,' said he. 'I think I can do this job alone, but I take you as a precaution. I am going to have a little talk with Bellingham. If I have only him to deal with, I won't, of course, need you. If I shout, however, up you come, and lam out with your whip as hard as you can lick. Do you understand?'

'All right. I'll come if I hear you bellow.'

'Stay here, then. I may be a little time, but don't budge until I come down.'

'I'm a fixture.'

Smith ascended the stairs, opened Bellingham's door and stepped in. Bellingham was seated behind his table, writing. Beside him, among his litter of strange possessions, towered the mummy case, with its sale number 249 still stuck upon its front, and its hideous occupant stiff and stark within it. Smith looked very deliberately round him, closed the door, and then, stepping across to the fireplace, struck a match and set the fire alight. Bellingham sat staring, with amazement and rage upon his bloated face.

'Well, really now, you make yourself at home,' he gasped.

Smith sat himself deliberately down, placing his watch upon the table, drew out his pistol, cocked it, and laid it in his lap. Then he took the long amputating knife from his bosom, and threw it down in front of Bellingham.

'Now, then,' said he, 'just get to work and cut up that mummy.'

'Oh, is that it?' said Bellingham with a sneer.

'Yes, that is it. They tell me that the law can't touch you. But I have a law that will set matters straight. If in five minutes you have not set to work, I swear by the God who made me that I will put a bullet through your brain!'

'You would murder me?'

Bellingham had half-risen, and his face was the colour of putty.

'Yes.'

'And for what?'

'To stop your mischief. One minute has gone.'

'But what have I done?'

'I know and you know.'

'This is mere bullying.'

'Two minutes are gone.'

'But you must give reasons. You are a madman—a dangerous madman. Why should I destroy my own property? It is a valuable mummy.'

'You must cut it up, and you must burn it.

'I will do no such thing.'

'Four minutes are gone.'

Smith took up the pistol and he looked towards Bellingham with an inexorable face. As the second-hand stole round, he raised his hand, and the finger twitched upon the trigger.

'There! there! I'll do it!' screamed Bellingham.

In frantic haste he caught up the knife and hacked at the figure of the mummy, ever glancing round to see the eye and the weapon of his terrible visitor bent upon him. The creature crackled and snapped under every stab of the keen blade. A thick, yellow dust rose up from it. Spices and dried essences rained down upon the floor. Suddenly, with a rending crack, its backbone snapped asunder, and it fell, a brown heap of sprawling limbs, upon the floor.

'Now into the fire!' said Smith.

The flames leaped and roared as the dried and tinder-like debris was piled upon it. The little room was like the stoke-hole of a steamer* and the sweat ran down the faces of the two men; but still the one stooped and worked, while the other sat watching him with a set face. A thick, fat smoke oozed out from the fire, and a heavy smell of burned resin and singed hair filled the air. In a quarter of an hour a few charred and brittle sticks were all that was left of Lot No. 249.

'Perhaps that will satisfy you,' snarled Bellingham, with hate and fear in his little grey eyes as he glanced back at his tormentor.

'No; I must make a clean sweep of all your materials. We must have no more devil's tricks. In with all these leaves! They may have something to do with it.'

'And what now?' asked Bellingham, when the leaves also had been added to the blaze.

'Now the roll of papyrus which you had on the table that night. It is in that drawer, I think.'

'No, no,' shouted Bellingham. 'Don't burn that! Why, man, you don't know what you do. It is unique; it contains wisdom which is nowhere else to be found.'

'Out with it!'

'But look here, Smith, you can't really mean it. I'll share the knowledge with you. I'll teach you all that is in it. Or, stay, let me only copy it before you burn it!'

Smith stepped forward and turned the key in the drawer. Taking out the yellow, curled roll of paper, he threw it into the fire, and pressed it down with his heel. Bellingham screamed, and grabbed at it; but Smith pushed him back and stood over it until it was reduced to a formless, grey ash.

'Now, Master B.,' said he, 'I think I have pretty well drawn your teeth. You'll hear from me again, if you return to your old tricks. And now good morning, for I must go back to my studies.'

And such is the narrative of Abercrombie Smith as to the singular events which occurred in Old College, Oxford, in the spring of '84. As Bellingham left the university immediately afterwards, and was last heard of in the Soudan,* there is no one who can contradict his statement. But the wisdom of men is small, and the ways of Nature are strange, and who shall put a bound to the dark things which may be found by those who seek for them?

THE LOS AMIGOS FIASCO

I USED to be the leading practitioner of Los Amigos. Of course,
every one has heard of the great electrical generating gear there.
The town is widespread, and there are dozens of little townlets and
villages all around, which receive their supply from the same centre,
so that the works are on a very large scale. The Los Amigos folk say
that they are the largest upon earth, but then we claim that for
everything in Los Amigos except the gaol and the death-rate. Those
are said to be the smallest.

Now, with so fine an electrical supply, it seemed to be a sinful waste
of hemp that the Los Amigos criminals should perish in the old-
fashioned manner. And then came the news of the electrocutions in
the East,* and how the results had not after all been so instantaneous
as had been hoped. The Western engineers raised their eyebrows
when they read of the puny shocks by which these men had perished,
and they vowed in Los Amigos that when an irreclaimable* came their
way he should be dealt handsomely by, and have the run of, all the big
dynamos. There should be no reserve, said the engineers, but he
should have all that they had got. And what the result of that would
be none could predict, save that it must be absolutely blasting and
deadly. Never before had a man been so charged with electricity as
they would charge him. He was to be smitten by the essence of ten
thunderbolts. Some prophesied combustion, and some disintegration
and disappearance. They were waiting eagerly to settle the question
by actual demonstration, and it was just at that moment that Duncan
Warner came that way.

Warner had been wanted by the law, and by nobody else, for many
years. Desperado, murderer, train robber and road agent, he was
a man beyond the pale of human pity. He had deserved a dozen deaths,
and the Los Amigos folk grudged him so gaudy a one as that. He
seemed to feel himself to be unworthy of it, for he made two frenzied
attempts at escape. He was a powerful, muscular man, with a lion
head, tangled black locks, and a sweeping beard which covered his
broad chest. When he was tried, there was no finer head in all the
crowded court. It's no new thing to find the best face looking from the

dock. But his good looks could not balance his bad deeds. His advocate did all he knew, but the cards lay against him, and Duncan Warner was handed over to the mercy of the big Los Amigos dynamos.

I was there at the committee meeting when the matter was discussed. The town council had chosen four experts to look after the arrangements. Three of them were admirable. There was Joseph M'Connor, the very man who had designed the dynamos, and there was Joshua Westmacott, the chairman of the Los Amigos Electrical Supply Company, Limited. Then there was myself as the chief medical man, and lastly an old German of the name of Peter Stulpnagel. The Germans were a strong body at Los Amigos, and they all voted for their man. That was how he got on the committee. It was said that he had been a wonderful electrician at home, and he was eternally working with wires and insulators and Leyden jars;* but, as he never seemed to get any further, or to have any results worth publishing, he came at last to be regarded as a harmless crank, who had made science his hobby. We three practical men smiled when we heard that he had been elected as our colleague, and at the meeting we fixed it all up very nicely among ourselves without much thought of the old fellow who sat with his ears scooped forward in his hands, for he was a trifle hard of hearing, taking no more part in the proceedings than the gentlemen of the press who scribbled their notes on the back benches.

We did not take long to settle it all. In New York a strength of some two thousand volts had been used, and death had not been instantaneous.* Evidently their shock had been too weak. Los Amigos should not fall into that error. The charge should be six times greater, and therefore, of course, it would be six times more effective. Nothing could possibly be more logical. The whole concentrated force of the great dynamos should be employed on Duncan Warner.

So we three settled it, and had already risen to break up the meeting, when our silent companion opened his mouth for the first time.

'Gentlemen,' said he, 'you appear to me to show an extraordinary ignorance upon the subject of electricity. You have not mastered the first principles of its actions upon a human being.'

The committee was about to break into an angry reply to this brusque comment, but the chairman of the Electrical Company tapped his forehead to claim its indulgence for the crankiness of the speaker.

'Pray tell us, sir,' said he, with an ironical smile, 'what is there in our conclusions with which you find fault?'

'With your assumption that a large dose of electricity will merely increase the effect of a small dose. Do you not think it possible that it might have an entirely different result? Do you know anything, by actual experiment, of the effect of such powerful shocks?'

'We know it by analogy,' said the chairman pompously. 'All drugs increase their effect when they increase their dose; for example—for example——'

'Whisky,' said Joseph M'Connor.

'Quite so. Whisky. You see it there.'

Peter Stulpnagel smiled and shook his head.

'Your argument is not very good,' said he. 'When I used to take whisky, I used to find that one glass would excite me, but that six would send me to sleep, which is just the opposite. Now, suppose that electricity were to act in just the opposite way also, what then?'

We three practical men burst out laughing. We had known that our colleague was queer, but we never had thought that he would be as queer as this.

'What then?' repeated Peter Stulpnagel.

'We'll take our chances,' said the chairman.

'Pray consider,' said Peter, 'that workmen who have touched the wires, and who have received shocks of only a few hundred volts, have died instantly. The fact is well known. And yet when a much greater force was used upon a criminal at New York, the man struggled for some little time. Do you not clearly see that the smaller dose is the more deadly?'

'I think, gentlemen, that this discussion has been carried on quite long enough,' said the chairman, rising again. 'The point, I take it, has already been decided by the majority of the committee, and Duncan Warner shall be electrocuted on Tuesday by the full strength of the Los Amigos dynamos. Is it not so?'

'I agree,' said Joseph M'Connor.

'I agree,' said I.

'And I protest,' said Peter Stulpnagel.

'Then the motion is carried, and your protest will be duly entered in the minutes,' said the chairman, and so the sitting was dissolved.

The attendance at the electrocution was a very small one. We four members of the committee were, of course, present with the executioner, who was to act under their orders. The others were the United States Marshal, the governor of the gaol, the chaplain, and three members of the press. The room was a small, brick chamber, forming an out-house to the Central Electrical station. It had been used as a laundry, and had an oven and copper* at one side, but no other furniture save a single chair for the condemned man. A metal plate for his feet was placed in front of it, to which ran a thick, insulated wire. Above, another wire depended from the ceiling, which could be connected with a small, metallic rod projecting from a cap which was to be placed upon his head. When this connection was established Duncan Warner's hour was come.

There was a solemn hush as we waited for the coming of the prisoner. The practical engineers looked a little pale, and fidgeted nervously with the wires. Even the hardened Marshal was ill at ease, for a mere hanging was one thing, and this blasting of flesh and blood a very different one. As to the pressmen, their faces were whiter than the sheets which lay before them. The only man who appeared to feel none of the influence of these preparations was the little German crank, who strolled from one to the other with a smile on his lips and mischief in his eyes. More than once he even went so far as to burst into a shout of laughter, until the chaplain sternly rebuked him for his ill-timed levity.

'How can you so far forget yourself, Mr Stulpnagel,' said he, 'as to jest in the presence of death?'

But the German was quite unabashed.

'If I were in the presence of death I should not jest,' said he, 'but since I am not I may do what I choose.'

This flippant reply was about to draw another and a sterner reproof from the chaplain, when the door was swung open and two warders entered leading Duncan Warner between them. He glanced round him with a set face, stepped resolutely forward, and seated himself upon the chair.

'Touch her off!' said he.

It was barbarous to keep him in suspense. The chaplain murmured a few words in his ear, the attendant placed the cap upon his head, and then, while we all held our breath, the wire and the metal were brought in contact.

'Great Scott!' shouted Duncan Warner.

He had bounded in his chair as the frightful shock crashed through his system. But he was not dead. On the contrary, his eyes gleamed far more brightly than they had done before. There was only one change, but it was a singular one. The black had passed from his hair and beard as the shadow passes from a landscape. They were both as white as snow. And yet there was no other sign of decay. His skin was smooth and plump and lustrous as a child's.

The Marshal looked at the committee with a reproachful eye.

'There seems to be some hitch here, gentlemen,' said he.

We three practical men looked at each other.

Peter Stulpnagel smiled pensively.

'I think that another one should do it,' said I.

Again the connection was made, and again Duncan Warner sprang in his chair and shouted, but, indeed, were it not that he still remained in the chair none of us would have recognised him. His hair and his beard had shredded off in an instant, and the room looked like a barber's shop on a Saturday night. There he sat, his eyes still shining, his skin radiant with the glow of perfect health, but with a scalp as bald as a Dutch cheese, and a chin without so much as a trace of down. He began to revolve one of his arms, slowly and doubtfully at first, but with more confidence as he went on.

'That jint,'* said he, 'has puzzled half the doctors on the Pacific Slope.* It's as good as new, and as limber as a hickory twig.'

'You are feeling pretty well?' asked the old German.

'Never better in my life,' said Duncan Warner cheerily.

The situation was a painful one. The Marshal glared at the committee. Peter Stulpnagel grinned and rubbed his hands. The engineers scratched their heads. The bald-headed prisoner revolved his arm and looked pleased.

'I think that one more shock——' began the chairman.

'No sir,' said the Marshal; 'we've had foolery enough for one morning. We are here for an execution, and an execution we'll have.'

'What do you propose?'

'There's a hook handy upon the ceiling. Fetch a rope, and we'll soon set this matter straight.'

There was another awkward delay while the warders departed for the cord. Peter Stulpnagel bent over Duncan Warner, and whispered something in his ear. The desperado stared in surprise.

'You don't say?' he asked.

The German nodded.

'What! No ways?'

Peter shook his head, and the two began to laugh as though they shared some huge joke between them.

The rope was brought, and the Marshal himself slipped the noose over the criminal's neck. Then the two warders, the assistant and he swung their victim into the air. For half an hour he hung—a dreadful sight—from the ceiling. Then in solemn silence they lowered him down, and one of the warders went out to order the shell to be brought round. But as he touched ground again what was our amazement when Duncan Warner put his hands up to his neck, loosened the noose, and took a long, deep breath.

'Paul Jefferson's sale is goin' well,' he remarked. 'I could see the crowd from up yonder,' and he nodded at the hook in the ceiling.

'Up with him again!' shouted the Marshal, 'we'll get the life out of him somehow.'

In an instant the victim was up at the hook once more.

They kept him there for an hour, but when he came down he was perfectly garrulous.

'Old man Plunket goes too much to the Arcady Saloon,' said he. 'Three times he's been there in an hour; and him with a family. Old man Plunket would do well to swear off.'

It was monstrous and incredible, but there it was. There was no getting round it. The man was there talking when he ought to have been dead. We all sat staring in amazement, but United States Marshal Carpenter was not a man to be euchred so easily. He motioned the others to one side, so that the prisoner was left standing alone.

'Duncan Warner,' said he slowly, 'you are here to play your part, and I am here to play mine. Your game is to live if you can, and my game is to carry out the sentence of the law. You've beat us on electricity. I'll give you one there. And you've beat us on hanging, for you seem to thrive on it. But it's my turn to beat you now, for my duty has to be done.'

He pulled a six-shooter from his coat as he spoke, and fired all the shots through the body of the prisoner. The room was so filled with smoke that we could see nothing, but when it cleared the prisoner was still standing there, looking down in disgust at the front of his coat.

'Coats must be cheap where you come from,' said he. 'Thirty dollars it cost me, and look at it now. The six holes in front are bad enough, but four of the balls have passed out, and a pretty fine state the back must be in.'

The Marshal's revolver fell from his hand, and he dropped his arms to his sides, a beaten man.

'Maybe some of you gentlemen can tell me what this means,' said he, looking helplessly at the committee.

Peter Stulpnagel took a step forward.

'I'll tell you all about it,' said he.

'You seem to be the only person who knows anything.'

'I *am* the only person who knows anything. I should have warned these gentlemen; but, as they would not listen to me, I have allowed them to learn by experience. What you have done with your electricity is that you have increased the man's vitality until he can defy death for centuries.'

'Centuries!'

'Yes, it will take the wear of hundreds of years to exhaust the enormous nervous energy with which you have drenched him. Electricity is life, and you have charged him with it to the utmost. Perhaps in fifty years you might execute him, but I am not sanguine about it.'

'Great Scott! What shall I do with him?' cried the unhappy Marshal.

Peter Stulpnagel shrugged his shoulders.

'It seems to me that it does not much matter what you do with him now,' said he.

'Maybe we could drain the electricity out of him again. Suppose we hang him up by the heels?'

'No, no, it's out of the question.'

'Well, well, he shall do no more mischief in Los Amigos anyhow,' said the Marshal, with decision. 'He shall go into the new gaol. The prison will wear him out.'

'On the contrary,' said Peter Stulpnagel, 'I think that it is much more probable that he will wear out the prison.'

It was rather a fiasco, and for years we didn't talk more about it than we could help, but it's no secret now, and I thought you might like to jot down the facts in your case-book.

THE CASE OF LADY SANNOX

HE relations between Douglas Stone and the notorious Lady Sannox were very well known both among the fashionable circles of which she was a brilliant member, and the scientific bodies which numbered him among their most illustrious *confrères*.* There was naturally, therefore, a very widespread interest when it was announced one morning that the lady had absolutely and for ever taken the veil, and that the world would see her no more. When, at the very tail of this rumour, there came the assurance that the celebrated operating surgeon, the man of steel nerves, had been found in the morning by his valet, seated on one side of his bed, smiling pleasantly upon the universe, with both legs jammed into one side of his breeches and his great brain about as valuable as a cap full of porridge, the matter was strong enough to give quite a little thrill of interest to folk who had never hoped that their jaded nerves were capable of such a sensation.

Douglas Stone in his prime was one of the most remarkable men in England. Indeed, he could hardly be said to have ever reached his prime, for he was but nine-and-thirty at the time of this little incident. Those who knew him best were aware that famous as he was as a surgeon, he might have succeeded with even greater rapidity in any of a dozen lines of life. He could have cut his way to fame as a soldier, struggled to it as an explorer, bullied for it in the courts, or built it out of stone and iron as an engineer. He was born to be great, for he could plan what another man dare not do, and he could do what another man dare not plan. In surgery none could follow him. His nerve, his judgment, his intuition, were things apart. Again and again his knife cut away death, but grazed the very springs of life in doing it, until his assistants were as white as the patient. His energy, his audacity, his full-blooded self-confidence—does not the memory of them still linger to the south of Marylebone Road and the north of Oxford Street?*

His vices were as magnificent as his virtues, and infinitely more picturesque. Large as was his income, and it was the third largest of all professional men in London, it was far beneath the luxury of his living. Deep in his complex nature lay a rich vein of sensualism, at the sport of which he placed all the prizes of his life. The eye, the ear, the touch, the palate, all were his masters. The bouquet of old vintages, the scent of rare exotics, the curves and tints of the daintiest potteries of Europe, it was to these that the quick-running stream of gold was transformed. And then there came his sudden mad passion for Lady Sannox, when a single interview with two challenging glances and a whispered word set him ablaze. She was the loveliest woman in London and the only one to him. He was one of the handsomest men in London, but not the only one to her. She had a liking for new experiences, and was gracious to most men who wooed her. It may have been cause or it may have been effect that Lord Sannox looked fifty, though he was but six-and-thirty.

He was a quiet, silent, neutral-tinted man, this lord, with thin lips and heavy eyelids, much given to gardening, and full of home-like habits. He had at one time been fond of acting, had even rented a theatre in London, and on its boards had first seen Miss Marion Dawson, to whom he had offered his hand, his title, and the third of a county. Since his marriage this early hobby had become distasteful to him. Even in private theatricals it was no longer possible to persuade him to exercise the talent which he had often shown that he possessed. He was happier with a spud* and a watering-can among his orchids and chrysanthemums.

It was quite an interesting problem whether he was absolutely devoid of sense, or miserably wanting in spirit. Did he know his lady's ways and condone them, or was he a mere blind, doting fool? It was a point to be discussed over the teacups in snug little drawing-rooms, or with the aid of a cigar in the bow windows of clubs. Bitter and plain were the comments among men upon his conduct. There was but one who had a good word to say for him, and he was the most silent member in the smoking-room. He had seen him break in a horse at the University, and it seemed to have left an impression upon his mind.

But when Douglas Stone became the favourite all doubts as to Lord Sannox's knowledge or ignorance were set for ever at rest. There was no subterfuge about Stone. In his high-handed, impetuous fashion, he set all caution and discretion at defiance. The scandal became notorious. A learned body intimated that his name had been struck from the list of its vice-presidents. Two friends implored him to consider his professional credit. He cursed them all three, and spent forty guineas on a bangle to take with him to the lady. He was at her house every evening, and she drove in his carriage in the afternoons. There was not an attempt on either side to conceal their relations; but there came at last a little incident to interrupt them.

It was a dismal winter's night, very cold and gusty, with the wind whooping in the chimneys and blustering against the window-panes. A thin spatter of rain tinkled on the glass with each fresh sough of the gale, drowning for the instant the dull gurgle and drip from the eaves. Douglas Stone had finished his dinner, and sat by his fire in the study, a glass of rich port upon the malachite* table at his elbow. As he raised it to his lips, he held it up against the lamplight, and watched with the eye of a connoisseur the tiny scales of beeswing* which floated in its rich ruby depths. The fire, as it spurted up, threw fitful lights upon his bold, clear-cut face, with its widely-opened grey eyes, its thick and yet firm lips, and the deep, square jaw, which had something Roman in its strength and its animalism. He smiled from time to time as he nestled back in his luxurious chair. Indeed, he had a right to feel well pleased, for, against the advice of six colleagues, he had performed an operation that day of which only two cases were on record, and the result had been brilliant beyond all expectation. No other man in London would have had the daring to plan, or the skill to execute, such a heroic measure.

But he had promised Lady Sannox to see her that evening and it was already half-past eight. His hand was outstretched to the bell to order the carriage when he heard the dull thud of the knocker. An instant later there was the shuffling of feet in the hall, and the sharp closing of a door.

'A patient to see you, sir, in the consulting room,' said the butler.

'About himself?'

'No, sir; I think he wants you to go out.'

'It is too late,' cried Douglas Stone peevishly. 'I won't go.'

'This is his card, sir.'

The butler presented it upon the gold salver which had been given to his master by the wife of a Prime Minister.

' "Hamil Ali, Smyrna."* Hum! The fellow is a Turk, I suppose.'

'Yes, sir. He seems as if he came from abroad, sir. And he's in a terrible way.'

'Tut, tut! I have an engagement. I must go somewhere else. But I'll see him. Show him in here, Pim.'

A few moments later the butler swung open the door and ushered in a small and decrepit man, who walked with a bent back and with the forward push of the face and blink of the eyes which goes with extreme short sight. His face was swarthy, and his hair and beard of the deepest black. In one hand he held a turban of white muslin striped with red, in the other a small chamois leather bag.

'Good evening,' said Douglas Stone, when the butler had closed the door. 'You speak English, I presume?'

'Yes, sir. I am from Asia Minor,* but I speak English when I speak slow.'

'You wanted me to go out, I understand?'

'Yes, sir. I wanted very much that you should see my wife.'

'I could come in the morning, but I have an engagement which prevents me from seeing your wife to-night.'

The Turk's answer was a singular one. He pulled the string which closed the mouth of the chamois leather bag, and poured a flood of gold on to the table.

'There are one hundred pounds there,' said he, 'and I promise you that it will not take you an hour. I have a cab ready at the door.'

Douglas Stone glanced at his watch. An hour would not make it too late to visit Lady Sannox. He had been there later. And the fee was an extraordinarily high one. He had been pressed by his creditors lately, and he could not afford to let such a chance pass. He would go.

'What is the case?' he asked.

'Oh, it is so sad a one! So sad a one! You have not, perhaps, heard of the daggers of the Almohades?'*

'Never.'

'Ah, they are Eastern daggers of a great age and of a singular shape, with the hilt like what you call a stirrup. I am a curiosity dealer, you understand, and that is why I have come to England from Smyrna, but next week I go back once more. Many things I brought with me, and I have a few things left, but among them, to my sorrow, is one of these daggers.'

'You will remember that I have an appointment, sir,' said the surgeon, with some irritation; 'pray confine yourself to the necessary details.'

'You will see that it is necessary. To-day my wife fell down in a faint in the room in which I keep my wares, and she cut her lower lip upon this cursed dagger of Almohades.'

'I see,' said Douglas Stone, rising. 'And you wish me to dress the wound?'

'No, no, it is worse than that.'

'What then?'

'These daggers are poisoned.'

'Poisoned!'

'Yes, and there is no man, East or West, who can tell now what is the poison or what the cure. But all that is known I know, for my father was in this trade before me, and we have had much to do with these poisoned weapons.'

'What are the symptoms?'

'Deep sleep, and death in thirty hours.'

'And you say there is no cure. Why then should you pay me this considerable fee?'

'No drug can cure, but the knife may.'

'And how?'

'The poison is slow of absorption. It remains for hours in the wound.'

'Washing, then, might cleanse it?'

'No more than in a snake bite. It is too subtle and too deadly.'

'Excision of the wound, then?'

'That is it. If it be on the finger, take the finger off. So said my father always. But think of where this wound is, and that it is my wife. It is dreadful!'

But familiarity with such grim matters may take the finer edge from a man's sympathy. To Douglas Stone this was already an interesting case, and he brushed aside as irrelevant the feeble objections of the husband.

'It appears to be that or nothing,' said he brusquely. 'It is better to lose a lip than a life.'

'Ah, yes, I know that you are right. Well, well, it is kismet, and it must be faced. I have the cab, and you will come with me and do this thing.'

Douglas Stone took his case of bistouries* from a drawer, and placed it with a roll of bandage and a compress of lint in his pocket. He must waste no more time if he were to see Lady Sannox.

'I am ready,' said he, pulling on his overcoat. 'Will you take a glass of wine before you go out into this cold air?'

His visitor shrank away, with a protesting hand upraised.

'You forget that I am a Mussulman,* and a true follower of the

Prophet,' said he. 'But tell me what is the bottle of green glass which you have placed in your pocket?'

'It is chloroform.'*

'Ah, that also is forbidden to us. It is a spirit, and we make no use of such things.'

'What! You would allow your wife to go through an operation without an anæsthetic?'

'Ah! she will feel nothing, poor soul. The deep sleep has already come on, which is the first working of the poison. And then I have given her of our Smyrna opium. Come, sir, for already an hour has passed.'

As they stepped out into the darkness, a sheet of rain was driven in upon their faces, and the hall lamp, which dangled from the arm of a marble Caryatid,* went out with a fluff. Pim, the butler, pushed the heavy door to, straining hard with his shoulder against the wind, while the two men groped their way towards the yellow glare which showed where the cab was waiting. An instant later they were rattling upon their journey.

'Is it far?' asked Douglas Stone.

'Oh, no. We have a very little quiet place off the Euston Road.'*

The surgeon pressed the spring of his repeater* and listened to the little tings which told him the hour. It was a quarter past nine. He calculated the distances, and the short time which it would take him to perform so trivial an operation. He ought to reach Lady Sannox by ten o'clock. Through the fogged windows he saw the blurred gas lamps dancing past, with occasionally the broader glare of a shop front. The rain was pelting and rattling upon the leathern top of the carriage, and the wheels swashed as they rolled through puddle and mud. Opposite to him the white headgear of his companion gleamed faintly through the obscurity. The surgeon felt in his pockets and arranged his needles, his ligatures and his safety-pins, that no time might be wasted when they arrived. He chafed with impatience and drummed his foot upon the floor.

But the cab slowed down at last and pulled up. In an instant Douglas Stone was out, and the Smyrna merchant's toe was at his very heel.

'You can wait,' said he to the driver.

It was a mean-looking house in a narrow and sordid street. The surgeon, who knew his London well, cast a swift glance into the shadows, but there was nothing distinctive—no shop, no movement, nothing but a double line of dull, flat-faced houses, a double stretch of wet flagstones which gleamed in the lamplight, and a double rush of water in the gutters which swirled and gurgled towards the sewer gratings. The door which faced them was blotched and discoloured, and a faint light in the fan pane above it served to show the dust and the grime which covered it. Above, in one of the bedroom windows, there was a dull yellow glimmer. The merchant knocked loudly, and, as he turned his dark face towards the light, Douglas Stone could see that it was contracted with anxiety. A bolt was drawn, and an elderly woman with a taper stood in the doorway, shielding the thin flame with her gnarled hand.

'Is all well?' gasped the merchant.

'She is as you left her, sir.'

'She has not spoken?'

'No, she is in a deep sleep.'

The merchant closed the door, and Douglas Stone walked down the narrow passage, glancing about him in some surprise as he did so. There was no oil-cloth, no mat, no hat-rack. Deep grey dust and heavy festoons of cobwebs met his eyes everywhere. Following the old woman up the winding stair, his firm footfall echoed harshly through the silent house. There was no carpet.

The bedroom was on the second landing. Douglas Stone followed the old nurse into it, with the merchant at his heels. Here, at least, there was furniture and to spare. The floor was littered and the corners piled with Turkish cabinets, inlaid tables, coats of chain mail, strange pipes, and grotesque weapons. A single small lamp stood upon a bracket on the wall. Douglas Stone took it down, and picking his way among the lumber, walked over to a couch in the corner, on which lay a woman dressed in the Turkish fashion, with yashmak and veil. The lower part of the face was exposed, and the surgeon saw a jagged cut which zigzagged along the border of the under lip.

'You will forgive the yashmak,' said the Turk. 'You know our views about woman in the East.'

But the surgeon was not thinking about the yashmak. This was no longer a woman to him. It was a case. He stooped and examined the wound carefully.

'There are no signs of irritation,' said he. 'We might delay the operation until local symptoms develop.'

The husband wrung his hands in uncontrollable agitation.

'Oh! sir, sir,' he cried. 'Do not trifle. You do not know. It is deadly. I know, and I give you my assurance that an operation is absolutely necessary. Only the knife can save her.'

'And yet I am inclined to wait,' said Douglas Stone.

'That is enough,' the Turk cried, angrily. 'Every minute is of importance, and I cannot stand here and see my wife allowed to sink. It only remains for me to give you my thanks for having come, and to call in some other surgeon before it is too late.'

Douglas Stone hesitated. To refund that hundred pounds was no pleasant matter. But of course if he left the case he must return the money. And if the Turk were right and the woman died, his position before a coroner might be an embarrassing one.

'You have had personal experience of this poison?' he asked.

'I have.'

'And you assure me that an operation is needful.'

'I swear it by all that I hold sacred.'

'The disfigurement will be frightful.'

'I can understand that the mouth will not be a pretty one to kiss.'

Douglas Stone turned fiercely upon the man. The speech was a brutal one. But the Turk has his own fashion of talk and of thought, and there was no time for wrangling. Douglas Stone drew a bistoury from his case, opened it and felt the keen straight edge with his forefinger. Then he held the lamp closer to the bed. Two dark eyes were gazing up at him through the slit in the yashmak. They were all iris, and the pupil was hardly to be seen.

'You have given her a very heavy dose of opium.'

'Yes, she has had a good dose.'

He glanced again at the dark eyes which looked straight at his own. They were dull and lustreless, but, even as he gazed, a little shifting sparkle came into them, and the lips quivered.

'She is not absolutely unconscious,' said he.

'Would it not be well to use the knife while it will be painless?'

The same thought had crossed the surgeon's mind. He grasped the wounded lip with his forceps, and with two swift cuts he took out a broad V-shaped piece. The woman sprang up on the couch with a dreadful gurgling scream. Her covering was torn from her face. It was a face that he knew. In spite of that protruding upper lip and that slobber of blood, it was a face that he knew. She kept on putting her

hand up to the gap and screaming. Douglas Stone sat down at the foot
of the couch with his knife and his forceps. The room was whirling
round, and he had felt something go like a ripping seam behind his
ear. A bystander would have said that his face was the more ghastly of
the two. As in a dream, or as if he had been looking at something at
the play, he was conscious that the Turk's hair and beard lay upon the
table, and that Lord Sannox was leaning against the wall with his
hand to his side, laughing silently. The screams had died away now,
and the dreadful head had dropped back again upon the pillow, but
Douglas Stone still sat motionless, and Lord Sannox still chuckled
quietly to himself.

'It was really very necessary for Marion, this operation,' said he,
'not physically, but morally, you know, morally.'

Douglas Stone stooped forwards and began to play with the fringe
of the coverlet. His knife tinkled down upon the ground, but he still
held the forceps and something more.

'I had long intended to make a little example,' said Lord Sannox,
suavely. 'Your note of Wednesday miscarried, and I have it here
in my pocket-book. I took some pains in carrying out my idea. The
wound, by the way, was from nothing more dangerous than my signet
ring.'

He glanced keenly at his silent companion, and cocked the small
revolver which he held in his coat pocket. But Douglas Stone was still
picking at the coverlet.

'You see you have kept your appointment after all,' said Lord
Sannox.

And at that Douglas Stone began to laugh. He laughed long and
loudly. But Lord Sannox did not laugh now. Something like fear sharpened and hardened his features. He walked from the room, and he
walked on tiptoe. The old woman was waiting outside.

'Attend to your mistress when she awakes,' said Lord Sannox.

Then he went down to the street. The cab was at the door, and the
driver raised his hand to his hat.

'John,' said Lord Sannox, 'you will take the doctor home first. He
will want leading downstairs, I think. Tell his butler that he has been
taken ill at a case.'

'Very good, sir.'

'Then you can take Lady Sannox home.'

'And how about yourself, sir?'

'Oh, my address for the next few months will be Hotel di Roma, Venice.* Just see that the letters are sent on. And tell Stevens to exhibit all the purple chrysanthemums next Monday, and to wire me the result.'

THE LORD OF CHÂTEAU NOIR

IT was in the days when the German armies had broken their
way across France, and when the shattered forces of the young
Republic had been swept away to the north of the Aisne and to the
south of the Loire.* Three broad streams of armed men had rolled
slowly but irresistibly from the Rhine, now meandering to the north,
now to the south, dividing, coalescing, but all uniting to form one
great lake round Paris. And from this lake there welled out smaller
streams, one to the north, one southward to Orleans, and a third west-
ward to Normandy. Many a German trooper saw the sea for the first
time when he rode his horse girth-deep into the waves at Dieppe.*

Black and bitter were the thoughts of Frenchmen when they saw
this weal of dishonour slashed across the fair face of their country.
They had fought and they had been overborne. That swarming cavalry, those countless footmen, the masterful guns—they had tried
and tried to make head against them. In battalions their invaders were
not to be beaten; but man to man, or ten to ten, they were their equals.
A brave Frenchman might still make a single German rue the day that
he had left his own bank of the Rhine. Thus, unchronicled amid the
battles and the sieges, there broke out another war, a war of individuals, with foul murder upon the one side and brutal reprisal on the
other.

Colonel von Gramm, of the 24th Posen* Infantry, had suffered
severely during this new development. He commanded in the little
Norman town of Les Andelys,* and his outposts stretched amid the
hamlets and farmhouses of the district round. No French force was
within fifty miles of him, and yet morning after morning he had to
listen to a black report of sentries found dead at their posts, or of
foraging parties which had never returned. Then the Colonel would
go forth in his wrath, and farmsteadings would blaze and villages
tremble; but next morning there was still that same dismal tale to be
told. Do what he might, he could not shake off his invisible enemies.
And yet, it should not have been so hard, for from certain signs
in common, in the plan and in the deed, it was certain that all these
outrages came from a single source.

Colonel von Gramm had tried violence and it had failed. Gold might be more successful. He published it abroad over the countryside that five hundred francs would be paid for information. There was no response. Then eight hundred. The peasants were incorruptible. Then, goaded on by a murdered corporal, he rose to a thousand, and so bought the soul of François RcJane, farm labourer, whose Norman avarice was a stronger passion than his French hatred.

'You say that you know who did these crimes?' asked the Prussian Colonel, eyeing with loathing the blue-bloused, rat-faced creature before him.

'Yes, Colonel.'

'And it was——?'

'Those thousand francs, Colonel——'

'Not a sou until your story has been tested. Come! Who is it who has murdered my men?'

'It is Count Eustace of Château Noir.'

'You lie!' cried the Colonel, angrily. 'A gentleman and a nobleman could not have done such crimes.'

The peasant shrugged his shoulders.

'It is evident to me that you do not know the Count. It is this way, Colonel. What I tell you is the truth, and I am not afraid that you should test it. The Count of Château Noir is a hard man: even at the best time he was a hard man. But of late he has been terrible. It was his son's death, you know. His son was under Douay,* and he was taken, and then in escaping from Germany he met his death. It was the Count's only child, and indeed we all think that it has driven him mad. With his peasants he follows the German armies. I do not know how many he has killed, but it is he who cuts the cross upon the foreheads, for it is the badge of his house.'

It was true. The murdered sentries had each had a saltire cross* slashed across their brows, as by a hunting-knife. The Colonel bent his stiff back and ran his forefinger over the map which lay upon the table.

'The Château Noir is not more than four leagues,' he said.

'Three and a kilometre,* Colonel.'

'You know the place?'

'I used to work there.'

Colonel von Gramm rang the bell.

'Give this man food and detain him,' said he to the sergeant.

'Why detain me, Colonel? I can tell you no more.'

'We shall need you as guide.'

'As guide! But the Count? If I were to fall into his hands? Ah, Colonel——'

The Prussian commander waved him away.

'Send Captain Baumgarten to me at once.' said he.

The officer who answered the summons was a man of middle age, heavy-jawed, blue-eyed, with a curving yellow moustache, and a brick-red face which turned to an ivory white where his helmet had sheltered it. He was bald, with a shining, tightly-stretched scalp, at the back of which, as in a mirror, it was a favourite mess-joke of the subalterns to trim their moustaches. As a soldier he was slow, but reliable and brave. The Colonel could trust him where a more dashing officer might be in danger.

'You will proceed to Château Noir to-night, Captain,' said he. 'A guide has been provided. You will arrest the Count and bring him back. If there is an attempt at rescue, shoot him at once.'

'How many men shall I take, Colonel?'

'Well, we are surrounded by spies, and our only chance is to pounce upon him before he knows that we are on the way. A large force will attract attention. On the other hand, you must not risk being cut off.'

'I might march north, Colonel, as if to join General Goeben.* Then I could turn down this road which I see upon your map, and get to Château Noir before they could hear of us. In that case, with twenty men——'

'Very good, Captain. I hope to see you with your prisoner to-morrow morning.'

* * *

It was a cold December night when Captain Baumgarten marched out of Les Andelys with his twenty Poseners, and took the main road to the north-west. Two miles out he turned suddenly down a narrow, deeply-rutted track, and made swiftly for his man. A thin, cold rain was falling, swishing among the tall poplar trees and rustling in the fields on either side. The Captain walked first with Moser, a veteran sergeant, beside him. The sergeant's wrist was fastened to that of the French peasant, and it had been whispered in his ear that in case of an ambush the first bullet fired would be through his head. Behind them the twenty infantrymen plodded along through the darkness with their faces sunk to the rain, and their boots squeaking in the soft, wet clay. They knew where they were going and why, and the thought upheld them, for they were bitter at the loss of their comrades. It was a cavalry job, they knew, but the cavalry were all on with the advance, and, besides, it was more fitting that the regiment should avenge its own dead men.

It was nearly eight when they left Les Andelys. At half-past eleven their guide stopped at a place where two high pillars, crowned with some heraldic stonework, flanked a huge iron gate. The wall in which it had been the opening had crumbled away, but the great gate still towered above the brambles and weeds which had overgrown its base. The Prussians made their way round it, and advanced stealthily, under the shadow of a tunnel of oak branches, up the long avenue, which was still cumbered by the leaves of last autumn. At the top they halted and reconnoitred.

The black château lay in front of them. The moon had shone out between two rain-clouds, and threw the old house into silver and shadow. It was shaped like an L, with a low arched door in front, and lines of small windows like the open ports of a man-of-war. Above was a dark roof breaking at the corners into little round overhanging turrets, the whole lying silent in the moonshine, with a drift of ragged clouds blackening the heavens behind it. A single light gleamed in one of the lower windows.

The Captain whispered his orders to his men. Some were to creep to the front door, some to the back. Some were to watch the east, and some the west. He and the sergeant stole on tiptoe to the lighted window.

It was a small room into which they looked, very meanly furnished. An elderly man in the dress of a menial was reading a tattered paper by the light of a guttering candle. He leaned back in his wooden chair with his feet upon a box, while a bottle of white wine stood with a half-filled tumbler upon a stool beside him. The sergeant thrust his needle-gun through the glass, and the man sprang to his feet with a shriek.

'Silence, for your life! The house is surrounded and you cannot escape. Come round and open the door, or we will show you no mercy when we come in.'

'For God's sake, don't shoot! I will open it! I will open it!' He rushed from the room with his paper still crumpled up in his hand. An instant later, with a groaning of old locks and a rasping of bars, the low door swung open, and the Prussians poured into the stone-flagged passage.

'Where is Count Eustace de Château Noir?'

'My master! He is out, sir.'

'Out at this time of night? Your life for a lie!'

'It is true, sir. He is out!'

'Where?'

'I do not know.'

'Doing what?'

'I cannot tell. No, it is no use your cocking your pistol, sir. You may kill me, but you cannot make me tell you that which I do not know.'

'Is he often out at this hour?'

'Frequently.'

'And when does he come home?'

'Before daybreak.'

Captain Baumgarten rasped out a German oath. He had had his journey for nothing, then. The man's answers were only too likely to be true. It was what he might have expected. But at least he would search the house and make sure. Leaving a picket at the front door and another at the back, the sergeant and he drove the trembling butler in front of them—his shaking candle sending strange, flickering shadows over the old tapestries and the low, oak-raftered ceilings. They searched the whole house, from the huge, stone-flagged kitchen below to the dining-hall on the second floor with its gallery for musicians, and its panelling black with age, but nowhere was there a living creature. Up above in an attic they found Marie, the elderly wife of the butler; but the owner kept no other servants, and of his own presence there was no trace.

It was long, however, before Captain Baumgarten had satisfied himself upon the point. It was a difficult house to search. Thin stairs, which only one man could ascend at a time, connected lines of tortuous corridors. The walls were so thick that each room was cut off from its neighbour. Huge fireplaces yawned in each, while the windows were six feet deep in the wall. Captain Baumgarten stamped with his feet, and tore down curtains, and struck with the pommel of his sword. If there were secret hiding-places, he was not fortunate enough to find them.

'I have an idea,' said he, at last, speaking in German to the sergeant. 'You will place a guard over this fellow, and make sure that he communicates with no one.'

'Yes, Captain.'

'And you will place four men in ambush at the front and at the back. It is likely enough that about daybreak our bird may return to the nest.'

'And the others, Captain?'

'Let them have their suppers in the kitchen. This fellow will serve you with meat and wine. It is a wild night, and we shall be better here than on the country road.'

'And yourself, Captain?'

'I will take my supper up here in the dining-hall. The logs are laid and we can light the fire. You will call me if there is any alarm. What can you give me for supper—you?'

'Alas, monsieur, there was a time when I might have answered, "What you wish!" but now it is all that we can do to find a bottle of new claret and a cold pullet.'*

'That will do very well. Let a guard go about with him, sergeant, and let him feel the end of a bayonet if he plays us any tricks.'

Captain Baumgarten was an old campaigner. In the Eastern provinces, and before that in Bohemia, he had learned the art of quartering himself upon the enemy. While the butler brought his supper he occupied himself in making his preparations for a comfortable night. He lit the candelabrum of ten candles upon the centre table. The fire was already burning up, crackling merrily, and sending spurts of blue, pungent smoke into the room. The Captain walked to the window and looked out. The moon had gone in again, and it was raining heavily. He could hear the deep sough of the wind and see the dark loom of the trees, all swaying in the one direction. It was a sight which gave a zest to his comfortable quarters, and to the cold fowl and the bottle of wine which the butler had brought up for him. He was tired and hungry after his long tramp, so he threw his sword, his helmet, and his revolver-belt down upon a chair, and fell to eagerly upon his supper. Then, with his glass of wine before him and his cigar between his lips, he tilted his chair back and looked about him.

He sat within a small circle of brilliant light which gleamed upon his silver shoulder-straps, and threw out his terra-cotta face, his heavy eyebrows, and his yellow moustache. But outside that circle things were vague and shadowy in the old dining-hall. Two sides were oak-panelled and two were hung with faded tapestry, across which huntsmen and dogs and stags were still dimly streaming. Above the fireplace were rows of heraldic shields with the blazonings of the family and of its alliances, the fatal saltire cross breaking out on each of them.

Four paintings of old seigneurs of Château Noir faced the fireplace, all men with hawk noses and bold, high features, so like each other that only the dress could distinguish the Crusader from the Cavalier of the Fronde.* Captain Baumgarten, heavy with his repast, lay back in his chair looking up at them through the clouds of his tobacco smoke, and pondering over the strange chance which had sent him, a man from the Baltic coast,* to eat his supper in the ancestral hall of these proud Norman chieftains. But the fire was hot, and the Captain's eyes were heavy. His chin sank slowly upon his chest, and the ten candles gleamed upon the broad white scalp.

Suddenly a slight noise brought him to his feet. For an instant it seemed to his dazed senses that one of the pictures opposite had walked from its frame. There, beside the table, and almost within arm's length of him, was standing a huge man, silent, motionless, with no sign of life save his fierce, glinting eyes. He was black-haired, olive-skinned, with a pointed tuft of black beard, and a great, fierce nose, towards which all his features seemed to run. His cheeks were wrinkled like a last year's apple, but his sweep of shoulder, and bony, corded hands, told of a strength which was un-sapped by age. His arms were folded across his arching chest, and his mouth was set in a fixed smile.

'Pray do not trouble yourself to look for your weapons,' he said, as the Prussian cast a swift glance at the empty chair in which they had been laid. 'You have been, if you will allow me to say so, a little indiscreet to make yourself so much at home in a house every wall of which is honeycombed with secret passages. You will be amused to hear that forty men were watching you at your supper. Ah! what then?'

Captain Baumgarten had taken a step forward with clenched fists. The Frenchman held up the revolver which he grasped in his right hand, while with the left he hurled the German back into his chair.

'Pray keep your seat,' said he. 'You have no cause to trouble about your men. They have already been provided for. It is astonishing with these stone floors how little one can hear what goes on beneath. You have been relieved of your command, and have now only to think of yourself. May I ask what your name is?'

'I am Captain Baumgarten, of the 24th Posen Regiment.'

'Your French is excellent, though you incline, like most of your countrymen, to turn the "p" into a "b." I have been amused to hear them cry "avez bitié sur moi!"* You know, doubtless, who it is who addresses you.'

'The Count of Château Noir.'

'Precisely. It would have been a misfortune if you had visited my château and I had been unable to have a word with you. I have had to do with many German soldiers, but never with an officer before. I have much to talk to you about.'

Captain Baumgarten sat still in his chair. Brave as he was, there was something in this man's manner which made his skin creep with apprehension. His eyes glanced to right and to left, but his weapons were gone, and in a struggle he saw that he was but a child to this gigantic adversary. The Count had picked up the claret bottle, and held it to the light:

'Tut! tut!' said he. 'And was this the best that Pierre could do for you? I am ashamed to look you in the face, Captain Baumgarten. We must improve upon this.'

He blew a call upon a whistle, which hung from his shooting-jacket. The old man-servant was in the room in an instant.

'Chambertin* from bin 15!' he cried, and a minute later a grey bottle streaked with cobwebs was carried in as a nurse bears an infant. The Count filled two glasses to the brim.

'Drink!' said he. 'It is the very best in my cellars, and not to be matched between Rouen* and Paris. Drink, sir, and be happy! There are cold joints below. There are two lobsters fresh from Honfleur.* Will you not venture upon a second and more savoury supper?'

The German officer shook his head. He drained the glass, however, and his host filled it once more, pressing him to give an order for this or that dainty.

'There is nothing in my house which is not at your disposal. You have but to say the word. Well, then, you will allow me to tell you a story while you drink your wine. I have so longed to tell it to some German officer. It is about my son, my only child, Eustace, who was taken and died in escaping. It is a curious little story, and I think that I can promise you that you will never forget it.

'You must know, then, that my boy was in the artillery, a fine young fellow, Captain Baumgarten, and the pride of his mother. She died within a week of the news of his death reaching us. It was brought by a brother officer who was at his side throughout, and who escaped while my lad died. I want to tell you all that he told me.

'Eustace was taken at Weissenburg* on the 4th of August. The prisoners were broken up into parties, and sent back into Germany by different routes. Eustace was taken upon the 5th to a village called Lauterburg,* where he met with kindness from the German officer in command. This good Colonel had the hungry lad to supper, offered him the best he had, opened a bottle of good wine, as I have tried to do for you, and gave him a cigar from his own case. Might I entreat you to take one from mine?'

The German again shook his head. His horror of his companion had increased as he sat watching the lips that smiled and the eyes that glared.

'The Colonel, as I say, was good to my boy. But, unluckily, the prisoners were moved next day across the Rhine to Ettlingen.* They were not equally fortunate there. The officer who guarded them was a ruffian and a villain, Captain Baumgarten. He took a pleasure in humiliating and ill-treating the brave men who had fallen into his power. That night, upon my son answering fiercely back to some taunt of his, he struck him in the eye, like this!'

The crash of the blow rang through the hall. The German's face fell forward, his hand up, and blood oozing through his fingers. The Count settled down in his chair once more.

'My boy was disfigured by the blow, and this villain made his appearance the object of his jeers. By the way, you look a little comical yourself at the present moment, Captain, and your Colonel would certainly say that you had been getting into mischief. To continue, however, my boy's youth and his destitution—for his pockets were empty—moved the pity of a kind-hearted major, and he advanced him ten Napoleons from his own pocket without security of any kind. Into your hands, Captain Baumgarten, I return these ten gold pieces, since I cannot learn the name of the lender. I am grateful from my heart for this kindness shown to my boy.

'The vile tyrant who commanded the escort accompanied the prisoners to Durlach, and from there to Carlsruhe.* He heaped every outrage upon my lad, because the spirit of the Châteaux Noirs would not stoop to turn away his wrath by a feigned submission. Ay, this cowardly villain, whose heart's blood shall yet clot upon this hand, dared to strike my son with his open hand, to kick him, to tear hairs from his moustache—to use him thus—and thus—and thus!'

The German writhed and struggled. He was helpless in the hands of this huge giant whose blows were raining upon him. When at last, blinded and half-senseless, he staggered to his feet, it was only to be hurled back again into the great oaken chair. He sobbed in his impotent anger and shame.

'My boy was profoundly moved to tears by the humiliation of his position,' continued the Count. 'You will understand me when I say that it is a bitter thing to be helpless in the hands of an insolent and remorseless enemy. On arriving at Carlsruhe, however, his face, which had been wounded by the brutality of his guard, was bound up by a young Bavarian subaltern who was touched by his appearance. I regret to see that your eye is bleeding so. Will you permit me to bind it with my silk handkerchief?'

He leaned forward, but the German dashed his hand aside.

'I am in your power, you monster!' he cried; 'I can endure your brutalities, but not your hypocrisy.'

The Count shrugged his shoulders. 'I am taking things in their order, just as they occurred,' said he. 'I was under vow to tell it to the first German officer with whom I could talk *tête-à-tête*. Let me see, I had got as far as the young Bavarian at Carlsruhe. I regret extremely that you will not permit me to use such slight skill in surgery as I possess. At Carlsruhe, my lad was shut up in the old caserne,* where he remained for a fortnight. The worst pang of his captivity was that some unmannerly curs in the garrison would taunt him with his position as he sat by his window in the evening. That reminds me, Captain, that you are not quite situated upon a bed of roses yourself, are you, now? You came to trap a wolf, my man, and now the beast has you down with his fangs in your throat. A family man, too, I should judge, by that well-filled tunic. Well, a widow the more will make little matter, and they do not usually remain widows long. Get back into the chair, you dog!

'Well, to continue my story—at the end of a fortnight my son and his friend escaped. I need not trouble you with the dangers which they ran, or with the privations which they endured. Suffice it that to disguise themselves they had to take the clothes of two peasants, whom they waylaid in a wood. Hiding by day and travelling by night, they had got as far into France as Remilly,* and were within a mile— a single mile, Captain—of crossing the German lines when a patrol of Uhlans* came right upon them. Ah! it was hard, was it not, when they had come so far and were so near to safety?'

The Count blew a double call upon his whistle, and three hard-faced peasants entered the room.

'These must represent my Uhlans,' said he. 'Well then, the Captain in command, finding that these men were French soldiers in civilian dress within the German lines, proceeded to hang them without trial or ceremony. I think, Jean, that the centre beam is the strongest.'

The unfortunate soldier was dragged from his chair to where a noosed rope had been flung over one of the huge oaken rafters which spanned the room. The cord was slipped over his head, and he felt its harsh grip round his throat. The three peasants seized the other end, and looked to the Count for his orders. The officer, pale, but firm, folded his arms and stared defiantly at the man who tortured him.

'You are now face to face with death, and I perceive from your lips that you are praying. My son was also face to face with death, and he prayed, also. It happened that a general officer came up, and he heard the lad praying for his mother, and it moved him so—he being himself a father—that he ordered his Uhlans away, and he remained with his aide-de-camp only, beside the condemned men. And when he heard all the lad had to tell, that he was the only child of an old family, and that his mother was in failing health, he threw off the rope as I throw off this, and he kissed him on either cheek, as I kiss you, and he bade him go, as I bid you go, and may every kind wish of that noble General, though it could not stave off the fever which slew my son, descend now upon your head.'

And so it was that Captain Baumgarten, disfigured, blinded, and bleeding, staggered out into the wind and the rain of that wild December dawn.

THE THIRD GENERATION

SCUDAMORE LANE, sloping down riverwards from just behind the Monument,* lies, at night, in the shadow of two black and monstrous walls which loom high above the glimmer of the scattered gas-lamps. The footpaths are narrow, and the causeway is paved with rounded cobblestones so that the endless drays roar along it like so many breaking waves. A few old-fashioned houses lie scattered among the business premises, and in one of these—half-way down on the left-hand side—Dr Horace Selby conducts his large practice. It is a singular street for so big a man, but a specialist who has a European reputation can afford to live where he likes. In his particular branch, too, patients do not always consider seclusion to be a disadvantage.*

It was only ten o'clock. The dull roar of the traffic which converged all day upon London Bridge* had died away now to a mere confused murmur. It was raining heavily, and the gas shone dimly through the streaked and dripping glass, throwing little yellow circles upon the glistening cobblestones. The air was full of the sounds of rain, the thin swish of its fall, the heavier drip from the eaves, and the swirl and gurgle down the two steep gutters and through the sewer grating. There was only one figure in the whole length of Scudamore Lane. It was that of a man, and it stood outside the door of Dr Horace Selby.

He had just rung and was waiting for an answer. The fanlight beat full upon the gleaming shoulders of his waterproof and upon his upturned features. It was a wan, sensitive, clear-cut face, with some subtle, nameless peculiarity in its expression—something of the startled horse in the white-rimmed eye, something, too, of the helpless child in the drawn cheek and the weakening of the lower lip. The man-servant knew the stranger as a patient at a bare glance at those frightened eyes. Such a look had been seen at that door before.

'Is the doctor in?'

The man hesitated.

'He has had a few friends to dinner, sir. He does not like to be disturbed outside his usual hours, sir.'

'Tell him that I *must* see him. Tell him that it is of the very first importance. Here is my card.' He fumbled with his trembling fingers in trying to draw one from the case. 'Sir Francis Norton is the name. Tell him that Sir Francis Norton of Deane Park must see him at once.'

'Yes, sir.' The butler closed his fingers upon the card and the half-sovereign which accompanied it. 'Better hang your coat up here in the hall. It is very wet. Now, if you will wait here in the consulting-room I have no doubt that I shall be able to send the doctor in to you.'

It was a large and lofty room in which the young baronet found himself. The carpet was so soft and thick that his feet made no sound as he walked across it. The two gas-jets were turned only half-way up, and the dim light with the faint, aromatic smell which filled the air had a vaguely religious suggestion. He sat down in a shining, leather arm-chair by the smouldering fire and looked gloomily about him. Two sides of the room were taken up with books, fat and sombre, with broad, gold lettering upon their backs. Beside him was the high, old-fashioned mantelpiece of white marble, the top of it strewed with cotton wadding and bandages, graduated measures and little bottles. There was one with a broad neck, just above him, containing blue-stone, and another narrower one with what looked like the ruins of a broken pipe-stem, and 'Caustic'* outside upon a red label. Thermometers, hypodermic syringes, bistouries* and spatulas were scattered thickly about, both on the mantelpiece and on the central table on either side of the sloping desk. On the same table to the right stood copies of the five books which Dr Horace Selby had written upon the subject with which his name is peculiarly associated, while on the left, on the top of a red medical directory, lay a huge glass model of a human eye, the size of a turnip, which opened down the centre to expose the lens and double chamber within.

Sir Francis Norton had never been remarkable for his powers of observation, and yet he found himself watching these trifles with the keenest attention. Even the corrosion of the cork of an acid bottle caught his eye and he wondered that the doctor did not use glass stoppers. Tiny scratches where the light glinted off the table, little stains upon the leather of the desk, chemical formulæ scribbled upon the labels of some of the phials—nothing was too slight to arrest his attention. And his sense of hearing was equally alert. The heavy ticking of the solemn, black clock above the fireplace struck quite painfully upon his ears. Yet, in spite of it, and in spite also of the thick, old-fashioned wooden partition walls, he could hear the voices of men talking in the next room and could even catch scraps of their conversation. 'Second hand was bound to take it.' 'Why, you drew the last of them yourself.' 'How could I play the queen when I knew the ace was against me?' The phrases came in little spurts, falling back into the dull murmur of conversation. And then suddenly he heard a creaking of a door, and a step in the hall, and knew with a tingling mixture of impatience and horror that the crisis of his life was at hand.

Dr Horace Selby was a large, portly man, with an imposing presence. His nose and chin were bold and pronounced, yet his features were puffy— a combination which would blend more freely with the wig and cravat of the early Georges,* than with the close cropped hair and black frockcoat of the end of the nineteenth century. He was clean shaven, for his mouth was too good to cover, large, flexible and sensitive, with a kindly human softening at either corner, which, with his brown, sympathetic eyes, had drawn out many a shame-struck sinner's secret. Two masterful, little, bushy, side whiskers bristled out from under his ears, spindling away upwards to merge in the thick curves of his brindled hair. To his patients there was something reassuring in the mere bulk and dignity of the man. A high and easy bearing in medicine, as in war, bears with it a hint of victories in the past, and a promise of others to come. Dr Horace Selby's face was a consolation, and so, too, were the large, white, soothing hands, one of which he held out to his visitor.

'I am sorry to have kept you waiting. It is a conflict of duties, you perceive. A host to his guests and an adviser to his patient. But now I am entirely at your disposal, Sir Francis. But, dear me, you are very cold.'

'Yes, I am cold.'

'And you are trembling all over. Tut, tut, this will never do. This miserable night has chilled you. Perhaps some little stimulant——'

'No, thank you. I would really rather not. And it is not the night which has chilled me. I am frightened, doctor.'

The doctor half turned in his chair and patted the arch of the young man's knee as he might the neck of a restless horse.

'What, then?' he asked, looking over his shoulder at the pale face with the startled eyes.

Twice the young man parted his lips. Then he stooped with a sudden gesture and turning up the right leg of his trousers he pulled down his sock and thrust forward his shin. The doctor made a clicking noise with his tongue as he glanced at it.

'Both legs?'

'No, only one.'

'Suddenly?'

'This morning.'

'Hum!' The doctor pouted his lips, and drew his finger and thumb down the line of his chin. 'Can you account for it?' he said briskly.

'No.'

A trace of sternness came into the large, brown eyes.

'I need not point out to you that unless the most absolute frankness——'

The patient sprang from his chair.

'So help me God, doctor,' he cried, 'I have nothing in my life with which to reproach myself. Do you think that I would be such a fool as to come here and tell you lies? Once for all, I have nothing to regret.'

He was a pitiful, half-tragic and half-grotesque figure as he stood with one trouser leg rolled to his knee, and that ever-present horror still lurking in his eyes. A burst of merriment came from the card-players in the next room and the two looked at each other in silence.

'Sit down!' said the doctor abruptly. 'Your assurance is quite sufficient.' He stooped and ran his finger down the line of the young man's shin, raising it at one point. 'Hum! Serpiginous!' he murmured, shaking his head; 'any other symptoms?'

'My eyes have been a little weak.'

'Let me see your teeth!' He glanced at them, and again made the gentle clicking sound of sympathy and disapprobation.

'Now the eye!' He lit a lamp at the patient's elbow, and holding a small, crystal lens to concentrate the light, he threw it obliquely upon the patient's eye. As he did so a glow of pleasure came over his large, expressive face, a flush of such enthusiasm as the botanist feels when he packs the rare plant into his tin knapsack, or the astronomer when the long-sought comet first swims into the field of his telescope.

'This is very typical—very typical indeed,' he murmured, turning to his desk and jotting down a few memoranda upon a sheet of paper. 'Curiously enough I am writing a monograph upon the subject. It is singular that you should have been able to furnish so well-marked a case.'

He had so forgotten the patient in his symptom that he had assumed an almost congratulatory air towards its possessor. He reverted to human sympathy again as his patient asked for particulars.

'My dear sir, there is no occasion for us to go into strictly professional details together,' said he soothingly. 'If, for example, I were to say that you have interstitial keratitis, how would you be the wiser? There are indications of a strumous diathesis. In broad terms I may say that you have a constitutional and hereditary taint.'*

The young baronet sank back in his chair and his chin fell forward upon his chest. The doctor sprang to a side-table and poured out a half glass of liqueur brandy which he held to his patient's lips. A little fleck of colour came into his cheeks as he drank it down.

'Perhaps I spoke a little abruptly,' said the doctor. 'But you must have known the nature of your complaint, why otherwise should you have come to me?'

'God help me, I suspected it—but only to-day when my leg grew bad. My father had a leg like this.'

'It was from him, then?'

'No, from my grandfather. You have heard of Sir Rupert Norton, the great Corinthian?'*

The doctor was a man of wide reading with a retentive memory. The name brought back to him instantly the remembrance of the sinister reputation of its owner—a notorious buck of the thirties, who had gambled and duelled and steeped himself in drink and debauchery until even the vile set with whom he consorted had shrunk away from him in horror, and left him to a sinister old age with the barmaid wife whom in some drunken frolic he had espoused. As he looked at the young man still leaning back in the leather chair, there seemed for the instant to flicker up behind him some vague presentiment of that foul old dandy with his dangling seals,* many-wreathed scarf, and dark, satyric face. What was he now? An armful of bones in a mouldy box? But his deeds—they were living and rotting the blood in the veins of an innocent man.

'I see that you have heard of him,' said the young baronet. 'He died horribly, I have been told, but not more horribly than he had lived. My father was his only son. He was a studious man, fond of books and canaries and the country. But his innocent life did not save him.'

'His symptoms were cutaneous, I understand.'

'He wore gloves in the house. That was the first thing I can remember. And then it was his throat, and then his legs. He used to ask me so often about my own health, and I thought him so fussy, for how could I tell what the meaning of it was? He was always watching me—always with a sidelong eye fixed upon me. Now at last I know what he was watching for.'

'Had you brothers or sisters?'

'None, thank God!'

'Well, well, it is a sad case, and very typical of many which come in my way. You are no lonely sufferer, Sir Francis. There are many thousands who bear the same cross as you do.'

'But where's the justice of it, doctor?' cried the young man, springing from the chair and pacing up and down the consulting-room. 'If I were heir to my grandfather's sins as well as to their results I could understand it, but I am of my father's type; I love all that is gentle and beautiful, music and poetry and art. The coarse and animal is abhorrent to me. Ask any of my friends and they would tell you that. And now that this vile, loathsome thing—Ach, I am polluted to the marrow, soaked in abomination! And why? Haven't I a right to ask why? Did I do it? Was it my fault? Could I help being born? And look at me now, blighted and blasted, just as life was at its sweetest! Talk about the sins of the father! How about the sins of the Creator!'

He shook his two clenched hands in the air, the poor, impotent atom with his pin-point of brain caught in the whirl of the infinite.

The doctor rose and placing his hands upon his shoulders he pressed him back into his chair again.

'There, there, my dear lad,' said he. 'You must not excite yourself! You are trembling all over. Your nerves cannot stand it. We must take these great questions upon trust. What are we after all? Half-evolved creatures in a transition stage; nearer, perhaps, to the medusa on the one side than to perfected humanity on the other. With half a complete brain we can't expect to understand the whole of a complete fact, can we, now? It is all very dim and dark, no doubt, but I think Pope's famous couplet* sums the whole matter up, and from my heart, after fifty years of varied experience, I can say that——'

But the young baronet gave a cry of impatience and disgust.

'Words, words, words! You can sit comfortably there in your chair and say them—and think them, too, no doubt. You've had your life. But I've never had mine. You've healthy blood in your veins. Mine is putrid. And yet I am as innocent as you. What would words do for you if you were in this chair and I in that? Ah, it's such a mockery and a make-belief. Don't think me rude, though, doctor. I don't mean to be that. I only say that it is impossible for you or any man to realise it.

But I've a question to ask you, doctor. It's one on which my whole life must depend.'

He writhed his fingers together in an agony of apprehension.

'Speak out, my dear sir. I have every sympathy with you.'

'Do you think—do you think the poison has spent itself on me? Do you think if I had children that they would suffer?'

'I can only give one answer to that. "The third and fourth genera-tion,"* says the trite old text. You may in time eliminate it from your system, but many years must pass before you can think of marriage.'

'I am to be married on Tuesday,' whispered the patient.

It was Dr Horace Selby's turn to be thrilled with horror. There were not many situations which would yield such a sensation to his well-seasoned nerves. He sat in silence while the babble of the card-table broke in again upon them. 'We had a double ruff if you had returned a heart.' 'I was bound to clear the trumps.' They were hot and angry about it.

'How could you?' cried the doctor severely. 'It was criminal.'

'You forget that I have only learned how I stand to-day.' He put his two hands to his temples and pressed them convulsively. 'You are a man of the world, Doctor Selby. You have seen or heard of such things before. Give me some advice. I'm in your hands. It is all very sudden and horrible, and I don't think I am strong enough to bear it.'

The doctor's heavy brows thickened into two straight lines and he bit his nails in perplexity.

'The marriage must not take place.'

'Then what am I to do?'

'At all costs it must not take place.'

'And I must give her up?'

'There can be no question about that!'

The young man took out a pocket-book and drew from it a small photograph, holding it out towards the doctor. The firm face softened as he looked at it.

'It is very hard on you, no doubt. I can appreciate it more now that I have seen that. But there is no alternative at all. You must give up all thought of it.'

'But this is madness, doctor—madness, I tell you. No, I won't raise my voice! I forgot myself! But realise it, man! I am to be married on Tuesday—this coming Tuesday, you know. And all the world knows it. How can I put such a public affront upon her? It would be monstrous.'

'None the less it must be done. My dear sir, there is no way out of it.'

'You would have me simply write brutally and break the engagement at this last moment without a reason? I tell you I couldn't do it.'

'I had a patient once who found himself in a somewhat similar situation some years ago,' said the doctor thoughtfully. 'His device was a singular one. He deliberately committed a penal offence and so compelled the young lady's people to withdraw their consent to the marriage.'

The young baronet shook his head.

'My personal honour is as yet unstained,' said he. 'I have little else left, but that at least I will preserve.'

'Well, well, it's a nice dilemma and the choice lies with you.'

'Have you no other suggestion?'

'You don't happen to have property in Australia?'

'None.'

'But you have capital?'

'Yes.'

'Then you could buy some—to-morrow morning, for example. A thousand mining shares would do. Then you might write to say that urgent business affairs have compelled you to start at an hour's notice to inspect your property. That would give you six months at any rate.'

'Well, that would be possible—yes, certainly it would be possible. But think of her position—the house full of wedding presents— guests coming from a distance. It is awful. And you say there is no alternative.'

The doctor shrugged his shoulders.

'Well, then, I might write it now, and start to-morrow—eh? Perhaps you would let me use your desk. Thank you! I am so sorry to keep you from your guests so long. But I won't be a moment now.' He wrote an abrupt note of a few lines. Then, with a sudden impulse, he tore it to shreds and flung it into the fireplace. 'No, I can't sit down and tell her a lie, doctor,' said he rising. 'We must find some other way out of this. I will think it over, and let you know my decision. You must allow me to double your fee as I have taken such an unconscionable time. Now, good-bye, and thank you a thousand times for your sympathy and advice.'

'Why, dear me, you haven't even got your prescription yet. This is the mixture, and I should recommend one of these powders every morning and the chemist will put all directions upon the ointment box. You are placed in a cruel situation, but I trust that these may be but passing clouds. When may I hope to hear from you again?'

'To-morrow morning.'

'Very good. How the rain is splashing in the street. You have your waterproof there. You will need it. Good-bye, then, until to-morrow.'

He opened the door. A gust of cold, damp air swept into the hall. And yet the doctor stood for a minute or more watching the lonely figure which passed slowly through the yellow splotches of the gas-lamps and into the broad bars of darkness between. It was but his own shadow which trailed up the wall as he passed the lights, and yet it looked to the doctor's eye as though some huge and sombre figure walked by a manikin's* side, and led him silently up the lonely street.

Doctor Horace Selby heard again of his patient next morning and rather earlier than he had expected. A paragraph in the *Daily News** caused him to push away his breakfast untasted, and turned him sick and faint while he read it. 'A Deplorable Accident' it was headed, and it ran in this way:—

'A fatal accident of a peculiarly painful character is reported from King William Street.* About eleven o'clock last night a young man was observed, while endeavouring to get out of the way of a hansom, to slip and fall under the wheels of a heavy two-horse dray. On being picked up, his injuries were found to be of a most shocking character, and he expired while being conveyed to the hospital. An examination of his pocket-book and card-case shows beyond any question that the deceased is none other than Sir Francis Norton of Deane Park, who has only within the last year come into the baronetcy. The accident is made the more deplorable as the deceased, who was only just of age, was on the eve of being married to a young lady belonging to one of the oldest families in the south. With his wealth and his talents the ball of fortune was at his feet, and his many friends will be deeply grieved to know that his promising career has been cut short in so sudden and tragic a fashion.'

THE STRIPED CHEST

***

'**W**HAT do you make of her, Allardyce?' I asked.

My second mate was standing beside me upon the poop, with his short, thick legs astretch, for the gale had left a considerable swell behind it, and our two quarter-boats* nearly touched the water with every roll. He steadied his glass against the mizzen-shrouds,* and he looked long and hard at this disconsolate stranger every time she came reeling up on to the crest of a roller and hung balanced for a few seconds before swooping down upon the other side. She lay so low in the water that I could only catch an occasional glimpse of a pea-green line of bulwark.

She was a brig,* but her mainmast had been snapped short off some ten feet above the deck, and no effort seemed to have been made to cut away the wreckage, which floated, sails and yards, like the broken wing of a wounded gull, upon the water beside her. The fore-mast was still standing, but the fore-topsail was flying loose, and the headsails* were streaming out in long white pennons in front of her. Never have I seen a vessel which appeared to have gone through rougher handling.

But we could not be surprised at that, for there had been times during the last three days when it was a question whether our own barque would ever see land again. For thirty-six hours we had kept her nose to it, and if the *Mary Sinclair* had not been as good a sea-boat as ever left the Clyde,* we could not have gone through. And yet here we were at the end of it with the loss only of our gig and of part of the starboard bulwark.* It did not astonish us, however, when the smother* had cleared away, to find that others had been less lucky, and that this mutilated brig, staggering about upon a blue sea, and under a cloudless sky, had been left, like a blinded man after a light-ning flash, to tell of the terror which is past.

Allardyce, who was a slow and methodical Scotchman, stared long and hard at the little craft, while our seamen lined the bulwark or clustered upon the fore shrouds to have a view of the stranger. In latitude 20° and longitude 10°,* which were about our bearings, one becomes a little curious as to whom one meets, for one has left the main lines of Atlantic commerce to the north. For ten days we had been sailing over a solitary sea.

'She's derelict, I'm thinking,' said the second mate.

I had come to the same conclusion, for I could see no sign of life upon her deck, and there was no answer to the friendly wavings from our seamen. The crew had probably deserted her under the impression that she was about to founder.

'She can't last long,' continued Allardyce, in his measured way. 'She may put her nose down and her tail up any minute. The water's lipping up to the edge of her rail.'

'What's her flag?' I asked.

'I'm trying to make out. It's got all twisted and tangled with the halyards.* Yes, I've got it now, clear enough. It's the Brazilian flag, but it's wrong side up.'

She had hoisted a signal of distress, then, before her people had abandoned her. Perhaps they had only just gone. I took the mate's glass and looked round over the tumultuous face of the deep blue Atlantic, still veined and starred with white lines and spoutings of foam. But nowhere could I see anything human beyond ourselves.

'There may be living men aboard,' said I.

'There may be salvage,' muttered the second mate.

'Then we will run down upon her lee side,* and lie to.'

We were not more than a hundred yards from her when we swung our foreyard aback, and there we were, the barque and the brig, ducking and bowing like two clowns in a dance.

'Drop one of the quarter-boats,' said I. 'Take four men, Mr Allardyce, and see what you can learn of her.'

But just at that moment my first officer, Mr Armstrong, came on deck, for seven bells* had struck, and it was but a few minutes off his watch. It would interest me to go myself to this abandoned vessel and to see what there might be aboard of her. So, with a word to Armstrong, I swung myself over the side, slipped down the falls,* and took my place in the sheets of the boat.

It was but a little distance, but it took some time to traverse, and so heavy was the roll, that often, when we were in the trough of the sea, we could not see either the barque which we had left or the brig which we were approaching. The sinking sun did not penetrate down there, and it was cold and dark in the hollows of the waves, but each passing billow heaved us up into the warmth and the sunshine once more.

At each of these moments, as we hung upon a white-capped ridge between the two dark valleys, I caught a glimpse of the long, pea-green line, and the nodding foremast of the brig, and I steered so as to come round by her stern, so that we might determine which was the best way of boarding her. As we passed her we saw the name *Nossa Senhora da Vittoria** painted across her dripping counter.

'The weather side, sir,' said the second mate. 'Stand by with the boathook, carpenter!' An instant later we had jumped over the bulwarks, which were hardly higher than our boat, and found ourselves upon the deck of the abandoned vessel.

Our first thought was to provide for our own safety in case—as seemed very probable—the vessel should settle down beneath our feet. With this object two of our men held on to the painter* of the boat, and fended her off from the vessel's side, so that she might be ready in case we had to make a hurried retreat. The carpenter was sent to find out how much water there was, and whether it was still gaining, while the other seaman, Allardyce and myself, made a rapid inspection of the vessel and her cargo.

The deck was littered with wreckage and with hencoops, in which the dead birds were washing about. The boats were gone, with the exception of one, the bottom of which had been stove, and it was certain that the crew had abandoned the vessel. The cabin was in a deck house, one side of which had been beaten in by a heavy sea. Allardyce and I entered it, and found the captain's table as he had left it, his books and papers—all Spanish or Portuguese—scattered over it, with piles of cigarette ash everywhere. I looked about for the log, but could not find it.

'As likely as not he never kept one,' said Allardyce.

'Things are pretty slack aboard a South American trader, and they don't do more than they can help. If there was one it must have been taken away with him in the boat.'

'I should like to take all these books and papers,' said I. 'Ask the carpenter how much time we have.'

His report was reassuring. The vessel was full of water, but some of the cargo was buoyant, and there was no immediate danger of her sinking. Probably she would never sink, but would drift about as one of those terrible, unmarked reefs which have sent so many stout vessels to the bottom.

'In that case there is no danger in your going below, Mr Allardyce,' said I. 'See what you can make of her, and find out how much of her cargo may be saved. I'll look through these papers while you are gone.'

The bills of lading,* and some notes and letters which lay upon the desk, sufficed to inform me that the Brazilian brig *Nossa Senhora da* ~~Tᵤₘₐᵢ ₕₐd ₗₑft Bₐₕᵢₐ ₐ ₘₒₙₜₕ~~ before. The name of the captain was Texeira, but there was no record as to the number of the crew. She was bound for London, and a glance at the bills of lading was sufficient to show me that we were not likely to profit much in the way of salvage. Her cargo consisted of nuts, ginger, and wood, the latter in the shape of great logs of valuable tropical growths. It was these, no doubt, which had prevented the ill-fated vessel from going to the bottom, but they were of such a size as to make it impossible for us to extract them. Besides these, there were a few fancy goods, such as a number of ornamental birds for millinery purposes, and a hundred cases of preserved fruits. And then, as I turned over the papers, I came upon a short note in English, which arrested my attention.

'It is requested,' said the note, 'that the various old Spanish and Indian curiosities, which came out of the Santarem collection, and which are consigned to Prontfoot and Neuman, of Oxford Street, London, should be put in some place where there may be no danger of these very valuable and unique articles being injured or tampered with. This applies most particularly to the treasure-chest of Don Ramirez di Leyra, which must on no account be placed where anyone can get at it.'

The treasure-chest of Don Ramirez! Unique and valuable articles! Here was a chance of salvage after all! I had risen to my feet with the paper in my hand, when my Scotch mate appeared in the doorway.

'I'm thinking all isn't quite as it should be aboard of this ship, sir,' said he. He was a hard-faced man, and yet I could see that he had been startled.

'What's the matter?'

'Murder's the matter, sir. There's a man here with his brains beaten out.'

'Killed in the storm?' said I.

'Maybe so, sir. But I'll be surprised if you think so after you have seen him.'

'Where is he, then?'

'This way, sir; here in the main-deck house.'

There appeared to have been no accommodation below in the brig, for there was the afterhouse for the captain, another by the main hatchway with the cook's galley attached to it, and a third in the forecastle for the men. It was to this middle one that the mate led me. As you entered, the galley, with its litter of tumbled pots and dishes, was upon the right, and upon the left was a small room with two bunks for the officers. Then beyond there was a place about twelve feet square, which was littered with flags and spare canvas. All round the walls were a number of packets done up in coarse cloth and carefully lashed to the woodwork. At the other end was a great box, striped red and white, though the red was so faded and the white so dirty that it was only where the light fell directly upon it that one could see the colouring. The box was, by subsequent measurement, four feet three inches in length, three feet two inches in height, and three feet across—considerably larger than a seaman's chest.

But it was not to the box that my eyes or my thoughts were turned as I entered the store-room. On the floor, lying across the litter of bunting, there was stretched a small, dark man with a short, curling beard. He lay as far as it was possible from the box, with his feet towards it and his head away. A crimson patch was printed upon the white canvas on which his head was resting, and little red ribbons wreathed themselves round his swarthy neck and trailed away on to the floor, but there was no sign of a wound that I could see, and his face was as placid as that of a sleeping child.

It was only when I stooped that I could perceive his injury, and then I turned away with an exclamation of horror. He had been poleaxed; apparently by some person standing behind him. A frightful blow had smashed in the top of his head and penetrated deeply into his brain. His face might well be placid, for death must have been absolutely instantaneous, and the position of the wound showed that he could never have seen the person who had inflicted it.

'Is that foul play or accident, Captain Barclay?' asked my second mate, demurely.

'You are quite right, Mr Allardyce. The man has been murdered, struck down from above by a sharp and heavy weapon. But who was he, and why did they murder him?'

'He was a common seaman, sir,' said the mate. 'You can see that if you look at his fingers.' He turned out his pockets as he spoke and brought to light a pack of cards, some tarred string, and a bundle of Brazilian tobacco.

'Hullo, look at this!' said he.

It was a large, open knife with a stiff spring blade which he had picked up from the floor. The steel was shining and bright, so that we could not associate it with the crime, and yet the dead man had apparently held it in his hand when he was struck down, for it still lay within his grasp.

'It looks to me, sir, as if he knew he was in danger, and kept his knife handy,' said the mate. 'However, we can't help the poor beggar now. I can't make out these things that are lashed to the wall. They seem to be idols and weapons and curios of all sorts done up in old sacking.'

'That's right,' said I. 'They are the only things of value that we are likely to get from the cargo. Hail the barque and tell them to send the other quarter-boat to help us to get the stuff aboard.'

While he was away I examined this curious plunder which had come into our possession. The curiosities were so wrapped up that I could only form a general idea as to their nature, but the striped box stood in a good light where I could thoroughly examine it. On the lid, which was clamped and cornered with metal-work, there was engraved a complex coat of arms, and beneath it was a line of Spanish which I was able to decipher as meaning, 'The treasure-chest of Don Ramirez di Leyra, Knight of the Order of Saint James, Governor and Captain-General of Terra Firma and of the Province of Veraquas.'* In one corner was the date 1606, and on the other a large white label, upon which was written in English, 'You are earnestly requested, upon no account, to open this box.' The same warning was repeated underneath in Spanish. As to the lock, it was a very complex and heavy one of engraved steel, with a Latin motto, which was above a seaman's comprehension.

By the time I had finished this examination of the peculiar box, the other quarter-boat with Mr Armstrong, the first officer, had come alongside, and we began to carry out and place in her the various curiosities which appeared to be the only objects worth moving from the derelict ship. When she was full I sent her back to the barque, and then Allardyce and I, with a carpenter and one seaman, shifted the striped box, which was the only thing left, to our boat, and lowered it over, balancing it upon the two middle thwarts, for it was so heavy that it would have given the boat a dangerous tilt had we placed it at either end. As to the dead man, we left him where we had found him.

The mate had a theory that, at the moment of the desertion of the ship, this fellow had started plundering, and that the captain in an attempt to preserve discipline, had struck him down with a hatchet or some other heavy weapon. It seemed more probable than any other explanation, and yet it did not entirely satisfy me either. But the ocean is full of mysteries, and we were content to leave the fate of the dead seaman of the Brazilian brig to be added to that long list which every sailor can recall.

The heavy box was slung up by ropes on to the deck of the *Mary Sinclair*, and was carried by four seamen into the cabin, where, between the table and the after-lockers, there was just space for it to stand. There it remained during supper, and after that meal the mates remained with me, and discussed over a glass of grog the event of the day. Mr Armstrong was a long, thin, vulture-like man, an excellent seaman, but famous for his nearness* and cupidity. Our treasure-trove had excited him greatly, and already he had begun with glistening eyes to reckon up how much it might be worth to each of us when the shares of the salvage came to be divided.

'If the paper said that they were unique, Mr Barclay, then they may be worth anything that you like to name. You wouldn't believe the sums that the rich collectors give. A thousand pounds is nothing to them. We'll have something to show for our voyage, or I am mistaken.'

'I don't think that,' said I. 'As far as I can see they are not very different from any other South American curios.'

'Well, sir, I've traded there for fourteen voyages, and I have never seen anything like that chest before. That's worth a pile of money, just as it stands. But it's so heavy, that surely there must be something valuable inside it. Don't you think that we ought to open it and see?'

'If you break it open you will spoil it, as likely as not,' said the second mate.

Armstrong squatted down in front of it, with his head on one side, and his long, thin nose within a few inches of the lock.

'The wood is oak,' said he, 'and it has shrunk a little with age. If I had a chisel or a strong-bladed knife I could force the lock back without doing any damage at all.'

The mention of a strong-bladed knife made me think of the dead seaman upon the brig.

'I wonder if he could have been on the job when someone came to interfere with him,' said I.

'I don't know about that, sir, but I am perfectly certain that I could open the box. There's a screwdriver here in the locker. Just hold the lamp, Allardyce, and I'll have it done in a brace of shakes.'

'Wait a bit,' said I, for already, with eyes which gleamed with curiosity and with avarice, he was stooping over the lid. 'I don't see that there is any hurry over this matter. You've read that card which warns us not to open it. It may mean anything or it may mean nothing, but somehow I feel inclined to obey it. After all, whatever is in it will keep, and if it is valuable it will be worth as much if it is opened in the owner's offices as in the cabin of the *Mary Sinclair*.'

The first officer seemed bitterly disappointed at my decision.

'Surely, sir, you are not superstitious about it,' said he, with a slight sneer upon his thin lips. 'If it gets out of our own hands, and we don't see for ourselves what is inside it, we may be done out of our rights; besides——'

'That's enough, Mr Armstrong,' said I, abruptly. 'You may have every confidence that you will get your rights, but I will not have that box opened to-night.'

'Why, the label itself shows that the box has been examined by Europeans,' Allardyce added. 'Because a box is a treasure-box is no reason that it has treasures inside it now. A good many folk have had a peep into it since the days of the old Governor of Terra Firma.'

Armstrong threw the screwdriver down upon the table and shrugged his shoulders.

'Just as you like,' said he; but for the rest of the evening, although we spoke upon many subjects, I noticed that his eyes were continually coming round, with the same expression of curiosity and greed, to the old striped box.

And now I come to that portion of my story which fills me even now with a shuddering horror when I think of it. The main cabin had the rooms of the officers round it, but mine was the farthest away from it at the end of the little passage which led to the companion. No regular watch was kept by me, except in cases of emergency, and the three mates divided the watches among them. Armstrong had the middle watch, which ends at four in the morning, and he was relieved by Allardyce. For my part I have always been one of the soundest of sleepers, and it is rare for anything less than a hand upon my shoulder to arouse me.

And yet I was aroused that night, or rather in the early grey of the morning. It was just half-past four by my chronometer when something caused me to sit up in my berth wide awake and with every nerve tingling. It was a sound of some sort, a crash with a human cry at the end of it, which still jarred upon my ears. I sat listening, but all was now silent. And yet it could not have been imagination, that hideous cry, for the echo of it still rang in my head, and it seemed to have come from some place quite close to me. I sprang from my bunk, and, pulling on some clothes, I made my way into the cabin.

At first I saw nothing unusual there. In the cold, grey light I made out the red-clothed table, the six rotating chairs, the walnut lockers, the swinging barometer, and there, at the end, the big striped chest. I was turning away with the intention of going upon deck and asking the second mate if he had heard anything, when my eyes fell suddenly upon something which projected from under the table. It was the leg of a man—a leg with a long sea-boot upon it. I stooped, and there was a figure sprawling upon his face, his arms thrown forward and his body twisted. One glance told me that it was Armstrong, the first officer, and a second that he was a dead man. For a few moments I stood gasping. Then I rushed on to the deck, called Allardyce to my assistance, and came back with him into the cabin.

Together we pulled the unfortunate fellow from under the table, and as we looked at his dripping head we exchanged glances, and I do not know which was the paler of the two.

'The same as the Spanish sailor,' said I.

'The very same. God preserve us! It's that infernal chest! Look at Armstrong's hand!'

He held up the mate's right hand, and there was the screwdriver which he had wished to use the night before.

'He's been at the chest, sir. He knew that I was on deck and you asleep. He knelt down in front of it, and he pushed the lock back with that tool. Then something happened to him, and he cried out so that you heard him.'

'Allardyce,' I whispered, 'what *could* have happened to him?'

The second mate put his hand upon my sleeve and drew me into his cabin.

'We can talk here, sir, and we don't know who may be listening to us in there. What do you suppose is in that box, Captain Barclay?'

'I give you my word, Allardyce, that I have no idea.'

'Well, I can only find one theory which will fit all the facts. Look at the size of the box. Look at all the carving and metal-work which may conceal any number of holes. Look at the weight of it; it took four men to carry it. On the top of that, remember that two men have tried to open it, and both have come to their end through it. Now, sir, what can it mean except one thing?'

'You mean there is a man in it?'

'Of course there is a man in it. You know how it is in these South American States, sir. A man may be President one week and hunted like a dog the next. They are for ever flying for their lives. My idea is that there is some fellow in hiding there, who is armed and desperate, and who will fight to the death before he is taken.'

'But his food and drink?'

'It's a roomy chest, sir, and he may have some provisions stowed away. As to his drink, he had a friend among the crew upon the brig who saw that he had what he needed.'

'You think, then, that the label asking people not to open the box was simply written in his interest?'

'Yes, sir, that is my idea. Have you any other way of explaining the facts?'

I had to confess that I had not.

'The question is what are we to do?' I asked.

'The man's a dangerous ruffian who sticks at nothing. I'm thinking it wouldn't be a bad thing to put a rope round the chest and tow it alongside for half an hour; then we could open it at our ease. Or if we just tied the box up and kept him from getting any water maybe that would do as well. Or the carpenter could put a coat of varnish over it and stop all the blowholes.'

'Come, Allardyce,' said I, angrily. 'You don't seriously mean to say that a whole ship's company are going to be terrorized by a single man in a box. If he's there, I'll engage to fetch him out!' I went to my room and came back with my revolver in my hand.

'Now, Allardyce,' said I. 'Do you open the lock, and I'll stand on guard.'

'For God's sake, think what you are doing, sir!' cried the mate. 'Two men have lost their lives over it, and the blood of one not yet dry upon the carpet.'

'The more reason why we should revenge him.'

'Well, sir, at least let me call the carpenter. Three are better than two, and he is a good stout man.'

He went off in search of him, and I was left alone with the striped chest in the cabin. I don't think that I'm a nervous man, but I kept the table between me and this solid old relic of the Spanish Main.* In the growing light of morning the red and white striping was beginning to appear, and the curious scrolls and wreaths of metal and carving which showed the loving pains which cunning craftsmen had expended upon it. Presently the carpenter and the mate came back together, the former with a hammer in his hand.

'It's a bad business, this, sir,' said he, shaking his head, as he looked at the body of the mate. 'And you think there's someone hiding in the box?'

'There's no doubt about it,' said Allardyce, picking up the screwdriver and setting his jaw like a man who needs to brace his courage. 'I'll drive the lock back if you will both stand by. If he rises let him have it on the head with your hammer, carpenter! Shoot at once, sir, if he raises his hand. Now!'

He had knelt down in front of the striped chest, and passed the blade of the tool under the lid. With a sharp snick the lock flew back. 'Stand by!' yelled the mate, and with a heave he threw open the massive top of the box. As it swung up, we all three sprang back, I with my pistol levelled, and the carpenter with the hammer above his head. Then, as nothing happened, we each took a step forward and peeped in. The box was empty.

Not quite empty either, for in one corner was lying an old yellow candlestick, elaborately engraved, which appeared to be as old as the box itself. Its rich yellow tone and artistic shape suggested that it was an object of value. For the rest there was nothing more weighty or valuable than dust in the old striped treasure-chest.

'Well, I'm blessed!' cried Allardyce, staring blankly into it. 'Where does the weight come in, then?'

'Look at the thickness of the sides and look at the lid. Why, it's five inches through. And see that great metal spring across it.'

'That's for holding the lid up,' said the mate. 'You see, it won't lean back. What's that German printing on the inside?'

'It means that it was made by Johann Rothstein of Augsburg,* in 1606.'

'And a solid bit of work, too. But it doesn't throw much light on what has passed, does it, Captain Barclay? That candlestick looks like gold. We shall have something for our trouble after all.'

He leant forward to grasp it, and from that moment I have never doubted as to the reality of inspiration, for on the instant I caught him by the collar and pulled him straight again. It may have been some story of the Middle Ages which had come back to my mind, or it may have been that my eye had caught some red which was not that of rust upon the upper part of the lock, but to him and to me it will always seem an inspiration, so prompt and sudden was my action.

'There's devilry here,' said I. 'Give me the crooked stick from the corner.'

It was an ordinary walking cane with a hooked top. I passed it over the candlestick and gave it a pull. With a flash a row of polished steel fangs shot out from below the upper lip, and the great striped chest snapped at us like a wild animal. Clang came the huge lid into its place, and the glasses on the swinging rack sang and tinkled with the shock. The mate sat down on the edge of the table and shivered like a frightened horse.

'You've saved my life, Captain Barclay!' said he.

So this was the secret of the striped treasure-chest of old Don Ramirez di Leyra, and this was how he preserved his ill-gotten gains from the Terra Firma and the Province of Veraquas. Be the thief ever so cunning he could not tell that golden candlestick from the other articles of value, and the instant that he laid hand upon it the terrible spring was unloosed and the murderous steel spikes were driven into his brain, while the shock of the blow sent the victim backwards and enabled the chest to automatically close itself. How many, I wondered, had fallen victims to the ingenuity of the Mechanic of Augsburg. And as I thought of the possible history of that grim striped chest my resolution was very quickly taken.

'Carpenter, bring three men and carry this on deck.'

'Going to throw it overboard, sir?'

'Yes, Mr Allardyce. I'm not superstitious as a rule, but there are some things which are more than a sailor can be called upon to stand.'

'No wonder that brig made heavy weather, Captain Barclay, with such a thing on board. The glass is dropping fast, sir, and we are only just in time.'

So we did not even wait for the three sailors, but we carried it out, the mate, the carpenter, and I, and we pushed it with our own hands over the bulwarks. There was a white spout of water, and it was gone. There it lies, the striped chest, a thousand fathoms deep, and if, as they say, the sea will some day be dry land, I grieve for the man who finds that old box and tries to penetrate into its secret.

THE FIEND OF THE COOPERAGE

Ｔ was no easy matter to bring the *Gamecock* up to the island, for the river had swept down so much silt that the banks extended for many miles out into the Atlantic. The coast was hardly to be seen when the first white curl of the breakers warned us of our danger, and from there onwards we made our way very carefully under mainsail and jib,* keeping the broken water well to the left, as is indicated on the chart. More than once her bottom touched the sand (we were drawing something under six feet at the time), but we had always way enough and luck enough to carry us through. Finally, the water shoaled, very rapidly, but they had sent a canoe from the factory, and the Krooboy* pilot brought us within two hundred yards of the island. Here we dropped our anchor, for the gestures of the negro indicated that we could not hope to get any farther. The blue of the sea had changed to the brown of the river, and, even under the shelter of the island, the current was singing and swirling round our bows. The stream appeared to be in spate,* for it was over the roots of the palm trees, and everywhere upon its muddy greasy surface we could see logs of wood and debris of all sorts which had been carried down by the flood.

When I had assured myself that we swung securely at our moorings, I thought it best to begin watering at once, for the place looked as if it reeked with fever. The heavy river, the muddy, shining banks, the bright poisonous green of the jungle, the moist steam in the air, they were all so many danger signals to one who could read them. I sent the long-boat off, therefore, with two large hogsheads, which should be sufficient to last us until we made St Paul de Loanda.* For my own part I took the dinghy and rowed for the island, for I could see the Union Jack fluttering above the palms to mark the position of Armitage and Wilson's trading station.

When I had cleared the grove, I could see the place, a long, low, whitewashed building, with a deep verandah in front, and an immense pile of palm-oil barrels heaped upon either flank of it. A row of surf boats and canoes lay along the beach, and a single small jetty projected into the river. Two men in white suits with red cummerbunds round their waists were waiting upon the end of it to receive me. One was a large portly fellow with a greyish beard. The other was slender and tall, with a pale pinched face, which was half-concealed by a great mushroom-shaped hat.

'Very glad to see you,' said the latter, cordially. 'I am Walker, the agent of Armitage and Wilson. Let me introduce Doctor Severall of the same company. It is not often we see a private yacht in these parts.'

She's the *Gamecock*,' I explained. 'I'm owner; and captain—Meldrum is the name.'

'Exploring?' he asked.

'I'm a lepidopterist—a butterfly-catcher. I've been doing the west coast from Senegal downwards.'

'Good sport?' asked the Doctor, turning a slow yellow-shot eye upon me.

'I have forty cases full. We came in here to water, and also to see what you have in my line.'

These introductions and explanations had filled up the time whilst my two Krooboys were making the dinghy fast. Then I walked down the jetty with one of my new acquaintances upon either side, each plying me with questions, for they had seen no white man for months.

'What do we do?' said the Doctor, when I had begun asking questions in my turn. 'Our business keeps us pretty busy, and in our leisure time we talk politics.'

'Yes, by the special mercy of Providence Severall is a rank Radical, and I am a good stiff Unionist, and we talk Home Rule* for two solid hours every evening.'

'And drink quinine* cocktails,' said the Doctor. 'We're both pretty well salted now, but our normal temperature was about 103 last year. I shouldn't, as an impartial adviser, recommend you to stay here very long unless you are collecting bacilli as well as butterflies. The mouth of the Ogowai River* will never develop into a health resort.'

There is nothing finer than the way in which these outlying pickets of civilization distil a grim humour out of their desolate situation, and turn not only a bold, but a laughing face upon the chances which their lives may bring. Everywhere from Sierra Leone downwards I had found the same reeking swamps, the same isolated fever-racked communities, and the same bad jokes. There is something approaching to the divine in that power of man to rise above his conditions and to use his mind for the purpose of mocking at the miseries of his body.

'Dinner will be ready in about half an hour, Captain Meldrum,' said the Doctor. 'Walker has gone in to see about it; he's the house-keeper this week. Meanwhile, if you like, we'll stroll round and I'll show you the sights of the island.'

The sun had already sunk beneath the line of palm trees, and the great arch of the heaven above our head was like the inside of a huge shell, shimmering with dainty pinks and delicate iridescence. No one who has not lived in a land where the weight and heat of a napkin become intolerable upon the knees can imagine the blessed relief which the coolness of evening brings along with it. In this sweeter and purer air the Doctor and I walked round the little island, he pointing out the stores, and explaining the routine of his work.

'There's a certain romance about the place,' said he, in answer to some remark of mine about the dullness of their lives. 'We are living here just upon the edge of the great unknown. Up there,' he contin-ued, pointing to the north-east, 'Du Chaillu penetrated, and found the home of the gorilla. That is the Gaboon* country—the land of the great apes. In this direction,' pointing to the south-east, 'no one has been very far. The land which is drained by this river is practically unknown to Europeans. Every log which is carried past us by the cur-rent has come from an undiscovered country. I've often wished that I was a better botanist when I have seen the singular orchids and curious-looking plants which have been cast up on the eastern end of the island.'

The place which the Doctor indicated was a sloping brown beach, freely littered with the flotsam of the stream. At each end was a curved point, like a little natural breakwater, so that a small shallow bay was left between. This was full of floating vegetation, with a single huge splintered tree lying stranded in the middle of it, the current rippling against its high black side.

'These are all from up country,' said the Doctor. 'They get caught in our little bay, and then when some extra freshet comes they are washed out again and carried out to sea.'

'What is the tree?' I asked.

'Oh, some kind of teak, I should imagine, but pretty rotten by the look of it. We get all sorts of big hardwood trees floating past here, to say nothing of the palms. Just come in here, will you?'

He led the way into a long building with an immense quantity of barrel staves and iron hoops littered about in it.

'This is our cooperage,' said he. 'We have the staves sent out in bundles, and we put them together ourselves. Now, you don't see anything particularly sinister about this building, do you?'

I looked round at the high corrugated iron roof, the white wooden walls, and the earthen floor. In one corner lay a mattress and a blanket.

'I see nothing very alarming,' said I.

'And yet there's something out of the common, too,' he remarked. 'You see that bed? Well, I intend to sleep there to-night. I don't want to buck, but I think it's a bit of a test for nerve.'

'Why?'

'Oh, there have been some funny goings on. You were talking about the monotony of our lives, but I assure you that they are sometimes quite as exciting as we wish them to be. You'd better come back to the house now, for after sundown we begin to get the fever-fog up from the marshes. There, you can see it coming across the river.'

I looked and saw long tentacles of white vapour writhing out from among the thick green underwood and crawling at us over the broad swirling surface of the brown river. At the same time the air turned suddenly dank and cold.

'There's the dinner gong,' said the Doctor. 'If this matter interests you I'll tell you about it afterwards.'

It did interest me very much, for there was something earnest and subdued in his manner as he stood in the empty cooperage, which appealed very forcibly to my imagination. He was a big, bluff, hearty man, this Doctor, and yet I had detected a curious expression in his eyes as he glanced about him—an expression which I would not describe as one of fear, but rather that of a man who is alert and on his guard.

'By the way,' said I, as we returned to the house, 'you have shown me the huts of a good many of your native assistants, but I have not seen any of the natives themselves.'

'They sleep in the hulk over yonder,' the Doctor answered, pointing over to one of the banks.

'Indeed. I should not have thought in that case they would need the huts.'

'Oh, they used the huts until quite recently. We've put them on the hulk until they recover their confidence a little. They were all half mad with fright, so we let them go, and nobody sleeps on the island except Walker and myself.'

'What frightened them?' I asked.

'Well, that brings us back to the same story. I suppose Walker has no objection to your hearing all about it. I don't know why we should make any secret about it, though it is certainly a pretty bad business.'

He made no further allusion to it during the excellent dinner which had been prepared in my honour. It appeared that no sooner had the little white topsail of the *Gamecock* shown round Cape Lopez than these kind fellows had begun to prepare their famous pepper-pot—which is the pungent stew peculiar to the West Coast—and to boil their yams and sweet potatoes. We sat down to as good a native dinner as one could wish, served by a smart Sierra Leone waiting boy. I was just remarking to myself that he at least had not shared in the general flight when, having laid the dessert and wine upon the table, he raised his hand to his turban.

'Anyting else I do, Massa Walker?' he asked.

'No, I think that is all right, Moussa,' my host answered. 'I am not feeling very well to-night, though, and I should much prefer if you would stay on the island.'

I saw a struggle between his fears and his duty upon the swarthy face of the African. His skin had turned of that livid purplish tint which stands for pallor in a negro, and his eyes looked furtively about him.

'No, no, Massa Walker,' he cried, at last, 'you better come to the hulk with me, sah. Look after you much better in the hulk, sah!'

'That won't do, Moussa. White men don't run away from the posts where they are placed.'

Again I saw the passionate struggle in the negro's face, and again his fears prevailed.

'No use, Massa Walker, sah!' he cried. 'S'elp me, I can't do it. If it was yesterday or if it was tomorrow, but this is the third night, sah, an' it's more than I can face.'

Walker shrugged his shoulders.

'Off with you then!' said he. 'When the mail-boat comes you can get back to Sierra Leone, for I'll have no servant who deserts me when I need him most. I suppose this is all mystery to you, or has the Doctor told you, Captain Meldrum?'

'I showed Captain Meldrum the cooperage, but I did not tell him anything,' said Doctor Severall. 'You're looking bad, Walker,' he added, glancing at his companion. 'You have a strong touch coming on you.'

'Yes, I've had the shivers all day, and now my head is like a cannon-ball. I took ten grains of quinine, and my ears are singing like a kettle. But I want to sleep with you in the cooperage to-night.'

'No, no, my dear chap. I won't hear of such a thing. You must get to bed at once, and I am sure Meldrum will excuse you. I shall sleep in the cooperage, and I promise you that I'll be round with your medicine before breakfast.'

It was evident that Walker had been struck by one of those sudden and violent attacks of remittent fever* which are the curse of the West Coast. His sallow cheeks were flushed and his eyes shining with fever, and suddenly as he sat there he began to croon out a song in the high-pitched voice of delirium.

'Come, come, we must get you to bed, old chap,' said the Doctor, and with my aid he led his friend into his bedroom. There we un-dressed him and presently, after taking a strong sedative, he settled down into a deep slumber.

'He's right for the night,' said the Doctor, as we sat down and filled our glasses once more. 'Sometimes it is my turn and sometimes his, but, fortunately, we have never been down together. I should have been sorry to be out of it to-night, for I have a little mystery to unravel. I told you that I intended to sleep in the cooperage.'

'Yes, you said so.'

'When I said sleep I meant watch, for there will be no sleep for me. We've had such a scare here that no native will stay after sundown, and I mean to find out to-night what the cause of it all may be. It has always been the custom for a native watchman to sleep in the cooper-age, to prevent the barrel hoops being stolen. Well, six days ago the fellow who slept there disappeared, and we have never seen a trace of him since. It was certainly singular, for no canoe had been taken, and these waters are too full of crocodiles for any man to swim to shore. What became of the fellow, or how he could have left the island is a complete mystery. Walker and I were merely surprised, but the blacks were badly scared and queer Voodoo tales began to get about amongst them. But the real stampede broke out three nights ago, when the new watchman in the cooperage also disappeared.'

'What became of him?' I asked.

'Well, we not only don't know, but we can't even give a guess which would fit the facts. The niggers swear there is a fiend in the cooper-age who claims a man every third night. They wouldn't stay in the

island—nothing could persuade them. Even Moussa, who is a faithful boy enough, would, as you have seen, leave his master in a fever
rather than remain for the night. If we are to continue to run this
place we must reassure our niggers, and I don't know any better way
of doing it than by putting in a night there myself. This is the third
night, you see, so I suppose the thing in the, wherever it may be.'

'Than you no clue?' I asked. 'Was there no mark of violence, no
blood-stain, no footprints, nothing to give a hint as to what kind of
danger you may have to meet?'

'Absolutely nothing. The man was gone and that was all. Last time
it was old Ali, who has been wharf tender here since the place was
started. He was always as steady as a rock, and nothing but foul play
would take him from his work.'

'Well,' said I, 'I really don't think that this is a one-man job. Your
friend is full of laudanum,* and come what might he can be of no
assistance to you. You must let me stay and put in a night with you at
the cooperage.'

'Well, now, that's very good of you, Meldrum,' said he heartily,
shaking my hand across the table. 'It's not a thing that I should have
ventured to propose, for it is asking a good deal of a casual visitor, but
if you really mean it——'

'Certainly I mean it. If you will excuse me a moment, I will hail the
Gamecock and let them know that they need not expect me.'

As we came back from the other end of the little jetty we were both
struck by the appearance of the night. A huge blue-black pile of clouds
had built itself up upon the landward side, and the wind came from it
in little hot pants, which beat upon our faces like the draught from
a blast furnace. Under the jetty the river was swirling and hissing,
tossing little white spurts of spray over the planking.

'Confound it!' said Doctor Severall. 'We are likely to have a flood
on the top of all our troubles. That rise in the river means heavy rain
up-country, and when it once begins you never know how far it will
go. We've had the island nearly covered before now. Well, we'll just go
and see that Walker is comfortable, and then if you like we'll settle
down in our quarters.'

The sick man was sunk in a profound slumber, and we left him
with some crushed limes in a glass beside him in case he should awake
with the thirst of fever upon him. Then we made our way through the
unnatural gloom thrown by that menacing cloud. The river had risen

so high that the little bay which I have described at the end of the island had become almost obliterated through the submerging of its flanking peninsula. The great raft of driftwood, with the huge black tree in the middle, was swaying up and down in the swollen current.

'That's one good thing a flood will do for us,' said the Doctor. 'It carries away all the vegetable stuff which is brought down on to the east end of the island. It came down with the freshet* the other day, and here it will stay until a flood sweeps it out into the main stream. Well, here's our room, and here are some books and here is my tobacco pouch, and we must try and put in the night as best we may.'

By the light of our single lantern the great lonely room looked very gaunt and dreary. Save for the piles of staves and heaps of hoops there was absolutely nothing in it, with the exception of the mattress for the Doctor, which had been laid in the corner. We made a couple of seats and a table out of the staves, and settled down together for a long vigil. Severall had brought a revolver for me and was himself armed with a double-barrelled shot-gun. We loaded our weapons and laid them cocked within reach of our hands. The little circle of light and the black shadows arching over us were so melancholy that he went off to the house, and returned with two candles. One side of the cooperage was pierced, however, by several open windows, and it was only by screening our lights behind staves that we could prevent them from being extinguished.

The Doctor, who appeared to be a man of iron nerves, had settled down to a book, but I observed that every now and then he laid it upon his knee, and took an earnest look all round him. For my part, although I tried once or twice to read, I found it impossible to concentrate my thoughts upon the book. They would always wander back to this great empty silent room, and to the sinister mystery which overshadowed it. I racked my brains for some possible theory which would explain the disappearance of these two men. There was the black fact that they were gone, and not the least tittle of evidence as to why or whither. And here we were waiting in the same place—waiting without an idea as to what we were waiting for. I was right in saying that it was not a one-man job. It was trying enough as it was, but no force upon earth would have kept me there without a comrade.

What an endless, tedious night it was! Outside we heard the lapping and gurgling of the great river, and the soughing* of the rising wind. Within, save for our breathing, the turning of the Doctor's pages, and the high, shrill ping of an occasional mosquito, there was a heavy silence. Once my heart sprang into my mouth as Severall's book suddenly fell to the ground and he sprang to his feet with his eyes on one of the windows.

'Did you see anything, Meldrum?'

'No, did you?'

'Well, I had a vague sense of movement outside that window.' He caught up his gun and approached it. 'No, there's nothing to be seen, and yet I could have sworn that something passed slowly across it.'

'A palm leaf, perhaps,' said I, for the wind was growing stronger every instant.

'Very likely,' said he, and settled down to his book again, but his eyes were for ever darting little suspicious glances up at the window. I watched it also, but all was quiet outside.

And then suddenly our thoughts were turned into a new direction by the bursting of the storm. A blinding flash was followed by a clap which shook the building. Again and again came the vivid white glare with thunder at the same instant, like the flash and roar of a monstrous piece of artillery. And then down came the tropical rain, crashing and rattling on the corrugated iron roofing of the cooperage. The big hollow room boomed like a drum. From the darkness arose a strange mixture of noises, a gurgling, splashing, tinkling, bubbling, washing, dripping—every liquid sound that nature can produce from the thrashing and swishing of the rain to the deep steady boom of the river. Hour after hour the uproar grew louder and more sustained.

'My word,' said Severall, 'we are going to have the father of all the floods this time. Well, here's the dawn coming at last and that is a blessing. We've about exploded the third night superstition, anyhow.'

A grey light was stealing through the room, and there was the day upon us in an instant. The rain had eased off, but the coffee-coloured river was roaring past like a waterfall. Its power made me fear for the anchor of the *Gamecock*.

'I must get aboard,' said I. 'If she drags she'll never be able to beat up the river again.'

'The island is as good as a breakwater,' the Doctor answered. 'I can give you a cup of coffee if you will come up to the house.'

I was chilled and miserable, so the suggestion was a welcome one. We left the ill-omened cooperage with its mystery still unsolved, and we splashed our way up to the house.

'There's the spirit lamp,' said Severall. 'If you would just put a light to it, I will see how Walker feels this morning.'

He left me, but was back in an instant with a dreadful face.

'He's gone!' he cried hoarsely.

The words sent a thrill of horror through me. I stood with the lamp in my hand, glaring at him.

'Yes, he's gone!' he repeated. 'Come and look!'

I followed him without a word, and the first thing that I saw as I entered the bedroom was Walker himself lying huddled on his bed in the grey flannel sleeping suit in which I had helped to dress him on the night before.

'Not dead, surely!' I gasped.

The Doctor was terribly agitated. His hands were shaking like leaves in the wind.

'He's been dead some hours.'

'Was it fever?'

'Fever! Look at his foot!'

I glanced down and a cry of horror burst from my lips. One foot was not merely dislocated, but was turned completely round in a most grotesque contortion.

'Good God!' I cried. 'What can have done this?'

Severall had laid his hand upon the dead man's chest.

'Feel here,' he whispered.

I placed my hand at the same spot. There was no resistance. The body was absolutely soft and limp. It was like pressing a sawdust doll.

'The breast-bone is gone,' said Severall in the same awed whisper. 'He's broken to bits. Thank God that he had the laudanum. You can see by his face that he died in his sleep.'

'But who can have done this?'

'I've had about as much as I can stand,' said the Doctor, wiping his forehead. 'I don't know that I'm a greater coward than my neighbours, but this gets beyond me. If you're going out to the *Gamecock*——'

'Come on!' said I, and off we started. If we did not run it was be-cause each of us wished to keep up the last shadow of his self-respect before the other. It was dangerous in a light canoe on that swollen river, but we never paused to give the matter a thought. He bailing and I paddling we kept her above water, and gained the deck of the yacht. There, with two hundred yards of water between us and this cursed island we felt that we were our own men once more.

'We'll go back in an hour or so,' said he. 'But we need have a little time to steady ourselves. I wouldn't have had the niggers see me as I was just now for a year's salary.'

'I've told the steward to prepare breakfast. Then we shall go back,' said I. 'But in God's name, Doctor Severall, what do you make of it all?'

'It beats me—beats me clean. I've heard of Voodoo devilry, and I've laughed at it with the others. But that poor old Walker, a decent, God-fearing, nineteenth-century, Primrose-League* Englishman should go under like this without a whole bone in his body—it's given me a shake, I won't deny it. But look there, Meldrum, is that hand of yours mad or drunk, or what is it?'

Old Patterson, the oldest man of my crew, and as steady as the Pyramids, had been stationed in the bows with a boat-hook to fend off the drifting logs which came sweeping down with the current. Now he stood with crooked knees, glaring out in front of him, and one forefinger stabbing furiously at the air.

'Look at it!' he yelled. 'Look at it!'

And at the same instant we saw it.

A huge black tree trunk was coming down the river, its broad glistening back just lapped by the water. And in front of it—about three feet in front—arching upwards like the figure-head of a ship, there hung a dreadful face, swaying slowly from side to side. It was flattened, malignant, as large as a small beer-barrel, of a faded fungoid colour, but the neck which supported it was mottled with a dull yellow and black. As it flew past the *Gamecock* in the swirl of the waters I saw two immense coils roll up out of some great hollow in the tree, and the villainous head rose suddenly to the height of eight or ten feet, looking with dull, skin-covered eyes at the yacht. An instant later the tree had shot past us and was plunging with its horrible passenger towards the Atlantic.

'What was it?' I cried.

'It is our fiend of the cooperage,' said Doctor Severall, and he had become in an instant the same bluff, self-confident man that he had been before. 'Yes, that is the devil who has been haunting our island. It is the great python of the Gaboon.'*

I thought of the stories which I had heard all down the coast of the monstrous constrictors of the interior, of their periodical appetite, and of the murderous effects of their deadly squeeze. Then it all took shape in my mind. There had been a freshet the week before. It had brought down this huge hollow tree with its hideous occupant. Who knows from what far distant tropical forest it may have come! It had been stranded on the little east bay of the island. The cooperage had been the nearest house. Twice with the return of its appetite it had carried off the watchman. Last night it had doubtless come again, when Severall had thought he saw something move at the window, but our lights had driven it away. It had writhed onwards and had slain poor Walker in his sleep.

'Why did it not carry him off?' I asked.

'The thunder and lightning must have scared the brute away. There's your steward, Meldrum. The sooner we have breakfast and get back to the island the better, or some of those niggers might think that we had been frightened.'

THE BEETLE-HUNTER

A CURIOUS experience? said the Doctor. Yes, my friends, I have had one very curious experience. I never expect to have another, for it is against all doctrines of chances that two such events would befall any one man in a single lifetime. You may believe me or not, but the thing happened exactly as I tell it.

I had just become a medical man, but I had not started in practice, and I lived in rooms in Gower Street.* The street has been renumbered since then, but it was in the only house which has a bow-window, upon the left-hand side as you go down from the Metropolitan Station.* A widow named Murchison kept the house at that time, and she had three medical students and one engineer as lodgers. I occupied the top room, which was the cheapest, but cheap as it was it was more than I could afford. My small resources were dwindling away, and every week it became more necessary that I should find something to do. Yet I was very unwilling to go into general practice, for my tastes were all in the direction of science, and especially of zoology, towards which I had always a strong leaning. I had almost given the fight up and resigned myself to being a medical drudge for life, when the turning-point of my struggles came in a very extraordinary way.

One morning I had picked up the *Standard** and was glancing over its contents. There was a complete absence of news, and I was about to toss the paper down again, when my eyes were caught by an advertisement at the head of the personal column. It was worded in this way:

'Wanted for one or more days the services of a medical man. It is essential that he should be a man of strong physique, of steady nerves, and of a resolute nature. Must be an entomologist—coleopterist* preferred. Apply, in person, at 77B, Brook Street.* Application must be made before twelve o'clock to-day.'

Now, I have already said that I was devoted to zoology. Of all branches of zoology, the study of insects was the most attractive to me, and of all insects beetles were the species with which I was most familiar. Butterfly collectors are numerous, but beetles are far more varied, and more accessible in these islands than are butterflies. It was this fact which had attracted my attention to them, and I had myself made a collection which numbered some hundred varieties. As to the other requisites of the advertisement, I knew that my nerves could be depended upon, and I had won the weight-throwing competition at the inter-hospital sports. Clearly, I was the very man for the vacancy. Within five minutes of my having read the advertisement I was in a cab and on my way to Brook Street.

As I drove, I kept turning the matter over in my head and trying to make a guess as to what sort of employment it could be which needed such curious qualifications. A strong physique, a resolute nature, a medical training, and a knowledge of beetles—what connection could there be between these various requisites? And then there was the disheartening fact that the situation was not a permanent one, but terminable from day to day, according to the terms of the advertisement. The more I pondered over it the more unintelligible did it become; but at the end of my meditations I always came back to the ground fact that, come what might, I had nothing to lose, that I was completely at the end of my resources, and that I was ready for any adventure, however desperate, which would put a few honest sovereigns into my pocket. The man fears to fail who has to pay for his failure, but there was no penalty which Fortune could exact from me. I was like the gambler with empty pockets, who is still allowed to try his luck with the others.

No. 77B, Brook Street, was one of those dingy and yet imposing houses, dun-coloured and flat-faced, with the intensely respectable and solid air which marks the Georgian builder. As I alighted from the cab, a young man came out of the door and walked swiftly down the street. In passing me, I noticed that he cast an inquisitive and somewhat malevolent glance at me, and I took the incident as a good omen, for his appearance was that of a rejected candidate, and if he resented my application it meant that the vacancy was not yet filled up. Full of hope, I ascended the broad steps and rapped with the heavy knocker.

A footman in powder and livery opened the door. Clearly I was in touch with people of wealth and fashion.

'Yes, sir?' said the footman.

'I came in answer to——'

'Quite so, sir,' said the footman. 'Lord Linchmere will see you at once in the library.'

Lord Linchmere! I had vaguely heard the name, but could not for the instant recall anything about him. Following the footman, I was shown into a large, book-lined room in which there was seated behind a writing-desk a small man with a pleasant, clean-shaven, mobile face, and long hair shot with grey, brushed back from his forehead. He looked me up and down with a very shrewd, penetrating glance, holding the card which the footman had given him in his right hand. Then he smiled pleasantly, and I felt that externally at any rate I possessed the qualifications which he desired.

'You have come in answer to my advertisement, Dr Hamilton?' he asked.

'Yes, sir.'

'Do you fulfil the conditions which are there laid down?'

'I believe that I do.'

'You are a powerful man, or so I should judge from your appearance.'

'I think that I am fairly strong.'

'And resolute?'

'I believe so.'

'Have you ever known what it was to be exposed to imminent danger?'

'No, I don't know that I ever have.'

'But you think you would be prompt and cool at such a time?'

'I hope so.'

'Well, I believe that you would. I have the more confidence in you because you do not pretend to be certain as to what you would do in a position that was new to you. My impression is that, so far as personal qualities go, you are the very man of whom I am in search. That being settled, we may pass on to the next point.'

'Which is?'

'To talk to me about beetles.'

I looked across to see if he was joking, but, on the contrary, he was leaning eagerly forward across his desk, and there was an expression of something like anxiety in his eyes.

'I am afraid that you do not know about beetles,' he cried.

'On the contrary, sir, it is the one scientific subject about which I feel that I really do know something.'

'I am overjoyed to hear it. Please talk to me about beetles.'

I talked. I do not profess to have said anything original upon the subject, but I gave a short sketch of the characteristics of the beetle, and ran over the more common species, with some allusions to the specimens in my own little collection and to the article upon 'Burying Beetles' which I had contributed to the *Journal of Entomological Science*.*

'What! not a collector?' cried Lord Linchmere. 'You don't mean that you are yourself a collector?' His eyes danced with pleasure at the thought.

'You are certainly the very man in London for my purpose. I thought that among five millions of people there must be such a man, but the difficulty is to lay one's hands upon him. I have been extraordinarily fortunate in finding you.'

He rang a gong upon the table, and the footman entered.

'Ask Lady Rossiter to have the goodness to step this way,' said his lordship, and a few moments later the lady was ushered into the room. She was a small, middle-aged woman, very like Lord Linchmere in appearance, with the same quick, alert features and grey-black hair. The expression of anxiety, however, which I had observed upon his face was very much more marked upon hers. Some great grief seemed to have cast its shadow over her features. As Lord Linchmere presented me she turned her face full upon me, and I was shocked to observe a half-healed scar extending for two inches over her right eyebrow. It was partly concealed by plaster, but none the less I could see that it had been a serious wound and not long inflicted.

'Dr Hamilton is the very man for our purpose, Evelyn,' said Lord Linchmere. 'He is actually a collector of beetles, and he has written articles upon the subject.'

'Really!' said Lady Rossiter. 'Then you must have heard of my husband. Everyone who knows anything about beetles must have heard of Sir Thomas Rossiter.'

For the first time a thin little ray of light began to break into the obscure business. Here, at last, was a connection between these people and beetles. Sir Thomas Rossiter—he was the greatest authority upon the subject in the world. He had made it his life-long study, and had written a most exhaustive work upon it. I hastened to assure her that I had read and appreciated it.

'Have you met my husband?' she asked.

'No, I have not.'

'But you shall,' said Lord Linchmere, with decision.

The lady was standing beside the desk, and she put her hand upon his shoulder. It was obvious to me as I saw their faces together that they were brother and sister.

'Are you really prepared for this, Charles? It is noble of you, but you fill me with fears.' Her voice quavered with apprehension, and he appeared to me to be equally moved, though he was making strong efforts to conceal his agitation.

'Yes, yes, dear; it is all settled, it is all decided; in fact, there is no other possible way, that I can see.'

'There is one obvious way.'

'No, no, Evelyn, I shall never abandon you—never. It will come right—depend upon it; it will come right, and surely it looks like the interference of Providence that so perfect an instrument should be put into our hands.'

My position was embarrassing, for I felt that for the instant they had forgotten my presence. But Lord Linchmere came back suddenly to me and to my engagement.

'The business for which I want you, Dr Hamilton, is that you should put yourself absolutely at my disposal. I wish you to come for a short journey with me, to remain always at my side, and to promise to do without question whatever I may ask you, however unreasonable it may appear to you to be.'

'That is a good deal to ask,' said I.

'Unfortunately I cannot put it more plainly, for I do not myself know what turn matters may take. You may be sure, however, that you will not be asked to do anything which your conscience does not approve; and I promise you that, when all is over, you will be proud to have been concerned in so good a work.'

'If it ends happily,' said the lady.

'Exactly; if it ends happily,' his lordship repeated.

'And terms?' I asked.

'Twenty pounds a day.'

I was amazed at the sum, and must have showed my surprise upon my features.

'It is a rare combination of qualities, as must have struck you when you first read the advertisement,' said Lord Linchmere; 'such varied gifts may well command a high return, and I do not conceal from you that your duties might be arduous or even dangerous. Besides, it is possible that one or two days may bring the matter to an end.'

'Please God!' sighed his sister.

'So now, Dr Hamilton, may I rely upon your aid?'

'Most undoubtedly,' said I. 'You have only to tell me what my duties are.'

'Your first duty will be to return to your home. You will pack up whatever you may need for a short visit to the country. We start together from Paddington Station* at 3.40 this afternoon.'

'Do we go far?'

'As far as Pangbourne.* Meet me at the bookstall at 3.30. I shall have the tickets. Good-bye, Dr Hamilton! And, by the way, there are two things which I should be very glad if you would bring with you, in case you have them. One is your case for collecting beetles, and the other is a stick, and the thicker and heavier the better.'

* * *

You may imagine that I had plenty to think of from the time that I left Brook Street until I set out to meet Lord Linchmere at Paddington. The whole fantastic business kept arranging and rearranging itself in kaleidoscopic forms inside my brain, until I had thought out a dozen explanations, each of them more grotesquely improbable than the last. And yet I felt that the truth must be something grotesquely improbable also. At last I gave up all attempts at finding a solution, and contented myself with exactly carrying out the instructions which I had received. With a hand valise, specimen-case, and a loaded cane, I was waiting at the Paddington bookstall when Lord Linchmere arrived. He was an even smaller man than I had thought—frail and peaky, with a manner which was more nervous than it had been in the morning. He wore a long, thick travelling ulster,* and I observed that he carried a heavy blackthorn cudgel in his hand.

'I have the tickets,' said he, leading the way up the platform. 'This is our train. I have engaged a carriage, for I am particularly anxious to impress one or two things upon you while we travel down.'

And yet all that he had to impress upon me might have been said in a sentence, for it was that I was to remember that I was there as a protection to himself, and that I was not on any consideration to leave him for an instant. This he repeated again and again as our journey drew to a close, with an insistence which showed that his nerves were thoroughly shaken.

'Yes,' he said at last, in answer to my looks rather than to my words, 'I *am* nervous, Dr Hamilton. I have always been a timid man, and my timidity depends upon my frail physical health. But my soul is firm, and I can bring myself up to face a danger which a less-nervous man might shrink from. What I am doing now is done from no compulsion, but entirely from a sense of duty, and yet it is, beyond doubt, a desperate risk. If things should go wrong, I will have some claims to the title of martyr.'

This eternal reading of riddles was too much for me. I felt that I must put a term to it.

'I think it would be very much better, sir, if you were to trust me entirely,' said I. 'It is impossible for me to act effectively, when I do not know what are the objects which we have in view, or even where we are going.'

'Oh, as to where we are going, there need be no mystery about that,' said he; 'we are going to Delamere Court, the residence of Sir Thomas Rossiter, with whose work you are so conversant. As to the exact object of our visit, I do not know that at this stage of the proceedings anything would be gained, Dr Hamilton, by taking you into my complete confidence. I may tell you that we are acting—I say "we," because my sister, Lady Rossiter, takes the same view as myself—with the one object of preventing anything in the nature of a family scandal. That being so, you can understand that I am loth to give any explanations which are not absolutely necessary. It would be a different matter, Dr Hamilton, if I were asking your advice. As matters stand, it is only your active help which I need, and I will indicate to you from time to time how you can best give it.'

There was nothing more to be said, and a poor man can put up with a good deal for twenty pounds a day, but I felt none the less that Lord Linchmere was acting rather scurvily towards me. He wished to convert me into a passive tool, like the blackthorn in his hand. With his sensitive disposition I could imagine, however, that scandal would be abhorrent to him, and I realized that he would not take me into his confidence until no other course was open to him. I must trust to my own eyes and ears to solve the mystery, but I had every confidence that I should not trust to them in vain.

Delamere Court lies a good five miles from Pangbourne Station, and we drove for that distance in an open fly.* Lord Linchmere sat in deep thought during the time, and he never opened his mouth until we were close to our destination. When he did speak it was to give me a piece of information which surprised me.

'Perhaps you are not aware,' said he, 'that I am a medical man like yourself?'

'No, sir, I did not know it.'

'Yes, I qualified in my younger days, when there were several lives between me and the peerage. I have not had occasion to practise, but I have found it a useful education, all the same. I never regretted the years which I devoted to medical study. These are the gates of Delamere Court.'

We had come to two high pillars crowned with heraldic monsters which flanked the opening of a winding avenue. Over the laurel bushes and rhododendrons I could see a long, many-gabled mansion, girdled with ivy, and toned to the warm, cheery, mellow glow of old brick-work. My eyes were still fixed in admiration upon this delightful house when my companion plucked nervously at my sleeve.

'Here's Sir Thomas,' he whispered. 'Please talk beetle all you can.'

A tall, thin figure, curiously angular and bony, had emerged through a gap in the hedge of laurels. In his hand he held a spud,* and he wore gauntleted gardener's gloves. A broad-brimmed, grey hat cast his face into shadow, but it struck me as exceedingly austere, with an ill-nourished beard and harsh, irregular features. The fly pulled up and Lord Linchmere sprang out.

'My dear Thomas, how are you?' said he, heartily.

But the heartiness was by no means reciprocal. The owner of the grounds glared at me over his brother-in-law's shoulder, and I caught broken scraps of sentences—'well-known wishes ... hatred of strangers ... unjustifiable intrusion ... perfectly inexcusable.' Then there was a muttered explanation, and the two of them came over together to the side of the fly.

'Let me present you to Sir Thomas Rossiter, Dr Hamilton,' said Lord Linchmere. 'You will find that you have a strong community of tastes.'

I bowed. Sir Thomas stood very stiffly, looking at me severely from under the broad brim of his hat.

'Lord Linchmere tells me that you know something about beetles,' said he. 'What do you know about beetles?'

'I know what I have learned from your work upon the coleoptera, Sir Thomas,' I answered.

'Give me the names of the better-known species of the British scarabæi,'* said he.

I had not expected an examination, but fortunately I was ready for one. My answers seemed to please him, for his stern features relaxed.

'You appear to have read my book with some profit, sir,' said he. 'It is a rare thing for me to meet anyone who takes an intelligent interest in such matters. People can find time for such trivialities as sport or society, and yet the beetles are overlooked. I can assure you that the greater part of the idiots in this part of the country are unaware that I have ever written a book at all—I, the first man who ever described the true function of the elytra.* I am glad to see you, sir, and I have no doubt that I can show you some specimens which will interest you.' He stepped into the fly and drove up with us to the house, expounding to me as we went some recent researches which he had made into the anatomy of the lady-bird.

I have said that Sir Thomas Rossiter wore a large hat drawn down over his brows. As he entered the hall he uncovered himself, and I was at once aware of a singular characteristic which the hat had concealed. His forehead, which was naturally high, and higher still on account of receding hair, was in a continual state of movement. Some nervous weakness kept the muscles in a constant spasm, which sometimes produced a mere twitching and sometimes a curious rotary movement unlike anything which I had ever seen before. It was strikingly visible as he turned towards us after entering the study, and seemed the more singular from the contrast with the hard, steady, grey eyes which looked out from underneath those palpitating brows.

'I am sorry,' said he, 'that Lady Rossiter is not here to help me to welcome you. By the way, Charles, did Evelyn say anything about the date of her return?'

'She wished to stay in town for a few more days,' said Lord Linchmere. 'You know how ladies' social duties accumulate if they have been for some time in the country. My sister has many old friends in London at present.'

'Well, she is her own mistress, and I should not wish to alter her plans, but I shall be glad when I see her again. It is very lonely here without her company.'

'I was afraid that you might find it so, and that was partly why I ran down. My young friend, Dr Hamilton, is so much interested in the subject which you have made your own, that I thought you would not mind his accompanying me.'

'I lead a retired life, Dr Hamilton, and my aversion to strangers grows upon me,' said our host. 'I have sometimes thought that my nerves are not so good as they were. My travels in search of beetles in my younger days took me into many malarious and unhealthy places. But a brother coleopterist like yourself is always a welcome guest, and I shall be delighted if you will look over my collection, which I think that I may without exaggeration describe as the best in Europe.'

And so no doubt it was. He had a huge, oaken cabinet arranged in shallow drawers, and here, neatly ticketed and classified, were beetles from every corner of the earth, black, brown, blue, green, and mottled. Every now and then as he swept his hand over the lines and lines of impaled insects he would catch up some rare specimen, and, handling it with as much delicacy and reverence as if it were a precious relic, he would hold forth upon its peculiarities and the circumstances under which it came into his possession. It was evidently an unusual thing for him to meet with a sympathetic listener, and he talked and talked until the spring evening had deepened into night, and the gong announced that it was time to dress for dinner. All the time Lord Linchmere said nothing, but he stood at his brother-in-law's elbow, and I caught him continually shooting curious, little, questioning glances into his face. And his own features expressed some strong emotion, apprehension, sympathy, expectation: I seemed to read them all. I was sure that Lord Linchmere was fearing something and awaiting something, but what that something might be I could not imagine.

The evening passed quietly but pleasantly, and I should have been entirely at my ease if it had not been for that continual sense of tension upon the part of Lord Linchmere. As to our host, I found that he improved upon acquaintance. He spoke constantly with affection of his absent wife, and also of his little son, who had recently been sent to school. The house, he said, was not the same without them. If it were not for his scientific studies, he did not know how he could get through the days. After dinner we smoked for some time in the billiard-room, and finally went early to bed.

And then it was that, for the first time, the suspicion that Lord Linchmere was a lunatic crossed my mind. He followed me into my bedroom, when our host had retired.

'Doctor,' said he, speaking in a low, hurried voice, 'you must come with me. You must spend the night in my bedroom.'

'What do you mean?'

'I prefer not to explain. But this is part of your duties. My room is close by, and you can return to your own before the servant calls you in the morning.'

'But why?' I asked.

'Because I am not fond of being alone,' said he. 'That's the reason, since you must have a reason.'

It seemed rank lunacy, but the argument of those twenty pounds would overcome many objections. I followed him to his room.

'Well,' said I, 'there's only room for one in that bed.'

'Only one shall occupy it,' said he.

'And the other?'

'Must remain on watch.'

'Why?' said I. 'One would think you expected to be attacked.'

'Perhaps I do.'

'In that case, why not lock your door?'

'Perhaps I *want* to be attacked.'

It looked more and more like lunacy. However, there was nothing for it but to submit. I shrugged my shoulders and sat down in the arm-chair beside the empty fireplace.

'I am to remain on watch, then?' said I, ruefully.

'We will divide the night. If you will watch until two, I will watch the remainder.'

'Very good.'

'Call me at two o'clock, then.'

'I will do so.'

'Keep your ears open, and if you hear any sounds wake me instantly—instantly, you hear?'

'You can rely upon it.' I tried to look as solemn as he did.

'And for God's sake don't go to sleep,' said he, and so, taking off only his coat, he threw the coverlet over him and settled down for the night.

It was a melancholy vigil, and made more so by my own sense of its folly. Supposing that by any chance Lord Linchmere had cause to suspect that he was subject to danger in the house of Sir Thomas Rossiter, why on earth could he not lock his door and so protect himself? His own answer that he might wish to be attacked was absurd. Why should he possibly wish to be attacked? And who would wish to attack him? Clearly, Lord Linchmere was suffering from some singular delusion, and the result was that on an imbecile pretext I was to be deprived of my night's rest. Still, however absurd, I was determined to carry out his injunctions to the letter as long as I was in his employment. I sat, therefore, beside the empty fireplace, and listened to a sonorous chiming clock somewhere down the passage, which gurgled and struck every quarter of an hour. It was an endless vigil. Save for that single clock, an absolute silence reigned throughout the great house. A small lamp stood on the table at my elbow, throwing a circle of light round my chair, but leaving the corners of the room draped in shadow. On the bed Lord Linchmere was breathing peacefully. I envied him his quiet sleep, and again and again my own eyelids drooped, but every time my sense of duty came to my help, and I sat up, rubbing my eyes and pinching myself with a determination to see my irrational watch to an end.

And I did so. From down the passage came the chimes of two o'clock, and I laid my hand upon the shoulder of the sleeper. Instantly he was sitting up, with an expression of the keenest interest upon his face.

'You have heard something?'

'No, sir. It is two o'clock.'

'Very good. I will watch. You can go to sleep.'

I lay down under the coverlet as he had done and was soon unconscious. My last recollection was of that circle of lamplight, and of the small, hunched-up figure and strained, anxious face of Lord Linchmere in the centre of it.

How long I slept I do not know; but I was suddenly aroused by a sharp tug at my sleeve. The room was in darkness, but a hot smell of oil told me that the lamp had only that instant been extinguished.

'Quick! Quick!' said Lord Linchmere's voice in my ear.

I sprang out of bed, he still dragging at my arm.

'Over here!' he whispered, and pulled me into a corner of the room. 'Hush! Listen!'

In the silence of the night I could distinctly hear that someone was coming down the corridor. It was a stealthy step, faint and intermittent, as of a man who paused cautiously after every stride. Sometimes for half a minute there was no sound, and then came the shuffle and creak which told of a fresh advance. My companion was trembling with excitement. His hand, which still held my sleeve, twitched like a branch in the wind.

'What is it?' I whispered.

'It's he!'

'Sir Thomas?'

'Yes.'

'What does he want?'

'Hush! Do nothing until I tell you.'

I was conscious now that someone was trying the door. There was the faintest little rattle from the handle, and then I dimly saw a thin slit of subdued light. There was a lamp burning somewhere far down the passage and it just sufficed to make the outside visible from the darkness of our room. The greyish slit grew broader and broader, very gradually, very gently, and then outlined against it I saw the dark figure of a man. He was squat and crouching, with the silhouette of a bulky and misshapen dwarf. Slowly the door swung open with this ominous shape framed in the centre of it. And then, in an instant, the crouching figure shot up, there was a tiger spring across the room and thud, thud, thud, came three tremendous blows from some heavy object upon the bed.

I was so paralysed with amazement that I stood motionless and staring until I was aroused by a yell for help from my companion. The open door shed enough light for me to see the outline of things, and there was little Lord Linchmere with his arms round the neck of his brother-in-law, holding bravely on to him like a game bull-terrier with its teeth into a gaunt deerhound. The tall, bony man dashed himself about, writhing round and round to get a grip upon his assailant; but the other, clutching on from behind, still kept his hold, though his shrill, frightened cries showed how unequal he felt the contest to be. I sprang to the rescue, and the two of us managed to throw Sir Thomas to the ground, though he made his teeth meet in my shoulder. With all my youth and weight and strength, it was a desperate struggle before we could master his frenzied struggles; but at last we secured his arms with the waist-cord of the dressing-gown which he was wearing. I was holding his legs while Lord Linchmere was endeavouring to relight the lamp, when there came the pattering of many feet in the passage, and the butler and two footmen, who had been alarmed by the cries, rushed into the room. With their aid we had no further difficulty in securing our prisoner, who lay foaming and glaring upon the ground. One glance at his face was enough to prove that he was a dangerous maniac, while the short, heavy hammer which lay beside the bed showed how murderous had been his intentions.

'Do not use any violence!' said Lord Linchmere, as we raised the struggling man to his feet. 'He will have a period of stupor after this excitement. I believe that it is coming on already.' As he spoke the convulsions became less violent, and the madman's head fell forward upon his breast, as if he were overcome by sleep. We led him down the passage and stretched him upon his own bed, where he lay unconscious, breathing heavily.

'Two of you will watch him,' said Lord Linchmere. 'And now, Dr Hamilton, if you will return with me to my room, I will give you the explanation which my horror of scandal has perhaps caused me to delay too long. Come what may, you will never have cause to regret your share in this night's work.

'The case may be made clear in a very few words,' he continued, when we were alone. 'My poor brother-in-law is one of the best fellows upon earth, a loving husband and an estimable father, but he comes from a stock which is deeply tainted with insanity. He has more than once had homicidal outbreaks, which are the more painful because his inclination is always to attack the very person to whom he is most attached. His son was sent away to school to avoid this danger, and then came an attempt upon my sister, his wife, from which she escaped with injuries that you may have observed when you met her in London. You understand that he knows nothing of the matter when he is in his sound senses, and would ridicule the suggestion that he could under any circumstances injure those whom he loves so dearly. It is often, as you know, a characteristic of such maladies that it is absolutely impossible to convince the man who suffers from them of their existence.

'Our great object was, of course, to get him under restraint before he could stain his hands with blood, but the matter was full of difficulty. He is a recluse in his habits, and would not see any medical man. Besides, it was necessary for our purpose that the medical man should convince himself of his insanity; and he is sane as you or I, save on these very rare occasions. But, fortunately, before he has these attacks he always shows certain premonitory symptoms, which are providential danger-signals, warning us to be upon our guard. The chief of these is that nervous contortion of the forehead which you must have observed. This is a phenomenon which always appears from three to four days before his attacks of frenzy. The moment it showed itself his wife came into town on some pretext, and took refuge in my house in Brook Street.

'It remained for me to convince a medical man of Sir Thomas's insanity, without which it was impossible to put him where he could do no harm. The first problem was how to get a medical man into his house. I bethought me of his interest in beetles, and his love for anyone who shared his tastes. I advertised, therefore, and was fortunate enough to find in you the very man I wanted. A stout companion was necessary, for I knew that the lunacy could only be proved by a murderous assault, and I had every reason to believe that that assault would be made upon myself, since he had the warmest regard for me in his moments of sanity. I think your intelligence will supply all the rest. I did not know that the attack would come by night, but I thought it very probable, for the crises of such cases usually do occur in the early hours of the morning. I am a very nervous man myself, but I saw no other way in which I could remove this terrible danger from my sister's life. I need not ask you whether you are willing to sign the lunacy papers.'

'Undoubtedly. But *two* signatures are necessary.'*

'You forget that I am myself a holder of a medical degree. I have the papers on a side-table here, so if you will be good enough to sign them now, we can have the patient removed in the morning.'

* * *

So that was my visit to Sir Thomas Rossiter, the famous beetle-hunter, and that was also my first step upon the ladder of success, for Lady Rossiter and Lord Linchmere have proved to be staunch friends, and they have never forgotten my association with them in the time of their need. Sir Thomas is out and said to be cured, but I still think that if I spent another night at Delamere Court, I should be inclined to lock my door upon the inside.

THE SEALED ROOM

⁂

𝕬 SOLICITOR of an active habit and athletic tastes who is compelled by his hopes of business to remain within the four walls of his office from ten till five must take what exercise he can in the evenings. Hence it was that I was in the habit of indulging in very long nocturnal excursions, in which I sought the heights of Hampstead and Highgate in order to cleanse my system from the impure air of Abchurch Lane.* It was in the course of one of these aimless rambles that I first met Felix Stanniford, and so led up to what has been the most extraordinary adventure of my lifetime.

One evening—it was in April or early May of the year 1894—I made my way to the extreme northern fringe of London, and was walking down one of those fine avenues of high brick villas which the huge city is for ever pushing farther and farther out into the country. It was a fine, clear spring night, the moon was shining out of an unclouded sky, and I, having already left many miles behind me, was inclined to walk slowly and look about me. In this contemplative mood, my attention was arrested by one of the houses which I was passing.

It was a very large building, standing in its own grounds, a little back from the road. It was modern in appearance, and yet it was far less so than its neighbours, all of which were crudely and painfully new. Their symmetrical line was broken by the gap caused by the laurel-studded lawn, with the great, dark, gloomy house looming at the back of it. Evidently it had been the country retreat of some wealthy merchant, built perhaps when the nearest street was a mile off, and now gradually overtaken and surrounded by the red brick tentacles of the London octopus. The next stage, I reflected, would be its digestion and absorption, so that the cheap builder might rear a dozen eighty-pound-a-year villas upon the garden frontage. And then, as all this passed vaguely through my mind, an incident occurred which brought my thoughts into quite another channel.

A four-wheeled cab, that opprobrium of London, was coming jolting and creaking in one direction, while in the other there was a yellow glare from the lamp of a cyclist. They were the only moving objects in the whole long, moonlit road, and yet they crashed into each other with that malignant accuracy which brings two ocean liners together in the broad waste of the Atlantic. It was the cyclist's fault. He tried to cross in front of the cab, miscalculated his distance, and was knocked sprawling by the horse's shoulder. He rose, snarling; the cabman swore back at him, and then, realizing that his number had not yet been taken, lashed his horse and lumbered off. The cyclist caught at the handles of his prostrate machine, and then suddenly sat down with a groan. 'Oh, Lord!' he said.

I ran across the road to his side. 'Any harm done?' I asked.

'It's my ankle,' said he. 'Only a twist, I think; but it's pretty painful. Just give me your hand, will you?'

He lay in the yellow circle of the cycle lamp, and I noted as I helped him to his feet that he was a gentlemanly young fellow, with a slight dark moustache and large, brown eyes, sensitive and nervous in appearance, with indications of weak health upon his sunken cheeks. Work or worry had left its traces upon his thin, yellow face. He stood up when I pulled his hand, but he held one foot in the air, and he groaned as he moved it.

'I can't put it to the ground,' said he.

'Where do you live?'

'Here!' he nodded his head towards the big, dark house in the garden. 'I was cutting across to the gate when that confounded cab ran into me. Could you help me so far?'

It was easily done. I put his cycle inside the gate, and then I supported him down the drive, and up the steps to the hall door. There was not a light anywhere, and the place was as black and silent as if no one had ever lived in it.

'That will do. Thank you very much,' said he, fumbling with his key in the lock.

'No, you must allow me to see you safe.'

He made some feeble, petulant protest, and then realised that he could really do nothing without me. The door had opened into a pitch-dark hall. He lurched forward, with my hand still on his arm.

'This door to the right,' said he, feeling about in the darkness.

I opened the door, and at the same moment he managed to strike a light. There was a lamp upon the table, and we lit it between us. 'Now, I'm all right. You can leave me now! Good-bye!' said he, and with the words he sat down in the arm-chair and fainted dead away.

It was a queer position for me. The fellow looked so ghastly, that really I was not sure that he was not dead. Presently his lips quivered and his breast heaved, but his eyes were two white slits and his colour was horrible. The responsibility was more than I could stand. I pulled at the bell-rope, and heard the bell ringing furiously far away. But no one came in response. The bell tinkled away into silence, which no murmur or movement came to break. I waited, and rang again, with the same result. There must be someone about. This young gentleman could not live all alone in that huge house. His people ought to know of his condition. If they would not answer the bell, I must hunt them out myself. I seized the lamp and rushed from the room.

What I saw outside amazed me. The hall was empty. The stairs were bare, and yellow with dust. There were three doors opening into spacious rooms, and each was uncarpeted and undraped, save for the grey webs which drooped from the cornice, and rosettes of lichen which had formed upon the walls. My feet reverberated in those empty and silent chambers. Then I wandered on down the passage, with the idea that the kitchens, at least, might be tenanted. Some caretaker might lurk in some secluded room. No, they were all equally desolate. Despairing of finding any help, I ran down another corridor, and came on something which surprised me more than ever.

The passage ended in a large, brown door, and the door had a seal of red wax the size of a five-shilling piece over the key-hole. This seal gave me the impression of having been there for a long time, for it was dusty and discoloured. I was still staring at it, and wondering what that door might conceal, when I heard a voice calling behind me, and, running back, found my young man sitting up in his chair and very much astonished at finding himself in darkness.

'Why on earth did you take the lamp away?' he asked.

'I was looking for assistance.'

'You might look for some time,' said he. 'I am alone in the house.'

'Awkward if you get an illness.'

'It was foolish of me to faint. I inherit a weak heart from my mother, and pain or emotion has that effect upon me. It will carry me off some day, as it did her. You're not a doctor, are you?'

'No, a lawyer. Frank Alder is my name.'

'Mine is Felix Stanniford. Funny that I should meet a lawyer, for my friend, Mr Perceval, was saying that we should need one soon.'

'Very happy, I am sure.'

'Well, that will depend upon him, you know. Did you say that you had run with that lamp all over the ground floor?'

'Yes.'

'*All* over it?' he asked, with emphasis, and he looked at me very hard.

'I think so. I kept on hoping that I should find someone.'

'Did you enter *all* the rooms?' he asked, with the same intent gaze.

'Well, all that I could enter.'

'Oh, then you *did* notice it!' said he, and he shrugged his shoulders with the air of a man who makes the best of a bad job.

'Notice what?'

'Why, the door with the seal on it.'

'Yes, I did.'

'Weren't you curious to know what was in it?'

'Well, it did strike me as unusual.'

'Do you think you could go on living alone in this house, year after year, just longing all the time to know what is at the other side of that door, and yet not looking?'

'Do you mean to say,' I cried, 'that you don't know yourself?'

'No more than you do.'

'Then why don't you look?'

'I mustn't,' said he.

He spoke in a constrained way, and I saw that I had blundered on to some delicate ground. I don't know that I am more inquisitive than my neighbours, but there certainly was something in the situation which appealed very strongly to my curiosity. However, my last excuse for remaining in the house was gone now that my companion had recovered his senses. I rose to go.

'Are you in a hurry?' he asked.

'No; I have nothing to do.'

'Well, I should be very glad if you would stay with me a little. The fact is that I live a very retired and secluded life here. I don't suppose there is a man in London who leads such a life as I do. It is quite unusual for me to have anyone to talk with.'

I looked round at the little room, scantily furnished, with a sofa-bed at one side. Then I thought of the great, bare house, and the sinister door with the discoloured red seal upon it. There was something queer and grotesque in the situation, which made me long to know a little more. Perhaps I should, if I waited. I told him that I should be very happy.

'You will find the spirits and a siphon upon the side-table. You must forgive me if I cannot act as host, but I can't get across the room. Those are cigars in the tray there. I'll take one myself, I think. And so you are a solicitor, Mr Alder?'

'Yes.'

'And I am nothing. I am that most helpless of living creatures, the son of a millionaire. I was brought up with the expectation of great wealth; and here I am, a poor man, without any profession at all. And then, on the top of it all, I am left with this great mansion on my hands, which I cannot possibly keep up. Isn't it an absurd situation? For me to use this as my dwelling is like a coster* drawing his barrow with a thoroughbred. A donkey would be more useful to him, and a cottage to me.'

'But why not sell the house?' I asked.

'I mustn't.'

'Let it, then?'

'No, I mustn't do that either.'

I looked puzzled, and my companion smiled.

'I'll tell you how it is, if it won't bore you,' said he.

'On the contrary, I should be exceedingly interested.'

'I think, after your kind attention to me, I cannot do less than relieve any curiosity that you may feel. You must know that my father was Stanislaus Stanniford, the banker.'

Stanniford, the banker! I remembered the name at once. His flight from the country some seven years before had been one of the scandals and sensations of the time.

'I see that you remember,' said my companion. 'My poor father left the country to avoid numerous friends, whose savings he had invested in an unsuccessful speculation. He was a nervous, sensitive man, and the responsibility quite upset his reason. He had committed no legal offence. It was purely a matter of sentiment. He would not even face his own family, and he died among strangers without ever letting us know where he was.'

'He died!' said I.

'We could not prove his death, but we know that it must be so, because the speculations came right again, and so there was no reason why he should not look any man in the face. He would have returned if he were alive. But he must have died in the last two years.'

'Why in the last two years?'

'Because we heard from him two years ago.'

'Did he not tell you then where he was living?'

'The letter came from Paris, but no address was given. It was when my poor mother died. He wrote to me then, with some instructions and some advice, and I have never heard from him since.'

'Had you heard before?'

'Oh, yes, we had heard before, and that's where our mystery of the sealed door upon which you stumbled to-night, has its origin. Pass me that desk, if you please. Here I have my father's letters, and you are the first man except Mr Perceval who has seen them.'

'Who is Mr Perceval, may I ask?'

'He was my father's confidential clerk, and he has continued to be the friend and adviser of my mother and then of myself. I don't know what we should have done without Perceval. He saw the letters, but no one else. This is the first one, which came on the very day when my father fled, seven years ago. Read it to yourself.'

This is the letter which I read:

'MY EVER DEAREST WIFE, —

'Since Sir William told me how weak your heart is, and how harmful any shock might be, I have never talked about my business affairs to you. The time has come when at all risks I can no longer refrain from telling you that things have been going badly with me. This will cause me to leave you for a little time, but it is with the absolute assurance that we shall see each other very soon. On this you can thoroughly rely. Our parting is only for a very short time, my own darling, so don't let it fret you, and above all don't let it impair your health, for that is what I want above all things to avoid.

'Now, I have a request to make, and I implore you by all that binds us together to fulfil it exactly as I tell you. There are some things which I do not wish to be seen by anyone in my dark room—the room which I use for photographic purposes at the end of the garden passage. To prevent any painful thoughts, I may assure you once for all, dear, that it is nothing of which I need be ashamed. But still I do not wish you or Felix to enter that room. It is locked, and I implore you when you receive this to at once place a seal over the lock, and leave it so. Do not sell or let the house, for in either case my secret will be discovered. As long as you or Felix are in the house, I know that you will comply with my wishes. When Felix is twenty-one he may enter the room—not before.

'And now, good-bye, my own best of wives. During our short separation you can consult Mr Perceval on any matters which may arise. He has my complete confidence. I hate to leave Felix and you—even for a time—but there is really no choice.

'Ever and always your loving husband,
'STANISLAUS STANNIFORD.
'*June 4th*, 1887.'

'These are very private family matters for me to inflict upon you,' said my companion apologetically. 'You must look upon it as done in your professional capacity. I have wanted to speak about it for years.'

'I am honoured by your confidence,' I answered, 'and exceedingly interested by the facts.'

'My father was a man who was noted for his almost morbid love of truth. He was always pedantically accurate. When he said, therefore, that he hoped to see my mother very soon, and when he said that he had nothing to be ashamed of in that dark room, you may rely upon it that he meant it.'

'Then what can it be?' I ejaculated.

'Neither my mother nor I could imagine. We carried out his wishes to the letter, and placed the seal upon the door; there it has been ever since. My mother lived for five years after my father's disappearance, although at the time all the doctors said that she could not survive long. Her heart was terribly diseased. During the first few months she had two letters from my father. Both had the Paris post-mark, but no address. They were short and to the same effect: that they would soon be reunited, and that she should not fret. Then there was a silence, which lasted until her death; and then came a letter to me of so private a nature that I cannot show it to you, begging me never to think evil of him, giving me much good advice, and saying that the sealing of the room was of less importance now than during the lifetime of my mother, but that the opening might still cause pain to others, and that, therefore, he thought it best that it should be postponed until my twenty-first year, for the lapse of time would make things easier. In the meantime, he committed the care of the room to me; so now you can understand how it is that, although I am a very poor man, I can neither let nor sell this great house.'

'You could mortgage it.'

'My father had already done so.'

'It is a most singular state of affairs.'

'My mother and I were gradually compelled to sell the furniture and to dismiss the servants, until now, as you see, I am living unattended in a single room. But I have only two more months.'

'What do you mean?'

'Why, that in two months I come of age. The first thing that I do will be to open that door; the second, to get rid of the house.'

'Why should your father have continued to stay away when these investments had recovered themselves?'

'He must be dead.'

'You say that he had not committed any legal offence when he fled the country?'

'None.'

'Why should he not take your mother with him?'

'I do not know.'

'Why should he conceal his address?'

'I do not know.'

'Why should he allow your mother to die and be buried without coming back?'

'I do not know.'

'My dear sir,' said I, 'if I may speak with the frankness of a professional adviser, I should say that it is very clear that your father had the strongest reasons for keeping out of the country, and that, if nothing has been proved against him, he at least thought that something might be, and refused to put himself within the power of the law. Surely that must be obvious, for in what other possible way can the facts be explained?'

My companion did not take my suggestion in good part.

'You had not the advantage of knowing my father, Mr Alder,' he said coldly. 'I was only a boy when he left us, but I shall always look upon him as my ideal man. His only fault was that he was too sensitive and too unselfish. That anyone should lose money through him would cut him to the heart. His sense of honour was most acute, any theory of his disappearance which conflicts with that is a mistaken one.'

It pleased me to hear the lad speak out so roundly, and yet I knew that the facts were against him, and that he was incapable of taking an unprejudiced view of the situation.

'I only speak as an outsider,' said I. 'And now I must leave you, for I have a long walk before me. Your story has interested me so much that I should be glad if you could let me know the sequel.'

'Leave me your card,' said he; and so, having bade him 'good night,' I left him.

I heard nothing more of the matter for some time, and had almost feared that it would prove to be one of those fleeting experiences which drift away from our direct observation and end only in a hope or a suspicion. One afternoon, however, a card bearing the name of Mr J. H. Perceval was brought up to my office in Abchurch Lane, and its bearer, a small dry, bright-eyed fellow of fifty, was ushered in by the clerk.

'I believe, sir,' said he, 'that my name has been mentioned to you by my young friend, Mr Felix Stanniford?'

'Of course,' I answered, 'I remember.'

'He spoke to you, I understand, about the circumstances in connection with the disappearance of my former employer, Mr Stanislaus Stanniford, and the existence of a sealed room in his former residence.'

'He did.'

'And you expressed an interest in the matter.'

'It interested me extremely.'

'You are aware that we hold Mr Stanniford's permission to open the door on the twenty-first birthday of his son?'

'I remember.'

'The twenty-first birthday is to-day.'

'Have you opened it?' I asked eagerly.

'Not yet, sir,' said he gravely. 'I have reason to believe that it would be well to have witnesses present when that door is opened. You are a lawyer, and you are acquainted with the facts. Will you be present on the occasion?'

'Most certainly.'

'You are employed during the day, and so am I. Shall we meet at nine o'clock at the house?'

'I will come with pleasure.'

'Then you will find us waiting for you. Good-bye, for the present.' He bowed solemnly, and took his leave.

I kept my appointment that evening, with a brain which was weary with fruitless attempts to think out some plausible explanation of the mystery which we were about to solve. Mr Perceval and my young acquaintance were waiting for me in the little room. I was not surprised to see the young man looking pale and nervous, but I was rather astonished to find the dry little City man in a state of intense, though partially suppressed, excitement. His cheeks were flushed, his hands twitching, and he could not stand still for an instant.

Stanniford greeted me warmly, and thanked me many times for having come. 'And now, Perceval,' said he to his companion, 'I suppose there is no obstacle to our putting the thing through without delay? I shall be glad to get it over.'

The banker's clerk took up the lamp and led the way. But he paused in the passage outside the door, and his hand was shaking, so that the light flickered up and down the high, bare walls.

'Mr Stanniford,' said he, in a cracking voice, 'I hope you will prepare yourself in case any shock should be awaiting you when that seal is removed and the door is opened.'

'What could there be, Perceval? You are trying to frighten me.'

'No, Mr Stanniford; but I should wish you to be ready...to be braced up...not to allow yourself....' He had to lick his dry lips between every jerky sentence, and I suddenly realised, as clearly as if he had told me, that he knew what was behind that closed door, and that it *was* something terrible. 'Here are the keys, Mr Stanniford, but remember my warning!'

He had a bunch of assorted keys in his hand, and the young man snatched them from him. Then he thrust a knife under the discoloured seal and jerked it off. The lamp was rattling and shaking in Perceval's hands, so I took it from him and held it near the keyhole while Stanniford tried key after key. At last one turned in the lock, the door flew open, he took one step into the room, and then, with a horrible cry, the young man fell senseless at our feet.

If I had not given heed to the clerk's warning, and braced myself for a shock, I should certainly have dropped the lamp. The room, windowless and bare, was fitted up as a photographic laboratory, with a tap and sink at the side of it. A shelf of bottles and measures stood at one side, and a peculiar, heavy smell, partly chemical, partly animal, filled the air. A single table and chair were in front of us, and at this, with his back turned towards us, a man was seated in the act of writing. His outline and attitude were as natural as life; but as the light fell upon him, it made my hair rise to see that the nape of his neck was black and wrinkled, and no thicker than my wrist. Dust lay upon him—thick, yellow dust—upon his hair, his shoulders, his shrivelled, lemon-coloured hands. His head had fallen forward upon his breast. His pen still rested upon a discoloured sheet of paper.

'My poor master! My poor, poor master!' cried the clerk, and the tears were running down his cheeks.

'What!' I cried, 'Mr Stanislaus Stanniford!'

'Here he has sat for seven years. Oh, why would he do it? I begged him, I implored him, I went on my knees to him, but he would have his way. You see the key on the table. He had locked the door upon the inside. And he has written something. We must take it.'

'Yes, yes, take it, and for God's sake, let us get out of this,' I cried; 'the air is poisonous. Come, Stanniford, come!' Taking an arm each, we half led and half carried the terrified man back to his own room.

'It was my father!' he cried, as he recovered his consciousness. 'He is sitting there dead in his chair. You knew it, Perceval! This was what you meant when you warned me.'

'Yes, I knew it, Mr Stanniford. I have acted for the best all along, but my position has been a terribly difficult one. For seven years I have known that your father was dead in that room.'

'You knew it, and never told us!'

'Don't be harsh with me, Mr Stanniford, sir! Make allowance for a man who has had a hard part to play.'

'My head is swimming round. I cannot grasp it!' He staggered up, and helped himself from the brandy bottle. 'These letters to my mother and to myself—were they forgeries?'

'No, sir; your father wrote them and addressed them, and left them in my keeping to be posted. I have followed his instructions to the very letter in all things. He was my master, and I have obeyed him.'

The brandy had steadied the young man's shaken nerves. 'Tell me about it. I can stand it now,' said he.

'Well, Mr Stanniford, you know that at one time there came a period of great trouble upon your father, and he thought that many poor people were about to lose their savings through his fault. He was a man who was so tender-hearted that he could not bear the thought. It worried him and tormented him, until he determined to end his life. Oh, Mr Stanniford, if you knew how I have prayed him and wrestled with him over it, you would never blame me! And he in turn prayed me as no man has ever prayed me before. He had made up his mind, and he would do it in any case, he said; but it rested with me whether his death should be happy and easy or whether it should be most miserable. I read in his eyes that he meant what he said. And at last I yielded to his prayers, and I consented to do his will.

'What was troubling him was this. He had been told by the first doctor in London that his wife's heart would fail at the slightest shock. He had a horror of accelerating her end, and yet his own existence had become unendurable to him. How could he end himself without injuring her?

'You know now the course that he took. He wrote the letter which she received. There was nothing in it which was not literally true. When he spoke of seeing her again so soon, he was referring to her own approaching death, which he had been assured could not be delayed more than a very few months. So convinced was he of this, that he only left two letters to be forwarded at intervals after his death. She lived five years, and I had no letters to send.

'He left another letter with me to be sent to you, sir, upon the occasion of the death of your mother. I posted all these in Paris to sustain the idea of his being abroad. It was his wish that I should say nothing, and I have said nothing. I have been a faithful servant. Seven years after his death, he thought no doubt that the shock to the feelings of his surviving friends would be lessened. He was always considerate for others.'

There was a silence for some time. It was broken by young Stanniford.

'I cannot blame you, Perceval. You have spared my mother a shock, which would certainly have broken her heart. What is that paper?'

'It is what your father was writing, sir. Shall I read it to you?'

'Do so.'

'I have taken the poison, and I feel it working in my veins. It is strange, but not painful. When these words are read I shall, if my wishes have been faithfully carried out, have been dead many years. Surely no one who has lost money through me will still bear me animosity. And you, Felix, you will forgive me this family scandal. May God find rest for a sorely wearied spirit!'

'Amen!' we cried, all three.

THE BRAZILIAN CAT

⸻❦⸻

IT is hard luck on a young fellow to have expensive tastes, great expectations, aristocratic connections, but no actual money in his pocket, and no profession by which he may earn any. The fact was that my father, a good, sanguine, easy-going man, had such confidence in the wealth and benevolence of his bachelor elder brother, Lord Southerton, that he took it for granted that I, his only son, would never be called upon to earn a living for myself. He imagined that if there were not a vacancy for me on the great Southerton Estates, at least there would be found some post in that diplomatic service which still remains the special preserve of our privileged classes. He died too early to realize how false his calculations had been. Neither my uncle nor the State took the slightest notice of me, or showed any interest in my career. An occasional brace of pheasants, or basket of hares, was all that ever reached me to remind me that I was heir to Otwell House and one of the richest estates in the country. In the meantime, I found myself a bachelor and man about town, living in a suite of apartments in Grosvenor Mansions, with no occupation save that of pigeon-shooting and polo-playing at Hurlingham.* Month by month I realized that it was more and more difficult to get the brokers to renew my bills, or to cash any further post-obits upon an unentailed property.* Ruin lay right across my path, and every day I saw it clearer, nearer, and more absolutely unavoidable.

What made me feel my own poverty the more was that, apart from the great wealth of Lord Southerton, all my other relations were fairly well-to-do. The nearest of these was Everard King, my father's nephew and my own first cousin, who had spent an adventurous life in Brazil, and had now returned to this country to settle down on his fortune. We never knew how he made his money, but he appeared to have plenty of it, for he bought the estate of Greylands, near Clipton-on-the-Marsh,* in Suffolk. For the first year of his residence in England he took no more notice of me than my miserly uncle; but at last one summer morning, to my very great relief and joy, I received a letter asking me to come down that very day and spend a short visit at Greylands Court. I was expecting a rather long visit to Bankruptcy

Court* at the time, and this interruption seemed almost providential. If I could only get on terms with this unknown relative of mine, I might pull through yet. For the family credit he could not let me go entirely to the wall. I ordered my valet to pack my valise, and I set off the same evening for Clipton-on-the-Marsh.

After changing at Ipswich, a little local train deposited me at a small, deserted station lying amidst a rolling grassy country, with a sluggish and winding river curving in and out amidst the valleys, between high, silted banks, which showed that we were within reach of the tide. No carriage was awaiting me (I found afterwards that my telegram had been delayed), so I hired a dog-cart at the local inn. The driver, an excellent fellow, was full of my relative's praises, and I learned from him that Mr Everard King was already a name to conjure with in that part of the country. He had entertained the school-children, he had thrown his grounds open to visitors, he had subscribed to charities—in short, his benevolence had been so universal that my driver could only account for it on the supposition that he had Parliamentary ambitions.

My attention was drawn away from my driver's panegyric by the appearance of a very beautiful bird which settled on a telegraph-post beside the road. At first I thought that it was a jay, but it was larger, with a brighter plumage. The driver accounted for its presence at once by saying that it belonged to the very man whom we were about to visit. It seems that the acclimatization of foreign creatures was one of his hobbies, and that he had brought with him from Brazil a number of birds and beasts which he was endeavouring to rear in England. When once we had passed the gates of Greylands Park we had ample evidence of this taste of his. Some small spotted deer, a curious wild pig known, I believe, as a peccary, a gorgeously feathered oriole, some sort of armadillo, and a singular lumbering intoed beast like a very fat badger,* were among the creatures which I observed as we drove along the winding avenue.

Mr Everard King, my unknown cousin, was standing in person upon the steps of his house, for he had seen us in the distance, and guessed that it was I. His appearance was very homely and benevolent, short and stout, forty-five years old, perhaps, with a round, good-humoured face, burned brown with the tropical sun, and shot with a thousand wrinkles. He wore white linen clothes, in true planter style, with a cigar between his lips, and a large Panama hat upon the

back of his head. It was such a figure as one associates with a ver-
andahed bungalow, and it looked curiously out of place in front of this
broad, stone English mansion, with its solid wings and its Palladio
pillars* before the door-way.

'My dear!' he cried, glancing over his shoulder; 'my dear, here is
our guest! Welcome, welcome to Greylands! I am delighted to make
your acquaintance, Cousin Marshall, and I take it as a great compliment that you should honour this sleepy little country place with your
presence.'

Nothing could be more hearty than his manner, and he set me at
my ease in an instant. But it needed all his cordiality to atone for the
frigidity and even rudeness of his wife, a tall, haggard woman, who
came forward at his summons. She was, I believe, of Brazilian extrac-
tion, though she spoke excellent English, and I excused her manners
on the score of her ignorance of our customs. She did not attempt to
conceal, however, either then or afterwards, that I was no very welcome visitor at Greylands Court. Her actual words were, as a rule,
courteous, but she was the possessor of a pair of particularly expressive dark eyes, and I read in them very clearly from the first that she
heartily wished me back in London once more.

However, my debts were too pressing and my designs upon my
wealthy relative were too vital for me to allow them to be upset by the
ill-temper of his wife, so I disregarded her coldness and reciprocated
the extreme cordiality of his welcome. No pains had been spared by
him to make me comfortable. My room was a charming one. He
implored me to tell him anything which could add to my happiness. It
was on the tip of my tongue to inform him that a blank cheque would
materially help towards that end, but I felt that it might be premature
in the present state of our acquaintance. The dinner was excellent,
and as we sat together afterwards over his Havanas and coffee, which
latter he told me was specially prepared upon his own plantation, it
seemed to me that all my driver's eulogies were justified, and that
I had never met a more large-hearted and hospitable man.

But, in spite of his cheery good nature, he was a man with a strong
will and a fiery temper of his own. Of this I had an example upon the
following morning. The curious aversion which Mrs Everard King
had conceived towards me was so strong, that her manner at breakfast
was almost offensive. But her meaning became unmistakable when
her husband had quitted the room.

'The best train in the day is at twelve fifteen,' said she.

'But I was not thinking of going to-day,' I answered, frankly—perhaps even defiantly, for I was determined not to be driven out by this woman.

'Oh, if it rests with you——' said she, and stopped with a most insolent expression in her eyes.

'I am sure,' I answered, 'that Mr Everard King would tell me if I were outstaying my welcome.'

'What's this? What's this?' said a voice, and there he was in the room. He had overheard my last words, and a glance at our faces had told him the rest. In an instant his chubby, cheery face set into an expression of absolute ferocity.

'Might I trouble you to walk outside, Marshall?' said he. (I may mention that my own name is Marshall King.)

He closed the door behind me, and then, for an instant, I heard him talking in a low voice of concentrated passion to his wife. This gross breach of hospitality had evidently hit upon his tenderest point. I am no eavesdropper, so I walked out on to the lawn. Presently I heard a hurried step behind me, and there was the lady, her face pale with excitement, and her eyes red with tears.

'My husband has asked me to apologize to you, Mr Marshall King,' said she, standing with downcast eyes before me.

'Please do not say another word, Mrs King.'

Her dark eyes suddenly blazed out at me.

'You fool!' she hissed, with frantic vehemence, and turning on her heel swept back to the house.

The insult was so outrageous, so insufferable, that I could only stand staring after her in bewilderment. I was still there when my host joined me. He was his cheery, chubby self once more.

'I hope that my wife has apologized for her foolish remarks,' said he.

'Oh, yes—yes, certainly!'

He put his hand through my arm and walked with me up and down the lawn.

'You must not take it seriously,' said he. 'It would grieve me inexpressibly if you curtailed your visit by one hour. The fact is—there is no reason why there should be any concealment between relatives—that my poor dear wife is incredibly jealous. She hates that anyone—male or female—should for an instant come between us. Her ideal is a desert island and an eternal *tête-à-tête*. That gives you the clue to her actions, which are, I confess, upon this particular point, not very far removed from mania. Tell me that you will think no more of it.'

'No, no; certainly not.'

'Then light this cigar and come round with me and see my little menagerie.'

The whole afternoon was occupied by this inspection, which included all the birds, beasts, and even reptiles which he had imported. Some were free, some in cages, a few actually in the house. He spoke with enthusiasm of his successes and his failures, his births and his deaths, and he would cry out in his delight, like a schoolboy, when, as we walked, some gaudy bird would flutter up from the grass, or some curious beast slink into the cover. Finally he led me down a corridor which extended from one wing of the house. At the end of this there was a heavy door with a sliding shutter in it, and beside it there projected from the wall an iron handle attached to a wheel and a drum. A line of stout bars extended across the passage.

'I am about to show you the jewel of my collection,' said he. 'There is only one other specimen in Europe, now that the Rotterdam cub is dead. It is a Brazilian cat.'

'But how does that differ from any other cat?'

'You will soon see that,' said he, laughing. 'Will you kindly draw that shutter and look through?'

I did so, and found that I was gazing into a large, empty room, with stone flags, and small, barred windows upon the farther wall. In the centre of this room, lying in the middle of a golden patch of sunlight, there was stretched a huge creature, as large as a tiger, but as black and sleek as ebony. It was simply a very enormous and very well-kept black cat, and it cuddled up and basked in that yellow pool of light exactly as a cat would do. It was so graceful, so sinewy, and so gently and smoothly diabolical, that I could not take my eyes from the opening.

'Isn't he splendid?' said my host, enthusiastically.

'Glorious! I never saw such a noble creature.'

'Some people call it a black puma, but really it is not a puma at all.* That fellow is nearly eleven feet from tail to tip. Four years ago he was a little ball of black fluff, with two yellow eyes staring out of it. He was sold me as a new-born cub up in the wild country at the head-waters of the Rio Negro.* They speared his mother to death after she had killed a dozen of them.'

'They are ferocious, then?'

'The most absolutely treacherous and bloodthirsty creatures upon earth. You talk about a Brazilian cat to an up-country Indian, and see him get the jumps. They prefer humans to game. This fellow has never tasted living blood yet, but when he does he will be a terror. At present he won't stand anyone but me in his den. Even Baldwin, the groom, dare not go near him. As to me, I am his mother and father in one.'

As he spoke he suddenly, to my astonishment, opened the door and slipped in, closing it instantly behind him. At the sound of his voice the huge, lithe creature rose, yawned and rubbed its round, black head affectionately against his side, while he patted and fondled it.

'Now, Tommy, into your cage!' said he.

The monstrous cat walked over to one side of the room and coiled itself up under a grating. Everard King came out, and taking the iron handle which I have mentioned, he began to turn it. As he did so the line of bars in the corridor began to pass through a slot in the wall and closed up the front of this grating, so as to make an effective cage. When it was in position he opened the door once more and invited me into the room, which was heavy with the pungent, musty smell peculiar to the great carnivora.

'That's how we work it,' said he. 'We give him the run of the room for exercise, and then at night we put him in his cage. You can let him out by turning the handle from the passage, or you can, as you have seen, coop him up in the same way. No, no, you should not do that!'

I had put my hand between the bars to pat the glossy, heaving flank. He pulled it back, with a serious face.

'I assure you that he is not safe. Don't imagine that because I can take liberties with him anyone else can. He is very exclusive in his friends—aren't you. Tommy? Ah, he hears his lunch coming to him! Don't you, boy?'

A step sounded in the stone-flagged passage, and the creature had sprung to his feet, and was pacing up and down the narrow cage, his yellow eyes gleaming, and his scarlet tongue rippling and quivering over the white line of his jagged teeth. A groom entered with a coarse joint upon a tray, and thrust it through the bars to him. He pounced lightly upon it, carried it off to the corner, and there, holding it between his paws, tore and wrenched at it, raising his bloody muzzle every now and then to look at us. It was a malignant and yet fascinating sight.

'You can't wonder that I am fond of him, can you?' said my host, as we left the room, 'especially when you consider that I have had the rearing of him. It was no joke bringing him over from the centre of South America; but here he is safe and sound—and, as I have said, far the most perfect specimen in Europe. The people at the Zoo are dying to have him, but I really can't part with him. Now, I think that I have inflicted my hobby upon you long enough, so we cannot do better than follow Tommy's example, and go to our lunch.'

My South American relative was so engrossed by his grounds and their curious occupants, that I hardly gave him credit at first for having any interests outside them. That he had some, and pressing ones, was soon borne in upon me by the number of telegrams which he received. They arrived at all hours, and were always opened by him with the utmost eagerness and anxiety upon his face. Sometimes I imagined that it must be the Turf,* and sometimes the Stock Exchange, but certainly he had some very urgent business going forwards which was not transacted upon the Downs of Suffolk. During the six days of my visit he had never fewer than three or four telegrams a day, and sometimes as many as seven or eight.

I had occupied these six days so well, that by the end of them I had succeeded in getting upon the most cordial terms with my cousin. Every night we had sat up late in the billiard-room, he telling me the most extraordinary stories of his adventures in America—stories so desperate and reckless, that I could hardly associate them with the brown little, chubby man before me. In return, I ventured upon some of my own reminiscences of London life, which interested him so much, that he vowed he would come up to Grosvenor Mansions and stay with me. He was anxious to see the faster side of city life, and certainly, though I say it, he could not have chosen a more competent guide. It was not until the last day of my visit that I ventured to approach that which was on my mind. I told him frankly about my pecuniary difficulties and my impending ruin, and I asked his advice—though I hoped for something more solid. He listened attentively, puffing hard at his cigar.

'But surely,' said he, 'you are the heir of our relative, Lord Southerton?'

'I have every reason to believe so, but he would never make me any allowance.'

'No, no, I have heard of his miserly ways. My poor Marshall, your position has been a very hard one. By the way, have you heard any news of Lord Southerton's health lately?'

'He has always been in a critical condition ever since my childhood.'

'Exactly—a creaking hinge, if ever there was one. Your inheritance may be a long way off. Dear me, how awkwardly situated you are!'

'I had some hopes, sir, that you, knowing all the facts, might be inclined to advance——'

'Don't say another word, my dear boy,' he cried, with the utmost cordiality; 'we shall talk it over to-night, and I give you my word that whatever is in my power shall be done.'

I was not sorry that my visit was drawing to a close, for it is unpleasant to feel that there is one person in the house who eagerly desires your departure. Mrs King's sallow face and forbidding eyes had become more and more hateful to me. She was no longer actively rude—her fear of her husband prevented her—but she pushed her insane jealousy to the extent of ignoring me, never addressing me, and in every way making my stay at Greylands as uncomfortable as she could. So offensive was her manner during that last day, that I should certainly have left had it not been for that interview with my host in the evening which would, I hoped, retrieve my broken fortunes.

It was very late when it occurred, for my relative, who had been receiving even more telegrams than usual during the day, went off to his study after dinner, and only emerged when the household had retired to bed. I heard him go round locking the doors, as his custom was of a night, and finally he joined me in the billiard-room. His stout figure was wrapped in a dressing-gown, and he wore a pair of red Turkish slippers without any heels. Settling down into an arm-chair, he brewed himself a glass of grog, in which I could not help noticing that the whisky considerably predominated over the water.

'My word!' said he, 'what a night!'

It was, indeed. The wind was howling and screaming round the house, and the latticed windows rattled and shook as if they were coming in. The glow of the yellow lamps and the flavour of our cigars seemed the brighter and more fragrant for the contrast.

'Now, my boy,' said my host, 'we have the house and the night to ourselves. Let me have an idea of how your affairs stand, and I will see what can be done to set them in order. I wish to hear every detail.'

Thus encouraged, I entered into a long exposition, in which all my tradesmen and creditors from my landlord to my valet figured in turn. I had notes in my pocket-book, and I marshalled my facts, and gave, I flatter myself, a very business-like statement of my own un-businesslike ways and lamentable position. I was depressed, however, to notice that my companion's eyes were vacant and his attention else-where. When he did occasionally throw out a remark it was so entirely perfunctory and pointless, that I was sure he had not in the least fol-lowed my remarks. Every now and then he roused himself and put on some show of interest, asking me to repeat or to explain more fully, but it was always to sink once more into the same brown study. At last he rose and threw the end of his cigar into the grate.

'I'll tell you what, my boy,' said he. 'I never had a head for figures, so you will excuse me. You must jot it all down upon paper, and let me have a note of the amount. I'll understand it when I see it in black and white.'

The proposal was encouraging. I promised to do so.

'And now it's time we were in bed. By Jove, there's one o'clock striking in the hall.'

The tingling of the chiming clock broke through the deep roar of the gale. The wind was sweeping past with the rush of a great river.

'I must see my cat before I go to bed,' said my host. 'A high wind excites him. Will you come?'

'Certainly,' said I.

'Then tread softly and don't speak, for everyone is asleep.'

We passed quietly down the lamp-lit Persian-rugged hall, and through the door at the farther end. All was dark in the stone corri-dor, but a stable lantern hung on a hook, and my host took it down and lit it. There was no grating visible in the passage, so I knew that the beast was in its cage.

'Come in!' said my relative, and opened the door.

A deep growling as we entered showed that the storm had really excited the creature. In the flickering light of the lantern, we saw it, a huge black mass coiled in the corner of its den and throwing a squat, uncouth shadow upon the whitewashed wall. Its tail switched angrily among the straw.

'Poor Tommy is not in the best of tempers,' said Everard King, holding up the lantern and looking in at him. 'What a black devil he looks, doesn't he? I must give him a little supper to put him in a better humour. Would you mind holding the lantern for a moment?'

I took it from his hand and he stepped to the door.

'His larder is just outside here,' said he. 'You will excuse me for an instant, won't you?' He passed out, and the door shut with a sharp metallic click behind him.

That hard crisp sound made my heart stand still. A sudden wave of terror passed over me. A vague perception of some monstrous treachery turned me cold. I sprang to the door, but there was no handle upon the inner side.

'Here!' I cried. 'Let me out!'

'All right! Don't make a row!' said my host from the passage. 'You've got the light all right.'

'Yes, but I don't care about being locked in alone like this.'

'Don't you?' I heard his hearty, chuckling laugh. 'You won't be alone long.'

'Let me out, sir!' I repeated angrily. 'I tell you I don't allow practical jokes of this sort.'

'Practical is the word,' said he, with another hateful chuckle. And then suddenly I heard, amidst the roar of the storm, the creak and whine of the winch-handle turning, and the rattle of the grating as it passed through the slot. Great God, he was letting loose the Brazilian cat!

In the light of the lantern I saw the bars sliding slowly before me. Already there was an opening a foot wide at the farther end. With a scream I seized the last bar with my hands and pulled with the strength of a madman. I *was* a madman with rage and horror. For a minute or more I held the thing motionless. I knew that he was straining with all his force upon the handle, and that the leverage was sure to overcome me. I gave inch by inch, my feet sliding along the stones, and all the time I begged and prayed this inhuman monster to save me from this horrible death. I conjured him by his kinship. I reminded him that I was his guest; I begged to know what harm I had ever done him. His only answers were the tugs and jerks upon the handle, each of which, in spite of all my struggles, pulled another bar through the opening. Clinging and clutching, I was dragged across the whole front of the cage, until at last, with aching wrists and lacerated fingers, I gave up the hopeless struggle. The grating clanged back as I released it, and an instant later I heard the shuffle of the Turkish slippers in the passage, and the slam of the distant door. Then everything was silent.

The creature had never moved during this time. He lay still in the corner, and his tail had ceased switching. This apparition of a man adhering to his bars and dragged screaming across him had apparently filled him with amazement. I saw his great eyes staring steadily at me. I had dropped the lantern when I seized the bars, but it still burned upon the floor, and I made a movement to grasp it, with some idea that its light might protect me. But the instant I moved, the beast gave a deep and menacing growl. I stopped and stood still, quivering with fear in every limb. The cat (if one may call so fearful a creature by so homely a name) was not more than ten feet from me. The eyes glimmered like two disks of phosphorus in the darkness. They appalled and yet fascinated me. I could not take my own eyes from them. Nature plays strange tricks with us at such moments of intensity, and those glimmering lights waxed and waned with a steady rise and fall. Sometimes they seemed to be tiny points of extreme brilliancy—little electric sparks in the black obscurity—then they would widen and widen until all that corner of the room was filled with their shifting and sinister light. And then suddenly they went out altogether.

The beast had closed its eyes. I do not know whether there may be any truth in the old idea of the dominance of the human gaze, or whether the huge cat was simply drowsy, but the fact remains that, far from showing any symptom of attacking me, it simply rested its sleek, black head upon its huge forepaws and seemed to sleep. I stood, fearing to move lest I should rouse it into malignant life once more. But at least I was able to think clearly now that the baleful eyes were off me. Here I was shut up for the night with the ferocious beast. My own instincts, to say nothing of the words of the plausible villain who laid this trap for me, warned me that the animal was as savage as its master. How could I stave it off until morning? The door was hopeless, and so were the narrow, barred windows. There was no shelter anywhere in the bare, stone-flagged room. To cry for assistance was absurd. I knew that this den was an outhouse, and that the corridor which connected it with the house was at least a hundred feet long. Besides, with that gale thundering outside, my cries were not likely to be heard. I had only my own courage and my own wits to trust to.

And then, with a fresh wave of horror, my eyes fell upon the lantern. The candle had burned low, and was already beginning to gutter. In ten minutes it would be out. I had only ten minutes then in which to do something, for I felt that if I were once left in the dark with that fearful beast I should be incapable of action. The very thought of it paralysed me. I cast my despairing eyes round this chamber of death, and they rested upon one spot which seemed to promise I will not say safety, but less immediate and imminent danger than the open floor.

I have said that the cage had a top as well as a front, and this top was left standing when the front was wound through the slot in the wall. It consisted of bars at a few inches' interval, with stout wire-netting between, and it rested upon a strong stanchion at each end. It stood now as a great barred canopy over the crouching figure in the corner. The space between this iron shelf and the roof may have been from two to three feet. If I could only get up there, squeezed in between bars and ceiling, I should have only one vulnerable side. I should be safe from below, from behind, and from each side. Only on the open face of it could I be attacked. There, it is true, I had no protection whatever; but, at least, I should be out of the brute's path when he began to pace about his den. He would have to come out of his way to reach me. It was now or never, for if once the light were out it would be impossible. With a gulp in my throat I sprang up, seized the iron edge of the top, and swung myself panting on to it. I writhed in face downwards, and found myself looking straight into the terrible eyes and yawning jaws of the cat. Its fetid breath came up into my face like the steam from some foul pot.

It appeared, however, to be rather curious than angry. With a sleek ripple of its long, black back it rose, stretched itself, and then rearing itself on its hind legs, with one forepaw against the wall, it raised the other, and drew its claws across the wire meshes beneath me. One sharp, white hook tore through my trousers—for I may mention that I was still in evening dress—and dug a furrow in my knee. It was not meant as an attack, but rather as an experiment, for upon my giving a sharp cry of pain he dropped down again, and springing lightly into the room, he began walking swiftly round it, looking up every now and again in my direction. For my part I shuffled backwards until I lay with my back against the wall, screwing myself into the smallest space possible. The farther I got the more difficult it was for him to attack me.

He seemed more excited now that he had begun to move about, and he ran swiftly and noiselessly round and round the den, passing continually underneath the iron couch upon which I lay. It was wonderful to see so great a bulk passing like a shadow, with hardly the softest thudding of velvety pads. The candle was burning low—so low that I could hardly see the creature. And then, with a last flare and splutter it went out altogether. I was alone with the cat in the dark!

It helps one to face a danger when one knows that one has done all that possibly can be done. There is nothing for it then but to quietly await the result. In this case, there was no chance of safety anywhere except the precise spot where I was. I stretched myself out, therefore, and lay silently, almost breathlessly, hoping that the beast might forget my presence if I did nothing to remind him. I reckoned that it must already be two o'clock. At four it would be full dawn. I had not more than two hours to wait for daylight.

Outside, the storm was still raging, and the rain lashed continually against the little windows. Inside, the poisonous and fetid air was overpowering. I could neither hear nor see the cat. I tried to think about other things—but only one had power enough to draw my mind from my terrible position. That was the contemplation of my cousin's villainy, his unparalleled hypocrisy, his malignant hatred of me. Beneath that cheerful face there lurked the spirit of a mediæval assassin. And as I thought of it I saw more clearly how cunningly the thing had been arranged. He had apparently gone to bed with the others. No doubt he had his witnesses to prove it. Then, unknown to them, he had slipped down, had lured me into this den and abandoned me. His story would be so simple. He had left me to finish my cigar in the billiard-room. I had gone down on my own account to have a last look at the cat. I had entered the room without observing that the cage was opened, and I had been caught. How could such a crime be brought home to him? Suspicion, perhaps—but proof, never!

How slowly those dreadful two hours went by! Once I heard a low, rasping sound, which I took to be the creature licking its own fur. Several times those greenish eyes gleamed at me through the darkness, but never in a fixed stare, and my hopes grew stronger that my presence had been forgotten or ignored. At last the least faint glimmer of light came through the windows—I first dimly saw them as two grey squares upon the black wall, then grey turned to white, and I could see my terrible companion once more. And he, alas, could see me!

It was evident to me at once that he was in a much more dangerous and aggressive mood than when I had seen him last. The cold of the

morning had irritated him, and he was hungry as well. With a continual growl he paced swiftly up and down the side of the room which
was farthest from my refuge, his whiskers bristling angrily, and his
tail switching and lashing. As he turned at the corners his savage eyes
always looked upwards at me with a dreadful menace. I knew then
that he meant to kill me. Yet I found myself even at that moment
admiring the sinuous grace of the devilish thing, its long, undulating,
rippling movements, the gloss of its beautiful flanks, the vivid, palpitating scarlet of the glistening tongue which hung from the jet-black
muzzle. And all the time that deep, threatening growl was rising and
rising in an unbroken crescendo. I knew that the crisis was at hand.

It was a miserable hour to meet such a death—so cold, so comfort-
less, shivering in my light dress clothes upon this gridiron of torment
upon which I was stretched. I tried to brace myself to it, to raise my
soul above it, and at the same time, with the lucidity which comes to
a perfectly desperate man, I cast round for some possible means of
escape. One thing was clear to me. If that front of the cage was only
back in its position once more, I could find a sure refuge behind it.
Could I possibly pull it back? I hardly dared to move for fear of bringing the creature upon me. Slowly, very slowly, I put my hand forward
until it grasped the edge of the front, the final bar which protruded
through the wall. To my surprise it came quite easily to my jerk. Of
course the difficulty of drawing it out arose from the fact that I was
clinging to it. I pulled again, and three inches of it came through. It
ran apparently on wheels. I pulled again...and then the cat sprang!

It was so quick, so sudden, that I never saw it happen. I simply
heard the savage snarl, and in an instant afterwards the blazing yellow
eyes, the flattened black head with its red tongue and flashing teeth,
were within reach of me. The impact of the creature shook the bars
upon which I lay, until I thought (as far as I could think of anything at
such a moment) that they were coming down. The cat swayed there
for an instant, the head and front paws quite close to me, the hind
paws clawing to find a grip upon the edge of the grating. I heard the
claws rasping as they clung to the wire-netting, and the breath of the
beast made me sick. But its bound had been miscalculated. It could
not retain its position. Slowly, grinning with rage, and scratching
madly at the bars, it swung backwards and dropped heavily upon the
floor. With a growl it instantly faced round to me and crouched for
another spring.

I knew that the next few moments would decide my fate. The creature had learned by experience. It would not miscalculate again. I must act promptly, fearlessly, if I were to have a chance for life. In an instant I had formed my plan. Pulling off my dress-coat, I threw it down over the head of the beast. At the same moment I dropped over the edge, seized the end of the front grating, and pulled it frantically out of the wall.

It came more easily than I could have expected. I rushed across the room, bearing it with me; but, as I rushed, the accident of my position put me upon the outer side. Had it been the other way, I might have come off scathless. As it was, there was a moment's pause as I stopped it and tried to pass in through the opening which I had left. That moment was enough to give time to the creature to toss off the coat with which I had blinded him and to spring upon me. I hurled myself through the gap and pulled the rails to behind me, but he seized my leg before I could entirely withdraw it. One stroke of that huge paw tore off my calf as a shaving of wood curls off before a plane. The next moment, bleeding and fainting, I was lying among the foul straw with a line of friendly bars between me and the creature which ramped so frantically against them.

Too wounded to move, and too faint to be conscious of fear, I could only lie, more dead than alive, and watch it. It pressed its broad, black chest against the bars and angled for me with its crooked paws as I have seen a kitten do before a mouse-trap. It ripped my clothes, but, stretch as it would, it could not quite reach me. I have heard of the curious numbing effect produced by wounds from the great carnivora, and now I was destined to experience it, for I had lost all sense of personality, and was as interested in the cat's failure or success as if it were some game which I was watching. And then gradually my mind drifted away into strange vague dreams, always with that black face and red tongue coming back into them, and so I lost myself in the nirvana of delirium, the blessed relief of those who are too sorely tried.

Tracing the course of events afterwards, I conclude that I must have been insensible for about two hours. What roused me to consciousness once more was that sharp metallic click which had been the precursor of my terrible experience. It was the shooting back of the spring lock. Then, before my senses were clear enough to entirely apprehend what they saw, I was aware of the round, benevolent face of my cousin peering in through the open door. What he saw evidently amazed him.

There was the cat crouching on the floor. I was stretched upon my back in my shirt-sleeves within the cage, my trousers torn to ribbons and a great pool of blood all round me. I can see his amazed face now, with the morning sunlight upon it. He peered at me, and peered again. Then he closed the door behind him, and advanced to the cage to see if I were really dead.

I cannot undertake to say what happened. I was not in a fit state to witness or to chronicle such events. I can only say that I was suddenly conscious that his face was away from me—that he was looking towards the animal.

'Good old Tommy!' he cried. 'Good old Tommy!'

Then he came near the bars, with his back still towards me.

'Down, you stupid beast!' he roared. 'Down, sir! Don't you know your master?'

Suddenly even in my bemuddled brain a remembrance came of those words of his when he had said that the taste of blood would turn the cat into a fiend. My blood had done it, but he was to pay the price.

'Get away!' he screamed. 'Get away, you devil! Baldwin! Baldwin! Oh, my God!'

And then I heard him fall, and rise, and fall again, with a sound like the ripping of sacking. His screams grew fainter until they were lost in the worrying snarl. And then, after I thought that he was dead, I saw, as in a nightmare, a blinded, tattered, blood-soaked figure running wildly round the room—and that was the last glimpse which I had of him before I fainted once again.

* * *

I was many months in my recovery—in fact, I cannot say that I have ever recovered, for to the end of my days I shall carry a stick as a sign of my night with the Brazilian cat. Baldwin, the groom, and the other servants could not tell what had occurred, when, drawn by the death-cries of their master, they found me behind the bars, and his remains—or what they afterwards discovered to be his remains—in the clutch of the creature which he had reared. They stalled him off with hot irons and afterwards shot him through the loophole of the door before they could finally extricate me. I was carried to my bedroom, and there, under the roof of my would-be murderer, I remained between life and death for several weeks. They had sent for a surgeon from Clipton and a nurse from London, and in a month

I was able to be carried to the station, and so conveyed back once more to Grosvenor Mansions.

I have one remembrance of that illness, which might have been part of the ever-changing panorama conjured up by a delirious brain were it not so definitely fixed in my memory. One night, when the nurse was absent, the door of my chamber opened, and a tall woman in blackest mourning slipped into the room. She came across to me, and as she bent her sallow face I saw by the faint gleam of the night-light that it was the Brazilian woman whom my cousin had married. She stared intently into my face, and her expression was more kindly than I had ever seen it.

'Are you conscious?' she asked.

I feebly nodded—for I was still very weak.

'Well, then, I only wished to say to you that you have yourself to blame. Did I not do all I could for you? From the beginning I tried to drive you from the house. By every means, short of betraying my husband, I tried to save you from him. I knew that he had a reason for bringing you here. I knew that he would never let you get away again. No one knew him as I knew him, who had suffered from him so often. I did not dare to tell you all this. He would have killed me. But I did my best for you. As things have turned out, you have been the best friend that I have ever had. You have set me free, and I fancied that nothing but death would do that. I am sorry if you are hurt, but I cannot reproach myself. I told you that you were a fool—and a fool you have been.' She crept out of the room, the bitter, singular woman, and I was never destined to see her again. With what remained from her husband's property she went back to her native land, and I have heard that she afterwards took the veil at Pernambuco.*

It was not until I had been back in London for some time that the doctors pronounced me to be well enough to do business. It was not a very welcome permission to me, for I feared that it would be the signal for an inrush of creditors; but it was Summers, my lawyer, who first took advantage of it.

'I am very glad to see that your lordship is so much better,' said he. 'I have been waiting a long time to offer my congratulations.'

'What do you mean, Summers? This is no time for joking.'

'I mean what I say,' he answered. 'You have been Lord Southerton for the last six weeks, but we feared that it would retard your recovery if you were to learn it.'

Lord Southerton! One of the richest peers in England! I could not believe my ears. And then suddenly I thought of the time which had elapsed, and how it coincided with my injuries.

'Then Lord Southerton must have died about the same time that I was hurt?'

'His death occurred upon that very day.' Summers looked hard at me as I spoke, and I am convinced—for he was a very shrewd fellow—that he had guessed the true state of the case. He paused for a moment as if awaiting a confidence from me, but I could not see what was to be gained by exposing such a family scandal.

'Yes, a very curious coincidence,' he continued, with the same knowing look. 'Of course, you are aware that your cousin Everard King was the next heir to the estates. Now, if it had been you instead of him who had been torn to pieces by this tiger, or whatever it was, then of course he would have been Lord Southerton at the present moment.'

'No doubt,' said I.

'And he took such an interest in it,' said Summers. 'I happen to know that the late Lord Southerton's valet was in his pay, and that he used to have telegrams from him every few hours to tell him how he was getting on. That would be about the time when you were down there. Was it not strange that he should wish to be so well informed, since he knew that he was not the direct heir?'

'Very strange,' said I. 'And now, Summers, if you will bring me my bills and a new cheque-book, we will begin to get things into order.'

THE NEW CATACOMB

'Look here, Burger,' said Kennedy, 'I do wish that you would confide in me.'

The two famous students of Roman remains sat together in Kennedy's comfortable room overlooking the Corso.* The night was cold, and they had both pulled up their chairs to the unsatisfactory Italian stove which threw out a zone of stuffiness rather than of warmth. Outside under the bright winter stars lay the modern Rome, the long, double chain of the electric lamps, the brilliantly lighted cafés, the rushing carriages, and the dense throng upon the footpaths. But inside, in the sumptuous chamber of the rich young English archæologist, there was only old Rome to be seen. Cracked and time-worn friezes hung upon the walls, grey old busts of senators and soldiers with their fighting heads and their hard, cruel faces peered out from the corners. On the centre table, amidst a litter of inscriptions, fragments, and ornaments, there stood the famous reconstruction by Kennedy of the Baths of Caracalla,* which excited such interest and admiration when it was exhibited in Berlin. Amphoræ hung from the ceiling, and a litter of curiosities strewed the rich red Turkey carpet. And of them all there was not one which was not of the most unimpeachable authenticity, and of the utmost rarity and value; for Kennedy, though little more than thirty, had a European reputation in this particular branch of research, and was, moreover, provided with that long purse which either proves to be a fatal handicap to the student's energies, or, if his mind is still true to its purpose, gives him an enormous advantage in the race for fame. Kennedy had often been seduced by whim and pleasure from his studies, but his mind was an incisive one, capable of long and concentrated efforts which ended in sharp reactions of sensuous languor. His handsome face, with its high, white forehead, its aggressive nose, and its somewhat loose and sensual mouth, was a fair index of the compromise between strength and weakness in his nature.

Of a very different type was his companion, Julius Burger. He came of a curious blend, a German father and an Italian mother, with the robust qualities of the North mingling strangely with the softer graces of the South. Blue Teutonic eyes lightened his sun-browned face, and above them rose a square, massive forehead, with a fringe of close yellow curls lying round it. His strong, firm jaw was clean-shaven, and his companion had frequently remarked how much it suggested those old Roman busts which peered out from the shadows in the corners of his chamber. Under its bluff German strength there lay always a suggestion of Italian subtlety, but the smile was so honest, and the eyes so frank, that one understood that this was only an indication of his ancestry, with no actual bearing upon his character. In age and in reputation, he was on the same level as his English companion, but his life and his work had both been far more arduous. Twelve years before, he had come as a poor student to Rome, and had lived ever since upon some small endowment for research which had been awarded to him by the University of Bonn. Painfully, slowly, and doggedly, with extraordinary tenacity and single-mindedness, he had climbed from rung to rung of the ladder of fame, until now he was a member of the Berlin Academy,* and there was every reason to believe that he would shortly be promoted to the Chair of the greatest of German Universities. But the singleness of purpose which had brought him to the same high level as the rich and brilliant Englishman, had caused him in everything outside their work to stand infinitely below him. He had never found a pause in his studies in which to cultivate the social graces. It was only when he spoke of his own subject that his face was filled with life and soul. At other times he was silent and embarrassed, too conscious of his own limitations in larger subjects, and impatient of that small talk which is the conventional refuge of those who have no thoughts to express.

And yet for some years there had been an acquaintanceship which appeared to be slowly ripening into a friendship between these two very different rivals. The base and origin of this lay in the fact that in their own studies each was the only one of the younger men who had knowledge and enthusiasm enough to properly appreciate the other. Their common interests and pursuits had brought them together, and each had been attracted by the other's knowledge. And then gradually something had been added to this. Kennedy had been amused by the frankness and simplicity of his rival, while Burger in turn had been fascinated by the brilliancy and vivacity which had made Kennedy such a favourite in Roman society. I say 'had,' because just at the moment the young Englishman was somewhat under a cloud.

A love-affair, the details of which had never quite come out, had indicated a heartlessness and callousness upon his part which shocked many of his friends. But in the bachelor circles of students and artists in which he preferred to move there is no very rigid code of honour in such matters, and though a head might be shaken or a pair of shoulders shrugged over the flight of two and the return of one, the general sentiment was probably one of curiosity and perhaps of envy rather than of reprobation.

'Look here, Burger,' said Kennedy, looking hard at the placid face of his companion, 'I do wish that you would confide in me.'

As he spoke he waved his hand in the direction of a rug which lay upon the floor. On the rug stood a long, shallow fruit-basket of the light wicker-work which is used in the Campagna,* and this was heaped with a litter of objects, inscribed tiles, broken inscriptions, cracked mosaics, torn papyri, rusty metal ornaments, which to the uninitiated might have seemed to have come straight from a dustman's bin, but which a specialist would have speedily recognized as unique of their kind. The pile of odds and ends in the flat wicker-work basket supplied exactly one of those missing links of social development which are of such interest to the student. It was the German who had brought them in, and the Englishman's eyes were hungry as he looked at them.

'I won't interfere with your treasure-trove, but I should very much like to hear about it,' he continued, while Burger very deliberately lit a cigar. 'It is evidently a discovery of the first importance. These inscriptions will make a sensation throughout Europe.'

'For every one here there are a million there!' said the German. 'There are so many that a dozen savants might spend a lifetime over them, and build up a reputation as solid as the Castle of St Angelo.'*

Kennedy sat thinking with his fine forehead wrinkled and his fingers playing with his long, fair moustache.

'You have given yourself away, Burger!' said he at last. 'Your words can only apply to one thing. You have discovered a new catacomb.'

'I had no doubt that you had already come to that conclusion from an examination of these objects.'

'Well, they certainly appeared to indicate it, but your last remarks make it certain. There is no place except a catacomb which could contain so vast a store of relics as you describe.'

'Quite so. There is no mystery about that. I *have* discovered a new catacomb.'

'Where?'

'Ah, that is my secret, my dear Kennedy. Suffice it that it is so situated that there is not one chance in a million of anyone else coming upon it. Its date is different from that of any known catacomb, and it has been reserved for the burial of the highest Christians, so that the remains and the relics are quite different from anything which has ever been seen before. If I was not aware of your knowledge and of your energy, my friend, I would not hesitate, under the pledge of secrecy, to tell you everything about it. But as it is I think that I must certainly prepare my own report of the matter before I expose myself to such formidable competition.'

Kennedy loved his subject with a love which was almost a mania— a love which held him true to it, amidst all the distractions which come to a wealthy and dissipated young man. He had ambition, but his ambition was secondary to his mere abstract joy and interest in everything which concerned the old life and history of the city. He yearned to see this new underworld which his companion had discovered.

'Look here, Burger,' said he, earnestly, 'I assure you that you can trust me most implicitly in the matter. Nothing would induce me to put pen to paper about anything which I see until I have your express permission. I quite understand your feeling and I think it is most natural, but you have really nothing whatever to fear from me. On the other hand, if you don't tell me I shall make a systematic search, and I shall most certainly discover it. In that case, of course, I should make what use I liked of it, since I should be under no obligation to you.'

Burger smiled thoughtfully over his cigar.

'I have noticed, friend Kennedy,' said he, 'that when I want information over any point you are not always so ready to supply it.'

'When did you ever ask me anything that I did not tell you? You remember, for example, my giving you the material for your paper about the temple of the Vestals.'

'Ah, well, that was not a matter of much importance. If I were to question you upon some intimate thing would you give me an answer, I wonder! This new catacomb is a very intimate thing to me, and I should certainly expect some sign of confidence in return.'

'What you are driving at I cannot imagine,' said the Englishman, 'but if you mean that you will answer my question about the catacomb if I answer any question which you may put to me I can assure you that I will certainly do so.'

'Well, then,' said Burger, leaning luxuriously back in his settee, and puffing a blue tree of cigar-smoke into the air, 'tell me all about your relations with Miss Mary Saunderson.'

Kennedy sprang up in his chair and glared angrily at his impassive companion.

'What the devil do you mean?' he cried. 'What sort of a question is this? You may mean it as a joke, but you never made a worse one.'

'No, I don't mean it as a joke,' said Burger, simply. 'I am really rather interested in the details of the matter. I don't know much about the world and women and social life and that sort of thing, and such an incident has the fascination of the unknown for me. I know you, and I knew her by sight—I had even spoken to her once or twice. I should very much like to hear from your own lips exactly what it was which occurred between you.'

'I won't tell you a word.'

'That's all right. It was only my whim to see if you would give up a secret as easily as you expected me to give up my secret of the new catacomb. You wouldn't, and I didn't expect you to. But why should you expect otherwise of me? There's Saint John's clock* striking ten. It is quite time that I was going home.'

'No; wait a bit, Burger,' said Kennedy; 'this is really a ridiculous caprice of yours to wish to know about an old love-affair which has burned out months ago. You know we look upon a man who kisses and tells as the greatest coward and villain possible.'

'Certainly,' said the German, gathering up his basket of curiosities, 'when he tells anything about a girl which is previously unknown he must be so. But in this case, as you must be aware, it was a public matter which was the common talk of Rome, so that you are not really doing Miss Mary Saunderson any injury by discussing her case with me. But still, I respect your scruples, and so good night!'

'Wait a bit, Burger,' said Kennedy, laying his hand upon the other's arm; 'I am very keen upon this catacomb business, and I can't let it drop quite so easily. Would you mind asking me something else in return—something not quite so eccentric this time?'

'No, no; you have refused, and there is an end of it,' said Burger, with his basket on his arm. 'No doubt you are quite right not to answer, and no doubt I am quite right also—and so again, my dear Kennedy, good night!'

The Englishman watched Burger cross the room, and he had his hand on the handle of the door before his host sprang up with the air of a man who is making the best of that which cannot be helped.

'Hold on, old fellow,' said he; 'I think you are behaving in a most ridiculous fashion; but still, if this is your condition, I suppose that I must submit to it. I hate saying anything about a girl, but, as you say, it is all over Rome and I don't suppose I can tell you anything which you do not know already. What was it you wanted to know?'

The German came back to the stove, and, laying down his basket, he sank into his chair once more.

'May I have another cigar?' said he. 'Thank you very much! I never smoke when I work, but I enjoy a chat much more when I am under the influence of tobacco. Now, as regards this young lady, with whom you had this little adventure. What in the world has become of her?'

'She is at home with her own people.'

'Oh, really—in England?'

'Yes.'

'What part of England—London?'

'No, Twickenham.'*

'You must excuse my curiosity, my dear Kennedy, and you must put it down to my ignorance of the world. No doubt it is quite a simple thing to persuade a young lady to go off with you for three weeks or so, and then to hand her over to her own family at—what did you call the place?'

'Twickenham.'

'Quite so—at Twickenham. But it is something so entirely outside my own experience that I cannot even imagine how you set about it. For example, if you had loved this girl your love could hardly disappear in three weeks, so I presume that you could not have loved her at all. But if you did not love her why should you make this great scandal which has damaged you and ruined her?'

Kennedy looked moodily into the red eye of the stove.

'That's a logical way of looking at it, certainly,' said he. 'Love is a big word, and it represents a good many different shades of feeling. I liked her, and—well, you say you've seen her—you know how charming she could look. But still I am willing to admit, looking back, that I could never have really loved her.'

'Then, my dear Kennedy, why did you do it?'

'The adventure of the thing had a great deal to do with it.'

'What! You are so fond of adventures!'

'Where would the variety of life be without them? It was for an adventure that I first began to pay my attentions to her. I've chased a good deal of game in my time, but there's no chase like that of a pretty woman. There was the piquant difficulty of it also, for, as she was the companion of Lady Emily Rood, it was almost impossible to see her alone. On the top of all the other obstacles which attracted me, I learned from her own lips very early in the proceedings that she was engaged.'

'Mein Gott! To whom?'

'She mentioned no names.'

'I do not think that anyone knows that. So that made the adventure more alluring, did it?'

'Well, it did certainly give a spice to it. Don't you think so?'

'I tell you that I am very ignorant about these things.'

'My dear fellow, you can remember that the apple you stole from your neighbour's tree was always sweeter than that which fell from your own. And then I found that she cared for me.'

'What—at once?'

'Oh, no, it took about three months of sapping* and mining. But at last I won her over. She understood that my judicial separation from my wife made it impossible for me to do the right thing by her—but she came all the same, and we had a delightful time, as long as it lasted.'

'But how about the other man?'

Kennedy shrugged his shoulders.

'I suppose it is the survival of the fittest,'* said he. 'If he had been the better man she would not have deserted him. Let's drop the subject, for I have had enough of it!'

'Only one other thing. How did you get rid of her in three weeks?'

'Well, we had both cooled down a bit, you understand. She absolutely refused, under any circumstances, to come back to face the people she had known in Rome. Now, of course, Rome is necessary to me, and I was already pining to be back at my work—so there was one obvious cause of separation. Then, again, her old father turned up at the hotel in London, and there was a scene, and the whole thing became so unpleasant that really—though I missed her dreadfully at first—I was very glad to slip out of it. Now, I rely upon you not to repeat anything of what I have said.'

'My dear Kennedy, I should not dream of repeating it. But all that you say interests me very much, for it gives me an insight into your way of looking at things, which is entirely different from mine, for I have seen so little of life. And now you want to know about my new catacomb. There's no use my trying to describe it, for you would never find it by that. There is only one thing, and that is for me to take you there.'

'That would be splendid.'

'When would you like to come?'

'The sooner the better. I am all impatience to see it.'

'Well, it is a beautiful night—though a trifle cold. Suppose we start in an hour. We must be very careful to keep the matter to ourselves. If anyone saw us hunting in couples they would suspect that there was something going on.'

'We can't be too cautious,' said Kennedy. 'Is it far?'

'Some miles.'

'Not too far to walk?'

'Oh, no, we could walk there easily.'

'We had better do so, then. A cabman's suspicions would be aroused if he dropped us both at some lonely spot in the dead of the night.'

'Quite so. I think it would be best for us to meet at the Gate of the Appian Way* at midnight. I must go to my lodgings for the matches and candles and things.'

'All right, Burger! I think it is very kind of you to let me into this secret, and I promise you that I will write nothing about it until you have published your report. Good-bye for the present! You will find me at the Gate at twelve.'

The cold, clear air was filled with the musical chimes from that city of clocks as Burger, wrapped in an Italian overcoat, with a lantern hanging from his hand, walked up to the rendezvous. Kennedy stepped out of the shadow to meet him.

'You are ardent in work as well as in love!' said the German, laughing.

'Yes; I have been waiting here for nearly half an hour.'

'I hope you left no clue as to where we were going.'

'Not such a fool! By Jove, I am chilled to the bone! Come on, Burger, let us warm ourselves by a spurt of hard walking.'

Their footsteps sounded loud and crisp upon the rough stone paving of the disappointing road which is all that is left of the most famous highway of the world. A peasant or two going home from the wine-shop, and a few carts of country produce coming up to Rome, were the only things which they met. They swung along, with the huge tombs looming up through the darkness upon each side of them, until they had come as far as the Catacombs of St Calixtus, and saw against a rising moon the great circular bastion of Cecilia Metella* in front of them. Then Burger stopped with his hand to his side.

'Your legs are longer than mine, and you are more accustomed to walking,' said he, laughing. 'I think that the place where we turn off is somewhere here. Yes, this is it, round the corner of the trattoria.* Now, it is a very narrow path, so perhaps I had better go in front and you can follow.'

He had lit his lantern, and by its light they were enabled to follow a narrow and devious track which wound across the marshes of the Campagna. The great Aqueduct* of old Rome lay like a monstrous caterpillar across the moon-lit landscape, and their road led them under one of its huge arches, and past the circle of crumbling bricks which marks the old arena. At last Burger stopped at a solitary wooden cow-house, and he drew a key from his pocket.

'Surely your catacomb is not inside a house!' cried Kennedy.

'The entrance to it is. That is just the safeguard which we have against anyone else discovering it.'

'Does the proprietor know of it?'

'Not he. He had found one or two objects which made me almost certain that his house was built on the entrance to such a place. So I rented it from him, and did my excavations for myself. Come in, and shut the door behind you.'

It was a long, empty building, with the mangers of the cows along one wall. Burger put his lantern down on the ground, and shaded its light in all directions save one by draping his overcoat round it.

'It might excite remark if anyone saw a light in this lonely place,' said he. 'Just help me to move this boarding.'

The flooring was loose in the corner, and plank by plank the two savants raised it and leaned it against the wall. Below there was a square aperture and a stair of old stone steps which led away down into the bowels of the earth.

'Be careful!' cried Burger, as Kennedy, in his impatience, hurried down them. 'It is a perfect rabbits'-warren below, and if you were once to lose your way there the chances would be a hundred to one against your ever coming out again. Wait until I bring the light.'

'How do you find your own way if it is so complicated?'

'I had some very narrow escapes at first, but I have gradually learned to go about. There is a certain system to it, but it is one which a lost man, if he were in the dark, could not possibly find out. Even now I always spin out a ball of string behind me when I am going far into the catacomb. You can see for yourself that it is difficult, but every one of these passages divides and subdivides a dozen times before you go a hundred yards.'

They had descended some twenty feet from the level of the byre, and they were standing now in a square chamber cut out of the soft tufa.* The lantern cast a flickering light, bright below and dim above, over the cracked brown walls. In every direction were the black openings of passages which radiated from this common centre.

'I want you to follow me closely, my friend,' said Burger. 'Do not loiter to look at anything upon the way, for the place to which I will take you contains all that you can see, and more. It will save time for us to go there direct.'

He led the way down one of the corridors, and the Englishman followed closely at his heels. Every now and then the passage bifurcated, but Burger was evidently following some secret marks of his own, for he neither stopped nor hesitated. Everywhere along the walls, packed like the berths upon an emigrant ship, lay the Christians of old Rome. The yellow light flickered over the shrivelled features of the mummies, and gleamed upon rounded skulls and long, white armbones crossed over fleshless chests. And everywhere as he passed Kennedy looked with wistful eyes upon inscriptions, funeral vessels, pictures, vestments, utensils, all lying as pious hands had placed them so many centuries ago. It was apparent to him, even in those hurried, passing glances, that this was the earliest and finest of the catacombs, containing such a storehouse of Roman remains as had never before come at one time under the observation of the student.

'What would happen if the light went out?' he asked, as they hurried onwards.

'I have a spare candle and a box of matches in my pocket. By the way, Kennedy, have you any matches?'

'No; you had better give me some.'

'Oh, that is all right. There is no chance of our separating.'

'How far are we going? It seems to me that we have walked at least a quarter of a mile.'

'More than that, I think. There is really no limit to the tombs—at least, I have never been able to find any. This is a very difficult place, so I think that I will use our ball of string.'

He fastened one end of it to a projecting stone and he carried the coil in the breast of his coat, paying it out as he advanced. Kennedy saw that it was no unnecessary precaution, for the passages had become more complex and tortuous than ever, with a perfect network of intersecting corridors. But these all ended in one large circular hall with a square pedestal of tufa topped with a slab of marble at one end of it.

'By Jove!' cried Kennedy in an ecstasy, as Burger swung his lantern over the marble. 'It is a Christian altar—probably the first one in existence. Here is the little consecration cross* cut upon the corner of it. No doubt this circular space was used as a church.'

'Precisely,' said Burger. 'If I had more time I should like to show you all the bodies which are buried in these niches upon the walls, for they are the early popes and bishops of the Church, with their mitres, their croziers, and full canonicals.* Go over to that one and look at it!'

Kennedy went across, and stared at the ghastly head which lay loosely on the shredded and mouldering mitre.

'This is most interesting,' said he, and his voice seemed to boom against the concave vault. 'As far as my experience goes, it is unique. Bring the lantern over, Burger, for I want to see them all.'

But the German had strolled away, and was standing in the middle of a yellow circle of light at the other side of the hall.

'Do you know how many wrong turnings there are between this and the stairs?' he asked. 'There are over two thousand. No doubt it was one of the means of protection which the Christians adopted. The odds are two thousand to one against a man getting out, even if he had a light; but if he were in the dark it would, of course, be far more difficult.'

'So I should think.'

'And the darkness is something dreadful. I tried it once for an experiment. Let us try it again!' He stooped to the lantern, and in an instant it was as if an invisible hand was squeezed tightly over each of Kennedy's eyes. Never had he known what such darkness was. It seemed to press upon him and to smother him. It was a solid obstacle against which the body shrank from advancing. He put his hands out to push it back from him.

'That will do, Burger,' said he, 'let's have the light again.'

But his companion began to laugh, and in that circular room the sound seemed to come from every side at once.

'You seem uneasy, friend Kennedy,' said he.

'Go on, man, light the candle!' said Kennedy impatiently.

'It's very strange, Kennedy, but I could not in the least tell by the sound in which direction you stand. Could you tell where I am?'

'No; you seem to be on every side of me.'

'If it were not for this string which I hold in my hand I should not have a notion which way to go.'

'I dare say not. Strike a light, man, and have an end of this nonsense.'

'Well, Kennedy, there are two things which I understand that you are very fond of. The one is an adventure, and the other is an obstacle to surmount. The adventure must be the finding of your way out of this catacomb. The obstacle will be the darkness and the two thousand wrong turns which make the way a little difficult to find. But you need not hurry, for you have plenty of time, and when you halt for a rest now and then, I should like you just to think of Miss Mary Saunderson, and whether you treated her quite fairly.'

'You devil, what do you mean?' roared Kennedy. He was running about in little circles and clasping at the solid blackness with both hands.

'Good-bye,' said the mocking voice, and it was already at some distance. 'I really do not think, Kennedy, even by your own showing that you did the right thing by that girl. There was only one little thing which you appeared not to know, and I can supply it. Miss Saunderson was engaged to a poor ungainly devil of a student, and his name was Julius Burger.'

There was a rustle somewhere, the vague sound of a foot striking a stone, and then there fell silence upon that old Christian church— a stagnant, heavy silence which closed round Kennedy and shut him in like water round a drowning man.

* * *

Some two months afterwards the following paragraph made the round of the European Press:—

'One of the most interesting discoveries of recent years is that of the new catacomb in Rome, which lies some distance to the east of the well-known vaults of St Calixtus. The finding of this important burial-place, which is exceeding rich in most interesting early Christian remains, is due to the energy and sagacity of Dr Julius Burger, the young German specialist, who is rapidly taking the first place as an authority upon ancient Rome. Although the first to publish his discovery, it appears that a less fortunate adventurer had anticipated Dr Burger. Some months ago Mr Kennedy, the well-known English student, disappeared suddenly from his rooms in the Corso, and it was conjectured that his association with a recent scandal had driven him to leave Rome. It appears now that he had in reality fallen a victim to that fervid love of archæology which had raised him to a distinguished place among living scholars. His body was discovered in the heart of the new catacomb, and it was evident from the condition of his feet and boots that he had tramped for days through the tortuous corridors which make these subterranean tombs so dangerous to explorers. The deceased gentleman had, with inexplicable rashness, made his way into this labyrinth without, as far as can be discovered, taking with him either candles or matches, so that his sad fate was the natural result of his own temerity. What makes the matter more painful is that Dr Julius Burger was an intimate friend of the deceased. His joy at the extraordinary find which he has been so fortunate as to make has been greatly marred by the terrible fate of his comrade and fellow-worker.'

THE RETIREMENT OF SIGNOR LAMBERT

IR WILLIAM SPARTER was a man who had raised himself in the course of a quarter of a century from earning four-and-twenty shillings a week as a fitter in Portsmouth Dockyard to being the owner of a yard and a fleet of his own. The little house in Lake Road, Landport,* where he, an obscure mechanic, had first conceived the idea of the boilers which are associated with his name, is still pointed out to the curious. But now, at the age of fifty, he owned a mansion in Leinster Gardens, a country house at Taplow, and a shooting in Argyleshire,* with the best stable, the choicest cellars, and the prettiest wife in town.

As untiring and inflexible as one of his own engines, his life had been directed to the one purpose of attaining the very best which the world had to give. Square-headed and round-shouldered, with massive, clean-shaven face and slow deep-set eyes, he was the very embodiment of persistency and strength. Never once from the beginning of his career had public failure of any sort tarnished its brilliancy.

And yet he had failed in one thing, and that the most important of all. He had never succeeded in gaining the affection of his wife. She was the daughter of a surgeon and the belle of a northern town when he married her. Even then he was rich and powerful, which made her overlook the twenty years which divided them. But he had come on a long way since then. His great Brazilian contract, his conversion into a company, his baronetcy—all these had been since his marriage. Only in the one thing he had never progressed. He could frighten his wife, he could dominate her, he could make her admire his strength and respect his consistency, he could mould her to his will in every other direction, but, do what he would he could not make her love him.

But it was not for want of trying. With the unrelaxing patience which made him great in business, he had striven, year in and year out, to win her affection. But the very qualities which had helped him in his public life made him unendurable in private. He was tactless, unsympathetic, overbearing, almost brutal sometimes, and utterly unable to think out those small attentions in word and deed which women value far more than the larger material benefits. The hundred pound cheque tossed across a breakfast table is a much smaller thing to a woman than the five-shilling charm which represents some thought and some trouble upon the part of the giver.

Sparter failed to understand this. With his mind full of the affairs of his firm, he had little time for the delicacies of life, and he endeavoured to atone by periodical munificence. At the end of five years he found that he had lost rather than gained in the lady's affections. Then at this unwonted sense of failure the evil side of the man's nature began to stir, and he became dangerous. But he was more dangerous still when a letter of his wife came, through the treachery of a servant, into his hands, and he realised that if she was cold to him she had passion enough for another. His firm, his ironclads, his patents, everything was dropped, and he turned his huge energies to the undoing of the man who had wronged him.

He had been cold and silent during dinner that evening, and she had wondered vaguely what had occurred to change him. He had said nothing while they sat together over their coffee in the drawing-room. Once or twice she had glanced at him in surprise, and had found those deep-set grey eyes fixed upon her with an expression which was new to her. Her mind had been full of someone else, but gradually her husband's silence and the inscrutable expression of his face forced themselves upon her attention.

'You don't seem yourself, to-night, William. What is the matter?' she asked. 'I hope there has been nothing to trouble you.'

He was still silent, and leant back in his armchair watching her beautiful face, which had turned pale with the sense of some impending catastrophe.

'Can I do anything for you, William?'

'Yes, you can write a letter.'

'What is the letter?'

'I will tell you presently.'

The last murmur died away in the house, and they heard the discreet step of Peterson, the butler, and the snick of the lock as he made all secure for the night. Sir William Sparter sat listening for a little. Then he rose.

'Come into my study,' said he.

The room was dark, but he switched on the green-shaded electric lamp which stood upon the writing-table.

'Sit here at the table,' said he. He closed the door and seated himself beside her. 'I only wanted to tell you, Jacky, that I know all about Lambert and the Warburton Street studio.'

She gasped and shivered, flinching away from him with her hands out as if she feared a blow.

'Yes, I know everything,' said he, and his quiet tone carried such conviction with it that she could not question what he said. She made no reply, but sat with her eyes fixed upon his grave, impassive face. A clock ticked loudly upon the mantelpiece, but everything else was silent in the house. She had never noticed that ticking before, but now it was like the hammering of a nail into her head. He rose and put a sheet of paper before her. Then he drew one from his own pocket and flattened it out upon the corner of the table.

'I have a rough draft here of the letter which I wish you to copy,' said he. 'I will read it to you if you like. "My own dearest Cecil,—I will be at No. 29 at half-past six, and I particularly wish you to come before you go down to the Opera. Don't fail me, for I have the very strongest reasons for wishing to see you. Ever yours, Jacqueline." Take up a pen, and copy that letter.'

'William, you are plotting some revenge. Oh, Willie, if I have wronged you, I am so sorry—'

'Copy that letter!'

'How can you be so harsh to me, William. You know very well—'

'Copy that letter!'

'I begin to hate you, William. I believe that it is a fiend, not a man, that I have married.'

'Copy that letter!'

Gradually the inflexible will and the unfaltering purpose began to prevail over the creature of nerves and moods. Reluctantly, mutinously, she took the pen in her hand.

'You wouldn't harm him, William!'

'Copy the letter!'

'Will you promise to forgive me, if I do?'

'Copy it!'

She looked at him with the intention of defying him, but those masterful, grey eyes dominated her. She was like a half-hypnotised creature, resentful, and yet obedient.

'There, will that satisfy you?'

He took the note from her and placed it in an envelope.

'Now address it to him!'

She wrote 'Cecil Lambert, Esq., 133B, Half Moon Street, W.,'* in a straggling agitated hand. Her husband very deliberately blotted it and placed it carefully in his pocket-book.

'I hope that you are satisfied now,' said she with weak petulance.

'Quite,' said he gravely. 'You can go to your room. Mrs McKay has my orders to sleep with you, and to see that you write no letters.'

'Mrs McKay! Do you expose me to the humiliation of being watched by my own servants!'

'Go to your room.'

'If you imagine that I am going to be under the orders of the house-keeper—'

'Go to your room.'

'Oh, William, who would have thought in the old days that you could ever have treated me like this. If my mother had ever dreamed—'

He took her by the arm, and led her to the door.

'Go to your room!' said he, and she passed out into the darkened hall. He closed the door and returned to the writing-table. Out of a drawer he took two things which he had purchased that day, the one a paper and the other a book. The former was a recent number of the 'Musical Record,'* and it contained a biography and picture of the famous Signor Lambert, whose wonderful tenor voice had been the delight of the public and the despair of his rivals. The picture was that of a good-natured, self-satisfied creature, young and handsome, with a full eye, a curling moustache, and a bull neck. The biography explained that he was only in his twenty-seventh year, that his career had been one continued triumph, that he was devoted to his art, and that his voice was worth to him, at a very moderate computation, some twenty thousand pounds a year. All this Sir William Sparter read very carefully, with his great brows drawn down, and a furrow like a gash between them, as his way was when his attention was concentrated. Then he folded the paper up again, and he opened the book.

It was a curious work for such a man to select for his reading— a technical treatise upon the organs of speech and voice-production. There were numerous coloured illustrations, to which he paid particular attention. Most of them were of the internal anatomy of the larynx, with the silvery vocal chords shining from under the pink aretenoid cartilages.* Far into the night Sir William Sparter, with those great virile eyebrows still bunched together, pored over these irrelevant pictures, and read and re-read the text in which they were explained.

* * *

Dr Manifold Ormonde, the famous throat specialist, of Cavendish Square,* was surprised next morning when his butler brought the card of Sir William Sparter into his consulting room. He had met him at dinner at the table of Lord Marvin a few nights before, and it had struck him at the time that he had seldom seen a man who looked such a type of rude, physical health. So he thought again, as the square, thick-set figure of the shipbuilder was ushered in to him.

'Glad to meet you again, Sir William,' said the specialist. 'I hope there is nothing wrong with your health.'

'Nothing, thank you.'

'Or with Lady Sparter's?'

'She is quite well.'

He sat down in the chair which the Doctor had indicated, and he ran his eyes slowly and deliberately round the room. Dr Ormonde watched him with some curiosity, for he had the air of a man who looks for something which he had expected to see.

'No, I didn't come about my health,' said he at last. 'I came for information.'

'Whatever I can give you is entirely at your disposal.'

'I have been studying the throat a little of late. I read McIntyre's book about it. I suppose that is all right.'

'An elementary treatise, but accurate as far as it goes.'

'I had an idea that you would be likely to have a model or something of the kind.'

For answer the Doctor unclasped the lid of a yellow, shining box upon his consulting-room table, and turned it back upon the hinge. Within was a very complete model of the human vocal organs.

'You are right, you see,' said he.

Sir William Sparter stood up, and bent over the model.

'It's a neat little bit of work,' said he, looking at it with the critical eyes of an engineer. 'This is the glottis, is it not? And here is the epiglottis.'

'Precisely. And here are the cords.'

'What would happen if you cut them?'

'Cut what?'

'These things—the vocal cords.'

'But you could not cut them. They are out of the reach of all accident.'

'But if such a thing did happen?'

'There is no such case upon record, but of course, the person would become dumb—for the time, at any rate.'

'You have a large practice among singers, have you not?'

'The largest in London.'

'I suppose you agree with what this man McIntyre says, that a fine voice depends partly upon the cords.'

'The volume of sound would depend upon the lung capacity, but the clearness of the note would correspond with the complete control which the singer exercised over the cords.'

'Any roughness or notching of the cords would ruin the voice?'

'For singing purposes, undoubtedly—but your researches seem to be taking a very curious direction.'

'Yes,' said Sir William, as he picked up his hat, and laid a fee upon the corner of the table. 'They *are* a little out of the common, are they not?'

* * *

Warburton Street is one of the network of thoroughfares which connect Chelsea with Kensington,* and it is chiefly remarkable for a number of studios, in which it is rumoured that other arts besides that of painting are occasionally cultivated. The possession of a comfortable room, easily accessible and at a moderate rent, may be useful to other people besides artists amid the publicity of London. At any rate, Signor Cecil Lambert, the famous tenor, owned such an apartment, and his neat little dark green brougham* might have been seen several times a week waiting at the head of the long passage which led down to the chambers in question.

When Sir William Sparter, muffled in his overcoat, and carrying a small black leather bag in his hand, turned the corner he saw the lamps of the carriage against the kerb, and knew that the man whom he had come to see was already at the place of assignation. He passed the empty brougham, and walked up the tile-paved passage with the yellow gas lamp shining at the far end of it.

The door was open, and led into a large empty hall, laid down with cocoa-nut matting and stained with many footmarks. The place was a rabbit warren by daylight, but now, when the working hours were over, it was deserted. A house-keeper in the basement was the only permanent resident. Sir William paused, but everything was silent and everything was dark, save for one door which was outlined in thin yellow slashes. He pushed it open and entered. Then he locked it upon the inside and put the key in his pocket.

It was a large room scantily furnished, and lit by a single oil lamp upon a centre table. A gaunt easel kept up appearances in the corner, and three studies of antique figures hung upon unpapered walls. For the rest a couple of comfortable chairs, a cupboard, and a settee made up the whole of the furniture. There was no carpet, but the windows were discreetly draped. On one of the chairs at the further side of a table a man had been sitting, who had sprung to his feet with an exclamation of joy, which had changed into one of surprise, and culminated in an oath.

'What the devil do you mean by locking that door? Unlock it again, sir, this instant!'

Sir William did not even answer him. He took off his overcoat and laid it over the back of a chair. Then he advanced to the table, opened his bag, and began to take out all sorts of things—a green bottle, a dentist's gag, an inhaler, a pair of forceps, a curved bistoury,* and a curious pair of scissors. Signor Lambert stood staring at him in a paralysis of rage and astonishment.

'You infernal scoundrel; who are you, and what do you want?'

Sir William had emptied his bag, and now for the first time he turned his eyes upon the singer. He was a taller man than himself, but far slighter and weaker. The engineer, though short, was exceedingly powerful, with muscles which had been toughened by hard, physical work. His broad shoulders, arching chest, and great gnarled hands gave him the outline of a gorilla. Lambert shrunk away from him, frightened by his sinister figure and by his cold, inexorable eyes.

'Have you come to rob me?' he gasped.

'I have come to speak to you. My name is Sparter.'

Lambert tried to retain his grasp upon the self-possession which was rapidly slipping away from him.

'Sparter!' said he, with an attempt at jauntiness. 'Sir William Sparter, I presume? I have had the pleasure of meeting Lady Sparter, and I have heard her mention you. May I ask the object of this visit?' He buttoned up his coat with twitching fingers, and tried to look fierce over his high collar.

'I've come,' said Sparter, jerking some fluid from the green bottle into the inhaler, 'to treat your voice.'

'To treat my voice?'

'Precisely.'

'You are a madman! What do you mean?'

'Kindly lie back upon the settee.'

'You are raving! I see it all. You wish to bully me. You have some motive in this. You imagine that there are relations between Lady Sparter and me. I do assure you that your wife—'

'My wife has nothing to do with the matter either now or hereafter. Her name does not appear at all. My motives are musical—purely musical, you understand. I don't like your voice. It wants treatment. Lie back upon the settee!'

'Sir William, I give you my word of honour—'

'Lie back!'

'You're choking me! It's chloroform!* Help, help, help! You brute! Let me go! Let me go, I say! Oh please! Lemme—Lemme—Lem—!' His head had fallen back, and he muttered into the inhaler. Sir William pulled up the table which held the lamp and the instruments.

* * *

It was some minutes after the gentleman with the overcoat and the bag had emerged that the coachman outside heard a voice shouting, and shouting very hoarsely and angrily, within the building. Presently came the sounds of unsteady steps, and his master, crimson with rage, stumbled out into the yellow circle thrown by the carriage lamps.

'You, Holden!' he cried, 'you leave my service to-night. Did you not hear me calling? Why did you not come?'

The man looked at him in bewilderment, and shuddered at the colour of his shirt-front.

'Yes, sir, I heard someone calling,' he answered, 'but it wasn't you sir. *It was a voice that I had never heard before*.'

* * *

'Considerable disappointment was caused at the Opera last week,' said one of the best informed of our musical critics, 'by the fact that Signor Cecil Lambert was unable to appear in the various roles which had been announced. On Tuesday night it was only at the very last instant that the management learned of the grave indisposition which had overtaken him, and had it not been for the presence of Jean Caravatti, who had understudied the part, the piece must have been abandoned. Since then we regret to hear that Signor Lambert's seizure was even more severe than was originally thought, and that it consists of an acute form of laryngitis, spreading to the vocal cords, and involving changes which may permanently affect the quality of his voice. All lovers of music will hope that these reports may prove to be pessimistic, and that we may soon be charmed once more by the finest tenor which we have heard for many a year upon the London operatic stage.'

THE BROWN HAND

EVERYONE knows that Sir Dominick Holden, the famous Indian surgeon, made me his heir, and that his death changed me in an hour from a hard-working and impecunious medical man to a well-to-do landed proprietor. Many know also that there were at least five people between the inheritance and me, and that Sir Dominick's selection appeared to be altogether arbitrary and whimsical. I can assure them, however, that they are quite mistaken, and that, although I only knew Sir Dominick in the closing years of his life, there were, none the less, very real reasons why he should show his goodwill towards me. As a matter of fact, though I say it myself, no man ever did more for another than I did for my Indian uncle. I cannot expect the story to be believed, but it is so singular that I should feel that it was a breach of duty if I did not put it upon record—so here it is, and your belief or incredulity is your own affair.

Sir Dominick Holden, CB, KCSI,* and I don't know what besides, was the most distinguished Indian surgeon of his day. In the Army originally, he afterwards settled down into civil practice in Bombay, and visited, as a consultant, every part of India. His name is best remembered in connection with the Oriental Hospital which he founded and supported. The time came, however, when his iron constitution began to show signs of the long strain to which he had subjected it, and his brother practitioners (who were not, perhaps, entirely disinterested upon the point) were unanimous in recommending him to return to England. He held on as long as he could, but at last he developed nervous symptoms of a very pronounced character, and so came back, a broken man, to his native county of Wiltshire. He bought a considerable estate with an ancient manor-house upon the edge of Salisbury Plain, and devoted his old age to the study of Comparative Pathology, which had been his learned hobby all his life, and in which he was a foremost authority.

We of the family were, as may be imagined, much excited by the news of the return of this rich and childless uncle to England. On his part, although by no means exuberant in his hospitality, he showed some sense of his duty to his relations, and each of us in turn had an invitation to visit him. From the accounts of my cousins it appeared to be a melancholy business, and it was with mixed feelings that I at last received my own summons to appear at Rodenhurst. My wife was so carefully excluded in the invitation that my first impulse was to refuse it, but the interests of the children had to be considered, and so, with her consent, I set out one October afternoon upon my visit to Wiltshire, with little thought of what that visit was to entail.

My uncle's estate was situated where the arable land of the plains begins to swell upwards into the rounded chalk hills which are characteristic of the county. As I drove from Dinton* Station in the waning light of that autumn day, I was impressed by the weird nature of the scenery. The few scattered cottages of the peasants were so dwarfed by the huge evidences of prehistoric life,* that the present appeared to be a dream and the past to be the obtrusive and masterful reality. The road wound through the valleys, formed by a succession of grassy hills, and the summit of each was cut and carved into the most elaborate fortifications, some circular, and some square, but all on a scale which has defied the winds and the rains of many centuries. Some call them Roman and some British, but their true origin and the reasons for this particular tract of country being so interlaced with entrenchments have never been finally made clear. Here and there on the long, smooth, olive-coloured slopes there rose small, rounded barrows or tumuli. Beneath them lie the cremated ashes of the race which cut so deeply into the hills, but their graves tell us nothing save that a jar full of dust* represents the man who once laboured under the sun.

It was through this weird country that I approached my uncle's residence of Rodenhurst, and the house was, as I found, in due keeping with its surroundings. Two broken and weather-stained pillars, each surmounted by a mutilated heraldic emblem, flanked the entrance to a neglected drive. A cold wind whistled through the elms which lined it, and the air was full of the drifting leaves. At the far end, under the gloomy arch of trees, a single yellow lamp burned steadily. In the dim half-light of the coming night I saw a long, low building stretching out two irregular wings, with deep eaves, a sloping gambrel roof,* and walls which were criss-crossed with timber balks in the fashion of the Tudors. The cheery light of a fire flickered in the broad, latticed window to the left of the low-porched door, and this, as it proved, marked the study of my uncle, for it was thither that I was led by his butler in order to make my host's acquaintance.

He was cowering over his fire, for the moist chill of an English autumn had set him shivering. His lamp was unlit, and I only saw the red glow of the embers beating upon a huge, craggy face, with a Red Indian nose and cheek, and deep furrows and seams from eye to chin, the sinister marks of hidden volcanic fires. He sprang up at my entrance with something of an old-world courtesy and welcomed me warmly to Rodenhurst. At the same time I was conscious, as the lamp was carried in, that it was a very critical pair of light-blue eyes which looked out at me from under shaggy eyebrows, like scouts beneath a bush, and that this outlandish uncle of mine was carefully reading off my character with all the ease of a practised observer and an experienced man of the world.

For my part I looked at him, and looked again, for I had never seen a man whose appearance was more fitted to hold one's attention. His figure was the framework of a giant, but he had fallen away until his coat dangled straight down in a shocking fashion from a pair of broad and bony shoulders. All his limbs were huge and yet emaciated, and I could not take my gaze from his knobby wrists, and long, gnarled hands. But his eyes—those peering, light-blue eyes—they were the most arrestive of any of his peculiarities. It was not their colour alone, nor was it the ambush of hair in which they lurked; but it was the expression which I read in them. For the appearance and bearing of the man were masterful, and one expected a certain corresponding arrogance in his eyes, but instead of that I read the look which tells of a spirit cowed and crushed, the furtive, expectant look of the dog whose master has taken the whip from the rack. I formed my own medical diagnosis upon one glance at those critical and yet appealing eyes. I believed that he was stricken with some mortal ailment, that he knew himself to be exposed to sudden death, and that he lived in terror of it. Such was my judgment—a false one, as the event showed; but I mention it that it may help you to realize the look which I read in his eyes.

My uncle's welcome was, as I have said, a courteous one, and in an hour or so I found myself seated between him and his wife at a comfortable dinner, with curious, pungent delicacies upon the table, and a stealthy, quick-eyed Oriental waiter behind his chair. The old couple had come round to that tragic imitation of the dawn of life when husband and wife, having lost or scattered all those who were their intimates, find themselves face to face and alone once more, their work done, and the end nearing fast. Those who have reached that stage in sweetness and love, who can change their winter into a gentle, Indian summer, have come as victors through the ordeal of life. Lady Holden was a small, alert woman with a kindly eye, and her expression as she glanced at him was a certificate of character to her husband. And yet, though I read a mutual love in their glances, I read also mutual horror, and recognized in her face some reflection of that stealthy fear which I had detected in his. Their talk was sometimes merry and sometimes sad, but there was a forced note in their merriment and a naturalness in their sadness which told me that a heavy heart beat upon either side of me.

We were sitting over our first glass of wine, and the servants had left the room, when the conversation took a turn which produced a remarkable effect upon my host and hostess. I cannot recall what it was which started the topic of the supernatural, but it ended in my showing them that the abnormal in psychical experiences was a subject to which I had, like many neurologists, devoted a great deal of attention. I concluded by narrating my experiences when, as a member of the Psychical Research Society,* I had formed one of a committee of three who spent the night in a haunted house. Our adventures were neither exciting nor convincing, but, such as it was, the story appeared to interest my auditors in a remarkable degree. They listened with an eager silence, and I caught a look of intelligence between them which I could not understand. Lady Holden immediately afterwards rose and left the room.

Sir Dominick pushed the cigar-box over to me, and we smoked for some little time in silence. That huge, bony hand of his was twitching as he raised it with his cheroot to his lips, and I felt that the man's nerves were vibrating like fiddle-strings. My instincts told me that he was on the verge of some intimate confidence, and I feared to speak lest I should interrupt it. At last he turned towards me with a spasmodic gesture like a man who throws his last scruple to the winds.

'From the little that I have seen of you it appears to me, Dr Hardacre,' said he, 'that you are the very man I have wanted to meet.'

'I am delighted to hear it, sir.'

'Your head seems to be cool and steady. You will acquit me of any desire to flatter you, for the circumstances are too serious to permit of insincerities. You have some special knowledge upon these subjects, and you evidently view them from that philosophical stand-point which robs them of all vulgar terror. I presume that the sight of an apparition would not seriously discompose you?'

'I think not, sir.'

'Would even interest you, perhaps?'

'Most intensely.'

'As a psychical observer, you would probably investigate it in as impersonal a fashion as an astronomer investigates a wandering comet?'

'Precisely.'

He gave a heavy sigh.

'Believe me, Dr Hardacre, there was a time when I could have spoken as you do now. My nerve was a byword in India. Even the Mutiny* never shook it for an instant. And yet you see what I am reduced to—the most timorous man, perhaps, in all this county of Wiltshire. Do not speak too bravely upon this subject, or you may find yourself subjected to as long-drawn a test as I am—a test which can only end in the madhouse or the grave.'

I waited patiently until he should see fit to go farther in his confidence. His preamble had, I need not say, filled me with interest and expectation.

'For some years, Dr Hardacre,' he continued, 'my life and that of my wife have been made miserable by a cause which is so grotesque that it borders upon the ludicrous. And yet familiarity has never made it more easy to bear—on the contrary, as time passes my nerves become more worn and shattered by the constant attrition. If you have no physical fears, Dr Hardacre, I should very much value your opinion upon this phenomenon which troubles us so.'

'For what it is worth my opinion is entirely at your service. May I ask the nature of the phenomenon?'

'I think that your experiences will have a higher evidential value if you are not told in advance what you may expect to encounter. You are yourself aware of the quibbles of unconscious cerebration and subjective impressions with which a scientific sceptic may throw a doubt upon your statement. It would be as well to guard against them in advance.'

'What shall I do, then?'

'I will tell you. Would you mind following me this way?' He led me out of the dining-room and down a long passage until we came to a terminal door. Inside there was a large, bare room fitted as a laboratory, with numerous scientific instruments and bottles. A shelf ran along one side, upon which there stood a long line of glass jars containing pathological and anatomical specimens.

'You see that I still dabble in some of my old studies,' said Sir Dominick. 'These jars are the remains of what was once a most excellent collection, but unfortunately I lost the greater part of them when my house was burned down in Bombay in '92. It was a most unfortunate affair for me—in more ways than one. I had examples of many rare conditions, and my splenic collection* was probably unique. These are the survivors.'

I glanced over them, and saw that they really were of a very great value and rarity from a pathological point of view: bloated organs, gaping cysts, distorted bones, odious parasites—a singular exhibition of the products of India.

'There is, as you see, a small settee here,' said my host. 'It was far from our intention to offer a guest so meagre an accommodation, but since affairs have taken this turn, it would be a great kindness upon your part if you would consent to spend the night in this apartment. I beg that you will not hesitate to let me know if the idea should be at all repugnant to you.'

'On the contrary,' I said, 'it is most acceptable.'

'My own room is the second on the left, so that if you should feel that you are in need of company a call would always bring me to your side.'

'I trust that I shall not be compelled to disturb you.'

'It is unlikely that I shall be asleep. I do not sleep much. Do not hesitate to summon me.'

And so with this agreement we joined Lady Holden in the drawing-room and talked of lighter things.

It was no affectation upon my part to say that the prospect of my night's adventure was an agreeable one. I have no pretence to greater physical courage than my neighbours, but familiarity with a subject robs it of those vague and undefined terrors which are the most appalling to the imaginative mind. The human brain is capable of only one strong emotion at a time, and if it be filled with curiosity or scientific enthusiasm, there is no room for fear. It is true that I had my uncle's assurance that he had himself originally taken this point of view, but I reflected that the break-down of his nervous system might be due to his forty years in India as much as to any psychical experiences which had befallen him. I at least was sound in nerve and brain, and it was with something of the pleasurable thrill of anticipation with which the sportsman takes his position beside the haunt of his game that I shut the laboratory door behind me, and partially undressing, lay down upon the rug-covered settee.

It was not an ideal atmosphere for a bedroom. The air was heavy with many chemical odours, that of methylated spirit predominating. Nor were the decorations of my chamber very sedative. The odious line of glass jars with their relics of disease and suffering stretched in front of my very eyes. There was no blind to the window, and a three-quarter moon streamed its white light into the room, tracing a silver square with filigree lattices upon the opposite wall. When I had extinguished my candle this one bright patch in the midst of the general gloom had certainly an eerie and discomposing aspect. A rigid and absolute silence reigned throughout the old house, so that the low swish of the branches in the garden came softly and smoothly to my ears. It may have been the hypnotic lullaby of this gentle susurrus, or it may have been the result of my tiring day, but after many dozings and many efforts to regain my clearness of perception, I fell at last into a deep and dreamless sleep.

I was awakened by some sound in the room, and I instantly raised myself upon my elbow on the couch. Some hours had passed, for the square patch upon the wall had slid downwards and sideways until it lay obliquely at the end of my bed. The rest of the room was in deep shadow. At first I could see nothing, presently, as my eyes became accustomed to the faint light, I was aware, with a thrill which all my scientific absorption could not entirely prevent, that something was moving slowly along the line of the wall. A gentle, shuffling sound, as of soft slippers, came to my ears, and I dimly discerned a human figure walking stealthily from the direction of the door. As it emerged into the patch of moonlight I saw very clearly what it was and how it was employed. It was a man, short and squat, dressed in some sort of dark-grey gown, which hung straight from his shoulders to his feet. The moon shone upon the side of his face, and I saw that it was chocolate-brown in colour, with a ball of black hair like a woman's at the back of his head. He walked slowly, and his eyes were cast upwards towards the line of bottles which contained those gruesome remnants of humanity. He seemed to examine each jar with attention, and then to pass on to the next. When he had come to the end of the line, immediately opposite my bed, he stopped, faced me, threw up his hands with a gesture of despair, and vanished from my sight.

I have said that he threw up his hands, but I should have said his arms, for as he assumed that attitude of despair I observed a singular peculiarity about his appearance. He had only one hand! As the sleeves drooped down from the upflung arms I saw the left plainly, but the right ended in a knobby and unsightly stump. In every other way his appearance was so natural, and I had both seen and heard him so clearly, that I could easily have believed that he was an Indian servant of Sir Dominick's who had come into my room in search of something. It was only his sudden disappearance which suggested anything more sinister to me. As it was I sprang from my couch, lit a candle, and examined the whole room carefully. There were no signs of my visitor, and I was forced to conclude that there had really been something outside the normal laws of Nature in his appearance. I lay awake for the remainder of the night, but nothing else occurred to disturb me.

I am an early riser, but my uncle was an even earlier one, for I found him pacing up and down the lawn at the side of the house. He ran towards me in his eagerness when he saw me come out from the door.

'Well, well!' he cried. 'Did you see him?'

'An Indian with one hand?'

'Precisely.'

'Yes, I saw him'—and I told him all that occurred. When I had finished, he led the way into his study.

'We have a little time before breakfast,' said he. 'It will suffice to give you an explanation of this extraordinary affair—so far as I can explain that which is essentially inexplicable. In the first place, when I tell you that for four years I have never passed one single night, either in Bombay, aboard ship, or here in England without my sleep being broken by this fellow, you will understand why it is that I am a wreck of my former self. His programme is always the same. He appears by my bedside, shakes me roughly by the shoulder, passes from my room into the laboratory, walks slowly along the line of my bottles, and then vanishes. For more than a thousand times he has gone through the same routine.'

'What does he want?'

'He wants his hand.'

'His hand?'

'Yes, it came about in this way. I was summoned to Peshawur* for a consultation some ten years ago, and while there I was asked to look at the hand of a native who was passing through with an Afghan caravan. The fellow came from some mountain tribe living away at the back of beyond somewhere on the other side of Kaffiristan. He talked a bastard Pushtoo,* and it was all I could do to understand him. He was suffering from a soft sarcomatous swelling of one of the meta-carpal joints,* and I made him realize that it was only by losing his hand that he could hope to save his life. After much persuasion he consented to the operation, and he asked me, when it was over, what fee I demanded. The poor fellow was almost a beggar, so that the idea of a fee was absurd, but I answered in jest that my fee should be his hand, and that I proposed to add it to my pathological collection.

'To my surprise he demurred very much to the suggestion, and he explained that according to his religion it was an all-important matter that the body should be reunited after death, and so make a perfect dwelling for the spirit. The belief is, of course, an old one, and the mummies of the Egyptians arose from an analogous superstition. I answered him that his hand was already off, and asked him how he intended to preserve it. He replied that he would pickle it in salt and carry it about with him. I suggested that it might be safer in my keep-ing than his, and that I had better means than salt for preserving it. On realizing that I really intended to carefully keep it, his opposition vanished instantly. "But remember, sahib," said he, "I shall want it back when I am dead." I laughed at the remark, and so the matter ended. I returned to my practice, and he no doubt in the course of time was able to continue his journey to Afghanistan.

'Well, as I told you last night, I had a bad fire in my house at Bombay. Half of it was burned down, and, among other things, my pathological collection was largely destroyed. What you see are the poor remains of it. The hand of the hillman went with the rest, but I gave the matter no particular thought at the time. That was six years ago.

'Four years ago—two years after the fire—I was awakened one night by a furious tugging at my sleeve. I sat up under the impression that my favourite mastiff was trying to arouse me. Instead of this, I saw my Indian patient of long ago, dressed in the long, grey gown which was the badge of his people. He was holding up his stump and looking reproachfully at me. He then went over to my bottles, which at that time I kept in my room, and he examined them carefully, after which he gave a gesture of anger and vanished. I realized that he had just died, and that he had come to claim my promise that I should keep his limb in safety for him.

'Well, there you have it all, Dr Hardacre. Every night at the same hour for four years this performance has been repeated. It is a simple thing in itself, but it has worn me out like water dropping on a stone. It has brought a vile insomnia with it, for I cannot sleep now for the expectation of his coming. It has poisoned my old age and that of my wife, who has been the sharer in this great trouble. But there is the breakfast gong, and she will be waiting impatiently to know how it fared with you last night. We are both much indebted to you for your gallantry, for it takes something from the weight of our misfortune when we share it, even for a single night, with a friend, and it reassures us to our sanity, which we are sometimes driven to question.'

This was the curious narrative which Sir Dominick confided to me—a story which to many would have appeared to be a grotesque impossibility, but which, after my experience of the night before, and my previous knowledge of such things, I was prepared to accept as an absolute fact. I thought deeply over the matter, and brought the whole range of my reading and experience to bear upon it. After breakfast, I surprised my host and hostess by announcing that I was returning to London by the next train.

'My dear doctor,' cried Sir Dominick in great distress, 'you make me feel that I have been guilty of a gross breach of hospitality in intruding this unfortunate matter upon you. I should have borne my own burden.'

'It is, indeed, that matter which is taking me to London,' I answered; 'but you are mistaken, I assure you, if you think that my experience of last night was an unpleasant one to me. On the contrary, I am about to ask your permission to return in the evening and spend one more night in your laboratory. I am very eager to see this visitor once again.'

My uncle was exceedingly anxious to know what I was about to do, but my fears of raising false hopes prevented me from telling him. I was back in my own consulting-room a little after luncheon, and was confirming my memory of a passage in a recent book upon occultism which had arrested my attention when I read it.

'In the case of earth-bound spirits,' said my authority, 'some one dominant idea obsessing them at the hour of death is sufficient to hold them in this material world. They are the amphibia of this life and of the next, capable of passing from one to the other as the turtle passes from land to water. The causes which may bind a soul so

strongly to a life which its body has abandoned are any violent emotion. Avarice, revenge, anxiety, love and pity have all been known to
have this effect. As a rule it springs from some unfulfilled wish, and
when the wish has been fulfilled the material bond relaxes. There are
many cases upon record which show the singular persistence of these
visitors, and also their disappearance when their wishes have been
fulfilled, or in some cases when a reasonable compromise has been
effected.'

'*A reasonable compromise effected*'—those were the words which
I had brooded over all the morning, and which I now verified in the
original. No actual atonement could be made here—but a reasonable
compromise! I made my way as fast as a train could take me to the
Shadwell Seamen's Hospital,* where my old friend Jack Hewett was
house-surgeon. Without explaining the situation I made him understand what it was that I wanted.

'A brown man's hand!' said he, in amazement. 'What in the world
do you want that for?'

'Never mind. I'll tell you some day. I know that your wards are full
of Indians.'

'I should think so. But a hand——' He thought a little and then
struck a bell.

'Travers,' said he to a student-dresser, 'what became of the hands
of the Lascar which we took off yesterday? I mean the fellow from the
East India Dock* who got caught in the steam winch.'

'They are in the *post-mortem* room, sir.'

'Just pack one of them in antiseptics and give it to Dr Hardacre.'

And so I found myself back at Rodenhurst before dinner with
this curious outcome of my day in town. I still said nothing to Sir
Dominick, but I slept that night in the laboratory, and I placed the
Lascar's hand in one of the glass jars at the end of my couch.

So interested was I in the result of my experiment that sleep was
out of the question. I sat with a shaded lamp beside me and waited
patiently for my visitor. This time I saw him clearly from the first. He
appeared beside the door, nebulous for an instant, and then hardening into as distinct an outline as any living man. The slippers beneath
his grey gown were red and heelless, which accounted for the low,
shuffling sound which he made as he walked. As on the previous night
he passed slowly along the line of bottles until he paused before
that which contained the hand. He reached up to it, his whole figure

quivering with expectation, took it down, examined it eagerly, and then, with a face which was convulsed with fury and disappointment, he hurled it down on the floor. There was a crash which resounded through the house, and when I looked up the mutilated Indian had disappeared. A moment later my door flew open and Sir Dominick rushed in.

'You are not hurt?' he cried.

'No—but deeply disappointed.'

He looked in astonishment at the splinters of glass, and the brown hand lying upon the floor.

'Good God!' he cried. 'What is this?'

I told him my idea and its wretched sequel. He listened intently, but shook his head.

'It was well thought of,' said he, 'but I fear that there is no such easy end to my sufferings. But one thing I now insist upon. It is that you shall never again upon any pretext occupy this room. My fears that something might have happened to you—when I heard that crash—have been the most acute of all the agonies which I have undergone. I will not expose myself to a repetition of it.'

He allowed me, however, to spend the remainder of that night where I was, and I lay there worrying over the problem and lamenting my own failure. With the first light of morning there was the Lascar's hand still lying upon the floor to remind me of my fiasco. I lay looking at it—and as I lay suddenly an idea flew like a bullet through my head and brought me quivering with excitement out of my couch. I raised the grim relic from where it had fallen. Yes, it was indeed so. The hand was the *left* hand of the Lascar.

By the first train I was on my way to town, and hurried at once to the Seamen's Hospital. I remembered that both hands of the Lascar had been amputated, but I was terrified lest the precious organ which I was in search of might have been already consumed in the crematory. My suspense was soon ended. It had still been preserved in the *post-mortem* room. And so I returned to Rodenhurst in the evening with my mission accomplished and the material for a fresh experiment.

But Sir Dominick Holden would not hear of my occupying the laboratory again. To all my entreaties he turned a deaf ear. It offended his sense of hospitality, and he could no longer permit it. I left the hand, therefore, as I had done its fellow the night before, and I occupied a comfortable bedroom in another portion of the house, some distance from the scene of my adventures.

But in spite of that my sleep was not destined to be uninterrupted. In the dead of night my host burst into my room, a lamp in his hand. His huge, gaunt figure was enveloped in a loose dressing-gown, and his whole appearance might certainly have seemed more formidable to a weak-nerved man than that of the Indian of the night before. But it was not his entrance so much as his expression which amazed me. He had turned suddenly younger by twenty years at the least. His eyes were shining, his features radiant, and he waved one hand in triumph over his head. I sat up astounded, staring sleepily at this extraordinary visitor. But his words soon drove the sleep from my eyes.

'We have done it! We have succeeded!' he shouted. 'My dear Hardacre, how can I ever in this world repay you?'

'You don't mean to say that it is all right?'

'Indeed I do. I was sure that you would not mind being awakened to hear such blessed news.'

'Mind! I should think not indeed. But is it really certain?'

'I have no doubt whatever upon the point. I owe you such a debt, my dear nephew, as I have never owed a man before, and never expected to. What can I possibly do for you that is commensurate? Providence must have sent you to my rescue. You have saved both my reason and my life, for another six months of this must have seen me either in a cell or a coffin. And my wife—it was wearing her out before my eyes. Never could I have believed that any human being could have lifted this burden off me.' He seized my hand and wrung it in his bony grip.

'It was only an experiment—a forlorn hope—but I am delighted from my heart that it has succeeded. But how do you know that it is all right? Have you seen something?'

He seated himself at the foot of my bed.

'I have seen enough,' said he. 'It satisfies me that I shall be troubled no more. What has passed is easily told. You know that at a certain hour this creature always comes to me. To-night he arrived at the usual time, and aroused me with even more violence than is his custom. I can only surmise that his disappointment of last night increased the bitterness of his anger against me. He looked angrily at me, and then went on his usual round. But in a few minutes I saw him, for the first time since this persecution began, return to my chamber. He was smiling. I saw the gleam of his white teeth through the dim light. He stood facing me at the end of my bed, and three times he made the low, Eastern salaam* which is their solemn leave-taking. And the third time that he bowed he raised his arms over his head, and I saw his *two* hands outstretched in the air. So he vanished, and, as I believe, for ever.'

*　*　*

So that is the curious experience which won me the affection and the gratitude of my celebrated uncle, the famous Indian surgeon. His anticipations were realised, and never again was he disturbed by the visits of the restless hillman in search of his lost member. Sir Dominick and Lady Holden spent a very happy old age, unclouded, so far as I know, by any trouble, and they finally died during the great influenza epidemic* within a few weeks of each other. In his lifetime he always turned to me for advice in everything which concerned that English life of which he knew so little; and I aided him also in the purchase and development of his estates. It was no great surprise to me, therefore, that I found myself eventually promoted over the heads of five exasperated cousins, and changed in a single day from a hard-working country doctor into the head of an important Wiltshire family. I, at least, have reason to bless the memory of the man with the brown hand, and the day when I was fortunate enough to relieve Rodenhurst of his unwelcome presence.

PLAYING WITH FIRE

I CANNOT pretend to say what occurred on the 14th of April last at No. 17, Badderly Gardens. Put down in black and white, my surmise might seem too crude, too grotesque, for serious consideration. And yet that something did occur, and that it was of a nature which will leave its mark upon every one of us for the rest of our lives, is as certain as the unanimous testimony of five witnesses can make it. I will not enter into any argument or speculation. I will only give a plain statement, which will be submitted to John Moir, Harvey Deacon, and Mrs Delamere, and withheld from publication unless they are prepared to corroborate every detail. I cannot obtain the sanction of Paul Le Duc, for he appears to have left the country.

It was John Moir (the well-known senior partner of Moir, Moir, and Sanderson) who had originally turned our attention to occult subjects. He had, like many very hard and practical men of business, a mystic side to his nature, which had led him to the examination, and eventually to the acceptance, of those elusive phenomena which are grouped together with much that is foolish, and much that is fraudulent, under the common heading of spiritualism.* His researches, which had begun with an open mind, ended unhappily in dogma, and he became as positive and fanatical as any other bigot. He represented in our little group the body of men who have turned these singular phenomena into a new religion.*

Mrs Delamere, our medium, was his sister, the wife of Delamere, the rising sculptor. Our experience had shown us that to work on these subjects without a medium was as futile as for an astronomer to make observations without a telescope. On the other hand, the introduction of a paid medium was hateful to all of us. Was it not obvious that he or she would feel bound to return some result for money received, and that the temptation to fraud would be an overpowering one? No phenomena could be relied upon which were produced at a guinea an hour. But, fortunately, Moir had discovered that his sister was mediumistic—in other words, that she was a battery of that animal magnetic force* which is the only form of energy which is subtle enough to be acted upon from the spiritual plane as well as from our own material one. Of course, when I say this, I do not mean to beg the question; but I am simply indicating the theories upon which we were ourselves, rightly or wrongly, explaining what we saw. The lady came, not altogether with the approval of her husband, and though she never gave indications of any very great psychic force, we were able, at least, to obtain those usual phenomena of mere table-tilting which are at the same time so puerile and so inexplicable. Every Sunday evening we met in Harvey Deacon's studio at Badderly Gardens, the next house to the corner of Merton Park Road.*

Harvey Deacon's imaginative work in art would prepare anyone to find that he was an ardent lover of everything which was *outré* and sensational. A certain picturesqueness in the study of the occult had been the quality which had originally attracted him to it, but his attention was speedily arrested by some of those phenomena to which I have referred, and he was coming rapidly to the conclusion that what he had looked upon as an amusing romance and an after-dinner entertainment was really a very formidable reality. He is a man with a remarkably clear and logical brain—a true descendant of his ancestor, the well-known Scotch professor*—and he represented in our small circle the critical element, the man who has no prejudices, is prepared to follow facts as far as he can see them, and refuses to theorise in advance of his data. His caution annoyed Moir as much as the latter's robust faith amused Deacon, but each in his own way was equally keen upon the matter.

And I? What am I to say that I represented? I was not the devotee. I was not the scientific critic. Perhaps the best that I can claim for myself is that I was the dilettante man about town, anxious to be in the swim of every fresh movement, thankful for any new sensation which would take me out of myself and open up fresh possibilities of existence. I am not an enthusiast myself, but I like the company of those who are. Moir's talk, which made me feel as if we had a private passkey through the door of death, filled me with a vague contentment. The soothing atmosphere of the séance with the darkened lights was delightful to me. In a word, the thing amused me, and so I was there.

It was, as I have said, upon the 14th of April last that the very singular event which I am about to put upon record took place. I was the first of the men to arrive at the studio, but Mrs Delamere was already there, having had afternoon tea with Mrs Harvey Deacon. The two ladies and Deacon himself were standing in front of an unfinished picture of his upon the easel. I am not an expert in art, and I have never professed to understand what Harvey Deacon meant by his pictures; but I could see in this instance that it was all very clever and imaginative, fairies and animals and allegorical figures of all sorts. The ladies were loud in their praises, and indeed the colour effect was a remarkable one.

'What do you think of it, Markham?' he asked.

'Well, it's above me,' said I. 'These beasts—what are they?'

'Mythical monsters, imaginary creatures, heraldic emblems—a sort of weird, bizarre procession of them.'

'With a white horse in front!'

'It's not a horse,' said he, rather testily—which was surprising, for he was a very good-humoured fellow as a rule, and hardly ever took himself seriously.

'What is it, then?'

'Can't you see the horn in front? It's a unicorn. I told you they were heraldic beasts. Can't you recognize one?'

'Very sorry, Deacon,' said I, for he really seemed to be annoyed.

He laughed at his own irritation.

'Excuse me, Markham!' said he; 'the fact is that I have had an awful job over the beast. All day I have been painting him in and painting him out, and trying to imagine what a real live, ramping unicorn would look like. At last I got him, as I hoped; so when you failed to recognise it, it took me on the raw.'

'Why, of course it's a unicorn,' said I, for he was evidently depressed at my obtuseness. 'I can see the horn quite plainly, but I never saw a unicorn except beside the Royal Arms, and so I never thought of the creature. And these others are griffins and cockatrices, and dragons of sorts?'

'Yes, I had no difficulty with them. It was the unicorn which bothered me. However, there's an end of it until to-morrow.' He turned the picture round upon the easel, and we all chatted about other subjects.

Moir was late that evening, and when he did arrive he brought with him, rather to our surprise, a small, stout Frenchman, whom he introduced as Monsieur Paul Le Duc. I say to our surprise, for we held a theory that any intrusion into our spiritual circle deranged the conditions, and introduced an element of suspicion. We knew that we could trust each other, but all our results were vitiated by the presence of an outsider. However, Moir soon reconciled us to the innovation.

Monsieur Paul Le Duc was a famous student of occultism, a seer, a medium, and a mystic. He was travelling in England with a letter of introduction to Moir from the President of the Parisian brothers of the Rosy Cross.* What more natural than that he should bring him to our little séance, or that we should feel honoured by his presence?

He was, as I have said, a small, alert man, undistinguished in appearance, with a broad, smooth, clean-shaven face, remarkable only for a pair of large, brown, velvety eyes, staring vaguely out in front of him. He was well dressed, with the manners of a gentleman, and his curious little turns of English speech set the ladies smiling. Mrs Deacon had a prejudice against our researches and left the room, upon which we lowered the lights, as was our custom, and drew up our chairs to the square mahogany table which stood in the centre of the studio. The light was subdued, but sufficient to allow us to see each other quite plainly. I remember that I could even observe the curious, podgy little square-topped hands which the Frenchman laid upon the table.

'What a fun!' said he. 'It is many years since I have sat in this fashion, and it is to me amusing. Madame is medium. Does madame make the trance?'

'Well, hardly that,' said Mrs Delamere. 'But I am always conscious of extreme sleepiness.'

'It is the first stage. Then you encourage it, and there comes the trance. When the trance comes, then out jumps your little spirit and in jumps another little spirit, and so you have direct talking or writing.* You leave your machine to be worked by another. *Hein?** But what have unicorns to do with it?'

Harvey Deacon started in his chair. The Frenchman was moving his head slowly round and staring into the shadows which draped the walls.

'What a fun!' said he. 'Always unicorns. Who has been thinking so hard upon a subject so bizarre?'

'This is wonderful!' cried Deacon. 'I have been trying to paint one all day. But how could you know it?'

'You have been thinking of them in this room.'

'Certainly.'

'But thoughts are things, my friend. When you imagine a thing you make a thing. You did not know it, *hein?* But I can see your unicorns because it is not only with my eye that I can see.'

'Do you mean to say that I create a thing which has never existed by merely thinking of it?'

'But certainly. It is the fact which lies under all other facts. That is why an evil thought is also a danger.'

'They are, I suppose, upon the astral plane?'* said Moir.

'Ah, well, these are but words, my friends. They are there—somewhere—everywhere—I cannot tell myself. I see them. I could touch them.'

'You could not make *us* see them.'

'It is to materialise them. Hold! It is an experiment. But the power is wanting. Let us see what power we have, and then arrange what we shall do. May I place you as I wish?'

'You evidently know a great deal more about it than we do,' said Harvey Deacon; 'I wish that you would take complete control.'

'It may be that the conditions are not good. But we will try what we can do. Madame will sit where she is, I next, and this gentleman beside me. Meester Moir will sit next to madame, because it is well to have blacks and blondes in turn. So! And now with your permission I will turn the lights all out.'

'What is the advantage of the dark?' I asked.

'Because the force with which we deal is a vibration of ether* and so also is light. We have the wires all for ourselves now—*hein?* You will not be frightened in the darkness, madame? What a fun is such a séance!'

At first the darkness appeared to be absolutely pitchy, but in a few minutes our eyes became so far accustomed to it that we could just make out each other's presence—very dimly and vaguely, it is true. I could see nothing else in the room—only the black loom of the motionless figures. We were all taking the matter much more seriously than we had ever done before.

'You will place your hands in front. It is hopeless that we touch, since we are so few round so large a table. You will compose yourself, madame, and if sleep should come to you you will not fight against it. And now we sit in silence and we expect—*hein?*'

So we sat in silence and expected, staring out into the blackness in front of us. A clock ticked in the passage. A dog barked intermittently far away. Once or twice a cab rattled past in the street, and the gleam of its lamps through the chink in the curtains was a cheerful break in that gloomy vigil. I felt those physical symptoms with which previous séances had made me familiar—the coldness of the feet, the tingling in the hands, the glow of the palms, the feeling of a cold wind upon the back. Strange little shooting pains came in my forearms, especially as it seemed to me in my left one, which was nearest to our visitor—due no doubt to disturbance of the vascular system, but worthy of some attention all the same. At the same time I was conscious of a strained feeling of expectancy which was almost painful. From the rigid, absolute silence of my companions I gathered that their nerves were as tense as my own.

And then suddenly a sound came out of the darkness—a low, sibilant sound, the quick, thin breathing of a woman. Quicker and thinner yet it came, as between clenched teeth, to end in a loud gasp with a dull rustle of cloth.

'What's that? Is all right?' someone asked in the darkness.

'Yes, all is right,' said the Frenchman. 'It is madame. She is in her trance. Now, gentlemen, if you will wait quiet you will see something, I think, which will interest you much.'

Still the ticking in the hall. Still the breathing, deeper and fuller now, from the medium. Still the occasional flash, more welcome than ever, of the passing lights of the hansoms. What a gap we were bridging, the half-raised veil of the eternal on the one side and the cabs of London on the other. The table was throbbing with a mighty pulse. It swayed steadily, rhythmically, with an easy swooping, scooping motion under our fingers. Sharp little raps and cracks came from its substance, file-firing, volley-firing, the sounds of a fagot burning briskly on a frosty night.

'There is much power,' said the Frenchman. 'See it on the table!'

I had thought it was some delusion of my own, but all could see it now. There was a greenish-yellow phosphorescent light—or I should say a luminous vapour rather than a light—which lay over the surface of the table. It rolled and wreathed and undulated in dim glimmering folds, turning and swirling like clouds of smoke. I could see the white, square-ended hands of the French medium in this baleful light.

'What a fun!' he cried. 'It is splendid!'

'Shall we call the alphabet?'* asked Moir.

'But no—for we can do much better,' said our visitor. 'It is but a clumsy thing to tilt the table for every letter of the alphabet, and with such a medium as madame we should do better than that.'

'Yes, you will do better,' said a voice.

'Who was that? Who spoke? Was that you, Markham?'

'No, I did not speak.'

'It was madame who spoke.'

'But it was not her voice.'

'Is that you, Mrs Delamere?'

'It is not the medium, but it is the power which uses the organs of the medium,' said the strange, deep voice.

'Where is Mrs Delamere? It will not hurt her, I trust.'

'The medium is happy in another plane of existence. She has taken my place, as I have taken hers.'

'Who are you?'

'It cannot matter to you who I am. I am one who has lived as you are living, and who has died as you will die.'

We heard the creak and grate of a cab pulling up next door. There was an argument about the fare, and the cabman grumbled hoarsely down the street. The green-yellow cloud still swirled faintly over the table, dull elsewhere, but glowing into a dim luminosity in the direction of the medium. It seemed to be piling itself up in front of her. A sense of fear and cold struck into my heart. It seemed to me that lightly and flippantly we had approached the most real and august of sacraments, that communion with the dead of which the fathers of the Church had spoken.*

'Don't you think we are going too far? Should we not break up this séance?' I cried.

But the others were all earnest to see the end of it. They laughed at my scruples.

'All the powers are made for use,' said Harvey Deacon. 'If we *can* do this, we *should* do this. Every new departure of knowledge has been called unlawful in its inception. It is right and proper that we should inquire into the nature of death.'

'It is right and proper,' said the voice.

'There, what more could you ask?' cried Moir, who was much excited. 'Let us have a test. Will you give us a test that you are really there?'

'What test do you demand?'

'Well, now—I have some coins in my pocket. Will you tell me how many?'

'We come back in the hope of teaching and of elevating, and not to guess childish riddles.'

'Ha, ha, Meester Moir, you catch it that time,' cried the Frenchman. 'But surely this is very good sense what the Control* is saying.'

'It is a religion, not a game,' said the cold, hard voice.

'Exactly—the very view I take of it,' cried Moir, 'I am sure I am very sorry if I have asked a foolish question. You will not tell me who you are?'

'What does it matter?'

'Have you been a spirit long?'

'Yes.'

'How long?'

'We cannot reckon time as you do. Our conditions are different.'

'Are you happy?'

'Yes.'

'You would not wish to come back to life?'

'No—certainly not.'

'Are you busy?'

'We could not be happy if we were not busy.'

'What do you do?'

'I have said that the conditions are entirely different.'

'Can you give us no idea of your work?'

'We labour for our own improvement and for the advancement of others.'*

'Do you like coming here to-night?'

'I am glad to come if I can do any good by coming.'

'Then to do good is your object?'

'It is the object of all life on every plane.'

'You see, Markham, that should answer your scruples.'

It did, for my doubts had passed and only interest remained.

'Have you pain in your life?' I asked.

'No; pain is a thing of the body.'

'Have you mental pain?'

'Yes; one may always be sad or anxious.'

'Do you meet the friends whom you have known on earth?'

'Some of them.'

'Why only some of them?'

'Only those who are sympathetic.'

'Do husbands meet wives?'

'Those who have truly loved.'

'And the others?'

'They are nothing to each other.'

'There must be a spiritual connection?'

'Of course.'

'Is what we are doing right?'

'If done in the right spirit.'

'What is the wrong spirit?'

'Curiosity and levity.'

'May harm come of that?'

'Very serious harm.'

'What sort of harm?'

'You may call up forces over which you have no control.'

'Evil forces?'

'Undeveloped forces.'*

'You say they are dangerous. Dangerous to body or mind?'

'Sometimes to both.'

There was a pause, and the blackness seemed to grow blacker still, while the yellow-green fog swirled and smoked upon the table.

'Any questions you would like to ask, Moir?' said Harvey Deacon.

'Only this—do you pray in your world?'

'One should pray in every world.'

'Why?'

'Because it is the acknowledgment of forces outside ourselves.'

'What religion do you hold over there?'

'We differ exactly as you do.'

'You have no certain knowledge?'

'We have only faith.'

'These questions of religion,' said the Frenchman, 'they are of interest to you serious English people, but they are not so much fun. It seems to me that with this power here we might be able to have some great experience—*hein?* Something of which we could talk.'

'But nothing could be more interesting than this,' said Moir.

'Well, if you think so, that is very well,' the Frenchman answered, peevishly. 'For my part, it seems to me that I have heard all this before, and that to-night I should weesh to try some experiment with all this force which is given to us. But if you have other questions, then ask them, and when you are finish we can try something more.'

But the spell was broken. We asked and asked, but the medium sat silent in her chair. Only her deep, regular breathing showed that she was there. The mist still swirled upon the table.

'You have disturbed the harmony. She will not answer.'

'But we have learned already all that she can tell—*hein?* For my part I wish to see something that I have never seen before.'

'What then?'

'You will let me try?'

'What would you do?'

'I have said to you that thoughts are things. Now I wish to prove it to you, and to show you that which is only a thought. Yes, yes, I can do it and you will see. Now I ask you only to sit still and say nothing, and keep ever your hands quiet upon the table.'

The room was blacker and more silent than ever. The same feeling of apprehension which had lain heavily upon me at the beginning of the séance was back at my heart once more. The roots of my hair were tingling.

'It is working! It is working!' cried the Frenchman, and there was a crack in his voice as he spoke which told me that he also was strung to his tightest.

The luminous fog drifted slowly off the table, and wavered and flickered across the room. There in the farther and darkest corner it gathered and glowed, hardening down into a shining core—a strange, shifty, luminous, and yet non-illuminating patch of radiance, bright itself, but throwing no rays into the darkness. It had changed from a greenish-yellow to a dusky sullen red. Then round this centre there coiled a dark, smoky substance, thickening, hardening, growing denser and blacker. And then the light went out, smothered in that which had grown round it.

'It has gone.'

'Hush—there's something in the room.'

We heard it in the corner where the light had been, something which breathed deeply and fidgeted in the darkness.

'What is it? Le Duc, what have you done?'

'It is all right. No harm will come.' The Frenchman's voice was treble with agitation.

'Good heavens, Moir, there's a large animal in the room. Here it is, close by my chair! Go away! Go away!'

It was Harvey Deacon's voice, and then came the sound of a blow upon some hard object. And then...And then...how can I tell you what happened then?

Some huge thing hurtled against us in the darkness, rearing, stamping, smashing, springing, snorting. The table was splintered. We were scattered in every direction. It clattered and scrambled amongst us, rushing with horrible energy from one corner of the room to another. We were all screaming with fear, grovelling upon our hands and knees to get away from it. Something trod upon my left hand, and I felt the bones splinter under the weight.

'A light! A light!' someone yelled.

'Moir, you have matches, matches!'

'No, I have none. Deacon, where are the matches? For God's sake, the matches!'

'I can't find them. Here, you Frenchman, stop it!'

'It is beyond me. Oh, *mon Dieu*, I cannot stop it. The door! Where is the door?'

My hand, by good luck, lit upon the handle as I groped about in the darkness. The hard-breathing, snorting, rushing creature tore past me and butted with a fearful crash against the oaken partition. The instant that it had passed I turned the handle, and next moment we were all outside, and the door shut behind us. From within came a horrible crashing and rending and stamping.

'What is it? In Heaven's name, what is it?'

'A horse. I saw it when the door opened. But Mrs Delamere——?'

'We must fetch her out. Come on, Markham; the longer we wait the less we shall like it.'

He flung open the door and we rushed in. She was there on the ground amidst the splinters of her chair. We seized her and dragged her swiftly out, and as we gained the door I looked over my shoulder into the darkness. There were two strange eyes glowing at us, a rattle of hoofs, and I had just time to slam the door when there came a crash upon it which split it from top to bottom.

'It's coming through! It's coming!'

'Run, run for your lives!' cried the Frenchman.

Another crash, and something shot through the riven door. It was a long white spike, gleaming in the lamp-light. For a moment it shone before us, and then with a snap it disappeared again.

'Quick! Quick! This way!' Harvey Deacon shouted. 'Carry her in! Here! Quick!'

We had taken refuge in the dining-room, and shut the heavy oak door. We laid the senseless woman upon the sofa, and as we did so, Moir, the hard man of business, drooped and fainted across the hearthrug. Harvey Deacon was as white as a corpse, jerking and twitching like an epileptic. With a crash we heard the studio door fly to pieces, and the snorting and stamping were in the passage, up and down, up and down, shaking the house with their fury. The Frenchman had sunk his face on his hands, and sobbed like a frightened child.

'What shall we do?' I shook him roughly by the shoulder. 'Is a gun any use?'

'No, no. The power will pass. Then it will end.'

'You might have killed us all—you unspeakable fool—with your infernal experiments.'

'I did not know. How could I tell that it would be frightened? It is mad with terror. It was his fault. He struck it.'

Harvey Deacon sprang up. 'Good heavens!' he cried.

A terrible scream sounded through the house.

'It's my wife! Here, I'm going out. If it's the Evil One himself I am going out!'

He had thrown open the door and rushed out into the passage. At the end of it, at the foot of the stairs, Mrs Deacon was lying senseless, struck down by the sight which she had seen. But there was nothing else.

With eyes of horror we looked about us, but all was perfectly quiet and still. I approached the black square of the studio door, expecting with every slow step that some atrocious shape would hurl itself out of it. But nothing came, and all was silent inside the room. Peeping and peering, our hearts in our mouths, we came to the very threshold, and stared into the darkness. There was still no sound, but in one direction there was also no darkness. A luminous, glowing cloud, with an incandescent centre, hovered in the corner of the room. Slowly it dimmed and faded, growing thinner and fainter, until at last the same dense, velvety blackness filled the whole studio. And with the last flickering gleam of that baleful light the Frenchman broke into a shout of joy.

'What a fun!' he cried. 'No one is hurt, and only the door broken, and the ladies frightened. But, my friends, we have done what has never been done before.'

'And as far as I can help,' said Harvey Deacon, 'it will certainly never be done again.'

And that was what befell on the 14th of April last at No. 17 Badderly Gardens. I began by saying that it would seem too grotesque to dogmatise as to what it was which actually did occur; but I give my impressions, *our* impressions (since they are corroborated by Harvey Deacon and John Moir), for what they are worth. You may, if it pleases you, imagine that we were the victims of an elaborate and extraordinary hoax. Or you may think with us that we underwent a very real and a very terrible experience. Or perhaps you may know more than we do of such occult matters, and can inform us of some similar occurrence. In this latter case a letter to William Markham, 146M, The Albany,* would help to throw a light upon that which is very dark to us.

THE LEATHER FUNNEL

My friend, Lionel Dacre, lived in the Avenue de Wagram, Paris.* His house was that small one, with the iron railings and grass plot in front of it, on the left-hand side as you pass down from the Arc de Triomphe.* I fancy that it had been there long before the avenue was constructed, for the grey tiles were stained with lichens, and the walls were mildewed and discoloured with age. It looked a small house from the street, five windows in front, if I remember right, but it deepened into a single long chamber at the back. It was here that Dacre had that singular library of occult literature, and the fantastic curiosities which served as a hobby for himself, and an amusement for his friends. A wealthy man of refined and eccentric tastes, he had spent much of his life and fortune in gathering together what was said to be a unique private collection of Talmudic, cabalistic, and magical works,* many of them of great rarity and value. His tastes leaned toward the marvellous and the monstrous, and I have heard that his experiments in the direction of the unknown have passed all the bounds of civilization and of decorum. To his English friends he never alluded to such matters, and took the tone of the student and *virtuoso*; but a Frenchman whose tastes were of the same nature has assured me that the worst excesses of the black mass have been perpetrated in that large and lofty hall, which is lined with the shelves of his books, and the cases of his museum.

Dacre's appearance was enough to show that his deep interest in these psychic matters was intellectual rather than spiritual. There was no trace of asceticism upon his heavy face, but there was much mental force in his huge, dome-like skull, which curved upward from amongst his thinning locks, like a snow-peak above its fringe of fir trees. His knowledge was greater than his wisdom, and his powers were far superior to his character. The small bright eyes, buried deeply in his fleshy face, twinkled with intelligence and an unabated curiosity of life, but they were the eyes of a sensualist and an egotist. Enough of the man, for he is dead now, poor devil, dead at the very time that he had made sure that he had at last discovered the elixir of life. It is not with his complex character that I have to deal, but with the very strange and inexplicable incident which had its rise in my visit to him in the early spring of the year '82.

I had known Dacre in England, for my researches in the Assyrian Room of the British Museum had been conducted at the time when he was endeavouring to establish a mystic and esoteric meaning in the Babylonian tablets, and this community of interests had brought us together. Chance remarks had led to daily conversation, and that to something verging upon friendship. I had promised him that on my next visit to Paris I would call upon him. At the time when I was able to fulfil my compact I was living in a cottage at Fontainebleau,* and as the evening trains were inconvenient, he asked me to spend the night in his house.

'I have only that one spare couch,' said he, pointing to a broad sofa in his large salon; 'I hope that you will manage to be comfortable there.'

It was a singular bedroom, with its high walls of brown volumes, but there could be no more agreeable furniture to a bookworm like myself, and there is no scent so pleasant to my nostrils as that faint, subtle reek which comes from an ancient book. I assured him that I could desire no more charming chamber, and no more congenial surroundings.

'If the fittings are neither convenient nor conventional, they are at least costly,' said he, looking round at his shelves. 'I have expended nearly a quarter of a million of money upon these objects which sur-round you. Books, weapons, gems, carvings, tapestries, images—there is hardly a thing here which has not its history, and it is generally one worth telling.'

He was seated as he spoke at one side of the open fireplace, and I at the other. His reading-table was on his right, and the strong lamp above it ringed it with a very vivid circle of golden light. A half-rolled palimpsest lay in the centre, and around it were many quaint articles of bric-à-brac. One of these was a large funnel, such as is used for filling wine casks. It appeared to be made of black wood, and to be rimmed with discoloured brass.

'That is a curious thing,' I remarked. 'What is the history of that?'

'Ah!' said he, 'it is the very question which I have had occasion to ask myself. I would give a good deal to know. Take it in your hands and examine it.'

I did so, and found that what I had imagined to be wood was in reality leather, though age had dried it into an extreme hardness.

It was a large funnel, and might hold a quart* when full. The brass rim encircled the wide end, but the narrow was also tipped with metal.

'What do you make of it?' asked Dacre.

'I should imagine that it belonged to some vintner or maltster in the Middle Ages,' said I. 'I have seen in England leathern drinking flagons of the seventeenth century—"blook jacks"' as they were called which were of the same colour and hardness as this filler.'

'I dare say the date would be about the same,' said Dacre, 'and, no doubt, also, it was used for filling a vessel with liquid. If my suspicions are correct, however, it was a queer vintner who used it, and a very singular cask which was filled. Do you observe nothing strange at the spout end of the funnel.'

As I held it to the light I observed that at a spot some five inches above the brass tip the narrow neck of the leather funnel was all haggled and scored, as if someone had notched it round with a blunt knife. Only at that point was there any roughening of the dead black surface.

'Someone has tried to cut off the neck.'

'Would you call it a cut?'

'It is torn and lacerated. It must have taken some strength to leave these marks on such tough material, whatever the instrument may have been. But what do you think of it? I can tell that you know more than you say.'

Dacre smiled, and his little eyes twinkled with knowledge.

'Have you included the psychology of dreams among your learned studies?' he asked.

'I did not even know that there was such a psychology.'*

'My dear sir, that shelf above the gem case is filled with volumes, from Albertus Magnus* onward, which deal with no other subject. It is a science in itself.'

'A science of charlatans.'

'The charlatan is always the pioneer. From the astrologer came the astronomer, from the alchemist the chemist, from the mesmerist the experimental psychologist. The quack of yesterday is the professor of tomorrow. Even such subtle and elusive things as dreams will in time be reduced to system and order. When that time comes the researches of our friends on the bookshelf yonder will no longer be the amusement of the mystic, but the foundations of a science.'

'Supposing that is so, what has the science of dreams to do with a large, black, brass-rimmed funnel?'

'I will tell you. You know that I have an agent who is always on the lookout for rarities and curiosities for my collection. Some days ago he heard of a dealer upon one of the Quais who had acquired some old rubbish found in a cupboard in an ancient house at the back of the Rue Mathurin, in the Quartier Latin.* The dining-room of this old house is decorated with a coat of arms, chevrons, and bars rouge upon a field argent,* which prove, upon inquiry, to be the shield of Nicholas de la Reynie, a high official of King Louis XIV.* There can be no doubt that the other articles in the cupboard date back to the early days of that king. The inference is, therefore, that they were all the property of this Nicholas de la Reynie, who was, as I understand, the gentleman specially concerned with the maintenance and execution of the Draconic laws* of that epoch.'

'What then?'

'I would ask you now to take the funnel into your hands once more and to examine the upper brass rim. Can you make out any lettering upon it?'

There were certainly some scratches upon it, almost obliterated by time. The general effect was of several letters, the last of which bore some resemblance to a B.

'You make it a B?'

'Yes, I do.'

'So do I. In fact, I have no doubt whatever that it is a B.'

'But the nobleman you mentioned would have had R for his initial.'

'Exactly! That's the beauty of it. He owned this curious object, and yet he had someone else's initials upon it. Why did he do this?'

'I can't imagine; can you?'

'Well, I might, perhaps, guess. Do you observe something drawn a little farther along the rim?'

'I should say it was a crown.'

'It is undoubtedly a crown; but if you examine it in a good light, you will convince yourself that it is not an ordinary crown. It is a heraldic crown—a badge of rank, and it consists of an alternation of four pearls and strawberry leaves, the proper badge of a marquis.* We may infer, therefore, that the person whose initials end in B was entitled to wear that coronet.'

'Then this common leather filler belonged to a marquis?'

Dacre gave a peculiar smile.

'Or to some member of the family of a marquis,' said he. 'So much we have clearly gathered from this engraved rim.'

'But what has all this to do with dreams?' I do not know whether it was from a look upon Dacre's face, or from some subtle suggestion in his manner, but a feeling of repulsion, of unreasoning horror, came upon me as I looked at the gnarled old lump of leather.

'I have more than once received important information through my dreams,' said my companion in the didactic manner which he loved to affect. 'I make it a rule now when I am in doubt upon any material point to place the article in question beside me as I sleep, and to hope for some enlightenment. The process does not appear to me to be very obscure, though it has not yet received the blessing of orthodox science. According to my theory, any object which has been intimately associated with any supreme paroxysm of human emotion, whether it be joy or pain, will retain a certain atmosphere or association which it is capable of communicating to a sensitive mind. By a sensitive mind I do not mean an abnormal one, but such a trained and educated mind as you or I possess.'

'You mean, for example, that if I slept beside that old sword upon the wall, I might dream of some bloody incident in which that very sword took part?'*

'An excellent example, for, as a matter of fact, that sword was used in that fashion by me, and I saw in my sleep the death of its owner, who perished in a brisk skirmish, which I have been unable to identify, but which occurred at the time of the wars of the Frondists.* If you think of it, some of our popular observances show that the fact has already been recognized by our ancestors, although we, in our wisdom, have classed it among superstitions.'

'For example?'

'Well, the placing of the bride's cake beneath the pillow in order that the sleeper may have pleasant dreams. That is one of several instances which you will find set forth in a small *brochure* which I am myself writing upon the subject. But to come back to the point, I slept one night with this funnel beside me, and I had a dream which certainly throws a curious light upon its use and origin.'

'What did you dream?'

'I dreamed—' He paused, and an intent look of interest came over his massive face. 'By Jove, that's well thought of,' said he. 'This really will be an exceedingly interesting experiment. You are yourself a psychic subject—with nerves which respond readily to any impression.'

'I have never tested myself in that direction.'

'Then we shall test you to-night. Might I ask you as a very great favour, when you occupy that couch to-night, to sleep with this old funnel placed by the side of your pillow?'

The request seemed to me a grotesque one; but I have myself, in my complex nature, a hunger after all which is bizarre and fantastic. I had not the faintest belief in Dacre's theory, nor any hopes for success in such an experiment; yet it amused me that the experiment should be made. Dacre, with great gravity, drew a small stand to the head of my settee, and placed the funnel upon it. Then, after a short conversation, he wished me good night and left me.

* * *

I sat for some little time smoking by the smouldering fire, and turning over in my mind the curious incident which had occurred, and the strange experience which might lie before me. Sceptical as I was, there was something impressive in the assurance of Dacre's manner, and my extraordinary surroundings, the huge room with the strange and often sinister objects which were hung round it, struck solemnity into my soul. Finally I undressed, and turning out the lamp, I lay down. After long tossing I fell asleep. Let me try to describe as accurately as I can the scene which came to me in my dreams. It stands out now in my memory more clearly than anything which I have seen with my waking eyes.

There was a room which bore the appearance of a vault. Four spandrels* from the corners ran up to join a sharp, cup-shaped roof. The architecture was rough, but very strong. It was evidently part of a great building.

Three men in black, with curious, top-heavy, black velvet hats, sat in a line upon a red-carpeted dais. Their faces were very solemn and sad. On the left stood two long-gowned men with portfolios in their hands, which seemed to be stuffed with papers. Upon the right, looking toward me, was a small woman with blonde hair and singular, light-blue eyes—the eyes of a child. She was past her first youth, but could not yet be called middle-aged. Her figure was inclined to stoutness and her bearing was proud and confident. Her face was pale, but serene. It was a curious face, comely and yet feline, with a subtle suggestion of cruelty about the straight, strong little mouth and chubby jaw. She was draped in some sort of loose, white gown. Beside her stood a thin, eager priest, who whispered in her ear, and continually raised a crucifix before her eyes. She turned her head and looked fixedly past the crucifix at the three men in black, who were, I felt, her judges.

As I gazed the three men stood up and said something, but I could distinguish no words, though I was aware that it was the central one who was speaking. They then swept out of the room, followed by the two men with the papers. At the same instant several rough-looking fellows in stout jerkins came bustling in and removed first the red carpet, and then the boards which formed the dais, so as to entirely clear the room. When this screen was removed I saw some singular articles of furniture behind it. One looked like a bed with wooden rollers at each end, and a winch handle to regulate its length. Another was a wooden horse. There were several other curious objects, and a number of swinging cords which played over pulleys. It was not unlike a modern gymnasium.

When the room had been cleared there appeared a new figure upon the scene. This was a tall, thin person clad in black, with a gaunt and austere face. The aspect of the man made me shudder. His clothes were all shining with grease and mottled with stains. He bore himself with a slow and impressive dignity, as if he took command of all things from the instant of his entrance. In spite of his rude appearance and sordid dress, it was now *his* business, *his* room, his to command. He carried a coil of light ropes over his left forearm. The lady looked him up and down with a searching glance, but her expression was unchanged. It was confident—even defiant. But it was very different with the priest. His face was ghastly white, and I saw the moisture glisten and run on his high, sloping forehead. He threw up his hands in prayer and he stooped continually to mutter frantic words in the lady's ear.

The man in black now advanced, and taking one of the cords from his left arm, he bound the woman's hands together. She held them meekly toward him as he did so. Then he took her arm with a rough grip and led her toward the wooden horse, which was little higher than her waist. On to this she was lifted and laid, with her back upon it, and her face to the ceiling, while the priest, quivering with horror, had rushed out of the room. The woman's lips were moving rapidly, and though I could hear nothing I knew that she was praying. Her feet hung down on either side of the horse, and I saw that the rough varlets in attendance had fastened cords to her ankles and secured the other ends to iron rings in the stone floor.

My heart sank within me as I saw these ominous preparations, and yet I was held by the fascination of horror, and I could not take my eyes from the strange spectacle. A man had entered the room with a bucket of water in either hand. Another followed with a third bucket. They were laid beside the wooden horse. The second man had a wooden dipper—a bowl with a straight handle—in his other hand. This he gave to the man in black. At the same moment one of the varlets approached with a dark object in his hand, which even in my dream filled me with a vague feeling of familiarity. It was a leathern filler. With horrible energy he thrust it—but I could stand no more. My hair stood on end with horror. I writhed, I struggled, I broke through the bonds of sleep, and I burst with a shriek into my own life, and found myself lying shivering with terror in the huge library, with the moonlight flooding through the window and throwing strange silver and black traceries upon the opposite wall. Oh, what a blessed relief to feel that I was back in the nineteenth century—back out of that mediæval vault into a world where men had human hearts within their bosoms. I sat up on my couch, trembling in every limb, my mind divided between thankfulness and horror. To think that such things were ever done—that they *could* be done without God striking the villains dead. Was it all a fantasy, or did it really stand for something which had happened in the black, cruel days of the world's history? I sank my throbbing head upon my shaking hands. And then, suddenly, my heart seemed to stand still in my bosom, and I could not even scream, so great was my terror. Something was advancing toward me through the darkness of the room.

It is a horror coming upon a horror which breaks a man's spirit. I could not reason, I could not pray; I could only sit like a frozen image, and glare at the dark figure which was coming down the great room. And then it moved out into the white lane of moonlight, and I breathed once more. It was Dacre, and his face showed that he was as frightened as myself.

'Was that you? For God's sake what's the matter?' he asked in a husky voice.

'Oh, Dacre, I am glad to see you! I have been down into hell. It was dreadful.'

'Then it was you who screamed?'

'I dare say it was.'

'It rang through the house. The servants are all terrified.' He struck a match and lit the lamp. 'I think we may get the fire to burn up again,' he added, throwing some logs upon the embers. 'Good God, my dear chap, how white you are! You look as if you had seen a ghost.'

'So I have — several ghosts.'

'The leather funnel has acted, then?'

'I wouldn't sleep near the infernal thing again for all the money you could offer me.'

Dacre chuckled.

'I expected that you would have a lively night of it,' said he. 'You took it out of me in return, for that scream of yours wasn't a very pleasant sound at two in the morning. I suppose from what you say that you have seen the whole dreadful business.'

'What dreadful business?'

'The torture of the water—the "Extraordinary Question,"* as it was called in the genial days of "Le Roi Soleil." Did you stand it out to the end?'

'No, thank God, I awoke before it really began.'

'Ah! it is just as well for you. I held out till the third bucket. Well, it is an old story, and they are all in their graves now anyhow, so what does it matter how they got there? I suppose that you have no idea what it was that you have seen?'

'The torture of some criminal. She must have been a terrible malefactor indeed if her crimes are in proportion to her penalty.'

'Well, we have that small consolation,' said Dacre, wrapping his dressing-gown round him and crouching closer to the fire. 'They *were* in proportion to her penalty. That is to say, if I am correct in the lady's identity.'

'How could you possibly know her identity?'

For answer Dacre took down an old vellum-covered volume from the shelf.

'Just listen to this,' said he; 'it is in the French of the seventeenth century, but I will give a rough translation as I go. You will judge for yourself whether I have solved the riddle or not.'

'"The prisoner was brought before the Grand Chambers and Tournelles of Parliament, sitting as a court of justice, charged with the murder of Master Dreux d'Aubray, her father, and of her two brothers, MM* d'Aubray, one being civil lieutenant, and the other a counsellor of Parliament. In person it seemed hard to believe that she had really done such wicked deeds, for she was of a mild appearance, and of short stature, with a fair skin and blue eyes. Yet the Court, having found her guilty, condemned her to the ordinary* and to the extraordinary question in order that she might be forced to name her accomplices, after which she should be carried in a cart to the Place de Grève,* there to have her head cut off, her body being afterwards burned and her ashes scattered to the winds."

'The date of this entry is July 16, 1676.'

'It is interesting,' said I, 'but not convincing. How do you prove the two women to be the same?'

'I am coming to that. The narrative goes on to tell of the woman's behaviour when questioned. "When the executioner approached her she recognized him by the cords which he held in his hands, and she at once held out her own hands to him, looking at him from head to foot without uttering a word." How's that?'

'Yes, it was so.'

'"She gazed without wincing upon the wooden horse and rings which had twisted so many limbs and caused so many shrieks of agony. When her eyes fell upon the three pails of water, which were all ready for her, she said with a smile, 'All that water must have been brought here for the purpose of drowning me, Monsieur. You have no idea, I trust, of making a person of my small stature swallow it all.'" Shall I read the details of the torture?'

'No, for Heaven's sake, don't.'

'Here is a sentence which must surely show you that what is here recorded is the very scene which you have gazed upon to-night: "The good Abbé Pirot, unable to contemplate the agonies which were suffered by his penitent, had hurried from the room." Does that convince you?'

'It does entirely. There can be no question that it is indeed the same event. But who, then, is this lady whose appearance was so attractive and whose end was so horrible?'

For answer Dacre came across to me, and placed the small lamp upon the table which stood by my bed. Lifting up the ill-omened filler, he turned the brass rim so that the light fell full upon it. Seen in this way the engraving seemed clearer than on the night before.

'We have already agreed that this is the badge of a marquis or of a marquise,' said he. 'We have also settled that the last letter is B.'

'It is undoubtedly so.'

'I now suggest to you that the other letters from left to right are, M, M, a small d, A, a small d, and then the final B.'

'Yes, I am sure that you are right. I can make out the two small d's quite plainly.'

'What I have read to you to-night,' said Dacre, 'is the official record of the trial of Marie Madeleine d'Aubray, Marquise de Brinvilliers,* one of the most famous poisoners and murderers of all time.'

I sat in silence, overwhelmed at the extraordinary nature of the incident, and at the completeness of the proof with which Dacre had exposed its real meaning. In a vague way I remembered some details of the woman's career, her unbridled debauchery, the cold-blooded and protracted torture of her sick father, the murder of her brothers for motives of petty gain. I recollected also that the bravery of her end had done something to atone for the horror of her life, and that all Paris had sympathised with her last moments, and blessed her as a martyr within a few days of the time when they had cursed her as a murderess. One objection, and one only, occurred to my mind.

'How came her initials and her badge of rank upon the filler? Surely they did not carry their mediæval homage to the nobility to the point of decorating instruments of torture with their titles?'

'I was puzzled with the same point,' said Dacre, 'but it admits of a simple explanation. The case excited extraordinary interest at the time, and nothing could be more natural than that La Reynie, the head of the police, should retain this filler as a grim souvenir. It was not often that a marchioness of France underwent the extraordinary question. That he should engrave her initials upon it for the information of others was surely a very ordinary proceeding upon his part.'

'And this?' I asked, pointing to the marks upon the leathern neck.

'She was a cruel tigress,' said Dacre, as he turned away. 'I think it is evident that like other tigresses her teeth were both strong and sharp.'

THE POT OF CAVIARE

⸺⧯⸺

J T was the fourth day of the siege. Ammunition and provisions were both nearing an end. When the Boxer insurrection* had suddenly flamed up, and roared, like a fire in dry grass, across Northern China, the few scattered Europeans in the outlying provinces had huddled together at the nearest defensible post and had held on for dear life until rescue came—or until it did not. In the latter case, the less said about their fate the better. In the former, they came back into the world of men with that upon their faces which told that they had looked very closely upon such an end as would ever haunt their dreams.

Ichau was only fifty miles from the coast, and there was a European squadron in the Gulf of Liantong.* Therefore the absurd little garrison, consisting of native Christians and railway men, with a German officer to command them and five civilian Europeans to support him, held on bravely with the conviction that help must soon come sweeping down to them from the low hills to eastward. The sea was visible from those hills, and on the sea were their armed countrymen. Surely, then, they could not feel deserted. With brave hearts they manned the loopholes in the crumbling brick walls outlining the tiny European quarter, and they fired away briskly, if ineffectively, at the rapidly advancing sangars* of the Boxers. It was certain that in another day or so they would be at the end of their resources, but then it was equally certain that in another day or so they must be relieved. It might be a little sooner or it might be a little later, but there was no one who ever ventured to hint that the relief would not arrive in time to pluck them out of the fire. Up to Tuesday night there was no word of discouragement.

It was true that on the Wednesday their robust faith in what was going forward behind those eastern hills had weakened a little. The grey slopes lay bare and unresponsive while the deadly sangars pushed ever nearer, so near that the dreadful faces which shrieked imprecations at them from time to time over the top could be seen in every hideous feature. There was not so much of that now since young Ainslie, of the Diplomatic service, with his neat little .303 sporting rifle, had settled down in the squat church tower, and had devoted his days to abating the nuisance. But a silent sangar is an even more impressive thing than a clamorous one, and steadily, irresistibly, inevitably, the lines of brick and rubble drew closer. Soon they would be so near that one rush would assuredly carry the frantic swordsmen over the frail entrenchment. It all seemed very black upon the Wednesday evening. Colonel Dresler, the German ex-infantry soldier, went about with an imperturbable face, but a heart of lead. Ralston, of the railway, was up half the night writing farewell letters. Professor Mercer, the old entomologist, was even more silent and grimly thoughtful than ever. Ainslie had lost some of his flippancy. On the whole, the ladies— Miss Sinclair, the nurse of the Scotch Mission, Mrs Patterson, and her pretty daughter Jessie—were the most composed of the party. Father Pierre, of the French Mission, was also unaffected, as was natural to one who regarded martyrdom as a glorious crown. The Boxers yelling for his blood beyond the walls disturbed him less than his forced association with the sturdy Scotch Presbyterian presence of Mr Patterson, with whom for ten years he had wrangled over the souls of the natives. They passed each other now in the corridors as dog passes cat, and each kept a watchful eye upon the other lest even in the trenches he might filch some sheep from the rival fold, whispering heresy in his ear.

But the Wednesday night passed without a crisis, and on the Thursday all was bright once more. It was Ainslie up in the clock tower who had first heard the distant thud of a gun. Then Dresler heard it, and within half an hour it was audible to all—that strong iron voice, calling to them from afar and bidding them to be of good cheer, since help was coming. It was clear that the landing party from the squadron was well on its way. It would not arrive an hour too soon. The cartridges were nearly finished. Their half-rations of food would soon dwindle to an even more pitiful supply. But what need to worry about that now that relief was assured? There would be no attack that day, as most of the Boxers could be seen streaming off in the direction of the distant firing, and the long lines of sangars were silent and deserted. They were all able, therefore, to assemble at the lunch-table, a merry, talkative party, full of that joy of living which sparkles most brightly under the imminent shadow of death.

'The pot of caviare!' cried Ainslie. 'Come, Professor, out with the pot of caviare!'

'Potz-tausend!* yes,' grunted old Dresler. 'It is certainly time that we had that famous pot.'

The ladies joined in, and from all parts of the long, ill-furnished table there came the demand for caviare.

It was a strange time to ask for such a delicacy, but the reason is soon told. Professor Mercer, the old Californian entomologist, had received a jar of caviare in a hamper of goods from San Francisco, arriving a day or two before the outbreak. In the general pooling and distribution of provisions this one dainty and three bottles of Lachryma Christi* from the same hamper had been excepted and set aside. By common consent they were to be reserved for the final joyous meal when the end of their peril should be in sight. Even as they sat the thud-thud of the relieving guns came to their ears—more luxurious music to their lunch than the most sybaritic restaurant of London could have supplied. Before evening the relief would certainly be there. Why, then, should their stale bread not be glorified by the treasured caviare?

But the Professor shook his gnarled old head and smiled his inscrutable smile.

'Better wait,' said he.

'Wait! Why wait?' cried the company.

'They have still far to come,' he answered.

'They will be here for supper at the latest,' said Ralston, of the railway—a keen, bird-like man, with bright eyes and long, projecting nose. 'They cannot be more than ten miles from us now. If they only did two miles an hour it would make them due at seven.'

'There is a battle on the way,' remarked the Colonel. 'You will grant two hours or three hours for the battle.'

'Not half an hour,' cried Ainslie. 'They will walk through them as if they were not there. What can these rascals with their matchlocks* and swords do against modern weapons?'

'It depends on who leads the column of relief,' said Dresler. 'If they are fortunate enough to have a German officer——'

'An Englishman for my money!' cried Ralston.

'The French commodore is said to be an excellent strategist,' remarked Father Pierre.

'I don't see that it matters a toss,' cried the exuberant Ainslie. 'Mr Mauser and Mr Maxim* are the two men who will see us through, and with them on our side no leader can go wrong. I tell you they will just brush them aside and walk through them. So now, Professor, come on with that pot of caviare!'

But the old scientist was unconvinced.

'We shall reserve it for supper,' said he.

'After all,' said Mr Patterson, in his slow, precise Scottish intonation, 'it will be a courtesy to our guests—the officers of the relief if we have some palatable food to lay before them. I'm in agreement with the Professor that we reserve the caviare for supper.'

The argument appealed to their sense of hospitality. There was something pleasantly chivalrous, too, in the idea of keeping their one little delicacy to give a savour to the meal of their preservers. There was no more talk of the caviare.

'By the way, Professor,' said Mr Patterson, 'I've only heard to-day that this is the second time that you have been besieged in this way. I'm sure we should all be very interested to hear some details of your previous experience.'

The old man's face set very grimly.

'I was in Sung-tong, in South China,* in 'eighty-nine,' said he.

'It's a very extraordinary coincidence that you should twice have been in such a perilous situation,' said the missionary. 'Tell us how you were relieved at Sung-tong.'

The shadow deepened upon the weary face.

'We were not relieved,' said he.

'What! the place fell?'

'Yes, it fell.'

'And you came through alive.'

'I am a doctor as well as an entomologist. They had many wounded; they spared me.'

'And the rest?'

'Assez! assez!' cried the little French priest, raising his hand in protest. He had been twenty years in China. The professor had said nothing, but there was something, some lurking horror, in his dull, grey eyes which had turned the ladies pale.

'I am sorry,' said the missionary. 'I can see that it is a painful subject. I should not have asked.'

'No,' the Professor answered, slowly. 'It is wiser not to ask. It is better not to speak about such things at all. But surely those guns are very much nearer?'

There could be no doubt of it. After a silence the thud-thud had recommenced with a lively ripple of rifle-fire playing all round that deep bass master-note. It must be just at the farther side of the nearest hill. They pushed back their chairs and ran out to the ramparts. The silent-footed native servants came in and cleared the scanty remains from the table. But after they had left, the old Professor sat on there, his massive, grey-crowned head leaning upon his hands and the same pensive look of horror in his eyes. Some ghosts may be laid for years, but when they do rise it is not so easy to drive them back to their slumbers. The guns had ceased outside, but he had not observed it, lost as he was in the one supreme and terrible memory of his life.

His thoughts were interrupted at last by the entrance of the Commandant. There was a complacent smile upon his broad German face.

'The Kaiser will be pleased,' said he, rubbing his hands. 'Yes, certainly it should mean a decoration. "Defence of Ichau against the Boxers by Colonel Dresler, late Major of the 114th Hanoverian Infantry. Splendid resistance of small garrison against overwhelming odds." It will certainly appear in the Berlin papers.'

'Then you think we are saved?' said the old man, with neither emotion nor exultation in his voice.

The Colonel smiled.

'Why, Professor,' said he, 'I have seen you more excited on the morning when you brought back *Lepidus Mercerensis** in your collecting box.'

'The fly was safe in my collecting-box first,' the entomologist answered. 'I have seen so many strange turns of Fate in my long life that I do not grieve nor do I rejoice until I know that I have cause. But tell me the news.'

'Well,' said the Colonel, lighting his long pipe, and stretching his gaitered legs in the bamboo chair, 'I'll stake my military reputation that all is well. They are advancing swiftly, the firing has died down to show that resistance is at an end, and within an hour we'll see them over the brow. Ainslie is to fire his gun three times from the church tower as a signal, and then we shall make a little sally on our own account.'

'And you are waiting for this signal?'

'Yes, we are waiting for Ainslie's shots. I thought I would spend the time with you, for I had something to ask you.'

'What was it?'

'Well, you remember your talk about the other siege—the siege of

Sung-tong. It interests me very much from a professional point of view. Now that the ladies and civilians are gone you will have no objection to discussing it.'

'It is not a pleasant subject.'

'No, I dare say not. Mein Gott! it was indeed a tragedy. But you have seen how I have conducted the defence here. Was it good? Was it would? Was it worthy of the traditions of the German army?'

'I think you could have done no more.'

'Thank you. But this other place, was it as ably defended? To me a comparison of this sort is very interesting. Could it have been saved?'

'No; everything possible was done—save only one thing.'

'Ah! there was one omission. What was it?'

'No one—above all, no woman —should have been allowed to fall alive into the hands of the Chinese.'*

The Colonel held out his broad red hand and enfolded the long, white, nervous fingers of the Professor.

'You are right—a thousand times right. But do not think that this has escaped my thoughts. For myself I would die fighting, so would Ralston, so would Ainslie. I have talked to them, and it is settled. But the others, I have spoken with them, but what are you to do? There are the priest, and the missionary, and the women?'

'Would they wish to be taken alive?'

'They would not promise to take steps to prevent it. They would not lay hands on their own lives. Their consciences would not permit it. Of course, it is all over now, and we need not speak of such dreadful things. But what would you have done in my place?'

'Kill them.'

'Mein Gott! You would murder them?'

'In mercy I would kill them. Man, I have been through it. I have seen the death of the hot eggs; I have seen the death of the boiling kettle;* I have seen the women—my God! I wonder that I have ever slept sound again.' His usually impassive face was working and quivering with the agony of the remembrance. 'I was strapped to a stake with thorns in my eyelids to keep them open, and my grief at their torture was a less thing than my self-reproach when I thought that I could with one tube of tasteless tablets have snatched them at the last instant from the hands of their tormentors. Murder! I am ready to stand at the Divine bar and answer for a thousand murders such as that! Sin! Why, it is such an act as might well cleanse the stain of real sin from the soul. But if, knowing what I do, I should have failed this second time to do it, then, by Heaven! there is no hell deep enough or hot enough to receive my guilty craven spirit.'

The Colonel rose, and again his hand clasped that of the Professor. 'You speak sense,' said he. 'You are a brave, strong man, who know your own mind. Yes, by the Lord! you would have been my great help had things gone the other way. I have often thought and wondered in the dark, early hours of the morning, but I did not know how to do it. But we should have heard Ainslie's shots before now; I will go and see.'

Again the old scientist sat alone with his thoughts. Finally, as neither the guns of the relieving force nor yet the signal of their approach sounded upon his ears, he rose, and was about to go himself upon the ramparts to make inquiry when the door flew open, and Colonel Dresler staggered into the room. His face was of a ghastly yellow-white, and his chest heaved like that of a man exhausted with running. There was brandy on the side-table, and he gulped down a glassful. Then he dropped heavily into a chair.

'Well,' said the Professor, coldly, 'they are not coming?'

'No, they cannot come.'

There was silence for a minute or more, the two men staring blankly at each other.

'Do they all know?'

'No one knows but me.'

'How did you learn?'

'I was at the wall near the postern gate*—the little wooden gate that opens on the rose garden. I saw something crawling among the bushes. There was a knocking at the door. I opened it. It was a Christian Tartar,* badly cut about with swords. He had come from the battle. Commodore Wyndham, the Englishman, had sent him. The relieving force had been checked. They had shot away most of their ammunition. They had entrenched themselves and sent back to the ships for more. Three days must pass before they could come. That was all. Mein Gott! it was enough.'

The Professor bent his shaggy grey brows.

'Where is the man?' he asked.

'He is dead. He died of loss of blood. His body lies at the postern gate.'

'And no one saw him?'

'Not to speak to.'

'Oh! they did see him, then?'

'Ainslie must have seen him from the church tower. He must know that I have had tidings. He will want to know what they are. If I tell him they must all know.'

'How long can we hold out?'

'An hour or two at the most.'

'Is that absolutely certain?'

'I pledge my credit as a soldier upon it.'

'Then we must fall?'

'Yes, we must fall.'

'There is no hope for us?'

'None.'

The door flew open and young Ainslie rushed in. Behind him crowded Ralston, Patterson, and a crowd of white men and of native Christians.

'You've had news, Colonel?'

Professor Mercer pushed to the front.

'Colonel Dresler has just been telling me. It is all right. They have halted, but will be here in the early morning. There is no longer any danger.'

A cheer broke from the group in the doorway. Everyone was laughing and shaking hands.

'But suppose they rush us before to-morrow morning?' cried Ralston, in a petulant voice. 'What infernal fools these fellows are not to push on! Lazy devils, they should be court-martialled, every man of them.'

'It's all safe,' said Ainslie. 'These fellows have had a bad knock. We can see their wounded being carried by the hundred over the hill. They must have lost heavily. They won't attack before morning.'

'No, no,' said the Colonel; 'it is certain that they won't attack before morning. None the less, get back to your posts. We must give no point away.' He left the room with the rest, but as he did so he looked back, and his eyes for an instant met those of the old Professor. 'I leave it in your hands,' was the message which he flashed.

A stern set smile was his answer.

The afternoon wore away without the Boxers making their last attack. To Colonel Dresler it was clear that the unwonted stillness meant only that they were reassembling their forces from their fight with the relief column, and were gathering themselves for the inevitable and final rush. To all the others it appeared that the siege was indeed over, and that the assailants had been crippled by the losses which they had already sustained. It was a joyous and noisy party, therefore, which met at the supper-table, when the three bottles of Lachryma Christi were uncorked and the famous pot of caviare was finally opened. It was a large jar, and, though each had a tablespoonful of the delicacy, it was by no means exhausted. Ralston, who was an epicure, had a double allowance. He pecked away at it like a hungry bird. Ainslie, too, had a second helping, The Professor took a large spoonful himself, and Colonel Dresler, watching him narrowly, did the same. The ladies ate freely, save only pretty Miss Patterson, who disliked the salty, pungent taste. In spite of the hospitable entreaties of the Professor, her portion lay hardly touched at the side of her plate.

'You don't like my little delicacy. It is a disappointment to me when I had kept it for your pleasure,' said the old man. 'I beg that you will eat the caviare.'

'I have never tasted it before. No doubt I should like it in time.'

'Well, you must make a beginning. Why not start to educate your taste now? Do, please!'

Pretty Jessie Patterson's bright face shone with her sunny, boyish smile.

'Why, how earnest you are!' she laughed. 'I had no idea you were so polite, Professor Mercer. Even if I do not eat it I am just as grateful.'

'You are foolish not to eat it,' said the Professor, with such intensity that the smile died from her face and her eyes reflected the earnestness of his own. 'I tell you it is foolish not to eat caviare to-night.'

'But why—why?' she asked.

'Because you have it on your plate. Because it is sinful to waste it.'

'There! there!' said stout Mrs Patterson, leaning across. 'Don't trouble her any more. I can see that she does not like it. But it shall not be wasted.' She passed the blade of her knife under it, and scraped it from Jessie's plate on to her own. 'Now it won't be wasted. Your mind will be at ease, Professor.'

But it did not seem at ease. On the contrary his face was agitated like that of a man who encounters an unexpected and formidable obstacle. He was lost in thought.

The conversation buzzed cheerily. Everyone was full of his future plans.

'No, no, there is no holiday for me,' said Father Pierre. 'We priests don't get holidays. Now that the mission and school are formed I am to leave it to Father Amiel, and to push westwards to found another.'

'You are leaving?' said Mr Patterson. 'You don't mean that you are going away from Ichau?'

Father Pierre shook his venerable head in waggish reproof. 'You must not look so pleased, Mr Patterson.'

'Well, well, our views are very different,' said the Presbyterian, 'but there is no personal feeling towards you, Father Pierre. At the same time, how any reasonable educated man at this time of the world's history can teach these poor benighted heathen that——'

A general buzz of remonstrance silenced the theology.

'What will you do yourself, Mr Patterson?' asked someone.

'Well, I'll take three months in Edinburgh to attend the annual meeting. You'll be glad to do some shopping in Princes Street,* I'm thinking, Mary. And you, Jessie, you'll see some folk your own age. Then we can come back in the fall, when your nerves have had a rest.'

'Indeed, we shall all need it,' said Miss Sinclair, the mission nurse. 'You know, this long strain takes me in the strangest way. At the present moment I can hear such a buzzing in my ears.'

'Well, that's funny, for it's just the same with me,' cried Ainslie. 'An absurd up-and-down buzzing, as if a drunken bluebottle were trying experiments on his register. As you say, it must be due to nervous strain. For my part I am going back to Peking, and I hope I may get some promotion over this affair. I can get good polo here, and that's as fine a change of thought as I know. How about you, Ralston?'

'Oh, I don't know. I've hardly had time to think. I want to have a real good sunny, bright holiday and forget it all. It was funny to see all the letters in my room. It looked so black on Wednesday night that I had settled up my affairs and written to all my friends. I don't quite know how they were to be delivered, but I trusted to luck. I think I will keep those papers as a souvenir. They will always remind me of how close a shave we have had.'

'Yes, I would keep them,' said Dresler.

His voice was so deep and solemn that every eye was turned upon him.

'What is it, Colonel? You seem in the blues tonight.' It was Ainslie who spoke.

'No, no; I am very contented.'

'Well, so you should be when you see success in sight. I am sure we are all indebted to you for your science and skill. I don't think we could have held the place without you. Ladies and gentlemen, I ask you to drink to the health of Colonel Dresler, of the Imperial German army. Er soll leben—hoch!'*

They all stood up and raised their glasses to the soldier, with smiles and bows.

His pale face flushed with professional pride.

'I have always kept my books with me. I have forgotten nothing,' said he. 'I do not think that more could be done. If things had gone wrong with us and the place had fallen you would, I am sure, have freed me from any blame or responsibility.' He looked wistfully round him.

'I'm voicing the sentiments of this company, Colonel Dresler,' said the Scotch minister, 'when I say——but, Lord save us! what's amiss with Mr Ralston?'

He had dropped his face upon his folded arms and was placidly sleeping.

'Don't mind him,' said the Professor, hurriedly. 'We are all in a stage of reaction now. I have no doubt that we are all liable to collapse. It is only to-night that we shall feel what we have gone through.'

'I'm sure I can fully sympathize with him,' said Mrs Patterson. 'I don't know when I have been more sleepy. I can hardly hold my own head up.' She cuddled back in her chair and shut her eyes.

'Well, I've never known Mary do that before,' cried her husband, laughing heartily. 'Gone to sleep over her supper! Whatever will she think when we tell her of it afterwards? But the air does seem hot and heavy. I can certainly excuse anyone who falls asleep to-night. I think that I shall turn in early myself.'

Ainslie was in a talkative, excited mood. He was on his feet once more with his glass in his hand.

'I think that we ought to have one drink all together, and then sing "Auld Lang Syne," ' said he, smiling round at the company. 'For a week we have all pulled in the same boat, and we've got to know each other as people never do in the quiet days of peace. We've learned to appreciate each other, and we've learned to appreciate each other's nations. There's the Colonel here stands for Germany. And Father Pierre is for France. Then there's the Professor for America. Ralston and I are Britishers. Then there's the ladies, God bless 'em! They have been angels of mercy and compassion all through the siege.

I think we should drink the health of the ladies. Wonderful thing—the quiet courage, the patience, the—what shall I say?—the fortitude, the—the—by George, look at the Colonel! He's gone to sleep, too— most infernal sleepy weather.' His glass crashed down upon the table, and he sank back, mumbling and muttering, into his seat. Miss Sinclair, the pale mission nurse, had dropped off also. She lay like a broken lily across the arm of her chair. Mr Patterson looked round him and sprang to his feet. He passed his hand over his flushed forehead.

'This isn't natural, Jessie,' he cried. 'Why are they all asleep? There's Father Pierre—he's off too. Jessie, Jessie, your mother is cold. Is it sleep? Is it death? Open the windows! Help! help! help!' He staggered to his feet and rushed to the windows, but midway his head spun round, his knees sank under him, and he pitched forward upon his face.

The young girl had also sprung to her feet. She looked round her with horror-stricken eyes at her prostrate father and the silent ring of figures.

'Professor Mercer! What is it? What is it?' she cried. 'Oh, my God, they are dying! They are dead!'

The old man had raised himself by a supreme effort of his will, though the darkness was already gathering thickly round him.

'My dear young lady,' he said, stuttering and stumbling over the words, 'we would have spared you this. It would have been painless to mind and body. It was cyanide. I had it in the caviare. But you would not have it.'

'Great Heaven!' She shrank away from him with dilated eyes. 'Oh, you monster! You monster! You have poisoned them!'

'No! no! I saved them. You don't know the Chinese. They are hor- rible. In another hour we should all have been in their hands. Take it now, child.' Even as he spoke a burst of firing broke out under the very windows of the room. 'Hark! There they are! Quick, dear, quick, you may cheat them yet!' But his words fell upon deaf ears, for the girl had sunk back senseless in her chair. The old man stood listening for an instant to the firing outside. But what was that? Merciful Father, what was that? Was he going mad? Was it the effect of the drug? Surely it was a European cheer? Yes, there were sharp orders in English. There was the shouting of sailors. He could no longer doubt it. By some miracle the relief had come after all. He threw his long arms upwards in his despair. 'What have I done? Oh, good Lord, what *have* I done?' he cried.

It was Commodore Wyndham himself who was the first, after his desperate and successful night attack, to burst into that terrible supper-room. Round the table sat the white and silent company. Only in the young girl who moaned and faintly stirred was any sign of life to be seen. And yet there was one in the circle who had the energy for a last supreme duty. The Commodore, standing stupefied at the door, saw a grey head slowly lifted from the table, and the tall form of the Professor staggered for an instant to its feet.

'Take care of the caviare! For God's sake don't touch the caviare!' he croaked.

Then he sank back once more and the circle of death was complete.

THE SILVER MIRROR

—∞∞∞—

AN. 3.—This affair of White and Wotherspoon's accounts proves to be a gigantic task. There are twenty thick ledgers to be examined and checked. Who would be a junior partner? However, it is the first big bit of business which has been left entirely in my hands. I must justify it. But it has to be finished so that the lawyers may have the result in time for the trial. Johnson said this morning that I should have to get the last figure out before the twentieth of the month. Good Lord! Well, have at it, and if human brain and nerve can stand the strain, I'll win out at the other side. It means office-work from ten to five, and then a second sitting from about eight to one in the morning. There's drama in an accountant's life. When I find myself in the still early hours, while all the world sleeps, hunting through column after column for those missing figures which will turn a respected alderman into a felon, I understand that it is not such a prosaic profession after all.

On Monday I came on the first trace of defalcation.* No heavy game hunter ever got a finer thrill when first he caught sight of the trail of his quarry. But I look at the twenty ledgers and think of the jungle through which I have to follow him before I get my kill. Hard work—but rare sport, too, in a way! I saw the fat fellow once at a City dinner, his red face glowing above a white napkin. He looked at the little pale man at the end of the table. He would have been pale, too, if he could have seen the task that would be mine.

Jan. 6.—What perfect nonsense it is for doctors to prescribe rest when rest is out of the question! Asses! They might as well shout to a man who has a pack of wolves at his heels that what he wants is absolute quiet. My figures must be out by a certain date; unless they are so, I shall lose the chance of my lifetime, so how on earth am I to rest? I'll take a week or so after the trial.

Perhaps I was myself a fool to go to the doctor at all. But I get nervous and highly strung when I sit alone at my work at night. It's not a pain—only a sort of fullness of the head with an occasional mist over the eyes. I thought perhaps some bromide, or chloral,* or something of the kind might do me good. But stop work? It's absurd to ask such a thing. It's like a long-distance race. You feel queer at first and your heart thumps and your lungs pant, but if you have only the pluck to keep on, you get your second wind. I'll stick to my work and wait for my second wind. If it never comes—all the same, I'll stick to my work. Two ledgers are done, and I am well on in the third. The rascal has covered his tracks well, but I pick them up for all that.

Jan. 9.—I had not meant to go to the doctor again. And yet I have had to. 'Straining my nerves, risking a complete breakdown, even endangering my sanity.' That's a nice sentence to have fired off at one. Well, I'll stand the strain and I'll take the risk, and so long as I can sit in my chair and move a pen I'll follow the old sinner's slot.

By the way, I may as well set down here the queer experience which drove me this second time to the doctor. I'll keep an exact record of my symptoms and sensations, because they are interesting in them-selves—'a curious psycho-physiological study,' says the doctor—and also because I am perfectly certain that when I am through with them they will all seem blurred and unreal, like some queer dream betwixt sleeping and waking. So now, while they are fresh, I will just make a note of them if only as a change of thought after the endless figures.

There's an old silver-framed mirror in my room. It was given me by a friend who had a taste for antiquities, and he, as I happen to know, picked it up at a sale and had no notion where it came from. It's a large thing—three feet across and two feet high—and it leans at the back of a side-table on my left as I write. The frame is flat, about three inches across, and very old; far too old for hall-marks or other meth-ods of determining its age. The glass part projects, with a bevelled edge, and has the magnificent reflecting power which is only, as it seems to me, to be found in very old mirrors. There's a feeling of perspective when you look into it such as no modern glass can ever give.

The mirror is so situated that as I sit at the table I can usually see nothing in it but the reflection of the red window curtains. But a queer thing happened last night. I had been working for some hours, very much against the grain, with continual bouts of that mistiness of which I had complained. Again and again I had to stop and clear my eyes. Well, on one of these occasions I chanced to look at the mirror. It had the oddest appearance. The red curtains which should have been reflected in it were no longer there, but the glass seemed to be clouded and steamy, not on the surface, which glittered like steel, but deep down in the very grain of it. This opacity, when I stared hard at it, appeared to slowly rotate this way and that, until it was a thick, white cloud swirling in heavy wreaths. So real and solid was it, and so reasonable was I, that I remember turning, with the idea that the curtains were on fire. But everything was deadly still in the room—no sound save the ticking of the clock, no movement save the slow gyration of that strange woolly cloud deep in the heart of the old mirror.

Then, as I looked, the mist, or smoke, or cloud, or whatever one may call it, seemed to coalesce and solidify at two points quite close together, and I was aware, with a thrill of interest rather than of fear, that these were two eyes looking out into the room. A vague outline of a head I could see—a woman's by the hair, but this was very shadowy. Only the eyes were quite distinct; such eyes—dark, luminous, filled with some passionate emotion, fury or horror, I could not say which. Never have I seen eyes which were so full of intense, vivid life. They were not fixed upon me, but stared out into the room. Then as I sat erect, passed my hand over my brow, and made a strong conscious effort to pull myself together, the dim head faded into the general opacity, the mirror slowly cleared, and there were the red curtains once again.

A sceptic would say, no doubt, that I had dropped asleep over my figures, and that my experience was a dream. As a matter of fact, I was never more vividly awake in my life. I was able to argue about it even as I looked at it, and to tell myself that it was a subjective impression—a chimera of the nerves—begotten by worry and insomnia. But why this particular shape? And who is the woman, and what is the dreadful emotion which I read in those wonderful brown eyes? They come between me and my work. For the first time I have done less than the daily tally which I had marked out. Perhaps that is why I have had no abnormal sensations to-night. To-morrow I must wake up, come what may.

Jan. 11.—All well, and good progress with my work. I wind the net, coil after coil, round that bulky body. But the last smile may remain with him if my own nerves break over it. The mirror would seem to be a sort of barometer which marks my brain pressure. Each night I have observed that it had clouded before I reached the end of my task.

Dr Sinclair (who is, it seems, a bit of a psychologist) was so interested in my account that he came round this evening to have a look at the mirror. I had observed that something was scribbled in crabbed old characters upon the metal work at the back. He examined this with a lens, but could make nothing of it. 'Sanc. X. Pal.' was his final reading of it, but that did not bring us any further. He advised me to put it away into another room; but, after all, whatever I may see in it is, by his own account, only a symptom. It is in the cause that the danger lies. The twenty ledgers—not the silver mirror—should be packed away if I could only do it. I'm at the eighth now, so I progress.

Jan. 13.—Perhaps it would have been wiser after all if I had packed away the mirror. I had an extraordinary experience with it last night. And yet I find it so interesting, so fascinating, that even now I will keep it in its place. What on earth is the meaning of it all?

I suppose it was about one in the morning, and I was closing my books preparatory to staggering off to bed, when I saw her there in front of me. The stage of mistiness and development must have passed unobserved, and there she was in all her beauty and passion and distress, as clear-cut as if she were really in the flesh before me. The figure was small, but very distinct—so much so that every feature, and every detail of dress, are stamped in my memory. She is seated on the extreme left of the mirror. A sort of shadowy figure crouches down beside her—I can dimly discern that it is a man—and then behind them is cloud, in which I see figures—figures which move. It is not a mere picture upon which I look. It is a scene in life, an actual episode. She crouches and quivers. The man beside her cowers down. The vague figures make abrupt movements and gestures. All my fears were swallowed up in my interest. It was maddening to see so much and not to see more.

But I can at least describe the woman to the smallest point. She is very beautiful and quite young—not more than five-and-twenty, I should judge. Her hair is of a very rich brown, with a warm chestnut shade fining into gold at the edges. A little flat-pointed cap comes to an angle in front and is made of lace edged with pearls. The forehead is high, too high perhaps for perfect beauty; but one would not have it otherwise, as it gives a touch of power and strength to what would otherwise be a softly feminine face. The brows are most delicately curved over heavy eyelids, and then come those wonderful eyes—so large, so dark, so full of overmastering emotion, of rage and horror, contending with a pride of self-control which holds her from sheer frenzy! The cheeks are pale, the lips white with agony, the chin and throat most exquisitely rounded. The figure sits and leans forward in the chair, straining and rigid, cataleptic with horror. The dress is black velvet, a jewel gleams like a flame in the breast, and a golden crucifix smoulders in the shadow of a fold. This is the lady whose image still lives in the old silver mirror. What dire deed could it be which has left its impress there so that now, in another age, if the spirit of a man be but worn down to it, he may be conscious of its presence?

One other detail: On the left side of the skirt of the black dress was, as I thought at first, a shapeless bunch of white ribbon. Then, as I looked more intently or as the vision defined itself more clearly, I perceived what it was. It was the hand of a man, clenched and knotted in agony, which held on with a convulsive grasp to the fold of the dress. The rest of the crouching figure was a mere vague outline, but that strenuous hand shone clear on the dark background, with a sinister suggestion of tragedy in its frantic clutch. The man is frightened—horribly frightened. That I can clearly discern. What has terrified him so? Why does he grip the woman's dress? The answer lies amongst those moving figures in the background. They have brought danger both to him and to her. The interest of the thing fascinated me. I thought no more of its relation to my own nerves. I stared and stared as if in a theatre. But I could get no further. The mist thinned. There were tumultuous movements in which all the figures were vaguely concerned. Then the mirror was clear once more.

The doctor says I must drop work for a day, and I can afford to do so, for I have made good progress lately. It is quite evident that the visions depend entirely upon my own nervous state, for I sat in front of the mirror for an hour to-night, with no result whatever. My soothing day has chased them away. I wonder whether I shall ever penetrate what they all mean? I examined the mirror this evening under a good light, and besides the mysterious inscription 'Sanc. X. Pal.,' I was able to discern some signs of heraldic marks, very faintly visible upon the silver. They must be very ancient, as they are almost obliterated. So far as I could make out, they were three spear-heads, two above and one below.* I will show them to the doctor when he calls to-morrow.

Jan. 14.—Feel perfectly well again, and I intend that nothing else shall stop me until my task is finished. The doctor was shown the marks on the mirror and agreed that they were armorial bearings. He is deeply interested in all that I have told him, and cross-questioned me closely on the details. It amuses me to notice how he is torn in two by conflicting desires—the one that his patient should lose his symptoms, the other that the medium—for so he regards me—should solve this mystery of the past. He advised continued rest, but did not oppose me too violently when I declared that such a thing was out of the question until the ten remaining ledgers have been checked.

Jan. 17.—For three nights I have had no experiences—my day of rest has borne fruit. Only a quarter of my task is left, but I must make a forced march, for the lawyers are clamouring for their material. I will give them enough and to spare. I have him fast on a hundred counts. When they realise what a slippery, cunning rascal he is, I should gain some credit from the case. False trading accounts, false balance-sheets, dividends drawn from capital,* losses written down as profits, suppression of working expenses, manipulation of petty cash—it is a fine record!

Jan. 18.—Headaches, nervous twitches, mistiness, fullness of the temples—all the premonitions of trouble, and the trouble came sure enough. And yet my real sorrow is not so much that the vision should come as that it should cease before all is revealed.

But I saw more to-night. The crouching man was as visible as the lady whose gown he clutched. He is a little swarthy fellow, with a black, pointed beard. He has a loose gown of damask* trimmed with fur. The prevailing tints of his dress are red. What a fright the fellow is in, to be sure! He cowers and shivers and glares back over his shoulder. There is a small knife in his other hand, but he is far too tremulous and cowed to use it. Dimly now I begin to see the figures in the background. Fierce faces, bearded and dark, shape themselves out of the mist. There is one terrible creature, a skeleton of a man, with hollow cheeks and eyes sunk in his head. He also has a knife in his hand. On the right of the woman stands a tall man, very young, with flaxen hair, his face sullen and dour. The beautiful woman looks up at him in appeal. So does the man on the ground. This youth seems to be the arbiter of their fate. The crouching man draws closer and hides himself in the woman's skirts. The tall youth bends and tries to drag her away from him. So much I saw last night before the mirror cleared. Shall I never know what it leads to and whence it comes? It is not a mere imagination, of that I am very sure. Somewhere, some time, this scene has been acted, and this old mirror has reflected it. But when—where?

Jan. 20.—My work draws to a close, and it is time. I feel a tenseness within my brain, a sense of intolerable strain, which warns me that something must give. I have worked myself to the limit. But to-night should be the last night. With a supreme effort I should finish the final ledger and complete the case before I rise from my chair. I will do it. I will.

Feb. 7.—I did. My God, what an experience! I hardly know if I am strong enough yet to set it down.

Let me explain in the first instance that I am writing this in Dr Sinclair's private hospital some three weeks after the last entry in my diary. On the night of January 20 my nervous system finally gave way, and I remembered nothing afterwards until I found myself, three days ago, in the home of rest. And I can rest with a good conscience. My work was done before I went under. My figures are in the solicitors' hands. The hunt is over.

And now I must describe that last night. I had sworn to finish my work, and so intently did I stick to it, though my head was bursting, that I would never look up until the last column had been added. And yet it was fine self-restraint, for all the time I knew that wonderful things were happening in the mirror. Every nerve in my body told me so. If I looked up there was an end of my work. So I did not look up till all was finished. Then, when at last with throbbing temples I threw down my pen and raised my eyes, what a sight was there!

The mirror in its silver frame was like a stage, brilliantly lit, in which a drama was in progress. There was no mist now. The oppression of my nerves had wrought this amazing clarity. Every feature, every movement, was as clear-cut as in life. To think that I, a tired accountant, the most prosaic of mankind, with the account-books of a swindling bankrupt before me, should be chosen of all the human race to look upon such a scene!

It was the same scene and the same figures, but the drama had advanced a stage. The tall young man was holding the woman in his arms. She strained away from him and looked up at him with loathing in her face. They had torn the crouching man away from his hold upon the skirt of her dress. A dozen of them were round him—savage men, bearded men. They hacked at him with knives. All seemed to strike him together. Their arms rose and fell. The blood did not flow from him—it squirted. His red dress was dabbled in it. He threw himself this way and that, purple upon crimson, like an over-ripe plum. Still they hacked, and still the jets shot from him. It was horrible—horrible! They dragged him kicking to the door. The woman looked over her shoulder at him and her mouth gaped. I heard nothing, but I knew that she was screaming. And then whether it was this nerve-racking vision before me, or whether, my task finished, all the overwork of the past weeks came in one crushing weight upon me, the room danced round me, the floor seemed to sink away beneath my feet, and I remembered no more. In the early morning my landlady found me stretched senseless before the silver mirror, but I knew nothing myself until three days ago I awoke in the deep peace of the doctor's nursing home.

Feb. 9.—Only to-day have I told Dr Sinclair my full experience. He had not allowed me to speak of such matters before. He listened with an absorbed interest. 'You don't identify this with any well-known scene in history?' he asked, with suspicion in his eyes. I assured him that I knew nothing of history. 'Have you no idea whence that mirror came and to whom it once belonged?' he continued. 'Have you?' I asked, for he spoke with meaning. 'It's incredible,' said he, 'and yet how else can one explain it? The scenes which you described before suggested it, but now it has gone beyond all range of coincidence. I will bring you some notes in the evening.'

Later.—He has just left me. Let me set down his words as closely as I can recall them. He began by laying several musty volumes upon my bed.

'These you can consult at your leisure,' said he. 'I have some notes here which you can confirm. There is not a doubt that what you have seen is the murder of Rizzio by the Scottish nobles in the presence of Mary, which occurred in March 1566. Your description of the woman is accurate. The high forehead and heavy eyelids combined with great beauty could hardly apply to two women. The tall young man was her husband, Darnley. Rizzio, says the chronicle, "was dressed in a loose dressing-gown of furred damask, with hose of russet velvet." With one hand he clutched Mary's gown, with the other he held a dagger. Your fierce, hollow-eyed man was Ruthven,* who was new-risen from a bed of sickness. Every detail is exact.'

'But why to me?' I asked, in bewilderment. 'Why of all the human race to me?'

'Because you were in the fit mental state to receive the impression. Because you chanced to own the mirror which gave the impression.'

'The mirror! You think, then, that it was Mary's mirror—that it stood in the room where the deed was done?'

'I am convinced that it was Mary's mirror. She had been Queen of France. Her personal property would be stamped with the Royal arms. What you took to be three spear-heads were really the lilies of France.'

'And the inscription?'

'"Sanc. X. Pal." You can expand it into Sanctæ Crucis Palatium. Someone has made a note upon the mirror as to whence it came. It was the Palace of the Holy Cross.'

'Holyrood!'* I cried.

'Exactly. Your mirror came from Holyrood. You have had one very singular experience, and have escaped. I trust that you will never put yourself into the way of having such another.'

THE TERROR OF BLUE JOHN GAP

⁂

HE following narrative was found among the papers of Dr James Hardcastle, who died of phthisis* on February 4, 1908, at 36, Upper Coventry Flats, South Kensington. Those who knew him best, while refusing to express an opinion upon this particular statement, are unanimous in asserting that he was a man of a sober and scientific turn of mind, absolutely devoid of imagination, and most unlikely to invent any abnormal series of events. The paper was contained in an envelope, which was docketed, 'A Short Account of the Circumstances which occurred near Miss Allerton's Farm in North-West Derbyshire* in the Spring of Last Year.' The envelope was sealed, and on the other side was written in pencil—

'DEAR SEATON,—

'It may interest, and perhaps pain you, to know that the incredulity with which you met my story has prevented me from ever opening my mouth upon the subject again. I leave this record after my death, and perhaps strangers may be found to have more confidence in me than my friend.'

Inquiry has failed to elicit who this Seaton may have been. I may add that the visit of the deceased to Allerton's Farm, and the general nature of the alarm there, apart from his particular explanation, have been absolutely established. With this foreword I append his account exactly as he left it. It is in the form of a diary, some entries in which have been expanded, while a few have been erased.

* * *

April 17.—Already I feel the benefit of this wonderful upland air. The farm of the Allertons lies fourteen hundred and twenty feet above sea-level, so it may well be a bracing climate. Beyond the usual morning cough I have very little discomfort, and, what with the fresh milk and the home-grown mutton, I have every chance of putting on weight. I think Saunderson will be pleased.

The two Miss Allertons are charmingly quaint and kind, two dear little hard-working old maids, who are ready to lavish all the heart which might have gone out to husband and to children upon an invalid stranger. Truly, the old maid is a most useful person, one of the reserve forces of the community. They talk of the superfluous woman, but what would the poor superfluous man do without her kindly presence? By the way, in their simplicity they very quickly let out the reason why Saunderson recommended their farm. The Professor rose from the ranks himself, and I believe that in his youth he was not above scaring crows in these very fields.

It is a most lonely spot, and the walks are picturesque in the extreme. The farm consists of grazing land lying at the bottom of an irregular valley. On each side are the fantastic limestone hills, formed of rock so soft that you can break it away with your hands. All this country is hollow. Could you strike it with some gigantic hammer it would boom like a drum, or possibly cave in altogether and expose some huge subterranean sea. A great sea there must surely be, for on all sides the streams run into the mountain itself, never to reappear. There are gaps everywhere amid the rocks, and when you pass through them you find yourself in great caverns, which wind down into the bowels of the earth. I have a small bicycle lamp, and it is a perpetual joy to me to carry it into these weird solitudes, and to see the wonderful silver and black effects when I throw its light upon the stalactites which drape the lofty roofs. Shut off the lamp, and you are in the blackest darkness. Turn it on, and it is a scene from the Arabian Nights.*

But there is one of these strange openings in the earth which has a special interest, for it is the handiwork, not of nature, but of man. I had never heard of Blue John when I came to these parts. It is the name given to a peculiar mineral of a beautiful purple shade, which is only found at one or two places in the world.* It is so rare that an ordinary vase of Blue John would be valued at a great price. The Romans, with that extraordinary instinct of theirs, discovered that it was to be found in this valley, and sank a horizontal shaft deep into the mountain side. The opening of their mine has been called Blue John Gap, a clean-cut arch in the rock, the mouth all overgrown with bushes. It is a goodly passage which the Roman miners have cut, and it intersects some of the great water-worn caves, so that if you enter Blue John Gap you would do well to mark your steps and to have a good store of candles, or you may never make your way back to the daylight again. I have not yet gone deeply into it, but this very day

I stood at the mouth of the arched tunnel, and peering down into the black recesses beyond, I vowed that when my health returned I would devote some holiday to exploring those mysterious depths and finding out for myself how far the Roman had penetrated into the Derbyshire hills.

Strange how superstitious these countrymen are! I should have thought better of young Armitage, for he is a man of some education and character, and a very fine fellow for his station in life. I was standing at the Blue John Gap when he came across the field to me.

'Well, doctor,' said he, 'you're not afraid, anyhow.'

'Afraid!' I answered. 'Afraid of what?'

'Of it,' said he, with a jerk of his thumb towards the black vault, 'of the Terror that lives in the Blue John Cave.'

How absurdly easy it is for a legend to arise in a lonely countryside! I examined him as to the reasons for his weird belief. It seems that from time to time sheep have been missing from the fields, carried bodily away, according to Armitage. That they could have wandered away of their own accord and disappeared among the mountains was an explanation to which he would not listen. On one occasion a pool of blood had been found, and some tufts of wool. That also, I pointed out, could be explained in a perfectly natural way. Further, the nights upon which sheep disappeared were invariably very dark, cloudy nights with no moon. This I met with the obvious retort that those were the nights which a commonplace sheep-stealer would naturally choose for his work. On one occasion a gap had been made in a wall, and some of the stones scattered for a considerable distance. Human agency again, in my opinion. Finally, Armitage clinched all his arguments by telling me that he had actually heard the Creature—indeed, that anyone could hear it who remained long enough at the Gap. It was a distant roaring of an immense volume. I could not but smile at this, knowing, as I do, the strange reverberations which come out of an underground water system running amid the chasms of a limestone formation. My incredulity annoyed Armitage so that he turned and left me with some abruptness.

And now comes the queer point about the whole business. I was still standing near the mouth of the cave turning over in my mind the various statements of Armitage, and reflecting how readily they could be explained away, when suddenly, from the depth of the tunnel beside me, there issued a most extraordinary sound. How shall

I describe it? First of all, it seemed to be a great distance away, far down in the bowels of the earth. Secondly, in spite of this suggestion of distance, it was very loud. Lastly, it was not a boom nor a crash, such as one would associate with falling water or tumbling rock, but it was a high whine, tremulous and vibrating, almost like the whinnying of a horse. It was certainly a most remarkable experience, and one which for a moment, I must admit, gave a new significance to Armitage's words. I waited by the Blue John Gap for half an hour or more, but there was no return of the sound, so at last I wandered back to the farmhouse, rather mystified by what had occurred. Decidedly I shall explore that cavern when my strength is restored. Of course, Armitage's explanation is too absurd for discussion, and yet that sound was certainly very strange. It still rings in my ears as I write.

April 20.—In the last three days I have made several expeditions to the Blue John Gap, and have even penetrated some short distance, but my bicycle lantern is so small and weak that I dare not trust myself very far. I shall do the thing more systematically. I have heard no sound at all, and could almost believe that I had been the victim of some hallucination suggested, perhaps, by Armitage's conversation. Of course, the whole idea is absurd, and yet I must confess that those bushes at the entrance of the cave do present an appearance as if some heavy creature had forced its way through them. I begin to be keenly interested. I have said nothing to the Miss Allertons, for they are quite superstitious enough already, but I have bought some candles, and mean to investigate for myself.

I observed this morning that among the numerous tufts of sheep's wool which lay among the bushes near the cavern there was one which was smeared with blood. Of course, my reason tells me that if sheep wander into such rocky places they are likely to injure themselves, and yet somehow that splash of crimson gave me a sudden shock, and for a moment I found myself shrinking back in horror from the old Roman arch. A fetid breath seemed to ooze from the black depths into which I peered. Could it indeed be possible that some nameless thing, some dreadful presence, was lurking down yonder? I should have been incapable of such feelings in the days of my strength, but one grows more nervous and fanciful when one's health is shaken.

For the moment I weakened in my resolution, and was ready to leave the secret of the old mine, if one exists, for ever unsolved. But to-night my interest has returned and my nerves grown more steady.

Tomorrow I trust that I shall have gone more deeply into this matter.

April 22.—Let me try and set down as accurately as I can my extraordinary experience of yesterday. I started in the afternoon, and made my way to the Blue John Gap. I confess that my misgivings returned as I gazed into its depths, and I wished that I had brought a companion to share my exploration. Finally, with a return of resolution, I lit my candle, pushed my way through the briars, and descended into the rocky shaft.

It went down at an acute angle for some fifty feet, the floor being covered with broken stone. Thence there extended a long, straight passage cut in the solid rock. I am no geologist, but the lining of this corridor was certainly of some harder material than limestone, for there were points where I could actually see the tool-marks which the old miners had left in their excavation, as fresh as if they had been done yesterday. Down this strange, old-world corridor I stumbled, my feeble flame throwing a dim circle of light around me, which made the shadows beyond the more threatening and obscure. Finally, I came to a spot where the Roman tunnel opened into a water-worn cavern—a huge hall, hung with long white icicles of lime deposit. From this central chamber I could dimly perceive that a number of passages worn by the subterranean streams wound away into the depths of the earth. I was standing there wondering whether I had better return, or whether I dare venture farther into this dangerous labyrinth, when my eyes fell upon something at my feet which strongly arrested my attention.

The greater part of the floor of the cavern was covered with boulders of rock or with hard incrustations of lime, but at this particular point there had been a drip from the distant roof, which had left a patch of soft mud. In the very centre of this there was a huge mark—an ill-defined blotch, deep, broad and irregular, as if a great boulder had fallen upon it. No loose stone lay near, however, nor was there anything to account for the impression. It was far too large to be caused by any possible animal, and besides, there was only the one, and the patch of mud was of such a size that no reasonable stride could have covered it. As I rose from the examination of that singular mark and then looked round into the black shadows which hemmed me in, I must confess that I felt for a moment a most unpleasant sinking of my heart, and that, do what I could, the candle trembled in my outstretched hand.

I soon recovered my nerve, however, when I reflected how absurd it was to associate so huge and shapeless a mark with the track of any known animal. Even an elephant could not have produced it. I determined, therefore, that I would not be scared by vague and senseless fears from carrying out my exploration. Before proceeding, I took good note of a curious rock formation in the wall by which I could recognise the entrance of the Roman tunnel. The precaution was very necessary, for the great cave, so far as I could see it, was intersected by passages. Having made sure of my position, and reassured myself by examining my spare candles and my matches, I advanced slowly over the rocky and uneven surface of the cavern.

And now I come to the point where I met with such sudden and desperate disaster. A stream, some twenty feet broad, ran across my path, and I walked for some little distance along the bank to find a spot where I could cross dry-shod. Finally, I came to a place where a single flat boulder lay near the centre, which I could reach in a stride. As it chanced, however, the rock had been cut away and made top-heavy by the rush of the stream, so that it tilted over as I landed on it and shot me into the ice-cold water. My candle went out, and I found myself floundering about in utter and absolute darkness.

I staggered to my feet again, more amused than alarmed by my adventure. The candle had fallen from my hand, and was lost in the stream, but I had two others in my pocket, so that it was of no importance. I got one of them ready, and drew out my box of matches to light it. Only then did I realize my position. The box had been soaked in my fall into the river. It was impossible to strike the matches.

A cold hand seemed to close round my heart as I realized my position. The darkness was opaque and horrible. It was so utter that one put one's hand up to one's face as if to press off something solid. I stood still, and by an effort I steadied myself. I tried to reconstruct in my mind a map of the floor of the cavern as I had last seen it. Alas! the bearings which had impressed themselves upon my mind were high on the wall, and not to be found by touch. Still, I remembered in a general way how the sides were situated, and I hoped that by groping my way along them I should at last come to the opening of the Roman tunnel. Moving very slowly, and continually striking against the rocks, I set out on this desperate quest.

But I very soon realized how impossible it was. In that black, velvety darkness one lost all one's bearings in an instant. Before I had made a dozen paces, I was utterly bewildered as to my whereabouts. The rippling of the stream, which was the one sound audible, showed me where it lay, but the moment that I left its bank I was utterly lost. The idea of finding my way back in absolute darkness through that limestone labyrinth was clearly an impossible one.

I sat down upon a boulder and reflected upon my unfortunate plight. I had not told anyone that I proposed to come to the Blue John mine, and it was unlikely that a search party would come after me. Therefore I must trust to my own resources to get clear of the danger. There was only one hope, and that was that the matches might dry. When I fell into the river, only half of me had got thoroughly wet. My left shoulder had remained above the water. I took the box of matches, therefore, and put it into my left armpit. The moist air of the cavern might possibly be counteracted by the heat of my body, but even so, I knew that I could not hope to get a light for many hours. Meanwhile there was nothing for it but to wait.

By good luck I had slipped several biscuits into my pocket before I left the farm-house. These I now devoured, and washed them down with a draught from that wretched stream which had been the cause of all my misfortunes. Then I felt about for a comfortable seat among the rocks, and, having discovered a place where I could get a support for my back, I stretched out my legs and settled myself down to wait. I was wretchedly damp and cold, but I tried to cheer myself with the reflection that modern science prescribed open windows and walks in all weather for my disease. Gradually, lulled by the monotonous gurgle of the stream, and by the absolute darkness, I sank into an uneasy slumber.

How long this lasted I cannot say. It may have been for an hour, it may have been for several. Suddenly I sat up on my rock couch, with every nerve thrilling and every sense acutely on the alert. Beyond all doubt I had heard a sound—some sound very distinct from the gurgling of the waters. It had passed, but the reverberation of it still lingered in my ear. Was it a search party? They would most certainly have shouted, and vague as this sound was which had wakened me, it was very distinct from the human voice. I sat palpitating and hardly daring to breathe. There it was again! And again! Now it had become continuous. It was a tread—yes, surely it was the tread of some living creature. But what a tread it was! It gave one the impression of enormous weight carried upon sponge-like feet, which gave forth a muffled but ear-filling sound. The darkness was as complete as ever, but the tread was regular and decisive. And it was coming beyond all question in my direction.

My skin grew cold, and my hair stood on end as I listened to that steady and ponderous footfall. There was some creature there, and surely by the speed of its advance, it was one which could see in the dark. I crouched low on my rock and tried to blend myself with the stone. The steps grew nearer still, then stopped, and presently I was aware of a loud lapping and gurgling. The creature was drinking at the stream. Then again there was silence, broken by a succession of long sniffs and snorts of tremendous volume and energy. Had it caught the scent of me? My own nostrils were filled by a low fetid odour, mephitic* and abominable. Then I heard the steps again. They were on my side of the stream now. The stones rattled within a few yards of where I lay. Hardly daring to breathe, I crouched upon my rock. Then the steps drew away. I heard the splash as it returned across the river, and the sound died away into the distance in the direction from which it had come.

For a long time I lay upon the rock, too much horrified to move. I thought of the sound which I had heard coming from the depths of the cave, of Armitage's fears, of the strange impression in the mud, and now came this final and absolute proof that there was indeed some inconceivable monster, something utterly unearthly and dreadful, which lurked in the hollow of the mountain. Of its nature or form I could frame no conception, save that it was both light-footed and gigantic. The combat between my reason, which told me that such things could not be, and my senses, which told me that they were, raged within me as I lay. Finally, I was almost ready to persuade myself that this experience had been part of some evil dream, and that my abnormal condition might have conjured up an hallucination. But there remained one final experience which removed the last possibility of doubt from my mind.

I had taken my matches from my armpit and felt them. They seemed perfectly hard and dry. Stooping down into a crevice of the rocks, I tried one of them. To my delight it took fire at once. I lit the candle, and, with a terrified backward glance into the obscure depths of the cavern, I hurried in the direction of the Roman passage. As I did so I passed the patch of mud on which I had seen the huge imprint. Now I stood astonished before it, for there were three similar imprints upon its surface, enormous in size, irregular in outline, of a depth which indicated the ponderous weight which had left them. Then a great terror surged over me. Stooping and shading my candle with my hand, I ran in a frenzy of fear to the rocky archway, hastened up it, and never stopped until, with weary feet and panting lungs, I rushed up the final slope of stones, broke through the tangle of briars, and flung myself exhausted upon the soft grass under the peaceful light of the stars. It was three in the morning when I reached the farm-house, and to-day I am all unstrung and quivering after my terrific adventure. As yet I have told no one. I must move warily in the matter. What would the poor lonely women, or the uneducated yokels here think of it if I were to tell them my experience? Let me go to someone who can understand and advise.

April 25.—I was laid up in bed for two days after my incredible adventure in the cavern. I use the adjective with a very definite meaning, for I have had an experience since which has shocked me almost as much as the other. I have said that I was looking round for someone who could advise me. There is a Dr Mark Johnson who practises some few miles away, to whom I had a note of recommendation from Professor Saunderson. To him I drove, when I was strong enough to get about, and I recounted to him my whole strange experience. He listened intently, and then carefully examined me, paying special attention to my reflexes and to the pupils of my eyes. When he had finished, he refused to discuss my adventure, saying that it was entirely beyond him, but he gave me the card of a Mr Picton at Castleton,* with the advice that I should instantly go to him and tell him the story exactly as I had done to himself. He was, according to my adviser, the very man who was pre-eminently suited to help me. I went on to the station, therefore, and made my way to the little town, which is some ten miles away. Mr Picton appeared to be a man of importance, as his brass plate was displayed upon the door of a considerable building on the outskirts of the town. I was about to ring his bell, when some misgiving came into my mind, and, crossing to a neighbouring shop, I asked the man behind the counter if he could tell me anything of Mr Picton. 'Why,' said he, 'he is the best mad doctor in Derbyshire, and yonder is his asylum.' You can imagine that it was not long before I had shaken the dust of Castleton from my feet and returned to the farm, cursing all unimaginative pedants who cannot conceive that there may be things in creation which have never yet chanced to come across their mole's vision. After all, now that I am cooler, I can afford to admit that I have been no more sympathetic to Armitage than Dr Johnson has been to me.

April 27.—When I was a student I had the reputation of being a man of courage and enterprise. I remember that when there was a ghost-hunt at Coltbridge* it was I who sat up in the haunted house. Is it advancing years (after all, I am only thirty-five), or is it this physical malady which has caused degeneration? Certainly my heart quails when I think of that horrible cavern in the hill, and the certainty that it has some monstrous occupant. What shall I do? There is not an hour in the day that I do not debate the question. If I say nothing, then the mystery remains unsolved. If I do say anything, then I have the alternative of mad alarm over the whole countryside, or of absolute incredulity which may end in consigning me to an asylum. On the whole, I think that my best course is to wait, and to prepare for some expedition which shall be more deliberate and better thought out than the last. As a first step I have been to Castleton and obtained a few essentials—a large acetylene lantern for one thing, and a good double-barrelled sporting rifle for another. The latter I have hired, but I have bought a dozen heavy game cartridges, which would bring down a rhinoceros. Now I am ready for my troglodyte friend. Give me better health and a little spate of energy, and I shall try conclusions with him yet. But who and what is he? Ah! there is the question which stands between me and my sleep. How many theories do I form, only to discard each in turn! It is all so utterly unthinkable. And yet the cry, the footmark, the tread in the cavern—no reasoning can get past these. I think of the old-world legends of dragons and of other monsters.* Were they, perhaps, not such fairy-tales as we have thought? Can it be that there is some fact which underlies them, and am I, of all mortals, the one who is chosen to expose it?

May 3.—For several days I have been laid up by the vagaries of an English spring, and during those days there have been developments, the true and sinister meaning of which no one can appreciate save myself. I may say that we have had cloudy and moonless nights of late, which according to my information were the seasons upon which sheep disappeared. Well, sheep *have* disappeared. Two of Miss Allerton's, one of old Pearson's of the Cat Walk, and one of Mrs Moulton's. Four in all during three nights. No trace is left of them at all, and the countryside is buzzing with rumours of gipsies and of sheep-stealers.

But there is something more serious than that. Young Armitage has disappeared also. He left his moorland cottage early on Wednesday night and has never been heard of since. He was an unattached man, so there is less sensation than would otherwise be the case. The popular explanation is that he owes money, and has found a situation in some other part of the country, whence he will presently write for his belongings. But I have grave misgivings. Is it not much more likely that the recent tragedy of the sheep has caused him to take some steps which may have ended in his own destruction? He may, for example, have lain in wait for the creature and been carried off by it into the recesses of the mountains. What an inconceivable fate for a civilized Englishman of the twentieth century! And yet I feel that it is possible and even probable. But in that case, how far am I answerable both for his death and for any other mishap which may occur? Surely with the knowledge I already possess it must be my duty to see that something is done, or if necessary to do it myself. It must be the latter, for this morning I went down to the local police-station and told my story. The inspector entered it all in a large book and bowed me out with commendable gravity, but I heard a burst of laughter before I had got down his garden path. No doubt he was recounting my adventure to his family.

June 10.—I am writing this, propped up in bed, six weeks after my last entry in this journal. I have gone through a terrible shock both to mind and body, arising from such an experience as has seldom befallen a human being before. But I have attained my end. The danger from the Terror which dwells in the Blue John Gap has passed never to return. Thus much at least I, a broken invalid, have done for the common good. Let me now recount what occurred as clearly as I may.

The night of Friday, May 3, was dark and cloudy—the very night for the monster to walk. About eleven o'clock I went from the farmhouse with my lantern and my rifle, having first left a note upon the table of my bedroom in which I said that, if I were missing, search should be made for me in the direction of the Gap. I made my way to the mouth of the Roman shaft, and, having perched myself among the rocks close to the opening, I shut off my lantern and waited patiently with my loaded rifle ready to my hand.

It was a melancholy vigil. All down the winding valley I could see the scattered lights of the farm-houses, and the church clock of

Chapel-le-Dale* tolling the hours came faintly to my ears. These tokens of my fellow-men served only to make my own position seem the more lonely, and to call for a greater effort to overcome the terror which tempted me continually to get back to the farm, and abandon for ever this dangerous quest. And yet there lies deep in every man a rooted self-respect which makes it hard for him to turn back from that which he has once undertaken. This feeling of personal pride was my salvation now, and it was that alone which held me fast when every instinct of my nature was dragging me away. I am glad now that I had the strength. In spite of all that it has cost me, my manhood is at least above reproach.

Twelve o'clock struck in the distant church, then one, then two. It was the darkest hour of the night. The clouds were drifting low, and there was not a star in the sky. An owl was hooting somewhere among the rocks, but no other sound, save the gentle sough of the wind, came to my ears. And then suddenly I heard it! From far away down the tunnel came those muffled steps, so soft and yet so ponderous. I heard also the rattle of stones as they gave way under that giant tread. They drew nearer. They were close upon me. I heard the crashing of the bushes round the entrance, and then dimly through the darkness I was conscious of the loom of some enormous shape, some monstrous inchoate creature, passing swiftly and very silently out from the tunnel. I was paralysed with fear and amazement. Long as I had waited, now that it had actually come I was unprepared for the shock. I lay motionless and breathless, whilst the great dark mass whisked by me and was swallowed up in the night.

But now I nerved myself for its return. No sound came from the sleeping countryside to tell of the horror which was loose. In no way could I judge how far off it was, what it was doing, or when it might be back. But not a second time should my nerve fail me, not a second time should it pass unchallenged. I swore it between my clenched teeth as I laid my cocked rifle across the rock.

And yet it nearly happened. There was no warning of approach now as the creature passed over the grass. Suddenly, like a dark, drifting shadow, the huge bulk loomed up once more before me, making for the entrance of the cave. Again came that paralysis of volition which held my crooked forefinger impotent upon the trigger. But with a desperate effort I shook it off. Even as the brushwood rustled, and the monstrous beast blended with the shadow of the Gap, I fired at the retreating form. In the blaze of the gun I caught a glimpse of a great shaggy mass, something with rough and bristling hair of a withered grey colour, fading away to white in its lower parts, the huge body supported upon short, thick, curving legs. I had just that glance, and then I heard the rattle of the stones as the creature tore down into its burrow. In an instant, with a triumphant revulsion of feeling, I had cast my fears to the wind, and uncovering my powerful lantern, with my rifle in my hand, I sprang down from my rock and rushed after the monster down the old Roman shaft.

My splendid lamp cast a brilliant flood of vivid light in front of me, very different from the yellow glimmer which had aided me down the same passage only twelve days before. As I ran, I saw the great beast lurching along before me, its huge bulk filling up the whole space from wall to wall. Its hair looked like coarse faded oakum,* and hung down in long, dense masses which swayed as it moved. It was like an enormous unclipped sheep in its fleece, but in size it was far larger than the largest elephant, and its breadth seemed to be nearly as great as its height. It fills me with amazement now to think that I should have dared to follow such a horror into the bowels of the earth, but when one's blood is up, and when one's quarry seems to be flying, the old primeval hunting-spirit awakes and prudence is cast to the wind. Rifle in hand, I ran at the top of my speed upon the trail of the monster.

I had seen that the creature was swift. Now I was to find out to my cost that it was also very cunning. I had imagined that it was in panic flight, and that I had only to pursue it. The idea that it might turn upon me never entered my excited brain. I have already explained that the passage down which I was racing opened into a great central cave. Into this I rushed, fearful lest I should lose all trace of the beast. But he had turned upon his own traces, and in a moment we were face to face.

That picture, seen in the brilliant white light of the lantern, is etched for ever upon my brain. He had reared up on his hind legs as a bear would do, and stood above me, enormous, menacing—such a creature as no nightmare had ever brought to my imagination. I have said that he reared like a bear, and there was something bear-like—if one could conceive a bear which was tenfold the bulk of any bear seen upon earth—in his whole pose and attitude, in his great crooked forelegs with their ivory-white claws, in his rugged skin, and in his red, gaping mouth, fringed with monstrous fangs. Only in one point did he differ from the bear, or from any other creature which walks the earth, and even at that supreme moment a shudder of horror passed over me as I observed that the eyes which glistened in the glow of my lantern were huge, projecting bulbs, white and sightless. For a moment his great paws swung over my head. The next he fell for-ward upon me, and my broken lantern crashed to the earth, and I remember no more.

* * *

When I came to myself I was back in the farm-house of the Allertons. Two days had passed since my terrible adventure in the Blue John Gap. It seems that I had lain all night in the cave insensible from con-cussion of the brain, with my left arm and two ribs badly fractured. In the morning my note had been found, a search party of a dozen farm-ers assembled, and I had been tracked down and carried back to my bedroom, where I had lain in high delirium ever since. There was, it seems, no sign of the creature, and no bloodstain which would show that my bullet had found him as he passed. Save for my own plight and the marks upon the mud, there was nothing to prove that what I said was true.

Six weeks have now elapsed, and I am able to sit out once more in the sunshine. Just opposite me is the steep hillside, grey with shaly rock, and yonder on its flank is the dark cleft which marks the open-ing of the Blue John Gap. But it is no longer a source of terror. Never again through that ill-omened tunnel shall any strange shape flit out into the world of men. The educated and the scientific, the Dr Johnsons and the like, may smile at my narrative, but the poorer folk of the countryside had never a doubt as to its truth. On the day after my recovering consciousness they assembled in their hundreds round the Blue John Gap. As the *Castleton Courier* said:

'It was useless for our correspondent, or for any of the adventurous gentle-men who had come from Matlock, Buxton,* and other parts, to offer to descend, to explore the cave to the end, and to finally test the extraordinary narrative of Dr James Hardcastle. The country people had taken the matter into their own hands, and from an early hour of the morning they had worked hard in stopping up the entrance of the tunnel. There is a sharp slope where the shaft begins, and great boulders, rolled along by many willing hands, were thrust down it until the Gap was absolutely sealed. So ends the episode which has caused such excitement throughout the country. Local opinion is fiercely divided upon the subject. On the one hand are those who point to Dr Hardcastle's impaired health, and to the possibility of cerebral lesions of tubercular origin* giving rise to strange hallucinations. Some *idée fixe*, according to these gentlemen, caused the doctor to wander down the tunnel, and a fall among the rocks was sufficient to account for his injuries. On the other hand, a legend of a strange creature in the Gap has existed for some months back, and the farmers look upon Dr Hardcastle's narrative and his personal injuries as a final corroboration. So the matter stands, and so the matter will continue to stand, for no definite solution seems to us to be now possible. It transcends human wit to give any scientific explanation which could cover the alleged facts.'

Perhaps before the *Courier* published these words they would have been wise to send their representative to me. I have thought the matter out, as no one else has occasion to do, and it is possible that I might have removed some of the more obvious difficulties of the narrative and brought it one degree nearer to scientific acceptance. Let me then write down the only explanation which seems to me to elucidate what I know to my cost to have been a series of facts. My theory may seem to be wildly improbable, but at least no one can venture to say that it is impossible.

My view is—and it was formed, as is shown by my diary, before my personal adventure—that in this part of England there is a vast subterranean lake or sea, which is fed by the great number of streams which pass down through the limestone. Where there is a large collection of water there must also be some evaporation, mists or rain, and a possibility of vegetation. This in turn suggests that there may be animal life, arising, as the vegetable life would also do, from those seeds and types which had been introduced at an early period of the world's history, when communication with the outer air was more easy. This place had then developed a fauna and flora of its own, including such monsters as the one which I had seen, which may well have been the old cave-bear, enormously enlarged and modified by its new environment. For countless æons the internal and the external creation had kept apart, growing steadily away from each other. Then there had come some rift in the depths of the mountain which had enabled one creature to wander up and, by means of the Roman tunnel, to reach the open air. Like all subterranean life, it had lost the power of sight, but this had no doubt been compensated for by nature in other directions. Certainly it had some means of finding its way about, and of hunting down the sheep upon the hillside. As to its choice of dark nights, it is part of my theory that light was painful to those great white eyeballs, and that it was only a pitch-black world which it could tolerate. Perhaps, indeed, it was the glare of my lantern which saved my life at that awful moment when we were face to face. So I read the riddle. I leave these facts behind me, and if you can explain them, do so; or if you choose to doubt them, do so. Neither your belief nor your incredulity can alter them, nor affect one whose task is nearly over.

* * *

So ended the strange narrative of Dr James Hardcastle.

THROUGH THE VEIL

H E was a great shock-headed, freckle-faced Borderer, the lineal
descendant of a cattle-thieving clan in Liddesdale.* In spite of
his ancestry he was as solid and sober a citizen as one would wish
to see, a town councillor of Melrose,* an elder of the Church, and
the chairman of the local branch of the Young Men's Christian
Association.* Brown was his name—and you saw it printed up as
'Brown and Handiside' over the great grocery stores in the High
Street. His wife, Maggie Brown, was an Armstrong before her marriage, and came from an old farming stock in the wilds of Teviothead.*
She was small, swarthy, and dark-eyed, with a strangely nervous temperament for a Scotch woman. No greater contrast could be found
than the big, tawny man and the dark little woman, but both were of
the soil as far back as any memory could extend.

One day—it was the first anniversary of their wedding—they had
driven over together to see the excavations of the Roman Fort at
Newstead.* It was not a particularly picturesque spot. From the
northern bank of the Tweed,* just where the river forms a loop, there
extends a gentle slope of arable land. Across it run the trenches of the
excavators, with here and there an exposure of old stonework to show
the foundations of the ancient walls. It had been a huge place, for the
camp was fifty acres in extent, and the fort fifteen. However, it was all
made easy for them since Mr Brown knew the farmer to whom the
land belonged. Under his guidance they spent a long summer evening
inspecting the trenches, the pits, the ramparts and all the strange variety of objects which were waiting to be transported to the Edinburgh
Museum of Antiquities. The buckle of a woman's belt had been dug
up that very day, and the farmer was discoursing upon it when his
eyes fell upon Mrs Brown's face.

'Your good leddy's tired,' said he. 'Maybe you'd best rest a wee
before we gang further.'

Brown looked at his wife. She was certainly very pale, and her dark
eyes were bright and wild.

'What is it, Maggie? I've wearied you. I'm thinkin' it's time we
went back.'

'No, no, John, let us go on. It's wonderful! It's like a dreamland place. It all seems so close and so near to me. How long were the Romans here, Mr Cunningham?'

'A fair time, mam. If you saw the kitchen midden-pits* you would guess it took a long time to fill them.'

'And why did they leave?'

'Well, mum, by all accounts they left because they had to. The folk round could thole* them no longer, so they just up and burned the fort aboot their lugs. You can see the fire marks on the stanes.'

The woman gave a quick little shudder. 'A wild night—a fearsome night,' said she. 'The sky must have been red that night—and these grey stones, they may have been red also.'

'Aye, I think they were red,' said her husband. 'It's a queer thing, Maggie, and it may be your words that have done it; but I seem to see that business aboot as clear as ever I saw anything in my life. The light shone on the water.'

'Aye, the light shone on the water. And the smoke gripped you by the throat. And all the savages were yelling.'

The old farmer began to laugh. 'The leddy will be writin' a story aboot the old fort,' said he. 'I've shown many a one ower it, but I never heard it put so clear afore. Some folk have the gift.'

They had strolled along the edge of the foss, and a pit yawned upon the right of them.

'That pit was fourteen foot deep,' said the farmer. 'What d'ye think we dug oot from the bottom o't? Weel, it was just the skeleton of a man wi' a spear by his side. I'm thinkin' he was grippin' it when he died. Now, how cam' a man wi' a spear doon a hole fourteen foot deep. He wasna' buried there, for they aye burned their dead. What make ye o' that, mam?'

'He sprang doon to get clear of the savages,' said the woman.

'Weel, it's likely enough, and a' the professors from Edinburgh couldna gie a better reason. I wish you were aye here, mam, to answer a' oor deeficulties sae readily. Now, here's the altar that we foond last week. There's an inscreeption. They tell me it's Latin, and it means that the men o' this fort give thanks to God for their safety.'

They examined the old worn stone. There was a large, deeply cut 'VV' upon the top of it.

'What does "VV" stand for?' asked Brown.

'Naebody kens,' the guide answered.

'*Valeria Victrix*,'* said the lady softly. Her face was paler than ever, her eyes far away, as one who peers down the dim aisles of over-arching centuries.

'What's that?' asked her husband sharply.

She started as one who wakes from sleep. 'What were we talking about?' she asked.

'About this "VV" upon the stone.'

'No doubt it was just the name of the Legion which put the altar up.'

'Aye, but you gave some special name.'

'Did I? How absurd! How should I ken what the name was?'

'You said something—"*Victrix*," I think.'

'I suppose I was guessing. It gives me the queerest feeling, this place, as if I were not myself, but someone else.'

'Aye, it's an uncanny place,' said her husband, looking round with an expression almost of fear in his bold grey eyes. 'I feel it mysel'. I think we'll just be wishin' you good evenin', Mr Cunningham, and get back to Melrose before the dark sets in.'

Neither of them could shake off the strange impression which had been left upon them by their visit to the excavations. It was as if some miasma had risen from those damp trenches and passed into their blood. All the evening they were silent and thoughtful, but such remarks as they did make showed that the same subject was in the mind of each. Brown had a restless night, in which he dreamed a strange, connected dream, so vivid that he woke sweating and shivering like a frightened horse. He tried to convey it all to his wife as they sat together at breakfast in the morning.

'It was the clearest thing, Maggie,' said he. 'Nothing that has ever come to me in my waking life has been more clear than that. I feel as if these hands were sticky with blood.'

'Tell me of it—tell me slow,' said she.

'When it began, I was oot on a braeside. I was laying flat on the ground. It was rough, and there were clumps of heather. All round me was just darkness, but I could hear the rustle and the breathin' of men. There seemed a great multitude on every side of me, but I could see no one. There was a low chink of steel sometimes, and then a number of voices would whisper, "Hush!" I had a ragged club in my hand, and it had spikes o' iron near the end of it. My heart was beatin' quickly, and I felt that a moment of great danger and excitement was at hand. Once I dropped my club, and again from all round me the voices in the darkness cried, "Hush!" I put oot my hand, and it touched the foot of another man lying in front of me. There was someone at my very elbow on either side. But they said nothin'.

'Then we all began to move. The whole braeside* seemed to be crawlin' downwards. There was a river at the bottom and a high arched wooden bridge. Beyond the bridge were many lights—torches on a wall. The creepin' men all flowed towards the bridge. There had been no sound of any kind, just a velvet stillness. And then there was a cry in the darkness, the cry of a man who had been stabbed suddenly to the hairt. That one cry swelled out for a moment, and then the roar of a thoosand furious voices. I was runnin'. Everyone was runnin'. A bright red light shone out, and the river was a scarlet streak. I could see my companions now. They were more like devils than men, wild figures clad in skins, with their hair and beards streamin'. They were all mad with rage, jumpin' as they ran, their mouths open, their arms wavin', the red light beatin' on their faces. I ran, too, and yelled out curses like the rest. Then I heard a great cracklin' of wood, and I knew that the palisades were doon. There was a loud whistlin' in my ears, and I was aware that arrows were flying past me. I got to the bottom of a dyke, and I saw a hand stretched doon from above. I took it, and was dragged to the top. We looked doon, and there were silver men beneath us holdin' up their spears. Some of our folk sprang on to the spears. Then we others followed, and we killed the soldiers before they could draw the spears oot again. They shouted loud in some foreign tongue, but no mercy was shown them. We went ower them like a wave, and trampled them doon into the mud, for they were few, and there was no end to our numbers.

'I found myself among buildings, and one of them was on fire. I saw the flames spoutin' through the roof. I ran on, and then I was alone among the buildings. Someone ran across in front o' me. It was a woman. I caught her by the arm, and I took her chin and turned her face so as the light of the fire would strike it. Whom think you that it was, Maggie?'

His wife moistened her dry lips. 'It was I,' she said.

He looked at her in surprise. 'That's a good guess,' said he. 'Yes, it was just you. Not merely like you, you understand. It was you—you yourself. I saw the same soul in your frightened eyes. You looked white and bonnie and wonderful in the firelight. I had just one thought in my head—to get you awa' with me; to keep you all to mysel' in my own home somewhere beyond the hills. You clawed at my face with your nails. I heaved you over my shoulder, and I tried to find a way oot of the light of the burning hoose and back into the darkness.

'Then came the thing that I mind best of all. You're ill, Maggie. Shall I stop? My God! you have the very look on your face that you had last night in my dream. You screamed. He came runnin' in the fire-light. His head was bare; his hair was black and curled; he had a naked sword in his hand, short and broad, little more than a dagger. He stabbed at me, but he tripped and fell. I held you with one hand, and with the other—'

His wife had sprung to her feet with writhing features.

'Marcus!' she cried. 'My beautiful Marcus! Oh, you brute! you brute! you brute!' There was a clatter of tea-cups as she fell forward senseless upon the table.

* * *

They never talk about that strange, isolated incident in their married life. For an instant the curtain of the past had swung aside, and some strange glimpse of a forgotten life had come to them. But it closed down, never to open again. They live their narrow round—he in his shop, she in her household—and yet new and wider horizons have vaguely formed themselves around them since that summer evening by the crumbling Roman fort.

HOW IT HAPPENED

SHE was a writing medium,* This is what she wrote.

I can remember some things upon that evening most distinctly, and others are like some vague, broken dreams. That is what makes it so difficult to tell a connected story. I have no idea now what it was that had taken me to London and brought me back so late. It just merges into all my other visits to London. But from the time that I got out at the little country station everything is extraordinarily clear. I can live it again—every instant of it.

I remember so well walking down the platform and looking at the illuminated clock at the end which told me that it was half-past eleven. I remember also my wondering whether I could get home before midnight. Then I remember the big motor, with its glaring headlights and glitter of polished brass, waiting for me outside. It was my new thirty-horse-power Robur,* which had only been delivered that day. I remember also asking Perkins, my chauffeur, how she had gone, and his saying that he thought she was excellent.

'I'll try her myself,' said I, and I climbed into the driver's seat.

'The gears are not the same,' said he. 'Perhaps, sir, I had better drive.'

'No; I should like to try her,' said I.

And so we started on the five-mile drive for home.

My old car had the gears as they used always to be in notches on a bar. In this car you passed the gear-lever through a gate to get on the higher ones. It was not difficult to master, and soon I thought that I understood it. It was foolish, no doubt, to begin to learn a new system in the dark, but one often does foolish things, and one has not always to pay the full price for them. I got along very well until I came to Claystall Hill.* It is one of the worst hills in England, a mile and a half long and one in six in places, with three fairly sharp curves. My park gate stands at the very foot of it upon the main London road.

We were just over the brow of this hill, where the grade is steepest, when the trouble began. I had been on the top speed, and wanted to get her on the free;* but she stuck between gears, and I had to get her back on the top again. By this time she was going at a great rate, so

I clapped on both brakes, and one after the other they gave way. I didn't mind so much when I felt my footbrake snap, but when I put all my weight on my side-brake, and the lever clanged to its full limit without a catch, it brought a cold sweat out of me. By this time we were fairly tearing down the slope. The lights were brilliant, and I brought her round the first curve all right. Then we did the second one, though it was a close shave for the ditch. There was a mile of straight then with the third curve beneath it, and after that the gate of the park. If I could shoot into that harbour all would be well, for the slope up to the house would bring her to a stand.

Perkins behaved splendidly. I should like that to be known. He was perfectly cool and alert. I had thought at the very beginning of taking the bank, and he read my intention.

'I wouldn't do it, sir,' said he. 'At this pace it must go over and we should have it on the top of us.'

Of course he was right. He got to the electric switch and had it off, so we were in the free; but we were still running at a fearful pace. He laid his hands on the wheel.

'I'll keep her steady,' said he, 'if you care to jump and chance it. We can never get round that curve. Better jump, sir.'

'No,' said I; 'I'll stick it out. You can jump if you like.'

'I'll stick it with you, sir,' said he.

If it had been the old car I should have jammed the gear-lever into the reverse, and seen what would happen. I expect she would have stripped her gears or smashed up somehow, but it would have been a chance. As it was, I was helpless. Perkins tried to climb across, but you couldn't do it going at that pace. The wheels were whirring like a high wind and the big body creaking and groaning with the strain. But the lights were brilliant, and one could steer to an inch. I remember thinking what an awful and yet majestic sight we should appear to anyone who met us. It was a narrow road, and we were just a great, roaring, golden death to anyone who came in our path.

We got round the corner with one wheel three feet high upon the bank. I thought we were surely over, but after staggering for a moment she righted and darted onwards. That was the third corner and the last one. There was only the park gate now. It was facing us, but, as luck would have it, not facing us directly. It was about twenty yards to the left up the main road into which we ran. Perhaps I could have done it, but I expect that the steering-gear had been jarred when we ran on the bank. The wheel did not turn easily. We shot out of the lane. I saw the open gate on the left. I whirled round my wheel with all the strength of my wrists. Perkins and I threw our bodies across, and then the next instant, going at fifty miles an hour, my right wheel struck full on the right-hand pillar of my own gate. I heard the crash. I was conscious of flying through the air, and then and then !

* * *

When I became aware of my own existence once more I was among some brushwood in the shadow of the oaks upon the lodge side of the drive. A man was standing beside me. I imagined at first that it was Perkins, but when I looked again I saw that it was Stanley, a man whom I had known at college some years before, and for whom I had a really genuine affection. There was always something peculiarly sympathetic to me in Stanley's personality; and I was proud to think that I had some similar influence upon him. At the present moment I was surprised to see him, but I was like a man in a dream, giddy and shaken and quite prepared to take things as I found them without questioning them.

'What a smash!' I said. 'Good Lord, what an awful smash!'

He nodded his head, and even in the gloom I could see that he was smiling the gentle, wistful smile which I connected with him.

I was quite unable to move. Indeed, I had not any desire to try to move. But my senses were exceedingly alert. I saw the wreck of the motor lit up by the moving lanterns. I saw the little group of people and heard the hushed voices. There were the lodge-keeper and his wife, and one or two more. They were taking no notice of me, but were very busy round the car. Then suddenly I heard a cry of pain.

'The weight is on him. Lift it easy,' cried a voice.

'It's only my leg!' said another one, which I recognised as Perkins's. 'Where's master?' he cried.

'Here I am,' I answered, but they did not seem to hear me. They were all bending over something which lay in front of the car.

Stanley laid his hand upon my shoulder, and his touch was inexpressibly soothing. I felt light and happy, in spite of all.

'No pain, of course?' said he.

'None,' said I.

'There never is,' said he.

And then suddenly a wave of amazement passed over me. Stanley!

Stanley! Why, Stanley had surely died of enteric at Bloemfontein in the Boer War!*

'Stanley!' I cried, and the words seemed to choke my throat—'Stanley, you are dead.'

He looked at me with the same old gentle, wistful smile.

'So are you,' he answered.

THE HORROR OF THE HEIGHTS

(Which Includes the Manuscript Known
as the Joyce-Armstrong Fragment)

———⟨⟩———

THE idea that the extraordinary narrative which has been called the Joyce-Armstrong Fragment is an elaborate practical joke evolved by some unknown person, cursed by a perverted and sinister sense of humour, has now been abandoned by all who have examined the matter. The most *macabre* and imaginative of plotters would hesitate before linking his morbid fancies with the unquestioned and tragic facts which reinforce the statement. Though the assertions contained in it are amazing and even monstrous, it is none the less forcing itself upon the general intelligence that they are true, and that we must readjust our ideas to the new situation. This world of ours appears to be separated by a slight and precarious margin of safety from a most singular and unexpected danger. I will endeavour in this narrative, which reproduces the original document in its necessarily somewhat fragmentary form, to lay before the reader the whole of the facts up to date, prefacing my statement by saying that, if there be any who doubt the narrative of Joyce-Armstrong, there can be no question at all as to the facts concerning Lieutenant Myrtle, RN, and Mr Hay Connor, who undoubtedly met their end in the manner described.

The Joyce-Armstrong Fragment was found in the field which is called Lower Haycock, lying one mile to the westward of the village of Withyham,* upon the Kent and Sussex border. It was on the fifteenth of September last that an agricultural labourer, James Flynn, in the employment of Mathew Dodd, farmer, of the Chauntry Farm, Withyham, perceived a briar pipe lying near the footpath which skirts the hedge in Lower Haycock. A few paces farther on he picked up a pair of broken binocular glasses. Finally, among some nettles in the ditch, he caught sight of a flat, canvas-backed book, which proved to be a note-book with detachable leaves, some of which had come loose and were fluttering along the base of the hedge. These he collected, but some, including the first, were never recovered, and leave a deplorable hiatus in this all-important statement. The note-book was taken by the labourer to his master, who in turn showed it to Dr J. H. Atherton, of Hartfield.* This gentleman at once recognized the need for an expert examination, and the manuscript was forwarded to the Aero Club* in London, where it now lies.

The first two pages of the manuscript are missing. There is also one torn away at the end of the narrative, though none of these affect the general coherence of the story. It is conjectured that the missing opening is concerned with the record of Mr Joyce-Armstrong's qualifications as an aeronaut, which can be gathered from other sources and are admitted to be unsurpassed among the air-pilots of England. For many years he has been looked upon as among the most daring and the most intellectual of flying men, a combination which has enabled him to both invent and test several new devices, including the common gyroscopic attachment which is known by his name. The main body of the manuscript is written neatly in ink, but the last few lines are in pencil and are so ragged as to be hardly legible—exactly, in fact, as they might be expected to appear if they were scribbled off hurriedly from the seat of a moving aeroplane. There are, it may be added, several stains, both on the last page and on the outside cover which have been pronounced by the Home Office experts to be blood—probably human and certainly mammalian. The face that something closely resembling the organism of malaria was discovered in this blood, and that Joyce-Armstrong is known to have suffered from intermittent fever, is a remarkable example of the new weapons which modern science has placed in the hands of our detectives.

And now a word as to the personality of the author of this epoch-making statement. Joyce-Armstrong, according to the few friends who really knew something of the man, was a poet and a dreamer, as well as a mechanic and an inventor. He was a man of considerable wealth, much of which he had spent in the pursuit of his aeronautical hobby. He had four private aeroplanes in his hangars near Devizes,* and is said to have made no fewer than one hundred and seventy ascents in the course of last year. He was a retiring man with dark moods, in which he would avoid the society of his fellows. Captain Dangerfield, who knew him better than anyone, says that there were times when his eccentricity threatened to develop into something more serious. His habit of carrying a shot-gun with him in his aeroplane was one manifestation of it.

Another was the morbid effect which the fall of Lieutenant Myrtle had upon his mind. Myrtle, who was attempting the height record, fell from an altitude of something over thirty thousand feet.* Horrible to narrate, his head was entirely obliterated, though his body and limbs preserved their configuration. At every gathering of airmen, Joyce-Armstrong, according to Dangerfield, would ask, with an enigmatic smile: 'And where, pray, is Myrtle's head?'

On another occasion after dinner, at the mess of the Flying School on Salisbury Plain,* he started a debate as to what will be the most permanent danger which airmen will have to encounter. Having listened to successive opinions as to air-pockets, faulty construction, and over-banking, he ended by shrugging his shoulders and refusing to put forward his own views, though he gave the impression that they differed from any advanced by his companions.

It is worth remarking that after his own complete disappearance it was found that his private affairs were arranged with a precision which may show that he had a strong premonition of disaster. With these essential explanations I will now give the narrative exactly as it stands, beginning at page three of the blood-soaked notebook:—

* * *

'Nevertheless, when I dined at Rheims with Coselli and Gustav Raymond* I found that neither of them was aware of any particular danger in the higher layers of the atmosphere. I did not actually say what was in my thoughts, but I got so near to it that if they had any corresponding idea they could not have failed to express it. But then they are two empty, vainglorious fellows with no thought beyond seeing their silly names in the newspaper. It is interesting to note that neither of them had ever been much beyond the twenty-thousand-foot level. Of course, men have been higher than this both in balloons and in the ascent of mountains. It must be well above that point that the aeroplane enters the danger zone—always presuming that my premonitions are correct.

'Aeroplaning has been with us now for more than twenty years, and one might well ask: Why should this peril be only revealing itself in our day? The answer is obvious. In the old days of weak engines, when a hundred horse-power Gnome or Green* was considered ample for every need, the flights were very restricted. Now that three hundred horse-power is the rule rather than the exception, visits to the upper layers have become easier and more common. Some of us can remember how, in our youth, Garros* made a world-wide reputation by attaining nineteen thousand feet, and it was considered a remarkable achievement to fly over the Alps. Our standard now has been immeasurably raised, and there are twenty high flights for one in former years. Many of them have been undertaken with impunity. The thirty-thousand-foot level has been reached time after time with no discomfort beyond cold and asthma. What does this prove? A visitor might descend upon this planet a thousand times and never see a tiger. Yet tigers exist, and if he chanced to come down into a jungle he might be devoured. There are jungles of the upper air, and there are worse things than tigers which inhabit them. I believe in time they will map these jungles accurately out. Even at the present moment I could name two of them. One of them lies over the Pau–Biarritz* district of France. Another is just over my head as I write here in my house in Wiltshire. I rather think there is a third in the Homburg-Wiesbaden* district.

'It was the disappearance of the airmen that first set me thinking. Of course, everyone said that they had fallen into the sea, but that did not satisfy me at all. First, there was Verrier in France; his machine was found near Bayonne,* but they never got his body. There was the case of Baxter also, who vanished, though his engine and some of the iron fixings were found in a wood in Leicestershire. In that case, Dr Middleton, of Amesbury,* who was watching the flight with a telescope, declares that just before the clouds obscured the view he saw the machine, which was at an enormous height, suddenly rise perpendicularly upwards in a succession of jerks in a manner that he would have thought to be impossible. That was the last seen of Baxter. There was a correspondence in the papers, but it never led to anything. There were several other similar cases, and then there was the death of Hay Connor. What a cackle there was about an unsolved mystery of the air, and what columns in the halfpenny papers, and yet how little was ever done to get to the bottom of the business! He came down in a tremendous vol-plané* from an unknown height. He never got off his machine and died in his pilot's seat. Died of what? "Heart disease," said the doctors. Rubbish! Hay Connor's heart was as sound as mine is. What did Venables say? Venables was the only man who was at his side when he died. He said that he was shivering and looked like a man who had been badly scared. "Died of fright," said Venables, but could not imagine what he was frightened about. Only said one word to Venables, which sounded like "Monstrous." They could make nothing of that at the inquest. But I could make something of it. Monsters! That was the last word of poor Harry Hay Connor. And he *did* die of fright, just as Venables thought.

'And then there was Myrtle's head. Do you really believe—does anybody really believe—that a man's head could be driven clean into his body by the force of a fall? Well, perhaps it may be possible, but I, for one, have never believed that it was so with Myrtle. And the grease upon his clothes—"all slimy with grease," said somebody at the inquest. Queer that nobody got thinking after that! I did—but, then, I had been thinking for a good long time. I've made three ascents—how Dangerfield used to chaff me about my shot-gun—but I've never been high enough. Now, with this new, light Paul Veroner machine and its one hundred and seventy-five Robur, I should easily touch the thirty thousand to-morrow. I'll have a shot at the record. Maybe I shall have a shot at something else as well. Of course, it's dangerous. If a fellow wants to avoid danger he had best keep out of flying altogether and subside finally into flannel slippers and a dressing-gown. But I'll visit the air-jungle to-morrow—and if there's anything there I shall know it. If I return, I'll find myself a bit of a celebrity. If I don't, this note-book may explain what I am trying to do, and how I lost my life in doing it. But no drivel about accidents or mysteries, if *you* please.

'I chose my Paul Veroner* monoplane for the job. There's nothing like a monoplane when real work is to be done. Beaumont found that out in very early days. For one thing it doesn't mind damp, and the weather looks as if we should be in the clouds all the time. It's a bonny little model and answers my hand like a tender-mouthed horse. The engine is a ten-cylinder rotary Robur* working up to one hundred and seventy-five. It has all the modern improvements—enclosed fuselage, high-curved landing skids, brakes, gyroscopic steadiers, and three speeds, worked by an alteration of the angle of the planes upon the Venetian-blind principle. I took a shot-gun with me and a dozen cartridges filled with buck-shot. You should have seen the face of Perkins, my old mechanic, when I directed him to put them in. I was dressed like an Arctic explorer, with two jerseys under my overalls, thick socks inside my padded boots, a storm-cap with flaps, and my talc goggles.* It was stifling outside the hangars, but I was going for the summit of the Himalayas, and had to dress for the part. Perkins knew there was something on and implored me to take him with me. Perhaps I should if I were using the biplane, but a monoplane is a one-man show—if you want to get the last foot of lift out of it. Of course, I took an oxygen bag; the man who goes for the altitude record without one will either be frozen or smothered—or both.

'I had a good look at the planes, the rudder-bar, and the elevating lever before I got in. Everything was in order so far as I could see. Then I switched on my engine and found that she was running sweetly. When they let her go she rose almost at once upon the lowest speed. I circled my home field once or twice just to warm her up, and then, with a wave to Perkins and the others, I flattened out my planes and put her on her highest. She skimmed like a swallow down wind for eight or ten miles until I turned her nose up a little and she began to climb in a great spiral for the cloud-bank above me. It's all-important to rise slowly and adapt yourself to the pressure as you go.

'It was a close, warm day for an English September, and there was the hush and heaviness of impending rain. Now and then there came sudden puffs of wind from the south-west—one of them so gusty and unexpected that it caught me napping and turned me half-round for an instant. I remember the time when gusts and whirls and air-pockets used to be things of danger—before we learned to put an overmastering power into our engines. Just as I reached the cloud-banks, with the altimeter marking three thousand, down came the rain. My word, how it poured! It drummed upon my wings and lashed against my face, blurring my glasses so that I could hardly see. I got down on to a low speed, for it was painful to travel against it. As I got higher it became hail, and I had to turn tail to it. One of my cylinders was out of action—a dirty plug, I should imagine, but still I was rising steadily with plenty of power. After a bit the trouble passed, whatever it was, and I heard the full, deep-throated purr—the ten singing as one. That's where the beauty of our modern silencers comes in. We can at last control our engines by ear. How they squeal and squeak and sob when they are in trouble! All those cries for help were wasted in the old days, when every sound was swallowed up by the monstrous racket of the machine. If only the early aviators could come back to see the beauty and perfection of the mechanism which have been bought at the cost of their lives!

'About nine-thirty I was nearing the clouds. Down below me, all blurred and shadowed with rain, lay the vast expanse of Salisbury Plain. Half a dozen flying machines were doing hackwork at the thousand-foot level, looking like little black swallows against the green background. I dare say they were wondering what I was doing up in cloud-land. Suddenly a grey curtain drew across beneath me and the wet folds of vapours were swirling round my face. It was clammily cold and miserable. But I was above the hail-storm, and that was something gained. The cloud was as dark and thick as a London fog. In my anxiety to get clear, I cocked her nose up until the automatic alarm bell rang, and I actually began to slide backwards. My sopped and dripping wings had made me heavier than I thought, but presently I was in lighter cloud, and soon had cleared the first layer. There was a second—opal-coloured and fleecy—at a great height above my head, a white, unbroken ceiling above, and a dark, unbroken floor below, with the monoplane labouring upwards upon a vast spiral between them. It is deadly lonely in these cloud-spaces. Once a great flight of some small water-birds went past me, flying very fast to the westwards. The quick whir of their wings and their musical cry were cheery to my ear. I fancy that they were teal, but I am a wretched zoologist. Now that we humans have become birds we must really learn to know our brethren by sight.

'The wind down beneath me whirled and swayed the broad cloud plain. Once a great eddy formed in it, a whirlpool of vapour, and through it, as down a funnel, I caught sight of the distant world. A large white biplane was passing at a vast depth beneath me. I fancy it was the morning mail service betwixt Bristol and London. Then the drift swirled inwards again and the great solitude was unbroken.

'Just after ten I touched the lower edge of the upper cloud-stratum. It consisted of fine diaphanous vapour drifting swiftly from the west-ward. The wind had been steadily rising all this time and it was now blowing a sharp breeze—twenty-eight an hour by my gauge. Already it was very cold, though my altimeter only marked nine thousand. The engines were working beautifully, and we went droning steadily upwards. The cloud-bank was thicker than I had expected, but at last it thinned out into a golden mist before me, and then in an instant I had shot out from it, and there was an unclouded sky and a bril-liant sun above my head—all blue and gold above, all shining silver below, one vast, glimmering plain as far as my eyes could reach. It was a quarter past ten o'clock, and the barograph* needle pointed to twelve thousand eight hundred. Up I went and up, my ears concen-trated upon the deep purring of my motor, my eyes busy always with the watch, the revolution indicator, the petrol lever, and the oil pump.

No wonder aviators are said to be a fearless race. With so many things to think of there is no time to trouble about oneself. About this time I noted how unreliable is the compass when above a certain height from earth. At fifteen thousand feet mine was pointing east and a point south. The sun and the wind gave me my true bearings.

'I had hoped to reach an eternal stillness in these high altitudes, but with every thousand feet of ascent the gale grew stronger. My machine groaned and trembled in every joint and rivet as she faced it, and swept away like a sheet of paper when I banked her on the turn, skimming down wind at a greater pace, perhaps, than ever mortal man has moved. Yet I had always to turn again and tack up in the wind's eye, for it was not merely a height record that I was after. By all my calculations it was above little Wiltshire that my air-jungle lay, and all my labour might be lost if I struck the outer layers at some farther point.

'When I reached the nineteen-thousand-foot level, which was about midday, the wind was so severe that I looked with some anxiety to the stays of my wings, expecting momentarily to see them snap or slacken. I even cast loose the parachute behind me, and fastened its hook into the ring of my leathern belt, so as to be ready for the worst. Now was the time when a bit of scamped work by the mechanic is paid for by the life of the aeronaut. But she held together bravely. Every cord and strut was humming and vibrating like so many harp-strings, but it was glorious to see how, for all the beating and the buffeting, she was still the conqueror of Nature and the mistress of the sky. There is surely something divine in man himself that he should rise so superior to the limitations which Creation seemed to impose—rise, too, by such unselfish, heroic devotion as this air-conquest has shown. Talk of human degeneration!* When has such a story as this been written in the annals of our race?

'These were the thoughts in my head as I climbed that monstrous, inclined plane with the wind sometimes beating in my face and some-times whistling behind my ears, while the cloud-land beneath me fell away to such a distance that the folds and hummocks of silver had all smoothed out into one flat, shining plain. But suddenly I had a hor-rible and unprecedented experience. I have known before what it is to be in what our neighbours have called a *tourbillon*,* but never on such a scale as this. That huge, sweeping river of wind of which I have spoken had, as it appears, whirlpools within it which were as monstrous as itself. Without a moment's warning I was dragged suddenly into the heart of one. I spun round for a minute or two with such velocity that I almost lost my senses, and then fell suddenly, left wing foremost, down the vacuum funnel in the centre. I dropped like a stone, and lost nearly a thousand feet. It was only my belt that kept me in my seat, and the shock and breathlessness left me hanging half-insensible over the side of the fuselage. But I am always capable of a supreme effort— it is my one great merit as an aviator. I was conscious that the descent was slower. The whirlpool was a cone rather than a funnel, and I had come to the apex. With a terrific wrench, throwing my weight all to one side, I levelled my planes and brought her head away from the wind. In an instant I had shot out of the eddies and was skimming down the sky. Then, shaken but victorious, I turned her nose up and began once more my steady grind on the upward spiral. I took a large sweep to avoid the danger-spot of the whirlpool, and soon I was safely above it. Just after one o'clock I was twenty-one thousand feet above the sea-level. To my great joy I had topped the gale, and with every hundred feet of ascent the air grew stiller. On the other hand, it was very cold, and I was conscious of that peculiar nausea which goes with rarefaction of the air. For the first time I unscrewed the mouth of my oxygen bag and took an occasional whiff of the glorious gas. I could feel it running like a cordial through my veins, and I was exhilarated almost to the point of drunkenness. I shouted and sang as I soared upwards into the cold, still outer world.

'It is very clear to me that the insensibility which came upon Glaisher, and in a lesser degree upon Coxwell when, in 1862, they ascended in a balloon to the height of thirty thousand feet, was due to the extreme speed with which a perpendicular ascent is made. Doing it at an easy gradient and accustoming oneself to the lessened barometric pressure by slow degrees, there are no such dreadful symptoms. At the same great height I found that even without my oxygen inhaler I could breathe without undue distress. It was bitterly cold, however, and my thermometer was at zero, Fahrenheit. At one-thirty I was nearly seven miles above the surface of the earth, and still ascending steadily. I found, however, that the rarefied air was giving markedly less support to my planes, and that my angle of ascent had to be considerably lowered in consequence. It was already clear that even with my light weight and strong engine-power there was a point in front of me where I should be held. To make matters worse, one of my sparking-plugs was in trouble again and there was intermittent misfiring in the engine. My heart was heavy with the fear of failure.

'It was about that time that I had a most extraordinary experience. Something whizzed past me in a trail of smoke and exploded with a loud, hissing sound, sending forth a cloud of steam. For the instant I could not imagine what had happened. Then I remembered that the earth is for ever being bombarded by meteor stones, and would be hardly inhabitable were they not in nearly every case turned to vapour in the outer layers of the atmosphere. Here is a new danger for the high-altitude man, for two others passed me when I was nearing the forty-thousand-foot mark. I cannot doubt that at the edge of the earth's envelope the risk would be a very real one.

'My barograph needle marked forty-one thousand three hundred when I became aware that I could go no farther. Physically, the strain was not as yet greater than I could bear, but my machine had reached its limit. The attenuated air gave no firm support to the wings, and the least tilt developed into side-slip, while she seemed sluggish on her controls. Possibly, had the engine been at its best, another thousand feet might have been within our capacity, but it was still misfiring, and two out of the ten cylinders appeared to be out of action. If I had not already reached the zone for which I was searching then I should never see it upon this journey. But was it not possible that I had attained it? Soaring in circles like a monstrous hawk upon the forty-thousand-foot level I let the monoplane guide herself, and with my Mannheim glass* I made a careful observation of my surroundings. The heavens were perfectly clear; there was no indication of those dangers which I had imagined.

'I have said that I was soaring in circles. It struck me suddenly that I would do well to take a wider sweep and open up a new air-tract. If the hunter entered an earth-jungle he would drive through it if he wished to find his game. My reasoning had led me to believe that the air-jungle which I had imagined lay somewhere over Wiltshire. This should be to the south and west of me. I took my bearings from the sun, for the compass was hopeless and no trace of earth was to be seen—nothing but the distant, silver cloud-plain. However, I got my direction as best I might and kept her head straight to the mark. I reckoned that my petrol supply would not last for more than another hour or so, but I could afford to use it to the last drop, since a single magnificent vol-plané could at any time take me to the earth.

'Suddenly I was aware of something new. The air in front of me had lost its crystal clearness. It was full of long, ragged wisps of something which I can only compare to very fine cigarette-smoke. It hung about in wreaths and coils, turning and twisting slowly in the sunlight. As the monoplane shot through it, I was aware of a faint taste of oil upon my lips, and there was a greasy scum upon the woodwork of the machine. Some infinitely fine organic matter appeared to be suspended in the atmosphere. There was no life there. It was inchoate and diffuse, extending for many square acres and then fringing on into the void. No, it was not life. But might it not be the remains of life? Above all, might it not be the food of life, of monstrous life, even as the humble grease of the ocean is the food for the mighty whale? The thought was in my mind when my eyes looked upwards and I saw the most wonderful vision that ever man has seen. Can I hope to convey it to you even as I saw it myself last Thursday?

'Conceive a jelly-fish such as sails in our summer seas, bell-shaped and of enormous size—far larger, I should judge, than the dome of St Paul's. It was of a light pink colour veined with a delicate green, but the whole huge fabric so tenuous that it was but a fairy outline against the dark blue sky. It pulsated with a delicate and regular rhythm. From it there depended two long, drooping, green tentacles, which swayed slowly backwards and forwards. This gorgeous vision passed gently with noiseless dignity over my head, as light and fragile as a soap-bubble, and drifted upon its stately way.

'I had half-turned my monoplane, that I might look after this beautiful creature, when, in a moment, I found myself amidst a perfect fleet of them, of all sizes, but none so large as the first. Some were quite small, but the majority about as big as an average balloon, and with much the same curvature at the top. There was in them a delicacy of texture and colouring which reminded me of the finest Venetian glass.* Pale shades of pink and green were the prevailing tints, but all had a lovely iridescence where the sun shimmered through their dainty forms. Some hundreds of them drifted past me, a wonderful fairy squadron of strange, unknown argosies* of the sky—creatures whose forms and substance were so attuned to these pure heights that one could not conceive anything so delicate within actual sight or sound of earth.

'But soon my attention was drawn to a new phenomenon—the serpents of the outer air. These were long, thin, fantastic coils of vapour-like material, which turned and twisted with great speed, flying round and round at such a pace that the eyes could hardly follow them. Some of these ghost-like creatures were twenty or thirty feet long, but it was difficult to tell their girth, for their outline was so hazy that it seemed to fade away into the air around them. These air-snakes were of a very light grey or smoke colour, with some darker lines within, which gave the impression of a definite organism. One of them whisked past my very face, and I was conscious of a cold, clammy contact, but their composition was so unsubstantial that I could not connect them with any thought of physical danger, any more than the beautiful bell-like creatures which had preceded them. There was no more solidity in their frames than in the floating spume from a broken wave.

'But a more terrible experience was in store for me. Floating downwards from a great height there came a purplish patch of vapour, small as I saw it first, but rapidly enlarging as it approached me, until it appeared to be hundreds of square feet in size. Though fashioned of some transparent, jelly-like substance, it was none the less of much more definite outline and solid consistence than anything which I had seen before. There were more traces, too, of a physical organization, especially two vast, shadowy, circular plates upon either side, which may have been eyes, and a perfectly solid white projection between them which was as curved and cruel as the beak of a vulture.

'The whole aspect of this monster was formidable and threatening, and it kept changing its colour from a very light mauve to a dark, angry purple so thick that it cast a shadow as it drifted between my monoplane and the sun. On the upper curve of its huge body there were three great projections which I can only describe as enormous bubbles, and I was convinced as I looked at them that they were charged with some extremely light gas which served to buoy up the misshapen and semi-solid mass in the rarefied air. The creature moved swiftly along, keeping pace easily with the monoplane, and for twenty miles or more it formed my horrible escort, hovering over me like a bird of prey which is waiting to pounce, its method of progression—done so swiftly that it was not easy to follow—was to throw out a long, glutinous streamer in front of it, which in turn seemed to draw forward the rest of the writhing body. So elastic and gelatinous was it that never for two successive minutes was it the same shape, and yet each change made it more threatening and loathsome than the last.

'I knew that it meant mischief. Every purple flush of its hideous body told me so. The vague, goggling eyes which were turned always upon me were cold and merciless in their viscid hatred. I dipped the nose of my monoplane downwards to escape it. As I did so, as quick as a flash there shot out a long tentacle from this mass of floating blubber, and it fell as light and sinuous as a whip lash across the front of my machine. There was a loud hiss as it lay for a moment across the hot engine, and it whisked itself into the air again, while the huge, flat body drew itself together as if in sudden pain. I dipped to a vol-piqué,* but again a tentacle fell over the monoplane and was shorn off by the propeller as easily as it might have cut through a smoke wreath. A long, gliding, sticky, serpent-like coil came from behind and caught me round the waist, dragging me out of the fuselage. I tore at it, my fingers sinking into the smooth, glue-like surface, and for an instant I disengaged myself, but only to be caught round the boot by another coil, which gave me a jerk that tilted me almost on to my back.

'As I fell over I blazed off both barrels of my gun, though, indeed, it was like attacking an elephant with a pea-shooter to imagine that any human weapon could cripple that mighty bulk. And yet I aimed better than I knew, for, with a loud report, one of the great blisters upon the creature's back exploded with the puncture of the buck-shot. It was very clear that my conjecture was right, and that these vast, clear bladders were distended with some lifting gas, for in an instant the huge, cloud-like body turned sideways, writhing desperately to find its balance, while the white beak snapped and gaped in horrible fury. But already I had shot away on the steepest glide that I dared to attempt, my engine still full on, the flying propeller and the force of gravity shooting me downwards like an aerolite.* Far behind me I saw a dull, purplish smudge growing swiftly smaller and merging into the blue sky behind it. I was safe out of the deadly jungle of the outer air.

'Once out of danger I throttled my engine, for nothing tears a machine to pieces quicker than running on full power from a height. It was a glorious, spiral vol-plané from nearly eight miles of altitude—first, to the level of the silver cloud-bank, then to that of the storm-cloud beneath it, and finally, in beating rain, to the surface of the earth. I saw the Bristol Channel beneath me as I broke from the clouds, but, having still some petrol in my tank, I got twenty miles inland before I found myself stranded in a field half a mile from the village of Ashcombe.* There I got three tins of petrol from a passing motor-car, and at ten minutes past six that evening I alighted gently in my own home meadow at Devizes, after such a journey as no mortal upon earth has ever yet taken and lived to tell the tale. I have seen the beauty and I have seen the horror of the heights—and greater beauty or greater horror than that is not within the ken of man.

'And now it is my plan to go once again before I give my results to the world. My reason for this is that I must surely have something to show by way of proof before I lay such a tale before my fellow-men. It is true that others will soon follow and will confirm what I have said, and yet I should wish to carry conviction from the first. Those lovely iridescent bubbles of the air should not be hard to capture. They drift slowly upon their way, and the swift monoplane could intercept their leisurely course. It is likely enough that they would dissolve in the heavier layers of the atmosphere, and that some small heap of amorphous jelly might be all that I should bring to earth with me. And yet something there would surely be by which I could substantiate my story. Yes, I will go, even if I run a risk by doing so. These purple horrors would not seem to be numerous. It is probable that I shall not see one. If I do I shall dive at once. At the worst there is always the shot-gun and my knowledge of . . .'

Here a page of the manuscript is unfortunately missing. On the next page is written, in large, straggling writing:—

'Forty-three thousand feet. I shall never see earth again. They are beneath me, three of them. God help me; it is a dreadful death to die!'

Such in its entirety is the Joyce-Armstrong Statement. Of the man nothing has since been seen. Pieces of his shattered monoplane have been picked up in the preserves of Mr Budd-Lushington upon the borders of Kent and Sussex, within a few miles of the spot where the note-book was discovered. If the unfortunate aviator's theory is correct that this air-jungle, as he called it, existed only over the south-west of England, then it would seem that he had fled from it at the full speed of his monoplane, but had been overtaken and devoured by these horrible creatures at some spot in the outer atmosphere above the place where the grim relics were found. The picture of that monoplane skimming down the sky, with the nameless terrors flying as swiftly beneath it and cutting it off always from the earth while they gradually closed in upon their victim, is one upon which a man who valued his sanity would prefer not to dwell. There are many, as I am aware, who still jeer at the facts which I have here set down, but even they must admit that Joyce-Armstrong has disappeared, and I would commend to them his own words: 'This note-book may explain what I am trying to do, and how I lost my life in doing it. But no drivel about accidents or mysteries, if you please.'

THE BULLY OF BROCAS COURT

THAT year—it was in 1878—the South Midland Yeomanry were out near Luton,* and the real question which appealed to every man in the great camp was not how to prepare for a possible European war,* but the far more vital one how to get a man who could stand up for ten rounds to Farrier-Sergeant Burton. Slogger Burton was a fine upstanding fourteen stone of bone and brawn, with a smack in either hand which would leave any ordinary mortal senseless. A match must be found for him somewhere or his head would outgrow his dragoon helmet. Therefore Sir Fred. Milburn, better known as Mumbles, was dispatched to London to find if among the fancy there was no one who would make a journey in order to take down the number of the bold dragoon.

They were bad days, those, in the prize-ring. The old knuckle-fighting* had died out in scandal and disgrace, smothered by the pestilent crowd of betting men and ruffians of all sorts who hung upon the edge of the movement and brought disgrace and ruin upon the decent fighting men, who were often humble heroes whose gallantry has never been surpassed. An honest sportsman who desired to see a fight was usually set upon by villains, against whom he had no redress, since he was himself engaged on what was technically an illegal action.* He was stripped in the open street, his purse taken, and his head split open if he ventured to resist. The ringside could only be reached by men who were prepared to fight their way there with cudgels and hunting-crops. No wonder that the classic sport was attended now by those only who had nothing to lose.

On the other hand, the era of the reserved building and the legal glove-fight had not yet arisen, and the cult was in a strange intermediate condition. It was impossible to regulate it, and equally impossible to abolish it, since nothing appeals more directly and powerfully to the average Briton. Therefore there were scrambling contests in stableyards and barns, hurried visits to France, secret meetings at dawn in wild parts of the country, and all manner of evasions and experiments. The men themselves became as unsatisfactory as their surroundings. There could be no honest open contest, and the loudest bragger talked his way to the top of the list. Only across the Atlantic had the huge figure of John Lawrence Sullivan* appeared, who was destined to be the last of the earlier system and the first of the later one.

Things being in this condition, the sporting Yeomanry Captain found it no easy matter among the boxing saloons and sporting pubs of London to find a man who would be relied upon to give a good account of the huge Farrier-Sergeant. Heavy-weights were at a premium. Finally his choice fell upon Alf Stevens of Kentish Town,* an excellent rising middle-weight who had never yet known defeat and had indeed some claims to the championship. His professional experience and craft would surely make up for the three stone of weight which separated him from the formidable dragoon. It was in this hope that Sir Fred. Milburn engaged him, and proceeded to convey him in his dog-cart behind a pair of spanking greys to the camp of the Yeomen. They were to start one evening, drive up the Great North Road, sleep at St Albans,* and finish their journey next day.

The prize-fighter met the sporting Baronet at the Golden Cross,* where Bates, the little groom, was standing at the head of the spirited horses. Stevens, a pale-faced, clean-cut young fellow, mounted beside his employer and waved his hand to a little knot of fighting men, rough, collarless, reefer-coated* fellows who had gathered to bid their comrade good-bye. 'Good luck, Alf!' came in a hoarse chorus as the boy released the horses' heads and sprang in behind, while the high dog-cart swung swiftly round the curve into Trafalgar Square.

Sir Frederick was so busy steering among the traffic in Oxford Street and the Edgware Road that he had little thought for anything else, but when he got into the edges of the country near Hendon,* and the hedges had at last taken the place of that endless panorama of brick dwellings, he let his horses go easy with a loose rein while he turned his attention to the young man at his side. He had found him by correspondence and recommendation, so that he had some curiosity now in looking him over. Twilight was already falling and the light dim, but what the Baronet saw pleased him well. The man was a fighter every inch, clean-cut, deep-chested, with the long straight cheek and deep-set eye which goes with an obstinate courage. Above all, he was a man who had never yet met his master and was still upheld by the deep sustaining confidence which is never quite the same after a single defeat. The Baronet chuckled as he realized what a surprise packet was being carried north for the Farrier-Sergeant.

'I suppose you are in some sort of training, Stevens?' he remarked, turning to his companion.

'Yes, sir; I am fit to fight for my life.'

'So I should judge by the look of you.'

'I live regular all the time, sir, but I was matched against Mike Connor for this last week-end and scaled down to eleven four. Then he paid forfeit, and here I am at the top of my form.'

'That's lucky. You'll need it all against a man who has a pull of three stone and four inches.'

The young man smiled.

'I have given greater odds than that, sir.'

'I dare say. But he's a game man as well.'

'Well, sir, one can but do one's best.'

The Baronet liked the modest but assured tone of the young pugil- ist. Suddenly an amusing thought struck him, and he burst out laughing.

'By Jove!' he cried. 'What a lark if the Bully is out to-night!'

Alf Stevens pricked up his ears.

'Who might he be, sir?'

'Well, that's what the folk are asking. Some say they've seen him, and some say he's a fairy-tale, but there's good evidence that he is a real man with a pair of rare good fists that leave their marks behind him.'

'And where might he live?'

'On this very road. It's between Finchley and Elstree,* as I've heard. There are two chaps, and they come out on nights when the moon is at full and challenge the passers-by to fight in the old style. One fights and the other picks up. By George! the fellow *can* fight, too, by all accounts. Chaps have been found in the morning with their faces all cut to ribbons to show that the Bully had been at work upon them.'

Alf Stevens was full of interest.

'I've always wanted to try an old-style battle, sir, but it never chanced to come my way. I believe it would suit me better than the gloves.'

'Then you won't refuse the Bully?'

'Refuse him! I'd go ten mile to meet him.'

'By George! it would be great!' cried the Baronet. 'Well, the moon is at the full, and the place should be about here.'

'If he's as good as you say,' Stevens remarked, 'he should be known in the ring, unless he is just an amateur who amuses himself like that.'

'Some think he's an ostler, or maybe a racing man from the training stables over yonder. Where there are horses there is boxing. If you can believe the accounts, there is something a bit queer and outlandish about the fellow. Hi! Look out, damn you, look out!'

The Baronet's voice had risen to a sudden screech of surprise and of anger. At this point the road dips down into a hollow, heavily shaded by trees, so that at night it arches across like the mouth of a tunnel. At the foot of the slope there stand two great stone pillars, which, as viewed by daylight, are lichen-stained and weathered, with heraldic devices on each which are so mutilated by time that they are mere protuberances of stone. An iron gate of elegant design, hanging loosely upon rusted hinges, proclaims both the past glories and the present decay of Brocas Old Hall,* which lies at the end of the weed-encumbered avenue. It was from the shadow of this ancient gateway that an active figure had sprung suddenly into the centre of the road and had, with great dexterity, held up the horses, who ramped and pawed as they were forced back upon their haunches.

'Here, Rowe, you 'old the tits,* will ye?' cried a high strident voice. 'I've a little word to say to this 'ere slap-up Corinthian* before 'e goes any farther.'

A second man had emerged from the shadows and without a word took hold of the horses' heads. He was a short, thick fellow, dressed in a curious brown many-caped overcoat, which came to his knees, with gaiters and boots beneath it. He wore no hat, and those in the dog-cart had a view, as he came in front of the side-lamps, of a surly red face with an ill-fitting lower lip clean shaven, and a high black cravat swathed tightly under the chin. As he gripped the leathers his more active comrade sprang forward and rested a bony hand upon the side of the splashboard while he looked keenly up with a pair of fierce blue eyes at the faces of the two travellers, the light beating full upon his own features. He wore a hat low upon his brow, but in spite of its shadow both the Baronet and the pugilist could see enough to shrink from him, for it was an evil face, evil but very formidable, stern, craggy, high-nosed, and fierce, with an inexorable mouth which bespoke a nature which would neither ask for mercy nor grant it. As to his age, one could only say for certain that a man with such a face was young enough to have all his virility and old enough to have experienced all the wickedness of life. The cold, savage eyes took a deliberate survey, first of the Baronet and then of the young man beside him.

'Aye, Rowe, it's a slap-up Corinthian, same as I said,' he remarked over his shoulder to his companion. 'But this other is a likely chap. If 'e isn't a millin' cove* 'e ought to be. Any'ow, we'll try 'im out.'

'Look here,' said the Baronet, 'I don't know who you are, except that you are a damned impertinent fellow. I'd put the lash of my whip across your face for two pins!'

'Stow that gammon,* gov'nor! It ain't safe to speak to me like that.'

'I've heard of you and your ways!' cried the angry soldier. 'I'll teach you to stop my horses on the Queen's high road! You've got the wrong men this time, my fine fellow, as you will soon learn.'

'That's as it may be,' said the stranger. 'May'ap, master, we may all learn something before we part. One or other of you 'as got to get down and put up your 'ands before you get any farther.'

Stevens had instantly sprung down into the road.

'If you want a fight you've come to the right shop,' said he; 'it's my trade, so don't say I took you unawares.'

The stranger gave a cry of satisfaction.

'Blow my dickey!* he shouted. 'It *is* a millin' cove, Joe, same as I said. No more chaw-bacons* for us, but the real thing. Well, young man, you've met your master to-night. Happen you never 'eard what Lord Longmore* said o' me? 'A man must be made special to beat you,' says 'e. That's wot Lord Longmore said.'

'That was before the Bull came along,' growled the man in front, speaking for the first time.

'Stow your chaffing, Joe! A little more about the Bull and you and me will quarrel. 'E bested me once, but it's all betters and no takers that I glut 'im if ever we meet again. Well, young man, what d'ye think of me?'

'I think you've got your share of cheek.'

'Cheek. Wot's that?'*

'Impudence, bluff—gas, if you like.'

The last word had a surprising effect upon the stranger. He smote his leg with his hand and broke out into a high neighing laugh, in which he was joined by his gruff companion.

'You've said the right word, my beauty,' cried the latter, '"Gas" is the word and no error. Well, there's a good moon, but the clouds are comin' up. We had best use the light while we can.'

Whilst this conversation had been going on the Baronet had been looking with an ever-growing amazement at the attire of the stranger.

A good deal of it confirmed his belief that he was connected with some stables, though making every allowance for this his appearance was very eccentric and old-fashioned. Upon his head he wore a yellowish-white top-hat of long-haired beaver, such as is still affected by some drivers of four-in-hands, with a bell crown and a curling brim. His dress consisted of a short-waisted swallow-tail coat, snuff-coloured, with steel buttons. It opened in front to show a vest of striped silk, while his legs were encased in buff knee-breeches with blue stockings and low shoes. The figure was angular and hard, with a great suggestion of wiry activity. This Bully of Brocas was clearly a very great character, and the young dragoon officer chuckled as he thought what a glorious story he would carry back to the mess of this queer old-world figure and the thrashing which he was about to receive from the famous London boxer.

Billy, the little groom, had taken charge of the horses, who were shivering and sweating.

'This way!' said the stout man, turning towards the gate. It was a sinister place, black and weird, with the crumbling pillars and the heavy arching trees. Neither the Baronet nor the pugilist liked the look of it.

'Where are you going, then?'

'This is no place for a fight,' said the stout man. 'We've got as pretty a place as ever you saw inside the gate here. You couldn't beat it on Molesey Hurst.'*

'The road is good enough for me,' said Stevens.

'The road is good enough for two Johnny Raws,'* said the man with the beaver hat. 'It ain't good enough for two slap-up millin' coves like you an' me. You ain't afeard, are you?'

'Not of you or ten like you,' said Stevens, stoutly.

'Well, then, come with me and do it as it ought to be done.'

Sir Frederick and Stevens exchanged glances.

'I'm game,' said the pugilist.

'Come on, then.'

The little party of four passed through the gateway. Behind them in the darkness the horses stamped and reared, while the voice of the boy could be heard as he vainly tried to soothe them. After walking fifty yards up the grass-grown drive the guide turned to the right through a thick belt of trees, and they came out upon a circular plot of grass, white and clear in the moonlight. It had a raised bank, and on the farther side was one of those little pillared stone summer-houses beloved by the early Georgians.

'What did I tell you?' cried the stout man, triumphantly. 'Could you do better than this within twenty mile of town? It was made for it. Now, Tom, get to work upon him, and show us what you can do.'

It had all become like an extraordinary dream. The strange men, their odd dress, their queer speech, the moonlit circle of grass, and the pillared summer-house all wove themselves into one fantastic whole. It was only the sight of Alf Stevens's ill-fitting tweed suit, and his homely English face surmounting it, which brought the Baronet back to the workaday world. The thin stranger had taken off his beaver hat, his swallow-tailed coat, his silk waistcoat, and finally his shirt had been drawn over his head by his second. Stevens in a cool and leisurely fashion kept pace with the preparations of his antagonist. Then the two fighting men turned upon each other.

But as they did so Stevens gave an exclamation of surprise and horror. The removal of the beaver hat had disclosed a horrible mutilation of the head of his antagonist. The whole upper forehead had fallen in, and there seemed to be a broad red weal between his close-cropped hair and his heavy brows.

'Good Lord,' cried the young pugilist. 'What's amiss with the man?'

The question seemed to rouse a cold fury in his antagonist.

'You look out for your own head, master,' said he. 'You'll find enough to do, I'm thinkin', without talkin' about mine.'

This retort drew a shout of hoarse laughter from his second. 'Well said, my Tommy!' he cried. 'It's Lombard Street to a China orange on the one and only.'*

The man whom he called Tom was standing with his hands up in the centre of the natural ring. He looked a big man in his clothes, but he seemed bigger in the buff, and his barrel chest, sloping shoulders, and loosely-slung muscular arms were all ideal for the game. His grim eyes gleamed fiercely beneath his misshapen brows, and his lips were set in a fixed hard smile, more menacing than a scowl. The pugilist confessed, as he approached him, that he had never seen a more formidable figure. But his bold heart rose to the fact that he had never yet found the man who could master him, and that it was hardly credible that he would appear as an old-fashioned stranger on a country road. Therefore, with an answering smile, he took up his position and raised his hands.

But what followed was entirely beyond his experience. The stranger feinted quickly with his left, and sent in a swinging hit with his right, so quick and hard that Stevens had barely time to avoid it and to counter with a short jab as his opponent rushed in upon him. Next instant the man's bony arms were round him, and the pugilist was hurled into the air in a whirling cross-buttock,* coming down with a heavy thud upon the grass. The stranger stood back and folded his arms while Stevens scrambled to his feet with a red flush of anger upon his cheeks.

'Look here,' he cried. 'What sort of game is this?'

'We claim foul!' the Baronet shouted.

'Foul be damned! As clean a throw as ever I saw!' said the stout man. 'What rules do you fight under?'

'Queensberry, of course.'

'I never heard of it. It's London prize-ring* with us.'

'Come on, then!' cried Stevens, furiously. 'I can wrestle as well as another. You won't get me napping again.'

Nor did he. The next time that the stranger rushed in Stevens caught him in as strong a grip, and after swinging and swaying they came down together in a dog-fall.* Three times this occurred, and each time the stranger walked across to his friend and seated himself upon the grassy bank before he recommenced.

'What d'ye make of him?' the Baronet asked, in one of these pauses.

Stevens was bleeding from the ear, but otherwise showed no sign of damage.

'He knows a lot,' said the pugilist. 'I don't know where he learned it, but he's had a deal of practice somewhere. He's as strong as a lion and as hard as a board, for all his queer face.'

'Keep him at out-fighting.* I think you are his master there.'

'I'm not so sure that I'm his master anywhere, but I'll try my best.'

It was a desperate fight, and as round followed round it became clear, even to the amazed Baronet, that the middle-weight champion had met his match. The stranger had a clever draw and a rush which, with his springing hits, made him a most dangerous foe. His head and body seemed insensible to blows, and the horribly malignant smile never for one instant flickered from his lips. He hit very hard with fists like flints, and his blows whizzed up from every angle. He had one particularly deadly lead, an uppercut at the jaw, which again and again nearly came home, until at last it did actually fly past the guard and brought Stevens to the ground. The stout man gave a whoop of triumph.

'The whisker hit, by George! It's a horse to a hen on my Tommy! Another like that, lad, and you have him beat.'

'I say, Stevens, this is going too far,' said the Baronet, as he supported his weary man. 'What will the regiment say if I bring you up all knocked to pieces in a bye-battle!* Shake hands with this fellow and give him best, or you'll not be fit for your job.'

'Give him best? Not I!' cried Stevens, angrily. 'I'll knock that damned smile off his ugly mug before I've done.'

'What about the Sergeant?'

'I'd rather go back to London and never see the Sergeant than have my number taken down by this chap.'

'Well, 'ad enough?' his opponent asked, in a sneering voice, as he moved from his seat on the bank.

For answer young Stevens sprang forward and rushed at his man with all the strength that was left to him. By the fury of his onset he drove him back, and for a long minute had all the better of the exchanges. But this iron fighter seemed never to tire. His step was as quick and his blow as hard as ever when this long rally had ended. Stevens had eased up from pure exhaustion. But his opponent did not ease up. He came back on him with a shower of furious blows which beat down the weary guard of the pugilist. Alf Stevens was at the end of his strength and would in another instant have sunk to the ground but for a singular intervention.

It has been said that in their approach to the ring the party had passed through a grove of trees. Out of these there came a peculiar shrill cry, a cry of agony, which might be from a child or from some small woodland creature in distress. It was inarticulate, high-pitched and inexpressibly melancholy. At the sound the stranger, who had knocked Stevens on to his knees, staggered back and looked round him with an expression of helpless horror upon his face. The smile had left his lips and there only remained the loose-lipped weakness of a man in the last extremity of terror.

'It's after me again, mate!' he cried.

'Stick it out, Tom! You have him nearly beat! It can't hurt you.'

'It can 'urt me! It will 'urt me!' screamed the fighting man. 'My God! I can't face it! Ah, I see it! I see it!'

With a scream of fear he turned and bounded off into the brushwood.

His companion, swearing loudly, picked up the pile of clothes and darted after him, the dark shadows swallowing up their flying figures.

Stevens, half-senselessly, had staggered back and lay upon the grassy bank, his head pillowed upon the chest of the young Baronet, who was holding his flask of brandy to his lips. As they sat there they were both aware that the cries had become louder and shriller. Then from among the bushes there ran a small white terrier, nosing about as if following a trail and yelping most piteously. It squattered across the grassy sward, taking no notice of the two young men. Then it also vanished into the shadows. As it did so the two spectators sprang to their feet and ran as hard as they could tear for the gateway and the trap. Terror had seized them—a panic terror far above reason or control. Shivering and shaking, they threw themselves into the dog-cart, and it was not until the willing horses had put two good miles between that ill-omened hollow and themselves that they at last ventured to speak.

'Did you ever see such a dog?' asked the Baronet.

'No,' cried Stevens. 'And, please God, I never may again.'

Late that night the two travellers broke their journey at the Swan Inn, near Harpenden Common.* The landlord was an old acquaintance of the Baronet's, and gladly joined him in a glass of port after supper. A famous old sport was Mr Joc Horner, of the Swan, and he would talk by the hour of the legends of the ring, whether new or old. The name of Alf Stevens was well known to him, and he looked at him with the deepest interest.

'Why, sir, you have surely been fighting,' said he. 'I hadn't read of any engagement in the papers.'

'Enough said of that,' Stevens answered, in a surly voice.

'Well, no offence! I suppose'—his smiling face became suddenly very serious—'I suppose you didn't, by chance, see anything of him they call the Bully of Brocas as you came north?'

'Well, what if we did?'

The landlord was tense with excitement.

'It was him that nearly killed Bob Meadows. It was at the very gate of Brocas Old Hall that he stopped him. Another man was with him. Bob was game to the marrow, but he was found hit to pieces on the lawn inside the gate where the summer-house stands.'

The Baronet nodded.

'Ah, you've been there!' cried the landlord.

'Well, we may as well make a clean breast of it,' said the Baronet, looking at Stevens. 'We have been there, and we met the man you speak of—an ugly customer he is, too!'

'Tell me!' said the landlord, in a voice that sank to a whisper. 'Is it true what Bob Meadows says, that the men are dressed like our grand-fathers, and that the fighting man has his head all caved in?'

'Well, he was old-fashioned, certainly, and his head was the queer-est ever I saw.'

'God in Heaven!' cried the landlord. 'Do you know, sir, that Tom Hickman, the famous prize-fighter, together with his pal, Joe Rowe, a silversmith of the City, met his death at that very point in the year 1822, when he was drunk, and tried to drive on the wrong side of a wagon? Both were killed and the wheel of the wagon crushed in Hickman's forehead.'

'Hickman! Hickman!' said the Baronet. 'Not the gasman?'

'Yes, sir, they called him Gas. He won his fights with what they called the "whisker hit," and no one could stand against him until Neate—him that they called the Bristol Bull—brought him down.'

Stevens had risen from the table as white as cheese.

'Let's get out of this, sir. I want fresh air. Let us get on our way.'

The landlord clapped him on the back.

'Cheer up, lad! You've held him off, anyhow, and that's more than anyone else has ever done. Sit down and have another glass of wine, for if a man in England has earned it this night it is you. There's many a debt you would pay if you gave the Gasman a welting, whether dead or alive. Do you know what he did in this very room?'

The two travellers looked round with startled eyes at the lofty room, stone-flagged and oak-panelled, with great open grate at the farther end.

'Yes, in this very room. I had it from old Squire Scotter, who was here that very night. It was the day when Shelton beat Josh Hudson out St Albans way, and Gas had won a pocketful of money on the fight. He and his pal Rowe came in here upon their way, and he was mad-raging drunk. The folk fairly shrunk into the corners and under the tables, for he was stalkin' round with the great kitchen poker in his hand, and there was murder behind the smile upon his face. He was like that when the drink was in him—cruel, reckless, and a terror to the world. Well, what think you that he did at last with the poker? There was a little dog, a terrier as I've heard, coiled up before the fire, for it was a bitter December night. The Gasman broke its back with one blow of the poker. Then he burst out laughin', flung a curse or two at the folk that shrunk away from him, and so out to his high gig that was waiting outside. The next we heard was that he was carried down to Finchley with his head ground to a jelly by the wagon wheel. Yes, they do say the little dog with its bleeding skin and its broken back has been seen since then, crawlin' and yelpin' about Brocas Corner, as if it were lookin' for the swine that killed it. So you see, Mr Stevens, you were fightin' for more than yourself when you put it across the Gasman.'

'Maybe so,' said the young prize-fighter, 'but I want no more fights like that. The Farrier-Sergeant is good enough for me, sir, and if it is the same to you, we'll take a railway train back to town.'

THE NIGHTMARE ROOM

HE sitting-room of the Masons was a very singular apartment. At one end it was furnished with considerable luxury. The deep sofas, the low, luxurious chairs, the voluptuous statuettes, and the rich curtains hanging from deep and ornamental screens of metal-work made a fitting frame for the lovely woman who was the mistress of the establishment. Mason, a young but wealthy man of affairs, had clearly spared no pains and no expense to meet every want and every whim of his beautiful wife. It was natural that he should do so, for she had given up much for his sake. The most famous dancer in France, the heroine of a dozen extraordinary romances, she had resigned her life of glittering pleasure in order to share the fate of the young American, whose austere ways differed so widely from her own. In all that wealth could buy he tried to make amends for what she had lost. Some might perhaps have thought it in better taste had he not pro-claimed this fact—had he not even allowed it to be printed—but save for some personal peculiarities of the sort, his conduct was that of a husband who has never for an instant ceased to be a lover. Even the presence of spectators would not prevent the public exhibition of his overpowering affection.

But the room was singular. At first it seemed familiar, and yet a longer acquaintance made one realise its sinister peculiarities. It was silent—very silent. No footfall could be heard upon those rich car-pets and heavy rugs. A struggle—even the fall of a body—would make no sound. It was strangely colourless also, in a light which seemed always subdued. Nor was it all furnished in equal taste. One would have said that when the young banker had lavished thousands upon this boudoir, this inner jewel-case for his precious possession, he had failed to count the cost and had suddenly been arrested by a threat to his own solvency. It was luxurious where it looked out upon the busy street below. At the farther side it was bare, spartan, and reflected rather the taste of a most ascetic man than of a pleasure-loving woman. Perhaps that was why she only came there for a few hours, sometimes two, sometimes four, in the day, but while she was there she lived intensely, and within this nightmare room Lucille

Mason was a very different and a more dangerous woman than elsewhere.

Dangerous—that was the word. Who could doubt it who saw her delicate figure stretched upon the great bearskin which draped the sofa. She was leaning upon her right elbow, her delicate but determined chin resting upon her hand, while her eyes, large and languishing, adorable but inexorable, stared out in front of her with a fixed intensity which had in it something vaguely terrible. It was a lovely face—a child's face, and yet Nature had placed there some subtle mark, some indefinable expression, which told that a devil lurked within. It had been noticed that dogs shrank from her, and that children screamed and ran from her caresses. There are instincts which are deeper than reason.

Upon this particular afternoon something had greatly moved her. A letter was in her hand, which she read and re-read with a tightening of those delicate little eyebrows and a grim setting of those delicious lips. Suddenly she started, and a shadow of fear softened the feline menace of her features. She raised herself upon her arm, and her eyes were fixed eagerly upon the door. She was listening intently—listening for something which she dreaded. For a moment a smile of relief played over her expressive face. Then with a look of horror she stuffed her letter into her dress. She had hardly done so before the door opened, and a young man came briskly into the room. It was Archie Mason, her husband—the man whom she had loved, the man for whom she had sacrificed her European fame, the man whom now she regarded as the one obstacle to a new and wonderful experience.

* * *

The American was a man about thirty, clean-shaven, athletic, dressed to perfection in a closely-cut suit, which outlined his perfect figure. He stood at the door with his arms folded, looking intently at his wife, with a face which might have been a handsome, sun-tinted mask save for those vivid eyes. She still leaned upon her elbow, but her eyes were fixed on his. There was something terrible in the silent exchange. Each interrogated the other, and each conveyed the thought that the answer to their question was vital. He might have been asking, 'What have you done?' She in her turn seemed to be saying, 'What do you know?' Finally, he walked forward, sat down upon the bearskin beside her, and taking her delicate ear gently between his fingers, turned her face towards his.

'Lucille,' he said, 'are you poisoning me?'

She sprang back from his touch with horror in her face and protests upon her lips. Too moved to speak, her surprise and her anger showed themselves rather in her darting hands and her convulsed features. She tried to rise, but his grasp tightened upon her wrist. Again he asked a question, but this time it had deepened in its terrible significance.

'Lucille, why are you poisoning me?'

'You are mad, Archie! Mad!' she gasped.

His answer froze her blood. With pale parted lips and blanched cheeks she could only stare at him in helpless silence, whilst he drew a small bottle from his pocket and held it before her eyes.

'It is from your jewel-case!' he cried.

Twice she tried to speak and failed. At last the words came slowly one by one from her contorted lips:—

'At least I never used it.'

Again his hand sought his pocket. From it he drew a sheet of paper, which he unfolded and held before her.

'It is the certificate of Dr Angus. It shows the presence of twelve grains of antimony.* I have also the evidence of Du Val, the chemist who sold it.'

Her face was terrible to look at. There was nothing to say. She could only lie with that fixed hopeless stare like some fierce creature in a fatal trap.

'Well?' he asked.

There was no answer save a movement of desperation and appeal.

'Why?' he said. 'I want to know why.' As he spoke his eye caught the edge of the letter which she had thrust into her bosom. In an instant he had snatched it. With a cry of despair she tried to regain it, but he held her off with one hand while his eyes raced over it.

'Campbell!' he gasped. 'It was Campbell!'

She had found her courage again. There was nothing more to conceal. Her face set hard and firm. Her eyes were deadly as daggers.

'Yes,' she said, 'it is Campbell.'

'My God! Campbell of all men!'

He rose and walked swiftly about the room. Campbell, the grandest man that he had ever known, a man whose whole life had been one long record of self-denial, of courage, of every quality which marks the chosen man. And yet, he, too, had fallen a victim to this siren, and had been dragged down to such a level that he had betrayed, in intention if not in actual deed, the man whose hand he shook in friendship. It was incredible—and yet here was the passionate, pleading letter imploring his wife to fly and share the fate of a penniless man. Every word of the letter showed that Campbell had at least no thought of Mason's death, which would have removed all difficulties. That devilish solution was the outcome of the deep and wicked brain which brooded within that perfect habitation.

Mason was a man in a million, a philosopher, a thinker, with a broad and tender sympathy for others. For an instant his soul had been submerged in his bitterness. He could for that brief period have slain both his wife and Campbell, and gone to his own death with the serene mind of a man who has done his plain duty. But already, as he paced the room, milder thoughts had begun to prevail. How could he blame Campbell? He knew the absolute witchery of this woman. It was not only her wonderful physical beauty. She had a unique power of seeming to take an interest in a man, in writhing into his inmost conscience, in penetrating those parts of his nature which were too sacred for the world, and in seeming to stimulate him towards ambition and even towards virtue. It was just there that the deadly cleverness of her net was shown. He remembered how it had been in his own case. She was free then—or so he thought—and he had been able to marry her. But suppose she had not been free. Suppose she had been married. And suppose she had taken possession of his soul in the same way. Would he have stopped there? Would he have been able to draw off with his unfulfilled longings? He was bound to admit that with all his New England strength he could not have done so. Why, then, should he feel so bitter with his unfortunate friend who was in the same position? It was pity and sympathy which filled his mind as he thought of Campbell.

And she? There she lay upon the sofa, a poor broken butterfly, her dreams dispersed, her plot detected, her future dark and perilous. Even for her, poisoner as she was, his heart relented. He knew something of her history. He knew her as a spoiled child from birth, untamed, unchecked, sweeping everything easily before her from her cleverness, her beauty, and her charm. She had never known an obstacle. And now one had risen across her path, and she had madly and wickedly tried to remove it. But if she had wished to remove it, was not that in itself a sign that he had been found wanting—that he was not the man who could bring her peace of mind and contentment of heart? He was too stern and self-contained for that sunny volatile nature. He was of the North, and she of the South, drawn strongly together for a time by the law of opposites, but impossible for permanent union. He should have seen to this—he should have understood it. It was on him, with his superior brain, that the responsibility for the situation lay. His heart softened towards her as it would to a little child which was in helpless trouble. For a time he had paced the room in silence, his lips compressed, his hands clenched till his nails had marked his palms. Now with a sudden movement he sat beside her and took her cold and inert hand in his. One thought beat in his brain. 'Is it chivalry, or is it weakness?' The question sounded in his ears, it framed itself before his eyes, he could almost fancy that it materialised itself and that he saw it in letters which all the world could read.

It had been a hard struggle, but he had conquered.

'You shall choose between us, dear,' he said. 'If really you are sure—*sure*, you understand—that Campbell could make you happy as a husband, I will not be the obstacle.'

'A divorce!' she gasped.

His hand closed upon the bottle of poison. 'You can call it that,' said he.

A new strange light shone in her eyes as she looked at him. This was a man who had been unknown to her. The hard, practical American had vanished. In his place she seemed to have a glimpse of a hero, and a saint, a man who could rise to an inhuman height of unselfish virtue. Both her hands were round that which held the fatal phial.

'Archie,' she cried, 'you could forgive me even that!'

He smiled at her. 'You are only a little wayward kiddie after all.'

Her arms were outstretched to him when there was a tap at the door, and the maid entered in the strange silent fashion in which all things moved in that nightmare room. There was a card on the tray. She glanced at it.

'Captain Campbell! I will not see him.'

Mason sprang to his feet.

'On the contrary, he is most welcome. Show him up this instant.'

* * *

A few minutes later a tall, sun-burned young soldier had been ushered into the room. He came forward with a smile upon his pleasant features, but as the door closed behind him, and the faces before him resumed their natural expressions, he paused irresolutely and glanced from one to the other.

'Well?' he asked.

Mason stepped forward and laid his hand upon his shoulder.

'I bear no ill-will,' he said.

'Ill-will?'

'Yes, I know all. But I might have done the same myself had the position been reversed.'

Campbell stepped back and looked a question at the lady. She nodded and shrugged her graceful shoulders. Mason smiled.

'You need not fear that it is a trap for a confession. We have had a frank talk upon the matter. See, Jack, you were always a sportsman. Here's a bottle. Never mind how it came here. If one or other of us drink it, it would clear the situation.' His manner was wild, almost delirious. 'Lucille, which shall it be?'

There had been a strange force at work in the nightmare room. A third man was there, though not one of the three who had stood in the crisis of their life's drama had time or thought for him. How long he had been there—how much he had heard—none could say. In the corner farthest from the little group he lay crouched against the wall, a sinister snake-like figure, silent and scarcely moving save for a nervous twitching of his clenched right hand. He was concealed from view by a square case and by a dark cloth drawn cunningly above it, so as to screen his features. Intent, watching eagerly every new phase of the drama, the moment had almost come for his intervention. But the three thought little of that. Absorbed in the interplay of their own emotions they had lost sight of a force stronger than themselves— a force which might at any moment dominate the scene.

'Are you game, Jack?' asked Mason.

The soldier nodded.

'No!—for God's sake, no!' cried the woman.

Mason had uncorked the bottle, and turning to the side table he drew out a pack of cards. Cards and bottle stood together.

'We can't put the responsibility on her,' he said. 'Come, Jack, the best of three.'

The soldier approached the table. He fingered the fatal cards. The woman, leaning upon her hand, bent her face forward and stared with fascinated eyes.

* * *

Then and only then the bolt fell.

The stranger had risen, pale and grave.

All three were suddenly aware of his presence. They faced him with eager inquiry in their eyes. He looked at them coldly, sadly, with something of the master in his bearing.

'How is it?' they asked, all together.

'Rotten!' he answered. 'Rotten! We'll take the whole reel once more to-morrow.'

THE LIFT

FLIGHT-COMMANDER STANGATE should have been happy. He had come safely through the war without a hurt, and with a good name in the most heroic of services. He had only just turned thirty, and a great career seemed to lie ahead of him. Above all, beautiful Mary MacLean was walking by his side, and he had her promise that she was there for life. What could a young man ask for more? And yet there was a heavy load upon his heart.

He could not explain it himself, and endeavoured to reason himself out of it. There was the blue sky above him, the blue sea in front, the beautiful gardens with their throngs of happy pleasure-seekers around. Above all, there was that sweet face turned upon his with questioning concern. Why could he not raise himself to so joyful an environment? He made effort after effort, but they were not convincing enough to deceive the quick instinct of a loving woman.

'What is it, Tom?' she asked anxiously. 'I can see that something is clouding you. Do tell me if I can help you in any way.'

He laughed in shamefaced fashion.

'It is such a sin to spoil our little outing,' he said. 'I could kick myself round these gardens when I think of it. Don't worry, my darling, for I know the cloud will roll off. I suppose I am a creature of nerves, though I should have got past that by now. The Flying Service* is supposed either to break you or to warrant you for life.'

'It is nothing definite, then?'

'No, it is nothing definite. That's the worst of it. You could fight it more easily if it was. It's just a dead, heavy depression here in my chest and across my forehead. But do forgive me, dear girl! What a brute I am to shadow you like this.'

'But I love to share even the smallest trouble.'

'Well, it's gone—vamosed*—vanished. We will talk about it no more.'

She gave him a swift, penetrating glance.

'No, no, Tom; your brow shows, as well as feels. Tell me, dear, have you often felt like this? You really look very ill. Sit here, dear, in the shade and tell me of it.'

They sat together in the shadow of the great, latticed Tower* which reared itself six hundred feet high beside them.

'I have an absurd faculty,' said he; 'I don't know that I have ever mentioned it to anyone before. But when imminent danger is threatening me I get these strange forebodings. Of course it is absurd to-day in these peaceful surroundings. It only shows how queerly these things work. But it is the first time that it has deceived me.'

'When had you it before?'

'When I was a lad it seized me one morning. I was nearly drowned that afternoon. I had it when the burglar came to Morton Hall and I got a bullet through my coat. Then twice in the war when I was overmatched and escaped by a miracle, I had this strange feeling before ever I climbed into my machine. Then it lifts quite suddenly, like a mist in the sunshine. Why, it is lifting now. Look at me! Can't you see that it is so?'

She could indeed. He had turned in a minute from a haggard man to a laughing boy. She found herself laughing in sympathy. A rush of high spirits and energy had swept away his strange foreboding and filled his whole soul with the vivid, dancing joy of youth.

'Thank goodness!' he cried. 'I think it is your dear eyes that have done it. I could not stand that wistful look in them. What a silly, foolish nightmare it all has been! There's an end for ever in my belief in presentiments. Now, dear girl, we have just time for one good turn before luncheon. After that the gardens get so crowded that it is hopeless to do anything. Shall we have a side-show, or the great wheel, or the flying boat, or what?'

'What about the Tower?' she asked, glancing upwards. 'Surely that glorious air and the view from the top would drive the last wisps of cloud out of your mind.'

He looked at his watch.

'Well, it's past twelve, but I suppose we could do it all in an hour. But it doesn't seem to be working. What about it, conductor?'

The man shook his head and pointed to a little knot of people who were assembled at the entrance.

'They've all been waiting, sir. It's hung up, but the gear is being overhauled, and I expect the signal every minute. If you join the others I promise it won't be long.'

They had hardly reached the group when the steel face of the lift rolled aside—a sign that there was hope in the future. The motley crowd drifted through the opening and waited expectantly upon the wooden platform. They were not numerous, for the gardens are not crowded until the afternoon, but they were fair samples of the kindly, good-humoured north-country folk who take their annual holiday at Northam.* Their faces were all upturned now, and they were watching with keen interest a man who was descending the steel framework. It seemed a dangerous, precarious business, but he came as swiftly as an ordinary mortal upon a staircase.

'My word!' said the conductor, glancing up. 'Jim has got a move on this morning.'

'Who is he?' asked Commander Stangate.

'That's Jim Barnes, sir, the best workman that ever went on a scaffold. He fair lives up there. Every bolt and rivet are under his care. He's a wonder, is Jim.'

'But don't argue religion with him,' said one of the group.

The attendant laughed.

'Ah, you know him, then,' said he. 'No, don't argue religion with him.'

'Why not?' asked the officer.

'Well, he takes it very hard, he does. He's the shining light of his sect.'

'It ain't hard to be that,' said the knowing one. 'I've heard there are only six folk in the fold. He's one of those who picture heaven as the exact size of their own back street conventicle* and everyone else left outside it.'

'Better not tell him so while he's got that hammer in his hand,' said the conductor, in a hurried whisper. 'Hallo, Jim, how goes it this morning?'

The man slid swiftly down the last thirty feet, and then balanced himself on a cross-bar while he looked at the little group in the lift. As he stood there, clad in a leather suit, with his pliers and other tools dangling from his brown belt, he was a figure to please the eye of an artist. The man was very tall and gaunt, with great, straggling limbs and every appearance of giant strength. His face was a remarkable one, noble and yet sinister, with dark eyes and hair, a prominent, hooked nose, and a beard which flowed over his chest. He steadied himself with one knotted hand, while the other held a steel hammer dangling by his knee.

'It's all ready aloft,' said he. 'I'll go up with you if I may.' He sprang down from his perch and joined the others in the lift.

'I suppose you are always watching it,' said the young lady.

'That is what I am engaged for, miss. From morning to night, and often from night to morning, I am up here. There are times when I feel as if I were not a man at all, but a fowl of the air. They fly round me, the creatures, as I lie out on the girders, and they cry to me until I find myself crying back to the poor, soulless things.'

'It's a great charge,' said the Commander, glancing up at the wonderful tracery of steel outlined against the deep blue sky.

'Aye, sir, and there is not a nut nor a screw that is not in my keeping. Here's my hammer to ring them true and my spanner to wrench them tight. As the Lord over the earth, so am I—even I—over the Tower, with power of life and power of death, aye of death and of life.'

The hydraulic machinery had begun to work and the lift very slowly ascended. As it mounted, the glorious panorama of the coast and bay gradually unfolded itself. So engrossing was the view that the passengers hardly noticed it when the platform stopped abruptly between stages at the five hundred foot level. Barnes, the workman, muttered that something must be amiss, and springing like a cat across the gap which separated them from the trellis-work of metal he clambered out of sight. The motley little party, suspended in mid-air, lost something of their British shyness under such unwonted conditions and began to compare notes with each other. One couple, who addressed each other as Dolly and Billy, announced to the company that they were the particular stars of the Hippodrome* bill, and kept their neighbours tittering with their rather obvious wit. A buxom mother, her precocious son, and two married couples upon holiday formed an appreciative audience.

'You'd like to be a sailor, would you?' said Billy the comedian, in answer to some remark of the boy. 'Look 'ere, my nipper, you'll end up as a blooming corpse if you ain't careful. See 'im standin' at the edge. At this hour of the morning I can't bear to watch it.'

'What's the hour got to do with it?' asked a stout commercial traveller.

'My nerves are worth nothin' before midday. Why, lookin' down there, and seein' those folk like dots, puts me all in a twitter. My family is all alike in the mornin'.'

'I expect,' said Dolly, a high-coloured young woman, 'that they're all alike the evening before.'

There was a general laugh, which was led by the comedian.

'You got it across that time, Dolly. It's KO for Battling Billy*—still senseless when last heard of. If my family is laughed at I'll leave the room.'

'It's about time we did,' said the commercial traveller, who was a red-faced, choleric person. 'It's a disgrace the way they hold us up. I'll write to the company.'

'Where's the bell-push?' said Billy. 'I'm goin' to ring.'

'What for—the waiter?' asked the lady.

'For the conductor, the chauffeur, whoever it is that drives the old bus up and down. Have they run out of petrol, or broke the main-spring, or what?'

'We have a fine view, anyhow,' said the Commander.

'Well, I've had that,' remarked Billy. 'I'm done with it, and I'm for getting on.'

'I'm getting nervous,' cried the stout mother. 'I do hope there is nothing wrong with the lift.'

'I say, hold on to the slack of my coat, Dolly. I'm going to look over and chance it. Oh, Lord, it makes me sick and giddy! There's a horse down under, and it ain't bigger than a mouse. I don't see anyone lookin' after us. Where's old Isaiah the prophet* who came up with us?'

'He shinned out of it mighty quick when he thought trouble was coming.'

'Look here,' said Dolly, looking very perturbed, 'this is a nice thing, I don't think. Here we are five hundred foot up, and stuck for the day as like as not. I'm due for the *matinée* at the Hippodrome. I'm sorry for the company if they don't get me down in time for that. I'm billed all over the town for a new song.'

'A new one! What's that, Dolly?'

'A real pot o' ginger, I tell you. It's called "On the Road to Ascot." I've got a hat four foot across to sing it in.'

'Come on, Dolly, let's have a rehearsal while we wait.'

'No, no; the young lady here wouldn't understand.'

'I'd be very glad to hear it,' cried Mary MacLean. 'Please don't let me prevent you.'

'The words were written to the hat. I couldn't sing the verses with-out the hat. But there's a nailin' good chorus to it:

> ' "If you want a little mascot
> When you're on the way to Ascot,
> Try the lady with the cartwheel hat." '

She had a tuneful voice and a sense of rhythm which set everyone nodding. 'Try it now all together,' she cried; and the strange little haphazard company sang it with all their lungs.

'I say,' said Billy, 'that ought to wake somebody up. What? Let's try a shout all together.'

It was a fine effort, but there was no response. It was clear that the management down below was quite ignorant or impotent. No sound came back to them.

The passengers became alarmed. The commercial traveller was rather less rubicund. Billy still tried to joke, but his efforts were not well received. The officer in his blue uniform at once took his place as rightful leader in a crisis. They all looked to him and appealed to him.

'What would you advise, sir? You don't think there's any danger of it coming down, do you?'

'Not the least. But it's awkward to be stuck here all the same. I think I could jump across on to that girder. Then perhaps I could see what is wrong.'

'No, no, Tom; for goodness' sake, don't leave us!'

'Some people have a nerve,' said Billy. 'Fancy jumping across a five-hundred-foot drop!'

'I dare say the gentleman did worse things in the war.'

'Well, I wouldn't do it myself—not if they starred me in the bills. It's all very well for old Isaiah. It's his job, and I wouldn't do him out of it.'

Three sides of the lift were shut in with wooden partitions, pierced with windows for the view. The fourth side, facing the sea, was clear. Stangate leaned over as far as he could and looked upwards. As he did so there came from above him a peculiar, sonorous, metallic twang, as if a mighty harp-string had been struck. Some distance up—a hundred feet, perhaps—he could see a long, brown, corded arm, which was working furiously among the wire cordage above. The form was beyond his view, but he was fascinated by this bare, sinewy arm which tugged and pulled and sagged and stabbed.

'It's all right,' he said, and a general sigh of relief broke from his strange comrades at his words. 'There is someone above us setting things right.'

'It's old Isaiah,' said Billy, stretching his neck round the corner. 'I can't see him, but it's his arm for a dollar. What's he got in his hand? Looks like a screwdriver or something. No, by George, it's a file.'

As he spoke there came another sonorous twang from above. There was a troubled frown upon the officer's brow.

'I say, dash it all, that's the very sound our steel hawser made when it parted, strand by strand, at Dixmude. What the deuce is the fellow about? Heh, there! what are you trying to do?'

The man had ceased his work and was now slowly descending the iron trellis.

'All right, he's coming,' said Stangate to his startled companions. 'It's all right, Mary. Don't be frightened, any of you. It's absurd to suppose he would really weaken the cord that holds us.'

A pair of high boots appeared from above. Then came the leathern breeches, the belt with its dangling tools, the muscular form, and, finally, the fierce, swarthy, eagle face of the workman. His coat was off and his shirt open showing the hairy chest. As he appeared there came another sharp, snapping vibration from above. The man made his way down in leisurely fashion, and then, balancing himself upon the cross-girder and leaning against the side piece, he stood with folded arms, looking from under his heavy black brows at the huddled passengers upon the platform.

'Hallo!' said Stangate. 'What's the matter?'

The man stood impassive and silent, with something indescribably menacing in his fixed, unwinking stare.

The flying officer grew angry.

'Hallo! Are you deaf?' he cried. 'How long do you mean to have us stuck here?'

The man stood silent. There was something devilish in his appearance.

'I'll complain of you, my lad,' said Billy, in a quivering voice. 'This won't stop here, I can promise you.'

'Look here!' cried the officer. 'We have ladies here and you are alarming them. Why are we stuck here? Has the machinery gone wrong?'

'You are here,' said the man, 'because I have put a wedge against the hawser above you.'

'You fouled the line! How dared you do such a thing! What right have you to frighten the women and put us all to this inconvenience? Take that wedge out this instant, or it will be the worse for you.'

The man was silent.

'Do you hear what I say? Why the devil don't you answer? Is this a joke or what? We've had about enough of it, I tell you.'

Mary MacLean had gripped her lover by the arm in an agony of sudden panic.

'Oh, Tom!' she cried. 'Look at his eyes—look at his horrible eyes! The man is a maniac.'

The workman stirred suddenly into sinister life. His dark face broke into writhing lines of passion, and his fierce eyes glowed like embers, while he shook one long arm in the air.

'Behold,' he cried, 'those who are mad to the children of this world are in very truth the Lord's anointed and the dwellers in the inner temple. Lo, I am one who is prepared to testify even to the uttermost, for of a verity the day has now come when the humble will be exalted and the wicked will be cut off in their sins!'

'Mother! Mother!' cried the little boy, in terror.

'There, there! It's all right, Jack,' said the buxom woman, and then, in a burst of womanly wrath, 'What d'you want to make the child cry for? You're a pretty man, you are!'

'Better he should cry now than in the outer darkness. Let him seek safety while there is yet time.'

The officer measured the gap with a practised eye. It was a good eight feet across, and the fellow could push him over before he could steady himself. It would be a desperate thing to attempt. He tried soothing words once more.

'See here, my lad, you've carried this joke too far. Why should you wish to injure us? Just shin up and get that wedge out, and we will agree to say no more about it.'

Another rending snap came from above.

'By George, the hawser is going!' cried Stangate. 'Here! Stand aside! I'm coming over to see to it.'

The workman had plucked the hammer from his belt, and waved it furiously in the air.

'Stand back, young man! Stand back! Or come—if you would hasten your end.'

'Tom, Tom, for God's sake, don't spring! Help! Help!'

The passengers all joined in the cry for aid. The man smiled malignly as he watched them.

'There is no one to help. They could not come if they would. You would be wiser to turn to your own souls that ye be not cast to the burning. Lo, strand by strand the cable snaps which holds you. There is yet another, and with each that goes there is more strain upon the rest. Five minutes of time, and all eternity beyond.'

A moan of fear rose from the prisoners in the lift. Stangate felt a cold sweat upon his brow as he passed his arm round the shrinking girl. If this vindictive devil could only be coaxed away for an instant he would spring across and take his chance in a hand-to-hand fight.

'Look here, my friend! We give you best!' he cried. 'We can do nothing. Go up and cut the cable if you wish. Go on—do it now, and get it over!'

'That you may come across unharmed. Having set my hand to the work, I will not draw back from it.'

Fury seized the young officer.

'You devil!' he cried. 'What do you stand there grinning for? I'll give you something to grin about. Give me a stick, one of you.'

The man waved his hammer.

'Come, then! Come to judgment!' he howled.

'He'll murder you, Tom! Oh, for God's sake, don't! If we must die, let us die together.'

'I wouldn't try it, sir,' cried Billy. 'He'll strike you down before you get a footing. Hold up, Dolly, my dear! Faintin' won't 'elp us. You speak to him, miss. Maybe he'll listen to you.'

'Why should you wish to hurt us?' said Mary. 'What have we ever done to you? Surely you will be sorry afterwards if we are injured. Now do be kind and reasonable and help us to get back to the ground.'

For a moment there may have been some softening in the man's fierce eyes as he looked at the sweet face which was upturned to him. Then his features set once more into their grim lines of malice.

'My hand is set to the work, woman. It is not for the servant to look back from his task.'

'But why should this be your task?'

'Because there is a voice within me which tells me so. In the night-time I have heard it, and in the day-time, too, when I have lain out alone upon the girders and seen the wicked dotting the streets beneath me, each busy on his own evil intent. "John Barnes, John Barnes,"* said the voice. "You are here that you may give a sign to a sinful generation—such a sign as shall show them that the Lord liveth and that there is a judgment upon sin." Who am I that I should disobey the voice of the Lord?'

'The voice of the devil,' said Stangate. 'What is the sin of this lady, or of these others, that you should seek their lives?'

'You are as the others, neither better nor worse. All day they pass me, load by load, with foolish cries and empty songs and vain babble of voices. Their thoughts are set upon the things of the flesh. Too long have I stood aside and watched and refused to testify. But now the day of wrath is come and the sacrifice is ready. Think not that a woman's tongue can turn me from my task.'

'It is useless!' Mary cried. 'Useless! I read death in his eyes.'

Another cord had snapped.

'Repent! Repent!' cried the madman. 'One more, and it is over!'

Commander Stangate felt as if it were all some extraordinary dream—some monstrous nightmare. Could it be possible that he, after all his escapes of death in warfare, was now, in the heart of peaceful England, at the mercy of a homicidal lunatic, and that his dear girl, the one being whom he would shield from the very shadow of danger, was helpless before this horrible man? All his energy and manhood rose up in him for one last effort.

'Here, we won't be killed like sheep in the shambles!'* he cried, throwing himself against the wooden wall of the lift and kicking with all his force. 'Come on, boys! Kick it! Beat it! It's only match-boarding, and it is giving. Smash it down! Well done! Once more all together! There she goes! Now for the side! Out with it! Splendid!'

First the back and then the side of the little compartment had been knocked out, and the splinters dropped down into the abyss. Barnes danced upon his girder his hammer in the air.

'Strive not!' he shrieked. 'It avails not. The day is surely come.'

'It's not two feet from the side-girder,' cried the officer. 'Get across! Quick! Quick! All of you. I'll hold this devil off!' He had seized a stout stick from the commercial traveller and faced the madman, daring him to spring across.

'Your turn now, my friend!' he hissed. 'Come on, hammer and all! I'm ready for you.'

Above him he heard another snap, and the frail platform began to rock. Glancing over his shoulder, he saw that his companions were all safe upon the side-girder. A strange line of terrified castaways they appeared as they clung in an ungainly row to the trellis-work of steel. But their feet were on the iron support. With two quick steps and a spring he was at their side. At the same instant the murderer, hammer in hand, jumped the gap. They had one vision of him there— a vision which will haunt their dreams—the convulsed face, the blazing eyes, the wind-tossed, raven locks. For a moment he balanced himself upon the swaying platform. The next, with a rending crash, he and it were gone. There was a long silence and then, far down, the thud and clatter of a mighty fall

* * *

With white faces, the forlorn group clung to the cold steel bars and gazed down into the terrible abyss. It was the Commander who broke the silence.

'They'll send for us now. It's all safe,' he cried, wiping his brow. 'But, by Jove, it was a close call!'

EXPLANATORY NOTES

ACD   Arthur Conan Doyle
CDS   *The Conan Doyle Stories* (1929)
EB   *Encyclopædia Britannica*
GDS   *Green's Dictionary of Slang*
Lycett   Andrew Lycett, *Conan Doyle: The Man Who Created Sherlock Holmes* (London, 2007)
OED   *Oxford English Dictionary*
US   *The Unknown Conan Doyle: Uncollected Stories*, ed. John Michael Gibson and Roger Lancelyn Green (1982)

All references to Shakespeare are to *The Oxford Shakespeare: The Complete Works*, ed. Stanley Wells and Gary Taylor (2nd edn., Oxford, 2005); those to the Bible are to the King James Version unless otherwise stated.

THE AMERICAN'S TALE

First published in *London Society* (Christmas number, 1880). Reprinted in *US*. The text used here is the *London Society* original.

3 *Hudson Bay men*: Hudson Bay, in the far north-east of Canada, was named in honour of the explorer Henry Hudson (*c*.1565–*c*.1611), who discovered and sailed across the bay in 1610 while searching for the North-West Passage, a fabled trade route to the Orient. The Hudson's Bay Company, incorporated in 1670, controlled most of the trade and commerce in the Hudson Bay area.

4 *Walker's filibusters*: filibustering originally referred to the American practice of colonizing adjacent territories through privately financed endeavours. Jefferson Adams has served with the most notorious American filibuster, William Walker (1824–60), who organized invasions of Baja California (1853) and Nicaragua (1855), where he set himself up as a dictator and was briefly recognized as such by the American government. In contemporary parlance, a filibuster is a delaying tactic, generally in the American Senate, in which a politician stalls the passing of legislation by talking and refusing to leave the floor until the bill is timed out.

"Greasers": in this context, a greaser is 'A native Mexican or native Spanish American: originally applied contemptuously by Americans in the South Western United States to the Mexicans' (*OED*).

'*Dianœa muscipula*': the Venus flytrap, a carnivorous plant, originally native to the Carolinas in the USA. ACD's flytraps are gigantic exaggerations: the actual carnivorous leaves of the Venus flytrap rarely exceed 6 inches in length.

4 *out and outer*: 'a thoroughgoing criminal or cheat' (*OED*).

5 *Chartist*: a political radical. Chartism was a movement for British parliamentary reform, largely working-class, and named after the 'People's Charter', a bill drafted in 1838 by William Lovett. Chartism flourished across the 1840s, often attracting large-scale support. Many Chartist leaders were transported, imprisoned, or driven into exile.

bowie: a large hunting knife, double-edged near the point, named after the Texan revolutionary hero Jim Bowie (*c.*1796–1836), killed at the Battle of the Alamo.

iron: revolver.

6 *Derringer*: a small, short-range pistol, often carried as a concealed weapon; named after its inventor, the gunsmith Henry Derringer (1786–1868).

7 *serapé*: serape, 'A shawl or plaid worn by Spanish-Americans' (*OED*).

8 *Judge Lynch*: lynching is summary justice, generally hanging without trial. The term was named after John and Charles Lynch, who in 1757 founded the township of Lynchburg, Virginia, where Charles set up an irregular court dispensing anti-British justice. He is the original Judge Lynch.

THE CAPTAIN OF THE 'POLESTAR'

First published in *Temple Bar* (January 1883); reprinted in *Dreamland and Ghostland*, vol. iii (October 1887), in *'The Captain of the Pole-Star' and Other Tales* (London, 1890), and in *CDS*. The text here is taken from *CDS*.

10 *Lat. 81° 40′ N.; long. 2° E.*: the *Polestar* is in the far northern waters, in the middle of the Greenland Sea, about halfway between Greenland and Spitsbergen.

Amsterdam Island...Spitzbergen: Spitsbergen is the largest island in the Svalbard archipelago, lying some 500 miles off the northern coast of Norway. Its capital, Longyearbyen, is the northernmost city in the world. Amsterdam Island, as Doyle notes, is a tiny island off the north-west coast of Spitsbergen.

whaler: like John M'Allister, as a young medic in 1880 Doyle himself worked as a doctor on board a whaling ship, the *Hope*. 'The Captain of the "Polestar"' is in part the product of this whaling voyage, during which time he also worked on a lost story entitled 'A Journey to the Pole' (Lycett, 71).

11 *Dundee*: maritime city on the east coast of Scotland, and from 1753 one of the major centres of the Scottish whaling industry.

13 *Pepys*: Samuel Pepys (1633–1703), English diarist. Pepys habitually closed his diary entries with the phrase 'And so to bed.'

distrait: 'Distracted in mind; excessively perplexed or troubled' (*OED*).

'fey': generally means magical or fairylike, but with a particular Scots usage of 'Fated to die; doomed to death' (*OED*).

14 *chloral and bromide of potassium*: both chloral (trichloroacetaldehyde) and potassium bromide were widely used as sedatives in the nineteenth century.

four bells in the middle watch: shipboard time is traditionally told by the ringing of bells every half hour. A ship's middle watch runs from midnight to 4 a.m, 'Four bells in the middle watch' is 2 a.m.

fo'c'sle-head: the forecastle (pronounced fo'c'sle) is the ship's upper deck in front of the foreward mast; traditionally the quarters of ordinary seamen, hence the term 'before the mast'.

I'll stake my davy: 'I'll stake my word', or 'I'll stake my oath'; 'davy' is a shortening of 'affidavit'.

15 *Medusæ and sea-lemons*: a medusa is a kind of jellyfish; sea lemons are a variety of sea slug.

the last Russian and Turkish War: there were a number of Russo-Turkish wars, from the sixteenth to the twentieth centuries; this particular war is the Russo-Turkish War of 1877–8, which ended with Russian control of the Caucasus.

16 *impassable*: impassive.

17 *ratlines*: ropes or cords used to mark out an area.

19 *'Yon puir beastie . . . you nor me!'*: 'That poor creature knows more, yes, and sees more than either you or me!' (Scots).

Scotsman: influential Scottish daily newspaper, first published in Edinburgh in 1817, and still going strong.

20 *haricot mutton*: a hash of mutton and turnips.

piped: a ship's crew was traditionally summoned on deck by the blowing of the boatswain's pipe.

on the parish: in receipt of financial aid administered by the church.

21 *oleographs*: chromolithographs; a medium for the colour reproduction of photographs, developed across the nineteenth century.

æt.: a shortening of 'Anno aet'; 'aged'.

22 *Aristotle and Plato*: both Aristotle (384–322 BC) and Plato (*c.*428–*c.*348 BC) offered early arguments for the immortality of the soul, Aristotle in *De Anima* (*On the Soul*) and Plato in the *Phaedo*.

metempsychosis . . . Pythagoras: metempsychosis is the philosophical doctrine of the transmigration of souls, of which the Greek mathematician and philosopher Pythagoras of Samos (*c.*570–*c.*495 BC) was a celebrated advocate.

the impostures of Slade: Henry Slade (1835–1905), fraudulent American medium, whom ACD was later to defend in *The History of Spiritualism*.

Bogie: bogey; a goblin or other supernatural fiend.

22 *Peterhead*: fishing port in Aberdeenshire, Scotland. The *Hope* (see note to p. 52) sailed from Peterhead.

waur: worse (Scots).

clavers: idle stories (Scots); 'aud wives clavers' are 'old wives' tales', or gossip.

24 *quarter-boat*: a small boat hanging from the side of a ship.

tympanum: eardrum.

25 *skirling*: shrieking (Scots).

bladder-nosed seals: hooded seals of the genus *Cystaphora* ('bladder-bearer'), named after the inflatable bladder on the adult male's head.

26 *Jan Meyen*: Jan Mayen, a volcanic island south-west of Svalbard.

27 *I fear me*: 'I fear not', or 'I doubt it'.

choreic: Sydenham's chorea, popularly known as St Vitus's dance, is a convulsive disorder characterized by involuntary movement of the limbs.

poop: the poop deck is the rearmost part of a ship.

taffrail: the rearmost part of the poop deck.

31 *Saltash, in Devonshire*: the town of Saltash is actually just over the border, in Cornwall.

THE WINNING SHOT

First published in *Bow Bells*, 11 July 1883. Reprinted in *Dreamland and Ghostland*, vol. iii (October 1887). First book appearance in *US*. The text here is taken from *Bow Bells*.

32 *the pestilence that walketh at noonday*: an adaptation of Psalm 91:6: '*Nor* for the pestilence *that* walketh in darkness; nor for the destruction *that* wasteth at noonday.'

Lincoln's Inn: one of the four Inns of Court, the professional societies of barristers traditionally responsible for the teaching of law (the others are the Middle and Inner Temple and Gray's Inn). The Inns of Court are all near to the Royal Courts of Justice in Holborn, central London. Lincoln's Inn was founded *c.* 1422, and is believed to be named after Henry De Lacey, 3rd Earl of Lincoln.

33 *Roborough*: village in south Devon, near to the border with Cornwall.

Long Vacation: the summer vacation in universities and law courts.

Crockford's and Tattersall's: Crockford's was a gentleman's club in St James's, London, founded in 1823, and with a reputation for gambling. Crockford's itself closed in 1845, but from 1874 to 1976 its building (50 St James's Street) was home to the Devonshire Club. Given the location of the story, it is fitting that Nicholas Underwood should be a member of the

Devonshire Club. Tattersall's, founded in 1776, and now based in New-market, Suffolk, is the foremost British auctioneer of racehorses.

the Liberal Administration: specifically, this refers to the second Gladstone government of 1880–5. The Liberal politician William Ewart Gladstone (1809–98) was British prime minister four times (1868–74, 1880–5, 1886, 1892–4).

Irish question: Irish Home Rule, a political issue which was to occupy all four Gladstone governments. The second Gladstone government oversaw the passing of the Irish Coercion Act, which allowed for imprisonment without trial, the Kilmainham Treaty, in which the nationalist leader Charles Stewart Parnell and the Irish Land League secured important concessions for exploited tenant farmers, and the Phoenix Park Murders, in which senior British administrators were murdered by Fenian activists. The attempt to introduce the first Irish Home Rule Bill of 1886 brought down the third Gladstone government. ACD, of Irish Catholic parentage, was initially (and at the time of writing 'The Winning Shot') an opponent of Irish Home Rule, but modified his position later in life.

35 *gloaming*: twilight.

  Tavistock: market town on the edge of Dartmoor, Devon; 2 miles from Roborough.

36 *the moor*: Dartmoor, a large expanse of moorland in south Devon. The location of a number of stone circles and other prehistoric sites, Dartmoor has long been associated with folklore and supernatural activity. Most famously in the works of ACD, Dartmoor is the location for *The Hound of the Baskervilles*.

  Plymouth 'leat': (or Drake's Leat) a sixteenth-century watercourse built to supply water to Plymouth.

38 *Cape Blanco to Canary*: Ras Nouadhibou, formerly known as Cabo Blanco, or Cap Blanc, is a peninsula in what is now the disputed territory of Western Sahara, south of Morocco, on the north-west coast of Africa; the Canary Islands are off the coast of north-west Africa, some 500 miles north of Ras Nouadhibou.

39 *Upsala*: Uppsala, a medieval city in central Sweden.

41 *Crimea*: the Crimean Peninsula, on the Black Sea; as an important location for East–West trade routes, Crimea has long been, and remains, a disputed territory. Col. Pillar is a veteran of the Crimean War (1852–6), in which Britain and France both fought as part of a victorious alliance with the Ottoman Empire against the Russian Empire.

  Cantab: Cantabrigian, a member or graduate of Cambridge University.

42 *cicatrix*: cicatrice; scar.

45 *fête champêtre*: 'An outdoor entertainment, a rural festival' (*OED*).

  the Lover's Leap, or Black Tor, or Beer Ferris Abbey: all Dartmoor landmarks. Lover's Leap is a rapid on the River Dart. There are three Black Tors on Dartmoor, though this is most likely a reference to Black Tor near Walkhampton, on the south-west of the moor. Beer Ferris, properly Bere Ferrers, is also on the south-west of the moor. There is no abbey, though Bere Ferrers does have a celebrated medieval parish church.

47 *Tromsberg*: there is no Tromsberg, though ACD may have meant Tromsø, a port city on the northern coast of Norway.

chef-d'œuvre: masterpiece.

48 *Steinberg... Madame Crowe... Gustav von Spee... Home*: Catherine Crowe (1803–76) was an English novelist and writer on the supernatural, whose collection of supernatural lore, *The Night Side of Nature* (2 vols., 1848), was one of the most high-profile nineteenth-century studies of the supernatural. Daniel Dunglas Home (1833–86) was a Scottish medium, probably the most famous spiritualist of the Victorian era, allegedly able to perform feats of levitation, including reportedly levitating out of windows. Steinberg and Gustav von Spee are unidentified, and do not appear in any of ACD's later writings on spiritualism.

52 *hankey-pankey*: 'Jugglery, legerdemain; trickery, double-dealing, underhand dealing' (*OED*).

53 *as the cook says in 'Pickwick'*: a misremembered quotation from Charles Dickens's *Pickwick Papers* (1837–8). In chapter 23, Sam Weller says, 'It's over, and can't be helped, and that's one consolation, as they always says in Turkey, ven they cuts the wrong man's head off.'

54 *From the Eddystone to the Start*: Eddystone Rocks and Start Point are both lighthouses off the south Devon coast.

55 *sweetmeat*: as well as being the centre of a target, a bullseye was a large, round boiled sweet.

59 *een... moo*: eyes; mouth.

hydropathics: garbled version of hydrophobia, or rabies. Hydrophobia (fear of water) is one of the symptoms of the disease, which affects the throat, causing great difficulty and pain in swallowing.

60 *Martell's three-star brandy*: Martell, one of the major manufacturers of cognac, was founded by Jean Martell in 1715, and is still very much in business.

J. HABAKUK JEPHSON'S STATEMENT

First published in the *Cornhill Magazine* (January 1884). Reprinted in *Dreamland and Ghostland*, and in *The Captain of the 'Polestar'*. The text here is taken from *CDS*.

63 *Dei Gratia*: 'By the Grace of God'; traditionally, in accordance with the theory of the Divine Right of Kings, this phrase appears as part of the full title of a monarch. The *Dei Gratia* was indeed the name of the ship which discovered the *Mary Celeste* (see note to p. 105). Doyle is slightly wrong

about the location of the *Mary Celeste*: according to the mate of the *Dei Gratia*, Oliver Deceau, 'By my reckoning we were 38° 20´ North Latitude and 17° 15´ West Longitude by dead reckoning of our own ship': see James Briggs, 'In the Wake of the *Mary Celeste*', *Old Dartmouth Historical Sketches*, 74 (1944).

Marie Celeste: on 5 December 1872, the British merchant brigantine (two-masted sailing-ship) *Mary Celeste* was discovered some 600 miles off the coast of Portugal, sailing towards the Straits of Gibraltar, completely unmanned. What happened to the crew of the *Mary Celeste* remains a mystery, although one of the ship's lifeboats was missing. 'J. Habakuk Jephson' was highly influential in establishing the legend of the *Mary Celeste* in the popular imagination. Further, apocryphal details were to accrue to the legend, such as the belief that breakfast was still cooking, or that cups of tea were still warm, when the ship was boarded. In 1913, the *Strand* published 'The Story of Abel Fosdyk', purportedly a true documentary narrative of the fate of the *Mary Celeste*.

Gibraltar Gazette: actually the *Gibraltar Chronicle*, a long-running daily newspaper established in 1801.

Boston... October 16: the *Mary Celeste* actually set sail from New York on 5 November.

The boats were intact... davits: ACD seems to be the originator of the false legend that the *Mary Celeste*'s lifeboats were still on board when it was discovered. Davits are the cranes on the side of a ship, from which the lifeboats are hung, raised, and lowered.

64 *longitudinal striation*: streaks, running lengthwise.

a brigantine of 170 tons... J. W. Tibbs: all of this information is false: the *Mary Celeste* was 282 tons; it was owned by a consortium of four business-men; and its captain was Benjamin Briggs.

the war: the American Civil War (1861–5).

epitomised: abridged.

65 *monomaniac*: one fixated to the point of madness on a single subject.

Plymouth Brethren... Lowell: the Plymouth Brethren are a Nonconformist, Evangelical Christian community who believe in the absolute authority of the Bible and who conduct extensive missionary work. They trace their origins to Trinity College Dublin, but were formally founded in Plymouth, Devon, in 1831, and reached the US in 1860. Lowell is a city in Massachusetts.

'Where is thy Brother?' (Swarburgh, Lister & Co., 1859): a fictitious book from a fictitious publishing house, but with its origins in the Cain and Abel story: 'And the LORD said unto Cain, Where *is* Abel thy brother? and he said, I know not: *Am* I my brother's keeper?' (Genesis 4:9).

66 *Bull's Run... Gettysburg... Antietam*: all major battles of the American Civil War. The Second Battle of Bull Run was fought in Virginia on 28–30

August 1862, and resulted in a Confederate victory. The Battle of Gettysburg, 1–3 July 1863, was fought in Pennsylvania and was a Union victory. The Battle of Antietam, the bloodiest battle of the Civil War, was fought in Maryland on 17 September 1862. Although Antietam had no clear victor, it was a decisive moment in halting the northward advance of the Confederate army.

66 *Grant's*: Ulysses S. Grant (1822–85), commanding general of the Union army in the American Civil War, and later president of the United States (1869–77).

across the Jordan: the river Jordan marks the boundary between modern-day Israel and Jordan, the border of the biblical 'Promised Land', and was the site of the baptism of Christ. In Christian terms, 'crossing the Jordan' signifies the transition from this world to the next.

67 *New York Institute*: fictitious academic institution or learned society.

Richmond: capital of Virginia, and the capital of the Confederacy during the Civil War. Richmond fell to the Union army on 2 April 1865, marking the effective end of the war.

68 *apex of my left lung … state of consolidation*: the solidifying or compacting of a portion of the lung; pulmonary disorder.

quadroon: according to nineteenth-century racial classification, a quadroon was a person with one black grandparent—i.e. one-quarter black.

70 *Brussels carpet*: a form of machine-made carpet with uncut loops in its pile, particularly fashionable in the nineteenth century.

warps: nautical ropes used to haul vessels.

poop: see note to p. 69.

71 *dyspepsia*: indigestion, or more general digestive disorder.

cordage: 'the ropes in the rigging of a ship' (*OED*).

Maury's observations: Matthew Fontaine Maury (1807–73), American oceanographer, cartographer, and abolitionist; creator of the standard nineteenth-century oceanographic charts.

topsails and top-gallant sails: the topsails are generally the uppermost sails on a ship's mast; the topgallant sails are, on some ships, set further up again, above the topsails.

72 *catspaw*: in nautical terms, 'A slight and local breeze, which shows itself by rippling the surface of the sea' (*OED*).

73 *rorqual, or 'finner'*: rorquals in general are a family of large baleen whales, which includes the blue whale. A finner is a fin whale, the second-largest type of whale, and also a member of the rorqual family.

Montaigne's Essays: Michel de Montaigne (1533–92), French writer and intellectual. Montaigne pioneered the form of the essay as a medium for philosophical and self-analysis.

nightmare … cerebral hemispheres: nineteenth-century medicine, in which

ACD was trained, held that nightmares were caused by a lack of oxygen to the brain due to sleep apnoea (irregular or suspended breathing).

74 *chaffinches*: specifically, these are blue chaffinches, found only in the Canary Islands—another sign that the *Marie Celeste* is several hundred miles off course.

pertinacity: persistency or obstinacy.

77 *De Quincey*: Thomas De Quincey (1785–1859), English essayist and critic, author of *Confessions of an English Opium-Eater* (1821–2). Specifically, ACD is alluding here to De Quincey's essay 'On Murder Considered as One of the Fine Arts' (1827).

afterhold: space for storing cargo at the rear of a ship.

external iliac artery: the external iliac arteries are two major arteries in the pelvis.

four bells in the middle watch: 2 a.m. See note to p. 14.

78 *laudanum*: solution of opium, widely used as a painkiller in the nineteenth century.

Tagus: river running along the Spanish–Portuguese border, and flowing into the Atlantic near Lisbon.

79 *fo'c'sle-head*: see note to p. 14.

80 *Peak of Teneriffe*: Tenerife is the largest of the Canary Islands, rising to a volcanic peak.

81 *Cape Blanco*: see note to p. 38. It is possible that 'J. Habakuk Jephson' draws on the history of Captain James Riley (1777–1840), whose merchant ship *Commerce* was shipwrecked off Cape Blanco in 1815. Riley and his crew were enslaved in the Sahara and endured brutal treatment, as recorded in his memoir *Sufferings in Africa* (1817), which became an influential work for Abraham Lincoln, and for the abolitionist movement in general.

86 *Timbuctoo*: Timbuktu (Fr. Tombouctou), a famously remote Saharan city, in modern-day Mali, and long shrouded in legend. The first modern Western explorer to visit Timbuktu and return alive was René Caillié, who journeyed there disguised as an Arab in 1828.

87 *Cæsar...village in Gaul*: quote attributed to Julius Caesar (100–44 BC) by Plutarch: 'I prefer to be first in this place [a small village in Gaul (France)] than second in Rome.'

Mahomet...schism among his followers: the major schism in Islam, over issues of succession, took place in the aftermath of the prophet Muhammad's death in 632, with the religion dividing into its Sunni majority and Shia minority.

black stone of Mecca: al-Hajar al-Aswaad, the Black Stone placed as the eastern cornerstone of the Ka'aba, the black granite cube at the centre of the al-Masjid al-Haram mosque in Mecca, Saudi Arabia—the most holy site in the Islamic world. The origin of the Black Stone is mysterious, though it is widely believed to be a meteorite fragment.

87 *Barbary*: the Barbary (or Berber) Coast; the coast of North Africa, including Morocco, Algeria, Tunisia, and Libya.

88 *Fantee... Liberia*: the Fante region comprises the Ivory Coast and parts of modern Ghana. Liberia, in West Africa, was founded by the US in 1847 as an independent republic for freed slaves; its capital, Monrovia, is named in honour of US President James Monroe (1758–1831), a major supporter of the Liberian venture.

JOHN BARRINGTON COWLES

First published in *Cassell's Saturday Journal*, 12–19 April 1884. Reprinted in *The Captain of the 'Polestar'*: this is the text used here. Not in *CDS* or *US*.

91 *Northumberland Street*: street in the New Town of Edinburgh.

Sikh regiment: there were two Sikh regiments in the British Indian Army, the Regiment of Ferozepore and the Regiment of Ludhiana. Both were founded in 1846.

Velasquez-like: Diego Rodríguez de Silva y Velázquez (1599–1660), major Spanish painter. In this context, 'Velazquez-like' means having a Hispanic or Mediterranean complexion.

92 *the senior medal for anatomy... the Neil Arnott prize for Physics*: both genuine academic awards given by the University of Edinburgh. Neil Arnott (1788–1874) was a prominent Scottish physician, who donated £2,000 to each of the Scottish universities, and to the University of London, for outstanding achievement in science. In Edinburgh University, the Neil Arnott Scholarship for experimental physics, 'to the value of £250 per annum for two years, is awarded to the most distinguished student in the Physical Laboratory who must assist the Professor of Physics in the Laboratory during the ensuing session'.

Royal Scottish Academy: founded in 1826, the RSA is an organization for the promotion of Scottish art.

the real Greek type: following J. C. Nott and G. R. Gliddon's *Types of Mankind* (Philadelphia, 1854), nineteenth-century racial theory and physiognomy tended to privilege the 'Greek' countenance, as displayed in classical statuary (most notably the Apollo Belvedere), as the highest type of perfection in the human form.

93 *Noel Paton*: Sir Joseph Noël Paton (1821–1901), Scottish painter, specializing in large-scale historical works.

Princes Street: the main shopping street and thoroughfare of central Edinburgh.

94 *Abercrombie Place*: Abercromby Place, in the New Town of Edinburgh, not far from Northumberland Street.

95 *Queen's Park*: Holyrood Park, central Edinburgh.

St Margaret's Loch...St Anthony's Chapel: both in Holyrood Park. St Anthony's Chapel, now in ruins, probably dates from the early fifteenth century.

gin-palace: a large, ornate urban public house, generally Victorian in origin.

96 *vinegar to his temples*: vinegar was applied to cool fevered skin

97 *Peterhead*: see note to p. 52.

98 *Carlo*: common (or stereotypical) name for a dog in the nineteenth century.

100 *daguerreotype*: the most common form of nineteenth-century photography, developed by Louis Daguerre and Nicéphore Niépce in the 1820s and 1830s, and first publicly displayed in 1839.

Forty-first regiment: the 41st (Welch) Regiment of Foot, formed in 1719.

Persian War: the Anglo-Persian War of 1856–7 was one of a number of Victorian wars fought for control of Afghanistan, and ended with the retreat of the Persian army from the city of Herat, western Afghanistan. The 41st Regiment did not fight in the Anglo–Persian War.

102 *the Mutiny*: the Indian Rebellion of 1857–8, or First War of Indian Independence—formerly known as the Indian Mutiny, or the Sepoy Mutiny—was an unsuccessful rebellion against British imperial rule, focused on Delhi and central India. Although unsuccessful, it led to the downfall of the East India Company, which had formerly administered colonial rule, and the governing of India became conducted directly by the British government.

Hyderabad: large city in southern India.

Sobraon: the Battle of Sobraon took place in the Punjab on 10 February 1846, and was the decisive battle in the First Anglo–Sikh War of 1845–6, leading to British annexation of large parts of the Punjab.

the effects of mind upon matter: telepathy, a term coined in 1882 by the psychical researcher Frederic W. H. Myers, was central to late Victorian psychical research and spiritualism, and a particular field of interest for ACD himself.

eternal fire...sun-worshippers' temple: given the Afghan location, it seems likely that Captain Northcott was killed while desecrating a Zoroastrian temple in Herat, part of a region with ancient connections to the Zoroastrian religion. Eternal flames burned in Zoroastrian temples as symbols of the *Amesha Spenta*, the 'divine sparks' which are the emanations of the creator-spirit Ahura Mazda. The nineteenth-century philologist and mythographer Max Müller (1823–1900), who did important work on Sanskrit and on comparative religion, propounded the influential hypothesis that all religions had their origins in sun-worship.

103 *effete*: in this context, 'weak, ineffectual, degenerate' (*OED*).

animal magnetism and electro-biology: originally, animal magnetism referred to 'a supposed force or emanation to which the action of mesmerism is attributed' (*OED*); electrobiology was used in the nineteenth century as a synonym for mesmerism.

103 *legerdemain*: sleight of hand; trickery.

105 *caught a Tartar*: the phrase 'to catch a Tartar' was used from the seventeenth to the nineteenth century to mean 'to get hold of one who can neither be controlled nor got quit of; to tackle one who unexpectedly proves to be too formidable' (*OED*). The Tartars were the Mongols and other inhabitants of central Asia, legendary for their ferocity.

107 *Corstorphine*: a prosperous Edinburgh suburb.

108 *ghoul from the pit*: a corpse-eating spirit, specifically in Muslim countries.

wehr-wolves: interest in werewolves and other lycanthropes was intensified in nineteenth-century Britain following the publication of Sabine Baring-Gould's folkloric study *The Book of Were-Wolves* (1865).

in one of Marryat's books: Captain Frederick Marryat (1792–1948), novelist, best known for *The Children of the New Forest* (1847). The novel referred to here is *The Phantom Ship* (1839), which contains the interpolated story 'The White Wolf of the Hartz Mountains'.

laudanum: see note to p. 78.

109 *drachm*: an apothecaries' measure: 60 grains, or ⅛ oz. Colloquially, a drachm was used to mean a very small amount.

Isle of May ... Firth of Forth: the Firth of Forth is the estuary of the river Forth; Edinburgh is situated on the south bank of the Firth of Forth. The Isle of May is an uninhabited island and bird sanctuary at the mouth of the Firth of Forth.

solan geese: gannets.

110 *dark wrack*: clouds strung out, resembling seaweed, although wrack here carries a secondary meaning of disaster or catastrophe.

brae: a steep bank, frequently on the side of a river valley (Scots).

111 *Scotsman*: see note to p. 19.

UNCLE JEREMY'S HOUSEHOLD

First published in *Boy's Own Paper* (January–February 1887); reprinted in *US*. The text here is from the *Boy's Own Paper* original.

113 *Munchausen*: Baron Karl Friedrich Hieronymus von Münchhausen (1720–97), German soldier, storyteller, and fantasist, whose various tall tales about his military exploits first appeared in print in *Vademecum für lustige Leute* (*Manual for Merry Minds*, 1781–3), and were adapted and further fictionalized (in English) by Rudolf Erich Raspe (1737–94) under the title *Baron Munchausen's Narrative of his Travels and Campaigns in Russia* (1785, popularly known as *The Adventures of Baron Munchausen*).

This in turn was translated back into German in 1786, and considerably enlarged, by the poet Gottfried August Bürger (1747–94).

Dunkelthwaite: fictitious Yorkshire village.

Yorkshire Fells: the Yorkshire Dales, a highly picturesque area of uplands and valleys in the western part of North Yorkshire. The Dales contain many mountains which are called fells. The location of 'Uncle Jeremy's Household' is closely modelled on the area around Masongill in North Yorkshire, to which ACD was a frequent visitor: his mother, Mary, lived there from 1882 to 1917.

Baker Street: central London. Most famous in the work of ACD as the home of Sherlock Holmes, who lived in 221B Baker Street.

114 *"Universal Rhyming Dictionary"*: there have been a number of rhyming dictionaries published as aids to poetic composition. The most influential was *Walker's Rhyming Dictionary*, first published in 1775.

Caesar's prejudice against lean men: Shakespeare, *Julius Caesar*, I. ii. 191–2: 'Yond Cassius has a lean and hungry look; | He thinks too much: such men are dangerous.'

the way of all flesh: popular religious phrase, referring to the inevitability of death, adapted from the story of Noah, Genesis 6:12: 'And God looked upon the earth, and, behold, it was corrupt; for all flesh had corrupted his way upon the earth.' Most famously, *The Way of All Flesh* is the title of Samuel Butler's semi-autobiographical attack on Victorian hypocrisy, first published posthumously in 1903.

115 *the mutiny*: see note to p. 102.

Ingleton… Carnforth: Ingleton is a village in North Yorkshire, near the Lancashire border. Carnforth is a small town in northern Lancashire.

116 *Battle of the Standard*: or the Battle of Northallerton, 22 August 1138, in which a local Yorkshire militia army defeated an invading Scottish force under the command of King David I of Scotland.

117 *Pope*: Alexander Pope (1688–1744), English poet. Many of the most celebrated portraits of Pope, including those of Godfrey Kneller and William Hoare, depict him in various kinds of head-wrapping.

'"The Harrying of Borrodaile"': Uncle Jeremy's poem most likely refers to the 'Harrying of the North', a series of brutal campaigns to subjugate northern England, conducted in 1069–70. Borrowdale is in Cumbria, north of Lancashire.

118 *Rembrandt-like lights and shades*: Rembrandt van Rijn (1606–69), Dutch painter, and one of the great masters of chiaroscuro, the strong contrasting of light and shade in painting.

119 *Kirby Lonsdale*: Kirkby Lonsdale, a small town in southern Cumbria.

Nana… Cawnpore business: Kanpur (Cawnpore) is a large city in Uttar Pradesh, northern India. During the Indian rebellion, the British garrison at Kanpur was besieged for twenty-two days before surrendering to Indian forces under the command of the Indian nobleman Dhondhu Pant, known as Nana Sahib (1824–*c.*1857).

121 *Border poetry*: most likely Sir Walter Scott's influential collection of ballads, *Minstrelsy of the Scottish Borders* (1802–3).

strophe and antistrophe, like a Greek chorus: in classical Greek drama, the chorus acted as a commentary on the action of the play. The ode of a Greek chorus was traditionally divided into three parts, the strophe (during which the chorus moved from right to left across the stage), the antistrophe (in which they moved from left to right), and the epode (which completed the ode, and was chanted centre stage).

123 *Rajpoots*: Rajputs, members of the Hindu military caste.

128 *"Much learning hath made thee mad"*: Acts 26:24: 'And as he thus spake for himself, Festus said with a loud voice, Paul, thou art beside thyself; much learning doth make thee mad.'

bromide of potassium: see note to p. 14.

129 *Mr Thurston*: the *Boy's Own Paper* text has 'Mr Thornton' here, a mistake or mistranscription which ACD repeats.

131 *Dooab . . . Feringhees*: the Dooab, or Doab, lies between the rivers Ganges and Jumna in northern India. Feringhee was the Indian term for Europeans, specifically (but not exclusively) the Portuguese. 'Feringhea' was also the pseudonym of Syed Amir Ali, the Thug who turned King's evidence and provided William Henry Sleeman (see following note) with information on the cult. Feringhea also provided Philip Meadows Taylor with the source material for his bestselling novel *Confessions of a Thug* (1839); Taylor's work is in turn the source and inspiration for ACD here.

Borka: the standard account of the Thugs is the colonial administrator Sir William Henry Sleeman's *The Thugs or Phansigars of India* (London: Carey and Hart, 1839). Sleeman glosses 'Burka' as 'A leader or chief of Thugs, or one thoroughly instructed in the art' (i. 50).

Bhuttotee: Sleeman (*The Thugs*, i. 44) glosses 'Bhurtote' as 'A strangler', and 'Bhurtotee' as 'The office or duty of strangler. Thugs seldom attain this rank or office till they have been on many expeditions, and acquired the requisite courage or insensibility by slow degrees.'

roomal: originally, a rumal referred to any handkerchief, but specifically in this context, it refers to the handkerchief with which the Thugs strangled their victims.

Lughaees . . . Pilhaoo: Sleeman glosses 'Lugha' as 'A grave digger' (*The Thugs*, i. 86), and provides a long explanation of *Pilhaoo* (i. 94–5) as an important element on the Thugs' 'rules of augury': 'The appearance or voice of the animals from which the omens are taken, on the left.' If the *Pilhaoo* was propitious, it meant that 'The Deity has taken the gang [of Thugs] by the left arm'—that is, it was a good omen.

Dacoit: an Indian bandit.

Gooroo: in general, a guru is a Hindu spiritual leader or teacher, but specifically here Sleeman glosses 'gooroo' as the 'priest who teaches the use of the roomal in strangling' (*The Thugs*, i. 63).

133 *alkaloid*: an organic alkaline compound; specifically used to refer to poisons derived from plants.

134 *opium-eating Malay . . . De Quincey*: Thomas De Quincey's *Confessions of an English Opium Eater* (1821) recount the episode of a Malay sailor who knocks on De Quincey's door to beg for food while he is staying at a remote Scottish farmhouse, and to whom De Quincey gives a large amount of opium.

135 *Mahrattas*: (or Marathas) 'Of or relating to the princely and military classes of the former Hindu kingdom of Maharashtra in central India' (*OED*).

138 *Bhowanee*: 'Bhowanee or Davey, a female goddess, is the tutelary deity of the Thugs' (Sleeman, *The Thugs*, i. 120).

Gooroo Ramdeen Singh: fictitious Thug priest.

139 *Tupounee*: 'A sacrifice of goor to Bhowanee. This sacrifice is offered at the first convenient place after every murder. One rupee and four annas worth of goor, or coarse sugar, is purchased and put upon a blanket or sheet spread upon the cleanest place they can select. Near the pile of sugar and on the blanket they place the consecrated pickax, and a piece of silver, as a "Roop Darsun," or silver offering. The most esteemed leader of the gang who is supposed to be most in favour with the goddess, and best acquainted with the modes of propitiating her, is placed on the blanket with his face to the west. As many noted stranglers as it can conveniently contain, sit on each side of the leader, with their faces in the same direction' (Sleeman, *The Thugs*, i. 109).

Thugs: members of an Indian organization of professional assassins, bound together by religious rituals. The Thugs date back at least as far as the fourteenth century; estimates for the total numbers murdered by them vary between 50,000 and 2,000,000. The Thugs were suppressed and probably eradicated by British colonial rule under Sleeman's administration in the 1830s, and specifically by the Thuggee and Dacoity Suppression Acts, 1836–48.

140 *Jublepore*: Jabulpar, city in Madhya Pradesh, central India.

141 *Colonel Meadows Taylor*: Philip Meadows Taylor (1808–76), colonial administrator and novelist; author of *Confessions of a Thug* (1839) (see note to p. 131).

142 *cozened*: cheated or defrauded.

143 *Shelley's 'Cenci'*: The Cenci (1819) is a verse tragedy by Percy Bysshe Shelley (1792–1822), set in Renaissance Rome.

the Langham: a landmark hotel in Portland Place, central London, which opened in 1865.

145 *stertorous*: snoring (strictly, 'stertorous snoring' is a tautology).

148 *Dr B. C. Haller*: the name is an echo of Dr Bryan Waller, a close friend of ACD's mother, on whose estate in Masongill, North Yorkshire, she came to live in 1882.

sacred goor: coarse sugar (see note to p. 139).

149 *Thibaoo*: the counterpart to *Pilhaoo*. See note to p. 131.

Lieutenant Monsell, in 1812: ACD's source here is Meadows Taylor: 'In 1812, after the murder by Thugs of Lieut. Monsell, Mr Halhed, accompanied by a strong detachment, proceeded to the villages where the murderers were known to reside, and was resisted.' Taylor, *Confessions of a Thug* (London, 1839), vol. i, pp. xi–xii.

Colonel Sleeman: Sir William Henry Sleeman (1788–1856), colonial administrator. See note to p. 131.

THE RING OF THOTH

First published in the *Cornhill Magazine* (January 1890). Reprinted in *The Captain of the 'Polestar'*, and in *CDS*.

150 *[Title]*: Thoth was the Egyptian god of the moon, and also of knowledge and writing. He is represented as a human figure with the head of an ibis.

John Vansittart Smith, FRS...Gower Street: both 'The Ring of Thoth' and '"De Profundis"' have protagonists named John Vansittart, though there seems to be no relationship between them. The Vansittarts were a prominent Tory political dynasty in the eighteenth and nineteenth centuries. FRS is Fellow of the Royal Society, the major British scientific learned society, founded in 1660. Gower Street is in Bloomsbury, central London. It is the main location of University College London, and close to the British Museum.

Oriental Society...Hieroglyphic and Demotic inscriptions of El Kab: the Oriental Society is fictitious, but is most likely a conflation of the Royal Asiatic Society of Great Britain and Ireland, a learned society founded in 1824, and the affiliated Oriental Club, a gentleman's club also founded in 1824. El Kab is an ancient Egyptian archaeological site on the banks of the Nile, comprising the ruins of the city of Nekheb, which includes a notable necropolis and a temple dedicated to Thoth. In this context, demotic inscriptions are written in 'A simplified, cursive form of ancient Egyptian script' (*OED*), as opposed to the pictographic hieroglyphs.

sixth dynasty: the Sixth Dynasty of Egyptian pharaohs ran from *c.*2345–*c.*2181 BC.

Lepsius ...Champollion: Karl Richard Lepsius (1810–84), German Egyptologist, often considered the founder of modern archaeology. Jean-François Champollion (1790–1832), French Egyptologist and linguist, most famous for deciphering the Rosetta Stone in 1821–2, and thus decoding Egyptian hieroglyphics. Champollion's discoveries inaugurated the nineteenth-century fascination with Egypt, known as Egyptomania.

Egyptian collections of the Louvre: the Louvre Museum in Paris is home to one of the world's major collections of Egyptian antiquities, a collection founded in the aftermath of Champollion's translation of the Rosetta Stone.

Hôtel de France, in the Rue Laffitte, the Hotel de France was a celebrated hotel, frequently recommended in nineteenth-century guidebooks, on the Rue Laffitte in the 9th arrondissement of Paris.

151 *Boulevard des Italiens...Avenue de l'Opéra*: the Boulevard des Italiens is one of the great boulevards which run from east to west across central Paris; it intersects with the Rue Laffitte. The Avenue de l'Opéra runs from the Louvre to the Opéra (Palais Garnier).

Palais Royal: a large palace in the 1st arrondissement of Paris, opposite the Louvre; the Palais-Royal (originally Palais-Cardinal) was built from 1629, as Cardinal Richelieu's residence.

152 *Nature in some Maori mood*: Maori is used in this context to mean 'unkempt, neglected, disorderly' (*OED*).

Memphis: the ruins of Memphis, the ancient capital of Egypt, founded *c.*3000 BC, are on the west bank of the Nile, 12 miles south of Cairo. Modern excavations of Memphis began during Napoleon Bonaparte's Egyptian campaign of 1798. The French conversation in this passage translates as 'Where is the Memphis collection?' 'It's there.' 'You are an Egyptian, aren't you?' 'No, sir; I am French.'

vitreous: glassy.

153 *membrana nictitans*: nictating membrane, a translucent third eyelid found in birds, reptiles, and some mammals, drawn horizontally across the eye for moisturizing or protection.

Rue de Rivoli...Notre Dame: the Rue de Rivoli is one of the major thoroughfares and shopping streets of Paris. Notre-Dame de Paris, one of the world's greatest Gothic cathedrals, stands on the Île de la Cité in the river Seine. Its construction commenced in 1163.

154 *Thebes...Luxor...Heliopolis*: Thebes, otherwise known as Luxor, is in southern Egypt; the city dates from 3200 BC and was at various times the Egyptian capital. Luxor is one of the greatest of all Egyptian archaeological sites, and the location of the Valley of the Kings. Heliopolis, now a suburb of Cairo, was also an important ancient Egyptian city.

155 *cerecloths*: winding sheets, used for wrapping dead bodies, and generally waxed.

'Ma petite!' ... 'Ma pauvre petite!': 'My little one!...My poor little one!'

157 *hermetic philosophy*: 'works of revelation on occult, theological and philosophical subjects ascribed to the Egyptian God Thoth...who was believed to be the inventor of writing and patron of all the arts dependent

on writing' (*EB*). Hermetic philosophy was named after Hermes Trisme-gistus ('Thrice-Greatest Hermes'), a conflation of Thoth and the Greek messenger-god Hermes, though a later tradition believed him to be a human mage. The Hermetic Order of the Golden Dawn, founded in 1888, was the major occult society of the *fin de siècle*, attracting numerous high-profile adherents, including W. B. Yeats, Aleister Crowley, Arthur Machen, and Algernon Blackwood. Less successful was the Hermetic Brotherhood of Luxor, founded in 1884.

158 *truckle bed*: a low bed on casters, often stored beneath another bed.

Tuthmosis: or Thutmose, a pharaonic dynasty whose name means 'born of Thoth'. The specific pharaoh referred to here is probably Thutmose I (*c.*1500 BC).

Osiris...Abaris...Bubastic: in Egyptian mythology, Osiris was god of the underworld and ruler of the dead. Bubastis (modern-day Tall Baṣṭah) was an ancient Egyptian city on the banks of the Nile, north of Cairo. Abaris seems to be a mistake by ACD: there was an Abaris the Hyperborean, an ancient Greek sage and healer, but the deity of Bubastis was the cat-god Bastet.

mystic arts... Bible: in Exodus 7–8, the pharaoh's magicians cast enchantments which replicate some of the divine plagues foretold by Moses.

159 *Hyksos*: an Asiatic people who migrated into the Nile delta in the eight-eenth century BC, eventually establishing the Fifteenth Dynasty of the pharaohs (*c.*1630–1500 BC). The Hyksos worshipped the storm-god Seth.

160 *Horus*: the falcon-headed Egyptian sky-god, son of Isis and Osiris. After Seth killed Osiris, Horus avenged his father's death by killing Seth, though in the process lost his left eye (a symbol for the moon), which was healed by Thoth (hence the waxing and waning of the moon).

Chefru: Sneferu or Snefru, an Egyptian pharaoh reigning *c.*2600 BC. The tomb of Sneferu is in the necropolis of Dahshur, 25 miles south of Cairo: ACD is probably referring specifically to Sneferu's Red Pyramid, the third-largest Egyptian pyramid.

tirewomen: maids; specifically, maids assisting a lady's toilet.

white plague: tuberculosis.

161 *land with the narrow portal*: in Egyptian mythology, Duat, the land of the dead, was reached through a series of gates, each guarded by dangerous spirits.

Anubis: jackal-headed Egyptian god, protector of the dead and guardian of entry into the underworld. Anubis was also the god of embalming and mummification.

162 *Mount Harbal*: fictitious, but possibly a conflation of Mount Serbal and Mount Helal, both on the Sinai peninsula in Egypt.

163 *From the wilderness of Shur to the great, bitter lake*: Shur is mentioned sev-eral times in the Bible, and is identified in 1 Samuel 15:7 as being 'over

against Egypt'—that is, probably, the Arabian Desert. Here, ACD has Exodus 16:22–3 in mind: 'So Moses brought Israel from the Red sea, and they went into the wilderness of Shur; and they went three days in the wilderness, and found no water. | And when they came to Marah, they could not drink of the waters of Marah, for they *were* bitter.' Marah has been identified as the Small Bitter Lake, formerly a saltwater lake, and now a part of the Suez Canal, but if so, ACD is conflating it with its neighbour the Great Bitter Lake, now also incorporated into the Canal.

Euphrates: a river flowing through Mesopotamia (modern-day southern Turkey, Syria, and Iraq). The area surrounding the Euphrates and its neighbouring river, the Tigris, comprises the majority of the Fertile Crescent, the cradle of human civilization.

Herodotus: Greek historian (*c.*484–*c.*425 BC), author of the *Histories*, the foundational work of Western history. Born in Halicarnassus (modern-day Bodrum, Turkey), Herodotus was a very widely travelled man, who certainly visited Egypt.

164 *Boulak Museum…Mariette Bey*: the Egyptian Museum of Antiquities was housed in the Cairo district of Bulaq between 1852 and 1892, under the curatorship of the founding director of the Egyptian Antiquities Department, August Mariette (1821–81). Mariette, a French archaeologist, was awarded the titles of bey (chieftain) and pasha (lord) by the Egyptian government.

THE SURGEON OF GASTER FELL

First published in *Chambers's Journal*, 6–27 December 1890. Reprinted in *CDS*.

166 [*Title*]: Gaster Fell itself is fictitious, but is closely modelled on Masongill in North Yorkshire. See note to p. 113.

Kirkby-Malhouse: a fictitious Yorkshire village, probably based on Ingleton, near Masongill; there are various Kirkbys in Yorkshire, Lancashire, and Cumbria. Malhouse may have a metaphorical resonance here: 'bad house'.

Rippingille of Birmingham: Rippingille's Albion Lamp Company, Birmingham, a major nineteenth-century manufacturer of stoves.

a Pythagorean: a vegetarian, in keeping with the ascetic dietary regulations of the philosopher and mathematician Pythagoras of Sanos (*c.*570–*c.*495 BC) and his followers.

truckle-bed: see note to p. 158.

167 *arabesque pattern of dead gold*: arabesque design, very popular in the nineteenth century, incorporated flowing, intertwining branches, leaves, and flowers. Dead gold is 'Unburnished gold, or gold without lustre' (*OED*).

168 *Distrait*: see note to p. 55.

170 *effroyable*: dreadful, frightening, appalling.

170 *voilà tout*: 'that's all', or 'there you have it'.

O comme... ces collines!: Oh, how sad and wild they are, these hills!

175 *infernal machine*: bomb, explosive device.

176 *Memphis*: the ancient capital of Egypt. Upperton is a student of hermetic philosophy, and thus very possibly a member of the Hermetic Order of the Golden Dawn: see notes to pp. 152, 157.

178 *Pennigent*: Pen-y-ghent, a prominent peak in Ribblesdale, North Yorkshire.

179 *retorts, test tubes and condensers*: all types of chemical apparatus. A retort is a glass bulb with a long, downward-curving neck, used for distilling liquids in chemical experiments. A condenser cools vapour to its liquid or solid form.

181 *Iamblichus...not in genius*: Iamblichus (AD 250–330), Syrian philosopher; a major figure in the development of Neoplatonic philosophy. Emperor Julian (c.331–60), a great admirer, claimed that he would give all the gold of Lydia (a province of Anatolia in what is now western Turkey) for one epistle of Iamblichus.

184 *alienist*: nineteenth-century term for a psychiatrist.

A PASTORAL HORROR

First published in *People*, 21 December 1890. Reprinted in *US*. The text here is taken from *People*.

185 *Lake of Constance... Tyrolese Alps... Feldkirch... Jesuit school*: Lake Constance (Bodensee) is on the river Rhine, straddling the borders of Germany, Austria, and Switzerland. The Tyrol is a state in the western part of Austria. Feldkirch is a medieval Austrian city, on the border with Switzerland and Germany. ACD lived in Feldkirch in 1875–6 while studying at the Jesuit academy of Stella Matutina, founded in 1651.

Vorarlberg: the westernmost state in Austria, bordering Switzerland, Germany, and Liechtenstein.

Anspach: fictitious.

Laden: fictitious.

battle of Sadowa: the Battle of Königgrätz, 3 July 1866: the decisive battle of the Austro-Prussian War of 1866 (the Seven Weeks War), in which the Prussian army defeated the army of the Austrian Empire. Königgrätz, now known as Hradec Králové, is in the modern-day Czech Republic.

186 *the Gruner Mann and the Schwartzer Bar*: the Green Man and the Negro Bar.

Brixton: a suburb of south London, distinctly middle-class in the nineteenth century.

Von Ranke's: Leopold Van Ranke (1795–1885), German historian, whose

History of the Popes, their Church and their State in the Sixteenth and Seventeenth Centuries was published 1834–6.

the abortive insurrection at Berlin: the Berlin Insurrection was one of the general wave of European political upheavals, rebellions, and insurrections that took place in 1848, 'The Year of Revolutions'. Beginning in Sicily in January 1848, and soon spreading to France, the revolutions took place across much of the continent as well as North and Central America. Loosely affiliated, and generally disorganized, the 1848 revolutions called for the abolition of monarchy, and for greater participatory democracy. None of the revolutions achieved any long-term aims. The fighting in Berlin was particularly bloody, part of a movement to unite a German fatherland free from the influence of the Austrian Empire.

187 *Intendant*: 'One who has the charge, direction or superintendence of a department of public business, the affairs of a town or province . . . Used originally and chiefly for the title of certain public officers in France and elsewhere' (*OED*).

Lindau and Fredericshaven: both German towns on the shores of Lake Constance. Lindau is a town and island on the east side of the lake; Friedrichshafen is on the north shore.

188 *mattock*: 'A tool similar to a pick, but with a point or chisel at one end of the head and an adze-like blade at the other, used for breaking up hard ground' (*OED*).

maire: chief municipal officer.

190 *Guy's*: major London teaching hospital, in Southwark, central London, founded in 1721 by Thomas Guy.

191 *quinine . . . gulden*: quinine is an alkaloid found in the bark of the cincona tree, with various medical uses: it is best known as an antimalarial drug, but is also used as an anti-inflammatory, and to reduce fever. A gulden (guilder) was a German coin, originally gold.

192 *Gordon's translation of Tacitus*: Publius (or Gaius) Cornelius Tacitus (AD 56–120), Roman historian and senator, whose *Histories* and *Annals* are a major source for the history of the Roman Empire in the first century. The *Annals* give an account of the crucifixion of Christ. Thomas Gordon (*c.*1691–1750) published his translation of Tacitus in 1728.

Thalstadt: fictitious.

194 *carbines*: firearms, shorter than rifles but longer than pistols.

chamois: an antelope native to southern and central Europe, whose soft leather is used to make cleaning cloths.

butts: mounds upon which targets are placed for shooting or archery.

195 *magpie*: 'A shot from a rifle which strikes the outermost division but one of a target, and is signalled by a black and white flag' (*OED*).

196 *Klopstock's*: Friedrich Gottlieb Klopstock (1724–1803), German poet.

197 *'tapferer Engländer'*: 'brave [literally "braver"] Englishman'.

'DE PROFUNDIS'

First published in *The Idler* (March 1892); reprinted in *The Last Galley: Impressions and Tales* (1911) and in *CDS*.

201 [*Title*]: 'De profundis' ('From the depths') is the opening of the Vulgate (Latin) version of Psalm 130 (129 in the Vulgate), 'De profundis clamavi ad te, Domine', which the KJV translates as 'Out of the depths have I cried unto thee, O LORD'.

three-mile limit: traditionally, according to maritime law, the extent of a nation's territorial waters was 3 miles from its coastline.

Peshawur, and Umballah, and Korti, and Fort Pearson: Peshawar, in modern-day Pakistan, was formerly the capital of the North-West Frontier Province, and lies near the mouth of the strategically vital Khyber Pass, running between Afghanistan and Pakistan. It played a major role in the First War of Indian Independence (Indian Mutiny) of 1857. Ambala (Umballah) is a city in the Haryana region of northern India. Korti is in Sudan, and was a significant location in the Anglo-Sudanese Mahdist war of the 1880s. Fort Pearson, now Fort Kwamondi, is in modern-day KwaZulu Natal, South Africa, and was built by Colonel (later General Sir) Charles Knight Pearson during the Anglo-Zulu War of 1879.

202 *have even labelled it with a name*: telepathy. See note to p. 102.

John Vansittart . . . Island of Ceylon: for the Vansittart family, see note to p. 150. Ceylon (now Sri Lanka) is a large island in the Indian Ocean, just off the southern tip of India. Sri Lanka's major crop is tea, though it was until 1869 also a major producer of coffee (see note to p. 202).

cadet branch of the Hereford Lawsons: a cadet branch is a younger branch of a family, or the family of a younger son. Hereford is a cathedral city in the English West Midlands, not far from the Welsh border.

Colombo . . . barque-rigged: Colombo is the largest city in Sri Lanka, and its effective capital (the actual administrative capital, Sri Jayawardenepura Kotte, is essentially a suburb of Colombo). A barque-rigged ship is a small, three-masted sailing ship.

a single season and a rotting fungus: the coffee-blight *Hemilieia vastatrix*, colloquially known as 'Devastating Emily', effectively wiped out the Ceylonese coffee industry in 1869; many planters successfully switched their crops to tea. ACD has his dates wrong here, when he writes that 'in '72 there was no cloud yet above the skyline'.

the lion at Waterloo: the Lion's Mound is a large, artificial conical hill, topped with a statue of a lion, on the battle site at Waterloo, Belgium. Specifically, the statue commemorates not the Battle of Waterloo (18 June 1815) itself, but the wounding of Prince William II of Orange (1792–1849) at the battle: it marks the site where he was knocked off his horse by a musket ball in the shoulder.

204 *Falmouth*: a port town in Cornwall, celebrated for its deep natural harbour.

Royal Hotel: the former Royal Hotel is in Market Street, Falmouth. Built in the early nineteenth century, it is now a Grade II listed building.

theolologicians: the conflation of 'theologian' and 'logician' seems to be ACD's own coinage, used to register Vansittart's disordered state of mind.

shakedown: in this context, a makeshift bed.

prickly heat: *Lichen tropicus*, or miliaria: a skin rash brought on in hot countries by the blocking of the sweat glands.

206 *Madeira*: an island in the north Atlantic, now an autonomous region of Portugal.

207 *Funchal*: the capital of Madeira.

white stuff: ectoplasm, a viscous substance believed by spiritualists to emanate from the body of a medium, and 'the basis for all psychic phenomena' according to ACD's *History of Spiritualism* (London, 1926), i. 7.

208 *Los Desertos*: the Desertas Islands, an uninhabited archipelago south-east of Madeira.

209 *lat. 35 N. and long. 15 W.*: the north Atlantic, north of Madeira.

wraith: 'an immaterial or spectral appearance of a living being, freq. regarded as portending that person's death' (*OED*).

changes which fetch a body to the surface: the distension of the abdomen by gases produced by the normal decomposition of the human body can make corpses buried in water extremely buoyant.

LOT NO. 249

First published in *Harper's* (September 1892). Reprinted in *Round the Red Lamp* (1894) and *CDS*.

210 *Old's*: fictitious Oxford college, probably based either on University College (which has a claim to be the oldest Oxford college, founded 1249) or New College (founded 1379). ACD's reference to 'King's College' (see note to p. 226) might imply that he is using opposites: that Old's is New College and King's is Queen's College.

Plantagenet: English monarchical dynasty, also known as the house of Anjou or Angevin, comprising fourteen monarchs reigning from 1154 to 1485. The origin of the name Plantagenet is uncertain, but may be because the dynasty's founder, Geoffrey, Count of Anjou (d. 1151) wore a sprig of broom (Latin *planta genista*) as a family symbol.

211 *bend and saltire*: both examples of heraldic terminology. A bend is a band or strap running diagonally from the upper left (from the viewer's perspective) to the lower right of a shield or other heraldic design. A saltire is a diagonal cross.

briar-root pipe: a pipe made from the wood of the Mediterranean shrub *Erica arborea*, the tree heath, which is highly resistant to heat.

211 *single-sticks*: sticks designed for fencing practice, to be used with one hand.

sculls: rowing, with a pair of oars rather than a single oar.

212 *second cataract last long*: the Nile has six stretches of cataracts, or rapids. The second cataract, or Great Cataract, in Nubia (modern-day Sudan), is now part of the reservoir Lake Nasser. The long is the university long vacation, traditionally running approximately from the middle of June to the end of September.

Coptic to the Copts: the Copts are the Egyptian Christians. Their language, Coptic, is an Afro-Asiatic language dating from around the second century AD, and is based on ancient Egyptian, though using the Greek rather than the hieroglyphic alphabet. It is believed to have become extinct around the seventeenth century.

Dutch uncle: one who issues harsh or frank advice.

215 *pringled*: prickled.

bull-headed . . . statues: the ancient Egyptian bull-headed deity is Apis, god of fertility and strength. The stork-headed deity is Thoth, god of wisdom and writing, represented with the head of an ibis. The cat-headed god is Bast or Bastet, god of music and love. The owl-headed deity is probably the sky-god Horus, represented with the head of a falcon.

beetle-like deities . . . lapis lazuli: the ancient Egyptian beetle deity is Khepri, god of rebirth. Lapis lazuli is a semi-precious blue stone, much prized in ancient Egypt. The ancient Egyptians got their lapis lazuli from mines in Afghanistan, which remains the major source for the stone.

Horus and Isis and Osiris: major Egyptian gods. See notes to pp. 158 and 160.

216 *Saxon phlegm*: ancient medicine believed that the human personality was governed by four humours, or temperaments, each associated with bodily fluids and with the elements: sanguine (blood, air), choleric (yellow bile, fire), melancholy (black bile, earth), and phlegmatic (phlegm, water). Some of this language was adopted, semi-metaphorically, by nineteenth-century racial theory, in which ACD was very interested, and which understood the English (Saxons) as characterized by a phlegmatic temperament, as opposed to the 'melancholy' Celts.

217 *balsamic resin*: benzoin resin, from the bark of the *Styrax* trees and shrubs, commonly used in perfume and incense.

218 *eleventh dynasty*: the Eleventh Dynasty of the pharaohs of ancient Egypt ruled from Thebes in approximately 2200–2000 BC.

the embalmer had left his mark: in the process of mummification, the internal organs were removed and placed alongside the mummy itself, in Canopic jars.

myrrh and of cassia: both used as aromatics, in incense and perfume. Myrrh is the resin of the *commiphora* tree; cassia is a type of cinnamon.

219 *natron . . . hodsmen . . . bitumen*: natron is a mineral salt found in lake beds, used in mummification as a drying or dehydrating agent. Hodsmen, or

hod-carriers, are manual labourers who carry bricks and mortar on building sites. Bitumen, or asphalt, is a kind of tar or pitch, and was used as an embalming agent in mummification.

shakedown: temporary accommodation; a bed for the night.

221 *Beni Hassan*: Beni Hasan, an ancient Egyptian burial site located near modern-day Minya in central Egypt.

⁣ ⁣⁣ ⁣ ⁣⁣ ⁣⁣⁣ ⁣⁣ ⁣⁣⁣⁣ ⁣⁣ ⁣'a variety of manufactured tobacco, in which the ribs of the leaves are cut along with the fibre' (*OED*).

half-volleys and long hops… on a wet wicket: all the terminology in this passage refers to cricket, and most particularly to bowling actions.

High Street: street in central Oxford, which contains a number of the university's colleges.

true bill: 'a bill of indictment found by a Grand Jury to be supported by sufficient evidence to justify the hearing of a case' (*OED*).

224 *garrotter*: given ACD's interest in thuggee (see 'Uncle Jeremy's Household'), this may well be an allusion to Thug stranglers, who used handkerchiefs and other cloth garrottes to strangle their victims.

noddle: head.

on the raw: in a sore or sensitive spot.

Vice-Chancellor's pot: a sum of money or award specifically set aside by the vice chancellor of a university, in this case as a sporting prize.

225 *sport his oak*: university slang for closing the door to one's rooms.

Isis: the name given to the Thames as it flows through Oxford.

226 *steady thirty-six… jerky forty*: the number of strokes per minute made by a rower.

King's: fictitious: there is no King's College in Oxford, though there is a Queen's College. See also note to p. 210.

oleographs: see note to p. 21.

231 *blue pill… disordered liver*: the blue pill, or blue mass, was a mercury-based medicine, commonly prescribed for a variety of ailments across the nineteenth century.

237 *central-fire cartridges*: centrefire cartridges, the most common type of pistol and rifle ammunition, have a removable primer in the centre of the base, unlike rimfire cartridges, where the primer strikes the rim of the cartridge itself in order to fire.

Sporting Times: a weekly horse-racing paper that ran from 1865 to 1932, popularly known as 'The Pink 'Un', because it was printed on pink paper.

239 *stoke-hole of a steamer*: the aperture through which a steamship furnace is fed with coal; an extraordinarily hot place.

240 *the Soudan*: the implication here is that Bellingham has become involved in the anti-colonial Mahdist uprising in Sudan, which took place from

1881 to 1899, and thus was still ongoing when ACD wrote 'Lot No. 249'. Bellingham has become an enemy of the British Empire.

THE LOS AMIGOS FIASCO

First published in *The Idler* (December 1892). Reprinted in *Round the Red Lamp* and in *CDS*.

241 *electrocutions in the East*: the first execution by means of the electric chair was carried out in New York on 6 August 1890; the victim was William Kemmler, a convicted murderer.

irreclaimable: irredeemable.

242 *Leyden jars*: electrical instruments probably first created in the University of Leiden by the physicist Pieter van Musschenbroek in 1746. The Leyden jar was used to store static electricity, which could then be used to deliver an electric shock.

two thousand volts... death had not been instantaneous: in the first electrocution by electric chair (see note to p. 241), William Kemmler took eight minutes to die, even after the charge had been increased to 2,000 volts. Contemporary press coverage, which ACD had clearly read, described the execution as 'an awful spectacle, far worse than hanging' ('Far Worse Than Hanging', *New York Times*, 7 August 1890).

244 *copper*: a copper cauldron used for washing clothes.

245 *jint*: joint.

Pacific Slope: the territory west of the North American Continental Divide, from where the land slopes down to the Pacific Ocean. All rivers west of the Continental Divide flow into the Pacific, all those east of it into the Atlantic.

THE CASE OF LADY SANNOX

First published in *The Idler* (November 1893). Reprinted in *Round the Red Lamp* and *CDS*.

248 *confrères*: colleagues.

Marylebone Road... Oxford Street: major thoroughfares in central London. Marylebone Road runs from Paddington to the Euston Road and forms part of what was the New Road which opened in 1756 as the city's first traffic bypass. It intersects with Baker Street, where Sherlock Holmes lived. Oxford Street runs from Marble Arch to Tottenham Court Road.

249 *spud*: a narrow-bladed gardening implement, or fork, for digging or weeding.

250 *malachite*: hydrous carbonate of copper: a green mineral, used for decorative purposes to make vases or tables.

beeswing: a translucent crust which forms on vintage bottles of port and other wines.

Smyrna: ancient city on the Anatolian coast and the major trading port of the Ottoman Empire. Now known as Izmir and part of Turkey.

251 *Asia Minor*: the Anatolian Peninsula, covering the majority of modern Turkey. The westernmost point of the Asian land mass.

Almohads: the Almohad Empire was an Islamic empire covering North Africa and Spain, 1130–1262.

252 *bistouries*: scalpels.

Mussulman: Muslim.

253 *chloroform:* trichloromethane, a liquid once widely used as an anaesthetic.

Caryatid: a sculptured female form, used as an architectural column.

Euston Road: running from Marylebone Road to King's Cross in central London; formerly part of the New Road (see note to p. 248).

repeater: chiming pocketwatch.

257 *Hotel di Roma, Venice*: presumably in the Piazzale Roma, the major point of entry to Venice by land.

THE LORD OF CHÂTEAU NOIR

First published in the *Strand* (July 1894). Reprinted in *The Green Flag* (1900) and *CDS*.

258 *It was in the days . . . to the north of the Aisne and to the south of the Loire*: the story is set during the Franco-Prussian War of 1870. The river Aisne flows through north-eastern France, before joining the river Oise, which in turn joins the Seine. The Loire is the longest river in France, rising in the southern Massif Central mountains and flowing through central France before flowing into the Bay of Biscay at Saint-Nazaire.

Dieppe: port in northern France.

Posen: historically, a province of Prussia, centring on what is now the city of Poznań, Poland.

Les Andelys: small town in Haute-Normandie, northern France. ACD had family connections with Les Andelys: his mother and sister Annette were both educated at St Clotilde's academy in the town. Annette, in fact, was caught up in the Franco–Prussian War, as Prussian troops invaded Les Andelys in December 1870, while she was a student at St Clotilde's.

259 *Douay*: Abel Douay (1809–70), French general killed during the rout of the French army by Prussian forces at the Battle of Wissembourg, 4 August 1870.

saltire cross: a diagonal cross.

259 *four leagues... Three and a kilometre*: a league was an ancient unit of measurement, traditionally very loosely defined as the distance once could walk in an hour, or as approximately 3 miles, though the precise length of a league has varied dramatically across cultures and periods. Nevertheless, it remained in informal usage across the nineteenth century. Here, it is combined with the kilometre, a precise unit of measurement, and part of the metric system of weights and measures first introduced in France in 1795 in the wake of the French Revolution, and formally readopted there in 1837.

260 *General Goeben*: August Karl von Göben (1816–80), Prussian general, commander of the campaign in northern France during the Franco-Prussian War.

263 *pullet*: a young chicken, from the French *poulet*.

264 *the Fronde*: a series of civil wars that took place in France between 1648 and 1653, against the larger background of the Franco-Spanish War of 1635–59.

Baltic coast: at its height in the nineteenth century, Prussia encompassed the entire southern coast of the Baltic Sea.

265 *'avez bitié sur moi!'*: 'have pity on me!'; an attempt to render French as spoken in a German accent.

Chambertin: a 'Grand Cru' ('Great Growth') producer of Burgundy wine.

Rouen: city of northern France, on the banks of the river Seine.

Honfleur: port town in north-western France, on the Seine estuary.

266 *Weissenburg*: the Battle of Wissembourg. See note to p. 259.

Lauterburg: small town in Alsace, north-eastern France, on the border with modern Germany.

Ettlingen: town in south-western Germany, near the French border.

Durlach... Carlsruhe: Karlsruhe is a city in south-western Germany, near the French border; Durlach is a borough of Karlsruhe.

267 *caserne*: barracks.

Remilly: a village in Lorraine, north-eastern France.

Uhlans: Polish or Prussian lancers or light cavalry.

THE THIRD GENERATION

First published in *Round the Red Lamp*. Reprinted in *CDS*.

269 *Scudamore Lane... Monument*: the 202-foot Monument to the Great Fire of London was completed in 1671 and stands on the spot in Pudding Lane where the Great Fire of 1666 is believed to have started. The Monument was jointly designed by Robert Hooke and Sir Christopher Wren. Scudamore Lane in the City of London is fictitious, but given its proximity to the Monument, must be said to lie in London EC2.

In his particular branch... disadvantage: Dr Selby is a specialist in sexually transmitted diseases. The area around the Monument was in traditionally an unfashionable and unglamorous district of London, away from the city's social centre, and thus suitable for the discretion required by Dr Selby's particular medical practice.

London Bridge: just south of the Monument, and connecting the City of London on the north bank of the Thames with Southwark on the south.

270 *bluestone... 'Caustic'*: bluestone is copper sulphate, a chemical compound formerly used in medicine as an emetic. Sodium hydroxide, also known as caustic soda, is a powerful scouring agent, generally used in medicine for breaking down and dissolving tissue.

bistouries: see note to p. 252.

271 *the early Georges*: monarchs of the House of Hanover which reigned over Great Britain and Ireland from the accession of George I in 1714 to the death of Victoria in 1901. Specifically, a reference to the eighteenth-century monarchs Georges I, II, and III.

273 *interstitial keratisis... strumous diathesis... hereditary taint*: keratitis is inflammation of the cornea; strumous means affected with struma, 'A scrofulous swelling or tumour' (*OED*); diathesis is 'A permanent (hereditary or acquired) condition of the body which renders it liable to certain special diseases or affections; a constitutional predisposition or tendency' (*OED*). Sir Francis Norton has hereditary syphilis, originally contracted by his libertine grandfather. ACD wrote his MD thesis on the subject of syphilis, graduating in August 1885.

Corinthian: in this context, 'profligate. In 19th cent. use: given to elegant dissipation' (*OED*).

dangling seals: engraved seals hanging from a pocket watch.

274 *Pope's famous couplet*: this is very likely a reference to Alexander Pope's *An Essay on Man* (1733–4), which is full of observations on the imperfect intellectual state of humanity, and full of 'famous couplets'—though which particular couplet Dr Selby has in mind is unclear.

275 *"The third and fourth generation"*: Exodus 20:5: 'I the LORD thy God *am* a jealous God, visiting the iniquity of the fathers upon the children unto the third and fourth *generation* of them that hate me'. This passage, or passages very similar, recurs across the Old Testament, in Exodus 34:7 and Numbers 14:18.

277 *manikin's*: a manikin is 'a small representation or statue of a human figure' (*OED*).

Daily News: English newspaper, founded in 1846 by Charles Dickens, its first editor, and running till 1930.

King William Street: runs through the City of London, north from London Bridge to the Bank of England, passing very close to the Monument.

THE STRIPED CHEST

First published in *Pearson's Magazine* (July 1897). Reprinted in *The Green Flag* and *CDS*.

278 *poop ... quarter boats*: for poop, see note to p. 69; for quarter-boat, see note to p. 24.

mizzen-shrouds: rigging made of ropes, supporting a ship's main (mizzen) mast.

brig: brigantine, a two-masted sailing ship.

headsails: a sail set on or in front of a ship's forward mast.

Clyde: the river Clyde was the centre of the Glasgow shipbuilding industry.

bulwark: in this context, 'The raised woodwork running along the sides of a vessel above the level of the deck' (*OED*).

smother: suffocating smoke.

latitude 20° and longitude 10°: the ship is in the north Atlantic, off the coast of West Africa.

279 *halyards*: ropes used to lower sails.

lee side: the sheltered side of a ship.

seven bells: given that this episode takes place at sunset, this is likely to be seven bells in the last dog watch according to ship time—or 7.30 p.m.

falls: 'When we mention the Falls of a ship, it is meant by the raising or laying of some part of the Deck higher, or lower than the other' (H. Mainwaring, *Sea-mans Dictionary* (1644), in *OED*).

280 *Nossa Senhora da Vittoria*: Our Lady of Victory (Portuguese).

painter: the rope used to hold an anchor to the side of a ship, or a ship to the side of a quay.

281 *bills of lading*: a bill of lading is 'An official detailed receipt given by the master of a merchant vessel to the person consigning the goods, by which he makes himself responsible for their safe delivery to the consignee' (*OED*).

Bahia: a region of Brazil, on the Atlantic coast.

283 *Don Ramirez di Leyra ... Terra Firma ... Veraquas*: Don Ramirez di Leyra was the governor of what is modern-day Panama. The Spanish province of Tierra Firme comprised what is now Venezuela and Colombia, as well as Panama. Veraguas is a province of central Panama.

284 *nearness*: meanness, stinginess.

288 *Spanish Main*: the territories of North and South America surrounding the Caribbean coast and the Gulf of Mexico. This was the Spanish Empire in the New World, and proverbially a haunt of pirates.

Augsburg: city in southern Germany.

THE FIEND OF THE COOPERAGE

First published in the *Manchester Weekly Times* (1 October 1897). Reprinted in *Round the Fire Stories* (1908) and in *CDS*.

291 *jib*: triangular sail at or near the front of a ship's rigging.

Krooboy: or Kruboy; the Kru were Liberian seamen, celebrated for their skill in handling craft

in spate: in flood.

St Paul de Laonda: São Paolo da Assunção de Luana; modern-day Luanda, the capital city of Angola in West Africa.

292 *Home Rule*: the issue of Irish Home Rule split successive Gladstone governments across the 1880s and 1890s, leading to the prime minister's resignation after the failure of the Second Home Rule Bill in 1894. Though he was to modify his position later in life, when writing 'The Fiend of the Cooperage' in 1897, ACD was himself, like Walker, 'a good stiff Unionist'.

quinine: see note to p. 191.

Ogowai River: the Ogooué or Ogowe river flows through the centre of modern-day Gabon, West Africa, and out into the Atlantic.

293 *Du Chaillu... Gaboon*: Paul Du Chaillu (c.1831–1903), French-American explorer and anthropologist, who travelled extensively along the Ogooué river in Gabon (Gaboon) in the 1850s, and became the first European to confirm the existence of live gorillas.

296 *remittent fever*: 'a fever in which the patient's temperature periodically rises and falls without returning to normal' (*OED*).

297 *laudanum*: see note to p. 78.

298 *freshet*: a small stream of fresh water.

soughing: sighing.

301 *Primrose-League*: the Primrose League was a British Conservative political movement, founded in 1883, and named in honour of Benjamin Disraeli's favourite flower. Walker's membership of the Primrose League is consistent with his 'good stiff Unionist' stance on Home Rule.

the great python of the Gaboon: the African rock python, one of the world's longest snakes, reputed to grow up to 23 feet in length.

THE BEETLE-HUNTER

First published as 'The Story of the Beetle Hunter' in the *Strand Magazine* (June 1898). Reprinted in *Round the Fire Stories* and *CDS*.

303 *Gower Street*: see note to p. 150. ACD briefly lived and practised medicine in nearby Montague Place in 1891.

303 *Metropolitan Station*: the Metropolitan Railway, London's first underground line, opened in 1863, running between the City and the Middlesex suburbs. Gower Street was one of the original Metropolitan Railway stations, though it is now closed.

Standard: the *Evening Standard*, a London daily newspaper, founded in 1827 and still going strong.

coleopterist: a specialist in beetles.

Brook Street: in Mayfair, west London.

306 *'Burying Beetles'...Journal of Entomological Science*: burying beetles (*Nicrophorus*) are a type of carrion beetle, so called because they bury the corpses of small birds and rodents as food for their larvae. There are several *Journals of Entomological Science*, though none dating back as far as the nineteenth century.

308 *Paddington Station*: major London railway station, opened in 1838 as the terminus of Isambard Kingdom Brunel's Great Western Railway.

Pangbourne: Berkshire, west of London. Pangbourne Railway Station, part of the Great Western line, opened in 1840.

ulster: a long woollen overcoat with built-in cape across the shoulders.

309 *fly*: a one-horsed carriage.

310 *spud*: see note to p. 249.

scarabæi: scarabs; a large family of beetles, comprising over 30,000 species.

311 *elytra*: the hardened, shell-like forewings of beetles.

317 *two signatures are necessary*: from 1828 onwards, authorization from two qualified professionals was (and remains) necessary in order for a patient to be committed for psychiatric treatment, as a means of safeguarding against unjust committal. This was a particular anxiety in Victorian England, which saw a massive increase in psychiatric institutionalization, from 'no more than a few thousand' in 1800 to 100,000 in 1900: Roy Porter, *Madmen: A Social History of Madhouses, Mad-Doctors and Lunatics* (Stroud, 2004), 14. The theme of unjust committal to lunatic asylums was to animate a number of high-profile Victorian novels, notably Wilkie Collins's *The Woman in White* (1860) and Charles Reade's *Hard Cash* (1863).

THE SEALED ROOM

First published as 'The Story of the Sealed Room' in the *Strand Magazine* (September 1898). Reprinted in *Round the Fire Stories* and in *CDS*.

318 *Hampstead and Highgate...Abchurch Lane*: Hampstead and Highgate are prosperous north London suburbs. Abchurch Lane runs between Cannon Street and Lombard Street in the City of London, and contains Christopher Wren's church of St Mary Abchurch.

322 *coster*: costermonger; one who sells produce from a barrow.

THE BRAZILIAN CAT

First published as 'The Story of the Brazilian Cat', the *Strand Magazine* (December 1898). Reprinted in *Round the Fire Stories* and *CDS*.

330 *Grosvenor Mansions...Hurlingham*: Grosvenor Mansions, built in 1858, was a highly exclusive apartment block (residents included Sir Arthur Sullivan) on the corner of Palace Street and Victoria Street in central London. In the Sherlock Holmes story 'The Adventure of the Noble Bachelor', it is the London home of Lord St Simon. The Hurlingham Club, founded in 1869, is an exclusive sports club in Ranelagh Gardens, Fulham, London. It became and remained until the Second World War, the headquarters of polo for the British Empire, and a major location for clay pigeon shooting. In the Holmes story 'The Illustrious Client', we are told that the villainous Baron Adelbert Gruner 'has expensive tastes. He is a horse fancier. For a short time he played polo at Hurlingham.' *Sherlock Holmes: The Complete Short Stories* (London, 1928), 1094.

post-obits upon an unentailed property: a post-obit is 'A bond, given by the borrower, securing to the lender a sum of money to be paid on the death of a specific person from whom the borrower expects to inherit' (*OED*). A property which is an unentailed inheritance can be sold off by its possessor, unlike an entailed estate, which must be kept within a succession.

Clipton-on-the-Marsh: fictitious Suffolk town.

331 *Bankruptcy Court*: the Victorian Bankrupts' Court (built in 1820) stood in Basinghall Street in the City of London. It is now the Bankruptcy and Companies Court, a part of the Chancery Division of the High Court, and located in Fetter Lane, also in the City.

small spotted deer...peccary...oriole...armadillo...very fat badger: all South American species. The small spotted deer is the fawn of the white-tailed deer, which loses its spots as it ages. The peccary is a wild pig found throughout South America. There are numerous species of New World oriole, many of them 'gorgeously feathered'. There are some twenty species of armadillo, all native to South America. The creature resembling a 'very fat badger' might be a capybara, the largest species of rodent.

332 *Palladio pillars*: Andrea Palladio (Andrea di Pietro della Gondola, 1508–80), an enormously influential Italian architect credited with the reintroduction of classical architectural forms to Renaissance Europe, and thus with completely redefining the direction of European architecture. Pillars were a vital component of two of the most distinctive features of Palladian architecture: the portico at the front of a building, and the Palladian arch, or window.

334 *not a puma at all*: the cat is a black jaguar.

Rio Negro: river running 1,400 miles through Brazil before flowing into the Amazon. The headwaters of the Rio Negro are in far north-western Brazil, on the border with Colombia.

336　*Turf*: horse-racing bookmakers.

346　*Pernambuco*: a district of eastern Brazil.

THE NEW CATACOMB

First published under the title 'Burger's Secret' in *The Sunlight Yearbook* (1898). Reprinted, as 'The New Catacomb', in *The Green Flag* and *CDS*. The story is the imaginative fruit of ACD's first visit to Rome in April 1898.

348　*the Corso*: the Via del Corso, Rome's main thoroughfare, running in a straight line south through the old city, from its ancient northern gate, the Porta del Popolo, to the Piazza Venezia.

　　Baths of Caracalla: celebrated Roman baths, built between AD 212 and 216 by the emperor Antoninus, or Caracalla (188–217).

349　*Berlin Academy*: fictitious learned society, but probably based on the Prussian Academy of Sciences, founded in Berlin in 1700.

350　*Campagna*: the area surrounding Rome.

　　Castle of St Angelo: Castel Sant'Angelo, the mausoleum of the emperor Hadrian (built AD 123–39) in the Parco Adriano near the Vatican, Rome.

352　*Saint John's clock*: a cryptic reference. Given the location on the Via del Corso, this is unlikely to be a reference to either of Rome's two main churches of San Giovanni (St John): the cathedral of San Giovanni in Laterano and the church of San Giovanni dei Fiorentini are both some distance from the Via del Corso (and neither has a clock).

353　*Twickenham*: originally a village on the banks of the Thames some 10 miles from London, Twickenham expanded rapidly with the coming of the railway in the mid-nineteenth century, firmly establishing itself as a prosperous commuter suburb by 1900.

354　*sapping*: in this context, undermining (literally by water or glacial erosion).

　　survival of the fittest: a term coined by Herbert Spencer (1820–1903) in his *Principles of Biology* (1864), and adopted by Charles Darwin for later (1869 onwards) editions of *On the Origin of Species*. The term was used by Spencer in the context of the morality of laissez-faire economics, applying the principles of Darwinian natural selection to human society. In doing so, Spencer founded the school of thought which later became known as social Darwinism. This is the context in which Kennedy uses it here.

355　*Gate of the Appian Way*: the Appian Way is a road running between Rome and Brindisi in southern Italy. Construction began in 312 BC, and the road was named in honour of its designer, Appius Claudius Caecus. The Gate of the Appian Way is the Porta San Sebastiano, constructed around AD 275 as part of the city's Aurelian Walls.

356　*Catacombs of St Calixtus... Cecilia Metella*: Rome has some forty underground catacombs. The Catacombs of Callixtus are situated on the Appian

Way, and were probably built in the second century AD by the future Pope Callixtus I (died *c*.223). They contain the Crypt of the Popes, which houses the remains of several early popes, though not Callixtus himself. The castellated tomb of Cecilia Metella, dating from the first century BC, lies further along the Appian Way.

trattoria: the Trattoria Priscilla, then and now a restaurant situated in a sixteenth-century building near the Catacombs along the Appian Way.

Aqueduct: the Aqua Appia, the first Roman aqueduct, constructed in 312 BC to bring water to the city.

357 *soft tufa*: or tuff; porous rock, sometimes volcanic in origin.

358 *consecration cross*: a cross on the wall of a church, or as here on an altar, to mark the place where a bishop has consecrated the church by anointing it with holy water.

 full canonicals: full clerical dress.

THE RETIREMENT OF SIGNOR LAMBERT

First published in *Pearson's Magazine* (December 1898). Reprinted in *US*. The text here is taken from *Pearson's*.

361 *Lake Road, Landport*: Landport is a district of central Portsmouth, perhaps most famous as the birthplace of Charles Dickens. Lake Road runs through the middle of Landport. ACD lived and practised medicine in Portsmouth from 1882 to 1890.

 Leinster Gardens... Taplow... Argyleshire: Leinster Gardens is a street in the Bayswater district of west London, heavily developed in the nineteenth century. Taplow is a village in Buckinghamshire. Argyleshire, now more properly Argyll, is a county on the west coast of Scotland.

364 *Half Moon Street, W.*: Half Moon Street is off Piccadilly in Mayfair, west London. W. stands for 'Western District': in 1856, Sir Rowland Hill designed the first set of London postcodes, dividing the city into a circle comprised of eight districts.

 'Musical Record': fictitious music magazine.

 aretenoid cartilages: the two arytenoid cartilages are part of the larynx.

365 *Cavendish Square*: square at the intersection of Oxford and Regent Streets in the West End of London.

366 *Warburton Street... Chelsea with Kensington*: there is no Warburton Street in this district of London, though there is one in the London Fields area of east London.

 brougham: a one-horsed closed carriage.

367 *bistoury*: see note to p. 252.

368 *chloroform*: see note to p. 253.

THE BROWN HAND

First published as 'The Story of the Brown Hand' in the *Strand Magazine*, (May 1899). Reprinted in *Round the Fire Stories* and *CDS*.

370 *CB, KCSI*: Sir Dominick is a member of two chivalric orders. CB is Companion of the Order of the Bath, an order founded by George I in 1725, and generally awarded to recipients with distinguished military or civil service careers. KCSI is Knight Commander of the Star of India, an order founded by Queen Victoria in 1861, specifically to honour contributions to the British Empire in India.

371 *Dinton*: village in Wiltshire, some 8 miles west of Salisbury Plain.

the huge evidences of prehistoric life: specifically, a reference to Stonehenge, the celebrated Neolithic stone circle on Salisbury Plain, whose earliest sections date from *c.* 3000 BC, although Salisbury Plain contains numerous ancient monuments.

cremated ashes . . . jar full of dust: there are numerous records of cremations having taken place in Stonehenge, and on Salisbury Plain more generally, including pottery artefacts from the Neolithic Beaker Culture unearthed at nearby Boscombe Down.

gambrel roof: a roof both of whose sides are divided into two parts, with the upper part at a shallower angle than the lower; particularly characteristic of traditional New England architecture.

373 *Psychical Research Society*: the Society for Psychical Research (SPR), a high-profile organization dedicated to the investigation of various paranormal phenomena. Founded in 1882 by Frederic W. H. Myers, Henry Sidgwick, and others. ACD joined the SPR in January 1893, but became increasingly estranged from it in the 1920s following his public avowal of spiritualism.

374 *Mutiny*: see note to p. 102.

375 *splenic collection*: a collection of spleens.

377 *Peshawur*: see note to p. 201.

378 *Kaffiristan . . . Pushtoo*: Kafiristan or Kafirstan was historically a region in what is now the far east of Afghanistan, bordering modern-day Pakistan. Pushtoo, more properly Pashto, is the official language of Afghanistan.

soft sarcomatous swelling of one of the metacarpal joints: a cancerous tumour on the wrist.

380 *the Shadwell Seamen's Hospital*: the Albert Dock Seamen's Hospital was founded in 1890, not in Shadwell, but in nearby Greenwich. In 1899, it was the first site of the London School of Tropical Medicine.

Lascar . . . East India Dock: a lascar was an Indian sailor, originally specifically from the east coast of India. The East India Docks, set up in 1803, formerly stood in Blackwall, east London.

383 *salaam*: 'peace be upon you'; a ceremonial bow or salutation.

the great influenza epidemic: the Asiatic Flu pandemic of 1889–90, which killed approximately 1 million people.

PLAYING WITH FIRE

First published in the *Strand Magazine* (March 1900). Reprinted in *Round the Fire Stories* and *CDS*.

384 *spiritualism*: 'Playing with Fire' is the first ACD story to be engaged explicitly and at length with the subject of spiritualism, which was increasingly to preoccupy him for the remainder of his life. (See Introduction, pp. xxvii–xxxiii.)

a new religion: spiritualist churches became increasingly common in the late nineteenth and early twentieth centuries, particularly after the formation of the National Federation of Spiritualists (later renamed the Spiritualists' National Union) in 1891, and are still to be found in Britain and across the world. ACD himself remains the 'Honorary President-in-Spirit' of the Spiritualists' National Union.

animal magnetic force: see note to p. 103.

385 *Merton Park Road*: Merton Park is a suburb of south-west London, adjacent to Wimbledon. This kind of suburban setting is a characteristic one for spiritualism and seances. Although Badderly Gardens is a fictitious street, Lycett plausibly suggests that the setting is 'suggestive of Bedford Park in Chiswick, where Florence Farr and her fellow members of the Order of the Golden Dawn congregated' (250). The actress Florence Farr was one of a circle of members of the occult society the Hermetic Order of the Golden Dawn with whom ACD became acquainted at around the time he was writing 'Playing with Fire', and although *Memories and Adventures* records his belief that his mind was read by occultists from the Golden Dawn, their attempts to persuade him to join the Order were not successful.

the well-known Scotch professor: the reference here is unclear—there are no obvious Scottish Harveys or Deacons (or Deakins) who might be Harvey Deacon's 'well-known' ancestor. It may be that the reference is to one of ACD's own teachers at Edinburgh University, such as Dr Joseph Bell (often cited as a major inspiration for Sherlock Holmes) or the renowned toxicologist Sir Robert Christison, either of whom could certainly be described as 'a man with a remarkably clear and logical brain'.

387 *brothers of the Rosy Cross*: Rosicrucians; members of an esoteric society purportedly founded by the German mystic Christian Rosenkreuz (most likely a legendary character). Forerunners of Freemasonry, the Rosicrucians were originally a secret society who practised alchemy and occultism, and whose early members were said to have included the English scientist and philosopher Francis Bacon (1561–1626). A number of orders and societies styling themselves Rosicrucians exist to this day.

387 *direct talking or writing*: 'automatic writing', through the vehicle of a medium, was one of the major forms of spirit communication. See note to p. 384.

Hein?: French exclamation, roughly translating as 'eh?', or 'what?'.

388 *astral plane*: originally referring in Platonic philosophy to the stars, which were believed to be made from a 'fifth element' or 'quintessence' not found in the earthly, material world, the astral plane came to be understood in esoteric and spiritualist thought as the realm of the spirits.

a vibration of ether: according to premodern science, the æther was the 'quintessence' or fifth element, the material which comprised the celestial realm—which nineteenth-century spiritualism in turn took to be the world of the spirits, the ethereal realm (see note to p. 384). Communications of various kinds from the spirit world were often interpreted pseudoscientifically as vibrations in the ether.

389 *call the alphabet*: participants in seances would encourage spirit communication by reciting the alphabet: the spirits would knock on a certain letter, thus eventually forming words. By the time ACD wrote 'Playing with Fire', alphabet-calling had largely been superseded in seances by the rise in popularity of the planchette and Ouija board.

390 *communion with the dead of which the fathers of the Church had spoken*: a reference, probably recalled from ACD's Jesuit education, to 'the communion of saints' in the Apostolic Creed.

Control: specifically, in spiritualist discourse, a control was 'A spirit who controls the words and actions of a medium in a trance' (*OED*).

391 '*We labour for our own improvement and the advancement of others*': ACD's spirit is a characteristic Victorian, an adherent of the 'gospel of work' most famously articulated in the self-help philosophies of Samuel Smiles (1812–1904).

392 '*Undeveloped forces*': a term with a specific meaning in spiritualist discourse, as defined, for example, in Margaret Cameron's *The Seven Purposes: An Experience on Psychic Phenomena* (New York, 1918), 272: 'No forces of destruction comprehend construction. They are intelligent and wily in destruction, but fail to comprehend its futility.... They are sometimes found on your plane among the highly educated, learned, and powerful. Here [in the spirit world] we regard them as undeveloped forces, to be fought unceasingly until they consent to become constructive.' ACD makes frequent reference to these 'undeveloped forces' throughout his spiritualist writings.

396 *The Albany*: an exclusive mansion block in Piccadilly, London. Originally built in 1770–4 as a private residence for Viscount Melbourne, in 1802 the Albany was converted into what were initially bachelor apartments. Celebrated residents have included William Ewart Gladstone, Lord Byron, Edward Heath, Aldous Huxley, and J. B. Priestley. The Albany was something of a favourite fictional residence for ACD, recurring, for example, in

'The Jew's Breastplate', and most notably as Lord John Roxton's 'famous aristocratic rookery' in *The Lost World*. The Albany is also the residence of A. J. Raffles, the gentleman thief created by ACD's brother-in-law, E. W. Hornung.

THE LEATHER FUNNEL

First published in *McClure's* (November 1902). Reprinted in *Round the Fire Stories* and *CDS*.

397 *Lionel Dacre... Avenue de Wagram, Paris*: it has been suggested that Lionel Dacre is a fictional portrait of the high-profile occultist Aleister Crowley (1875–1947), of whom ACD would certainly have been aware at this time because of his association with members of the Hermetic Order of the Golden Dawn (see note to p. 157). There is, however, no real evidence that Dacre is modelled on Crowley: Lycett (287) suggests that 'Dacre was an imaginative literary composite drawn from the central characters in J. A. Huysmans's novels *À Rebours* and *Là Bas*'. Avenue de Wagram is a major Parisian boulevard, one of twelve streets which converge upon the Place Charles-de-Gaulle (formerly Place de l'Étoile). In 1876, the young ACD spent a month staying with his great-uncle Michael Conan at the latter's apartment at 65 Avenue de Wagram.

Arc de Triomphe: monument standing at the centre of the Place Charles-de-Gaulle (see immediately preceding note), standing 50 metres high, and contructed between 1806 and 1836 from an original design by Jean Chalgrin.

Talmudic, cabalistic, and magical works: the Talmud ('study') is a collection of ancient Jewish writings, comprised of two books, the Mishna ('repeated learning'), a collection of laws, and the Gemara ('completion'), a commentary on the laws. 'Cabalistic' in general means mysterious, or written in a private language, with its roots in the Kabbalah, a body of esoteric Jewish mysticism dating from the twelfth century onwards. ACD is using both 'Talmudic' and 'cabalistic' here to signify arcane or occult writings.

398 *Fontainebleau*: town some 40 miles south-east of Paris; home to a famous royal palace, the Château de Fontainebleau.

399 *quart*: ¼ gallon, or 2 pints.

"black jacks": large, tar-coated leather vessels for beer.

'I did not even know that there was such a psychology': the psychology of dreams was to take a central role in psychoanalysis following the publication of Sigmund Freud's *The Interpretation of Dreams* in 1899. Though 'The Leather Funnel' was published three years later, this is still too early for Freudian theory to have become widely established in the popular imagination.

Albertus Magnus: c.1200–80; Dominican friar and theologian, celebrated as an alchemist and magician. In a 1914 footnote to *The Interpretation of*

Dreams, Freud writes, 'The first hint at the factor of regression is to be found as far back as in Albertus Magnus. . . . The *"imaginatio"*, he tells us, constructs dreams out of the stored-up images of sensory objects, and the process is carried out in the reverse direction to that in waking life.' *The Interpretation of Dreams*, trans. James Strachey (London and Harmondsworth, 1976), 692 n. 14.

400 *the Quais . . . Rue Mathurin, in the Quartier Latin*: the Quais run along the banks of the river Seine through Paris. The Rue des Mathurins runs parallel to the Boulevard Haussmann, north of the Seine in central Paris. It does not run through the Latin Quarter, the student and bohemian district on the Left Bank of the Seine, which is south of the river.

chevrons and bars rouge upon a field argent: a chevron is heraldic insignia shaped like an inverted V, a bar is a horizontal stripe, a field argent is a silver background.

Nicholas de la Reynie, a high official of King Louis XIV: 'The Leather Funnel' is based upon the 'Affair of the Poisons' a sensational French scandal of 1677–82, in which a number of nobles and other high-profile citizens were implicated in charges of murder and witchcraft, culminating in the sentencing to death of thirty-four people, including the Marquise de Brinvilliers (see note to p. 407). The investigation into the case was conducted by the lieutenant-general of police, Gabriel-Nicolas de la Reynie (1625–1709). It is likely that ACD encountered the Affair of the Poisons in Alexandre Dumas's *La Marquise de Brinvilliers*, part of the 8-volume collection *Crimes célèbres* (Celebrated Crimes, 1839–41).

Draconic laws: Draconian laws; harsh or severe laws, named after the Athenian legislator Dracon (seventh century BC).

the proper badge of a marquis: according to heraldic tradition, in British and continental usage the coronet of a marquis contained a design incorporating four strawberry leaves and four pearls.

401 *some bloody incident in which that very sword took part*: the story revolves around a particular branch of psychical research known as psychometry, the belief that touching an object, or proximity to an object, could reveal its history.

Frondists: see note to p. 264.

402 *spandrels*: 'The triangular space between the outer curve of an arch and the rectangle formed by the mouldings enclosing it, frequently filled in with ornamental work' (*OED*).

405 *"Extraordinary Question"*: water torture; specifically, the forced drinking of 16 pints of water.

406 *MM*: 'Messieurs'.

ordinary: in water torture, the 'ordinary question' was the forced drinking of 8 pints of water. (See also note to p. 405.)

Place de Grève: public square in central Paris, renamed the Place de l'Hôtel de Ville in 1802; notoriously, the site of Parisian public executions.

Marie Madeleine d'Aubray, Marquise de Brinvilliers: Marie-Madeleine-Marguerite d'Aubray (1630–76), convicted as part of the Affair of the Poisons of poisoning her father and two of her brothers, in order to gain a family inheritance. Madame de Brinvilliers's confession was obtained under water torture; found guilty, she was beheaded, and her body was burned.

THE POT OF CAVIARE

First published in the *Strand Magazine* (March 1908). Reprinted in *Round the Fire Stories* and *CDS*. ACD described the story as 'very gloomy but of my best' (Lycett, 324).

408 *Boxer insurrection*: or Boxer Rebellion, a Chinese nationalist uprising of 1899–1901, whose aim was the expulsion of all foreigners from China. The Boxer Rebellion came to a head with the fifty-five-day siege of the International Legations (the site of the international diplomatic missions) of Beijing in July–August 1900. 'The Boxers' was the Western name given to the Yihequan secret society, which played a major role in the rebellion, and whose adherents practised martial arts which they believed made them impervious to Western weapons.

Ichau...Gulf of Liantong: Ichau is fictitious. The Gulf of Liantong is Liaodong Bay, a part of the Bohai Gulf of the Yellow Sea, 100 miles east of Beijing.

sangars: fortified lookout posts.

410 *Potz-tausend!*: German interjection, approximately translating as 'Good gracious!' or 'Upon my soul!'

Lachryma Christi: 'Tears of Christ'; a celebrated Neopolitan wine, produced in the region of Mount Vesuvius.

matchlocks: early firearms, produced between the fourteenth and sixteenth centuries, and named after their particular firing mechanism.

Mr Mauser and Mr Maxim: modern Edwardian weapons technology. Mr Mauser was Paul Mauser, the founder in 1870 of a German armaments manufacturer originally specializing in bolt-action rifles. Mr Maxim was Hiram Maxim, inventor in 1883 of the devastating Maxim Gun, a recoil-operated machine gun put to heavy use on the British imperial wars of the *fin de siècle*.

411 *Sung-tong, in South China*: Suntong is a small town in Guangdong Province, to the north of Hong Kong.

412 *Lepidus Mercerensis*: Professor Mercer has discovered a species of butterfly, which has been named after him.

413 *fall alive into the hands of the Chinese*: in the wake of the Boxer Rebellion, 'Yellow peril' narratives, of which 'The Pot of Caviare' is a mild example, began to proliferate, often highlighting the 'fiendish' cruelty of the Chinese. See John Kuo Wei Chen and Dylan Yeats (eds.), *The Yellow Peril: An Archive of Anti-Asian Fear* (London, 2013).

413 *the death of the hot eggs... the death of the boiling kettle*: colourfully named tortures such as these were a staple of Edwardian yellow peril narratives.

414 *postern gate*: side or back gate.

Tartar: Mongol. See note to p. 105.

417 *Princes Street*: see note to p. 93.

418 *Er soll leben—hoch!*: a German toast, translating literally as 'He shall live—high!', or 'He shall be celebrated'; often as part of a birthday song, 'Hoch soll er leben | Dreimal hoch' ('He shall be celebrated | Thrice cheers').

THE SILVER MIRROR

First published in the *Strand Magazine* (August 1908). Reprinted in *The Last Galley* and *CDS*.

421 *defalcation*: generally, the act of reduction by taking away a part, but in this context referring specifically to financial fraud.

bromide, or chloral: see note to p. 128.

425 *three spear-heads, two above and one below*: Mary Stuart (Mary Queen of Scots, 1542–87) inherited from her mother, Marie de Guise, Duchess of Longueville (1515–60), a coat of arms of three fleurs-de-lys, or spear-heads, against an azure (blue) background.

426 *dividends drawn from capital*: fraudulent dividents, which should be drawn from interest or profits.

damask: a rich, elaborately woven silk fabric, named after its origin in the city of Damascus, Syria.

428 *Darnley... Rizzio... Mary... Ruthven*: the scene depicts the murder on 9 March 1566 of the Italian musician, courtier, and favourite of Mary Queen of Scots, David Riccio (Davide Rizzio, *c.* 1533–66), at Holyrood Palace in Edinburgh. Mary's husband, Henry Stuart, Lord Darnley (1545–67), had grown jealous of Riccio, perhaps believing him to have been responsible for Mary's pregnancy. Riccio's murderers were led by the Protestant nobleman Patrick Ruthven, 3rd Lord Ruthven (1520–66), who immediately fled to England, and died shortly thereafter. ACD viewed 'The Silver Mirror' as an experiment in historical fiction: 'The idea', he wrote to Robertson Nicoll, 'is to stick very closely to the truth of history, and only to introduce the absolute minimum of fiction which enables you to get colour and human comment into your picture' (Lycett, 327). The story's account of Riccio's murder is historically accurate: Riccio sought to protect himself by holding onto Mary's gown, but was stabbed a reputed fifty-six times.

429 *Holyrood*: the Palace of Holyroodhouse (that is, the House of the Holy Cross), built in its modern form between 1671 and 1678, lies at the bottom of the Royal Mile in Edinburgh, and is the British monarch's official

residence in Scotland. Like the narrator of the story, ACD's father owned antique furniture originally belonging to Holyrood (Lycett, 326–7).

THE TERROR OF BLUE JOHN GAP

First published in the *Strand Magazine* (August 1910). Reprinted in *The Last Galley* and *GDS*.

430 *phthisis*: pulmonary tuberculosis; consumption.

North-West Derbyshire: 'The Terror of Blue John Gap' makes important use of its setting in the limestone caves of the Derbyshire Peak District, with which ACD became familiar while working as an assistant to Dr Charles Richardson in nearby Sheffield in 1878.

431 *the Arabian Nights*: *The Thousand and One Nights*, a collection of Middle Eastern and Indian folk tales, some of which date back at least as far as the tenth century, framed by the narrative of Sultan Shahriyar and his story-telling bride Scheherazade, and containing amongst others the narratives of Sindbad the Sailor, Ali Baba and the Forty Thieves, and Aladdin. *The Thousand and One Nights* gained particular popularity in late Victorian and Edwardian England due to the high-profile translation of Sir Richard Burton (16 vols., 1885–8).

Blue John . . . mineral . . . only found at one or two places in the world: Blue John, or Derbyshire spar, is an ornamental stone, a form of fluorite characterized by vivid purple or yellow bands, and highly prized for its rarity. Blue John itself is found only in two caves, Blue John Cavern and Treak Cliff Cavern, in the Derbyshire Peak District, although similar forms of blue fluorite are found in a tiny handful of other locations worldwide.

437 *mephitic*: foul-smelling or noxious.

438 *Castleton*: village in the Derbyshire Peak District. Blue John Cavern and Treak Cliff Cavern (see note to p. 431) are both nearby.

439 *Coltbridge*: a district of Edinburgh. Like ACD himself, James Hardcastle studied medicine at Edinburgh University.

old-world legends of dragons and other monsters: British and Irish folklore abounds in tales of dragons, worms, and serpents dwelling in caves. Bram Stoker's last novel, *The Lair of the White Worm* (1911), written around the same time as 'The Terror of Blue John Gap' and set in an identical location, the Derbyshire Peak District, draws heavily on its author's research into local dragon-lore, and provides an interesting companion-piece to ACD's story.

441 *Chapel-le-Dale*: there is a village of Chapel-le-Dale, near Ingleton, North Yorkshire, with which ACD was familiar as it is very near to his mother's home in Masongill. It seems likely that he is conflating this Yorkshire village with Chapel-en-le-Frith in the Derbyshire Peak District, a few miles from the location of the story.

442 *oakum*: coarse fibres made from untwisting the hemp of old ropes.

443 *Matlock, Buxton*: both towns in the Derbyshire Peak District.

444 *cerebral lesions of tuberculous origin*: tuberculomas or tubercoulous abscesses; lesions on the brain which occur, very uncommonly, as a consequence of tuberculosis.

THROUGH THE VEIL

First published in the *Strand Magazine* (November 1910). Reprinted in *The Last Galley* and *CDS*.

446 *Borderer... cattle-thieving clan in Liddesdale*: Liddesdale is a valley in the County of Roxburgh in southern Scotland. Liddesdale is very near the Scottish–English border, traditionally the location of the 'Border Reivers', a group of families and clans on either side of the border notorious for their raids on livestock and property.

Melrose: town in the County of Roxburgh on the Scottish–English border, not far from Liddesdale.

Young Men's Christian Association: more popularly, the YMCA; a Christian lay movement, founded in London in 1844 by the draper George Williams to promote moral and physical improvement in young men. Now a world-wide organization with headquarters in Geneva.

Teviothead: Scottish border village.

Roman Fort at Newstead: Newstead is a village in the Scottish Borders, very near to Melrose, and the site of the Roman garrison of Trimontium. In 1905, a rare cavalry helmet ('the Newstead Helmet') was excavated from the Trimontium site; it and other Roman artefacts now form the basis of the Newstead Collection at the Edinburgh National Museum.

the northern bank of the Tweed: the river Tweed historically marked the border between England and Scotland.

447 *midden-pits*: refuse pits.

thole: to bear or endure (Old English, but still in use in northern dialects).

448 *'Valeria Victrix'*: 'Victorious Valerian'; the name given to the 20th (Valerian) Legion of the Roman Army. The 20th Legion were stationed in Britain from the first to the fourth century AD, operating out of their major base in Chester (Deva). The Roman province of Valeria, where the 20th Legion originated, is in modern-day Hungary and Croatia.

449 *braeside*: hillside (Scots).

HOW IT HAPPENED

First published in the *Strand Magazine* (September 1913). Reprinted in *Danger! and Other Stories* (1918) and *CDS*.

451 *a writing medium*: automatic writing was a major form of spirit communication. In his spiritualist work *The New Revelation* (1918), ACD wrote that
evidence for the 'fresh doctrine' of spiritualism had come 'in the main
through automatic writing' (p. 30), though he noted that 'Of all forms of
mediumship, this seems to me the one which should be tested most rigidly,
as it lends itself very easily not so much to deception as to self-deception,
which is a more subtle and dangerous thing' (p. 26).

Robur. German automobile manufacturer. The specific car to which ACD
makes reference here is the 3-litre, 28 horsepower Phänomobil 10/28 PS,
manufactured between 1912 and 1919. Robur, situated after the Second
World War in East Germany, became a major manufacturer of trucks for the
Eastern bloc. The company closed soon after German reunification in 1990.

Claystall Hill: fictitious.

on the free: coasting downhill in a neutral gear.

454 *died of enteric at Bloemfontein in the Boer War*: enteric is typhoid fever.
Bloemfontein is the capital of the Free State, formerly the Orange Free
State, originally founded in 1854 as an independent Boer republic. The
failure of the Bloemfontein Conference (May–June 1899), convened to
discuss the status of British migrant workers in the Orange Free State, led
to the outbreak of the Boer War (1899–1902). While working as a doctor in
Bloemfontein during the Boer War, ACD found himself treating a virulent
outbreak of enteric fever: see Introduction, p. xvi.

THE HORROR OF THE HEIGHTS

First published in the *Strand Magazine* (November 1913). Reprinted in
Danger! and *CDS*.

455 *Withyham*: village in East Sussex, on the Weald, not far from the border
with Kent.

456 *Hartfield*: village in East Sussex, a few miles from Withyham.

Aero Club: from 1910 the Royal Aero Club, the governing body of sports
aviation in the United Kingdom, with its headquarters until 1961 at 119
Piccadilly, London W1.

Devizes: historic market town in Wiltshire, not far from Salisbury Plain.

457 *thirty thousand feet*: at the time of writing, the altitude record for a fixed-
wing aircraft was held by Roland Garros (1888–1918), whose monoplane
reached 18,405 feet on 11 September 1912, the event which most likely
inspired 'The Horror of the Heights'. The balloon altitude record of
39,000 feet, to which the story also refers, was set on 5 September 1862 by
Henry Coxwell and James Glaisher.

Flying School on Salisbury Plain: there have been a number of airbases on
Salisbury Plain: in 1910, the army established flying camps in Larkhill and

in Upavon, and in 1914 the Royal Flying Corps opened their training school in Netheravon. Given the date and the setting, ACD is most likely referring to Larkhill.

457 *at Rheims with Coselli and Gustav Raymond*: Reims is a city in the Champagne-Ardenne region of northern France, and its champagne-producing capital. Coselli and Gustav Raymond appear to be fictitious.

Gnome or Green: the Gnome was originally a single-cylinder motor engine; in 1905 the brothers Louis and Laurent Sequin founded the Gnome Motor Company, which soon found success manufacturing aircraft engines, and expanded in 1915 into the Gnome et Rhône company, which traded until 1945. Gustavus Green's Green Engine Company was a major British rival to Gnome as a manufacturer of aircraft engines in the early twentieth century.

Garros: Roland Garros. See note to p. 457.

458 *Pau-Biarritz*: both cities in the far south-west of France.

Homburg-Wiesbaden: both cities in the south-west of Germany.

Bayonne: city in the Basque County, south-west France, not far from Biarritz.

Amesbury: village in Wiltshire, very close to Stonehenge.

vol-plané: French for 'gliding flight'.

459 *Paul Veroner*: fictitious.

Robur: see note to p. 451.

talc goggles: goggles made of Muscovy glass, the mineral otherwise known as mica.

461 *barograph*: an aneroid barometer, for recording atmospheric pressure.

462 *Talk of human degeneration!*: 'degeneration theory' was a particularly prevalent cultural discourse around the *fin de siècle*, given especial impetus by the publication of Max Nordau's *Degeneration* in 1892.

tourbillon: a whirlwind.

464 *Mannheim glass*: the Mannheim Glass Works in Lancaster County, Pennsylvania, were opened by Henry William Stiegel, an immigrant from Cologne, in 1863.

465 *Venetian glass*: usually made on the island of Murano in the Venetian lagoon, this is high-class glassware, often highly coloured and artistic.

argosies: large merchant vessels, particularly associated with Venice.

467 *vol-piqué*: nosedive.

aerolite: meteorite.

Ashcombe: a village in south Devon.

THE BULLY OF BROCAS COURT

First published in the *Strand Magazine* (November 1921). Reprinted in *Tales of the Ring and the Camp* (1928) and *CDS*.

470 *South Midland Yeomanry...Luton*: the 'South Midland Yeomanry' is
probably the Warwickshire Yeomanry, a British army regiment first raised
in 1794. During the First World War, the Warwickshire Yeomanry was one
of a number of regiments brought together to make up the South Midland
Mounted Brigade. Luton is a large town in Bedfordshire, some 30 miles
north of London.

possible European war: there were innumerable European wars across the
nineteenth century, though this is most likely a reference to the Russo-
Turkish War of 1877–8.

The old knuckle-fighting: 'The Bully of Brocas Court' is heavily dependent
on a knowledge of the history of nineteenth-century prizefighting. The
Marquess of Queensberry Rules, first published in 1867, are in essence the
rules of modern boxing, stipulating three-minute rounds and the wearing
of gloves, and banning wrestling throws. These are the rules under which
Alf Stevens fights. The Bully fights under the rougher bare knuckle
London Prize-Ring Rules, first codified by Jack Broughton in 1743.

technically an illegal action: William Blackstone's definitive *Commentaries
in the Laws of England* (1765–9) decreed that 'a tilt or tournament, the
martial diversion of our ancestors, is an unlawful act: and so are boxing and sword-playing, the succeeding amusements of their posterity'
(*Encyclopædia Britannica*).

471 *John Lawrence Sullivan*: John L. Sullivan (1858–1918), American boxer,
whose career began in 1878, the year in which 'The Bully of Brocas Court'
is set; often considered the first modern boxer.

Kentish Town: north London suburb.

Great North Road...St Albans: the Great North Road was a coaching road
that ran from London to York, following approximately the same route as the
modern A1. St Albans is a market city in Hertfordshire, some 20 miles north
of London. Technically, St Albans did not lie on the Great North Road, but
on the Roman and Saxon road Watling Street, now parts of the A2 and A5.

Golden Cross: a coaching inn at Charing Cross, central London, dating
from the seventeenth century. The Golden Cross was the starting point for
many historic coaching-routes and one of Dickens's favourite locations,
making an appearance in *Sketches by Boz*, *The Pickwick Papers*, and *David
Copperfield*.

reefer-coated: a reefer jacket was 'a thick, close-fitting double-breasted
jacket' (*OED*).

Edgware Road...Hendon: the Edgware Road in London runs north-west
from Marble Arch to Edgware, and was originally a part of Watling Street
(see note to p. 471). Hendon is a suburb of north-west London.

472 *Finchley and Elstree*: Finchley is a suburb of north-west London; Elstree
is a few miles further up the A5 (Watling Street), in Hertfordshire.

473 *Brocas Old Hall*: fictitious, although the Brocas family, like the Doyles,
were prominent Irish artists and caricaturists.

473 *tits*: in this context, a slang word for horses.

Corinthian: a sporting amateur.

474 *millin' cove*: fighting man, boxer.

Stow that gammon: 'stop that nonsense'.

'Blow my dickey!': 'a general exclamation of surprise' (*GDS*).

chaw-bacons: a chaw-bacon is 'a rustic, a peasant; thus a fool' (*GDS*). That is, Alf Stevens is not an amateur, but a professional.

Lord Longmore: fictitious.

'Cheek. Wot's that?': according to the *OED*, the first recorded use of 'cheek' to mean 'impudence' was in Dickens's *Bleak House* (1853). Thus, the term did not exist during the Bully's lifetime.

475 *Molesey Hurst*: on the south bank of the river Thames in Surrey; a notable sporting venue in the nineteenth century.

Johnny Raws: novices.

476 *Lombard Street to a China orange on the one and only*: a gambling expression: 'Lombard Street, a centre of London banking since the 12C + *china orange*. The sweet orange (*Citrus aurantium*) was first sold in London in the mid-17C and by the 19C it was used figuratively to mean anything of minimal value. The bet wagers the wealth that is available in the street's banks against the almost valueless orange' (*GDS*). In this context, it means that the odds are heavily in the Bully's favour.

477 *cross-buttock*: a wrestling throw over the hip; outlawed in boxing under the Queenberry Rules.

Queensberry ... London prize-ring: see note to p. 470.

dog-fall: 'A fall in which both wrestlers touch the ground together' (*OED*).

out-fighting: fighting on the outside, at a distance from one's opponent.

478 *bye-battle*: a secondary or subsidiary fight.

479 *Harpenden Common*: Harpenden is a town near St Albans, Herefordshire.

THE NIGHTMARE ROOM

First published in the *Strand Magazine* (December 1921). Reprinted in *Tales of Terror and Mystery* (1922) and *CDS*.

484 *antimony*: chemical element extracted from the mineral stibnite, and most often used as an alloy with lead. In nineteenth-century medicine, antimony pills were used as an emetic or purgative.

THE LIFT

First published in the *Strand Magazine* (June 1922). Reprinted in *The Great Keinplatz Experiment and Other Tales of Twilight* (1925) and *CDS*.

489 *Flying Service*: Stangate has served in the First World War as a member of the Royal Naval Air Service, which merged with the Royal Flying Corps in 1918 to form the Royal Air Force.

vamosed: disappeared, from the popular American slang phrase 'vamoose!', which is in turn derived from the Spanish *vamos*, 'let us go'.

490 *Tower*: the story is set on Blackpool Tower, designed by James Maxwell and Charles Tuke and opened in 1894. Blackpool Tower stands 518 feet tall, and was inspired by the Eiffel Tower.

491 *Northam*: a thinly disguised Blackpool in Lancashire, a popular seaside resort, particularly for the north-west of England.

conventicle: a meeting or assembly; in this context, a small, private religious gathering.

492 *Hippodrome*: a popular Blackpool variety theatre, first opened in 1895 as the Blackpool Empire, and renamed the Hippodrome in 1900. After existing in a number of guises, the Hippodrome was demolished in 2014.

493 *It's KO for Battling Billy*: KO = 'knockout', music hall slang. Billy concedes the argument.

Isaiah the prophet: Old Testament prophet, eighth century BC. Jim Barnes is nicknamed Isaiah because of his stern Nonconformist religion, and because of his patriarchal appearance and prophetic cadences.

495 *Dixmude*: Diksmuide, city in the north-west of Belgium, and during the First World War the location of the Battle of the Yser (October 1914).

497 *'John Barnes, John Barnes'*: Barnes is referred to as 'Jim Barnes' at the beginning of the story. ACD was notoriously careless when it came to the names of his characters: see the 'John Thurston'/'John Thornton' confusion in 'Uncle Jeremy's Household' (p. 129). In the Holmes stories, Dr Watson is referred to as both John and James Watson, while Professor James Moriarty's brother is also called James.

498 *shambles*: slaughterhouse.